ADAPTED PHYSICAL EDUCATION AND SPORT

Joseph P. Winnick, EdD

Editor

State University of New York College at Brockport

Human Kinetics Books

Champaign, Illinois

Library of Congress Cataloging-in-Publication Data

Adapted physical education and sport / edited by Joseph P. Winnick.
    p.   cm.
  Includes bibliographies and index.
  ISBN 0-87322-258-X
  1. Physical education for handicapped persons. 2. Sports for the
handicapped.   I. Winnick, Joseph P.
  GV445.A3 1990
  371.9'04486--dc20   89-15283
                                                         CIP

ISBN: 0-87322-258-X

Developmental Editor: Marie Roy
Managing Editor: Holly Gilly
Assistant Editor: Timothy Ryan
Copyeditor: Jean Tucker
Proofreader: Mark Kmetzko
Production Director: Ernie Noa
Typesetters: Sandra Meier and Angela Snyder
Text Design: Keith Blomberg
Text Layout: Denise Lowry and Tara Welsch
Graphic Production: Kimberlie Henris, Tom Janowski, and Craig Ronto
Cover Design: Tim Offenstein
Cover Photo: PVA/Sports 'N Spokes, Curt Beamer
Printer: Versa Press

Printed in the United States of America

10 9 8 7 6 5 4 3

Human Kinetics Books
A Division of Human Kinetics Publishers, Inc.
Box 5076, Champaign, IL 61825-5076
1-800-747-4457

Canada Office:
Human Kinetics Publishers, Inc.
P.O. Box 2503, Windsor, ON N8Y 4S2
1-800-465-7301 (in Canada only)

Europe Office:
Human Kinetics Publishers (Europe) Ltd.
P.O. Box IW14
Leeds LS16 6TR
England
0532-781708

Contents

Preface

This book has been designed as both a text and a resource in adapted physical education and sport. As a text it can be used to prepare students majoring in physical education, recreation, sport management, special education, and related disciplines. As a resource it can serve a variety of individuals and groups: teachers, administrators, parents, coaches, volunteers, and other professionals.

The book comprises five major parts. Part I, "Foundational Topics in Adapted Physical Education and Sport," presents information that is introductory, general, foundational or that serves as a background for subsequent chapters. It includes a brief history and overview of adapted physical education and sport, the organization and management of programs, individual education programming, measurement and appraisal, affective considerations related to adapted physical education, behavior management, perceptual-motor development, and wheelchairs and other assistive devices.

Part II, "Learning and Teaching," includes separate chapters on factors that influence learning and teaching styles or approaches.

In Part III, "Children and Youth With Unique Needs," chapters are devoted to mental retardation, learning disabilities, behavioral disabilities, sensory impairments, orthopedic impairments, and other health conditions. One chapter includes non-handicapped youngsters with unique needs in physical education. A chapter in this part typically includes a brief introduction, definitions of terms, classifications, and statistics on incidence. Causes and types of handicapping conditions, and characteristics of affected groups are discussed as well. Part III presents specific methods that are particularly appropriate for teaching each of the groups and suggests appropriate activities in physical education and sport. (More detailed activity modifications are offered in Part IV.) Each chapter identifies assessment instruments appropriate for use with the population under discussion, although the tests themselves are generally described in detail in chapter 4, "Measurement and Appraisal."

Part IV, "Developmental Aspects of Adapted Physical Education," covers the topics of physical fitness, motor development, body mechanics, and posture. The chapters identify components associated with the developmental areas, explore the relationship of these components to physical education and sport experiences, and show how those experiences can stimulate development.

Part V, "Activities for Students With Unique Needs," deals with physical education and sport activities in school and community contexts. It includes separate chapters on elementary games and activities, developmental and remedial exercises, rhythms and dance, aquatics, team sports, individual and dual sports, and winter activities. A key aspect of these chapters is the presentation of specific activity modifications for the various populations involved in adapted physical education and sport.

Acknowledgments

The writing of a book is a team effort. All of the authors of this text are indebted to the special people who have contributed to the effort in so many ways. We thank the parents, coaches, and teachers who, directly or indirectly, have helped us make the book a success. We thank all those significant in our own lives for their support. The following are acknowledgments by individual authors.

Diane H. Craft, PhD—My thanks to the colleagues and students who continue to teach me. And my thanks to Craig Smith, my husband and friend, who gave generously of his time so that I could write the chapters.

Luke E. Kelly, PhD—I would like to thank Dr. Joseph P. Winnick for inviting me to participate in the writing of this book and for his inspiration and dedication to improving the quality of services provided in adapted physical education and sport. I would also like to thank my graduate students at the University of Virginia who have served as a sounding board for my ideas and who have spent countless hours reviewing the chapters I have written.

E. Michael Loovis, PhD—Several people and institutions have helped in obtaining pictures used in my chapters. I am indebted to Carolyn Ellison of Chagrin Valley Therapeutic Riding Center, Chagrin Falls, Ohio; Joseph P. Winnick, State University of New York, College at Brockport; Lea & Febiger of Philadelphia; and Emmett Anderson of the Freehanderson Company, Helena, Montana. Appreciation is extended to Instructional Media Services, Cleveland State University, for figure development and film processing.

E. Louise Priest, MS—My appreciation to Susan Grosse for reviewing and making suggestions on my chapter.

David L. Porretta, PhD—Special recognition goes to the Dallas Riders, Disabled Sports Association; to the McIver School, Greensboro, North Carolina; and to *Sports 'N Spokes* magazine for providing me with photos used in my chapters. My gratitude is also extended to people from East Carolina University who posed for a number of photographs.

Sarah M. Rich, PhD—I would like to thank Dr. Deborah Wuest of Ithaca College for her technical assistance in writing and Ms. Joannie Hill of Denton State School for providing the opportunity to photograph individuals in the Special Olympics program.

Francis X. Short, PED—Gratitude is extended to colleagues at the State University of New York, College at Brockport; to Jim Dusen and Richard Incardona for photographs and art work; and to the editor, Dr. Joseph P. Winnick, for guidance and feedback on the construction of my chapters.

Joseph P. Winnick, EdD—Thanks to Jim Dusen and Richard Incardona for preparing tables and figures. Appreciation is extended to Kathy Fiddler and Rikki Cannioto for a variety of services rendered. Thanks are extended to Tim and Tucker Short, Valerie and Jason Winnick, and other willing participants for posing for pictures.

Foundational Topics in Adapted Physical Education and Sport

Part I presents information that is introductory, general, or foundational and establishes a background for subsequent chapters. The first chapter offers a definition of adapted physical education and sport and a brief orientation concerning its history, legal basis, and professional resources. In chapter 2 the focus shifts to the organization and management of programs. Topics covered include programmatic and curricular direction in adapted physical education, guidelines for administrative procedures and program implementation, human resources necessary for adapted physical education and sport programs, and program evaluation. Chapter 3 is a detailed discussion of individualized education programs developed for students with unique needs. Important in the establishment of programs are several concepts related to measurement and appraisal. These concepts are treated in chapter 4, which discusses various types of tests and standards, purposes of measurement and evaluation, data collection instruments, awards, and computer software relevant to adapted physical education.

Chapters 5 through 7 deal with affective considerations related to adapted physical education and sport, behavior management, and perceptual-motor development. Chapter 5, on affective considerations, presents background material related to adapted physical education and sport with particular emphasis on socialization and self-concept. Much attention is given to humanistic and behavioral approaches related to the development of affective qualities. Chapter 6 presents basic concepts and approaches related to methods of managing behavior, with emphasis on behavior modification. Chapter 7 treats perceptual-motor development, particularly important in adapted physical education because the subdiscipline serves many individuals whose unique needs are associated with impaired sensory and perceptual systems. The chapter describes the perceptual-motor process, identifies perceptual-motor abilities, and explains how those abilities are involved and can be developed or remediated in physical education and sport activities. Chapter 8 provides basic information on wheelchairs and other assistive devices.

CHAPTER 1

History, Legislation, and Professional Resources

Joseph P. Winnick

Many individuals who pursue a career of teaching physical education and coaching sports are skilled performers in physical education and sport activities. They have experienced a great deal of success and have probably earned letters in high school and/or college athletics. Many have interacted with high-level performers in physical education and sports. As they prepare for careers in physical education, they often become aware for the first time of the existence of *adapted physical education and sport*, the aspect of physical education that provides services to persons with *unique needs*. Those with unique needs may be low performers or high performers who need activities adapted for them.

Although most individuals with unique needs in physical education and sport remain rather obscure, some have become celebrities in the world of sport. For example, Wilma Rudolph—despite birth defects and polio—was a triple gold medalist in the 100-m, 200-m, and 400-m relays in the 1960 Rome Olympics. Peter Gray, who had a right arm amputation, played center field for the St. Louis Browns in 1945. Other well-known sport figures include Harry Cordellos, a sightless distance runner who in 1975 ran the Boston Marathon with a sighted partner in 2 hr 57 min 42 s; Tom Dempsey, who was born with only half a right foot and set a National Football League record in 1970 for the longest field goal kicked (63 yd); and Jim

Abbott, an award-winning left-handed pitcher for the University of Michigan with an impaired right hand. As Figure 1.1 shows, individuals with unique needs are capable of feats that many people would not think possible.

Figure 1.1 An elite performer with a severe lower-limb impairment performing a handstand.

The Meaning of Adapted Physical Education

Because different terms and different definitions of the same term have been applied to the part of physical education that deals with programs specially designed to meet the unique needs of individuals, it is necessary to clarify some terms used in this book.

Adapted physical education is a diverse program of developmental activities, exercises, games, rhythms, and sports designed to meet the unique physical education needs of individuals. As a subdiscipline of physical education (PE), it includes instruction individually planned to meet the needs of students who require adaptations in physical education for safe, satisfying, and successful participation and developmental and/or remedial activities.

Adapted physical education is generally designed to meet *long-term* (more than 30 days) unique needs. It serves individuals with handicapping conditions as defined in *PL 94-142*, the *Education for All Handicapped Children Act of 1975* (Department of Health, Education, and Welfare, 1977a). According to this legislation, handicapped students include those who are mentally retarded, hard-of-hearing, deaf, speech impaired, visually handicapped, seriously emotionally disturbed, orthopedically impaired, other health impaired, deaf/blind, multi-handicapped, or affected by specific learning disabilities. Adapted physical education may also involve students who are not identified by a school district as handicapped under PL 94-142, but who may have conditions that affect functioning and result in a need for specially designed instruction. The latter group may include nonhandicapped students of low fitness (including exceptional leanness or obesity), inadequate motor development, or low skill, and those with poor functional posture. These individuals may require specially designed programming to habilitate or remediate physical and motor functions required for continued physical education, functional skills, and physical well-being.

According to PL 94-142, each handicapped student must have an *individualized education program* (IEP) developed by a planning committee. The IEP may include specially designed instruction in physical education. Although not required by federal law, an individualized physical education program (IPEP) may also be developed for those who have a unique need in physical education but have not been identified as handicapped by the school. It is recommended that each school have policies and procedures to guide the development of individualized physical education programs. Specifics on IEP and IPEP development are addressed in chapter 3.

Adapted physical education may take place in classes that range from *mainstreamed* (i.e., regular physical education) to *segregated* (i.e., including only students with unique needs). Although adapted physical education is individualized, it can be conducted in a group setting. It is geared to the needs, limitations, and abilities of each student.

Adapted physical education is an *active* program of physical activity rather than a *sedentary* alternative program; it supports the attainment of the benefits of physical activity by meeting the needs of students who might otherwise be relegated to passive experiences associated with physical education. In establishing adapted physical education programs, educators work together with parents, students, school teachers and administrators, and professionals in various disciplines and related services. Adapted physical education may have a developmental, community-based, or other orientation and may use a variety of teaching styles. It takes place in schools and other agencies with the responsibility of educating individuals. Although adapted physical education is *educational*, it draws upon *related* services, especially medically related services, to help meet instructional objectives and goals.

Adapted physical education can help to restore the capabilities of the individual. Although it may exceed the minimal time required by policies or laws, it should not be supplanted by related services, intramurals, sport days, athletics, or other experiences that are not primarily instructional.

Adapted Sport

Adapted sport consists of sport experiences modified or specially designed to meet the unique needs of individuals. The settings for adapted sport may range from integrated settings, where individuals with handicapping conditions or disabilities interact with able-bodied participants, to segregated environments in which play includes only people with handicapping conditions.

Adapted sport programs may be conducted in intramural, extramural, interschool, and community-related settings. Intramural activities are conducted within the school, involve only students enrolled in that school, and are organized to serve the entire school population. Extramural sport activities involve students from two or more schools and take place on play days or sport days at the end of instructional or intramural sessions. Interschool sports are based on competition between representatives of two or more schools and offer enriched opportunities for selected and more highly skilled individuals. Community-related sports are organized to offer individuals with unique needs an opportunity to enjoy the benefits of sport in out-of-school settings.

Although adapted sport is important, it should not supplant mainstreamed sport participation or required instruction in physical education.

Brief History
of Adapted Physical Education

In 1838, physical activity began receiving special attention at the Perkins school for visually handicapped pupils in Boston. According to Charles Buell (1983), a noted visually impaired physical educator (Figure 1.2), this special attention resulted from the fact that Samuel Gridley Howe, the school's director, was an advocate for the health benefits of physical activity. For the first eight years, physical education consisted of compulsory recreation in the open air. In 1840, when the school was moved to South Boston, boys par-

Figure 1.2 Charles Buell, a national leader on physical education and sport for visually impaired persons.

ticipated in gymnastic exercises and swimming. This was the first physical education program for blind students in America, and it was, by Buell's account, far ahead of most physical education in the public schools. Buell himself has been a leader in providing physical activity for blind persons and is the author of several books and articles.

Medical Orientation

Although physical education was provided to the blind and to individuals with other impairments in the early 1800s, most students of the history of adapted physical education generally recognize the medically oriented gymnastics and drill begun in the latter part of the 19th century as the forerunner of modern adapted physical education. Sherrill (1986) states that physical education prior to 1900 was medically oriented and preventive, developmental, or corrective in nature. Its purpose was to foster healthier bodies and improve posture. Strongly influencing this orientation was a system of medical gymnastics developed in Sweden by Per Henrick Ling and introduced in this country in 1884.

Shift to Sports and the Whole Person

Toward the end of the 19th century and into the 1930s, programs began to shift from medically oriented physical training to sports-centered physical education and concern for the whole child (Sherrill, 1986). This transition resulted in broad mandatory physical education programs consisting of games, sports, rhythmic activities, and calisthenics designed to meet the needs of the whole person. Individuals unable to participate in regular activities were provided corrective or remedial physical education. According to Sherrill (see Figure 1.3), a prominent historian of adapted physical education, physical education programs between the 1930s and the 1950s consisted of regular or corrective classes for students who today would be considered normal. Sherrill has succinctly described adapted physical education during this period as follows:

> Assignment to physical education was based upon a thorough medical examination by a physician who determined whether a student should participate in the regular or corrective program. Corrective classes were comprised primarily of limited, restricted, or modified activities related to health, posture, or fitness problems. In many schools students were excused from physical education. In others, the physical educator typically taught several sections of regular physical education each day. Leaders in corrective physical education continued to have strong backgrounds in medicine and/or physical therapy. Persons preparing to be physical education teachers generally completed one university course in corrective physical education.

Figure 1.3 Claudine Sherrill, a visionary leader on adapted physical education and sport. Dr. Sherrill has developed a comprehensive humanistic orientation to the field.

The Emerging Comprehensive Subdiscipline

During the 1950s and 1960s, more and more handicapped students were being served in public schools, and the outlook toward them was becoming increasingly humanistic. With the greater diversity in pupils came a greater diversity in programs to meet their needs. In 1952, the American Alliance for Health, Physical Education and Recreation (AAHPER) formed a Committee on Adapted Physical Education to define the subdiscipline and give direction and guidance to professionals. This committee defined adapted physical education as "a diversified program of developmental activities, games, sports, and rhythms suited to the interests, capacities, and limitations of students with disabilities who may not safely or successfully engage in unrestricted participation in the rigorous activities of the general physical education program" (Committee on Adapted Physical Education, 1952, p. 15). The definition retained the evolving diversity of physical education and specifically included students with disabilities. *Adapted physical education* and *special physical education* serve today as comprehensive terms for this subdiscipline.

According to Fait and Dunn (1989), special physical education is a particularly appropriate designation for this subdiscipline of physical education because of its connotation of meeting individual needs through special provisions in the physical education program.

Current Influences and Status

With the impetus provided by a more humanistic, more informed, and less discriminatory society, major advances in adapted physical education continued in the middle and late 1960s. Many of these advances were associated with the Joseph P. Kennedy family. In 1965, the Joseph P. Kennedy, Jr. Foundation awarded a grant to the American Alliance for Health, Physical Education, Recreation and Dance (AAHPERD) to launch the Project on Recreation and Fitness for the Mentally Retarded to advance physical education services for mentally retarded individuals. From this beginning, the project grew to encompass all special populations, and its name was changed in 1968 to the Unit on Programs for the Handicapped. The unit, eventually funded by AAHPERD, became engaged in several activities; a significant one was the development of the Information and Research Utilization Center (IRUC), supported by a grant from the Bureau of Education for the Handicapped (BEH), U.S. Office of Education. While assuming the directorship of the Unit on Programs for the Handicapped and the IRUC, Dr. Julian Stein (see Figure 1.4) was able to provide leadership in adapted physical education that had important impact throughout the United States at every level in the late 1960s and 1970s.

In 1968, the Kennedy Foundation exhibited further concern for the mentally retarded with the establishment of the Special Olympics. The Special Olympics movement grew rapidly, with

Figure 1.4 Julian (Buddy) Stein. Dr. Stein has provided sustained leadership in the field of adapted physical education and sport.

competition being held at local, state, national, and international levels in an ever-increasing list of sports.

During the mid-1960s, concern for emotionally disturbed and learning-disabled populations had a significant effect on adapted physical education. The importance of physical activity for the well-being of those with emotional problems was explicitly recognized by the National Institute of Mental Health (NIMH), U.S. Public Health Service, when it funded the Buttonwood Farms Project. This project was valuable for recognizing the importance of physical activity in the lives of persons with handicapping conditions, bringing the problems of seriously disturbed youngsters to the attention of educators, and developing curricular materials to prepare professionals in physical education and recreation for work with this population. Important contributors to the project were Harold Jack, Donald Hilsendager, and Lester Mann. During the same era, adapted physical education attracted much attention through the use of perceptual-motor activities as a basis or modality for academic and/or intellectual development—particularly with students with learning disabilities. Newell C. Kephart, Gerald N. Getman, Raymond

H. Barsch, Marianne Frostig, Phyllis Maslow, Bryant J. Cratty, and Jean A. Ayres were major authors who recommended motoric experiences as a basis or modality for perceptual and/or academic development. This influence was particularly strong in the 1970s and continues with varying degrees of emphasis today.

Contemporary direction and emphasis in adapted physical education are heavily associated with the individual's right to a free and appropriate education. Because of litigation and the passage of various federal laws and regulations (PL 94-142 in 1975, the rules and regulations of PL 93-112 in 1977, and PL 95-606 in 1978), change and progress have occurred in both adapted physical education and sport. The legal impetus has served to enhance individualized instruction, the development and use of testing and curricular materials, and the development of instructional models. Legislation has also resulted in more money for professional preparation, research, and other special projects relevant to the provision of full educational opportunity for persons with unique needs.

Litigation

Much has been and can be written about the impact of litigation on the guarantee of full educational opportunity. The most prominent of cases, which has served as an important precedent for civil litigation, was *Brown v. Board of Education* of Topeka, Kansas, in 1954. This case established that the doctrine of *separate but equal* in public education resulted in segregation that violated the constitutional rights of black persons. Two landmark cases also had heavy impact on the provision of free, appropriate public education for all handicapped children. The first was the class action suit of the *Pennsylvania Association for Retarded Children (PARC) v. Commonwealth of Pennsylvania* (1972). Equal protection and due process clauses associated with the Fifth and Fourteenth Amendments served as the constitutional basis for the court's rulings and agreements. The

following were among the rulings or agreements in the case:

- Labeling a child as mentally retarded or denying public education or placement in a regular setting without due process or hearing violated the rights of the individual.
- All mentally retarded persons are capable of benefiting from a program of education and training.
- Mental age may not be used to postpone or in any way deny access to a free public program of education and training.
- Having undertaken to provide a free, appropriate education to all its children, a state may not deny mentally retarded children the same.

A second important case was *Mills v. Board of Education* of the District of Columbia (1972). This action, brought on behalf of seven children, sought to restrain the District of Columbia from excluding children from public schools or denying them publicly supported education. The district court held that, by failing to provide the seven handicapped children and the class they represented with publicly supported specialized education, the district violated controlling statutes, its own regulations, and due process. The District of Columbia was required to provide a publicly supported education, appropriate equitable funding, and procedural due process rights to the seven children.

From 1972 to 1975, 46 right-to-education cases related to handicapped persons were tried in 28 different states. All these cases were important in providing the foundation for much of the legislation to be discussed in the next section.

Laws Important to Adapted Physical Education and Sport

Laws have had a tremendous influence on educational programs for individuals with handicapping conditions. With legislation supported by Senator Ted Kennedy in the late 1960s, the federal government began to provide funds for various projects in adapted physical education and therapeutic recreation. Since 1969, colleges and universities in many states have received federal funds for professional preparation, research, and other projects to enhance physical education and recreation programs for people with handicapping conditions. Although the amount of money made available has been relatively small, physical educators have gained a great deal from that support. Several well-known projects, which are mentioned later in this book, have been associated with federal funding.

A government agency that has been responsible for administering federally funded programs related to adapted physical education is the Bureau of Education for the Handicapped (BEH). Two advocates in this agency who have influenced physical education and recreation are William Hillman (professional preparation) and Mel Appell (research). When the Office of Education was given departmental status by President Carter, BEH became the Office of Special Education and Rehabilitative Services (OSERS).

PL 94-142

A major milestone in the education of the handicapped is PL 94-142, the Education for All Handicapped Children Act of 1975. This legislation was designed to assure that all handicapped children would have available to them a free, appropriate public education emphasizing *special education* and *related services* designed to meet their unique needs. PL 94-142 also ensures that the rights of handicapped children and their parents or guardians are protected and helps states and localities in providing education for all handicapped children (see Table 1.1). In the development of this legislation and its rules and regulations, the term *special education* was defined to mean specially designed instruction—including classroom instruction, instruction in physical education, home instruction, and instruction in hospitals and institutions—provided at no cost to parents or guardians to meet the unique

Table 1.1 Highlights of PL 94-142

PL 94-142 and its rules and regulations require

- a right to a free and appropriate education;
- physical education available to every handicapped student;
- equal opportunity in athletics and intramurals;
- an individualized education program (IEP) designed to meet unique needs;
- a program developed by a planning committee including parents and, if appropriate, the student;
- a program conducted in the least restrictive environment;
- nondiscriminatory testing and objective criteria for placement;
- due process; and
- related services to assist in special education.

needs of a handicapped child. The term *related services* was defined as transportation and such developmental, corrective, and other supportive services (including speech pathology and audiology, psychological services, physical and occupational therapy, recreation, and medical and counseling services) as may be required to help the handicapped child benefit from special education.

Definition and Requirements of Physical Education

To clarify the meaning of physical education, the rules and regulations implementing PL 94-142 defined *physical education* as *the development of physical and motor fitness, fundamental motor skills, and patterns, along with skills in aquatics, dance, and individual and group games and sports (including intramural and lifetime sports).* The rules and regulations state that the term includes *special physical education, adapted physical education, movement education, and motor development.*

Figure 1.5 Physical education is for all pupils.

PL 94-142 specifies that special education, including physical education, must be made available and that it must include physical education specially designed, if necessary, to meet unique needs. This federal legislation, together with state requirements for physical education, impacts significantly upon adapted physical education in schools (see Figure 1.5).

Free, Appropriate Public Education

The term *free, appropriate public education* means special education and related services that are provided at public expense in conformity with an individualized education program (or IEP), a written statement prepared for each handicapped child. The IEP is developed by a representative of the local education agency or an intermediate educational unit qualified to provide or supervise the provision of specially designed instruction and by the teacher, the parents or guardians, and— where appropriate—the child. The statement must include present levels of educational performance; annual goals (including short-term instructional objectives); specific educational services to be provided; the extent to which the child will be able to participate in regular educational programs; the projected date for initiation and anticipated duration of such services; and appropriate objective criteria and evaluation procedures and schedules for determining, on at least an annual basis, whether instructional objectives are being achieved. The development of an IEP, a crucial requirement of PL 94-142, is discussed in detail in chapter 3.

Least Restrictive Environment

PL 94-142 also requires that education be conducted in the least restrictive environment. According to the iaw, each handicapped child must have the opportunity to participate in the regular physical education program available to non-handicapped children, unless the child is enrolled full time in separate facilities or needs specially designed physical education as prescribed in the IEP.

Basic to education in the most appropriate setting is a continuum of alternative placements (see chapter 2), which range from a situation in which handicapped children are integrated into a regular class (mainstreamed setting) to a very restrictive setting (out-of-school segregated placement).

Focus on Student Needs and Opportunity

PL 94-142 has encouraged educators to focus on the educational needs of the student instead of on clinical or diagnostic labels. As the IEP is developed, concern is with present level of functioning, objectives, annual goals, and the like. PL 94-142 does not require that handicapping condition(s) be identified on an IEP. The associated rules and regulations also indicate that handicapped children must be provided *equal opportunity* for participation in nonacademic and extracurricular services and activities, including athletics, intramurals, and recreational services. The right of equal opportunity emerges from another legislative milestone which has had an impact on both adapted physical education and sport—Section 504 of the Rehabilitation Act of 1973, PL 93-112. Section 504 provides that ''no otherwise qualified handicapped individual . . . solely by reason of his handicap, be excluded from participation in, be denied the benefits of, or be subject to discrimination under any program or activity receiving federal financial assistance'' (Department of Health, Education, and Welfare, 1977b).

As identified in a position statement developed by Winnick, Auxter, Jansma, Sculli, Stein, and Weiss (1980), an important intent of Section 504 is to ensure that individuals with handicapping conditions receive intended benefits of *all* educational programs and extracurricular activities. Two conditions are prerequisite to the delivery of services that guarantee benefits to those individuals: Programs must be equally effective, and they must be conducted in the most normal and integrated settings possible. To be equally effective, a program must offer individuals with handicapping conditions *equal* opportunity to attain the same results, gain the same benefits, or reach the same levels of achievement as peers without handicapping conditions.

To illustrate the basic intent of Section 504, let us consider a totally blind student enrolled in a college course in which all other students are sighted. A written test given at the end of the semester would not provide the blind student equal oppor-

tunity to demonstrate knowledge of the material; this approach would not be equally effective. By contrast, on a test administered orally or in braille, the blind student would have an equal opportunity to attain the same results or benefits as the other students. In giving an oral exam, the instructor would be providing *equivalent*, as opposed to *identical*, service. (Merely identical services, in fact, would be considered discriminatory and not in accord with Section 504.) It is neither necessary nor possible to *guarantee* equal results; what is important is the *equal opportunity to attain* those results. Thus, for example, a recipient of federal funds offering basketball to the general student population must provide wheelchair basketball for students confined to wheelchairs, *if a need exists*.

A program is not equally effective if it results in indiscriminate isolation or segregation of individuals with handicapping conditions. To the maximum degree possible, those with handicapping conditions should participate in the *least restrictive environment* as represented by a continuum of alternative placements (see chapter 2).

Compliance with Section 504 requires *program accessibility*; its rules and regulations prohibit exclusion of individuals with handicapping conditions from federally assisted programs because of architectural or other environmental barriers. Common barriers to accessibility include facilities, finances, and transportation. Money available for athletics within a school district cannot be spent in a way that discriminates on the basis of handicapping conditions. If a district lacks sufficient funds, then it is not obligated to offer programs; however, it cannot fund programs in a discriminatory manner.

History of Adapted Sport

Deaf athletes were among the first people with handicapping conditions to become visible on the sport scene. In tracing the history of sport competition in the United States, Gannon (1981) reports considerable activity in the late 1800s on the part of deaf athletes. In the 1870s the state school in Ohio became the first school for the deaf to offer baseball, and the state school in Illinois introduced football in 1885. Football became a major sport in many schools for the deaf around the turn of the century, and basketball was introduced at the Wisconsin School for the Deaf in 1906. Since these beginnings, teams from schools for the deaf have continued to compete against each other and against athletes in regular schools.

Beyond these school-related programs, formal international competition was established in 1924. In that year, competitors from nine nations gathered in Paris for the First International Silent Games Competition (see milestones in Table 1.2). In 1945, the American Athletic Association for the Deaf (AAAD) was established to provide, sanction, and promote competitive sport opportunities for individuals with hearing impairments in the United States. In 1965, the United States hosted the international summer games for deaf athletes in Washington, D.C.

The earliest formal, recorded athletic competition in the United States for individuals with visual handicaps was a telegraphic track meet between the Overbrook and Baltimore Schools for the Blind in 1907. In a telegraphic meet, results obtained from athletes participating at the local level are mailed to a control committee, which makes comparisons and determines winners. In recognition of the need of blind athletes in the United States for an organization to sponsor and promote ath-

Table 1.2 Milestones in the Evolution of Adapted Sport

1870s	Schools for the deaf are involved in organized team sport competition.
1907	A telegraphic track meet is held between the Overbrook and Baltimore Schools for the Blind—earliest formal and recorded sports competition in the U.S. for individuals with visual handicaps.
1924	The first International Silent Games Competition is held at Pershing Stadium, Paris, France.
1945	The American Athletic Association for the Deaf (AAAD) is formed.
1949	The National Wheelchair Basketball Association (NWBA) is formed.
1952	The first international wheelchair games are held at Stoke Mandeville, England.
1956	The National Wheelchair Athletic Association is formed.
1960	The International Stoke Mandeville Games, called the Paralympic Games, are held in conjunction with the Olympic Games in Rome.
1967	The National Handicapped Sports and Recreation Association (NHSRA) is formed.
1968	Special Olympics is founded and the first international Special Olympic Games are held at Soldier Field, Chicago.
1975	PL 94-142 is passed, requiring equal opportunity for participation in athletics by handicapped children.
1977	The rules and regulations governing Section 504 of PL 93-112, The Rehabilitation Act of 1973, are written, requiring that handicapped children receive the benefits of all educational programs and educational activities.
1978	PL 95-606, the Amateur Sports Act, leads to the establishment of a Committee on Sports for the Disabled (COSD) within the U.S. Olympic Committee (USOC).
1978	The National Association of Sports for Cerebral Palsy (NASCP) is formed.
1981	The United States Amputee Athletic Association (USAAA) is formed.
1985	The United States Les Autres Sports Association (USLASA) is formed.

letic competition on regional, national, and international levels, the United States Association for Blind Athletes (USABA) was formed in 1976. Its first national championship meet was held from March 30 to April 2, 1977, at Western Illinois University in Macomb, Illinois.

World War Era

Since the 1900s, wars have provided great impetus for competitive sport opportunities for individuals with handicapping conditions. Sir Ludwig Guttman of Stoke Mandeville, England, is credited with introducing competitive sports as an integral part of the rehabilitation of disabled veterans; in the 1940s Stoke Mandeville Hospital sponsored the first recognized games for wheelchair athletes. In 1949, the University of Illinois organized the first national wheelchair basketball tournament in the United States; it resulted in the formation of the National Wheelchair Basketball Association (NWBA). To expand sport opportunities, Ben Lipton founded the National Wheelchair Athletic Association (NWAA) in the mid-1950s. This organization sponsors various competitive sports on state, regional, and national levels for the spinal cord–injured and the wheelchair-bound amputee.

In 1960, 8 years after the start of international competition for wheelchair athletes, the International Stoke Mandeville Games Federation (ISMGF) was formed to sanction annual international competition for individuals with spinal cord injuries. Since 1960, international competition for wheelchair athletes has been held at Stoke Mandeville annually and every fourth year in the city hosting the Olympic Games. This competition, designated in 1960 as the Paralympics, became the Olympics for the Disabled in 1980. The United States' involvement in these games dates back to 1960.

Recent Influences and Developments

A more recent advancement in the United States in the realm of adapted sport was the creation of the National Handicapped Sports and Recreation Association (NHSRA). The organization, formed by a small group of Vietnam veterans, has been dedicated since 1967 to providing year-round sports and recreation opportunities for people with orthopedic, spinal cord, neuromuscular, and visual impairments.

In 1968, Special Olympics, created by the Joseph P. Kennedy, Jr. Foundation, held its first international games at Soldier Field in Chicago. (A symbol of Special Olympics is shown in Figure 1.6.) This organization has served as the model sport organization for people with handicapping conditions through its contributions in direct service, research, training, advocacy, education, and organizational leadership.

Figure 1.6 A symbol of Special Olympics. Gift of the Union of Soviet Socialist Republics on the occasion of the 1979 International Special Olympic Games hosted by State University of New York, College at Brockport. The artist is Zurab Tsereteli.

To govern sport programs in the United States for individuals with cerebral palsy and similar neurological conditions, the National Association of Sports for Cerebral Palsy (NASCP) was formed in 1978. In that year, the first national cerebral palsy games were held in Detroit and the first U.S. team attended the fourth international games for individuals with cerebral palsy in Scotland. The United States Cerebral Palsy Athletic Association (USCPAA), which has replaced NASCP, currently organizes sports for cerebral-palsied athletes in the United States.

In 1981, a small group of amputee athletes founded the United States Amputee Athletic Association (USAAA). The organization sponsors national competition annually in a variety of events and cooperates with organizations providing international competition for the amputee athlete. The first national amputee games were held in Nashville, at the Tennessee State University campus in 1981.

Although evolving programs were increasingly meeting the needs of disabled athletes, there were still many youngsters not eligible for organized sport opportunities in the 1970s and 1980s. To address this situation, sport competition for Les Autres (the others) was developed for disabled athletes not eligible to participate in other programs. Athletes designated as Les Autres competed in the 1984 International Games for the Disabled and in the 1985 Cerebral Palsy/Les Autres games. The United States Les Autres Sports Association (USLASA) was founded in 1985 to meet the specific needs of its athletes.

In addition to the various sport programs leading to Olympic-level competition, there are several others national in scope. Most of these programs have provided services for a specific disability in a specific sport; they are discussed in other parts of this book.

Passed in the 1970s, PL 94-142 and Section 504 of PL 93-112 serve today as a legal impetus for the provision of equal opportunity for participation in athletics by handicapped persons in institutions receiving federal financial assistance. Subsequently, PL 95-606, the Amateur Sports Act of 1978, was passed to coordinate national efforts concerning amateur athletic activity, including competition for handicapped athletes. This legislation led to the establishment of the Committee on Sports for the Disabled (COSD), a standing committee of the United States Olympic Committee (USOC) that consists of representatives from several sport organizations serving athletes with handicapping conditions. In addition to its work coordinating and stimulating the sports movement for athletes with disabilities, the COSD has been active in obtaining facilities and other services for the training of disabled athletes.

In the past few years, much of the impetus for sports for disabled athletes has been provided by out-of-school sport organizations. Other opportunities have also begun to surface throughout the United States in association with public school programs. For example, the Special School District of St. Louis County, Missouri, has developed competitive athletic opportunities for individuals with handicapping conditions: Participants from various special schools are matched in competitions among similar populations during the school day. In 1981, the Minnesota Association for Adapted Athletes (MAAA) was established to provide athletic programs for students with disabilities.

In 1985, the first New York State Games for the Physically Challenged were conducted, with government financing. The games are an alternative to New York's Empire State Games for able-bodied athletes. Several states now provide statewide athletic competition for athletes with handicapping conditions.

Periodicals

The increased knowledge base and greater attention to adapted physical education and sport in recent years have been accompanied by the founding and development of several periodicals devoted to the subject. Among the most relevant of these are the *Adapted Physical Activity Quarterly*, *Palaestra*, and *Sports 'N Spokes* (Figure 1.7). It is through his role as editor of *Adapted Physical Activity Quarterly* that Dr. Geoffrey D. Broadhead has contributed significantly to the body of knowledge in adapted physical education (Figure 1.8).

Other periodicals that publish directly relevant

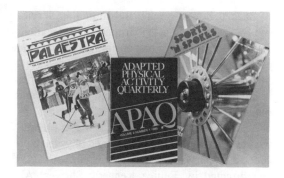

Figure 1.7 Three important periodicals in adapted physical education and sport.

Figure 1.8 Geoffrey D. Broadhead. Dr. Broadhead has contributed substantially to the body of knowledge in adapted physical education and sport as editor of the *Adapted Physical Activity Quarterly*.

information from time to time include *Journal of Physical Education, Recreation and Dance*; *Research Quarterly for Exercise and Sport*; *Journal of Visual Impairment and Blindness*; *Journal of Learning Disabilities; Exceptional Education Quarterly*; *American Annals of the Deaf*; *Teaching Exceptional Children*; *Exceptional Children*; *American Journal of Mental Deficiency*; *Journal of Special Education*; *Therapeutic Recreation Journal*; *Journal of the Association for the Severely Handicapped*; *Education and Training of the Mentally Retarded*; and *Clinical Kinesiology*, formerly the *American Corrective Therapy Journal*.

Organizations

The American Alliance for Health, Physical Education, Recreation and Dance (AAHPERD) is an important national organization that has made and continues to make significant contributions to programs for special populations. AAHPERD (previously AAHPER, before the dance discipline was added) has many members whose primary professional concern lies in adapted physical education. As mentioned earlier, it was members of this organization who established a definition of adapted physical education in 1952. AAHPERD is the organization that administered the Project on Recreation and Fitness for the Mentally Retarded and developed the Unit on Programs for the Handicapped. Over the years, its many publications, conferences, and conventions have focused much attention on adapted physical education—not only on the national level but within the organization's state, district, and local affiliates. The professional conferences and conventions that AAHPERD conducts on its many levels are among the best sources of information on adapted physical education and sport. At the national level, the organization continues to be a physical education and physical fitness advocate on behalf of handicapped persons. It has also been a leader in defining competencies required for quality professional preparation in adapted physical education. In the past few years AAHPERD has spent considerable attention on organizing itself to better serve handicapped persons. An organization within AAHPERD, the Adapted Physical Activity Council, is now directly associated with adapted physical education. It is expected that this council, established in 1985, will continue to provide key professional services and leadership in adapted physical education and sport.

In 1976, the National Consortium on Physical Education and Recreation for the Handicapped

(NCPERH, or the Consortium) was established to promote, stimulate, encourage, and conduct professional preparation and research in physical education and recreation for handicapped persons. The organization was started informally in the late 1960s by a small group of college and university directors of federally funded professional preparation and/or research projects seeking to share information. In 1973, this informal group formed the National Advisory Committee on Physical Education and Recreation for Handicapped Children and Youth; in 1976, it formed NCPERH. Since its initiation, the organization has been made up of individuals with extensive background and interest in adapted physical education and/or therapeutic recreation. They have provided leadership and counsel on national issues and concerns, including the development of PL 94-142 and its rules and regulations; federal funding for professional preparation, research, demonstration projects and other special projects; and the monitoring of legislation. In addition to a number of ongoing activities, the Consortium holds an annual meeting and publishes a newsletter.

A rapidly developing international organization created to enhance physical activity services for special populations is the International Federation for Adapted Physical Activity (IFAPA). IFAPA, which originated in the Canadian province of Quebec, has expanded to a worldwide organization with an international charter. Its primary service has been the sponsorship of an international adapted physical activity symposium held biannually. It has been held in Quebec (1977), Brussels (1979), New Orleans (1981), London (1983), Toronto (1985), Brisbane (1987), and Berlin (1989). The organization primarily solicits memberships from allied health therapists, therapeutic recreators, and adapted physical educators. With its international dimensions, IFAPA has the potential of disseminating valuable knowledge throughout the world.

A governmental agency with an important impact on adapted physical education is the Office of Special Education and Rehabilitation Service (OSERS) within the Department of Education. This federal agency is responsible for monitoring educational services for handicapped students and for providing grants to colleges and universities to fund professional preparation, research, and other special projects.

A private organization that has made a monumental contribution to both adapted physical education and sport is Special Olympics, Inc., founded and directed by Eunice Kennedy Shriver. Although its leadership in providing sport opportunities for the mentally retarded is well known, this organization has provided much more to adapted physical education and sport. Specifically, it has played a key role in the attention to physical education in federal legislation and the provision of federal funding for professional preparation, research, and other projects through its advocacy activities. The organization has provided a worldwide model for the provision of sport opportunities; its work is acknowledged in several sections of this book.

Many other organizations of a diverse nature have made and continue to make contributions to adapted physical education and sport. Some of these are mentioned earlier in this chapter; others are recognized elsewhere in this book. The appendix lists names and addresses of several sport organizations. Although space does not permit a detailed description of each one, they all provide valuable services and play important roles for adapted physical education and sport.

Summary

Gradually there has evolved an awareness that there are people with unique needs related to physical education and sport, needs that require special provisions or adaptations for fulfillment. This chapter has introduced adapted physical education and sport and highlighted factors that have affected their development.

Bibliography

Amateur Sports Act of 1978, § 36 U.S.C. § 371 (1978).

Brown v. Board of Education, 347 U.S. 483 (1954).

Buell, C.E. (1983). *Physical education for blind children* (2nd ed.). Springfield, IL: Charles C. Thomas.

Committee on Adapted Physical Education. (1952). Guiding principles for adapted physical education. *Journal of Health, Physical Education and Recreation*, **23**, 15.

Department of Health, Education, and Welfare (1977a). Education of handicapped children. *Federal Register*, **42**(163), 42434-42516.

Department of Health, Education, and Welfare (1977b). Nondiscrimination on basis of handicap. *Federal Register*, **42**(86), 22676-22702.

Fait, H.F., & Dunn, J.M. (1989). *Special physical education: Adapted, individualized, and developmental* (6th ed.). Dubuque, IA: Wm. C. Brown.

Gannon, J.R. (1981). *Deaf heritage: A narrative history of deaf America*. Silver Spring, MD: National Association for the Deaf.

Mills v. Board of Education of the District of Columbia, 348 F. Supp. 966 (1972).

The Pennsylvania Association for Retarded Children v. Commonwealth of Pennsylvania, U.S. District Court, 343 F. Supp. 279 (1972).

Sherrill, C. (1986). *Adapted physical education and recreation: A multidisciplinary approach* (3rd ed.). Dubuque, IA: Wm. C. Brown.

Winnick, J.P., Auxter, D., Jansma, P., Sculli, J., Stein, J., & Weiss, R.A. (1980). Implications of Section 504 of the Rehabilitation Act as related to physical education instructional, personnel preparation, intramural, and interscholastic/intercollegiate sport programs. *Practical Pointers*, **3**(11), 1-20.

Resources

The references just cited are excellent resources for more detailed and comprehensive information concerning the topics discussed in this chapter. Particularly recommended are Sherrill's definition of and orientation to adapted physical education (1986), Buell's writings on physical education for blind children (1983), and Gannon's (1981) book on sport for deaf athletes. Reading the position statement pertaining to Section 504 of PL 93-112 developed by Winnick, Auxter, Jansma, Sculli, Stein, and Weiss (1980) is also encouraged.

CHAPTER 2

Program Organization and Management

Joseph P. Winnick

For effective organization and management, schools are advised to develop written guidelines for their adapted physical education and sport programs or to include in general physical education plans detailed provisions related to adapted physical education and sport. The guidelines can serve as an operating code that reflects laws, regulations, policies, procedures, and practices. The information in this chapter can help schools develop guidelines and their own specific plans.

Programmatic and Curricular Direction

One necessary step in developing a school's adapted physical education program is to clearly identify programmatic and curricular direction. A framework for direction may include a philosophical statement, program aims, curricular goals, and curricular objectives. Because there is no universal model, each school or educational program must establish or adopt its own. A skeletal curricular framework (see Figure 2.1) can serve as a point of reference for school programs and as an organizational model for this book. This framework assumes that the program in adapted physical education is a part of the total physical education and sport program and that it contributes to the same programmatic aims. In essence, the program strives to develop each individual to the maximum so that the needs of the individual and of society can be served. This aim is primarily accomplished by development *of* and *through* the psychomotor domain.

The general content areas related to psychomotor development can be grouped in many ways. For this book, four general areas are identified: physical fitness, motor development, posture and body mechanics, and community- and sport-related activities (see Figure 2.1). Each of these content areas includes specific sport skills or developmental areas. For example, walking is a developmental area that can be included within the larger content area of motor development. Age-appropriate neighborhood skills like those shown in Figure 2.2 can be included in one or more of the content areas.

The general content areas or content goals shown in Figure 2.1 may serve as annual goals for individualized education programs, while specific skills and developmental areas associated with these goals may represent short-term objectives. For example, an annual goal in a student's IEP might be to improve physical fitness; the corresponding specific short-term objective might be to improve flexibility by obtaining a score of 25 cm on a sit-and-reach test. Objectives can be expressed on several levels to reflect the specificity desired by a teacher.

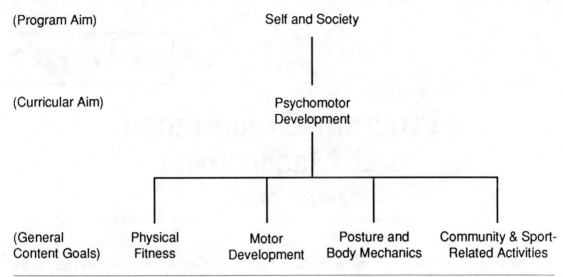

Figure 2.1 Aims and goals of an adapted physical education program.

Administrative Procedures and Program Implementation

Identifying Students for Adapted Physical Education

In identifying students for adapted physical education, it is important at the outset to determine who is qualified for the program. In some instances the decision is obvious, and an elaborate system of identification is not necessary. In other instances, students will have unique needs that are not readily apparent. Essentially, adapted physical education is for students with unique needs who require a specially designed program exceeding a duration of 30 consecutive calendar days. In the selection of candidates for such a program, procedures, criteria, and standards for determining unique needs are critical (they are discussed in chapters 3 and 4). Placement in the lowest 10th percentile on a physical fitness test is an example of one criterion and standard for establishing unique need.

Searching for adapted physical education stu-dents involves one or more important activities associated with *child find*. These include

- screening all new school entrants,
- screening students with handicapping conditions,
- annual screening of *all* students,
- screening referrals, and
- screening students requesting exemption from physical education.

Each child-find activity is discussed in more detail in the following paragraphs.

An important child-find activity is the screening of all new entrants to the school, those who are beginning their formal education or transferring to the school. For transfer students, records should be checked to determine whether unique needs in physical education have been identified. In the absence of such information, the school, as part of its procedures, may decide to administer a screening test if a unique physical education need is suspected.

A second child find source is a list of enrolled students who have been identified as handicapped in accord with PL 94-142. Every student who has

Figure 2.2 Age-appropriate neighborhood skills, an important part of physical education: a) pedaling the "Big Wheel," b) batting the ball, c) pushing the scooter, and d) riding the tricycle.

been so identified and whose handicapping condition is frequently associated with unique physical education needs should be routinely screened. In some school districts, all students identified as handicapped must undergo a screening test to determine if a unique physical education need exists. In other districts, only pupils who are mentally retarded or have orthopedic, visual, learning, or other health impairments are routinely tested. Thus, for example, a speech-impaired student classified as handicapped by a school district would not be routinely tested unless a unique need in physical education were suspected.

A third source of adapted physical education students is the annual screening of all those enrolled in the school. Such screening might involve informal observation as well as the administration of a screening test. Conditions that may be detected through informal screening and may warrant in-depth evaluation include (but are not limited to) handicapping conditions, obesity, clumsiness, aversion to physical activity, and postural deviations.

Many students are referred to adapted physical education. Guidelines should permit referrals from parents or persons in parental relationship; professional staff members in the school district; physicians; judicial offices or officers; representatives of public agencies with the responsibility for a student's welfare, health, or education; or the student if at least 18 years of age or an emancipated minor. Referrals for adapted physical education should be received by one designated person in the school.

Medical excuses or requests for exemption from physical education are a common source of adapted physical education referrals. When an excuse or request is made, immediate discussion with the family physician may be necessary to help determine the needed duration of the adaptation. For a period of fewer than 30 consecutive days, required adjustments can be determined by the regular physical education teacher following established local policies and procedures. If the period is longer than 30 consecutive days, the procedure for identifying students in adapted physical education should be followed.

Instructional Placements in Physical Education

Individuals who are referred or are otherwise identified as possibly requiring a specially designed program should undergo thorough assessment to determine whether unique needs exist. Chapters 3 and 4 deal with the procedures for assessment.

Once it is established that students have unique needs in physical education, they must be placed in appropriate instructional settings. To the extent possible, the most normal/integrated setting should be provided. Typical (though not all-inclusive) options on a continuum of instructional arrangements appear in Figure 2.3. The number of options available is less important than the concept that students will be educated in the environment most conducive to their advancement. The continuum clearly depicts more possibilities than regular or segregated adapted physical education. Although these two placements may be appropriate for some students with unique needs, they are not sufficient to meet the needs of all members of this population.

At the base of the cascade of instructional placement is regular class placement, Level 1, for students without unique needs or those whose short-term unique needs are met by the regular physical education teacher. This placement is also appropriate for individuals with long-term unique needs that can be met in the regular physical education setting.

Level 2 is for students whose unique needs can be met in regular class placement with support service assistance. For example, some students may function well in a regular class if consultation is available to teachers and parents. In another instance, regular class placement may be warranted if an aide can assist the individual with unique needs in a regular class.

Level 3 is regular class placement with supplementary and/or resource room assistance, as appropriate. Supplementary services can be provided each day or several times weekly, as a part of or in addition to the time scheduled for physical education. Where resource room assistance is indicated, the student may spend a portion of the physical education time in a resource room.

Students with unique needs who require part-time special class placement represent Level 4. Their needs might be met at times in a regular class

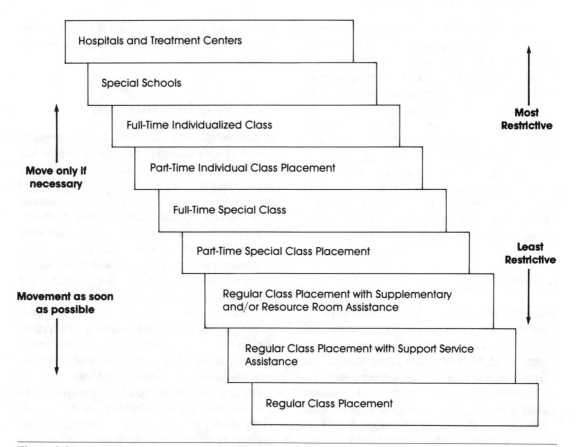

Figure 2.3 Continuum of instructional placements in physical education.

and at times in an adapted physical education class. To a great extent, the choice of setting would be determined by the nature of the class activity.

Level 5, full-time placement in a special class, is appropriate for those whose unique needs may not safely or successfully be met through unrestricted activity in the regular physical education program. Levels 6 and 7 are appropriate when part- or full-time individualized instruction is necessary because the individual's needs differ greatly from those of other students.

Levels 8 and 9 reflect instructional placements in which unique needs must be met outside the regular school. In Level 8, instruction is provided in special schools; in Level 9, instruction may be given in hospitals and/or treatment centers. Students in Levels 8 and 9 may be placed outside the school district. In such cases it is important to remember that the local school system is still responsible for ensuring that appropriate education is provided.

In addition to individual need, another variable that must be considered in placement is class size. For example, if students with unique needs are placed in regular classes with support service, those classes must be appropriately managed by the physical education teacher. Although no single teacher-student ratio can be prescribed, a reasonable guideline is not to exceed 25 students per class. This number should be reduced to equal

5 students for every individual with unique needs placed in a class. Thus, in a class including 3 students with long-term unique needs, the total number should not exceed 15. Special classes should not exceed 12 students; this number should be reduced to 6 homogeneous students when extraordinary needs are exhibited. In certain instances, individualized instruction may be warranted. Chronological age affects placement as well. *Age difference within a class should never exceed 3 years unless the students are 16 or older.* In any case, school officials should know and comply with their state laws and regulations governing class size and composition.

Scheduling

Scheduling becomes an important matter as placement decisions are made. There are many approaches to scheduling that can accommodate the variety of possible instructional arrangements. One effective method is to schedule supplementary and resource services and adapted physical education classes at the same time as regular physical education classes. A large school might have four physical education teachers assigned to four regular classes during a single period, with a fifth teacher assigned to adapted physical education. Other instructional arrangements might provide extra class time on alternate days from regular physical education classes, alternate periods, or opportunities during elective periods. In one scheduling technique used in elementary schools, a youngster placed in a special academic class joins an appropriate regular class for physical education. This arrangement meets that student's need to be mainstreamed in physical education while receiving a special support in academic areas. Too often, students who could have been integrated in a regular physical education class are placed in a special class primarily on the basis of academic or other performance unrelated to physical education. Schools in which students are permitted to elect physical education courses or units often find scheduling problems reduced because students

may choose activities in which they can participate with little or no adjustment and that fit their schedules.

Time Requirements

In adapted physical education, it is important to clearly specify time requirements (frequency and duration) for the instructional phase of the program. The frequency and duration of the required instructional program should at least equal those of the regular physical education program. If state time requirements for regular physical education are specified for various grade levels, and if adapted physical education students are placed in ungraded programs, the school's guidelines will need to express equivalent time requirements using chronological age as the common reference point. In accord with federal legislation, a local school district plan should state that physical education, specially designed, must be made available to all students identified as handicapped.

Physical education should be required of all students and should be adapted to meet the needs of those who are temporarily or permanently incapable of unrestricted participation in regular activities. In cases of temporary disability, it is important to ascertain how long the student will require adapted physical education and to set a standard to distinguish temporary and long-term conditions. For this book, a short-term condition lasts fewer than 30 consecutive days and can be accommodated by the regular classroom teacher. To the extent possible and reasonable, participation in physical activity rather than alternative, sedentary experiences should be required. For evaluation purposes, schools should set standards concerning the proportion of their students who participate in physical education but not in physical activity. When many students meet physical education requirements through inactivity, it is time to reassess the local program.

School districts also need to confront the issue of permitting participation in athletic activities as a substitute for physical education. Although coordination of instruction and sport participation (regular or adapted) is necessary, substitution should not be made unless it is approved in the student's IEP and the practice is in accord with the school district's overall physical education plan. Ordinarily, substitution of sport participation for physical education should not be permitted.

School districts must also clarify and coordinate instructional time requirements with related services. For instance, time spent in physical therapy should not supplant time in the physical education program. If appropriate guidelines are developed, few if any students will be exempt from physical education, physical education will mean physical activity, and physical education will not be replaced by related services or extracurricular activities.

Sports

Guidelines for Sport Participation

An adapted physical education plan should include general guidelines on sport participation and its relationship to the physical education program. In view of the detail involved in implementing a comprehensive extraclass sport program, a specific operating code should also be developed for local use. It is recommended that the extraclass program be established on the assumption that the sport program and the adapted physical education program are interrelated and interdependent. The sport program should build upon the basic instructional program in adapted physical education and should be educational in nature.

A sport program should emphasize the well-being of the participants in the context of games and sports. It is also important to assure participation to the extent possible and reasonable. Health examinations before participation in strenuous activities and periodically throughout the season, if necessary, will enhance safe participation. Athletes with handicapping conditions should receive, at minimum, the same medical safeguards as other athletes.

For an interscholastic program, it is important to have a written statement of the principal educational goals of the program as agreed to by the Board of Education, the school administration, and any other relevant individuals or groups. The statement should reflect a concern with the welfare of students, an interest in the educational aspects of athletic competition, and a commitment to the development of skills that will yield health and leisure benefits during as well as after the school years.

Integration Continuum

In the past few years, increasing attention has been given to providing sport opportunities for individuals with handicapping conditions or disabilities. In response to the intent of Section 504 of the Rehabilitation Act of 1973, educational and extracurricular opportunities must be provided in the least restrictive (most normal/integrated) setting possible, on the basis of a continuum of settings ranging from the most restrictive (segregated) to the least restrictive (integrated). Figure 2.4 presents a framework for a sport continuum to help enhance *integration* to the maximum extent possible, help guide decisions on sport participation, and help stimulate the provision of innovative opportunities along the continuum. The continuum and the related material in this section were published originally by Winnick (1987).

The continuum, which relates to the provision of programs in the least restrictive environment, encompasses opportunities in intramural, extramural, and interschool programs as well as out-of-school sport programs. (For this book, all are included under the designation of sport.) In the following paragraphs, levels on the continuum are explained in detail.

Levels 1 and 2 are essentially regular sport settings and are distinguished only by a need for accommodation. In regular sport the setting is integrated. Individuals with handicapping conditions should be given equal opportunity to qualify for participation at these levels. An example of Level 1 participation would be a mentally retarded

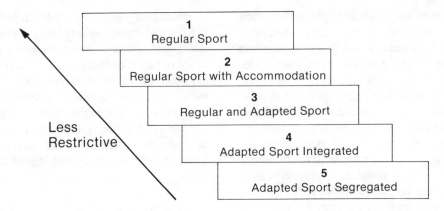

Figure 2.4 Sport integration continuum. *Note.* From "An Integration Continuum for Sport Participation" by J.P. Winnick, 1987, *Adapted Physical Activity Quarterly,* **4**, p. 158. Copyright 1987 by Human Kinetics. Reprinted by permission.

athlete running the dash for a regular high school track team. According to the framework, if that individual qualified for regular track competition, Special Olympics competition would be inappropriate because it would occur in a more segregated (restrictive) setting. Regular participation in a particular sport should not be supplemented or supplanted by more restrictive participation in the same sport.

In accord with Section 504, schools and agencies should provide modified or special activities only if (a) they operate programs and activities in the most normal and appropriate setting, (b) qualified students with handicapping conditions are not denied opportunity to participate in programs and activities that are not separate and different, (c) qualified students with handicapping conditions are able to participate in one or more regular programs and activities, and (d) students with handicapping conditions are appropriately placed full time in special facilities (Department of Health, Education, and Welfare, 1977; Winnick et al., 1980).

A blind bowler participating in regular sport competition with only the accommodation of a guide rail exemplifies Level 2. Section 504 rules and regulations require that any accommodation provided at this level be reasonable and allow in-

dividuals with handicapping conditions equal opportunity to gain the same benefits or results as other participants in a particular activity. At the same time, accommodation should not confer an unfair advantage on an individual with a handicapping condition. In the case of the blind bowler, the guide rail serves as a substitute for vision for the purpose of orientation to the target. Because the activity remains essentially unchanged for all participants and no undue advantage is given, this accommodation constitutes regular sport participation.

Level 3 includes both regular and adapted sport conducted in settings that are partly or fully integrated, or integrated part time. At this level, those with handicapping conditions may compete against or coact with all participants in a contest including both handicapped and able-bodied competitors. For instance, a handicapped athlete participating in a wheelchair (adapted sport) may compete against all runners in a marathon including able-bodied and handicapped athletes; able-bodied athletes run on foot (regular sport). In another Level 3 example, handicapped and able-bodied athletes may cooperate as doubles partners in wheelchair tennis. The able-bodied partner is permitted one bounce before returning a ball (regular sport), whereas the handicapped player is permitted two bounces (adapted sport) before returning a volley.

Level 3 also includes situations in which an athlete participates part time in regular sport and part time in adapted sport. For example, a blind person may participate in regular weight-lifting competition, but in adapted sport competition for goal ball. Level 3 activities show either (a) able-bodied and handicapped athletes integrated and participating in regular sport and adapted sport, respectively, or (b) handicapped athletes participating part time in adapted sport and part time in regular sport.

At Level 4 *both* able-bodied and handicapped athletes participate in a modified version of the sport. At this level, competition or coaction must include both a person with a handicapping condition and an able-bodied participant. One example is a game of tennis in which both able-bodied and handicapped athletes use wheelchairs in competing against opponents who are likewise in wheelchairs.

At Level 5, handicapped athletes participate in adapted sport in a totally segregated setting. A mentally retarded athlete participating in the Special Olympics program is an illustration. Two teams of blind youngsters competing in goal ball also exemplify Level 5.

The conceptual framework for the sport continuum is primarily based on degree of integration (with cooperator/coactor and/or competitor) and sport type (regular or adapted). The continuum stresses association or interaction between able-bodied and disabled athletes, the key ingredient in *integration*. To some extent, the continuum reflects severity of handicapping condition and ability to compete, but at other times it appears less responsive to this concern. This is because *nature* of handicapping condition and *ability* to perform, as related to a specific sport, are more important factors than *severity* of condition.

Facilities

The facilities available for adapted physical education and sport programs may significantly affect program quality. A school's overall athletic facilities should be operated in a way that makes them readily accessible to individuals with handicapping conditions. In fact, Section 504 rules and regulations prohibit exclusion of such individuals from federally assisted programs because of architectural, program, or other environmental barriers. Provision of access may dictate structural changes in existing facilities. All new facilities should be constructed to ensure accessibility and usability.

In planning facilities related to adapted physical education and sport, attention must be given to indoor and outdoor facilities, including teaching stations, lockers, and restrooms (see examples in Figures 2.5 and 2.6). Indoor facilities should have adequate activity space that is clear of hazards or impediments and is otherwise safe. The environment must have proper lighting, acoustics, and ventilation. Ceiling clearance should permit appropriate play. Floors should have a finish that permits ambulation in a variety of ways for individuals with handicapping conditions. When necessary, protective padding should be placed on walls. Space should be allotted for wheelchairs to pass and turn.

Like indoor areas, outdoor facilities should be accessible and properly surfaced. Facilities should

Figure 2.5 An accessible drinking fountain. Photograph courtesy of the New York State School for the Blind, Mr. Robert Seibold, Superintendent and Coordinator. Printed with permission.

Figure 2.6 Accessible sinks and a tilted mirror. Photograph courtesy of the New York State School for the Blind, Mr. Robert Seibold, Superintendent and Coordinator. Printed with permission.

be available and marked for a variety of activities, including special sports. Walkways leading to and from outdoor facilities should be smooth, firm, free of cracks, and at least 48 in. wide. Doorways to the facilities should have at least a 36-in. clearance. Doors should be light enough to be opened without undue effort; if possible, they should be automatically activitated. Water fountains with both hand and foot controls should be located conveniently for use by handicapped persons. Important signs should be in colors that aid the visually impaired individual. Tactual orientation maps of facilities should be posted where they will assist individuals with visual impairments.

Participants in adapted physical education and athletics need adequate space for dressing, showering, and drying. Space must be sufficient for peak load periods. The design of locker rooms should facilitate ambulation and the maintenance of safe and clean conditions; adequate ventilation, lighting, and heating are necessary. The shower room should be readily accessible and should provide a sufficient number of shower heads; the facilities should be equipped with grab rails. Locker rooms should include adequate benches, mirrors, and toilets. Handicapped users frequently prefer horizontal lockers and locks that are easy to manipulate. Planning must ensure that lockers are not obstructed by benches and other obstacles. All facilities should, of course, be in operable condition.

Well-designed restrooms have toilets at floor level, adequate space for manipulation of wheelchairs, easily activated foot and/or hand flush mechanisms, grab rails, and toilet and urinal levels that meet the needs of the varied school population.

Swimming pools are among the most important sport facilities. Pool design must provide for safe and quick entry into and exit from the water. Water depth and temperature should be adjustable to meet learning, recreational, therapeutic, and competitive athletic needs. Careful coordination of pool use is usually necessary to accommodate varying needs. Dressing, shower, and toilet facilities must be close by, with easy access to the pool.

Students in adapted physical education and sport programs must have equal opportunity to use normal/integrated facilities. Too often, physical education for individuals with handicapping conditions takes place in segregated areas not used by other pupils, like boiler rooms or hallways transformed for use as physical education teaching stations. Small class size should not be used as a reason to exclude persons with handicapping conditions from equitable use of facilities; such a practice is discriminatory and is demeaning to both students and school personnel.

Budget

If education is to be equitable, it will cost more to educate students with handicapping conditions than nonhandicapped students. To supplement local and state funds, the federal government, through a variety of programs, provides money for the education of people with unique needs. Funds associated with PL 94-142 are specifically earmarked for the education of this population. To ensure receipt of federal funds for physical education, planners must be sure that physical education is included in individualized education programs. This inclusion is more likely to occur if physical education personnel are involved in IEP development.

PL 94-142 funds are available to help meet excess costs of special education, that is, costs that exceed student expenditure in regular education. These funds flow through state education departments (which are permitted to keep a certain percentage) and on to local education agencies. The flow-through money can be used to help cover excess costs already met by the states. Because adapted physical education serves students who are not handicapped as well as those classified as handicapped, it is advantageous for schools to fund teachers in physical education, whether regular or adapted, from the same local funding source rather than to rely on PL 94-142 money. This is justifiable because states are responsible for the education of *all* their students.

In addition to meeting needs identified in IEPs, funding must support the preparation of teachers to provide quality services in adapted physical education and sport. For example, funds are needed for in-service education, workshops, clinics, local meetings, professional conferences and conventions, program visitation, and so on. Schools also need funds to maintain up-to-date libraries and other resources.

Interscholastic teams made up of students with handicapping conditions must receive equitable treatment in the allocation of equipment, supplies, travel expenses, officials, and the like. While the funding level for a local community is not externally dictated, available funds cannot be used in a discriminatory fashion—for example, made available to males but not to females, or made available to nonhandicapped but not handicapped students.

Human Resources

A quality program in adapted physical education and sport depends to a great extent on the availability of quality human resources and on the ability of involved personnel to perform effectively as members of a group. People are needed to plan, administer, manage, and coordinate services; fulfill technical and advocacy functions; and provide instruction. Many of these functions are carried out in important committees. In order to provide high-quality services in adapted physical education and sport, the physical educator must work with various school committees and IEP committees. In working with individuals and groups, it is helpful to know roles and responsibilities and to realize that the concern for students with unique needs is shared by many. This section identifies key personnel and discusses their primary roles and responsibilities. Many fulfill their responsibilities by serving on committees identified in chapter 3.

Director of Physical Education and Athletics

Although it is not a universal practice, it is desirable for all aspects of a school's physical education and sport program to be under the direction of an administrator certified in physical education. Such centralization enhances coordination and efficiency in regard to personnel, facilities and equipment, budgeting, professional development, and curriculum. The director of physical education and athletics should oversee all aspects of the program, including the work of the coordinator of adapted physical education if that position exists.

Because adapted physical education and sport are often in developmental stages and not a well-advocated part of the total physical education program, the director of physical education and athletics needs to demonstrate genuine commitment to this part of the program. A positive attitude will serve as a model for others to emulate. With the help of other administrative personnel, the director can help the program in adapted physical education and sport by ensuring adequate funding, employing qualified teachers, and providing support services. The director must also be knowledgeable about adapted physical education and sport in order to work effectively with individuals and groups outside the department. The director must relate with other athletic directors, coordinators, building principals, superintendents, and school boards, and must form positive professional relationships with medical personnel including physicians, nurses, and therapists. Other important relationships are those with parents, teachers, students with handicapping conditions, and advocacy groups. For this reason, it is important that the director of physical education and sport be informed about all students identified as having unique needs.

Adapted Physical Education and Sport Coordinator

In order to provide a quality, comprehensive program in adapted physical education and sport, schools are advised to name an individual as the adapted physical education and sport coordinator. In a small school, this might be a part-time position; in a larger school, a full-time adapted physical education coordinator may be needed. Although most states do not require a special endorsement, credential, or certification in adapted physical education, it is best to select an individual who has considerable professional preparation in adapted physical education. If possible, the coordinator should have completed a recognized specialization or concentration in adapted physical education and, where applicable, should meet the state competency requirements for certification. In 1981, an Adapted Physical Education Task Force within AAHPERD identified competencies needed by an adapted physical education specialist (Hurley, 1981); these serve as a reference for the development of professional preparation programs. A person demonstrating these competen-

cies is likely to be knowledgeable and genuinely interested in serving in that particular role. If a school cannot employ a person with preparation in adapted physical education, the coordinator's duties should be entrusted to someone who demonstrates genuine interest in serving in the position.

The particular role and functions of the coordinator will depend on the size of the school, the number and types of students with handicapping conditions within the school population, and the number and types of students in adapted physical education and sport. Generally, however, the coordinator will need to assume a leadership role in various functions associated with adapted physical education and sport. The specific functions often differ more in degree than in kind from those performed by regular physical educators. Table 2.1 identifies typical functions associated with adapted physical education and sport and indicates who is responsible for those functions. Functions may overlap or be shared; specific lines of demarcation will need to be drawn to suit local conditions.

Some schools may employ adapted physical education teachers who are not required to assume the position of adapted physical education and sport coordinator. Although these teachers certainly provide important support functions to the coordinator, they are primarily involved in carrying out instructional programs in more restrictive environments. In addition, they may help to implement adapted sport programs—for example, by developing and implementing sport days, arranging competition in out-of-school programs, preparing participants, and coaching teams. Most adapted physical education teachers will be heavily involved in working with IEP committees.

Regular Physical Educator

Although a school may employ adapted physical educators, the regular physical educator still has an important role and responsibility in implementing quality programs in adapted physical education and sport. Table 2.1 identifies several functions

Table 2.1 Primary Responsibility for Functions Relevant to Adapted Physical Education and Sport

Functions	Responsibility	
	Regular physical educator	Adapted physical educator/ coordinator
Measurement, assessment, evaluation		
Student screening	X	X
In-depth testing		X
Student assessment and evaluation		X
APE/S program evaluation		X
Teaching/coaching		
Implement instructional program for students with short-term unique needs	X	
Implement instructional program to meet long-term unique needs in mainstreamed environments	X	
Implement instructional program in segregated environments		X
Implement instructional and sport programs with guidance of adapted physical educator	X	
Implement adapted sport program		X
Management/leadership		
Consultation		X
In-service education		X
Advocacy/interpretation		X
Recruitment of aides/volunteers		X
Chair adapted physical education committee		X
Liaison with allied health professionals	X	X
Referral and placement	X	X
Organization of adapted sport program		X

that are shared or are the primary responsibility of regular physical educators. For example, regular teachers play an important role in screening. They may also be called on to implement instructional programs for students with short-term unique needs, to implement programs in mainstreamed environments, and to help in implementing sport programs. One of the most important tasks of the regular physical educator is referral. In the area of management/leadership, the regular physical educator will generally play a secondary role.

Nurse

An allied health professional with an important part in the successful development and implementation of adapted physical education and sport programs is the nurse. The school nurse must be knowledgeable about the adapted physical education and sport program and, ideally, should serve on the committee on adapted physical education. The nurse can be a valuable resource to that committee as well as to other committees and individuals. She or he can help in interpreting information that is required for IEP planning. If time permits, the school nurse can assist the physical education staff in testing students, particularly in the case of postural screening. The nurse can also provide valuable service in keeping medical records, communicating with physicians, and helping parents and students to understand the importance of exercise and physical activity.

Physicians

Physicians are among the allied health professionals who have an important relationship to the school's adapted physical education and sport program. The physician's role is so important that it is often addressed in federal, state, or local laws, rules, and regulations. In some instances, states look to the school physician for the final decision on participation in athletic opportunities. Above all, physicians provide and interpret medical information on which school programs can be based. Using this information, the groups responsible plan appropriate programs. In addition to providing and interpreting medical information and assisting in program development, the school physician has an important responsibility for interpreting the adapted physical education and sport program to family physicians and other medical personnel.

In states where physical education is required of all students, physicians must know and support laws and regulations. Also, they must be confident that if a student is unable to participate without restriction in a regular class, adaptation will be made for the youngster. Physicians should be aware that quality physical education and adapted physical education have changed considerably since many of them attended school, and they should understand the nature of these changes. In other words, they need to be aware of their role and responsibility in well-established modern programs.

One of a physician's important functions is to administer the physical examinations that are given periodically throughout the school career. Examination results are used as a basis for individualized student evaluation, program planning, placement, and determination of eligibility and qualification for athletic participation. It is desirable for each student to receive an exam every 3 years beginning in the first grade. Examinations should be annual for those assigned to adapted physical education because of medical referrals. School districts that do not provide physical examinations should require adequate examinations by family physicians. For athletic participation, annual exams should be required.

Coaches

Adapted sport programs should be operated under the direction of qualified school personnel. Where an adapted program includes interschool athletic teams, standards for coaches must be consistent with those for the regular interschool athletic program. Teachers certified in physical education should be permitted to coach any sport, including those whose participants have handicapping conditions. Ideally, coaches of teams composed primarily of individuals with unique needs should have additional expertise in adapted physical education.

Coaches must follow acceptable professional practices, including maintainence of a positive attitude; insistence on good sportsmanship, respect, and personal control; and willingness to improve professionally through in-service programs, workshops, and clinics.

Related Service Personnel

Under PL 94-142, related services are transportation and other developmental, corrective, and supportive services *that are required to assist a handicapped child to benefit from special education*. Related services include speech pathology and audiology, psychological services, physical and occupational therapy, recreation, early identification and assessment of disability in children, counseling services, and medical services for diagnostic or evaluation purposes. Related service providers with considerable importance for education are occupational and physical therapists. According to the rules and regulations for the implementation of PL 94-142, occupational therapy includes (a) improving, developing, or restoring functions impaired or lost through illness, injury, or deprivation; (b) improving ability to perform tasks for independent functioning when functions are impaired or lost; and (c) preventing, through early intervention, initial or further impairment or loss of functioning. The same rules and regulations define physical therapy as services provided by a qualified physical therapist. These services have traditionally included the provision of physical activities and other physical means for rehabilitation as prescribed by a physician. The rules and regulations specify that recreation includes assessment of leisure function, therapeutic recreation services, recreation programs in schools and community agencies, and leisure education.

Much has been written about the relationship between adapted physical education and the related services of physical and occupational therapy. Often the lines of responsibility among these areas are blurred. What is clear and not controversial is the fact that related services must be provided if a student *requires them to benefit from direct services*. For example, physical therapy and occupational therapy must be provided to the extent that the student needs them to benefit from physical education or other direct services in the school program. PL 94-142 specifies that physical education must be made available to individuals with handicapping conditions. Also, states have their own requirements concerning the provision of physical education. Clearly, physical therapy and adapted physical education are not identical, and related services *should not supplant* physical education or adapted physical education (which are direct services under PL 94-142).

Several assumptions about the role of physical education may underlie the assignment of responsibility within a particular educational setting. First, it is clearly the physical educator's responsibility to design programs to improve the physical fitness of students with handicapping conditions. Thus, the physical educator is involved with the development of strength, endurance, cardiorespiratory endurance, and flexibility (range of motion). His or her responsibility concerns *both* affected and nonaffected parts of the body. For example, individuals with cerebral palsy should be helped to maintain and develop their physical fitness. To deal with affected parts, the physical educator should cooperate with medical and/or related service personnel in program planning.

Sometimes improvements in physical development cannot be attained through the usual time allotments, methods, or activities associated with physical education. In such cases, the inclusion of physical or occupational therapy can enhance physical fitness development. Activities included in the physical education programs of youngters with handicapping conditions should be those that are typically *within the scope of physical education*. These are the kinds of activities subsumed under the definition of physical education in the rules and regulations of PL 94-142 and included in the scope of physical education as described in Figure 2.1. Although the physical educator involves children in exercise, it is important *not* to limit physical education to an exercise prescription program. Instead, a *broad* spectrum of activities should be offered. A youngster who requires a specific exercise to the extent that it would occupy an entire physical education period should meet this need in an extended physical education program or should receive related services. This approach would permit the use of a broad spectrum of activities within the regularly scheduled physical education class. Another important responsibility of the physical educator is to help individuals appropriately use wheelchairs and supportive devices in physical education activities. Physical educators must therefore be knowledgeable about wheelchairs and other assistive devices, although it is not their responsibility to provide functional training in the use of those aids for basic movement or ambulation.

It is vital that physical educators coordinate their programs with physicians and other medical personnel. It is important to establish and follow the procedures in a school district associated with planning programs as described in chapter 3 of this text.

Although much can be written and said concerning roles and responsibilities, very often the quality of services provided depends on the interpersonal relationships of the service providers. Successful situations are those in which the professionals have discussed roles and responsibilities and work hard to deliver supportive services to benefit students with unique needs.

Program Evaluation

At the beginning of this chapter, the importance of an adapted physical education and sport plan to serve as an operating code was stressed. Once in place, the plan can serve as a basis for program evaluation. The implementation aspects of adapted physical education should be evaluated annually and the total plan evaluated at 5-year intervals. Program evaluation should draw on data collected from a variety of relevant sources. Helpful to evaluation is use of a rating scale or checklist. Two rating scales (Sherrill & Megginson, 1984; Winnick, 1987) relevant to the concerns discussed in this chapter are listed in the resource section at the end of the chapter. These scales may be modified for local use or be used in their entirety. An instrument for evaluation is least threatening if used for self-appraisal. Evaluation provides a

point of departure for identifying and discussing strengths and weaknesses and for developing a schedule to remedy weaknesses.

Summary

Well-conducted programs in adapted physical education start with sound programmatic and curricular direction. They are also characterized by sound guidelines for student identification, placement, scheduling, participation, facilities, and budget. They depend on the cooperation of professionals from many disciplines working together toward the common goal of quality services. This chapter has discussed these elements of a good program, with the recommendation that schools develop written guidelines to help them improve organization and management, provide quality services, and evaluate program effectiveness.

Bibliography

Department of Health, Education, and Welfare. (1977). Nondiscrimination on basis of handicap. *Federal Register*, **42**(86), 22676-22702.

Hurley, D. (1981). Guidelines for adapted physical education. *Journal of Physical Education, Recreation and Dance,* **52**(6), 43-45.

Sherrill, C., & Megginson, N. (1984). A needs assessment instrument for local school district use in adapted physical education. *Adapted Physical Activity Quarterly*, **1**, 147-157.

Winnick, J.P. (1987). An integration continuum for sport participation. *Adapted Physical Activity Quarterly*, **4**, 157-161.

Winnick, J.P., Auxter, D., Jansma, P., Sculli, J., Stein, J., & Weiss, R.A. (1980). Implications of Section 504 of the Rehabilitation Act as related to physical education instructional, personnel preparation, intramural, and interscholastic/intercollegiate sport programs. *Practical Pointers*, **3**(11), 1-20.

Resources

Auxter, D., & Pyfer, J. (1989). *Principles and methods of adapted physical education and recreation* (6th ed.). St. Louis: Times Mirror/ Mosby College Publishing. This book describes and distinguishes developmental and community-based programming.

Flynn, R.B. (Ed.) (1985). *Planning facilities for athletics, physical education and recreation.* Reston, VA: American Alliance for Health, Physical Education, Recreation and Dance. This comprehensive resource for facilities planning includes one chapter on planning for handicapped populations and refers to adapted physical education in other chapters.

Seaman, J.A., & DePauw, K.P. (1989). *The new adapted physical education: A developmental approach.* Mountain View, CA: Mayfield. This book describes the developmental approach to programming.

Sherrill, C., & Megginson, N. (1984). A needs assessment instrument for local school district use in adapted physical education. *Adapted Physical Activity Quarterly*, **1**, 147-157. The article provides information on the Survey of Adapted Physical Education Needs (SAPEN) —an instrument that can be used for determining and prioritizing local school district adapted physical education needs. The survey itself may be procured from Dr. C. Sherrill, Department of Physical Education, Texas Woman's University, P.O. Box 23717, Denton, TX 76204.

Winnick, J.P. (1987). Rating scale for adapted physical education. This unpublished rating scale can be procured from Dr. J.P. Winnick, Department of Physical Education and Sport, SUNY, College at Brockport, Brockport, NY 14420. The survey presents criterion statements reflecting guidelines implicitly suggested in this chapter.

CHAPTER 3

Individualized Education Programs

Francis X. Short

When President Ford signed PL 94-142, the Education for All Handicapped Children Act of 1975, the provision of special education in the United States was significantly changed in a number of ways. One important change is the provision that every student with a handicapping condition must have an individualized education program, or as it is more commonly known, an IEP. An IEP is a written document that essentially describes the student's current level of educational achievement, identifies goals and objectives for the near future, and lists the educational services to be provided to meet those goals. According to the U.S. Department of Education, Office of Special Education (1980), the IEP

- serves as a focal point for parent-school communication and can be used as a tool in resolving differences between the two parties;
- lists the resources (special education and related services) that will be provided to the child and, as such, is used to determine the appropriate placement for the child as well as the appropriate curriculum;
- serves as a monitoring device for governmental agencies attempting to determine if a child is truly receiving a free, appropriate education; and
- serves as a basis for evaluation in determining the extent of the child's educational progress.

PL 94-142 addresses the needs of students who are identified as handicapped by a particular school district. Occasionally, however, there are students in a school setting who are not identified or labeled as handicapped under PL 94-142 but who have a unique need in physical education. Students recuperating from injuries or accidents; those convalescing from noncommunicable diseases; and students who are overweight or have low skill levels or low levels of physical fitness may fall into this second category. Schools, therefore, must have procedures for arranging appropriate physical education experiences for students who are not covered by PL 94-142 but who require an adapted physical education program.

This chapter discusses the development of individualized education programs in physical education. It addresses both requirements for the development of an IEP for a student with a handicapping condition, as set forth in PL 94-142, and recommendations for the development of an individualized program for a nonhandicapped student.

The Handicapped Student

The specially designed program for any child who has been identified as handicapped by the school district is dictated by the IEP. Local districts may determine and design their own IEP format. Consequently, it is not unusual for neighboring school districts to use different IEP forms.

Components of the IEP

While formats vary, each IEP form *must* contain the seven components listed in the following paragraphs. Sample physical education information that might be included in an IEP is shown in Figure 3.1.

1. Present Level of Performance (PLP)

The present level of performance component is the cornerstone of the IEP. The information presented in all subsequent components is related to the information set forth here. If the PLP is not adequately and properly determined, chances are the student's specially designed instructional program will not be the most appropriate. PLP statements should be objective, observable, and measurable; they should accurately reflect the child's current educational abilities. Ordinarily the PLP component will consist primarily of test results. These results could come from standardized tests with performance norms or criteria, or from less formal, teacher-constructed tests. Although both types of results are appropriately included in the IEP, it is recommended that, when possible, the PLP contain at least some standardized test results. Standardized results can help determine a "unique need" in a particular area and can provide stronger justification for an educational placement.

PLP information should be presented in a way that places the student on a continuum of achievement—that is, the test results shown should discriminate among levels of ability. For this reason, tests on which students attain either minimum (e.g., 0 out of 10) or maximum (e.g., 10 out of 10) scores are not helpful in determining PLP. Also, in situating a student on this continuum, the PLP component should note, to the extent possible, what the individual *can* do, not what he or she cannot do. Finally, PLP information should

be presented in a way that is immediately interpretable; it should not require additional explanation from the teacher. When standardized test results are included, percentiles (or other normative data) should be presented as well as the raw scores, and teacher-constructed tests should be adequately described so the conditions can be replicated at a later date. (See chapter 4 for more information on measurement in adapted physical education.)

2. Annual Goals

An annual goal is a broad or generic statement designed to give direction to the instructional program. Once the PLP information has been obtained and studied, the teacher should identify one or more content areas to be emphasized in the student's program. Usually an annual goal focuses on the student's area of weakness as identified in the PLP. In fact, this linkage is a key element in writing an annual goal statement: The annual goal must clearly relate to information presented in the PLP component. For instance, if the PLP contains only information on ball-handling skills, it would be inappropriate to write an annual goal for swimming, physical fitness, or any other content area of physical education unrelated to ball-handling skills. The need for emphasis on a particular content area in a child's program must be documented in the PLP.

3. Short-Term Objectives (STO)

While the annual goal is a broad or generic statement, a short-term objective is narrow and specific. An STO is a statement that describes a skill in terms of *action*, *condition*, and *criterion*. Action means the type of skill to be performed (e.g., *run*). Condition indicates the provisions under which the skill will be performed (e.g., run *50 yd*). Criterion refers to how well the skill is to be performed (e.g., run 50 yd *in 8.5 s*). Conditions and criteria used in physical education usually relate to such concepts as "how fast," "how long," "how far,"

Student's Name: Sammy   Age: 10

I. Present Level of Performance
   1. Catches a tennis ball (with hands only) 3 out of 10 times when tossed from a distance of 20 ft.
   2. Throws a tennis ball into a wall target (3 ft × 5 ft, 3 ft off the ground) 2 out of 10 times from a distance of 30 ft.
   3. Dribbles a basketball with right hand 5 consecutive times; 2 consecutive times with the left hand.
   4. Does 4 sit-ups in 60 s (0 percentile, Youth Fitness Test).
   5. Runs 50 yards in 9.9 s (5th percentile, Youth Fitness Test).
   6. Performs a standing broad jump of 48 in. (10th percentile, Youth Fitness Test).

II. Annual Goals
   1.0 Sammy will improve on selected eye-hand coordination skills.
   2.0 Sammy will improve his scores on selected measures of physical fitness.

III. Short-Term Objectives
   1.1 Sammy will catch a tennis ball (with hands only) 7 out of 10 times when tossed from a distance of 20 ft.
   1.2 Sammy will throw a tennis ball into a wall target (3 ft × 5 ft, 3 ft off the ground) 6 out of 10 times from a distance of 30 ft.
   1.3 Sammy will dribble a basketball 20 consecutive times with left hand.
   2.1 Sammy will do 15 sit-ups in 60 s.
   2.2 Sammy will run 50 yards in 9.0 s.
   2.3 Sammy will do a standing broad jump of 60 in.

IV. Statement of Services
   In addition to regular physical education (3 times per week) Sammy will attend adapted physical education 2 times per week. (No special materials or additional support personnel necessary.)

V. Schedule of Services
   Sammy will attend regular physical education from 9:00 to 9:45 on Monday, Tuesday, and Friday and adapted physical education from 11:30 to 12:15 on Wednesday and Thursday. This schedule will go into effect on October 6 and end on June 5.

VI. Extent of Mainstreaming
   Sixty percent of Sammy's physical education programming will be in an integrated situation, while 40% will be in a special or segregated situation.

VII. Criteria, Procedures, and Schedule for Evaluation
   Criteria for evaluation are specified under short-term objectives. Progress on objectives will be monitored periodically, and final evaluation on all objectives will be conducted during the week of June 8.

Figure 3.1 Sample IEP information prepared by the physical educator and presented to the IEP planning committee.

or "how many," although it is also appropriate to describe "how mature." For instance, a 10-year-old student may throw a ball into a wall target 9 out of 10 times from a certain distance. The teacher may be pleased with the accuracy score ("how many"), but if the student did not step with the opposite foot when throwing, the teacher may not be pleased with the quality of the movement pattern ("how mature"). In this case the teacher might write an STO that describes a movement pattern, rather than an accuracy score, to be attained.

Just as an annual goal must relate to PLP information, STOs must relate to an annual goal. If an annual goal stresses the content area of "eye-hand coordination," the STOs should include skills such as throwing, catching, and striking. Furthermore, it is important that the student's baseline (pretest) ability appear in the IEP, usually in the PLP component. For example, a short-term objective might specify that a student will be expected to do 15 sit-ups in 60 s at some future date; this statement has little meaning unless it is known how many sit-ups the student can do now. In fact, the easiest way to write an STO is to simply take a well-written PLP statement, copy the action and condition elements verbatim, and make a reasonable change in the criterion. (The teacher must use professional judgment to determine what constitutes a "reasonable" expectation for improvement.) It should be noted that, although STOs are helpful in identifying activities to be conducted in class, they are not meant to supplant daily, weekly, or monthly lesson plans.

4. Statement of Services

Once the present level of performance is determined and annual goals and short-term instructional objectives written, decisions must be made regarding the student's educational placement, additional services (if any) to be provided, and the use of special instructional media and materials as necessary. The placement agreed upon should be considered the least restrictive environment for the student.

In addition to appropriate placement, other special education and related services may be prescribed. A special education service is one that makes a direct impact on educational objectives— for example, physical education. Provisions for this service should be spelled out in this component of the IEP. A related service makes an indirect impact on educational objectives and, therefore, should be prescribed only to the extent that it will help the student benefit from a special education service. Examples of related services that may be prescribed in the IEP include physical therapy; therapeutic recreation; occupational therapy; psychological services; and speech, language, and/or hearing therapy.

In some cases special instructional materials may be required for the education of children with handicapping conditions. These materials should also be listed in the statement of services component. Modified pieces of equipment such as a beep baseball, an audible goal locator, a snap-handle bowling ball, or a bowling ramp are examples of special materials sometimes needed in physical education (see Figure 3.2).

5. Schedule of Services

The IEP must indicate when all special education and related services will begin and end, and how often they will be provided to the student.

6. Extent of Mainstreaming

The IEP must specify the extent to which the student with a handicap will be educated with nonhandicapped students. Often this is expressed as the percentage of time the student is educated in an integrated environment in a given subject area.

7. Criteria, Procedures, and Schedule for Evaluation

This component is used to specify how and when the student's progress will be evaluated. In most cases progress is determined by testing of the objectives written earlier. Evaluation can be sched-

Figure 3.2   Adapted equipment: audible goal locator, snap-handle bowling ball, and beep baseball.

uled to occur at any time within 1 year from the time the IEP takes effect; the IEP *must* be reviewed at least annually.

Development of the IEP

Procedures for developing an IEP vary slightly from state to state, but essentially the process involves two steps. The first is to determine if the student is eligible for special education services; if so, the second step is to develop the most appropriate program, including the establishment of goals and objectives and the determination of an appropriate placement. The process that results in development of an IEP usually begins with a referral. Any professional staff member at a particular school who suspects that a child might have a handicapping condition can refer the child for an evaluation to determine eligibility for special education. A referral should outline the reasons for it, including test results, records or reports, attempts to remediate the student's performance, and the extent of parental contact prior to the referral (The State Education Department, 1985). Parents may refer their own children for evalua-

tion when they suspect a problem. In fact, when parents enroll a youngster in a new school, the district will frequently ask them if they feel their child might possess a handicapping condition.

In many states a standing multidisciplinary team, consisting of a special educator, a psychologist, a physician, a parent, and/or other individuals concerned with the provision of special education, is charged with the responsibility of determining special education eligibility. (In other states the IEP Planning Committee performs this function.) This diagnostic team has different names in different states. In New York, for instance, it is called the Committee on Special Education (CSE), while in Louisiana the group that performs a similar function is known as the Pupil Appraisal Team. Regardless of name, however, the primary purpose of this special education diagnostic team is to determine if a particular student has a unique educational need (or needs) that cannot be addressed in the regular educational program. In many cases the diagnostic team will determine unique need by assessing the results of standardized tests administered to the student. But the team will also consider other information, including samples of current academic work and anecdotal accounts, before reaching a final decision. On the basis of the information gathered and the ensuing discussion, the diagnostic team will decide if the youngster qualifies for special education; if so, the team will recommend, in many states, a trial placement with an interim IEP. In this case, a time line for finalizing the IEP and determining final placement is established. This time line usually does not exceed 30 days from the beginning of the trial placement.

Whether or not a multidisciplinary diagnostic team is used to establish eligibility, the IEP Planning Committee has important responsibilities in developing the individualized education program. This committee is composed of the following members:

- a representative of the school district who is qualified to provide or supervise special education, or a designee (frequently this is a principal, a director of special education, or another professional with expertise in special education),

- the child's teacher (or teachers) who will have responsibility for implementing the IEP,
- one or both of the parents,
- the student, where appropriate, and
- other individuals at the discretion of the parents or the school. (The school might bring a member of the diagnostic team to the meeting, while the parents might invite a professional who has conducted a private evaluation of the child, or even a lawyer.)

When eligibility has already been established by a diagnostic team, the primary responsibilities of the IEP Planning Committee are to continue assessment at the site of the trial placement; to finalize the writing of the IEP; and, on the basis of the final IEP, to decide on the most appropriate placement for the youngster.

The IEP is a negotiated document; both the school and the parents have input into the development of the IEP and must agree on its content before it is signed and implemented. In the event the two parties cannot agree on the content of a child's

The IEP: Some Common Questions

1. *Must physical education (PE) be included in every handicapped child's IEP?*

In general the answer is yes. However, the kind and amount of information to be included in the IEP depends on the physical-motor needs of the individual child and the type of PE program that is to be provided. The following is a description of some of the different kinds of PE program arrangements:

- Regular PE with nonhandicapped students. If a handicapped child is enrolled in the regular PE program without any special adaptations, only the mainstreaming component of the IEP would have to be completed for physical education.
- Regular PE with adaptations. For these children, the IEP would (a) include under Present Level of Performance a brief statement of the physical-motor needs that require adapted PE, and (b) describe in the Statement of Services component the special adaptations that are necessary.
- Specially designed PE. For these students, the PE program would be included in *all* components of the IEP.
- PE in special settings (e.g., a special school). In this case, only minimal information is required in the IEP. For example, the IEP (a) would indicate that the child is participating in the basic PE program, and (b) could refer specifically to the parts of the PE curriculum that apply to the individual child. For children in special settings who have particular physical-motor needs, the IEP would include a statement of (a) the child's special needs and (b) the specific PE program and any other special education services that would be provided to meet those needs.

2. *For a handicapped child entering special education for the first time, when must an IEP be written— before placement or after placement?*

The IEP must be finalized before placement. An appropriate placement cannot be made until after the child's needs have been identified and services decided on. This requirement, however, does not preclude a trial placement as a formal part of the evaluation process.

3. *Must IEPs be reviewed or revised at the beginning of each school year?*

No. IEPs must *be in effect* at the beginning of each school year. An IEP must be reviewed or revised at least annually, but this can be done at other times during the school year (e.g., the anniversary date of the last IEP meeting, the child's birth date, or the end of the school year).

4. *Does the IEP list all special education and related services needed or only those available in the public school or agency?*

The IEP must include *all* specific special education and related services needed by the child as determined by the evaluation. This means that the services must be listed in the IEP even if they are not available in the local school or agency and must be provided through contract or other arrangements.

5. *Is the IEP a performance contract?*

The IEP is *not* a performance contract; PL 94-142 does not require that the school or agency, the teacher, or other persons be held accountable if the child does not achieve the growth projected in the IEP.

Note. Adapted from a U.S. Department of Education, Office of Special Education policy paper, *Individualized Education Programs (IEPs)*, May 23, 1980.

IEP, PL 94-142 provides procedures for resolving the disagreement. These *due process* procedures are designed to protect the rights of the child, the parents, and the school district (see Figure 3.3).

The Role of the Physical Educator

Historically, physical educators have not been actively involved in the IEP development process. Churton (1987) indicates that relatively few IEPs contain physical education entries. He points out that, according to 1980 Department of Education data, fewer than 3% of the IEPs surveyed mentioned physical education. It is clear that if students with handicapping conditions are to receive the free, appropriate education guaranteed by PL 94-142, physical education must be included in their IEPs. It is also clear that this will be accomplished only if physical educators make sure that they are involved in IEP development.

Ideally, a physical educator would serve on both the diagnostic team and the IEP Planning Committee. In many cases, however, students are placed in special education settings prior to a physical education assessment. This is particularly true in states that utilize a trial placement. In this instance, it is the responsibility of the physical educator to assess the student's ability in physical education, determine if the student has a unique need in the physical or motor area, recommend an appropriate placement (the least restrictive environment), and appropriately develop the physical education aspects of the IEP.

The assessment of the student should reflect as many content areas of physical education as possible. As you may recall from chapter 1, PL 94-142 defines physical education as follows: "The term means the development of a) physical and motor fitness, b) fundamental motor skills and patterns; and c) skills in aquatics, dance, and individual and group games and sports (including

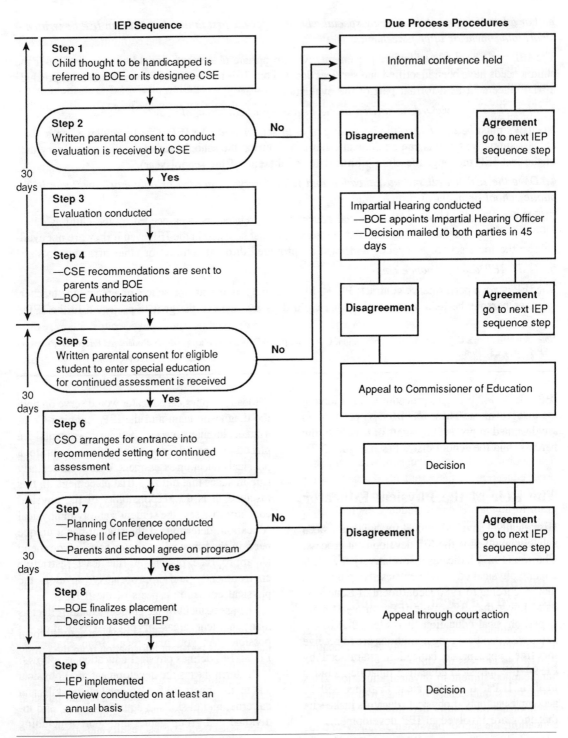

Figure 3.3 IEP development in New York State.

intramural and lifetime sports)'' (Federal Register, 1977, p. 424807). The physical educator, therefore, should select assessment instruments that reflect these components of physical education. Deficient scores on these tests would help the physical educator to determine unique need and justify an adapted physical education placement.

Although documentation of subaverage test performance is important in determining an adapted physical education placement, it is not the only criterion to use in making such a decision. For instance, an emotionally disturbed child might be placed in an adapted physical education class even though the child's physical and motor skills are age-appropriate. In this case, the placement might be justified on the basis of behavioral concerns; a large class size or an emphasis on competitive activities might make a regular physical education class placement inappropriate for such a child.

The Nonhandicapped Student With Unique Needs

As mentioned at the outset of this chapter, nonhandicapped students who have unique needs in physical education are not covered by PL 94-142. School districts, however, must provide an appropriate education for these students. Procedures for providing an appropriate physical education program to nonhandicapped students, including the establishment of a Committee on Adapted Physical Education, are described in this section.

Committee on Adapted Physical Education

It is recommended that school districts establish a Committee on Adapted Physical Education (CAPE) to address the unique needs of the nonhandicapped student in physical education. This committee should consist of at least four members: a school administrator, the director of physical education, the school physician or nurse, and the adapted physical educator. When possible, the stu-

dent's regular physical education teacher should also be a member of the committee. The function of CAPE is to determine the student's eligibility for an adapted program; define the nature of that program, including placement; and monitor the student's progress in the program.

Formulation of the Physical Education Program

A process for providing an appropriate adapted physical education program for nonhandicapped students is illustrated in Figure 3.4 and defined in the following paragraphs.

Step 1

Referrals to CAPE will ordinarily be made to the chairperson by a physical educator, a family physician, a parent, or even the student, when it is felt that the student's involvement in the regular program is inappropriate.

Step 2

The chairperson reviews the referral (or medical excuse) and makes a decision to consult with the student's family physician, the school physician, and/or the student's regular physical education teacher, depending on the nature of the referral.

Step 3

When a medical condition is involved, the CAPE chairperson may wish to consult with both the family physician and the school physician to determine the nature of the condition and its impact on physical activity. A sample physical activity form that requests pertinent information from the family physician is depicted in Figure 3.5. When a medical condition is not part of the referral, the chairperson consults with the student's regular physical education instructor. This consultation should include a discussion of test results and other related information.

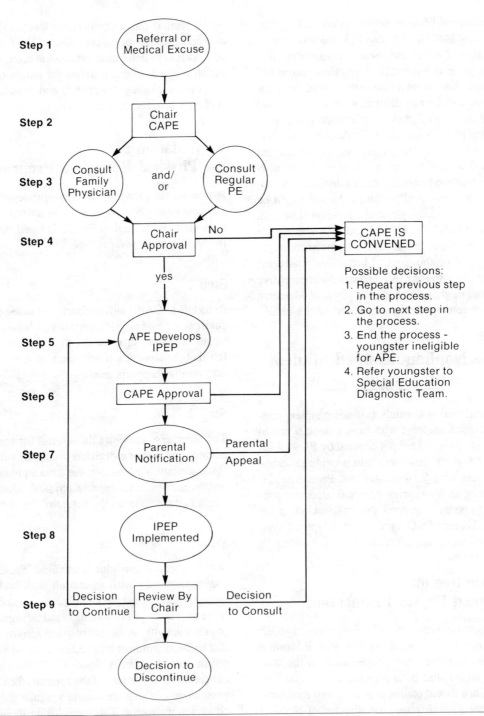

Figure 3.4 CAPE and the nonhandicapped pupil: a recommended procedure.

OCEAN BAY PARK CENTRAL SCHOOL DISTRICT
PHYSICAL ACTIVITY FORM

TO: _____ M.D.

FROM: _____ Chair, Committee on Adapted Physical
Education

_____
Address

RE: _____ _____
Name of Pupil   Grade in School

The Committee on Adapted Physical Education has received a medical excuse (or referral) regarding this student. All pupils registered in the schools of New York are required by the Education Law to attend courses of instruction in Physical Education. These courses are required to be adapted to meet individual pupil needs. This means that a pupil who is unable to participate in the entire program should have his/her activities modified to meet and/or improve the condition. The Physical Education classes are approximately _____ minutes in length and are held _____ times a week.

The final responsibility for the determination of a student's participation in the modified program rests with the Committee on Adapted Physical Education. Your recommendation will assist the Committee in making a decision. If further clarification is needed, the school physician will arrange a conference with you.

DIAGNOSIS: _____

SPECIFIC PHYSICAL LIMITATIONS: _____

_____

Within the physical limitations listed, this student can otherwise engage in: (check one)

_____ vigorous physical activity   _____ mild physical activity
_____ moderate physical activity   _____ minimal physical activity

Other recommendations for program adaptation: _____

_____

Do you wish student to return for re-evaluation? Yes _____ No _____
If so, when? _____

This is to certify that I have examined _____
and recommend that he/she participate in a physical education program within the guidelines specified above for a period of _____ weeks/months.

Physician's Signature: _____

Date: _____

White: APE   Yellow: CAPE File   Pink: Physician

Figure 3.5 Sample physicians' physical activity form.

Step 4

If, after appropriate consultation, the CAPE chairperson feels that the student is qualified for the program being considered, the process proceeds to Step 5. If, however, the chairperson does not consider the student qualified for the program in question or has other reservations or concerns about the referral, CAPE is convened. In considering a particular case, the committee has a number of options. It can request further consultation from the appropriate source (i.e., go back to Step 3); it can decide to continue the process (i.e., move to Step 5); it can decide to refer the student to the special education diagnostic team if there is reason to believe the student may have a handicapping condition; or it may decide that the student is not qualified for an adapted physical education program and terminate consideration at that time.

Step 5

The adapted physical education instructor develops an *individualized physical education program (IPEP)* for the student. The IPEP is analogous to the IEP, and much of the required information is similar. The IPEP should include the goals of the program, present levels of performance (including any medical limitations), short-term objectives, placement and schedule of services, and a schedule for review.

Step 6

CAPE must approve or modify the IPEP. For any student who is entering adapted physical education on a medically initiated referral, the school physician must approve the IPEP. School physician approval usually would not be required for an IPEP of a student entering adapted physical education on an educationally initiated referral.

Step 7

Once the IPEP is in place, parents or guardians are notified in writing of the school's intent to place the student in an adapted physical education program. The notification should include a letter of explanation and a copy of the completed IPEP. The student's regular physical education instructor and, in the case of a medically initiated referral, the physician are also notified at this point. If the parents do not agree with the decision or have any other concerns about their child's program, they may address the committee. Once again, CAPE has a number of options in resolving any problems. The committee can direct the adapted physical educator to modify the IPEP in some way, it can decide to proceed to the next step (implementation), it can decide to refer the pupil for special education evaluation, or it can decide to terminate the process. (The district should have in place due process procedures, comparable to those depicted in Figure 3.3, in the event CAPE and the parents cannot agree on the adapted program for the student.)

Step 8

The IPEP is implemented.

Step 9

The IPEP will be in effect for the period specified under "Schedule for Review." At the conclusion of this period, progress on the IPEP is reviewed by the CAPE chairperson. At this juncture the chairperson might decide to continue the adapted program, discontinue the program, or consult with CAPE before proceeding further.

In this model, CAPE serves primarily as a support group to its chairperson. The committee is convened when the chairperson wants to consult on a particular case, when conflicts arise, or when approval of the IPEP is sought. Ideally, CAPE can be scheduled to meet once a week at a predetermined time to consider the needs of nonhandicapped students for adapted physical education.

Summary

Students may be eligible for adapted physical education regardless of handicapping condition providing they exhibit a unique need in physical education. Procedures for program development for students who are labeled handicapped by a school district are governed by PL 94-142. These procedures include the determination of program eligibility and program design as defined by an individualized education program (IEP). Program development for students not designated as handicapped is not governed by federal legislation. Districts must establish their own procedures for determining program eligibility and design. It is recommended that districts establish a Committee on Adapted Physical Education (CAPE) to fulfill these functions, including the development of an individualized physical education program (IPEP) for each eligible nonhandicapped student.

Bibliography

Churton, M. (1987). Impact of the Education of the Handicapped Act on adapted physical education: A 10-year review. *Adapted Physical Activity Quarterly*, **4**, 1-8.

Federal Register. (1977, August 23). Final rules and regulations of Education of Handicapped Children, implementation of Part B of the Education of the Handicapped Act. Washington, DC: Department of Health, Education and Welfare.

The State Education Department. (1985). *Guidebook for committees on the handicapped in New York State*. Albany, NY: The University of the State of New York.

U.S. Education Department, Office of Special Education. (1980). *Individualized education programs (IEPs): OSE policy paper*. Washington, DC: Department of Health, Education and Welfare.

Resources

Written

American Alliance for Health, Physical Education and Recreation. *Update*. Answers to often-asked questions related to PL 94-142, especially concerning physical education. Relevant issues include November 1977, January 1978, February 1978, June 1978, October 1978, November 1978, January 1979, May 1979, and July-August 1979.

Audiovisual

Bowers, L., & Klesius, S. (1982). *I'm special* [videotape]. Tampa: The University of South Florida. A series of 15 videotapes produced by WUSF-TV related to adapted physical education. Modules 2 and 3, "Score One for Physical Education" and "On the Edge of Light," are specifically related to PL 94-142 and the IEP. Each module is approximately 15 min long.

CHAPTER 4

Measurement and Appraisal

Francis X. Short

Good teaching always begins with some form of measurement and appraisal, with measurement meaning the collection of data to describe a student characteristic or performance level and appraisal meaning the assessment of the data collected. Teaching cannot be consistently effective if the student's abilities are not clearly understood or if the student is assigned to an inappropriate educational placement. Instruction based on sound principles of measurement and appraisal is sometimes called diagnostic-prescriptive teaching. The acronym TAPE is frequently used to describe the diagnostic-prescriptive process: *t*est the student, *a*ssess the results obtained, *p*rescribe and implement a program related to the assessment, and *e*valuate the results. Good examples of the diagnostic-prescriptive method appear in chapter 10.

Concepts of measurement and appraisal related to adapted physical education are discussed in this chapter. Types of tests and standards, purposes of testing, tests for use in adapted physical education, award programs, and computer aids are the major topics covered.

Tests and Standards

Many types of tests with different types of standards are used in adapted physical education and sport as well as in other professional settings. Each test has its own relative strengths and weaknesses, and physical educators need to be aware of these characteristics before selecting a test instrument. Some of these strengths and weaknesses relate to the standards associated with a test. Three types of standards—norm referenced, content referenced, and criterion referenced—are discussed in the following paragraphs. Relative strengths and weaknesses of each are shown in Table 4.1.

Norm-Referenced Tests

A norm-referenced test provides the tester with standards that can be used to compare a particular individual's performance with the performance of other individuals from a specifically defined group. These standards, or norms, may be expressed in a variety of ways, although percentiles, standard scores, and age norms are the most popular. Relative strengths and weaknesses of these types of norms are presented in Table 4.2. Norms reflect research conducted by the test developer on a standardization sample. The sample is assumed to be representative of the population from which it was selected. Using scores obtained by the standardization sample, the test developer calculates and presents statistics (e.g., percentiles, standard scores, or age norms) to indicate certain levels of performance that are deemed appropriate for individuals with certain characteristics (e.g., age, gender, handicapping condition).

Table 4.1 Relative Strengths and Weaknesses of Tests With Three Types of Standards

Reference	Strengths	Weaknesses
Norm	Compares student scores with others from a similarly defined group; particularly helpful in summative evaluation (unique needs determination, placement, awards, etc.).	Teacher is limited to specific items on the test; therefore, strong relationship to the curriculum is not guaranteed; limited applicability for formative (ongoing or corrective) evaluation.
Content	Teacher-constructed; therefore test has the potential to be highly related to the curriculum; ideal for formative evaluation because it has day-to-day applicability.	Comparisons with established standards or performance are not possible; therefore, the *significance* of a test score may not be known.
Criterion	Teacher-constructed; therefore test has the potential to be highly related to the curriculum; ideal for formative evaluation; standards for "mastery" are provided.	If standards for "mastery" are established capriciously, interpretation of the significance of the score may be meaningless or erroneous.

Table 4.2 Relative Strengths and Weaknesses of Three Types of Norm-Referenced Standards

Standard	Strengths	Weaknesses
Percentiles	Easily interpreted by parents and other lay persons.	Percentiles are not averageable (unless first converted to a standard score) because the intervals between percentiles are not equal.
Standard scores	Individual scores can be added or averaged to yield a composite score.	Not usually well understood by parents because interpretation requires an understanding of the standard deviation.
Age norms	Easily interpreted by parents and other lay persons.	Usually associated with tests for youngsters 7 years of age and younger; therefore, have limited applicability in school settings.

Content-Referenced Tests

Content-referenced tests are used to place a student on a continuum of achievement; the significance of the test score is "interpreted in terms of perfor-mance at each point on the achievement continuum being measured" (Joint Committee, 1974, p. 19). In contrast to the norm-referenced test, the primary strength of a content-referenced test is flexibility. Unlike most norm-referenced tests, content-referenced tests are not "store bought." Content-referenced tests are developed by the user, who consequently has the flexibility to devise a test to measure exactly what is being taught in the gymnasium. Virtually any observable skill being taught in the curriculum can be measured with a content-referenced test. For instance, it is easy to test accuracy in shooting free throws by giving each student 20 shots from the foul line and counting how many go in the basket. Serving in volleyball can be measured in terms of the number of times out of 10 a student can serve the ball into the opponent's court. In this case, the continuum of achievement ranges from 0 to 10 successful serves; each student will fall somewhere along that continuum. The interpretation is that a higher score is associated with a more advanced level of functioning.

Criterion-Referenced Tests

Criterion-referenced tests are similar to content-referenced tests in that both types place individuals on an achievement continuum. The primary difference between the two is that criterion-referenced tests specify criteria that may be used to appraise performance. For instance, where a content-referenced test asks, "How far can you jump?" a criterion-referenced test asks, "Can you jump 30 in.?" The distance of 30 in. represents the criterion by which performance can be appraised. Behavioral objectives such as those found in an IEP, therefore, are essentially criterion-referenced tests. The objectives specify a level of mastery that the student must attain (e.g., "Ralph will make 5 out of 10 baskets from the free-throw line."). Criterion-referenced tests are popular in competency-based programs such as those sponsored by the American Red Cross. Participants must meet specific standards to gain Advanced Lifesaving or Water Safety Instructor certification. Criterion-referenced tests can also be arranged sequentially to yield a task analysis that can be used to develop a particular skill.

Test Applications

The usage in the present discussion of such terms as "norm-referenced test" and "criterion-referenced test" appears consistent with professional vocabulary. The reader should recognize, however, that the *test* per se is not norm referenced; rather, the *standards* are. It is possible, for instance, that a single test could be considered content referenced, criterion referenced, or norm referenced depending on the standards that are available and/or utilized by the teacher. As an example, consider a standing broad jump score of 35 in. If the teacher reports or utilizes only the raw score (35 in.), the standing broad jump becomes a content-referenced test. If the measurement of 35 in. is translated to a predetermined standard of competence (e.g., students who jump at least 35 in. qualify for the Kangaroo Klub), then it becomes a criterion-referenced test. And finally, if the teacher compares the score of 35 in. to scores obtained by other students who are similarly defined (by use of, say, a percentile table), the test is considered to be norm referenced.

Purposes
of Measurement and Appraisal

While assessment has numerous purposes in physical education in general (see Safrit, 1981), it has three primary purposes in adapted physical education: screening, determination of eligibility for adapted physical education services, and instruction. The relationship of measurement and appraisal to each of these functions is discussed next.

Screening

As discussed in the preceding chapters, students who are suspected of having unique physical and motor needs should be referred to the special education diagnostic team or the Committee on Adapted Physical Education (CAPE). A referral must document the reasons that the student should be considered for adapted physical education. Measurement and appraisal at the referral level is usually called screening. The primary purpose of screening is to document the need for an in-depth evaluation for adapted physical education services. A screening test can be any test that is routinely administered as part of the regular physical education program. Screening tests, therefore, can range from formal, norm-referenced tests to less formal, content-referenced tests.

Assessment for the purpose of screening also may include the use of checklists, rating scales, and informal observation techniques. Although each of these is typically less objective than tests with standardized conditions, directions, and scoring procedures, checklists and rating scales usually have more objectivity than informal observation because these techniques provide the tester with some guidelines for the evaluation of performance. In evaluating a volleyball serve with a 1-to-5 rating scale, for instance, the tester might award a 5 if the ball has good velocity *and* good placement or a 4 if the ball has good velocity *or* good placement. Still there is considerable subjectivity in this approach, because the tester must decide what constitutes good velocity and good placement.

With informal observation, teachers have no specific guidelines by which to judge performance; rather they must rely on their powers of observation and professional judgment. The good observer, for example, must know at what age a youngster should be able to perform a particular skill and must be able to detect deficiencies in mature movement patterns. Although largely subjective, informal observation is still an important assessment device, particularly in screening, for two reasons. First, observation can be unobtrusive; students can be observed in "natural" physical activity settings without feeling that they are being tested. A second reason is that a good observer can evaluate a relatively large number of students in a relatively short period of time. Formal assessment techniques, on the other hand, frequently require the construction of artificial conditions and one-to-one testing.

It is important to note that the purpose of screening is to guarantee the identification of *every* student who *might* be eligible for adapted physical education services. For this reason, information collected in a variety of formal and informal ways should be considered, and when standards are used for screening purposes they should be sufficiently high to prevent borderline students from "falling through the cracks." A school district might decide, for instance, to use a norm-referenced standard for screening and to refer any youngster who falls below the 25th percentile. Students identified in this preliminary step then receive a more extensive evaluation to determine if they are actually eligible for adapted physical education services.

Eligibility for Adapted Physical Education Services

In dealing with the question of eligibility, we must distinguish between an adapted physical education program and the placement to which a student is assigned. A student might qualify for an *adapted program*, but receive that program in a *regular class placement*. Placement, therefore, is established after the appropriate program has been determined. When a student is referred to CAPE or to the special education diagnostic team on the basis of preliminary screening, the committee must first determine if the student is eligible for the adapted physical education program. The adapted physical educator will probably need to conduct more assessment to determine whether the student has a unique need. A long-term unique need must be demonstrated in order for a student to qualify for adapted physical education.

In the absence of a medically based referral, the criteria for entry into the adapted program generally should be performance based. Measurement and appraisal for the purpose of determining program eligibility should usually focus, to the extent possible, on norm-referenced assessment. Because a change in program is a critical educational decision, the teacher should take the steps necessary to ensure that the student completely understands the test and any strategies that will enhance performance. Similarly, the teacher should stress the importance of the test and encourage the student to "try your best." In fact, when motivation appears to be a problem, the tester should consider a reward system to promote a "best effort."

A number of states, including Georgia, Minnesota, and Louisiana, have developed specific criteria for admission into adapted physical education. In the absence of such statewide criteria, it is recommended that school districts adopt local admission criteria. It is further recommended that districts consider the following standards for admission, based on results of tests that measure developmental aspects of physical education:

- The student scores below the 15th percentile when percentile ranks are used;
- the student scores more than 1 standard deviation below the mean (e.g., a T score less than 40) when standard scores are used; or
- the student exhibits a developmental delay of at least 2 years when age norms are used (although the use of age norms is not recommended for students beyond 7 years of age).

Inasmuch as formal testing often takes place under "artificial" conditions, districts might also consider additional criteria. For example, corroboration of test results through observational techniques or a temporary trial placement might also be required.

Although preference should be given to the use of norm-referenced standards in documenting unique need, criterion-referenced tests also can reflect unique need, particularly in competency-based programs. In Louisiana, for instance, failure to achieve 70% or more of the competencies in the physical education curriculum can serve as a criterion for entrance into adapted physical education. Whether norm-referenced or criterion-referenced standards are used, however, the objectives subsequently developed for the student in adapted physical education ordinarily will be different from those that have been established for the general population.

Once program eligibility is established, the most appropriate placement for attaining the student's goals and objectives must be selected. As placement is considered, *every effort should be made to keep the student in the regular class placement*. Teachers should attempt to modify activities and methodologies so that the student's objectives can be met in the regular class. While admission into the *program* depends on one primary criterion— performance—there are a number of considerations in the selection of the appropriate *placement*. For instance, students may require assignment to a more restrictive placement (see continuum of alternative placements, Figure 2.3) if they are unable to understand concepts or safety considerations being taught in the regular class, or if they are unable to maintain appropriate peer relations or engage in other forms of acceptable social behavior.

In instances where students are referred for behavioral reasons, measurement should focus on affective behaviors. These behaviors might include tantruming, physical aggression, or non-compliance. Once these behaviors are defined, baseline data can be collected to show how often a behavior occurs ("Joe averages 1.25 physical provocations a day in physical education."), how long it lasts ("Barbara's tantrums last, on the average, 4.5 min per occurrence."), or what percentage of the time it occurs ("Sean is compliant with teacher directions approximately 67% of the time.").

Placement also may depend, at least in part, on what is being taught in the regular class. A student who uses a wheelchair, for example, could probably meet appropriate goals and objectives for individual sports such as swimming, weight lifting, and track and field in a regular placement. Conversely, the same student might be assigned to a more restrictive setting when team sports such as basketball, soccer, or football are being taught in the regular class. A third important consideration in the selection of an appropriate placement is the input received from the student or the student's parents.

Instruction

The role of measurement and appraisal does not end with the student's assignment to an appropriate physical education program. Daily instruction should also be based on a sound assessment foundation.

Once present level of performance has been established, the teacher needs to select appropriate objectives for the student. Because the objectives for a student with unique needs ordinarily will differ from those for students in the regular program, they must be written individually. In some cases, objectives might be written for nontraditional physical activities such as high toss or precision beanbag (see Figure 4.1). Appropriate goals should be justified on the basis of performance in a general content area of physical education (e.g., physical fitness, swimming, fundamental movement patterns, etc.). The development of reasonable objectives will include the selection of appropriate performance criteria. While teachers will have to rely on their professional judgment in establishing these criteria, the standards should take into account the student's current level of performance. In some cases the teacher may wish to use normative data to help establish reasonable criteria. For instance, if a student has a visual impairment, the teacher might consult the percentile tables in the Project UNIQUE Physical Fitness Test (Winnick & Short, 1985) to answer the question "Given a visual impairment, what is a reasonable sit-up performance expectation for an 11-year-old boy?" The teacher may decide that the 50th percentile (in this case a test score of 30 sit-ups in 60 s) constitutes a reasonable expectation.

With the student's goals and objectives in place, appropriate activities are prescribed and implemented. Progress on the goals and objectives should be monitored closely. As suggested earlier in this chapter, content- or criterion-referenced tests can be designed and used for this purpose. Another technique, called *task analysis*, can help monitor progress during instruction. Although there are different approaches to task analysis, the

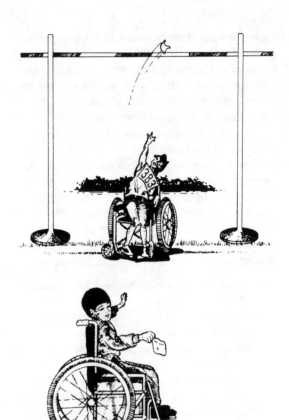

Figure 4.1 Measurement in adapted physical education might include evaluating high toss or precision beanbag performances. *Note.* From *Training Guide to Cerebral Palsy Sports* (pp. 104 and 218) by J.A. Jones (Ed.), 1988, Champaign, IL: Human Kinetics. Copyright 1988 by Jeffrey A. Jones. Reprinted by permission.

one most commonly used in physical education involves listing, usually in sequential order, the subtasks or subskills necessary for successful performance of the skill in question. When skills have been analyzed in this fashion, the teacher has essentially developed a criterion-referenced checklist that can be used in teaching and evaluating progress in a particular skill. Although teachers can develop their own task analyses, task-analytic curricula in physical education are available. (Chapter 10 presents more information on task analysis.)

At the conclusion of an instructional program or unit, the teacher should conduct final testing to determine the student's "exit abilities." In some cases, grades will be awarded on the basis of this final assessment. Whether the program is graded or nongraded, however, the teacher should evaluate progress in terms of the written objectives. As mentioned earlier, progress can be measured in a series of criterion-referenced tests. Occasionally teachers may wish to confer awards on the basis of students' final test performance. Some existing award programs are discussed later in this chapter.

Tests for Use in Adapted Physical Education

The problem of selecting a test or tests for use in adapted physical education is not insignificant. Davis (1984) has reported that over 250 tests exist for use in physical education assessment. In choosing test instruments, teachers should consider at least the following criteria:

- *Economy.* Tests selected should be economical in terms of both time and money.
- *Validity.* Test users should be provided with evidence that the test actually measures what it was designed to measure.
- *Reliability.* Teachers should have confidence that a test yields consistent scores.
- *Purpose.* When reflecting on this final criterion, teachers should consider *why* they are testing, *what* they are testing, and *whom* they are testing.

In regard to purpose, if the test is being conducted to determine eligibility for adapted physi-

cal education, the test selected should offer some external standards by which to judge performance. Norm-referenced measures are most applicable in this context, and content-referenced measures least. Whatever the purpose, the test selected should measure important aspects of physical education. According to PL 94-142, physical education involves physical and motor fitness; fundamental motor skills and patterns; and skills in aquatics, dance, games, and sports. Ideally, testing should sample as many of these content areas as possible. Minimally, information on physical fitness and motor ability should routinely be collected. After the "why" and "what" have been determined, the teacher must ascertain that the test is cognitively, affectively, and physically appropriate for the students being assessed. Teachers of students with physical handicaps, for example, should determine if students in wheelchairs or those who use crutches can participate in the test items. Similarly, teachers of students with mental retardation should make sure that the items or directions are not too difficult for their students.

While a test may not meet all the criteria listed here, it is critical that teachers understand the relative strengths and weaknesses of their assessment instruments and make educational decisions accordingly. The remainder of this section discusses selected tests that are generally appropriate for students with mild to moderate handicaps and for those with severe and profound handicaps. The mild-moderate and severe-profound categorization is somewhat arbitrary; readers are encouraged to judge the appropriateness of a test themselves, considering the criteria just presented.

Tests for Students With Mild and Moderate Handicaps

In many instances, students with mild to moderate handicapping conditions can take the same tests as their nonhandicapped peers. When the tests are norm referenced, however, and the teacher wants to account for the possible influence of the handicap, scores obtained by the student with a handicapping condition can be compared to norms established on a group with a similar handicapping condition.

Fitness Tests

The Youth Fitness Test (AAHPER, 1976b), the Health Related Test (AAHPERD, 1980), and the Presidential Fitness Award Test (President's Council on Physical Fitness and Sports, 1987) are examples of test batteries including items that may be appropriate for many youngsters with cognitive and sensory impairments. Norms associated with these tests, however, are provided only for the nonhandicapped person. Fitness tests with adapted norms are also available. The Special Fitness Test for Mildly Mentally Retarded Persons (AAHPER, 1976a), the Motor Fitness Test for the Moderately Mentally Retarded (Johnson & Londeree, 1976), and Buell's adaptation for the visually impaired (Buell, 1982) have items that are similar or identical to those on the Youth Fitness Test and have been normed on a specific population.

The Project UNIQUE Physical Fitness Test (Winnick & Short, 1985) is a more recent addition to the physical fitness testing literature. The UNIQUE test provides norms for nonhandicapped students as well as for those with selected physical and sensory handicaps. An advantage to this approach is that the teacher need not use more than one test to assess different students or to test for different purposes.

Physical fitness tests such as those mentioned here generally are similar in that most are considered product oriented (e.g., "How fast?" "How far?") and provide normative standards, usually percentile tables. Two recently developed tests, FITNESSGRAM (Institute for Aerobics Research, 1987) and Physical Best (AAHPERD, 1988) differ slightly: Although the items are product oriented, the standards are criterion referenced. These standards are test scores that represent minimal levels of performance thought to be associated with good health. Currently, criterion-referenced standards for these tests are available only for the nonhandicapped population, but FITNESSGRAM and Physical Best users have the flexibility of substituting their own standards on an individual basis for students with handicapping conditions.

Motor Ability Tests

There appears to be more variation in testing formats among tests of motor ability. For instance, there are product-oriented measures such as the Bruininks-Oseretsky Test of Motor Proficiency (Bruininks, 1978), as well as those considered to be qualitative or process-oriented measures of motor ability. Qualitative measures might compare performance to criteria that constitute a mature movement pattern, as in the Test of Gross Motor Development (Ulrich, 1985), or perhaps to a developmental level, as in the Ohio State SIGMA (Loovis & Ersing, 1979). In addition, tests of motor ability vary in that some are norm referenced (e.g., the Bruininks-Oseretsky); some are criterion referenced (e.g., the SIGMA); and at least one, the Test of Gross Motor Development, provides both norm- and criterion-referenced standards. Summary information on selected tests for students with mild to moderate handicaps is presented in Tables 4.3 to 4.5.

Tests for Students With Severe and Profound Handicaps

Students who have severe and profound handicaps frequently cannot be tested with the instruments discussed in the previous section. Regardless of chronological age, most individuals with severe and profound handicaps probably have a functional age of 0 to 2 years. Consequently, many of the instruments used to assess people in these classifications are also appropriate for nonhandicapped preschool children. The Denver Developmental Screening Test (Frankenburg, Dodds, & Fandal, 1973) and the Bayley Scales (Bayley, 1969) are examples of developmental instruments that are sometimes used with persons who are severely or profoundly handicapped. Task analytic approaches such as those found in the Data Based Gymnasium

Table 4.3 A Profile of Selected Norm-Referenced Tests of Physical Fitness

Name	Target population	Ages	No. of items	Components	Norms
Youth Fitness Test (AAHPER, 1976)	General	10-17	6	Arm and shoulder girdle strength, abdominal and hip flexor muscle efficiency, agility, power, speed, endurance	Percentiles by age and gender for each item
Health Related Physical Fitness Test (AAHPERD, 1980)	General	5-17	4	Body composition, abdominal and low back–hamstring musculoskeletal function; cardiorespiratory function	Percentiles by age and gender for each item
Special Fitness Test (AAHPER, 1976)	Mildly mentally retarded	8-18	7	Arm and shoulder girdle strength, abdominal and hip flexor muscle efficiency, agility, power, speed, cardiorespiratory efficiency, skill and coordination	Percentiles by age and gender for each item
Motor Fitness Test Manual for the Moderately Mentally Retarded (Johnson & Londeree, 1976)	Moderately mentally retarded	6-20	13	Muscular strength, power, and endurance; circulorespiratory endurance; flexibility; weight control; speed; developmental skill	Percentiles by age and gender for each item
Buell's Adaptation of the AAHPERD Tests (Buell, 1982)	Visually impaired	10-17	1	Speed (Buell recommends that visually impaired students be compared to nonhandicapped students on nonrunning items of the Youth Fitness and Health Related Tests)	Percentiles by age, gender, and severity of visual impairment for 50-yd dash
Fait Physical Fitness Test for Mildly and Moderately Mentally Retarded Students (Fait & Dunn, 1984)	Mildly and moderately retarded	9-20	6	Speed, static muscular endurance, dynamic muscular strength, static balance, agility, cardiorespiratory endurance	Cutoff scores for "low," "average," and "good" performances (provided by age and gender)

(Cont.)

Table 4.3 (Continued)

Name	Target population	Ages	No. of items	Components	Norms
Project ACTIVE Level II (Vodola, 1978b)	General, mentally retarded, learning disabled, emotionally disturbed	6-16	4	Arm and shoulder strength, abdominal strength, explosive leg power, cardiorespiratory endurance	National percentiles and stanines by age and gender; local and state norms also available; adapted norms by mental age
Project UNIQUE (Winnick & Short, 1985)	General, visually impaired, auditory impaired, cerebral palsied, spinally injured	10-17	4-6	Body composition, muscular strength and endurance, flexibility, cardiorespiratory endurance	Percentiles by age, gender, and population for each item (means and standard deviations also reported)
Presidential Physical Fitness Award Test (President's Council on Physical Fitness and Sports, 1987)	General	6-14	5	Abdominal strength and endurance; arm and shoulder strength and endurance; flexibility of lower back and posterior thighs; cardiorespiratory endurance; leg strength, endurance, power, and agility	85th percentile (award standard) by age and gender for each item

Table 4.4 A Profile of Selected Norm-Referenced Tests of Motor Ability and Perceptual-Motor Ability

Name	Target population	Ages	Number of items	Components	Norms
Bruininks-Oseretsky Test of Motor Proficiency (Bruininks, 1978)	General	4.5 - 14.5	46 (14 on short form)	Running speed and agility; balance; bilateral coordination; response speed; visual motor control; upper limb speed and dexterity	Standard scores and percentiles by age for each component (sex-differentiated adjustments can be made); means and standard deviations also provided
Test of Gross Motor Development (Ulrich, 1985)	General	3 - 10	12	Locomotion; object control	Standard scores and percentiles by age for each component (criterion referenced standards provided for each item)
Project ACTIVE Levels II & III (Vodola, 1974)	General, mentally retarded, learning disabled, and emotionally disturbed.	5 - 8 (Level II) 8-11 (Level III)	5	Gross body coordination; balance/postural orientation; eye-hand coordination; eye-hand accuracy; eye-foot accuracy	National percentiles and stanines by age and gender; local and state norms also available; adapted norms by mental age
Hughes Basic Gross Motor Assessment (Hughes, 1979)	General	6 - 12	8	Gross motor ability	Means and standard deviations by age and gender for total battery
Test of Motor Impairment (Stott, Moyes, & Henderson, 1984)	General	5 and up	32	Manual dexterity; ball skills; static balance; dynamic balance	Means and standard deviations by gender and age (5-12) based on Canadian and British standardization

(Cont.)

Table 4.4 (Continued)

Name	Target population	Ages	Number of items	Components	Norms
Cratty Six-Category Gross Motor Test (Cratty, 1969)	General, educable and trainable mentally retarded	4 - 11 (General) 5 - 20 (EMR) 5 - 24 (TMR)	6	Body perception; gross agility; balance; locomotor agility; ball throwing; ball tracking	Means and standard deviations by population, age, and gender
Basic Motor Ability Tests - Revised (Arnheim & Sinclair, 1979)	General	4 - 12	11	Small and large muscle control; static and dynamic balance; eye-hand coordination; flexibility	Percentiles by age and gender
Purdue Perceptual-Motor Survey (Roach & Kephart, 1966)	General	6 - 10	30	Balance and posture; body image and differentiation; perceptual-motor match; ocular control; form perception	Means and standard deviations by grade level (1 - 4)
Frostig Developmental Test of Visual Perception (Frostig, Lefever, & Whittlesey, 1966)	General	4 - 7	44 (paper/pencil)	Eye-motor coordination; figure-ground; constancy of shape; position in space; spatial relationships	"Perceptual age" equivalents and "perceptual quotients" may be calculated; percentile ranks of perceptual quotients provided

Table 4.5 A Profile of Selected Criterion-Referenced Tests

Name	Content evaluated				Method of evaluation
	Physical fitness	Fundamental movement patterns	Sports skills	Aquatics	
I CAN (Wessel, 1976)	X		X	X	Skills are task analyzed; teacher checks the qualitative components of the skill the student can perform. In some cases quantitative criteria are also required.
Kennedy Sports Skills Series (Special Olympics, 1982)			X	X	Assessment sheets allow for criterion-referenced testing on specific skills related to a given sport; scores can be added to identify current skill level ("Beginner," "Rookie," etc.); skill sheets are also provided to monitor daily progress on a task-analysis basis.
Test of Gross Motor Development (Ulrich, 1985)		X			Performance criteria are presented for each skill; 1 point is given for proper execution. Raw scores can be added to develop composite scores; normative data is also available.
Ohio State SIGMA (Loovis & Ersing, 1979)		X			Teacher identifies one of four levels that best describes student performance as defined by qualitative criteria for each skill.
Movement Pattern Evaluation (McClenaghan & Gallahue, 1978)		X			Teacher evaluates performance as either "Initial," "Elementary," or "Mature" as defined by specific qualitative criteria.
FITNESSGRAM (Institute for Aerobics Research, 1987)	X				Five health-related measures of physical fitness are administered. Raw scores are compared to criterion scores that are thought to represent minimal levels of performance associated with good health.

(Dunn et al., 1980) are also used with this population.

When working with students who have more severe handicaps, teachers may wish to collect information in addition to physical performance data. For instance, with the Data Based Gymnasium, teachers are encouraged to record data pertaining to the primary and social reinforcers that work well with the student, as well as the student's expressive and receptive language capabilities. Teachers may also record the type of cue or prompt that is necessary to obtain a response from the student. Physical assistance, visual demonstration, and verbal request constitute a hierarchy of teacher-generated prompts that can be another source of assessment information with this population. Table 4.6 gives examples of physical performance tests that can be used with students who have more serious handicaps.

Awards

Traditionally, teachers have used award programs to motivate students to improve their physical and motor performance or to attain standards of excellence. Awards range from a star placed next to a student's name on a chart in the gym to recognition reflecting the criteria of an established award program. AAHPERD provides awards in association with five of its currently available norm-referenced tests. Awards are available for the nonhandicapped as well as for those who are mildly or moderately mentally retarded or visually impaired. In addition to the AAHPERD awards, the Kennedy Foundation has established the CHAMP award to recognize elite performance among persons with mental retardation on the two relevant AAHPERD tests. Awards are also available through AAHPERD's Physical Best Program, and, although the test standards may not be appropriate for students with certain kinds of handicaps, awards for activity involvement and attainment of personal goals are appropriate for all, regardless of handicap or ability.

A relatively new and unique award program established in New York State is called *Be New York Fit* (Winnick & Short, 1986). To qualify a student for the *I Am New York Fit* award, a teacher must select, from a list of nine possibilities, the most appropriate test battery for that student. Six of the nine tests are normed for specific populations with handicapping conditions. In most cases, the award criterion is the 80th percentile. The program thus has rigorous standards but permits a great deal of flexibility in the selection of appropriate tests.

Computer Software

A complaint that physical educators sometimes voice about measurement and appraisal is that it takes a great deal of time, much of it after testing is complete. Certainly, the teacher who decides to provide sound instruction will invest more time than the teacher who elects to teach casually and haphazardly. The availability of the microcomputer in today's schools, however, can shrink the time investment substantially. Many companies and professionals have developed software for various aspects of physical education and sport, including measurement and appraisal.

A good example of the ways the computer can help the teacher organize data related to student performance and thereby become more accountable is the Physical Education Management System (PEMS) (Kelly, 1987). PEMS is an Apple-compatible software program that lets the teacher specify and define up to 15 objectives for each physical education class. For each objective the teacher assigns a "mastery level," which is the ultimate goal for every member of the class. For each student the teacher must enter "entry level" (i.e., present level of performance as noted on the IEP), "target exit" (i.e., short-term objective), and "actual exit" (i.e., performance at the end of the unit). With this data PEMS will calculate the extent of improvement on the objective ("net change"), judge whether the target exit was

Table 4.6 A Profile of Selected Tests Appropriate for the Severely and Profoundly Handicapped Student

Name	Content tested	Ages	Type of reference	Components
AMP Index #1 (Webb, Schultz, & McMahill, 1977)	Motor ability	Open	Criterion	Awareness, manipulation, posture, locomotion
Basic Movement Performance Profile (cited in Sherrill, 1986, pp. 472-473)	Motor ability	Open	Criterion	Locomotion, flexibility, eye-hand coordination, balance, eye-foot coordination, strength, agility
Bayley Schedules (The Motor Scale) (Bayley, 1969)	Motor ability	2 months-2 1/2 years	Norm	Posture, locomotion, fine motor coordination
Behavioral Characteristics Progression (psychomotor) (Vort, 1973, 1977)	Motor ability, physical fitness	Open	Criterion	Mobility, gross motor coordination, balance, strength, agility, swimming, posture, ambulation, flexibility, speed
Brigance Diagnostic Inventory of Early Development (motor) (Brigance, 1978)	Motor ability	0-7 years	Norm	Preambulatory skills, gross motor skills, fine motor skills
Callier-Azusa Scale (motor development) (Stillman, 1978)	Motor ability	0-7 years	Norm	Posture, locomotion, eye-limb coordination, balance, fine motor skills
Data Based Gymnasium (Dunn et al., 1980)	Motor ability, physical fitness	Open	Criterion	Movement concepts, basic game skills, physical fitness, leisure movement
Denver Developmental Screening Test (gross motor) (Frankenburg, Dodds, & Fandal, 1973)	Motor ability	2 weeks-6 years	Norm	Preambulatory, locomotion, balance, eye-foot coordination, eye-hand coordination
Early Intervention Developmental Profile (gross motor) (D'Eugenio & Rogers, 1976)	Motor ability	0-36 months	Norm	Locomotion, balance, eye-limb coordination, eye-hand coordination, reflexes

(Cont.)

Table 4.6 (Continued)

Name	Content tested	Ages	Type of reference	Components
Gesell Developmental Schedule (motor) (Gesell & Armatruda, 1974)	Motor ability	4 weeks-6 years	Norm	Posture, reflexes, locomotion, balance, eye-limb coordination, fine motor coordination
Learning Accomplishments Profile (motor) (Sanford, 1974)	Motor ability	1 mo-6 yrs.	Norm	Locomotion, balance, eye-limb coordination, rhythm
Portage Project Checklist (motor) (Bluma, Shearer, Frohman, & Hilliard, 1976)	Motor ability	0-6 years	Norm	Balance, posture, manipulation, fine motor locomotion, eye-hand coordination, strength
Teaching Research Scale (Fredericks, Baldwin, Doughty, & Walter, 1972)	Motor ability, physical fitness	3-18 years	Criterion	Posture, balance, locomotion, rhythm, imitation, eye-hand coordination, body awareness, fine motor, strength
Project ACTIVE Motor Ability Test for the Multihandicapped (Vodola, 1978a)	Motor ability	Open	Criterion	Gross body coordination, balance-posture orientation, eye-hand coordination

Note. Adapted from "Psychomotor Domain Tests for the Severely and Profoundly Handicapped" by P. Jansma, 1980, *Journal of the Association of the Severely Handicapped,* **5**(4), 368-381.

achieved, indicate how close the student is to the established mastery level (''% mastery to date''), calculate the class average on the objective, and indicate how this student compares to the class average. PEMS can generate individual and class reports and can perform some simple statistical analyses (e.g., correlation, t-test) as well.

Both AAHPERD and the Institute for Aerobics Research provide software to be used specifically with their health-related physical fitness tests. With the AAHPERD program, teachers can simply type in the four test scores from the Health Related Physical Fitness Test for each student and receive in return percentile ranks, an interpretation of the scores, and a short list of recommended activities. Software produced by the Institute for Aerobics Research will generate a FITNESSGRAM for each student after the five test scores have been entered. FITNESSGRAM is a ''report card'' that gives the five raw scores, a comparison of these scores to ''acceptable'' health standards (criterion referenced), and a short message to the student on the implications of the scores.

Summary

Measurement serves a number of functions in adapted physical education. It can take many forms, including the administration of tests with norm-referenced, content-referenced, and criterion-referenced standards as well as the use of task analyses, checklists, rating scales, and informal observation. These different approaches can also be combined to yield a more complete picture of the student. Careful observation by the tester, for example, might help to explain a curious test score on a norm-referenced test. Each approach has various strengths and weaknesses and should be selected in accord with the purpose of the assessment. Major purposes include preliminary screening, determination of program eligibility, and the establishment and maintenance of reasonable goals and objectives. Ordinarily measurement and appraisal will focus on physi-

cal fitness, motor ability, sport skills, aquatics, dance, and perceptual-motor ability. Occasionally it may be necessary to supplement this information with data from the affective and cognitive domains. Finally, it should be emphasized that, although some tests have been designed to serve a summative evaluation function, formative evaluation is critical, and teachers should make every effort to integrate measurement with their daily instruction.

Bibliography

American Alliance for Health, Physical Education and Recreation. (1976a). *Special fitness test for mildly mentally retarded persons*. Washington, DC: Author.

American Alliance for Health, Physical Education and Recreation. (1976b). *Youth fitness test*. Washington, DC: Author.

American Alliance for Health, Physical Education, Recreation and Dance. (1980). *Health related physical fitness*. Reston, VA: Author.

American Alliance for Health, Physical Education, Recreation and Dance. (1988). *Physical best*. Reston, VA: Author.

Arnheim, D., & Sinclair, W. (1979). *The clumsy child*. St. Louis: Mosby.

Bayley, N. (1969). *Manual for the Bayley scales of infant development*. New York: The Psychological Corporation.

Bluma, S., Shearer, M., Frohman, A., & Hilliard, J. (1976). *The Portage guide to early education*. Portage, WI: Cooperative Educational Service Agency #12.

Brigance, A. (1978). *The Brigance diagnostic inventory of early development*. Woburn, MA: Curriculum Associates.

Bruininks, R. (1978). *Bruininks-Oseretsky test of motor proficiency*. Circle Pines, MN: American Guidance Service.

Buell, C. (1982). *Physical education and recreation for the visually handicapped*. Reston, VA: American Alliance for Health, Physical Education, Recreation and Dance.

Cratty, B. (1969). *Motor activity and the education of retardates*. Philadelphia: Lea & Febiger.

Davis, W. (1984). Motor ability assessment of populations with handicapping conditions: Challenging basic assumptions. *Adapted Physical Activity Quarterly*, **2**, 125-140.

D'Eugenio, D., & Rogers, S. (1976). *Developmental screening of handicapped infants*. Ann Arbor: Institute for the Study of Mental Retardation and Related Disabilities, University of Michigan.

Dunn, J., Morehouse, J., Anderson, R., Fredericks, H., Baldwin, V., Blair, L., & Moore, W. (1980). *A data based gymnasium: A systematic approach to physical education for the handicapped*. Monmouth, OR: Instructional Development Corporation.

Fait, H., & Dunn, J. (1984). *Special physical education*. Philadelphia: Saunders.

Frankenburg, W., Dodds, J., & Fandal, A. (1973). *Denver developmental screening test*. Denver: LADOCA.

Fredericks, H., Baldwin, V., Doughty, P., & Walter, L. (1972). *The teaching research motor-development scale for moderately and severely retarded children*. Springfield, IL: Charles L. Thomas.

Frostig, M., Lefever, W., & Whittlesey, J. (1966). *Developmental test of visual perception*. Palo Alto, CA: Consulting Psychologists Press.

Gesell, A., & Armatruda, C. (1974). *Developmental diagnosis*. Hagerstown, MD: Harper & Row.

Hughes, J. (1979). *Hughes basic gross motor assessment*. Golden, CO: Author.

Institute for Aerobics Research. (1987). *FITNESSGRAM: User's Manual*. Dallas: Author.

Jansma, P. (1980). Psychomotor domain tests for the severely and profoundly handicapped. *Journal of the Association of the Severely Handicapped*, **5**(4), 368-381.

Johnson, L., & Londeree, B. (1976). *Motor fitness testing manual for the moderately mentally retarded*. Washington, DC: American Alliance for Health, Physical Education and Recreation.

Joint Committee of the American Psychological Association, the American Educational Research Association, and the National Council on Measurement in Education. (1974). *Standards for educational and psychological tests*. Washington, DC: American Psychological Association.

Kelly, L. (1987). Computer management of student performance. *Journal of Physical Education, Recreation and Dance*, **58**(8), 12-13, 82-85.

Loovis, M., & Ersing, W. (1979). *Assessing and programming gross motor development for children*. Cleveland Heights, OH: Ohio Motor Assessment Associates.

McClenaghan, B., & Gallahue, D. (1978). *Fundamental movement: A developmental and remedial approach*. Philadelphia: Saunders.

President's Council on Physical Fitness and Sports. (1987). *The presidential physical fitness award program: Instructor's guide*. Washington, DC: Author.

Roach, E., & Kephart, N. (1966). *The Purdue perceptual-motor survey*. Columbus, OH: Merrill.

Safrit, M. (1981). *Evaluation in physical education*. Englewood Cliffs, NJ: Prentice-Hall.

Sanford, A. (1974). *Learning accomplishment profile*. Chapel Hill: University of North Carolina.

Sherrill, C. (1986). *Adapted physical education and recreation: A multidisciplinary approach*. Dubuque, IA: Wm. C. Brown.

Special Olympics. (n.d.). *Sports skills instructional program*. Washington, DC: Kennedy Foundation.

Stillman, R. (Ed.) (1978). *The Callier-Azusa scale*. Dallas: Callier Center for Communication Disorders at the University of Texas.

Stott, D., Moyes, F., & Henderson, S. (1984). *Test of motor impairment*. San Antonio: The Psychological Corporation.

Ulrich, D. (1985). *Test of gross motor development*. Austin, TX: Pro-Ed.

Vodola, T. (1974). *Project ACTIVE level II-III motor ability tests*. Oakhurst, NJ: Township of Ocean School District.

Vodola, T. (1978a). *Basic motor ability test for seriously multi-handicapped individuals*. Oakhurst, NJ: Township of Ocean School District.

Vodola, T. (1978b). *Project ACTIVE level II physical fitness test*. Oakhurst, NJ: Township of Ocean School District.

Vort Corporation. (1973). *Behavioral characteristics progression*. Palo Alto, CA: Author.

Vort Corporation. (1977). *Behavioral characteristics progression method book #107—Motor skills*. Palo Alto, CA: Author.

Webb, R., Schultz, B., & McMahill, J. (1977). *AMP index #1*. Glenwood, IA: Glenwood State Hospital School.

Wessel, J. (1976). *I CAN*. Northbrook, IL: Hubbard Scientific.

Winnick, J., & Short, F. (1985). *Physical fitness testing of the disabled*. Champaign, IL: Human Kinetics.

Winnick, J., & Short, F. (1986). Be New York fit: A physical fitness award program for all students. *Palaestra*, **2**(3), 20-22.

Resources

Written

American Alliance for Health, Physical Education and Recreation. (n.d.). *Testing for impaired, disabled, and handicapped individuals*. Washington, DC: Author. This handbook provides an overview of testing and a summary of over 50 tests related to physical education.

Werder, J., & Kalakian, L. (1985). *Assessment in adapted physical education*. Minneapolis: Burgess. This textbook is designed to clarify "issues regarding the physical and motor assessment of students who are handicapped."

Software

Institute for Aerobics Research (1987). *FITNESSGRAM* [Computer program]. Dallas: Author. This computer software program will generate a fitness report card for each student in the class.

Kelly, L.E. (1987). *Physical education management system* [Computer program]. Northbrook, IL: Hubbard. This computer software program will manage data on up to 15 teacher-specified objectives for each class (see description in this chapter).

CHAPTER 5

Affective Dimensions

Joseph P. Winnick

Affective characteristics such as responsibility, control of one's feelings, cooperation, leadership, social interaction, competition, taking turns, and sportsmanship help determine the quantity and quality of people's involvement in physical education and sport activities. At the same time, the potential contribution of physical education and sport to the development of these qualities is acknowledged by many professionals. It is also generally accepted that affective development must often receive special attention in people with handicapping conditions. For example, children with emotional or behavioral disorders may reflect an extremely poor self-concept and demonstrate inability to follow rules, share or take turns, relate, or cooperate in a social situation. Thus, they lack the prerequisites for successful participation in activities requiring those affective abilities. Mentally retarded youngsters may exhibit social immaturity that may be overcome in physical education and sport settings. In many instances, physical education and sport provide an optimal laboratory for the "teachable" or "developmental" moment in which individuals can be encouraged to nurture positive affective qualities.

The Meaning of Affective Development

Affective development encompasses three interrelated concerns: socialization, self-concept, and moral development. *Socialization* is the process in which society prepares individuals to behave as mature adults; it requires development of both interpersonal skills and social competence. Interpersonal skills facilitate relations between individuals. Social competence facilitates effective functioning in society through the development of motor, writing, speaking, and other skills. Cooperation, competition, involvement, self-control, leadership, followership, responsibility, social awareness, sportsmanship, following rules, and taking turns are all components of socialization that are inherent in physical education and sport activities. *Self-concept* (opinion, attitude, and beliefs about oneself) is a second dimension of affective development that is related to socialization. Because of its importance and its stress on the self rather than on relationships to others, it warrants its own designation as a part of affective development. Underlying self-concept are self-confidence, self-worth, self-esteem, and body image. *Moral development*, which refers to one's conception of right and wrong, is the third area of affective development.

This chapter discusses areas of affective development considered particularly relevant to adapted physical education and sport and includes information that is foundational to subsequent chapters. Specifically, it emphasizes humanistic and behavioral orientations regarding affective development that currently appear to be very influential in the field of adapted physical education and sport.

Self-Actualization Theory

The self-actualization theory emerging from Maslow's (1970) hierarchy of human needs is relevant to affective development and to the entire field of adapted physical education and sport. In the hierarchy (Figure 5.1), five basic human needs are identified and arranged in ascending order, from the most basic to the most prepotent. According to this theory of motivation, the human, who seeks to meet unsatisfied needs, will satisfy lower-level needs first and then satisfy needs at progressively higher levels as lower ones are met. A person lacking food, safety, love, and esteem would most probably hunger for food more strongly than for anything else. But when the need for food was satisfied, the other needs would become stronger. In the needs hierarchy, self-actualization is the

fulfillment of one's highest potential. Maslow considered the following to be some of the attributes of self-actualized people: accepting, spontaneous, realistic, autonomous, appreciating, ethical, sympathetic, affectionate, helpful, intimate, democratic, sure about right and wrong, and creative.

Humanism, Adapted Physical Education, and Affective Development

Sherrill's Humanistic Orientation

In the third revision of her text on adapted physical education, Sherrill (1986) has drawn extensively and built upon self-actualization theory to guide

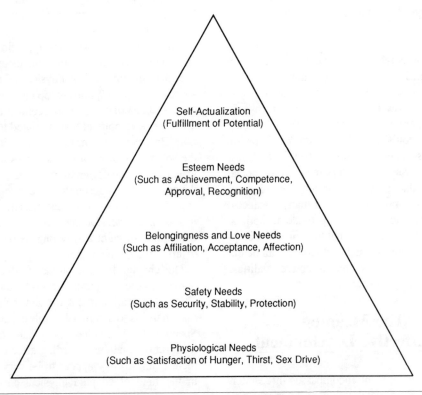

Figure 5.1 A model of Maslow's need hierarchy.

a humanistic orientation to adapted physical education in general, and to affective development in particular. She believes that the characteristics of a self-actualized person identified by Maslow are those that adapted physical educators should strive to develop in themselves and others through movement experiences. Sherrill holds that nondisabled children tend to develop these affective characteristics without concrete, specific help from teachers, but that children with handicapping conditions may need special help to develop these attributes. There are many reasons for this difference. In some cases, there may be less of the total physical self to be actualized, as in the case of amputation. In other cases, the process of becoming all one is capable of becoming (self-actualization) means conquering various problems or obstacles, such as clumsiness, perceptual or motor deficits, or health impairments. According to Sherrill, adapted physical educators need to help students develop positive self-concepts so that they will be intrinsically motivated to become all they can be in physical education and sport activities.

Humanistic physical education uses physical activity to assist people in developing self-esteem, self-understanding, and interpersonal relations—all important to affective development. A physical education program subscribing to humanistic principles strives to recognize and meet unique needs, abilities, and interests through individualized and personalized instruction that incorporates student choice. An important responsibility in physical education is to find games and sport activities that utilize students' abilities and help them develop their play potential.

According to Sherrill, affective domain goals include positive self-concept, social competency, and fun and tension release. Sherrill states that most adapted physical education specialists consider self-actualization, particularly as it relates to self-concept and body image, the most important goal of movement work with handicapped and/or clumsy students. She believes that humanistic teaching is least restrictive for the individual because it permits the individual to be and act most human. At the same time, Sherrill acknowledges

the need in certain instances for more restrictive approaches in adapted physical education. For example, she recognizes the value of behavioral approaches with severely or profoundly handicapped students. Central to humanistic teaching is communication with students to find out where they want to be, what they want to learn, and what goals they wish to undertake first.

For Sherrill, humanistic teaching is based on the assumption that students learn because they are responding to a teacher who relates to them with an attitude of acceptance, empathy, concreteness, and personal genuineness. The emphasis is not on telling students what to do but on guiding them toward making a personal decision to become healthy, fit, and happy individuals. In the humanistic gymnasium, students are taught to praise, encourage, and accept each other. The humanistic teacher values and respects individual differences and emphasizes the worth and dignity of all persons. Students develop their affective abilities largely by modeling behaviors of the teacher. The physical educator functioning within this theoretical framework is expected to combine *friendliness* and *warmth* in dealing with students, while exercising consistent enforcement of *controlled behavior*.

An affective domain goal important to the humanistic orientation is attainment of positive self-concept. Students need to feel good about themselves, and as shown in Figures 5.2 and 5.3, teachers play an important role in the development of this feeling. A success-oriented physical education program is instrumental in improving self-concept. Teachers can create a climate of success by adapting approaches and methods to meet the needs, interests, and abilities of all students and working out adaptations cooperatively with them. A successful experience is enhanced by positive social interaction (stressing the importance of genuineness and praise), effective use of task and activity analysis, assistance to help students perceive their skills and abilities, and leisure counseling to help them identify physical activities they would like to pursue.

Another key goal in a humanistic orientation is

Figure 5.2 Success is enhanced through positive interaction.

Figure 5.3 Responding to genuine warmth. Photo courtesy of CNCA: Frank Demma, photographer. Reprinted with permission.

the attainment of positive social competency. The physical education setting offers many opportunities to experience social responsibility and to develop a sense of responsibility in a positive way. A good classroom environment fosters the learning of cooperative and competitive behaviors as well as an understanding and appreciation of the rules that govern society.

Sherrill's approach to helping individuals reach their full potential includes making available learning, living, and working conditions as close as possible to the norms of society. At the same time, the availability of a continuum of services to meet the needs of all students is very much a part of the orientation.

According to Sherrill, teachers who desire to satisfy individual needs and differences should not feel obliged to introduce all students to the same progression of skills or test them on a particular movement pattern. When personalizing or individualizing instruction, it is important to arrange a progression of skills to suit the needs, interests, and abilities of the individual.

The recurring terms in Sherrill's text that serve to guide teachers in their relationship with students and with the environment they create include the following:

- Acceptance
- Genuineness
- Success
- Worth
- Appraisal
- Trust
- Warmth
- Individual
- Like
- Love
- Contact
- Facilitate
- Positive
- Privacy
- Empathy
- Equity
- Care
- Dignity
- Communication
- Subjectivity
- Personal
- Adapt
- Respect
- Interact
- Progress
- Confidence
- Rapport

Hellison's Goals and Humanistic Physical Education

For several years, Hellison has worked on conceptual frameworks in an attempt to portray the essence of humanistic physical education. He has developed a set of alternative goals for physical education (1985) that he believes focus on human needs and values rather than on fitness and sport skill development per se. The goals are developmental in nature and reflect a level-by-level progression of attitudes and behaviors (see Table 5.1). Specifically, they are self-control, involvement, self-responsibility, and caring for others. The goals are described in the following paragraphs.

Level I: Self-Control

The first level deals with the need for control of one's own behavior. Self-control should be the first goal, according to Hellison, because learning cannot take place effectively without it.

Level II: Involvement

Level II focuses on the need for physical activity and provides students one medium for personal stability through experiences that they can engage in as a regular part of their lives. Involvement includes playing, accepting challenges, practicing motor skills, and training for fitness under the teacher's supervision.

Level III: Self-Responsibility

Level III emphasizes the need for students to learn to take more responsibility for their choices and to link these choices with their own identities. Students at this level can work without direct supervision and can take responsibility for their intentions and actions. At this level, students begin to assume responsibility for the direction of their lives and to explore options in development of a strong and integrated personal identity.

Level IV: Caring

At Level IV students reach out beyond themselves to others, to commit themselves to caring about other people. Students are motivated to give support, cooperate, show concern, and help.

Hellison recognizes that the goals only provide a framework and that strategies must be employed to cause students to interact with self-control, involvement, self-responsibility, and caring on a regular basis. He suggests five general interaction

strategies to help reach the goals. These include *teacher talk* (what the teacher says to students), *modeling* (what the teacher does in the presence of students), *reinforcement* (what the teacher does to strengthen a specific attitude or behavior of an individual student), *reflection time* (time spent by students thinking about their attitudes and behaviors in relation to the goals), and *student sharing* (when students are asked to express their opinions about some aspect of the program). This last strategy gives students the opportunity to talk with the teacher about how best to encourage self-control, involvement, self-responsibility, and caring.

A sixth group of strategies suggested by Hellison are called *specific strategies*, which essentially deal with interaction at specific levels. An example, reciprocal teaching, in which students pair up and help each other to learn, may help them to function at Level IV, caring.

The intention of the strategies is to keep the goals of self-control, involvement, self-responsibility, and caring in front of students so that these qualities will eventually become viable choices in their lives both in and outside the gym. The interaction strategies are illustrated in Table 5.1. Hellison's text helps teachers fill in the blanks in the charts, suggesting interaction strategies that lead to the attainment of goals.

Behavioral Orientations and Affective Development

Behavior modification is another orientation used in adapted physical education to help students learn, control, and maintain appropriate behavior. Effective step-by-step strategies include

- defining a particular behavior to be developed or changed,
- determining baseline or present level of performance,
- establishing one or more terminal objectives, and

Table 5.1 General Interaction Strategies

	I. Self-control	II. Involvement	III. Self-responsibility	IV. Caring
Teacher talk	Teach Level I to students with examples from class.	Teach Level II to students with examples from class.	Teach Level III to students with examples from class.	Teach Level IV to students with examples from class.
Modeling (being)	Don't blow up!	Get involved with students in your lesson.	Keep your promises to students.	Be a caring teacher.
Reinforcement	Praise students for being under control without prompts.	If necessary, reward students to get them involved.	Give awards for independent work.	Praise students (gently and appropriately) who help others.
Reflection time	Require students to reflect on the extent of their self-control in class that day.	Require students to reflect on the extent of their involvement in class that day.	Require students to reflect on the extent of their responsible, self-directed behavior in class that day.	Require students to reflect on the extent that they helped or supported others.
Student sharing	Ask students how the class can do a better job of protecting everyone's rights.	Ask students what they want to learn.	Ask students if they want time to work independently.	Ask students whether they would like a more supportive environment in class.

Note. From *Goals and Strategies for Teaching Physical Education* (p. 24, 25) by D.R. Hellison, 1985, Champaign, IL: Human Kinetics. Copyright 1985 by Donald R. Hellison. Adapted by permission.

- implementing a behavioral intervention program.

Auxter and Pyfer (1985) are among the leaders in adapted physical education who suggest that social behavior can be changed through the application of behavioral principles. They make the assumption that, if the components of adaptive behavior can be defined and a behavior can be ascribed to its components, an intervention program applying behavioral principles can develop behavior that can be generalized to social abilities. Auxter and Pyfer have proposed a taxonomy that relates components of adaptive behavior to social traits and that can guide the design of inter-vention programs aimed at developing positive affective behavior. They hold that most games involving social interaction generate behavior that can contribute to both internal and external social traits. *Internal* traits that can be assessed and developed include delay of gratification, responsibility, reliability, pride in accomplishment, control of personal feelings for the good of the group, and delay of immediate needs and desires to reach long-range goals. *External* traits with a developmental structure that can be identified and remedied include response to authority, cooperation, competition, leadership, asocial behavior, and antisocial behavior.

Auxter and Pyfer situate games on a continuum

of social complexity to help meet social needs and permit an opportunity for development of social skills (see Tables 5.2 and 5.3). Some of the characteristics that make a game more or less socially complex include the level of motor skill required, the number of social interactions with others, the number of rules, the complexity of strategies, the interdependence of group members, the consequence of winning or losing, and the structure of training regimens. Table 5.2 ranks 40 social games in terms of difficulty on the basis of social demands, and Table 5.3 is a social games developmental scale reflecting the traits of competition, responsibility, response to authority, cooperation, and total score. The choice of games should take into account the social abilities of the participants as well as the complexity of the game.

In addition to their instructional model for the teaching of motor skills (the Data Based Gymnasium), Dunn, Morehouse, and Fredericks (1986) present an approach for the remediation of socialization and other inappropriate behaviors. The objective of socialization programs, according to these authors, is to teach students to engage in a variety of solitary and cooperative social activities at the appropriate times, places, and frequencies. Their approach is to task-analyze and teach social skills using instructional procedures based on behavioral principles. They group inappropriate behaviors into four major areas: self-indulgent, noncompliant, aggressive, and self-stimulatory or self-destructive. The authors suggest rule-of-thumb consequences for dealing with behaviors. If these are unsuccessful, a formal behavior program is implemented to change the behaviors. The formal program consists of several steps to improve socialization:

- Pinpointing and accurately defining the behavior,

Table 5.2   Difficulty Rating of Social Games

1. Movement Imitation	3.2	21. Fish Net	7.6
2. Simon Says	3.8	22. Scooter Relay	7.7
3. Hot Potato	3.8	23. Round the World	8.0
4. Duck, Duck, Goose	3.8	24. Four Square	8.0
5. Drop the Handkerchief	3.8	25. Club Guard	8.5
6. One, Two, Three	4.3	26. Tag End Person	8.5
7. Musical Chairs	4.5	27. Tug of War	8.9
8. Movement Imitation II	4.6	28. Wheelbarrow Relay	9.0
9. Squirrels and Trees	4.9	29. Whiffle Baseball	10.1
10. Cat and Mouse	5.0	30. Bowling	10.3
11. Hoop Tag	5.2	31. Air Ball	11.0
12. Jump the Brook	5.3	32. Kickball Soccer	11.9
13. Steal the Bacon	5.5	33. Scooter Basketball	12.4
14. Jump the Bean Bag	5.6	34. Scooter Soccer	12.7
15. Streets and Alleys	5.9	35. Kickball	12.8
16. Run and Catch	6.0	36. Badminton	12.9
17. Crows and Cranes	6.1	37. Dodge Ball	12.9
18. Running Bases	6.2	38. Keep Away	13.1
19. Sick Cat	6.6	39. Newcombe Volleyball	13.2
20. Circle Stride Ball	6.8	40. Basketball	14.4

Note. Reproduced by permission from: D. Auxter and J. Pyfer, *Principles and Methods of Adapted Physical Education and Recreation*, St. Louis, 1985, Times Mirror/Mosby College Publishing.

Table 5.3 Social Games Developmental Scale

Game	Total score	Competition	Responsibility	Response to authority	Cooperation
Hot Potato	2.7	0.0	1.5	0.5	1.0
Duck, Duck, Goose	2.0	0.0	0.5	0.5	1.0
Green Light	2.5	0.0	0.5	1.0	0.7
Squirrels and Trees	3.9	0.7	1.2	0.5	1.5
Hoop Tag	4.5	0.5	0.5	1.0	2.5
Steal the Bacon	4.8	0.3	0.5	1.0	3.0
Crows and Cranes	5.0	0.5	1.0	1.0	2.5
Scooter Relay	5.2	0.5	1.5	0.7	2.5
Streets and Alleys	6.3	2.0	2.0	1.0	1.3
Over and Under	7.5	1.5	2.0	1.5	2.5
Dodge Ball	7.5	1.0	1.3	1.7	3.5
Four Square	8.0	0.0	3.5	1.0	3.5
Tag End Person	9.3	2.5	2.5	1.3	3.0
Bowling	10.0	3.0	3.5	0.8	2.7
Newcombe Volleyball	12.5	3.5	3.0	2.5	3.5
Kickball	14.3	3.3	4.0	3.0	4.0
Scooter Soccer	15.5	4.0	4.5	3.0	4.0
Scooter Basketball	15.5	4.0	4.5	3.0	4.0

- collecting baseline data and establishing a terminal objective,
- designing and implementing the behavior program,
- analyzing the data,
- modifying the program, and
- maintaining the behavior change over time, as well as across settings and persons (Dunn, Morehouse, & Fredericks, 1986, p. 22).

Cooperative Play: An Emerging Concern

In the past 20 years, increasing attention has been given to the use of cooperative play and games in physical education to nurture cooperative behav-ior. Many who have written books on the subject have done so to supplement the competitive goals and activities that characterize many physical education programs. Seeing a need for attention to socialization and self-concept, they have provided cooperative game and play activities as an alternative to competitive ones. Several well-received books that include cooperative play and game activities appear in the resource section of this chapter.

Summary

Affective qualities are important in today's society and influence the quantity and quality of people's involvement in physical education and sport. Two theoretical orientations are particularly relevant to affective considerations in adapted physical education. The first is humanism, which is strongly rooted in Maslow's self-actualization theories. Sherrill and Hellison have formulated important implications for educators based on a humanistic orientation. Behavioral orientations have also had major impact on adapted physical education, especially for severely handicapped persons. Auxter and Pyfer (1985) have developed a taxonomy of components of adapted social behavior to enhance the design of instructional programs aimed at developing positive social behavior. Dunn, Morehouse, and Fredericks (1986) have developed an approach to the development and remediation of socialization problems and other inappropriate behaviors using behavioral principles as part of the Data Based Gymnasium. Finally, many writers have published books that encourage the nurturing of cooperation through games and play.

Bibliography

Auxter, D., & Pyfer, J. (1985). *Principles and methods of adapted physical education and recreation* (5th ed.). St. Louis: Times Mirror/ Mosby College Publishing.

Dunn, J.M., Morehouse, J.W., Jr., & Fredericks, H.D.B. (1986). *Physical education for the severely handicapped: A systematic approach to a data based gymnasium*. Austin, TX: Pro-Ed.

Hellison, D.R. (1985). *Goals and strategies for teaching physical education*. Champaign, IL: Human Kinetics.

Maslow, A.H. (1970). *Motivation and personality* (2nd ed.). New York: Harper & Row.

Sherrill, C. (1986). *Adapted physical education and recreation: A multidisciplinary approach* (3rd ed.). Dubuque, IA: Wm. C. Brown.

Resources

Auxter, D., Pyfer, J. (1989). *Principles and methods of adapted physical education and recreation*. St. Louis: Times Mirror/Mosby College Publishing. This book includes a chapter on psychosocial development, which presents an instructional process for socialization, techniques to promote socialization and change social misbehavior, and other topics relevant to psychosocial development.

Cratty, B.J. (1975). *Learning about human behavior through active games*. Englewood Cliffs, NJ: Prentice-Hall. This book helps to teach children important lessons about human behavior and about themselves through the constructive use of games.

Dunn, J.M., Morehouse, J.W., Jr., & Fredericks, H.D.B. (1986). *Physical education for the severely handicapped*. Austin, TX: Pro-Ed. This book presents a behavioral approach for teaching and programming socialization behaviors in physical education.

Fluegelman, A. (Ed.) (1976). *The new games book*. San Francisco: Headland Press. This book contains a variety of games and activities that encourage cooperative play.

Hellison, D.R. (1985). *Goals and strategies for teaching physical education*. Champaign, IL: Human Kinetics. This book provides strategies for the attainment of the goals of self-control, involvement, self-responsibility, and caring for others.

Orlick, T. (1978). *The cooperative sports & games book: Challenge without competition*. New York: Pantheon Books. This book contains many cooperative games that are relevant for affective stimulation.

Orlick, T. (1982). *The second cooperative sports & games book*. New York: Pantheon Books. Orlick's second book of cooperative games contains several hundred games different from those in the 1978 text and modifies and refines versions of games presented in the earlier work.

Rohnke, K. (1977). *Cowstails and cobras*. Hamilton, MA: Project Adventure. This book presents a broad range of natural outdoor activities, including cooperative group games and activities that may be selected to stimulate affective development. It also describes Project Adventure, a nationally validated project designed to further the spread of adventure programs throughout the country.

Rohnke, K. (1984). *Silver bullets: A guide to initiative problems, adventure games, stunts and trust activities*. Hamilton, MA: Project Adventure. This book presents innovative activities to bring people together and to build trust.

CHAPTER 6

Behavior Management Procedures

E. Michael Loovis

Lack of discipline continues to be one of the greatest problems in the public schools (Gallup & Clark, 1987). For years, educators confronting problems of inappropriate behavior have employed several remedial practices, including corporal punishment, behavior management techniques, suspension, and expulsion. In most cases use of these practices has been *reactive*: A particular method is applied after some misbehavior has occurred. However, many of the problems that educators face on a daily basis could be prevented if they took a more *proactive* stance toward managing the behavior of students. Implicit in this statement is the prevention of misbehavior before it occurs. For example, it will be difficult for the physical educator to establish an appropriate instructional climate in a self-contained class for students with behavior disabilities when several students persist in being verbally and physically abusive toward the teacher and other class members.

From another perspective, behavior management approaches have been used successfully to facilitate skill acquisition—either directly, through systematic manipulation of content, or indirectly, through arrangement of the consequences of performance to produce greater motivation on the part of the student. Thus, for example, a behavior management approach can help a physical educator to determine the appropriate level at which to begin instruction in golf with students who are moderately mentally retarded and to maintain the

students' enthusiasm for learning this activity over time. Behavior management has also been used to teach appropriate social behaviors considered essential to performance in school, at home, and in other significant environments. This chapter offers several proactive systems to help teachers and coaches achieve the goals and objectives of their programs in a positive learning environment.

Behavior Modification

Behavior modification is a systematic process in which the environment is arranged to facilitate skill acquisition and/or shape social behavior. More specifically, it is the application of reinforcement learning theory derived from operant psychology. Behavior modification includes such procedures as *respondent conditioning, operant conditioning, contingency management, behavioral modeling*, and *role playing*. All have one thing in common— the planned, systematic arrangement of consequences to alter an individual's response or at least the frequency of that response. In adapted physical education, this arrangement could involve the use of rewards to cause mentally retarded students to engage in sustained exercise behavior when riding stationary bicycles. It could mean establishing a contract with a student who has cerebral palsy to define a number of tasks to be completed in a unit on throwing and catching skills.

To understand behavior modification, it is necessary to know some basic terminology. On the assumption that behavior is controlled by its effect on the environment, the first step toward understanding the management of human behavior is to define the stimuli that influence people's behaviors. A measurable event that may have an influence on behavior is referred to as a *stimulus*. *Reinforcement* is a stimulus event that increases or maintains the frequency of a response. In physical education, reinforcement may be thought of as feedback provided directly or indirectly by the teacher or coach. Reinforcers can be physical, verbal, visual, edible, or active in nature. Examples of reinforcers include

- a pat on the back (physical),
- an approving comment like "Good job!" (verbal),
- a smile (visual),
- a piece of candy (edible), and
- a chance to bounce on a trampoline (active).

All of these examples are usually considered positive reinforcers. What would their negative or aversive counterparts be?

Positive reinforcers—or rewards, as they are commonly called—are stimuli that individuals perceive as good, that is, as something they want. If a response occurs and it is positively reinforced, the likelihood of its recurring under similar circumstances is maintained or increased. For example, a teacher might praise a student who demonstrates appropriate attending behavior during instruction in the gymnasium. If praise is positively reinforcing to that student, then the chances of the student's attending to instruction in the future are strengthened. This is *positive reinforcement*. Figure 6.1 illustrates the basic operant conditioning processes described in this section. The presence of aversive or "bad" stimuli—something that individuals wish to avoid—is commonly called *negative reinforcement*. If a response occurs and if it successfully averts a negative stimulus, the likelihood of the desired response recurring

OPERANT CONDITIONING PROCESSES

FUTURE LIKELIHOOD OF BEHAVIOR

	Strengthened	Weakened
Stimulus Added	Positive Reinforcement	Punishment
Stimulus Removed	Negative Reinforcement	Punishment
No Change		Extinction (Assuming that the behavior formerly was on a reinforcement contingency)

(left axis: **POST-BEHAVIOR ENVIRONMENT**)

Figure 6.1 Representation of operant conditioning processes. *Note.* From Cullinan/Epstein/Lloyd, BEHAVIOR DISORDERS OF CHILDREN AND ADOLESCENTS, © 1983, p. 78. Reprinted by permission of Prentice-Hall, Inc., Englewood Cliffs, New Jersey.

under similar circumstances is maintained or increased.

Because positive and negative reinforcement may produce similar results, the distinction between them may not be readily apparent. An example may clarify the difference. Suppose that the student mentioned in the previous paragraph had been talking to a friend while the teacher was explaining the lesson, and that this talking was distracting to the teacher and the rest of the class. If the teacher had warned that continual talking would result in after-school detention or a low grade for the day (possible aversive stimuli), and if the student perceived the stimuli as something to avoid, then the likelihood of the student's attending to instructions would increase. By listening in class, the student would have avoided staying after school or having the grade reduced. This is an example of negative reinforcement because the stimulus increased the likelihood of a desired behavior through the absence of an aversive consequence rather than the presence of a positive one.

Just as teachers and coaches seek to maintain or increase the frequency of some behaviors, they may wish to decrease the occurrence of others. When the consequence of a certain behavior has the effect of decreasing its frequency, the consequence is called *punishment*. Punishment can be either the presentation of an aversive stimulus or the removal of a positive stimulus. The intention of punishment is to weaken or eliminate a behavior. The following scenario illustrates the effect of punishment on the student in our previous example. The student has been talking during the instructional time. The teacher has warned the student that continued talking will result in detention or a grade reduction. The student ignores the warning and continues to talk. The consequence for talking when one is supposed to be listening, at least in this situation, will be the presentation of one of the two aversive stimuli.

A slightly different scenario illustrates the notion of punishment as the removal of a positive stimulus. Our student, still talking after the teacher's warning, is punished by being barred from a 5-minute free-time activity at the end of class—an activity perceived as a positive stimulus. The removal of this highly desirable activity fits the definition of punishment and will weaken or eliminate the disruptive behavior in future instructional episodes.

In contrast to punishment, *withholding of reinforcement* from a response that has previously been reinforced results in *extinction* or cessation of a behavior. Extinction differs from punishment in that no consequence follows the response; a stimulus (aversive or positive) is neither presented nor taken away. For example, teachers or coaches who pay attention to students when they clown around may be reinforcing the very behavior they would like to see extinguished. If they instead ignored (i.e., stopped reinforcing) the undesirable behavior, it would likely decrease in frequency.

Table 6.1 summarizes the basic principles of behavior modification. Each principle has a specific purpose; application of the principles requires that teachers or coaches analyze behaviors carefully before attempting to change them.

The examples just provided illustrate the range of learning principles available to teachers and coaches who wish to change the behavior of students. No one principle is necessarily the best choice all the time; the principle applied will depend on the specifics of the situation. Later in this chapter and again in chapter 13, recommendations are provided that originate from the work of Dunn, Morehouse, and Fredericks (1986). After reading the section on their rules of thumb, readers are encouraged to review Table 6.1 to better understand the place of selected learning principles in behavior change strategies.

Types of Reinforcers

Several types of reinforcers can be used in behavior management. Described in the following paragraphs, they include primary (unconditioned), secondary (conditioned), and vicarious reinforcers. Additionally, the use of highly preferred

Table 6.1 Behavior: Consequences, Classification, and Probable Effects

Behavior exhibited	Consequence	Classification	Effect
Jane pays attention during instruction.	Teacher praises Jane.	Positive reinforcement	Jane will continue to pay attention.
Bob forgets to wear his tennis shoes to gym.	Teacher suggests that next time Bob will lose 5 points.	Negative reinforcement	Bob wears his shoes.
Joyce fails to submit her class assignment on time.	Teacher deducts 5 points for late assignment.	Punishment	Joyce will not turn in late assignments.
Bill requests un-needed special help from the teacher every day.	Teacher ignores Bill's requests.	Extinction	Bill will stop requesting unneeded help.
Sue demonstrates poor sportsmanship during a game.	Teacher eliminates participation in free-time activity at end of class.	Punishment	Sue functions as a good sport.

Table 6.2 Intermittent Schedules of Reinforcement

Type	Operation	Effect on behavior	Example
		Ratio	
Fixed	Reinforcer is given after each predetermined response.	High response rate	Praise every second successful throw.
Variable	Reinforcer is given after x responses on the average.	High response rate	Praise every third successful throw on an average.
		Interval	
Fixed	Reinforcer is given after first response that occurs after each predetermined interval.	Cessation of response after reinforcement; high response rate just prior to time for next reinforcement	Praise first successful throw at end of each 1-min interval.
Variable	Reinforcer is given after first response that occurs after each predetermined interval on the average.	Consistent response rate	Praise first successful throw at end of an average 3-min interval.

activities to control the occurrence of less preferred responses, known as the Premack Principle, is discussed.

Primary Reinforcers

Primary or unconditioned reinforcers are stimuli that are necessary for survival. Examples include food, water, and other phenomena that satisfy biological needs such as the needs for sleep, warmth, and sexual stimulation.

Secondary Reinforcers

Secondary or conditioned reinforcers acquire their reinforcing properties through learning. A few examples are praise, grades, money, and completion of a task. Because secondary reinforcers must be learned, stimuli or events often must be paired repeatedly with other primary or secondary events before they become reinforcers in their own right.

Vicarious Reinforcers

The essence of vicarious reinforcement consists in observing the reinforcing or punishing consequences of another person's behavior. As a result of vicarious reinforcement, the observer will either engage in the behavior in order to receive the same positive reinforcement or avoid the behavior to avert punishment.

Premack Principle

According to the Premack Principle (Premack, 1965), activities that have a high probability of occurrence can be used to elicit low-probability behaviors. To state it in another way, Premack implies that activities in which an individual or group prefers to engage can be used as positive consequences or reinforcers for activities that are not especially favored.

Schedules of Reinforcement

When using the behavior modification approach, the teacher or coach must understand when to deliver a reinforcer to attain an optimal response. During the early stages of skill acquisition or behavior change, it is best to provide reinforcement after every occurrence of an appropriate response. This is called *continuous reinforcement*. After a behavior has been acquired, continuous reinforcement is no longer desirable or necessary. In fact, behavior is best maintained not through a process of continuous reinforcement but through a schedule of intermittent or partial reinforcement. Several types of reinforcement schedules exist; however, the two most commonly used are *ratio* and *interval* schedules.

In ratio schedules, reinforcement is applied after a specified number of "defined" responses occurs. Interval schedules, on the other hand, provide reinforcement when a specified time has elapsed since the previous reinforcement. A ratio schedule, therefore, is based on some pre-established number of responses, while an interval schedule is based on time between reinforcements. Associated with each of these major schedule types are two subtypes, *fixed* and *variable*. When these types and subtypes are combined, four alternatives for dispensing reinforcement are available. Table 6.2 presents the intermittent reinforcement schedules and provides a short description of their operation and possible effect on behavior.

Procedures
for Increasing Behavior

Once it is determined either that a behavior not currently in a student's repertoire is desired or that the frequency of a given behavior needs to be altered, it is necessary to define the targeted response in measurable and observable terms. That response will be an observable instance of performance having an effect on the environment. After clear identification has been made, behavioral intervention can begin. The following discussion highlights several of the more commonly used behavioral strategies. These include *shaping, prompting, fading, forward and backward chaining, modeling, token economy,* and *contingency management.*

Shaping

Shaping involves administering reinforcement contingent upon the learning and performing of sequential steps leading to development of the desired behavior. Shaping is most often employed in the teaching of a new skill. The use of shaping to teach a dive from a 1-m board could include the following progression of steps: kneeling dive from a 12-in. elevation, squat dive from a 12-in. elevation, standing modified dive from a 12-in. elevation, squat dive from the diving board, and standing modified forward dive from the diving board.

Prompting

Events that help initiate a response are called prompts. Prompts are cues, instructions, gestures, directions, examples, and models that act as antecedent events and trigger the desired response. In this way the frequency of responses and, subsequently, the chances of receiving reinforcement are increased. Prompting is very important in shaping and chaining procedures, as the discussion of chaining later in this section shows.

Fading

The ultimate goal of any procedure to increase the frequency of a response is for the response to occur without the need for a prompt or a reinforcer. The best way to reach this goal is with a procedure that removes or fades the prompts and reinforcers gradually over time. Fading rein-

forcers means stretching the schedule of reinforcement so that the individual has to perform more trials or demonstrate a significantly better response quality in order to receive reinforcement. For example, a person who has been receiving positive reinforcement for each successful basket must now make two baskets, then three baskets, and so forth before reinforcement is provided.

Chaining

Unlike shaping, which consists of reinforcing approximations of a new terminal behavior, chaining develops a series of discrete portions or links which, when tied together, lead to enhanced performance of a behavior. There are two types of chaining: forward and backward. In forward chaining, the most basic step in the behavioral sequence occurs first, followed by the next most basic step, and so on until the entire sequence has been learned. A student learning to execute a lay-up from three steps away from the basket would (a) take a step with the left foot, (b) take a step with the left foot while dribbling once with the right hand, (c) repeat both previous steps while adding a step with the right foot, and (d) repeat the previous three steps with an additional step and jump off the left foot up to the basket for the lay-up attempt. In some cases it is necessary to teach the last step in a behavioral sequence first, followed by the next-to-last step, and so on until the entire sequence is learned. This is called backward chaining.

Modeling

Modeling is a visual demonstration of a behavior that students are expected to perform. From a behavioral perspective, modeling (cf. vicarious reinforcement) is the process in which an individual watches someone else respond to a situation in a way that produces reinforcement or punishment. The observer thus learns vicariously.

Token Economy

Tokens are secondary reinforcers that are earned, collected, and subsequently redeemed for any of a variety of backup reinforcers. Tokens, which could be poker chips or checkmarks on a response tally sheet, are earned and exchanged for consumables, privileges, or activities—the backup reinforcers. A reinforcement system based on tokens is called a token economy. Establishment of a token economy includes a concise description of the targeted behavior or behaviors along with a detailed accounting of the numbers of tokens administered for performance of targeted behaviors.

Contingency Management

Contingency management means changing behavior by controlling and altering the relationship among the occasion when a response occurs, the response itself, and the reinforcing consequences (Rushall & Siedentop, 1972). The most sophisticated form of contingency management is the behavioral contract. Basically, the contract (which is an extension of the token economy) specifies the relationship between behaviors and their consequences. The well-developed contract contains five elements: (a) a detailed statement of what each party expects to happen; (b) targeted behaviors that are readily observable; (c) a statement of sanctions for failure to meet the terms of the contract; (d) a bonus clause, if desirable, to reinforce consistent compliance with the contract; and (e) a monitoring system to keep track of the rate of positive reinforcement given (Kazdin, 1984).

Procedures to Decrease Behavior

There will be occasions when some behavior of an individual or a group should be decreased. Traditionally, decreasing the frequency of behavior has been accomplished through extinction, punishment, reinforcement of alternative responses, and time out from reinforcement. This section will stress the management techniques that are positive in nature because they have been successful in reducing or eliminating a wide range of undesirable behaviors. Moreover, they model more socially appropriate ways of dealing with troublesome behaviors and are free of the undesirable side effects of punishment. Reinforcement is ordinarily thought of as a process to increase, rather than decrease, behavior. Consequently, extinction and punishment are most often mentioned as methods for decreasing behaviors. This section highlights the use of reinforcement techniques to decrease behavior.

Reinforcement of Other Behavior

Reinforcing an individual for engaging in any behavior other than the targeted behavior is known as differential reinforcement of other behavior. The reinforcer is delivered as long as the targeted behavior—for example, inappropriate running during the gym class—is not performed. This reinforcement has the effect of decreasing the targeted response.

Reinforcement of Incompatible Behavior

This technique reinforces behaviors that are directly incompatible with the targeted response. For example, a student has a difficult time engaging cooperatively in games during the physical education class. The opposite behavior is playing cooperatively. The effect of reinforcing cooperation during game playing is the elimination of the uncooperative response.

Reinforcement of Low Response Rates

With a technique known as differential reinforcement of low rates of responding, a student is reinforced for gradually reducing the frequency of an undesirable behavior or for increasing the amount of time during which the behavior does not occur. For instance, a student who swears on the average of five times per day would be reinforced for swearing only four times. This schedule would be followed until swearing was eliminated completely.

The three techniques just discussed use positive reinforcement to decrease the frequency of undesirable behavior. A description of the more traditional methods of decreasing such behaviors follows. They are included in recognition of the breadth and diversity of behavior management techniques.

Punishment

Normally, punishment is thought of as the presentation of an aversive consequence contingent upon the occurrence of an undesirable behavior. In the Skinnerian sense, punishment also includes the removal of a positively reinforcing stimulus or event, which is referred to as response cost. In either case, the individual is presented with a consequence that is not pleasing or is deprived of something that is very pleasing. The student who is kept after school for being disobedient is most likely experiencing punishment. Likewise, the student who has failed to fulfill a part of the contingency contract in the class and thus has lost some hard-earned tokens that would "buy" free time in the gymnasium is experiencing punishment. In each case the effect is to reduce the frequency of the undesirable behavior. Kazdin (1984) details the advantages and disadvantages of using punishment. One advantage is the immediacy of its effect: Usually there is an immediate reduction in the response rate. In addition, punishment can be effective when a disruptive behavior occurs with such frequency that reinforcement of an incompatible behavior is not possible. Punishment can also be effective for temporarily suppressing a behavior while another behavior is reinforced.

The disadvantages are several: undesirable emotional reactions, avoidance of the environment or the person producing the punishment, aggression toward the punishing individual, modeling of punishing techniques by the individual who is punished, and reinforcement for the person who is delivering the punishment.

Time-Out

Time-out is an extension of the punishment concept. We have mentioned that punishment often involves the removal of a positive event. The time-out procedure is based on the assumption that some positive reinforcer in the immediate environment is maintaining the undesirable behavior. In an effort to control the situation, the individual is physically removed from the environment and consequently deprived of all positive reinforcement for a specified time.

Implementing a Behavior Modification Program

On a daily basis, behavior modification is used in some form by most people—parents, teachers, co-workers, and students. In ordinary situations, however, its use may not be thorough and regular. On the other hand, the deliberate actual application of reinforcement learning principles in an attempt to change behavior is a systematic, step-by-step procedure. Minimally there are four steps that, if implemented correctly, provide a strong basis for either increasing or decreasing the frequency of a particular behavior.

Identifying the Behavior

The first step for any teacher or coach who wishes to change behavior is to identify the behavior in question. This is less easy than it might sound, because it entails fulfillment of two criteria. The first criterion is that the behavior must be observable; specifications that distinguish one behavior from another are clearly established. Measurability is the second criterion; it assumes that the frequency, intensity, and duration of a behavior can be quantified. Sportsmanship, for example, could be defined as the number of times students compliment their opponents for good performance during a game.

Establishing Baseline

With the targeted behavior identified, it is necessary to determine the frequency, intensity, and duration of its occurrence. This process, known as establishing baseline, consists of observing the individual or group in a natural setting with no behavioral intervention taking place. Baseline determination should occur across a minimum of three sessions, days, periods, classes, or trials. Baseline is important as the comparison against which any programmatic gains are measured; it requires precise and accurate recording based on the criteria described in the preceding step. There are several recording systems; the choice depends on the nature of the behavior being observed. The most frequently used recording systems note event, duration, and interval. Event recording entails counting the exact number of times a clearly defined behavior occurs during a given period, for example, the number of acts of good sportsmanship during a game or class period. Duration recording, on the other hand, measures the amount of time a student spends engaged in a particular behavior, for example, cumulative time demonstrating good sportsmanship during a game. When reliable estimates of behavior are desired and when observations are made during specific time periods, interval recording may be used. An example of interval recording is counting the number of 10-s intervals during which students demonstrate good sportsmanship, as defined in the first (identification) step of the behavior management program.

Choosing the Reinforcer

Once it has been determined that a behavior requires modification and the baseline data confirms this suspicion, it is essential to the success of the behavior modification program to choose the most effective reinforcer. Two important factors influence this choice. First, the type of reinforcer that will be effective in a given situation depends on the individual. Not all potential reinforcers work with all people; therefore, it is necessary to ascertain which of the potentially available reinforcers is best for a particular person or group. A second factor in the effectiveness of reinforcers is quantity. Within limits, more reinforcement is probably better. However, when teachers and coaches reinforce in excessive amounts, satiation results and the reinforcer loses its value and effectiveness.

Scheduling the Reinforcer

With the reinforcer chosen, the next step is to determine the schedule for its use. The previous discussion of schedules is applicable here, with one very important reminder. When initiating a behavior change strategy, it is advisable to reinforce continuously. Once the behavior has shown desired change, then the reinforcement schedule should be reduced gradually to an intermittent one. It is this shift that maintains the new behavior at a desirable rate. One last word on scheduling: The longer reinforcement is delayed, the less effective it becomes.

Uses in
Physical Education and Sport

Dunn and Fredericks (1985) suggest that there is evidence to support the use of behavior modification in both segregated and mainstreamed programs for students with special needs. Dunn, Morehouse, and Fredericks (1986) have developed a Data Based Gymnasium (DBG) for teaching severely and profoundly handicapped students in physical education. Successful implementation of the DBG program is dependent on systematic use of the behavioral principles discussed in this section. Additionally, the authors have provided rules of thumb that guide the use of behavioral techniques in teaching skills and/or changing social behaviors. These include the use of naturally occurring reinforcers such as social praise or extinction, that is, ignoring a behavior. Tangible reinforcers such as food, toys, or desirable activities, which are earned as part of a token economy system, are not instituted until it has been demonstrated that the consistent use of social reinforcement or extinction is ineffective.

In skill acquisition programs, task analytic phases and steps are individually determined, and students move through the sequence at a rate commensurate with their abilities. For example, a *phase* for kicking with the toe of the preferred foot consists of having the student "perform a kick by swinging the preferred leg backwards and then forwards, striking the ball with the toe of the foot, causing the ball to roll in the direction of the target" (Dunn, Morehouse, & Fredericks, 1986, p. 81). *Steps* represent distances, times, and/or numbers of repetitions that may further subdivide a particular phase—for example, kicking the ball with the toe of the preferred foot a distance of 10, 15, or 20 ft. Decisions about program modifications or changes in the use of behavioral strategies (rules of thumb) are made on an individual basis after review of each student's progress. Further discussion of the Data Based Gymnasium and the specific rules of thumb for managing inappropriate behavior in physical education with severely handicapped students are presented in chapter 13.

Advantages and Disadvantages

Advantages

The advantages of the use of behavior modification are many. Several important ones are that

(a) it considers only behaviors that are precisely defined and observable, (b) it assumes that knowing the cause of a particular behavior is not a prerequisite for changing it, (c) it encourages a thorough analysis of the environmental conditions and factors that may influence the behavior(s) in question, and (d) it requires precise measurement to demonstrate a cause-and-effect relationship between the behavioral intervention and the behavior that is changed.

Disadvantages

The following disadvantages should be considered before a behavior modification program is implemented: (a) Actual use of behavioral principles in a consistent and systematic manner is not as simple as it might seem; (b) behavioral techniques may fail because what is thought to be the controlling stimulus may not be so in reality; and (c) behavioral techniques may not work initially, requiring more thorough analysis by the teacher to determine if additional techniques would be useful and to implement a new approach immediately, if necessary.

Example of Behavior Analysis

The process for implementing a behavioral system, which is commonly referred to as behavior analysis, requires reasonably strict adherence to a number of well-defined steps. The following example illustrates the teaching of a skill using a limited number of concepts discussed in the previous section.

Skill: Standing long jump

Objective: When provided with appropriate visual and verbal descriptions of the standing long jump, the student will jump a minimum of 3 ft, demonstrating appropriate form on takeoff, in the air, and on landing.

Prompt: "Please stand behind this line, bend your knees, swing your arms backward and forward like this, and jump as far as possible.'' (verbal plus visual prompt)

Behavior: Student acknowledges prompts, correctly assumes long jump position, and executes long jump as intended.

Reinforcement: Teacher says, "Good job!" (verbal reinforcement)

Subsequent Behavior: Student is likely to maintain or improve on the performance as defined.

Other Approaches

The management of behavior has been the concern of individuals and groups with various theoretical and philosophical views. No fewer than five major approaches have been postulated to remediate problems associated with maladaptive behavior. One of these approaches, behavior modification, has already been discussed. Other interventions include the *psychodynamic, psychoeducational, psychoneurological,* and *humanistic* approaches. These interventions will be discussed only briefly here. Resources will be suggested for those who wish to further explore a particular intervention and its primary proponents.

Psychodynamic

Most closely associated with the work of Freud, the psychodynamic approach has evolved as a collection of many subtheories, each with its own discrete intervention. The focus of this approach, in any case, is psychological dysfunction. Specifically, the psychodynamic approach strives to improve emotional functioning by helping students understand *why* they are functioning inappropriately. This approach encourages teachers to accept students but not their undesirable behavior. It emphasizes helping students develop self-understanding through close and positive relationships with teachers. From the psychodynamic perspective, the development of a healthy self-concept, including the ability to trust others and

to have confidence in one's feelings, abilities, and emotions, is basic and integral to normal development. If the environment and the significant others in it are not supportive, then anxiety and depression may result. Self-perception as well as perceptions of others can become distorted, and the result can be impaired personal relationships, conflicting social values, inadequate self-concept, ability deficits, and maladaptive habits and attitudes.

In an attempt to identify the probable cause(s) of inappropriate behavior, the psychodynamic approach uses various diagnostic procedures such as projective techniques, case histories, interviews, observational measures of achievement, and measures of general and specific abilities. Through interpretation of diagnostic results and an analysis of prevailing symptoms, the cause of the psychic conflict is, ideally, identified. Once the primary locus of the emotional disturbance is known, an appropriate treatment can be determined.

Conventional *psychodynamic treatment modalities* include

- psychoanalysis,
- counseling interviews, and
- psychotherapeutic techniques (such as play therapy and group therapy).

Treatment sessions involve the student alone, though some therapists see only the parents. Recently, family therapy has become popular, with students and parents attending sessions together. However the session is configured, it is designed to help the student develop self-understanding. Two of the more commonly used and better understood interventions are reality therapy (Glasser, 1965, 1969) and transactional analysis (Harris, 1969). These interventions have been evaluated for use in adapted physical education by Jansma (1980) and by Jansma and French (1979), respectively.

The psychodynamic approach, including psychoanalysis and psychotherapy, is regarded as moderately effective. Its inadequacies include the following: (a) Diagnostic study is time-consuming and expensive; (b) the results of diagnostic study yield only possible causes for emotional conflict; and (c) therapeutic outcomes are similar regardless of the nature of the intervention—whether the students are seen alone or with their parents, or are seen in play therapy or in group counseling.

Teachers should be aware that implementation of psychodynamic theory as a means to manage behavior does not preclude working with groups. It need not have as its primary goal increasing students' personal awareness. It also does not imply that teachers should be permissively accepting, deal with the subconscious, or focus on problems other than those presenting real concerns in the present situation. The preceding are prevalent misconceptions about the psychodynamic approach.

Psychoeducational

The psychoeducational approach assumes that academic failure and misbehavior can be remediated directly if students are taught how to achieve and behave effectively. It balances the educational and psychological perspectives. This approach focuses on the affective and cognitive factors associated with development of appropriate social and academic readiness skills useful in home, school, and community. Its proponents recognize that some students do not understand why they behave as they do when their basic instincts, drives, and needs are not satisfied. The cause of inappropriate behavior, however, is of minimal importance in the psychoeducational approach; it is more important to identify students' potential for education and to emphasize their learning abilities. *Diagnostic procedures* used in this approach include

- case histories,
- observational data,
- measures of achievement,
- performance in specific situations requiring particular skills, and
- consideration of measures of general abilities.

The psychoeducational approach focuses on strengthening the person's ego and teaches self-control through self-understanding. This is accom-

plished through compensatory educational programs that encourage students to acknowledge that what they are doing is a problem, to understand their motivations for behaving in a certain way, observe the consequences of their behavior, and to plan alternate responses or ways of behaving in similar circumstances.

When a behavioral crisis occurs (or shortly thereafter), a teacher prepared in the psychoeducational approach conducts a life-space interview (LSI), a term first used by Redl and Wineman (1957). The purpose of the LSI is to help the student either overcome momentary difficulties or work through long-range goals.

The psychoeducational approach assumes that making students aware of their feelings and having them talk about the nature of their responses will give them insight into their behavior and help them develop control. This approach emphasizes the realistic demands of everyday functioning in school and home as they relate to the amelioration of inappropriate behavior.

There are several strategies that teachers can use to implement the psychoeducational approach. These include *self-instruction, modeling and rehearsal, self-determination of goals and reinforcement standards*, and *self-reward*.

Teachers are in an advantageous position to encourage students to use self-instructional strategies. This means helping students to reflect on the steps in good decision making when it is time to learn something new, solve a problem, or retain a concept. Fundamentally, the process involves teaching students to listen to their private speech—that is, those times when people talk either aloud or subvocally to themselves. For example, a person who makes a faulty ceiling shot in racquetball says, "Come on, reach out and hit the ball ahead of the body!" Self-instruction can be as simple as a checklist of questions for students to ask themselves when a decision is required. The following questions represent an example of the self-instructional process:

- What is my problem?
- How can I do it?

- Am I using my plan?
- How did I do?

In the modeling strategy, students who have a difficult time controlling their behavior watch others who have learned to deal with problems similar to their own. Beyond merely observing the behavior, the students can see how the models respond in a constructive manner to a problematic situation. Modeling could include the use of relaxation techniques and self-instruction. Students can also learn appropriate ways of responding when time is provided to mentally rehearse or practice successful management techniques.

Another strategy that has proven effective in helping students control their behavior works by including them in the establishment of goals, reinforcement contingencies, or standards. I observed this process as a group of adolescents with behavior disabilities determined which prosocial behaviors each member needed to concentrate on while on an overnight camping trip. Likewise, the group established the limits of inappropriate behavior and decided what the consequences would be if someone exceeded the goal.

A final strategy used in the psychoeducational approach is self-reward. It involves preparing students to reward themselves with some pre-established reinforcer. For example, a student who completes the prescribed tasks at a practice station immediately places a check on a recording sheet posted at that station. When the check marks total a specified number, the student will receive a certain reward. The student is thus instrumental not only in seeing that the goal of the lesson is achieved, but also in implementing the reinforcement process in an efficient manner.

Psychoneurological

The central focus of the psychoneurological approach is *neurophysiological dysfunction*. Identification of students with disabilities in this realm is made on the basis of general behavioral characteristics and specific functional deficits.

General behavioral characteristics include:

- hyperactivity,
- distractibility,
- impulsiveness, and
- emotional lability.

Specific functional deficits, on the other hand, include disorders in

- perception,
- language,
- motor ability, and
- concept formation and reasoning.

The manifestation of these characteristics and deficits is attributable to injury or damage to the central nervous system.

The psychoneurological approach places considerable importance on etiological factors. The integrity of the central nervous system is assessed on the basis of performance in selected activities or tests such as walking a line with eyes closed, touching finger to nose, and reacting to various stimuli such as pain, cold, and light. Additionally, a neurological examination including an electro-encephalogram (EEG) is often part of the diagnosis. Following diagnosis, treatment can include *drug therapy, surgical procedures, physical therapy, sensory integrative therapy*, and *developmental training*. The closest that physical education comes to applying the psychoneurological approach is in implementing perceptual-motor programs (e.g., Kephart, 1960, and Frostig, Lefever, Maslow, & Whittlesey, 1964). In such cases, the management of social behavior is secondary to the training program; however, an inability to control the behavior could reduce the effectiveness of the program considerably.

A major trend associated with the psychoneurological approach is drug therapy, although the use of drugs as a means of controlling or modifying behavior cuts across several behavioral approaches. Students are medicated for the management of such behaviors as short attention span, distractibility, impulsiveness, hyperactivity, visual motor impairments, and large motor coordination problems. Two major categories of drugs, psycho-tropic and anticonvulsant drugs, are used to manage the behavior of school-age children. According to Gadow (1980), the psychotropic drugs are prescribed primarily to alleviate certain behavior problems, improve academic perfor-mance, and enhance social behavior in school, whereas the anticonvulsant drugs are used to con-trol convulsive disorders. The most common categories of psychotropic drugs are stimulants, tranquilizers, and antidepressants.

Stimulants

Stimulants are administered primarily for the management of hyperactivity. Dexedrine and Ritalin, the most frequently prescribed stimulants, are adjunctive therapy and are used with students who experience moderate to severe hyperactivity, short attention span, distractibility, emotional lability, and impulsiveness. Possible side effects include loss of appetite, weight loss, and insomnia.

Tranquilizers

Tranquilizers are used to control bizarre behavior in psychotic adults. In children they are used to control hyperactivity, aggressivity, self-injurious acts, and stereotypic behavior. Tranquilizers are classified as either major or minor. Major tranquil-izers include such drugs as Mellaril and Thorazine, both of which are prescribed for the management of psychotic disorders, including severe behavior disorders marked by aggressiveness and comba-tiveness. Valium, Miltown, and Librium are con-sidered minor tranquilizers; they are used to relieve mild tension and anxiety in children (French & Jansma, 1981). Possible side effects of the major and minor tranquilizers include dizzi-ness, drowsiness, vertigo, fatigue, and diminished mental alertness that could impair performance in physical activities.

Antidepressants

Antidepressants are prescribed to adults to allevi-ate depression. In children they have a more diverse function, including the treatment of enuresis and, occasionally, hyperactivity. Perhaps because of the documented side effects of the antidepressant drugs—ataxia, muscle weakness, drowsiness, and mental dullness—physical educa-tors and coaches should know when students are receiving such medication (French & Jansma, 1981). Tofranil and Dilantin are two commonly used antidepressants; Dilantin is administered mainly as an anticonvulsant in grand mal epilepsy and psychomotor seizures.

Humanistic

Based on the work of Maslow (1962), the human-istic approach has as its major basis self-actualization theory (see chapter 5). Self-actualization, the apex of Maslow's hierarchy of human needs, is the process of becoming all that one is fully and humanly capable of becoming. In large measure, this is a natural development with nondisabled persons. Disabled persons, on the other hand, may not achieve the same relative status as their nondisabled peers because they may lack the intrinsic motivation to become all they are capable of becoming. The needed motivation can be supplied, at least initially, by others who care about disabled individuals first as people, and only secondarily as people with disabilities.

Perhaps no single professional in adapted physi-cal education and sport is a stronger advocate for this approach than Claudine Sherrill (1986). She is not only the spokesperson for the humanistic philosophy but also its instrumentalist in that she applies its concepts in the gymnasium and on the sports field. In an effort to demonstrate how the humanistic philosophy can be translated into action, Sherrill suggests that teachers and coaches of disabled students do the following:

1. To the degree possible, use a teaching style that encourages learners to make some of the major decisions during the learning process. This implies that students should be taught with the least restrictive teaching style or the one that most closely matches their learning styles.

2. Use assessment and instruction that are success oriented. No matter where students score in terms of the normal curve, they have worth as human beings and must be accepted as such.

3. Listen to and communicate with students in an effort to encourage them to take control of their lives and make personal decisions affecting their physical well-being. Counseling students to become healthy, fit, and self-actualized requires the skills of active listening, acceptance, empathy, and cooperative goal setting. Such interaction helps disabled persons reinforce their internal locus of control and take a step closer to self-actualization.

4. Use teaching practices that enhance self-concept. The following practices are recommended: (a) Show students that someone genuinely cares for them as human beings, (b) teach students to care about each other by modeling caring behavior in daily student and teacher interactions, (c) emphasize social interaction by using cooperative rather than competitive activities, and (d) build success into the instructional plan through the careful use of task and activity analysis.

Another physical educator who has been instrumental in disseminating the humanistic viewpoint is Hellison (1985). His primary concern is teaching students to be responsible, caring, and involved people who are capable of self-control. Hellison's model provides five interaction strategies to help teachers and students work together toward a primary goal. These strategies, which are elaborated upon in chapter 5 and discussed further in chapter 13, are teacher talk, modeling, reinforcement, reflection time, and student sharing.

Summary

Lack of discipline has been identified as one of the most significant problems confronting public school teachers. A number of behavior manage-ment systems are available that can significantly reduce the need to discipline students. If students with behavior disabilities are integrated into a regular class and demonstrate persistent disruptive behavior, a behavior management program designed to alleviate the problem might include any of the following: (a) behavior modification using a token economy system, (b) a psychoeducational approach using the life-space interview, (c) a psychodynamic approach incorporating play therapy, (d) a psychoneurological approach using medication, (e) a humanistic approach using listening and counseling skills, or (f) a combination of two or more approaches. Behavior management approaches have been used to promote skill acquisition and prosocial behaviors, as well.

Physical educators and coaches have traditionally employed an eclectic approach in managing behavior: They have chosen the best that each approach has to offer and modified it to suit their particular situations. It is not uncommon to see teachers and coaches with strong backgrounds in behavior modification, for example, who also draw on the humanistic skills of listening and counseling to manage the behavior of their students and players. The eclectic approach is less likely to be used in special schools or other specialized settings, such as hospitals, where a particular approach or management orientation is implemented by an entire staff.

Bibliography

Cullinan, D., Epstein, M.H., & Lloyd, J.W. (1983). *Behavior disorders of children and adolescents*. Englewood Cliffs, NJ: Prentice-Hall.

Dunn, J.M., & Fredericks, H.D.B. (1985). The utilization of behavior management in mainstreaming in physical education. *Adapted Physical Activity Quarterly*, **2**, 338-346.

Dunn, J.M., Morehouse, J.W., & Fredericks, H.D.B. (1986). *Physical education for the severely handicapped: A systematic approach to a data based gymnasium*. Austin, TX: Pro-Ed.

French, R., & Jansma, P. (1981). Medication, learning disabilities and physical education. *American Corrective Therapy Journal, 35*, 26-30.

Frostig, M., Maslow, P., Lefever, W., & Whittlesey, J. (1964). *The Marianne Frostig developmental test of visual perception.* Palo Alto, CA: Consulting Psychology Press.

Gadow, K.D. (1980). *Children on medication: A primer for school personnel.* Reston, VA: The Council for Exceptional Children.

Gallup, A.M., & Clark, D.L. (1987). The 19th annual Gallup poll of the public's attitudes toward the public schools. *Kappan, 69*(1), 17-30.

Glasser, W. (1965). *Reality therapy: A new approach to psychiatry.* New York: Harper & Row.

Glasser, W. (1969). *Schools without failure.* New York: Harper & Row.

Harris, T.A. (1969). *I'm OK—You're OK.* New York: Harper & Row.

Hellison, D.R. (1985). *Goals and strategies for teaching physical education.* Champaign, IL: Human Kinetics.

Jansma, P. (1980). Reality therapy: Another approach to managing inappropriate behavior. *American Corrective Therapy Journal, 34*, 64-69.

Jansma, P., & French, R. (1979). Transactional analysis: An alternative approach to managing inappropriate behavior. *American Corrective Therapy Journal, 33*, 155-162.

Kazdin, A.E. (1984). *Behavior modification in applied settings.* Homewood, IL: Dorsey Press.

Kephart, N. (1960). *The slow learner in the classroom.* Columbus, OH: Merrill.

Maslow, A.H. (1962). *Toward a psychology of being.* Princeton, NJ: Van Nostrand.

Premack, D. (1965). Reinforcement theory. In D. Levine (Ed.), *Nebraska symposium on motivation* (pp. 123-180). Lincoln, NE: University of Nebraska Press.

Redl, F., & Wineman, D. (1957). The life-space interview in the school setting. *American Journal of Orthopsychiatry, 29*, 367-379.

Rushall, B.S., & Siedentop, D. (1972). *The development and control of behavior in sport and physical education.* Philadelphia: Lea & Febiger.

Sherrill, C. (1986). *Adapted physical education and recreation: A multidisciplinary approach* (3rd ed.). Dubuque, IA: Wm. C. Brown.

Resources

Bell, D. (Producer). (1976). *Reality therapy approach* [Film]. Chicago: Film, Inc. This is a film about elementary school teachers successfully using concepts developed by Dr. William Glasser to achieve effective school discipline. It also includes a full explanation of Dr. Glasser's approach to discipline and of the seven steps of reality therapy.

Maslow, A. (Producer). (1968). *Maslow and self-actualization—Parts I & II* [Film]. Orange, CA: Psychological Films. Dr. Abraham Maslow discusses the dimension of self-actualization and elaborates on research and theory related to honesty, awareness, freedom, and trust.

O'Leary, K.D., & Schneider, M.R. (Producers). (1980). *Catch'em being good: Approaches to motivation and discipline* [Film]. Champaign, IL: Research Press. This film presents methods for helping children with emotional, behavioral, and academic problems and shares the more rewarding application of positive discipline based on warm teacher-child interaction.

CHAPTER 7

Perceptual-Motor Dimensions

Joseph P. Winnick

The ability to learn and function effectively is affected by perceptual-motor development. Perceptual-motor ability permits the human to receive, transmit, organize, integrate, and attach meaning to sensory information and to formulate appropriate responses. These responses are necessary for the individual to move, and to learn while moving, in a variety of environments. Thus, they have direct or indirect impact in physical education and sport.

Ordinarily, perceptual-motor development occurs without the need for formal intervention. In other instances, perceptual-motor abilities need attention because they have not developed satisfactorily. For example, deficits related to perceptual-motor ability are often named as characteristics of persons with learning disabilities. Such deficits include poor spatial orientation, poor body awareness, immature body image, clumsiness or awkwardness, coordination deficits, and poor balance. The higher incidence of perceptual deficits among people with cerebral palsy or mental retardation is well known. Perceptual-motor development is particularly important in cases where sensory systems are generally affected but residual abilities may be enhanced, and in cases where perceptual abilities must be developed to a greater degree to compensate for loss of sensory abilities. People with visual and/or auditory impairments exemplify these situations.

Assessment is important in identifying the specific nature of perceptual-motor deficit. Tests or parts of tests that physical educators may use to assess perceptual-motor abilities are described in chapter 4.

Overview of the Perceptual-Motor Process

Sensory Input

A simplified four-step schematic of perceptual-motor functioning is presented in Figure 7.1. The first step, *sensory input*, involves receiving energy forms from the environment and from within the body itself as sensory stimuli and processing this information for integration by the central nervous system. Visual (sight), auditory (hearing), kinesthetic (movement), vestibular (balance), and tactual (touch) sensory systems are important in physical education in providing raw data for the central nervous system. These sensory systems serve to gain information that is transmitted to the central nervous system through sensory (afferent) neurons.

Sensory Integration

The second step in the perceptual-motor process involves *sensory integration*, in which sensory stimuli received and processed enter the central nervous system for synthesis, comparison, and

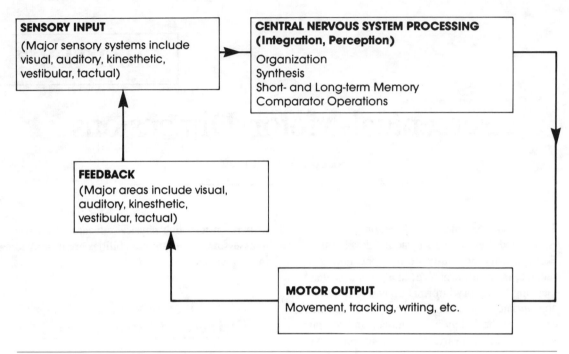

Figure 7.1   Perceptual-motor functioning.

storage. Present and past sensory information is integrated, compared, and stored in short- and/or long-term memory. An important phase occurs as the human organism selects and organizes an appropriate motor output based on the integration. The resultant decision becomes part of long-term memory, which is transmitted through the motor (efferent) mechanisms.

Motor Output

The third major step in the perceptual-motor process is *motor output*. This is the response step, in which overt movements occur as a result of commands from the central nervous system. As output occurs, information is also continually fed back as sensory input about the nature of the ongoing response by the human organism. This *feedback* constitutes step 4 and serves as sensory information to continue the process. As with sensory input, feedback in movement settings is usually kines-

thetic, tactual, visual, or auditory. During feedback, the adequacy or nature of the response is evaluated or judged. If it is judged inadequate, adjustments are made; if it is successful, adjustments are not required.

Terms Associated With the Process

Terms associated with the perceptual-motor process are used in a variety of ways; the following are definitions of some terms as used in this chapter. *Perception* is the monitoring and interpretation of sensory data resulting from the interaction between sensory and central nervous system processes. Perception occurs in the brain and enables the individual to derive meaning from sensory data. *Perceptual-motor development* is the process of enhancing the ability to integrate sensory stimuli arising from or relating to observable movement experiences. It involves the ability to combine kinesthetic and tactual perceptions with and for the development of other perceptions, the use of movement as a vehicle to explore the environment and develop perceptual abilities, and the ability to "perceive" tactually and kinesthetically. Perception occurs as sensory data or information is interpreted or given meaning. Because perceptual-motor includes both an individual's interpretation and response to sensory stimulation, it requires cognitive ability. On the other hand, *sensorimotor activity* occurs at a subcortical level and does not involve meaning, interpretation, or cortical level functioning. Sensorimotor activity is characterized by motor responses to sensory input. The sensory integration process results in perception and other types of synthesis of sensory data. Thus, perception is one aspect of sensory integration.

An Example of a Perceptual-Motor Skill

The perceptual-motor skill of batting a pitched softball can be used to illustrate these basic introductory concepts. As the pitched ball comes toward the plate, the batter focuses on the ball and tracks it. Information about speed, direction, spin, and other flight characteristics is picked up (stimulus reception) by the visual system (sensory input) for further processing. The information is transmitted via sensory neurons to the central nervous system, where it undergoes sensory integration. Because of various characteristics in the environment, the nature of the sensory information, and past experience, the incoming object is perceived as a softball (perception) to be struck (perceptual-motor). The batter's past experience will influence the ability to fixate and track the softball and process information about how to hit it. "How to hit it" involves comparative evaluations in which, for example, the arc of the ball is compared with that from previous instances in which the skill was performed.

The batter decides on the appropriate swing (decision about a motor behavior) on the basis of earlier steps in the process. This decision becomes part of the long-term memory, to be used for future reference. During the pitch, the brain is constantly kept informed about the position of the bat, and the body and will use this information to enhance the overt behavior of swinging the bat. Once the nature of the motor behavior or response has been determined, messages are sent to appropriate parts of the body to initiate the response (motor output or response). As the batter moves and completes the task, information is provided on which to judge whether the response is successful or inadequate (feedback). If the pitch was missed, the batter may decide that adjustments are necessary in similar future instances; this information is stored in long-term memory and serves as a basis for learning. Perceptual-motor functioning is concerned with the entire process depicted in Figure 7.1 and described in this example; batting is thus one type of perceptual-motor skill.

Perceptual-Motor Deficits

Because Figure 7.1 depicts perceptual-motor processing, it is a useful reference for breakdowns in the process—breakdowns at the input, integration, output, and feedback sites. A breakdown at the *input* site may occur for a variety of reasons. For example, individuals with sensory impairments like blindness or deafness may not be able to adequately pick up visual or auditory information from the environment, with the result that this information does not appropriately reach the central nervous system. Students diagnosed as retarded or autistic may not attend to and, thus, not receive relevant information. People with neuromuscular impairments may be inhibited by the lack of appropriate kinesthetic, vestibular, or tactual information basic to quality input.

Sensory *integration* may be affected by factors such as mental retardation or neurological conditions that impair the functioning of the central nervous system. Also, sensory integration may be influenced by the quality of information received during sensory input. Motor *output* can be affected by inappropriate functioning during previous steps as well as conditions influencing movement, including the transmission of information. Conditions associated with cerebral palsy, muscular dystrophy, and other neurological or orthopedic impairments are examples. Breakdowns at the *feedback* site can result from factors that affect earlier steps and any additional factors that bear on the ability to modify or correct behavior. The clumsy child, for example, may lack body awareness because of faulty kinesthetic perception; this would impair the adequacy of feedback.

Many of the factors causing perceptual-motor deficits are associated with handicapping conditions found in the school environment. Thus, physical educators may need to develop programs to nurture development or remediate performance. The nature of an individualized program will depend on the site of the perceptual-motor breakdown, the student's abilities, and the purpose of the program. In the case of a totally blind student, for example, it may be necessary to focus on heightening auditory perceptual-motor components to improve orientation to school grounds and to focus on kinesthetic perception to enhance efficient movement in the environment. Table 7.1 presents an analysis of prominent perceptual-motor need and deficit areas as a function of specific impairments.

Although technically there are many sensory systems associated with perceptual-motor development, the remainder of this chapter discusses visual, auditory, kinesthetic, and tactual perception.

Table 7.1 An Analysis of Prominent Perceptual-Motor Need and Deficit Areas

Impairment	Prominent need and deficit areas
Visual impairments (blind and partially sighted children)	Need to focus on the development of residual visual perceptual abilities and to help the child compensate for visual perceptual-motor deficits by enhancing auditory, vestibular, tactual, and kinesthetic perception. Give particular attention to input and feedback steps in the perceptual-motor process.
Auditory impairments (deaf and hard-of-hearing children)	Need to focus on the development of residual hearing and vestibular abilities (if affected) and help the child compensate by enhancing development associated with intact sensory systems. Give particular attention to input, integration, and feedback steps in the perceptual-motor process.
Haptic impairments (primarily the clumsy child; children with orthopedic, neuromuscular, or neurological impairments; etc.)	Need to focus on the development of vestibular, kinesthetic, and tactual perception and to integrate motor experiences with visual and auditory perception. There may be a particular need to focus on input, motor response, and feedback steps.
Mental or affective impairments (children with mental retardation, emotional disturbance, etc.)	Needs and focus based on assessment of perceptual-motor abilities. Involvement throughout the perceptual-motor process may exist.

Visual
Perceptual-Motor Development

Visual perceptual-motor abilities are important in academic, physical education, and sport settings. In the academic setting visual perceptual abilities are used in writing, drawing, reading, spelling, and arithmetic. In physical education and sport they are important for catching, throwing, and kicking of objects; playing tag; balancing; running; and performing fundamental movements. Age-appropriate visual perceptual-motor abilities are built on visual acuity, which affects the ability to see, fixate, track, and so forth, and thus is required for the input step. On the basis of input, the individual develops the abilities or components of visual perceptual-motor development associated with central nervous system processing and output. These components include visual figure-ground perception, spatial relationships, visual constancy, and visual-motor coordination.

Figure-Ground Perception

Figure-ground perception involves the ability to distinguish a figure from its background and give meaning to the forms or the combination of forms or elements that constitute the figure. It requires the ability to concentrate on, differentiate, and integrate parts of objects to form meaningful wholes and to appropriately shift attention and ignore irrelevant stimuli. Visual figure-ground perception is called on when students are asked to pick out a specific letter of the alphabet from a field of other, extraneous items. In sport, visual figure-ground perception is clearly demonstrated in baseball as a batter must distinguish a white ball from a background in attempting to hit it. Students with inadequate perception may exhibit difficulties in differentiating letters, numbers, and other geometric forms; combining parts of words to form an entire word; or sorting objects. In physical education, figure-ground perception is required

in games that depend on tracking moving objects and observing lines and boundaries, and in activities requiring concentration on relevant stimuli. These include activities in which children move under, over, through, and around perception boxes, tires, hoops, or playground equipment, as well as activities in which they follow or avoid the lines and shapes associated with obstacle courses, geometric figures, maps, mazes, hopscotch diagrams, or footprints.

Spatial Relationships

The perception of spatial relationships means locating objects in space relative to oneself (egocentric localization) and locating objects relative to each other (objective localization). *Egocentric localization*, often referred to as perception of position in space, is demonstrated as youngsters attempt to move through hoops without touching them. *Objective localization* is the ability to perceive the positions of two or more objects in space in relationship to each other. Objective localization is seen as a player attempts to complete a pass to a guarded teammate.

Spatial relationship, which affects virtually all aspects of academic learning, involves knowing direction, distance, and depth. Position in space is basic to the solution of reversal or directional problems (such as the ability to distinguish *d* and *b*, *p* and *q*, *36* and *63*, *saw* and *was*, *no* and *on*, etc.). Perception of spatial relationship also encompasses temporal ordering and sequencing. People who have difficulty putting objects in order will have difficulty in various academic areas, including arithmetic sequencing problems (performing operations in correct order) and writing and spelling (putting letters in correct order). Some authors have contended that spatial awareness is preceded by body awareness, that the awareness of relationships in space grows out of an awareness of relationships among the parts of one's own body.

Visual Perceptual Constancy

Perceptual constancy is the ability to recognize objects despite variations in their presentation. It entails recognizing the sameness of an object although the object may in actuality vary in appearance, size, color, texture, brightness, shape, and so on. For example, a football is recognized as having the same size even when seen from a distance. It has the same color in daylight as in twilight and maintains its shape even when only its tip is visible. Development of perceptual constancy involves seeing, feeling, manipulating, smelling, tasting, hearing, naming, classifying, and analyzing objects. Inadequate perceptual constancy affects the recognition of letters, numbers, shapes, and other symbols in different contexts. Physical education and sport provide a unique opportunity for the nurturing of constancy because objects are used and manipulated in a variety of ways and are viewed from many different perspectives.

Visual-Motor Coordination

Visual-motor coordination is the ability to coordinate vision with body movements. It is the aspect of visual perceptual-motor ability that combines visual with tactual and kinesthetic perception; thus, it is not an exclusively visual ability. Although coordination of vision and movement may involve many different parts of the body, eye-hand and eye-foot coordination are usually most important in physical education and sport activities. Effective eye-limb coordination is also important in academic pursuits, such as cutting, pasting, finger painting, drawing, tracing, coloring, scribbling, using the chalkboard, and manipulating clay and toys. In particular, it is important in writing. Effective eye-limb coordination is also necessary for such basic skills as putting on and tying shoes, putting on and buttoning clothes, eating or drinking without tipping glasses and plates, and using simple tools.

The Use and Development of Visual Perceptual-Motor Abilities

A wide variety of experiences in physical education and sport call on and may be used to stimulate visual perceptual-motor abilities. Although motor activities are not generally limited to the development of one specific ability, some activities are particularly well suited for figure-ground development. These include rolling, throwing, catching, kicking, striking, dodging, and chasing a variety of objects in a variety of ways; moving under, over, through, and around perception boxes, tires, hoops, geometric shapes, ropes, playground equipment, pieces of apparatus, and other "junk"; following or avoiding lines associated with obstacle courses, geometric shapes, maps, mazes, hopscotch games, or grids; stepping on or avoiding footprints, stones, animals, or shapes

Figure 7.2 Using a perception box to learn shapes and develop spatial abilities.

painted on outdoor hardtops or floors; imitating movements as in Leapfrog, Follow the Leader, or Simon Says; and doing simple rope activities, including moving under and over ropes and rope jumping.

Spatial relationships are involved in trampolining, tumbling, swimming, rope jumping, rhythms and dance, obstacle courses, and the like. Activities particularly useful in helping the individual to develop spatial abilities include moving through tunnels, tires, hoops, mazes, and perception boxes (Figure 7.2). Elementary games like dodgeball, tag, and Steal the Bacon, in which one must locate objects in space relative to oneself (egocentric localization) or relative to each other (objective localization), foster perception of spatial relationships as well.

Visual-motor coordination is clearly important in physical education and sport. Games that include throwing, catching, kicking, and striking of balls and other objects are among those activities requiring such coordination.

Auditory Perceptual-Motor Development

Age-appropriate auditory perceptual-motor abilities are built on auditory acuity. The ability to receive and transmit auditory stimuli as sensory input is the foundation for the development of auditory figure-ground perception, sound localization, discrimination, temporal auditory perception, and auditory-motor coordination. Educators should give much attention to auditory perception when working with students who have sensory impairments.

Figure-Ground Perception

Auditory figure-ground perception is the ability to distinguish and attend to relevant auditory stimuli against a background of general auditory stimuli. It includes the ability to ignore irrelevant stimuli (such as those in a noisy room or a room in which different activities are conducted simultaneously) and to attend to relevant stimuli. In situations where irrelevant stimuli are present, people with inadequate figure-ground perception may have difficulty concentrating on tasks at hand, responding to directions, and comprehending information received during the many listening activities of daily life. They may not attend to a honking horn, a shout, or a signaling whistle. Their problems in physical education and sport may be associated with occasions when beginning, changing, or ending activities are signaled through sound.

Auditory Discrimination

Auditory discrimination is the capacity to distinguish different frequencies, qualities, and amplitudes of sound. It involves the ability to recognize and discriminate among variations of auditory stimuli presented in a temporal series, as well as auditory perceptual constancy. The latter is the ability to recognize an auditory stimulus as the same under varying presentations. Auditory discrimination thus involves the ability to distinguish pitch, loudness, and constancy of auditory stimuli. People with inadequate auditory discrimination may exhibit problems in games, dances, and other rhythmic activities that depend on this ability.

Sound Localization

Sound localization is the ability to determine the source or direction of sounds in the environment. Sound localization is used on the basketball court to find the open player who is calling for the ball, and it is basic to goal ball, in which blindfolded players attempt to stop a ball emitting a sound. Sound localization is vital to orientation and mobility for people with visual impairments. Visually impaired individuals often need to further develop their ability to locate sounds; they may do so by reacting to a variety of stimuli (bells, voices, horns, etc.).

Temporal Auditory Perception

Temporal auditory perception involves the ability to recognize and discriminate among variations of auditory stimuli presented in time. It entails distinguishing rate, emphasis, tempo, and order of auditory stimuli. Individuals with inadequate temporal auditory perception may exhibit difficulties in rhythmic movement and dance, singing games, and other physical education activities.

Auditory-Motor Coordination

Auditory-motor coordination is the ability to coordinate auditory stimuli with body movements. This coordination is readily apparent when a person playing goal ball reaches for a rolling ball (ear-hand coordination) according to where the player believes the ball is located. Linking auditory and motor activities is also demonstrated when a person responds to a beat in music (ear-foot coordination) or to a particular cadence when football signals are called out. Auditory-motor coordination is evident as a skater or gymnast performs a routine to musical accompaniment.

Development of Auditory Perceptual Motor Abilities

Physical education and sport offer many opportunities to develop auditory perception. Participants may follow verbal directions or perform activities in response to tapes or records; the activities may be suggested by the music itself. For example, children may walk, run, skip, or gallop to a musical beat; they may imitate trains, airplanes, cars, or animals, as suggested by the music. Dances and rhythmic activities with variations in the rate and beat are useful, as are games and activities in which movements are begun, changed,

or stopped in response to various sounds. Blind or blindfolded children may move toward or be guided by audible goal locators or play with balls that have bells attached to them. Triangles, drums, bells, sticks, or whistles may direct children in movement or serve as play equipment. A teacher conducting such activities should minimize distracting stimuli and vary the rate, tempo, and loudness of sound. It may be necessary to speak softly at certain times so that the participants concentrate on listening.

Kinesthetic Perception

It is apparent even to the casual observer that we use information gained through auditory and visual receptors to move in and learn from the environment. Just as we can know a sight or a sound, we also have the ability to know a movement or body position. We can know an action before executing it, or feel the correctness of a movement. The awareness and memory of movement and position is kinesthetic perception. It develops from impulses that originate from the body's proprioceptors. Because kinesthetic perception is basic to all movement, it is associated with visual-motor and auditory-motor abilities.

Like all perceptions, kinesthetic perception is dependent on sensory input (including kinesthetic acuity) provided to the central nervous system. The central nervous system, in turn, processes this information in accord with the perceptual motor process. Certain diseases and conditions may cause kinesthetic perception to be impaired. For example, in the case of an amputee, all sensory information that would be normally processed by a particular extremity could be missing. Cerebral palsy, muscular dystrophy, and other diseases or conditions affecting the motor system may result in a pattern of input or output that is different from that of the able-bodied individual. A youngster with a learning disability may have difficulty selecting appropriate information from the many sources in the environment. Inadequate kinesthetic perception may manifest itself in clumsiness due to lack of opportunity for participation in motoric experiences. Two abilities closely associated with kinesthetic perception are body awareness and laterality.

Body Awareness

Body awareness is an elusive term that has been used in a variety of ways by writers representing different but related disciplines. Used here, it is a comprehensive term that includes body schema, body image, and body concept or knowledge. *Body schema* is the most basic component and is sometimes known as the sensorimotor component because it is dependent on information supplied through activity of the body itself. It involves awareness of the body's capabilities and limitations, including the ability to create appropriate muscular tensions in movement activities, and awareness of the position in space of the body and its parts. At basic levels, body schema helps the

individual know where the body ends and external space begins. Thus, an infant uses feedback from body actions to become aware of the dimensions and limitations of the physical being and begins to establish separateness of the body from external surroundings. As body schema evolves, higher levels of motor development and control appear and follow a continuous process of change throughout life.

Body image refers to the feelings one has about the body. It is affected by biological, intellectual, psychological, and social experiences. It includes the internal awareness of body parts and how they function. For example, people learn that they have two arms and two legs or two sides of the body and that, at times, these work in combination and at other times function independently of each other. Intellectual, social, and psychological factors enter into the perception of oneself as fast, slow, ugly, beautiful, weak, strong, masculine, feminine, and so forth.

Body concept, or body knowledge, is the verbalized knowledge one has about one's body. It

Figure 7.3   Developing body awareness with a partner.

includes the intellectual operation of naming body parts and the understanding of how the body and its parts move in space. Body concept builds on body schema and body image.

The importance of movement experiences for the stimulation and nurturing of body awareness and the importance of body awareness for movement are obvious. Movement experiences that may serve in the developmental years to enhance body awareness include those in which parts of the body are identified, named, pointed to, and innervated (Figure 7.3); imitation of movements; balance activities; rhythmic or dance activities; trampoline and scooter board activities; mimetic activities; movement exploration; swimming games and activities conducted in front of a mirror; stunts and tumbling; and a variety of exercises. Virtually all gross motor activities involve body awareness at some level.

Laterality and Directionality

Laterality is the internal awareness of right and left and, of course, is clearly associated with body awareness and kinesthetic perception. The concept of laterality received a great deal of attention following the work of Kephart (1960). He held that people develop laterality by experimenting with the two halves of the body, observing and comparing the differences, ascribing different qualities to each, and thus distinguishing the two sides. Kephart believed balance to be the primary pattern yielding the differentiation of the parts of the body, because balancing requires a postural adjustment (muscular tension) to keep the center of gravity over the base and helps the individual identify the midline of the body as a reference point for separating the two sides. These postural adjustments or muscular tensions, Kephart believed, help a child develop an internal awareness of right or left, that is, laterality. Because laterality is influenced by movement and may be treated as a goal in its own right, it is included here as a component of kinesthetic perception.

Although laterality can be considered a major motor goal to be pursued for its own sake, there is lack of agreement about its role in developing academic ability, particularly reading. According to Kephart, laterality is a basis for and leads to directionality, which, in his view, is laterality projected into space. Kephart associated problems in directionality with problems in the classroom. He considered directionality necessary for reading, writing, spelling, and other academic work, and blamed a deficiency in directionality for difficulties like discriminating between various letters of the alphabet. (Children lacking directionality might thus have difficulty distinguishing *b* and *d*, *24* and *42*, *was* and *say*, *p* and *q*, etc.) The notion that laterality serves as the basis for academic achievement has not been substantiated through research. However, it is known that movement activities help children develop laterality and directionality and that laterality and directionality depend on both maturation and experience.

Tactual Perception

Tactual perception is the ability to interpret sensations from the cutaneous surfaces of the body. Whereas kinesthetic perception is internally related, tactual perception is *externally* related and responds to touch, feel, and manipulation. Through these aspects of the tactile system, the human experiences a variety of sensations that contribute to a better understanding of the environment. For example, tactual perception enables one to distinguish wet from dry, hot from cold, soft from hard, and rough from smooth. The importance of tactual perception to the visually impaired is evident as a blind student feels a lacrosse stick to understand what it is, tries to stay on a cinder track while running, or learns to move through the environment using cane travel. For all youngsters, learning is enhanced when they touch, feel, hold, and manipulate objects. The term *soft* becomes more meaningful and tangible as the youngster feels something soft and distinguishes it from something hard.

Gross motor activities in physical education and sport offer many opportunities to exercise tactual perception. Relevant activities include those involving contact of the hands or the total body with a variety of surfaces. Tactual perception combines with kinesthetic sensations as youngsters crawl through a tunnel, walk along a balance beam, jump on a trampoline, climb a ladder, wrestle, or tumble. Individuals may walk barefoot on floors, lawns, beaches, balance beams, or mats or in swimming pools; they may climb ropes, cargo nets, ladders, and playground equipment. Swimming activities are particularly important because of the unique sensations that water provides.

Summary

Perceptual-motor development is a process of enhancing the ability to integrate sensory stimuli arising from or relating to observable movement experiences. Perceptual-motor development is associated with all the sensory systems. This chapter has discussed visual, auditory, kinesthetic, and tactual systems in regard to perceptual-motor development. It has delineated the importance of these systems and has presented examples of how each is involved in and can be enhanced through physical education and sport.

Bibliography

Kephart, N.C. (1960). *Slow learner in the classroom*. Columbus, OH: Merrill.

Resources

Capon, J. (1975). *Perceptual-motor lesson plans*. Byron, CA: Front Row Experience. Also, Capon, J. (1983). *Perceptual-motor lesson plans*. Byron, CA: Front Row Experience. This pair of books presents two levels of basic and practical lesson plans for perceptual-motor programs in preschool and elementary grades.

Cratty, B.J. (1986). *Perceptual and motor development in infants and children* (3rd ed.). Englewood Cliffs, NJ: Prentice-Hall. This is a comprehensive book providing a theoretical overview of perceptual-motor development and practical suggestions for programs.

CHAPTER 8

Wheelchairs and Assistive Devices

Luke E. Kelly

For many physically and orthopedically impaired individuals, a wheelchair or other assistive device (e.g., a cane or walker) will always be used for locomotion. In these cases, the wheelchair or assistive device becomes a relatively permanent extension of the body in the learning and performance of motor skills. Physical educators, therefore, should be thoroughly familiar with these devices so that they can capitalize on positive features and make accommodations for limitations. This chapter provides an introduction to the common types of wheelchairs and their features, as well as to orthoses and other assistive devices commonly used by physically impaired individuals.

Wheelchairs

There are four basic classifications of wheelchairs:

- standard hospital wheelchairs,
- adjustable modular chairs,
- sport chairs, and
- motorized wheelchairs.

The Everest & Jennings wheelchair, commonly seen in hospitals, is considered the standard wheelchair. These chairs typically weigh about 50 lb and fold when one pulls up on the center of the seat. Adjustable modular chairs include a wide variety of chairs designed by a number of companies to accommodate the special seating needs of children

and the more severely handicapped. These range from lightweight strollers to chairs with removable sections that can be used as car seats. Sport wheelchairs represent one of the newest and most rapidly growing areas in wheelchair design and manufacturing. Sport chairs are designed primarily to maximize performance in a given athletic event. Motorized wheelchairs, which are used by the more severely handicapped, are developed by a number of different companies and vary tremendously in terms of design, cost, and weight. Motorized chairs are usually powered by two 12-v car batteries and driven by some form of joystick that is manipulated by hand, mouth, or head controls. The combined weights of the batteries, the motor, and the frame required to support the other parts make motorized wheelchairs very heavy. They can range in weight from 100 to 250 lb.

Wheelchair Components

Given the wide variety of wheelchairs, the remainder of this chapter will focus on the common features of the standard wheelchair and, where appropriate, point out common differences found in sport chairs that physical educators might encounter in physical education or sport settings. Guidelines for wheelchair transfers and descriptions of important orthotic devices are also included in this chapter. Figure 8.1 illustrates the basic components of a standard wheelchair.

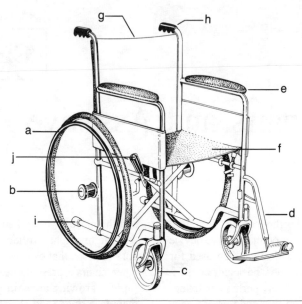

Figure 8.1 Components of a standard wheelchair: a) Drive wheel and handrim; b) Hub and axle (spokes not shown); c) Front caster wheel; d) Front rigging and foot plate; e) Armrest; f) Seat; g) Backrest; h) Push handles; i) Tipping lever; j) Lever brake.

Wheels

A wheelchair has two sets of wheels, the large drive wheels in the back and the much smaller front caster wheels. The drive wheels have four components: hub, spokes, tire (mounted to a rim), and handrim.

Hubs

The hub contains a set of ball bearings and an inner axle that attaches the drive wheel to the chair. The ball bearings should be kept clean and well lubricated. The nuts used to attach the axle to the hub and the axle to the chair should also be checked periodically to make sure they are secure. The nut that attaches the axle to the hub should be tightened to the point that there is no shimmying, but it should never be overtightened to the point that it restricts the movement of the wheel. On the standard wheelchair, the axle is mounted to a fixed position on the frame. On many newer modified and sport chairs, the axle is attached to a bracket that allows it to be placed in different vertical positions and/or moved horizontally so the wheel position can be adjusted in relation to the user's center of gravity.

Another modification often found on sport wheelchairs is *camber*, the angling of the drive wheels so that they are farther apart at the bottom where they contact the ground and closer together at the top. Cambering the wheels increases pushing efficiency, positions the user's elbows in a more comfortable position, and reduces the risk of abrasion caused by the upper arm rubbing against the wheel. Camber also increases chair maneuverability and speed, which makes it a common modification for basketball and track athletes. There is unfortunately no optimal camber; camber must be individually tailored according to the handrim diameter and the athlete's sitting height, arm length, and muscle function.

Spokes

The spokes attach the hub to the outer rim of the wheel. The spokes on most wheelchairs are similar to spokes on a bicycle wheel but are slightly thicker. The spokes can be tuned (tightened and loosened) to correct deviations in the rim. (Some newer wheelchairs have preformed plastic spokes and rims that cannot be adjusted.)

Tires

The standard wheelchair has solid, hard rubber tires mounted to 24-in. rims. These tires are durable and provide a good roll on hard, smooth surfaces. Solid rubber tires do not absorb the shock from bumps well, however, and are not very efficient on rough and/or soft surfaces like gravel, sand, and dirt. Most sport chairs employ pneumatic (air-filled) tires on a variety of rim sizes from 20 to 27 in. The size of the rim is matched to the sport activity and the size and ability of the user. Pneumatic tires have just the opposite features of hard rubber tires. Because they are softer than the solid rubber tires, they require more effort to propel on hard, smooth surfaces. Because pneumatic tires are not solid, they are also subject to greater wear and ultimately to flats. On the other hand, pneumatic tires are better designed for absorbing the shock of bumps and providing greater traction on irregular surfaces. Almost all sport wheelchairs use pneumatic tires. The type of tire is matched to the activity: Wheelchair basketball chairs use thicker tires with lower air pressure, while track racing chairs use very thin, high-pressure tires. The air pressure in pneumatic tires should be checked regularly; maintaining recommended pressure enhances efficiency and reduces abnormal tire wear due to underinflation.

Handrims

The final component of each drive wheel is the handrim, which is used to turn the wheel. Handrims vary in size from 12 to 22 in. and are matched to the nature of the activity and ability of the user. The size of the handrims directly affects the efficiency and speed with which the chair can be moved. Larger rims typically require less effort to overcome initial inertia and to accelerate the chair at low speeds but are inefficient for moving the chair at high speeds. Smaller handrims require greater force but can be used to generate greater speed. The standard wheelchair has large handrims, which are typically just smaller than the main wheelrims. Sport chairs tend to use smaller handrims. Handrims can be attached to the main rims or to the spokes with clamps. Many athletes change the handrims to suit their activities (e.g., larger rims for basketball and smaller rims for track). Some handrims have small handles (protruding rods) to assist individuals with poor arm and/or hand control. Wheelchairs can also be designed so that they can be propelled and steered by a handrim on only one side.

Front Caster Wheels

The front wheels on a wheelchair are usually 5 to 8 in. in diameter and are mounted to a universal joint, like a caster, which allows them to rotate 360°. The front wheels are typically made of hard rubber and are mounted to solid wheels that contain built-in bearings. The front wheels on many sport racing chairs can be moved forward or backward to adjust the maneuverability of the chair. The bearings on the front wheels usually require less maintenance but should be checked regularly and kept clean and well lubricated.

Frame

The frame of a standard wheelchair is usually made of stainless steel. Sport and modified chairs are frequently made from steel alloys and aluminum in an attempt to minimize weight while maximizing strength. The standard wheelchair and many modified chairs are generally made so that they can be folded for transporting, whereas most sport chairs and motorized chairs are not designed to be folded. Common attachments to the wheelchair frame are armrests, footplates, backrest, seat, push handles, and tipping levers. On the standard wheelchair, *armrests* and *footplates* are adjustable. Physical educators should know how to remove, replace, and adjust both the armrests and the footplates. These parts frequently need to be removed or adjusted to facilitate *transfers* from the wheelchair to other equipment and/or to facilitate performance of motor skills. Many folding sport wheelchairs also have an additional bar below the footplates that prevents the chair from folding when it is knocked over.

The *backrest* and *seat* of the standard wheelchair are made of canvas- or vinyl-covered upholstery. The material needs to be pliable so that the chair can be folded. The backrests and seats on standard chairs are usually not adjustable. Many spinal cord–impaired individuals place custom-made inserts or cushions on the seat, backrest, or both to provide support for correct posture and/or to help distribute the weight for proper seating, which prevents pressure sores. A number of belts or Velcro straps are also commonly attached to the frame of the seat and backrest to hold the user in the chair and maintain correct posture.

The standard wheelchair typically has *push handles* at the top of the backrest. The handles are designed to let an ambulatory person assist in moving the chair by either pushing or pulling. Many sport and modified wheelchairs have adjustable and/or modified backrests, which may or may not have push handles. When lifting or lowering a person (e.g., on stairs) in a wheelchair equipped with an adjustable backrest, take great care to ensure that the backrest is locked in place and can support the weight of the person being moved.

The standard wheelchair has two bars, called *tipping levers*, that protrude from the back bottom part of the frame. These levers are designed to give an assistant greater leverage to tip the chair back when traversing obstructions such as curbs. These should not be confused with the *antitip bars* frequently found on sport wheelchairs. Antitip bars are meant to prevent a chair from accidentally being tipped back too far.

Brakes

The final wheelchair component with which physical educators should be familiar is the brakes. The standard hospital chair employs a lever braking system; when the lever is fully engaged against the drive wheel, the wheel is immobilized. Immobilizing the chair is important for making transfers and for motor activities in which the user needs to work from the resistance provided by the chair. The lever can also be partially engaged to provide varying degrees of resistance that can be used to control the speed of the chair in descending a steep incline.

Wheelchair Assistance

The following procedures are recommended when a wheelchair user needs assistance to ascend or descend stairs and curbs. Two assistants are recommended for negotiating stairs. If there is any doubt that the assistant or assistants can safely lift a person in a wheelchair up or down a set of stairs, the lift should not be attempted. Whatever the number of assistants, one person should be in charge and direct all movements during a lift.

—— Wheelchair Assistance ——

Assist Up a Curb: Stand behind the wheelchair and point the front of the chair at the curb. Tip the chair back, using the tipping lever; roll the chair forward until the front wheels are over the curb and the back wheels are in contact with the curb. Lean the chair forward until the front wheels make contact, then push and lift on the push handles and roll the back wheels up and over the curb.

Assist Down a Curb: Turn the chair around so that the back of the chair is facing the curb. Step down the curb, using the push handles; pull the chair back slowly and allow the rear wheels to roll down the curb. As the rear wheels begin to roll down the curb, push in to the chair to control the speed; roll the chair backward until the front wheels clear the curb. Slowly lean the chair forward until the front wheels regain contact with the ground.

Assist Up Stairs: Turn the chair around so that the back is facing the stairs. Tip the chair back, using the tipping lever; pull the chair backward until contact is made with the first stair, then lift and pull on the push handles and roll the wheels up one step at a time. The lifter's back should remain as straight as possible, with the force coming from extending the legs. The second assistant, positioned in front of the chair, should hold the frame of the chair—not the footplates or front riggings—and should lift and push in unison with the first assistant.

Assist Down Stairs: Face the chair so that the front wheels are pointed toward the stairs to be descended. Tip the chair back, using the tipping lever; holding the push handles, roll the chair forward. As the rear wheels clear the edge of the step, pull back and allow the wheels to slowly roll down the step. The second assistant, positioned in front of the chair and holding the frame, should focus on maintaining the reclined angle of the chair and providing resistance as the chair rolls over the edge of each step, to control the speed of the roll.

Transfers

In addition to providing assistance with some difficult maneuvers, physical educators must know how to assist individuals in and out of their wheelchairs. The most common transfers involve moving a person from the wheelchair to a mat on the floor and then from the mat back into the chair. Most paraplegics are able to get in and out of their chairs independently or with minimal assistance. Quadriplegics, on the other hand, need greater if not total assistance with this maneuver. The following rules should guide the performance of transfers.

1. Prepare the chair first: Apply the brakes and remove or move the footplates and front riggings. If appropriate, have someone else hold the chair to provide additional stability.
2. Explain to the person being assisted exactly what is going to be done.
3. Bend your knees before lifting and do all lifting with your legs. When lifting from a mat, start with one knee on the mat and the other knee up.
4. Keep your lower back as straight as possible.
5. Hold the person as close to your body as possible.
6. Know your own strength, and do not attempt to lift anyone you cannot comfortably lift. As a general rule, do not attempt an individual lift of anyone who weighs more than a third of your weight.

When in doubt, use a two-person lift, performed with one assistant on each side of the person to be lifted. The person being assisted should be in a supine position (on the back, face up). Each assistant places one arm under the person's arm and around the back (under the shoulder blades) and then grasps the other assistant's wrist, forming an overlocking grip. The assistants then place their free arms under the person's thighs and grasp each other's wrists in an overlocking fashion. The lift should then be directed by one assistant and initiated on a set command.

Wheelchair Design and Propulsion Techniques

The Research and Training Center for the Physically Disabled at the University of Alberta, Edmonton, Canada, under the direction of Robert Steadward, has taken the lead in individually designing efficient wheelchairs for the nonambulatory athlete and in analyzing propulsion techniques for sprint and long-distance wheelchair racers. Studies at the University of Alberta (Steadward, 1979, 1980; Steadward, Koh, & Byrnes, 1983; Walsh, Marchiori, & Steadward, 1984) have determined that the optimum position of the wheelchair seat for track events should place the athlete's center of mass low to the ground and ensure that the greater trochanter be in line with, or slightly in front of, the wheel axle. This position permits the athlete to have the greatest amount of handrim contact and exert maximum trunk thrust.

Higgs (1983) studied 16 world-class, spinally paralyzed athletes (8 sprinters and 8 distance racers) during competition to ascertain the best hand pathways for sprinting and distance racing. Separate analyses were performed on the propulsive and recovery phases of the handrim stroke. During the propulsion phase, distance racers required earlier and longer contact with the handrim than did the sprinters. This produced a shuttle- (push-) type hand pathway for sprinters and a circular hand pathway for distance racers. In both cases, chair speed decreased as the length of the recovery phase increased.

There are basically two pushing techniques used to propel a wheelchair: the forward push and the full circular push. The forward push is the most common technique and the one used predominantly with standard wheelchairs. The full circular push, used primarily in wheelchair racing, requires specially fitted chairs and smaller, 12- to 16-in. handrims. The two pushing techniques are described and illustrated next. (The clock refer-

ences assume that the wheelchair is viewed from the right side.)

Forward Push Technique

1. Starting position: The back is straight and perpendicular to the ground. The hands grasp the handrims at around 11 o'clock. (See Figure 8.2a.)
2. Push phase: The handrims are pushed forward and down; near the end of the push, the trunk leans forward to increase the range of the push. (See Figure 8.2b.)
3. Recovery phase: The handrims are released at around 3 o'clock. The back is straightened to the upright position, and the hands regrasp the rims at around 11 o'clock. (See Figure 8.2c.)

Full Circular Push Technique

1. Starting position: The trunk is leaned forward approximately 30°. The hands grasp

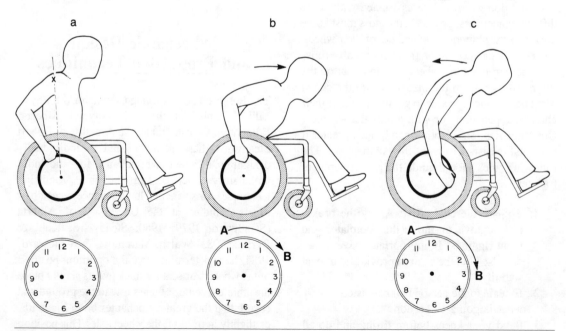

Figure 8.2 Illustration of the forward push technique: a) start, b) push, c) recovery.

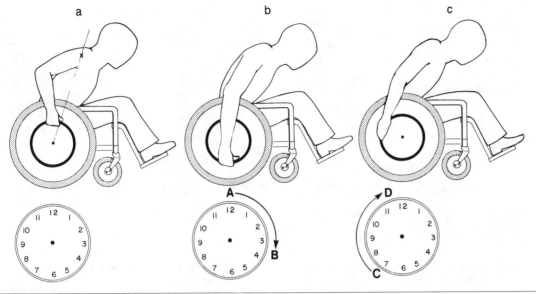

Figure 8.3 Illustration of the circular push technique: a) start, b) forward push phase, c) pull phase.

the handrims at the 12 o'clock position. (See Figure 8.3a.)

2. Push phase: The trunk position is held constant. The hands push forward and down on the handrims until around the 5 o'clock position. (See Figure 8.3b.)

3. Pull phase: The palms of the hands stay in contact with the handrims as the grip is changed and the rim is grasped again at 7 o'clock. The trunk position is held constant while the hands pull up on the handrims to the 11 o'clock position. The grip is then changed (palms remain in contact with the rims), and the next push phase begins when the hands reach the 12 o'clock position. (See Figure 8.3c.)

Orthotic Devices

Orthoses are a variety of splints and braces designed to provide support, improve positioning, correct or prevent deformities, and reduce or alleviate pain. Orthotic devices are prescribed by physicians and fitted by occupational therapists, who also instruct users in wearing and caring for the devices. Examples of the more common orthoses are shown in Figure 8.4. They are used both by ambulatory individuals to provide better stability and by wheelchair-bound individuals to prevent deformities. These devices are commonly referred to by abbreviations that describe the joints they cover: *AFO*—ankle-foot orthosis, *KAFO*—knee-ankle-foot orthosis, and *HKAFO*—hip-knee-ankle-foot orthosis.

Many of the newer plastic orthoses can be worn inside regular shoes and under clothing. Under normal circumstances, orthoses should be worn in all physical education activities with the exception of swimming. In vigorous activities, physical educators should periodically check that the straps are secure and that no abrasion or skin irritation is occurring where the orthosis or straps contact the skin.

Orthoses can also be used to improve positioning to maximize sensory input. Figure 8.5 shows a series of assistive devices often used with spina bifida children to position the head and body so that they parallel the postures through which a nonhandicapped child progresses. The last device

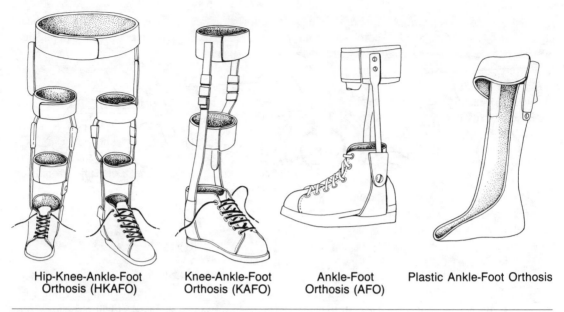

Hip-Knee-Ankle-Foot
Orthosis (HKAFO)

Knee-Ankle-Foot
Orthosis (KAFO)

Ankle-Foot
Orthosis (AFO)

Plastic Ankle-Foot Orthosis

Figure 8.4 Common orthotic devices worn by individuals with spinal cord impairments.

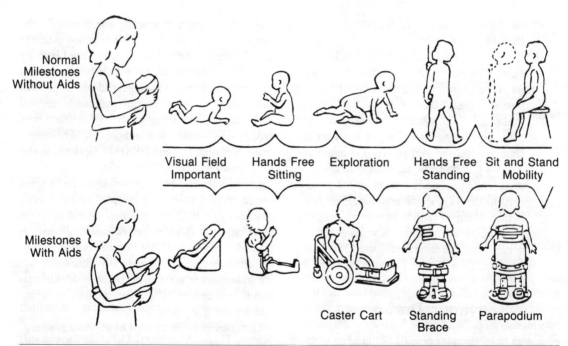

Normal
Milestones
Without Aids

Visual Field
Important

Hands Free
Sitting

Exploration

Hands Free
Standing

Sit and Stand
Mobility

Milestones
With Aids

Caster Cart

Standing
Brace

Parapodium

Figure 8.5 Illustration of the use of orthotic devices to help spina bifida children attain normal developmental postures. *Note.* From *Physically Handicapped Children* (p. 353) by E.E. Bleck and D.A. Nagel, 1982, New York: Grune & Stratton. Copyright 1982 by Grune & Stratton. Reprinted by permission.

shown in Figure 8.5 is a *parapodium*, or standing table. The parapodium allows individuals who otherwise could not stand to attain a standing position from which they can work and view the world. The parapodium frees the individual from the burden or inability to balance and bear weight and also affords complete use of the arms and hands. The parapodium can be used effectively in physical education to teach a number of skills such as table tennis. In recent years, several companies have devised ingenious modifications of the parapodium that can be easily adjusted to a number of vertical and horizontal positions. The Rochester parapodium has been designed to permit ambulation through twisting movements of the body (Lough & Nielsen, 1986).

A second category of orthotic devices includes canes and walkers that are used as assistive devices for ambulation. The *Lofstrand* or Canadian crutches are most commonly used by spina bifida and spinal cord–impaired people who ambulate with leg braces and crutches. Physical educators should be aware that a person using only one cane or crutch employs it on the strong side, thus immobilizing the better arm. This should be considered and appropriate modifications (i.e., to maintain balance) should be made for skills in which use of the better arm is desired.

Summary

To effectively teach motor skills to orthopedically impaired individuals, physical educators must be throroughly familiar with the wheelchairs and other assistive devices used by their students. A sound understanding of both the positive features and limitations associated with a wheelchair or assistive device will give the physical educator the information needed to task-analyze motor skills and modify sport and game activities. Physical educators must also stay abreast of the latest technological advances in wheelchairs and assistive devices so that they can disseminate this information to their students. This chapter has presented information that is basic to understanding wheelchairs and assistive devices as related to physical education and sport.

Acknowledgment

The author would like to acknowledge Patricia Krebs for her assistance with and contributions to the section "Wheelchair Design and Propulsion Techniques."

Bibliography

Higgs, C. (1983). An analysis of racing wheelchairs used at the 1980 Olympic Games for the Disabled. *Research Quarterly for Exercise and Sport*, **54**, 229-233.

Lough, L.K., & Nielsen, D.H. (1986). Ambulation of children with myelomeningocele: Parapodium versus parapodium with Orlau swivel modification. *Developmental Medicine and Child Neurology*, **28**, 489-497.

Steadward, R. D. (1979). Research on classifying wheelchair athletes. In R.D. Steadward (Ed.), *Proceedings of the First International Medical Congress on Sports for the Disabled* (pp. 36-41). Edmonton, Alberta, Canada: University of Alberta.

Steadward, R.D. (1980). Analysis of wheelchair sport events. In H. Natvig (Ed.), *Proceedings of the First International Medical Congress on Sports for the Disabled* (pp. 184-192). Oslo: Royal Ministry of Church and Education, State Office for Youth and Sport.

Steadward, R.D., Koh, S.M., & Byrnes, D.P. (1983). *A descriptive analysis of the competitive wheelchair stroke*. Manuscript submitted for publication.

Walsh, C.M., Marchiori, G.E., & Steadward, R.D. (1984). *Effect of feet position on maximal linear velocity in wheelchair sprints*. Manuscript submitted for publication.

Resources

Crase, N. (1987). 5th annual survey of light-weights. *Sports 'N Spokes*, **12**, 17-30. This article reviews the latest advances in wheelchairs made by 22 wheelchair manufacturers. Each chair is reviewed in terms of its cost, dimensions, weight, purpose for which it was designed, warranty, and procedures for ordering. A new review is released each year in the spring edition of *Sports 'N Spokes*.

LaMere, J., & Labanowich, S. (1984a). The history of sport wheelchairs—Part I: The development of the basketball wheelchair. *Sports 'N Spokes*, **9**, 6-9; LaMere, J., & Labanowich, S. (1984b). The history of sport wheelchairs—Part II: The racing wheelchair 1956-1975. *Sports 'N Spokes*, **10**(1), 12-14; *and* LaMere, J., & Labanowich, S. (1984c). The history of sport wheelchairs—Part III: The racing wheelchair 1976-1983. *Sports 'N Spokes*, **10**(2), 12-16. These three articles review the evolution that has led to today's sport wheelchairs. The articles highlight the individuals and the design features that were instrumental in the creation of each subsequent generation of sport wheelchairs, as well as the impact these new designs had on the sports competitions of the time.

Schuman, S. (1979). Wheelchair frame modifications. *Sports 'N Spokes*, **4**, 5-6. This short article discusses how a standard wheelchair can be modified into a sport chair. The two major modifications are the addition of position adaptors to relocate the rear axles and the addition of camber to the drive wheels of the chair.

Spooren, P. (1981). The technical characteristics of wheelchair racing. *Sports 'N Spokes*, **7**, 19-20. This article is a detailed analysis of the wheelchair design features relevant to wheelchair racing. The author addresses propulsion techniques as well as the features that should be considered in designing a chair to meet an athlete's specific needs.

Learning and Teaching

Part II focuses on the learner and the teacher. Chapter 9 begins with a brief review of the ways in which learning occurs, the stages of learning, and the sensory modes that are emphasized in physical education and sport. The discussion then turns to learning approaches, medical considerations, and environmental factors relevant to adapted physical education. The last part of the chapter treats motor learning and biomechanical and physiological principles as factors influencing successful learning. The chapter builds on the assumption that the effective educator must know the learner and the learning process in order to adapt or use the most appropriate teaching style or approach.

Chapter 10 discusses teaching styles and approaches that may be used in adapted physical education and sport, analyzing them in terms of various concerns. The chapter also includes techniques for individualizing and personalizing instruction and improving teaching effectiveness. The final section of the chapter describes established planning and instructional models that continue to be used in adapted physical education.

CHAPTER 9

Factors Influencing the Learning Process

Sarah M. Rich

To facilitate learning, the physical educator or coach must understand how individuals with unique needs learn most effectively and how the speed and success of learning can be influenced by the environment and other external factors such as medication. The best teaching is based on a sound knowledge of the scientific foundations of physical education, including motor learning, biomechanics, and exercise physiology. An understanding of the factors that affect learning helps teachers design optimal learning experiences that let students with unique needs achieve their maximum potential and satisfaction.

The Learning Process

The passing of knowledge from teacher to student underlies the educational process. True education does not occur by rote. Rather, it is influenced by initiative on the part of both the educator and the learner, and the learning of information and skills is enhanced by active communication. The teacher or coach of students with unique needs must understand the learning process so that the content to be learned can be easily assimilated by the learner.

Learning

Learning, as used here, is a change in behavior that usually occurs as a result of practice. Learning is typically regarded as occurring in three domains: the cognitive domain, the affective domain, and the psychomotor domain. Although the psychomotor domain is adapted physical education's main focus, the teacher can often enhance student achievement in the other domains as well. For example, a physical educator using colored hand- and footprints on a mat to teach laterality skills (psychomotor domain) to trainable mentally retarded students can also reinforce color identification (cognitive domain). Or, while helping emotionally disturbed children learn ball skills by throwing and catching with a partner, the physical educator can reinforce the need for sharing and cooperation (affective domain).

Although often equated, learning and performance are not synonymous. This is quite evident in some children with impairments. For example, on some days a child who has learned to swim using an appropriate elementary backstroke can perform the skill quite easily, indicating a high level of achievement. On other days environmental factors (e.g., water temperature) or individual limitations (e.g., spasticity or behavioral outbursts) may prevent successful performance of the skill. While performance is often an indicator of the extent of learning, it is not always a reliable measure of what an individual has learned, especially for those with unique learning requirements.

Information Processing Model

In order for learning to occur, an individual must process information so that decisions can be made about appropriate responses. The model for information processing is similar to the model for perceptual-motor functioning (see chapter 7, Figure 7.1). The information processing model, shown in Figure 9.1, has four components: input, decision making, output, and feedback. Input from the environment comes through many sensory channels or modes, including vision, hearing, smell, and touch. Input can also be provided via kinesthetic information. Input received from the various senses is processed in the brain, where incoming information is integrated with stored information from past experiences. The integrated information forms the basis for a judgment on the appropriate response or output. In responding, the individual receives feedback about the effectiveness of the response through the various sensory channels. The sequence of information processing steps is repeated; the next response may be adjusted on the basis of the feedback received. The four components of information processing can be affected by individual differences such as deficits in sensory ability, impairment of brain function,

limitations in the ability to execute motor skills, and variations in the ability to interpret the feedback provided.

A child preparing to catch a thrown playground ball illustrates the information processing model in action. Vision provides the child with information about the direction of the ball as well as its trajectory, speed, force, size, and shape. An individual who has a visual deficit may need to gather this information by auditory or other means. A sound-emitting ball is often used to provide this input for people with visual handicaps. Because auditory input cannot provide information about such qualities as size and shape, tactile information must be gathered in advance. The information gathered is integrated with previous experiences in the brain.

For example, if a child knows that the below-the-waist basket catch is the best way to catch a ball traveling in a high, arcing trajectory, and if the sensory input indicates that this is the trajectory of the approaching ball, then the child will normally decide to use the basket catch. If the child has a brain dysfunction such as a lesion or lacks long-term memory, the decision on how best to catch the ball will be difficult and may result in a lack of a motor response or an inappropriate or slow response. A child's motor responses may also be affected by physical ability, specifically, the limitations imposed by a handicapping condition. The ability to use feedback to improve future performance can be affected by deficits in any of the three other components of the model. (Information processing is discussed in detail in chapter 7.)

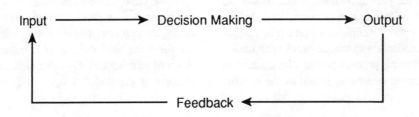

Figure 9.1 Information processing model.

Stages of Learning

The information processing model is applicable to the three stages of learning through which an individual progresses on the way to mastery of a skill. These stages are the cognitive stage, the associative stage, and the autonomic stage.

The *cognitive stage* is the level at which a child begins to understand the nature of a task. This understanding includes remembering the sequence of actions, the proper use of body parts, and the appropriate use of space and force to accomplish the task. During this stage, clear explanation and demonstration of the skill are extremely important. Adaptations for specific handicapping conditions and positive reinforcement must be provided so that the child will continue to progress to the next stage.

The *associative stage* is known as the practice stage, during which the child refines the skill,

correcting errors if necessary. Specific feedback and modeling help guide the efforts toward mastery.

The final or *autonomic stage* is reached when the child can perform the skill efficiently and with little thought to its elements (see Figure 9.2). It is at this level that the child can utilize the skill in various situations and can modify it, when necessary, to meet the demands of various conditions. Unfortunately, not all individuals, particularly those with handicaps, have the opportunity to reach this stage of learning characterized by skill mastery. However, if the educator is aware of the point in the information processing model at which the child experiences difficulties, opportunities for success can be maximized. One of the most pronounced areas of variance among children with handicaps is the input component of information processing, which relies heavily on various sensory abilities.

Figure 9.2   World Series beep baseball player exhibiting the autonomic stage of learning.

Sensory Modes

Not all children learn in the same manner or through the same channels. The four modes commonly used to obtain information about a task to be performed are *visual, auditory, tactile,* and *kinesthetic*. Dunn and Dunn (1979) reported that 40% of individuals are primarily visual learners, 20% to 30% are auditory learners, and the remaining 30% to 40% are tactile/kinesthetic or multisensory learners.

Visual

In visual learning, information is obtained through use of the eyes. Visual learners depend greatly on demonstration, visual aids, observation, and other visually dependent techniques as their primary source of information. This mode of learning is preferred by a majority of sighted people. However, in the case of individuals with visual or specific perceptual problems (e.g., nystagmus and tracking deficits), visual learning is not favored. Individuals with low intellectual functioning and/or poor body awareness may also have difficulty translating what they see into appropriate body movements.

Auditory

People who utilize their sense of hearing to gain the information to be learned are using the auditory mode. This method relies on explanation, questioning, and sound to transmit necessary information. Auditory learning is impossible or difficult for those with hearing impairment, a short attention span, a limited vocabulary, or low intellectual functioning.

Tactile

The tactile mode relies on the sense of touch to provide the necessary input for learning. A small percentage of individuals use this mode as their primary learning method. A form of tactile learning is the touching of a concrete object to under-

stand a concept—for example, when a child with no useful sight feels the starting blocks or the body position of a runner to help understand the requirements of a sprint start.

Kinesthetic

The kinesthetic mode of learning requires manual guidance of the learner through the desired movement. Guidance can be provided by a teacher, aide, or peer. This approach is often the primary learning style of individuals with visual deficits, multiple handicaps, or other profound impairments.

Multisensory

Because many people with handicapping conditions do not learn effectively using a single sensory channel, educators are advised to incorporate a multisensory approach in their teaching. By calling on all of the senses to convey the material to

Figure 9.3 Special Olympian being coached on a start using a multisensory approach. Photo courtesy of Denton State School Special Olympics.

be learned, the teacher or coach maximizes the chances for individuals with diverse learning styles and a wide range of abilities to learn desired skills. It is important that new material be clearly explained, demonstrated, and practiced—with hands-on direction if necessary (see Figure 9.3). Learning is facilitated when the educator knows the learning modes that are most effective for and preferred by individuals with specific handicapping conditions.

Learning Approaches

In addition to determining the preferred sensory learning modes of students with unique needs, the physical educator should also consider how to present the material to be learned. Material may be presented in one of three approaches: the *whole*, the *part-whole*, and the *progressive part*.

Whole Method

The whole method of learning should be used when the skill to be learned is relatively simple or made up of few parts. This method may be the preference of students who have difficulties in conceptual learning and are unable to relate the several parts of a skill to its whole. It is also the method of choice for students with short attention spans and those who best learn by imitation. However, one requirement of this method is that the learner be able to remember the skill to be learned, its specific movements, and its sequence. Motor skills that can be presented through the whole approach are running, catching, striking, and jumping.

Part-Whole Method

The part-whole method requires individuals to learn skills by practicing one part at a time. Once all the parts have been mastered, they are combined and practiced as a whole. This method works best for individuals who can concentrate on and accomplish small tasks. It may not be desirable for those who have difficulty integrating various

parts into a whole, even with the guidance of the instructor. In using this method, the physical educator breaks down the complete task into meaningful subtasks or parts; this process is task analysis. The teacher should make each part an end in itself, thus providing a sense of accomplishment even though the learner may not be able to master the entire task or terminal objective. An example of a skill that can be analyzed into meaningful tasks and thus is amenable to the part-whole method is the elementary backstroke in swimming. The skill can be divided into the back float, back glide, back glide with flutter kick, arm action, and leg action. Each of these tasks can give the learner a feeling of accomplishment and lead to successful movement in the water. Many individuals with handicapping conditions may not master the backstroke in its entirety, yet they can succeed in mastering its various elements.

Progressive-Part Method

The progressive-part approach involves teaching the most fundamental part of the skill first and then building on this base to present the next part (see Figure 9.4). When the first two parts are learned, they are combined and practiced in combination, and succeeding parts are added until the whole skill is mastered. Special Olympians might use this method in learning the triple jump. With the progressive-part method, the teacher or coach should be alert to problems that can occur if an individual fails to learn one part of the progression and should take care to provide the opportunity for success at each part level. This method lets individuals move toward the mastering of a skill at their own pace, practicing the most difficult parts while still progressing toward meeting the overall learning objective. Programs that incorporate these principles include the Data Based Gymnasium (Dunn, Morehouse, & Fredericks, 1986) and I CAN (Wessel, 1979).

On the basis of observations, interviews, and experimental studies completed over a 10-year period, Dunn and Dunn (1979) concluded that,

Figure 9.4 One-to-one instruction with positive reinforcement aid in learning to swim. Photo courtesy of Denton State School Special Olympics.

regardless of age, ability, achievement level, or socioeconomic status, "individuals respond uniquely to their immediate environment" (p. 239). Data supported the assertion that, when students were taught by methods that complemented their learning characteristics, they were more motivated and learned more easily. By understanding how a student learns best, the educator can facilitate the learning process considerably.

Medical Considerations

In addition to understanding the learning preferences and the social, physical, and motor characteristics of students with unique needs, physical educators and coaches should be knowledgeable about their students' medical conditions. They need to be aware of symptoms, associated medications, and limitations that may affect learning or performance.

Medical information that has a direct bearing on students' participation should be readily available to teachers (including substitute teachers) with the understanding that it is to be kept confidential. A simple way of identifying specific medical problems is through the use of subscripts in the roll book. A page in the front of the book should define what each subscript represents. A teacher's

failure to obtain and use medical information can cause unnecessary risk to the student and lead to a liability suit for the teacher and the school.

Many students enrolled in adapted physical education classes take medication to control their behavior and/or handicapping conditions. (Medications affecting behavior are discussed in detail in chapter 6.) The physical educator should be aware of the purpose of the medication and its possible side effects and should understand how the medication and physical activity interact. Medications are frequently prescribed for control of seizures; control of neuromuscular and orthopedic conditions; and management of hyperactivity, asthma, allergies, depression, emotional problems, diabetes, and eating disorders.

Environmental Factors

According to Dunn and Dunn (1979), the environmental factors that most affect learning are those associated with sound, light, and temperature. The organization of the environment also exerts a considerable influence on learning.

Sound

Sounds present in the learning environment can facilitate learning or hamper it, depending on an individual's needs and tolerances. Some people find it easier to concentrate on a learning task in a quiet environment. Extraneous sounds should be kept to a minimum for these individuals, as they might be distracted from the task by such sounds as an air conditioner motor, loudspeaker announcements, and the noise of classmates participating in class activities. These students usually learn best on a one-to-one basis. Other students can concentrate more easily when there is a constant background sound, such as music or "white noise," to mask more distracting noises. Background sound can also be used to influence the mood and activity level of the class. With still other students, sound level has no effect on learning.

Lighting

Illumination is a second environmental factor that can affect learning. Too much light can lead to overstimulation and hyperactive behavior. Lack of light tends to decrease the level of stimulation and produce a calmer environment. Consideration of the position and intensity of lighting is particularly important when the teacher is working with students who use light for self-stimulation.

Temperature

The temperature of the learning environment is another factor the physical educator must consider. In the gym, a mildly cool temperature is preferable. Too cold an environment tends to cause hyperactivity, poor attention, and muscle tightness; however, if the environment is too warm, students tend to be lethargic and drowsy. For swimming, a warmer climate and warm water usually provide a better instructional atmosphere. Warm water is especially important for individuals with Down syndrome and spastic cerebral palsy.

Organization

The final environmental factor that affects learning is the organization of the learning environment. Organization includes the size, color, and accessibility of the learning setting and the amount and placement of equipment. All of these factors must be weighed in the establishment of a safe, secure, barrier-free learning environment.

Application of Scientific Foundations

Application of the principles that form the scientific foundations of physical education can result in better learning experiences for children with unique needs. Particularly important are the principles governing motor learning, biomechanics, and exercise physiology. Using these principles, the physical educator or coach can modify the learning experience, taking into consideration the limitations and abilities associated with specific handicapping conditions in order to ensure optimum learning for each individual.

Motor Learning Principles

The area of motor learning focuses on the processes by which people acquire skills. Applying the principles of motor learning involves understanding the variables that enter into motor skill acquisition. Application of the principles can enhance the rate and quality of learning. The stages of skill learning, factors that affect learning, and the frequency and design of practice are of special concern to the teacher of students with unique needs.

The educator should follow the principles of motor learning to structure the environment so that each individual's learning opportunities are optimized. Principles that are particularly important in the teaching of handicapped students are discussed in the following paragraphs.

Guidelines —— of Motor Learning ——

1. Individual learning styles differ.

2. Individuals learn skills more easily when they have reached a state of neurological readiness.

3. Individuals who derive positive feelings from participation in an activity are more likely to continue participating in that activity.

4. Individuals who receive reinforcement for their efforts will be more motivated to continue participation.

5. Individual learning can be affected by the order in which skills are presented.

6. Individual performance will be affected by the amount and type of practice opportunities provided.

7. Individuals will vary in their rate of learning and the amount of learning that will occur.

8. Individuals who receive appropriate feedback will be encouraged to continue their efforts.

9. Individuals who have established predetermined goals will make better progress.

10. Individuals may or may not benefit from previously learned skills in the learning of new skills.

11. Individuals are more likely to retain skills that they have mastered or that have personal meaning to them.

Individual Differences

Individuals are different in the way they learn (method), the speed of their learning (rate), and what they learn (amount). Research indicates that these factors vary more among individuals with unique needs than among their nonhandicapped peers. Thus, it is crucial for physical educators to employ personalized and individualized approaches to ensure optimal opportunities for their students.

Readiness

Learning is easiest when there is a match between neurological capability and the demands of the skill to be learned. What is normally expected at a certain developmental level may not be attainable by an individual with motor or cognitive delays. While physical educators may typically introduce the skill of skipping to children between ages 5 and 7, they may find that some of their students with handicaps are still developing mature patterns of walking or running and will not be ready to skip for several more years.

Effect

The feelings individuals experience while participating in an activity can influence their learning. Someone who enjoys an activity or derives satisfaction and/or success from it is more likely to choose that activity than one that causes frustration. Designing learning activities that allow students to have fun and experience success should be an important aim of the educator. For example, students confined to wheelchairs may successfully play tennis if the rules of the game are modified or the equipment changed. Through the adaptations, these players experience success and are encouraged to continue improving their tennis skills.

Motivation

Drive, desire, and willingness to learn—in other words, motivation—greatly facilitate learning. Research indicates that people vary greatly in their *reasons for participation*. It is a challenge to the teacher to determine the best way to motivate students to perform and to maintain maximum effort. Motivation may also grow with an increase in skill; feelings of accomplishment motivate people to continue their efforts. Reinforcement plays a significant role in motivation, especially for individuals with unique needs. The use of praise, symbolic award systems like checklists or gold stars, and tangible rewards such as free time or special field trips may encourage learners to improve their performance.

Order of Learning

The sequence in which the teacher introduces skills to the learner is the order of learning. With young children and students who have handicapping conditions, it is important to present the principal focus of the task early in the lesson to take advantage of the learner's limited attention span. Research also indicates that tasks presented near the lesson's end are more likely to be retained than those presented in the middle of the lesson.

Practice

Improvement in motor skill performance occurs if an individual repeatedly performs the activity to be learned with attention to form and concentration on relevant cues. The length of practice and the amount of time between practices affect learning as well. To be most effective, practice should be specific to the task being learned. Thus, Special Olympians aspiring to participate in the softball throw should practice throwing for distance, including practicing throwing from behind a line.

Rate of Learning

The rate of learning varies among individuals. People tend to learn more rapidly and in larger increments as beginners. As they become more skillful, they progress more slowly. Often, after the initial learning phase, the learner reaches a plateau at which skill performance may stay the same or even decrease slightly in quality or quantity. Time spent on a plateau may be particularly frustrating. Creative teaching and analysis of skills into component parts help learners advance and encourage them to persist in their efforts toward skill mastery. In bowling, many students with handicaps are able to learn the gross motor pattern of rolling the ball. However, additional steps such as manual guidance, shortening the length of the alley, and allowing the child to roll the ball from a stride position may be necessary to bring about further skill development.

Feedback

Knowledge of results has long been recognized as one of the most critical factors in learning. In working with students with unique needs, it is im-

portant to provide meaningful, appropriate, and immediate feedback to reinforce individual efforts. In swimming, for example, verbal encouragement and nonverbal expressions of approval (e.g., enthusiastic clapping) can prompt students to continue their efforts. Corrective feedback, including kinesthetic manipulation and verbal guidance, can be used to modify performance when necessary.

Goal Setting

Individuals with specific goals make better progress in learning. Teachers and coaches must ensure that goals are concrete and easily understood and that progress toward the goal can be seen by the learner. Goals are more meaningful when the learners have had a role in determining them. Setting meaningful individual goals will also enhance the level of achievement.

Transfer

Skills learned previously may positively or negatively influence the learning of new ones. Often, little positive transfer occurs between one activity and another for individuals with handicapping conditions. The teacher can encourage transfer by drawing the student's attention to the elements common to the previously learned skill and the new task. Because transfer requires a high level of cognitive involvement, it may be especially difficult for those with mental deficits. It is also important that skills be practiced in the environment in which they are to be performed. For example, many Special Olympians may not perform at their optimal level if the practice track varies somewhat from the track on which they will compete.

Retention

Many factors can affect and enhance retention of learned material. Until an individual masters a skill, the chances of retention are less. Thus, a teacher can promote retention by providing enough practice opportunities that the student *overlearns* the task. Gross motor skills are generally retained more easily than fine motor skills. Skills with personal meaning to the learner are more likely to be retained than skills perceived as less important. Students should understand how and why the skills being learned may be carried over into everyday living or recreational activities. Reinforcement for a softball unit might include attending a local softball game or hosting a visit and demonstration by a professional athlete.

Biomechanical and Physiological Principles

Learners with unique needs will benefit from the physical educator's knowledge of biomechanical and physiological principles. Educators who can apply those principles in adapting activities to meet individual needs can significantly facilitate the acquisition of skills. The application of physiological principles is treated comprehensively in chapter 18, and the application of biomechanical principles is discussed in many chapters throughout this text.

Summary

To ensure successful learning, the physical educator or coach must understand the learning process, know how to adapt it to meet individual needs, and promote the learner's active involvement in the process. The educator must understand the learning sequence, the stages through which individuals progress in acquiring skills, and the sensory modalities involved in learning. By designing appropriate learning strategies and considering medical and environmental factors, the educator increases the probability of successful learning. Learning can also be enhanced through the application of the principles of motor learning, biomechanics, and exercise physiology. By understanding and applying these principles to the design of learning experiences, the teacher or coach may help students with unique needs to achieve their maximum potential.

Bibliography

Dunn, J., Morehouse, J., & Fredericks, H. (1986). *Physical education for the severely handicapped: A systematic approach to a data based gymnasium* (2nd ed.). Austin, TX: Pro-Ed.

Dunn, R., & Dunn, K. (1979). Learning styles/ teaching styles. Should they . . . can they be matched? *Educational Leadership*, **36**, 238-244.

Wessel, J. (1979). *I CAN—Sport, leisure, and recreation skills.* Northbrook, IL: Hubbard.

Resources

Gallahue, D.L. (1982). *Understanding motor development in children.* New York: Wiley. The development process from the prenatal period through age 12 is discussed. This book treats psychomotor, cognitive, and affective factors that influence the motor development of children. It would be helpful in working with developmentally delayed children.

Magill, R.A. (1985). *Motor learning: Concepts and applications.* Dubuque, IA: Wm. C. Brown. This book provides an understanding of the scientific foundations of motor learning while stressing practical applications. It offers an introduction to motor learning followed by information on both the learner and the learning environment.

CHAPTER 10

Teaching Styles and Approaches

Sarah M. Rich

This chapter discusses the factors that contribute to effective teaching in the realm of adapted physical education and sport. By understanding what is involved in successful teaching, the educator can better help students achieve their optimal level of learning and experience satisfaction and success. Effective teaching involves careful planning, selection of appropriate teaching strategies to attain the desired objectives, evaluation of student progress, and assessment of teacher effectiveness.

Teacher Effectiveness

Research has provided a profile of the characteristics shared by effective teachers. Rosenshine and Furst (1971) name five teacher characteristics consistently associated with student achievement. They are

- clearness of presentation,
- teacher enthusiasm,
- activity diversity,
- task-oriented behavior, and
- coverage of a high proportion of relevant content.

According to Siedentop (1983), effective teachers

- keep students appropriately engaged in relevant activities for a high percentage of the time,

- match classroom activities to student abilities, and
- establish a warm, positive learning climate.

Effective teaching in adapted physical education depends on a unique combination of factors that underlie successful interaction with a diversity of learners. These qualities include personal attributes and specialized knowledge and skills that help teachers maximize students' time on task, thus enhancing opportunity for success.

Personal Attributes

Although researchers have drawn no specific personality profile as a prototype of the ideal adapted physical educator, they have identified several characteristics that are desirable in those who teach learners with unique needs.

Creativity is an important quality that enables an educator to modify instruction, facilities, and equipment to meet the unique needs of each individual. Creative teachers approach most situations in a flexible manner, which enables them to easily modify their plans to maintain a positive class climate. They are able to design a variety of approaches to meet specific instructional goals.

Emotional maturity is another attribute that is particularly important in the adapted physical education setting. Emotional maturity is the ability to solve problems and adjust to unforeseen circumstances without undue emotional involvement or stress. Successful participation in physical education activities by students with unique needs depends in part on the teacher's ability to be a stabilizing influence.

Another quality that is particularly desirable in teachers of students with unique needs is the *ability to look beyond a handicap* and see each student as a person with needs similar to those of nonhandicapped people. Although individuals with handicaps often require special assistance to attain their goals, they also have the need to be as self-sufficient as possible (see Figure 10.1). A teacher who can understand this need is better able to develop an adapted physical education and sport program that fosters experiences of success and feelings of normalcy and independence.

Figure 10.1 An orthopedically impaired student enjoys participating in a "stream stroll" during an outdoor education unit.

Specialized Knowledge and Skills

Besides possessing certain personal attributes, educators of students with unique needs should have a foundation of specialized knowledge and skills. To help define the knowledge base relevant to adapted physical education, the American Alliance for Health, Physical Education, Recreation and Dance (AAHPERD) appointed a task force to establish guidelines for the preparation of physical education generalists and adapted physical education specialists (Hurley, 1981). The guidelines encompass biological, sociological, psychological, and historical-philosophical foundations as well as applied areas pertaining specifically to the role of the adapted physical educator. These applied areas are assessment and evaluation, curriculum planning and organization, and implementation of programs. While the competencies needed by generalists and specialists are similar, adapted physical education specialists require more specialized knowledge in order to serve individuals with a wider range of disabilities and with more severely handicapping conditions.

In addition to knowledge gained from professional preparation programs, skills and knowledge can be acquired through in-service programs, workshops, and on-the-job experience. For example, educators whose students are hearing impaired, autistic, and moderately to severely mentally retarded may find learning sign language to be an asset. For those working with visually impaired individuals, a familiarity with braille and mobility skill training techniques may be beneficial. Teachers of students who are physically impaired should master assistive and transfer techniques. It is highly recommended that educators possess up-to-date first aid and CPR skills. In addition, they may wish to have in-depth training in the management of seizures, the recognition and management of respiratory distress and insulin reactions, and the management of emotional outbursts. Educators should be familiar with the many high-technology aids available to assist the handicapped learner. Teachers and coaches should be able to make minor repairs to prostheses and wheelchairs. Any of these special skills can be incorporated into in-service workshop programs to enhance the specialized knowledge of adapted physical educators.

Education Approaches

Among the numerous educational approaches available, those most commonly used in adapted physical education today trace their origins to two major philosophical systems: *humanism* and *behaviorism*. To implement specific teaching styles and techniques most effectively, educators must understand the philosophical tenets that underlie them.

Humanism

Humanism is a philosophical approach that emphasizes the development of each individual to his or her fullest human potential. It is concerned with enhancing the quality of life and developing the maximum physical, mental, emotional, and social well-being of the individual. Humanistic teaching employs practices that are least restrictive to the individual while providing for self-direction and self-responsibility in learning. It values individualism and individual differences.

A physical education program based on a humanistic philosophy should strive to meet the unique needs and interests of each student through individualized instruction. The emphasis on sensitivity to individual differences and the development of the total person makes humanism a viable philosophy upon which to base adapted physical education programs.

Behaviorism

Organization of the environment to elicit the desired response is a major feature of the behaviorist philosophical model. This model is based on the premise that the teacher can best ensure that learning occurs by structuring the environment. The teacher's function is to identify the learning goals and involve students in educational activities that will enable them to achieve the goals. Behaviorism emphasizes the attainment of skills that will make an individual self-sufficient.

In the physical education setting, a behaviorist philosophy would emphasize a very goal-oriented, structured program. It would strive to minimize errors by directly engaging the student in appropriate behaviors. Behaviorism's emphasis on structured learning experiences that ensure success and its orientation toward functional skill development also make it an appropriate philosophical basis for adapted physical education programs.

Philosophical Integration

Both the humanistic and behavioristic philosophies are relevant to the educational process. However, the greatest value of these philosophies for adapted physical education can perhaps be realized by application of the best elements of each. At certain times the variety of individual needs makes a humanistic approach advisable; at other times the behavioristic approach is more expedient and effective. By integrating these philosophical bases, the educator can ensure that each student experiences success while facilitating optimal achievement for the individual.

Teaching Styles

Another choice crucial to successful instructional experiences is the selection of an appropriate teaching style. A teaching style is a method of presenting material to the learner. Mosston (1981) has described several strategies and classified them on a continuum, from direct teacher-centered styles to indirect student-centered styles. The continuum reflects the amount of decision-making responsibility allocated to the teacher and to the learner. In a teacher-centered approach, the teacher makes most of the decisions on such matters as the structure of the learning environment, lesson content, entry level of the students, and starting and stopping times. As one moves along the continuum, decision-making responsibility is shifted increasingly to the student. Decisions assumed by students include solutions to movement problems, beginning level for a task, and determination of the amount of time to be spent on each problem. While Mosston identified eight teaching styles, only four will be discussed in this chapter: command, task, guided discovery, and problem solving. These styles appear to have the greatest utility for providing adapted physical education students with a challenging learning experience.

The Command Style

The command style is probably the most commonly used teaching style in adapted physical education. Decisions are made predominately by the teacher concerning lesson content, organization of the learning content, organization of the learning environment, and acceptable standards of performance.

Use of the command style is illustrated in an adapted physical education setting with a class of wheelchair-bound students. The group is gathered around the teacher, who explains how to execute the overhand throw. A demonstration follows, with the teacher using a chair or wheelchair to make the demonstration more relevant for the class. The students are then sent to practice the skill using tethered balls or rebounders with ball returners attached, so that the individual can retrieve the ball easily and have maximum continuous practice of the throwing skill. The teacher moves from student to student, assisting each one with ball control, skill improvement, and motivation. At the end of the lesson, the teacher asks questions to review the major aspects of throwing and to measure the students' comprehension of the skill.

Advantages associated with the command style are

- teacher control,
- minimal investment of time in group organization, and
- knowledge of the expected outcome.

This is an effective style for use with large groups, in one-to-one instruction, or when the teacher wants all of the students to do the same task at the same time. It is particularly effective for children with behavioral problems, those with some degree of mental retardation, and those who require external control.

Disadvantages of the command style are

- little thought is required on the part of the learner,
- little creativity is permitted, and
- little variation of response is permitted.

Also, because this method stresses the attainment of one correct response, it is generally insensitive to individual differences. This is a severe limitation in working with individuals whose motor abilities may vary greatly or whose impairment inhibits production of the one correct response.

The Task Style

The task style of instruction requires the teacher to develop a series of tasks that progressively lead to the achievement of an instructional objective. The teacher develops task cards, which are given to the students. For learners who are unable to read, task cards can be made with pictures or braille writing, or even put on audio cassettes to meet individual needs. Additional resources such as filmstrips, posters, videotapes, books, and three-dimensional models can be provided to assist learners in mastering their tasks. The tasks must be presented in a manner that allows the learner to determine when the assignment has been successfully completed. For example, in a lesson using a task approach to teach dribbling, a task card may instruct the student to dribble through a five-cone obstacle course without losing control of the ball. After a successful evaluation is completed by the teacher, the learner, or a peer, the learner moves on to the next task in the sequence, for example, negotiating the same obstacle course while dribbling with the other hand. This method lets the teacher organize the learning setting so that all students can be working on tasks concurrently in a safe environment. Examples of the task method specifically designed for learners with handicapping conditions include the I CAN curriculum (Wessel, 1979), the Data Based Gymnasium (Dunn, Morehouse, & Fredericks, 1986), and the Special Olympics Sports Skills Series.

Advantages of the task method are numerous. This style

- encourages individuals to work at their own pace at tasks appropriate to their abilities,
- allows individuals to practice tasks appropriate to their abilities,
- diminishes competition with others,
- allows the teacher to control the difficulty of the task,
- ensures success for each student,
- enables the teacher to work with students on an individual basis, and
- encourages the maximum use of equipment, facilities, and aides or volunteers.

The task method can be used effectively with children who can work independently on their own, who may need extra time to master tasks, and who can be assisted in tasks by peers, aides, or paraprofessionals.

Disadvantages of the task style include

- reduction in the structure of the learning setting,
- possible increase in safety concerns,
- possible increase in distractions, and
- appearance of disorganization because many activities are going on simultaneously.

The Guided Discovery Style

Guided discovery uses teacher-designed movement challenges to help students attain a specified movement goal. Students are encouraged to discover movement solutions that must meet the criteria stated by the teacher. Using questions or short statements, the teacher guides the student in a progressive series of steps or subchallenges toward the desired outcome or challenge goal (Nichols, 1986).

Following is an example of the use of guided discovery in teaching a class of students with emotional disturbances to throw a softball for distance. The teacher breaks the skill down into subchallenges.

Challenge: "How far can you throw the softball using the overhand throw?"

> *Subchallenge 1.* "How should you stand to get the best possible distance?" If students do not respond motorically the teacher can cue the response by giving them ideas such as (a) feet together behind the line, (b) feet parallel but wide apart, or (c) stride position—"Which foot should be forward?"

> *Subchallenge 2.* "How high should the ball go to travel the farthest?" Possible cues for this subchallenge would be "Will it travel farther close to the ground?" "If you throw the ball as high as you can, will it travel a long distance?"

These are examples of subchallenges that would help a student find the movement solution that answers the teacher's challenge "How do you throw the softball the greatest distance?"

Advantages of the guided discovery style are that it

- encourages creativity,
- allows students to discover how various parts of the body contribute to movement patterns, and

- enhances self-concept as students receive positive feedback while shaping the response to obtain the desired outcome.

This method is appropriate with students whose cognitive ability permits the required thought processes.

Disadvantages of the guided discovery style are that it may require

- more time to achieve movement goals,
- more preparation on the part of the teacher, and
- more patience and a great deal of feedback to bring about the same level of performance as the command style.

The Problem-Solving Style

This method resembles the guided discovery method in presenting a series of movement challenges to the learner. However, in contrast to guided discovery where one specific movement is the goal, the problem-solving style emphasizes the development of multiple solutions to a given problem posed by the teacher. This style encourages students to develop as many solutions to the problem as possible, provided that the solutions meet the criteria stated by the teacher.

In an instructional episode in which students are encouraged to display different ways of rolling effectively, the teacher might pose the following challenges:

1. "Staying within the mat areas and not getting in another child's self-space, roll in as many different ways as you can."
2. "Roll with your body as long as possible."
3. "Can you find a way to roll with your arms out to the side?"
4. "Can you combine three different rolls and roll in a circle?"

After each challenge the teacher lets students experiment with a variety of movement solutions. Often, additional questions are needed to elicit a variety of responses, especially with students who learn primarily by imitation and those who have had limited motor experience (e.g., children who have spent most of their time in wheelchairs).

Advantages of the problem-solving style include

- wide allowances for individual differences,
- emphasis on cognitive processes and creativity, and
- acceptance of skill execution that varies from the expected norm.

It treats as correct any response to the movement challenge that meets the criteria; this is important in cases where handicapping conditions inhibit a particular response. Problem solving boosts learners' self-esteem by allowing them to experience success.

Disadvantages of the problem-solving style are

- the great amount of time required for students to fully explore possible movement solutions,
- the lack of structure, and
- the absence of an absolute outcome.

The range of instructional styles allows educators to teach the same content using a variety of methods. In selecting a style, the teacher should consider its appropriateness for the desired objectives. The choice of teaching style should also reflect such factors as the teacher's preferences and personality; the student's age, experience, learning style, and handicapping condition; the stage of learning; and the skills to be taught. The learning environment may also influence the choice of style. Practical considerations such as equipment, space, available time, and number of students may make one teaching style preferable to the others.

Individualized Learning

There are many ways to individualize the learning process to promote efficient learning and increase teacher effectiveness. *Task analysis* allows the teacher to use the task-specific approach by identifying the components inherent in various skills. *Activity analysis* helps the teacher select the activities that meet a student's needs. Once an appropriate activity has been selected, *activity or game modification* may be necessary to meet the special needs of the learner.

Organizational and methodological configurations may also assist the teacher in tailoring the learning environment to meet the specific needs of students. These include the use of team teaching, peer and cross-age teaching, and independent learning approaches such as individual learning packets, learning contracts, computer-assisted instructional modules, and independent study. The wise use of these techniques will help the educator not only to individualize but also to maximize learning by carefully matching objectives, organization, and methodology to the learners' abilities.

Task Analysis

A technique that can facilitate the acquisition of a skill by separating it into meaningful component parts is *task analysis*. The parts can be arranged in sequence, from easy to difficult, and can serve as the basis for short-term performance objectives. Before introducing a specific task, the teacher should determine where on the developmental continuum the learner is functioning and whether the child has met all relevant developmental prerequisites. Prerequisite skills should be included in the task analysis for a particular skill and should take into consideration developmental, environmental, and biomechanical factors. Task analysis provides a systematic, hierarchical method for analyzing skill mastery, from the fundamental level to the advanced level. It offers a way of breaking a skill down into its related subtasks, with each subtask more challenging than the previous one. In writing a task analysis, it is important to include all steps describing each component in observable, behavioral terms. This thoroughness will facilitate the identification of short-term behavioral objectives and thus simplify the process

TASK ANALYSIS

Identify skill to be learned.

↓

Determine prerequisite skills.

↓

Assess student's present level of functioning.

↓

Including prerequisite skill, develop a series of hierarchical tasks leading to the accomplishment of the skill.

↓

Write each task, specifying the observable behaviors to be achieved.

↓

Implement instructional program to achieve tasks.

Figure 10.2   Sequence for development of a task analysis.

of IEP development. The sequence of steps involved in a task analysis is shown in Figure 10.2, and an example of a task analysis of the overarm throw is presented in Figure 10.3.

Activity Analysis

Activity analysis is a technique for determining the basic characteristics of an activity and relating them to desired student outcomes. By breaking an activity down into its basic components, the teacher can better understand the specific value of a certain activity and modify the activity to fit an individual learner's needs, if necessary. Thus,

Skill: Overarm Throw

Prerequisite Skills: Ability to grasp a ball with one hand
Ability to sit or stand erect

Sequential Components:
1. Assume stance and grasp the ball.
2. Lift arm to throwing position.
3. Move arm forward and release the ball.
4. Transfer weight during the throwing process.
5. Step in opposition.
6. Rotate trunk to initiate throw.
7. Involve nonthrowing arm in the delivery.
8. Establish consistent release and follow-through.
9. Complete follow-through.

Figure 10.3 Task analysis of overarm throw.

once a student's needs have been determined, the teacher can use activity analysis to assess whether a specific activity can meet those needs.

Activity analysis facilitates the selection of program content to meet stated objectives. In making the analysis, the teacher must consider how the activity contributes to learning in the physical, cognitive, affective, and social domains. When analyzing an activity from a physiological perspective, the teacher should examine such factors as basic body positions required, body parts utilized, body actions performed, fundamental movement patterns incorporated, coordination needed, fitness level required, and sensory systems used. Cognitive factors that should be evaluated include the number and complexity of rules and the need for memorization, concentration, strategies, and perceptual and academic skills. Affective factors to consider in the activity analysis include the emotional effect of participation and the amount of emotional control required. The social interaction required for successful participation in the activity

must also be ascertained. Chapters 18 through 20 provide valuable information that can help educators identify developmental factors relevant to activity analysis.

Peterson and Gunn (1984) provide detailed forms that can be used in completing an activity

Table 10.1 Activity Analysis Guidelines

Activity _____

Physical demands:
1. Primary body position required?
2. Movement skills required?
3. Amount of fitness required?
   a. Strength
   b. Endurance
   c. Speed
   d. Flexibility
   e. Agility
4. Amount of coordination required?
5. Amount of energy required?

Social demands
1. Number of participants required?
2. Types of interaction?
3. Type of communication?
4. Type of leadership?
5. Is this a cooperative or competitive activity?
6. Amount of physical contact required?
7. Noise level?

Cognitive demands
1. Complexity of rules?
2. Level of strategy?
3. Concentration level?
4. Academic skills (reading, math, etc.) needed?
5. Verbal skills needed?
6. Directional concepts needed?
7. Complexity of scoring system?
8. Memory required?

Administrative demands
1. Time required?
2. Equipment needed?
3. Special facilities required?
4. Type of leadership required?
5. Safety factors to be considered?

analysis. Recently, interactive computer programs have also been designed to facilitate this task. A conceptual model for activity analysis developed by Berryman (1974) allows educators to analyze many activities and match activities to selected behavioral objectives. Table 10.1 provides an overview of the components that should be included in an activity analysis.

Activity Modification

Task analysis and activity analysis provide the basis for activity or game selection. After choosing the activities most appropriate to meet the individual's learning goals, the educator must then

Figure 10.4 A mentally handicapped individual learning softball skills which will enable her to participate in a community recreation league. Photo courtesy of Denton State School Special Olympics.

modify those activities to the extent necessary. A softball game in an adapted physical education class provides an example of *activity modification* to meet the diverse needs of individuals with various handicapping conditions (see Figure 10.4). Activity modification for students with below-average mental abilities may include simplifying the rules or practicing in lead-up activities. For those with visual impairments, the playing field might be made smaller, with base paths having a different texture than the field. Equipment might be adapted—for example, to include sound devices in the ball and in the bases to aid visually handicapped players and lighter balls and batting tees for those with physical disabilities. Modified rules for making ''outs'' or a change in the number of participants may be required for players with limited mobility. When modifying an activity, the educator should try to maintain its inherent nature so that it is as close to the traditional activity as possible.

Modifications need not affect every component of an activity; they should be limited to only those that are necessary to meet individual needs. It may be necessary to modify the rules of the activity to make them more easily understandable, the facilities to make them accessible, the equipment to allow for easy usage, the scoring to equalize competition, or the number of participants to ensure maximum participation.

Organizational and Methodological Techniques

Various *organizational and methodological techniques* may be employed to individualize instruction. They include team teaching, peer and cross-age tutoring, and independent learning.

Team Teaching

If there are individuals with unique needs in an adapted physical education class, it is often best for two or more teachers to instruct the class together so that individual differences can be accommodated. This approach, called team teaching, is especially important in settings where educators are not well prepared to work with students who have unique needs.

Peer and Cross-Age Tutoring

Peer tutoring involves calling on student peers to help with instruction. This technique is most successful in a class in which peer tutors can be used to reduce the student-teacher ratio. Cross-age tutoring programs enlist junior or senior high school students to work with elementary school children in physical education. Cross-age tutoring can provide satisfaction to the tutors while increasing the level of learning for handicapped students. A well-known program that utilizes peer teaching is PEOPEL (Physical Education Opportunity Program for Exceptional Learners) (Irmer, Cowger, Glasewapp, Arter, & Estes, 1977).

Independent Learning

Independent learning gives students the opportunity to work on their own and progress at their own rate. This technique is particularly useful when the educator is obliged to exclude a student from certain activities and, therefore, must provide instructional materials for the learner to use independently (Figure 10.5). Independent learning materials may take several forms. For example, the teacher may prepare and package a series of task cards specifying skills for learners to accomplish. Such an instructional packet usually is comprehensive, including directions, illustrations, progressions, self-evaluation tools, and supporting resources.

Sometimes the student and the educator might make a formal agreement designating the tasks the student must achieve to earn a certain grade. This is known as a learning contract. Learning contracts allow teachers to personalize grading to reflect the unique conditions of each individual learner.

Computer-assisted instructional modules are another resource that can allow students with handicapping conditions to learn at their own pace.

Figure 10.5 Use of a volunteer sighted guide allows a blind runner to move freely at her own pace.

These modules help individuals progress through the use of interactive episodes and programmed learning. Brasile, Conway-Callahan, Dager, and Klekner (1986) suggest that computer use can enhance manual dexterity, eye-hand coordination, knowledge, self-confidence, and relaxation. Computer programs such as *Beginning Tennis, Fitness—A State of Body and Mind*, and *Knowledge Pursuit* are examples of software useful in the adapted physical education setting (CompTech Systems Design, 1987). Computer programs can also assist the teacher with service delivery planning, assessment, and record keeping (Montelione & Davis, 1988).

Kelly (1981) was among the first to develop

computer software specifically for use in the adapted physical education setting. Using the I CAN program, he generated software to assist physical educators in writing IEPs. More recently, Kelly (1987) developed the Physical Education Management System (PEMS) to assist teachers in keeping records and writing progress reports.

Improvement of Teacher Effectiveness

Learning is enhanced when teacher effectiveness is improved. In order to become more effective, physical education teachers and coaches must be committed to observing and analyzing their own behaviors for the purpose of self-evaluation and improvement. Skilled observation by peers and supervisors may contribute to the improvement of teaching. Analysis of their teaching helps educators understand the relationship between their behavior and their students' learning. Also, supervisors and others involved in professional preparation can use teacher analysis to provide feedback and suggestions that lead to improved performance.

In an effort to improve teaching, various analytic techniques may be used to describe activities and behaviors in the physical education setting. The information thus collected can make teachers more aware of behaviors and events and can serve as a basis for the modification of teacher behaviors and instructional patterns. Teaching may be analyzed by traditional methods or by newer, more systematic methods of observation.

Methods of Analyzing Teaching Behavior

In the last two decades approaches to the analysis of teaching have changed dramatically. Before 1970, techniques such as ancedotal recording, checklists, and rating scales were commonly employed. Over the last 20 years a variety of systematic observation techniques have been developed

to provide teachers with specific, objective information about their teaching. Systematic observation instruments have been designed for use in the physical education setting. Darst, Zakrajsek, and Mancini (1989) provide a comprehensive collection of tools available for the systematic observation of instruction in physical education.

Each systematic instrument that serves to guide observation has a specific focus. Some instruments, such as Academic Learning Time—Physical Education (ALT-PE), concentrate on time–on–task, while others, such as Cheffers' Adaptation of Flanders' Interaction Analysis System (CAFIAS), focus on teacher-student interactions (Darst et al., 1989). These instruments provide well-defined categories for the classification of behaviors. Standardized coding procedures, coding rules, and training procedures are used to ensure the gathering of objective, valid, and reliable data about teacher performance (Darst et al., 1989).

In the adapted physical education setting, observers can use selected instruments to assess the frequency of specific events, such as how often a specific type of feedback is used or the number of trials that selected students experience during a specific time interval. It is also possible to measure the duration of events, such as the amount of class time spent on management, instruction, and activity, or the amount of time students are engaged in productive versus unproductive behaviors. Figure 10.6 provides an example of an observation form that may be used to evaluate teacher performance or provide feedback to volunteer aides. The form collects information about the use of cues and prompting to ensure that students receive appropriate reinforcement during the instructional episode.

Self-Analysis

Teachers may choose to analyze their own behavior by periodically reviewing their lesson plans, making notes about problems encountered, and listing suggestions for future improvement.

INSTRUCTION
OSU/TR Gymnasium Observation Form

Volunteer/Aide: _____ Observer: _____

Program: _____ Date: _____

Cue (verbal): _____ Time: _____

Instructional Setting: _____ Materials: _____

Describe Motor Response: _____ Criteria: _____

_____

KEY

	Code 1	Code 2	
	1 = Correct	1 = Correct	F = Fail To
	0 = Incorrect	D = Delay	C = Change
		W = Weak	Word
		R = Repeat	L = Level

Reinforcer and Schedule: _____

Correction Procedure: _____

Student	Program Cues — Verbal			Program Correction — Model			Program Correction — Physical Assistance			Behavior Cues and Consequences			Data
	Cue	Consequence +	−	Cue	Consequence +	−	Cue	Consequence +	−	Cue	+	−	
1													
2													
3													
4													
5													
6													
7													
8													
9													
10													
11													
12													

Comments:

Scores

Cues: $\dfrac{\text{Correct Cues}}{\text{Correct + Incorrect Cues}}$ = __/__ or ____ %

Consequences: $\dfrac{\text{Correct Consequences}}{\text{Correct + Incorrect Consequences}}$ = __/__ or ____ %

Data: $\dfrac{\text{Correct Data}}{\text{Correct + Incorrect Data}}$ = __/__ or ____ %

Criterion: Individual 90%, Agreement 85%

Figure 10.6 Data based gymnasium volunteer observation form. *Note.* From *OSU Data Based Gymnasium Workshop* by J. Dunn and J. Morehouse, 1985, Corvallis, OR: Oregon State University. Copyright 1985. Reprinted by permission of John M. Dunn.

Teachers may also employ group scanning techniques during the lesson to record behavioral information of interest, such as the number of students engaged in off-task behaviors. By wearing a small cassette recorder, teachers can audiotape their lessons for review at a later date. This allows them to assess the clarity of their explanations, monitor the length of time devoted to teacher talk versus student activity, and determine the amount and type of verbal feedback provided. Teachers may also elicit the assistance of colleagues to videotape their teaching, providing another opportunity to review verbal and nonverbal behaviors and identify areas needing improvement.

Periodic observations by supervisors and administrators may also utilize systematic observation instruments to provide teachers with feedback. Ideally, once teachers are comfortable with systematic feedback, they will use it to set specific objectives to improve their instructional effectiveness.

Prescriptive Planning and Instructional Models

Although the learning process has common elements for all individuals, certain models have proven successful in providing a quality physical education experience for individuals with handicapping conditions. These models, when used as guides for the instructional process, can help school districts to enhance the teaching process at various levels and ensure that students with unique needs are taught in an efficient and effective manner. The relevant instructional models include the Achievement-Based Curriculum developed by I CAN (Wessel & Kelly, 1985), the Data Based Gymnasium (Dunn et al., 1985), the PREP Program Instructional Model (Watkinson & Wall, 1979), and the TAPE instructional model advocated as part of Project ACTIVE (Vodola, 1976).

The Achievement-Based Curriculum Model and I CAN

The Achievement-Based Curriculum model (ABC) includes a systematic, sequential process that allows teachers to plan, implement, and evaluate instructional programs for individuals based on selected goals and objectives. Figure 10.7 represents the ABC model, developed by I CAN, which includes prescriptive methods for planning and programming.

The ABC model assists the teacher in developing instructional strategies in a systematic manner

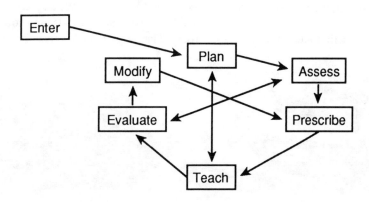

Figure 10.7 ABC Model used by I CAN. *Note.* Adapted for *Leadership Training Guide* by L. Burkett and J.A. Wessel, 1984, Tempe, AZ: Arizona State University, Department of Health and Physical Education. Reprinted with permission of Hubbard Publishing Company.

while being sensitive to the individual needs of the learner. The model involves five steps:

1. *Plan.* The planning step includes defining the program goals; determining community, school, and student interests; and creating a plan for what will be taught during the year. The final responsibility associated with this step is to plan a developmental sequence that will permit achievement of the stated goals.

2. *Assess.* Assessment is a continuous process that keeps the teacher informed about the present level of student performance. Criterion-referenced tests are used to assess the student's level of skill and to document improvement. Norm-referenced tests may also be employed to assess a student's performance in comparison with the performance of designated groups.

3. *Prescribe.* Using the assessment results, the teacher needs to select the specific skills to be included in the physical education program for each individual. Plans must also indicate what teaching methods, groupings, and equipment are necessary to ensure optimal student achievement.

4. *Teach.* Teaching is the implementation of the prescription. It is based on the instructional techniques previously discussed—motivation, feedback, maximizing on-task time, managing disruptive behaviors, and so on.

5. *Evaluate.* The evaluation step allows the teacher to determine the student's level of functioning at the completion of the instructional process. Evaluation gives the teacher an opportunity to modify expectations, teaching techniques, or the environment in an effort to improve future efforts and responses.

The ABC model is associated with I CAN (*I*ndividualize instruction, *C*reate social leisure competence, *A*ssociate all learnings, *N*arrow the gap between theory and practice). I CAN is a comprehensive physical education and leisure skills program appropriate for children with unique needs. It is developmental in nature and provides a continuum of skills, from preprimary motor and play skills to sport, leisure, and recreation skills. The I CAN program offers a balance between the development of psychomotor skills and affective and social development. It provides for individualized instruction at each individual's level of ability and lets learners progress at a rate and in a manner appropriate to their learning styles and motivational/interest levels. I CAN is particularly useful for children whose developmental growth is slower than average, including those with physical and mental disabilities as well as those with specific learning disabilities and social-emotional behavior problems.

The I CAN program comprises three major areas: Preprimary Motor and Play Skills; Primary Skills; and Sport, Leisure, and Recreation Skills (I CAN curricular materials are shown in Figure 10.8). The program is designed for use by physi-

Figure 10.8   Some available I CAN curriculum materials. *Note.* From Brochure No. 335, Northbrook, IL: Hubbard. Used with permission of Hubbard Publishing Company.

cal education specialists and special education or classroom teachers.

The Data Based Gymnasium Instructional Model

The Data Based Gymnasium (DBG) is an instructional model that emphasizes ways to initiate and analyze behavior and provide feedback, and recommends ways to manage the learning environment (Figure 10.9). Although it is similar in design to many other instructional models, it is unique in its specific delineation of behavior modification techniques as a means of accomplishing task and terminal objectives.

Originally, the Data Based Gymnasium model, illustrated in Figure 10.9, was designed to provide a physical education program for individuals with severe handicaps. However, its principles are applicable in some form to many instructional situations involving students with unique learning needs.

The Data Based Gymnasium emphasizes three essential elements:

1. *Cue.* The cue is a condition, signal, or request to the learner designed to influence the occurrence of a behavior. Cues can be verbal, like the command "Stand up," or nonverbal, like printed directions or a demonstration of the desired activity.
2. *Behavior.* Behavior is what a person does in response to a cue. In the DBG model,

it is a component of the task that the student is to learn or the skill that the student is being asked to master. The teacher presents cues that will result in the performance of the targeted behavior. If the desired terminal behavior is too complex for the student to achieve, it must be broken down into simpler, enabling behaviors. When the enabling behavior is accomplished (forward chaining), the student may then be capable of the more complex terminal behavior. With moderately and severely handicapped individuals, a reverse chaining sequence may be used. In the DBG model, this means providing assistance with the initial parts of the task but letting the student perform the last component independently. Progressing, the student is allowed to perform additional components of the task unaided. The sequence thus builds systematically from the final component to the initial one.

3. *Consequence.* The third major element in the DBG model is consequences, or feedback. After a behavior is performed, the student must receive information about its success or failure. Feedback or consequences can be positive or negative in nature. Positive feedback is called a reinforcer, while negative feedback is a punisher. The model stresses the delivery of appropriate positive consequences to increase the probability of a behavior's being repeated.

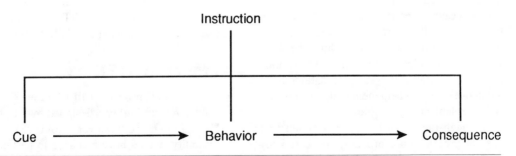

Figure 10.9 The data based gymnasium instructional process.

PROGRAM COVER SHEET

Pupil: Jim
Date Started: April 3, 1985
Date Completed:

Program: Leisure Skills, E.
Go Down a Slide

Verbal Cue:
"Jim, slide down the slide."

Materials:
1. clipboard
2. pencil
3. slide
4. reinforcer

Instructional Setting:
Position Jim so he can see the demonstration.

Reinforcement Procedure:
Give social reinforcement on completion of task.

Correction:
"No, Jim." Model, recue, mild social reinforcement if correct.
If not, go to next level of assistance.
"No, Jim."
Cue. "Jim, slide down the slide."
Physically assist Jim as he slides.
Socially reinforce on completion of the task.

Criterion:
Three consecutive correct responses before going to next step.

Figure 10.10 Example of the instructional procedure for teaching a skill according to the data based gymnasium model. *Note.* From *Physical Education for the Severely Handicapped: A Systematic Approach to a Data Based Gymnasium* by J. Dunn, J. Morehouse, and H.D. Fredericks (p. 53), 1986, Austin, TX: Pro-Ed. Copyright 1986 by Pro-Ed. Reprinted by permission.

The Data Based Gymnasium includes a task-analyzed game, exercise, and leisure sport curriculum. Figure 10.10 presents an example of the instructional procedures for teaching the skill of sliding down a slide. In addition, the DBG model provides examples of systematic data collection techniques that can help the instructor to successfully implement the program.

Although the I CAN and Data Based Gymnasium programs are probably the best known models, two other models should be included in an overview of quality instructional delivery systems. These models, which are also discussed in chapter 11, are Project ACTIVE (Vodola, 1976) and PREP (Watkinson & Wall, 1979).

Project ACTIVE

The ACTIVE program (*A*ll *C*hildren *T*otally *In*volved *E*xercising) was designed by Dr. Thomas Vodola to ensure that every child, regardless of disability, would have a chance to participate in a quality physical education program. This comprehensive program incorporates a test-assess-prescribe-evaluate planning process and includes normative as well as criterion-referenced tests in the areas of motor ability, nutrition, physical fitness, and posture. These specially designed instructional programs provide appropriate physical activity for individuals with mental retardation, learning disabilities, orthopedic impairments, sensory impairments, eating disorders, and breathing problems, as well as activities for postoperative convalescent children, normal children, and gifted individuals. Project ACTIVE is an innovative, cost-effective program that has been widely used throughout the United States.

PREP Play Program

The goal of the PREP Play Program, designed by Dr. Patricia Austin in 1974 in Edmonton, Alberta, Canada, is to develop the play skills of young, moderately mentally retarded children. It is based on the belief that improving individual play skills will enable children to participate more successfully in a nonstructured play environment.

The PREP Program is carried out during free play periods. The teacher interacts with one child at a time while the others continue their free play. Instructional episodes are short and focus on a specific task (e.g., learning to jump down). Although most of the teaching is done on a one-to-one basis, the teacher spends part of the time with small groups. These groups are composed of children with similar motor abilities and allow practice in a group context of the skills learned individually. An important underlying requirement of the PREP Program is a play environment that is conducive to stimulating and purposeful play.

The most helpful feature of the PREP Program is the set of task-analyzed, instructionally sequenced skills that are used for assessing the level of functioning of each individual, determining teaching objectives, and carrying out the instructional process. Figure 10.11 illustrates the PREP model. This model, if modified, can be employed in the teaching of other physical skills.

As shown in Figure 10.11, the instructional aspect of the PREP model incorporates three major phases designed to optimize individual instruction: the prompt, the behavior, and the feedback. After an assessment is completed, the play skills to be improved are identified. Using the task-analyzed instructional sequence for the identified skill, the teacher follows the prescribed routine while employing appropriate reinforcement and feedback techniques. Following each instructional episode, the teacher monitors the child's progress by recording performance on prepared forms. At regular intervals the performance is reviewed, and new target skills or instructional strategies are implemented. A major contribution of the PREP model is its description of the level of assistance

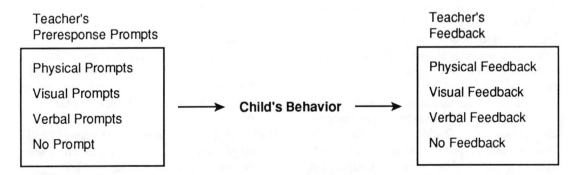

Figure 10.11 The PREP phases of instruction. *Note.* From *The PREP Play Program: Play Skill Instruction for Young Mentally Retarded Children* by E.J. Watkinson and A.E. Wall, 1979, Alberta, Canada: University of Canada.

a student needs to be successful. The assistance takes the form of prompts; the assistance required is categorized as "physical prompts," "verbal prompts," "visual prompts," or "no prompts."

The instructional systems just described are primarily behavioral in nature. Although there are also instructional systems based on humanistic principles, they have not yet been developed to the same extent. Some contributions of the humanistic orientation to the instructional planning process are discussed in chapter 5.

Summary

Many factors affect teaching effectiveness in the adapted physical education and sport setting. Educators' personal attributes and their specialized knowledge and skills contribute to their success in interacting with learners who have unique needs.

Educators who are capable of employing a variety of approaches and teaching methods and matching them to the learning needs of individuals can better structure the learning environment to ensure student satisfaction and success. Their flexibility permits them to teach the same content in different ways, thus allowing them to more fully adapt their teaching to meet individual needs.

Teachers can facilitate learning by employing task analysis, activity analysis, and activity modification. These techniques are valuable in helping educators to meet learners' goals and accommodate their needs. Organizational and methodological techniques allow teachers to maximize learning opportunities by decreasing the teacher-student ratio and structuring independent learning experiences.

Teacher effectiveness can be enhanced through the use of various observation techniques that provide teachers with feedback about their own behaviors. Self-evaluation and supervisory feedback using direct observation, audiotape, and videotape are excellent methods for promoting teacher improvement.

Several instructional planning models have been developed to meet the needs of unique individuals. They include the Achievement-Based Curriculum and the I CAN program, the Data Based Gymnasium instructional model, Project ACTIVE, and the PREP Play model. In addition to these behaviorally oriented models, teachers may draw on the humanistic orientation to physical education. These resources offer valuable assistance to physical educators in designing quality physical education programs to optimize learning for individuals with unique needs.

Bibliography

Berryman, D. (1974). *Systems utilization for comprehensive modular planning of therapeutic recreation services for disabled children and youth* (Final report BEH Grant OEG-0-73-5171). New York: New York University.

Brasile, F.M., Conway-Callagan, M.K., Dager, D., & Kleckner, D.J. (1986). Computer applications in therapeutic recreation. *Therapeutic Recreation Journal*, **10**(2), 8-18.

Burkett, L., & Wessel, J.A. (1984). *Leadership Training Guide*. Tempe, AZ: Department of Health and Physical Education, Arizona State University.

CompTech Systems Design. (1987). Catalog. Hastings, MN: CompTech Systems Design.

Darst, P.W., Zakrajsek, D.S., & Mancini, V.H. (1989). *Analyzing physical education and sport instruction*. Champaign, IL: Human Kinetics.

Dunn, J., Morehouse, J., & Fredericks, H. (1986). *Physical education for the severely handicapped: A systematic approach to a data based gymnasium* (2nd ed.). Austin, TX: Pro-Ed.

Hurley, D. (1981). Guidelines for adapted physical education. *Journal of Physical Education, Recreation and Dance*, **52**(6), 43-45.

Irmer, L., Cowger, B., Glasenapp, G., Arter, J., & Estes, G. (1977). *Physical education op-

portunity program for exceptional learners (PEOPEL): An administrative guide for secondary schools. Phoenix: Arizona Department of Education and Phoenix Union High School System.

Kelly, L.E. (1981). *Microcomputer assistance for educators in prescribing adapted physical education*. Unpublished doctoral dissertation, Texas Woman's University, Denton, TX.

Kelly, L.E. (1987, November). *Physical education management system*. Paper presented at the New York State Alliance for Health, Physical Education, Recreation and Dance Convention, Syracuse, NY.

Montelione, T., & Davis, R. (1988). The computer in adapted physical education professional preparation. In C. Sherrill (Ed.), *Leadership training in adapted physical education* (pp. 385-393). Champaign, IL: Human Kinetics.

Mosston, M. (1981). *Teaching physical education* (2nd ed.). Columbus, OH: Merrill.

Nichols, B. (1986). *Moving and learning: The elementary school physical education experience*. St. Louis: Times Mirror/Mosby.

Peterson, C.A., & Gunn, S.A. (1984). *Therapeutic recreation program design: Principles and procedures* (2nd ed.). Englewood Cliffs, NJ: Prentice-Hall.

Rosenshine, B., & Furst, N. (1971). Research in teacher performance criteria. In B. Smith (Ed.), *Research in teacher education* (pp. 370-391). Englewood Cliffs, NJ: Prentice-Hall.

Siedentop, D. (1983). *Developing teaching skills in physical education* (2nd ed.). Palo Alto, CA: Mayfield.

Vodola, T. (1976). *Project ACTIVE maxi-model: Nine training manuals*. Oakhurst, NJ: Project ACTIVE.

Watkinson, E.J., & Wall, A.E. (1979). *The PREP Play Program: Skill instruction for young mentally retarded children*. Edmonton, Alberta, Canada: Physical Education Department, University of Alberta.

Wessel, J.A. (1979). *I CAN—Sport, leisure and recreation skills*. Northbrook, IL: Hubbard.

Wessel, J.A., & Kelly, L. (1985). *Achievement-based curriculum development in physical education*. Philadelphia: Lea & Febiger.

Resources

Written

Auxter, D., & Pyfer, J. (1985). *Principles and methods of adapted physical education and recreation* (5th ed.). St. Louis: Times Mirror/Mosby. This book provides comprehensive information about adapted physical education and advocates the task-specific approach. It also provides various approaches to task analysis and compares the developmental and task-specific approaches.

Darst, P.W., Zakrajsek, D.B., & Mancini, V.H. (1989). *Analyzing physical education and sport instruction*. Champaign, IL: Human Kinetics. This book provides information about the most popular systematic observation instruments in physical education today. It includes a description of each instrument, coding procedures, data analysis procedures, and examples of possible uses.

Mosston, M., & Ashworth, S. (1986). *Teaching physical education* (3rd ed.). Columbus, OH: Merrill. This book provides a comprehensive discussion of various teaching styles as well as excellent examples of their application.

Sherrill, C. (1986). *Adapted physical education and recreation: A multidisciplinary approach* (3rd ed.). Dubuque, IA: Wm. C. Brown. This comprehensive book is an excellent source of information on the philosophy of humanism as it is applied to adapted physical education and the developmental approach to teaching. It also provides examples of teaching to meet individual needs through task analysis, activity modification, and activity analysis.

Siedentop, D. (1983). *Developing teaching skills in physical education* (2nd ed.). Palo Alto, CA: Mayfield. This book provides considerable information on teaching skills as well as on suggestions for their development.

Audiovisual

Bowers, L., & Klesius, S. (Directors). (1984). *I'm Special Instructional Modules* [Videotapes]. Tampa: Department of Professional Education, University of South Florida. Relevant modules include Module 6—Developmental Physical Education: Putting Principles into Action, Module 11—On the Move, Module 12—Reaching Out, and Module 13—Name of the Game.

Other

CompTech Systems Design, P.O. Box 516, Hastings, MN 55033. This company offers a wide variety of computer instructional software designed specifically for physical education.

Children and Youth With Unique Needs

Part III is devoted to major handicapping conditions, and one chapter relates to individuals with unique needs who have not been classified as handicapped according to PL 94-142. The handicapping conditions discussed in Part III include mental retardation, learning disabilities, behavior disabilities, sensory impairments, cerebral palsy, amputations, spinal cord impairments, and other health conditions. The chapters typically define terms and classifications, examine the causes of and types of conditions, and describe characteristics of affected groups. Particular attention is given to teaching methods and activities that meet a variety of unique needs.

CHAPTER 11

Mental Retardation

Patricia L. Krebs

Society's attitude toward individuals with mental retardation has, with time, become more humanistic. The possibility of educating people with mental retardation was not considered viable until 1798, when Dr. Jean Itard, Chief Medical Officer of the National Institute for the Deaf and Dumb in France, instructed an 11-year-old boy with severe retardation caught running wild. Known as the Wild Boy of Aveyron, the child had learned his behavior from the wild animals with whom he'd been raised. Fascinated by the work of Itard, Seguin, and Montessori, social scientists of the 1800s showed sporadic interest in educating people with mental retardation. Maria Montessori was the first to approach mental retardation as an educational problem rather than a medical problem.

Definition, Incidence, and Classification

There are as many different definitions of mental retardation as there are professional groups to serve individuals with mental retardation. However, the most commonly accepted definition of mental retardation was established by the American Association on Mental Deficiency (AAMD) and is reflected in PL 94-142. Section 121a.5(b) (4) states that "mental retardation refers to significantly subaverage general intellectual functioning existing concurrently with deficits in adaptive behavior and manifested during the developmental period" (Grossman, 1977, p. 11). It is important for the physical educator to understand the three criteria that must be met in order to determine whether an individual has mental retardation according to this definition.

Subaverage General Intellectual Functioning

The first criterion, "significantly subaverage general intellectual functioning," refers to a person's score on an intelligence test. There are two intelligence tests used extensively throughout the world: the Stanford-Binet Intelligence Scale and the Wechsler Intelligence Scale for Children-Revised (WISC-R).

The Stanford-Binet has a mean (average) score of 100 and a standard deviation (*SD*) of 16. Similarly, the WISC-R also has a mean score of 100 but a standard deviation of 15. Therefore, someone with significantly subaverage functioning functions at a level *two* or more standard deviations below the mean. Thus, an intelligence test score below 68 or 70, as measured by the Stanford-Binet or the WISC-R, respectively, denotes 2 standard deviations below the mean.

$$
\begin{array}{ll}
100 & \text{(Mean Stanford-Binet IQ)} \\
-32 & \text{(2 } SD \text{ Stanford-Binet)} \\
\hline
68 &
\end{array}
$$

$$
\begin{array}{ll}
100 & \text{(Mean WISC-R IQ)} \\
-30 & \text{(2 } SD \text{ WISC-R)} \\
\hline
70 &
\end{array}
$$

Table 11.1 The Normal Curve and Intelligence Quotient Scores

| | .13% | 2.15% | 13.59% | 34.14% | 34.14% | 13.59% | 2.15% | .13% |

SD	−3	−2	−1	0	1	2	3
Stanford Binet Score	52	68	84	100	116	132	148
Weschler Score	55	70	85	100	115	130	145

According to normal probability theory, it is estimated that 2.28% of the total population (with no known organic dysfunction) of any society has mental retardation (2.15% + .13% = 2.28%). It is also estimated that .76% of the total population has known organic dysfunctions that cause mental retardation. These figures (2.28% plus .76% rounded to 3.0%) are used to estimate the incidence of individuals with mental retardation in a particular geographic area (Table 11.1).

There are many systems for classifying mental retardation. Initially, those with mental retardation were classified by behavioral characteristics and etiology. With the advent of education for people with mental retardation, classification according to educational capacity has become the accepted standard. Table 11.2 contrasts the AAMD levels of mental retardation with another educational classification system preferred by Kirk (1972).

One problem with classification systems is that they label people with definitions that trigger absolute behavioral expectations and negative emotional reactions. Labels also provide preconceived ideas about individuals' abilities, disabilities, and potential. The educator must be prepared to accept the diversity of individuals with mental retardation.

Table 11.2 Levels of Mental Retardation and Associated IQ Ranges

Kirk (1972)	American Association on Mental Deficiency (Grossman, 1977)
Borderline or slow learner (80-90 IQ)	
Educable (50-55 to 75-79 IQ)	Mild (52-67 IQ)
Trainable (30-35 to 50-55 IQ)	Moderate (36-51 IQ)
Custodial or totally dependent or profound (25-30 IQ and below)	Severe (20-35 IQ)
	Profound (under 20 IQ)

Impairment in Adaptive Behavior

The second criterion, "impairment in adaptive behavior," refers to the individual's ability to mature personally and socially with age. Maturity is measured according to the development of sensorimotor abilities; self-help skills; communication; and academic, vocational, and socialization skills.

Origination During the Developmental Period

The third criterion, "originating during the developmental period," situates the period of development between conception and the 18th birthday. Retardation occurring after the 18th birthday is referred to as either neurological damage or brain damage.

Cognitive Development

The AAMD definition of mental retardation is psychometrically oriented. While this orientation is useful in determining individual differences in intelligence, it doesn't help in understanding the dynamic nature of intellectual functioning and how it changes from age to age in the developmental process. Such a developmental orientation toward intelligence facilitates effective instruction and programming.

In order to establish developmental orientation, it is necessary to draw on the extensive work of Piaget (1952). In his vast writing, Piaget proposed that children move through four stages of cognitive development: the sensorimotor stage (ages 0 to 2), the preoperational stage (ages 2 to 7), the stage of concrete operations (ages 7 to 11), and the stage of formal operations (age 11 or 12 to adulthood). These stages are depicted in Table 11.3.

Table 11.3   Stages of Cognitive and Play Development

Age (years)	Piagetian cognitive developmental stage	Type of play	Play group
0	Sensorimotor	Practice play and ritualization	Individual
1			
2	Preoperational	Symbolic	Egocentrism and parallel play
3			Reciprocal play
4			(progressive
5			reciprocity in
6			dyads, triads, etc.)
7	Concrete operations	Games with rules	Larger group play
8			
9			
10			
11	Formal operations		
12			
13			
14			
15			

Sensorimotor Stage

During the sensorimotor stage, children develop, use, and modify their first schemata. For Piaget, schema or schemata (plural) are forms of knowing that develop, change, expand, and adapt. A schema may be a simple response to a stimulus, an overt action, a means to an end, an end in itself, an internalized thought process, or a combination of overt actions and internalized thought processes. Examples of schemata include grasping, sucking, and tossing a ball. During the sensorimotor stage, for example, the child develops the schema of grasping, which is internally controlled and can be utilized in grasping the mother's finger, picking up different objects, or picking up an object from various angles. A schema often will function in combination or in sequence with other schemata, as when the child throws the ball. In this activity the child combines the schemata of grasping and releasing.

To a great extent, the sensorimotor period is one in which the child learns about the self and the environment through the sense modalities. A great deal of attention is given to physically manipulating and acting on objects and on observing the effects of such actions. The child is stimulated by objects in the environment and observes how objects react to actions applied to them. Through exploration, manipulation, and problem solving, children gain information about the properties of objects such as texture, size, weight, and resiliency as they drop, thrust, pull, push, bend, twist, punch, squeeze, or lift objects that have various properties. At this stage, the functioning of the individual is largely sensorimotor in nature, with only rudimentary ability to manipulate reality through symbolic thinking.

Preoperational Stage

The preoperational stage includes the preconceptual substage, which lasts to about the age of 4, and the substage of intuitive thought, which spans the ages of 4 to 7. Toward the end of the sensorimotor period, the child begins to develop the ability to symbolically represent actions before acting them out. However, the symbolic representation is primitive and limited to schemata associated with one's own actions. During the preoperational stage, progress occurs as the child is able to represent objects through language and use language in thinking. The child now can think about objects and activities and manipulate them verbally and symbolically.

Concrete Operations Stage

During the stage of concrete operations children achieve operational thought, which enables them to develop mental representations of the physical world and manipulate these representations in their minds (operations). The fact that operations are limited to those of action, to the "concrete," or to those that depend on perception distinguishes this stage from the stage of formal operations. The fact that the child is able to develop and manipulate mental representations of the physical world distinguishes this stage from earlier stages. In the stage of concrete operations, the child is able to mentally carry through a logical idea. The physical actions that predominated in earlier stages can now be internalized and manipulated as mental actions.

During the period of concrete operations, there is increased sophistication in the use of language and other signs. In the preoperational phase the child developed word definitions without full understanding of what the words meant. In the stage of concrete operations, language becomes a vehicle for the thinking process as well as a tool for verbal exchange. In this stage, children are able to analyze situations from perspectives other than their own. This decentering permits thinking to become more logical and the conception of the environment to be more coherently organized. During the period of concrete operations, children's thinking becomes more consistent, stabilized, and organized. At the same time, although children are able to perform the more complex operations just described, they are generally incapable of sustaining them when they cease to manipulate objects or when the operations are not tied to physical actions.

Formal Operations Stages

Children functioning at the stage of formal operations are not confined to concrete objects and events in their operations. They are able to think in terms of the hypothetical and to use abstractions to solve problems. They enter the world of ideas and can rely on pure symbolism instead of operating solely from physical reality. They are able to consider all of the possible ways a particular problem can be solved and to understand the effects of a particular variable on a problem. Individuals at this stage have the ability to isolate the elements of a problem and systematically explore possible solutions. Whereas children at the stage of concrete operations tend to deal largely with the present, those functioning at the formal operations stage are able to be concerned with the future, the remote, and the hypothetical. They can establish assumptions and hypotheses; test hypotheses; and formulate principles, theories, and laws. They are able not only to think, but to think about what they are thinking and why they are thinking it. During this stage, individuals are able to use systems of formal logic in their thinking.

Piaget and Play

Piaget calls behaviors related to play *ludic* behaviors, which are engaged in to amuse or excite the individual. He holds that behaviors become play when they are repeated for functional pleasure. Activities pursued for functional pleasure appear early in the sensorimotor period. According to Piaget, the most primitive type of play is practice play or exercise play. The child repeats clearly acquired skills (schemata) for the pleasure and joy of it. The infant repeats movements such as shaking a rattle over and over and exhibits pleasure in doing so. This type of play does not include symbolism or make-believe.

Later in the sensorimotor period, the play in which the child engages is called ritualization.

More and more schemata are developed and are used in new situations. Play becomes a happy display of mastered activities; gestures are repeated and combined as a ritual, and the child makes a motor game of them. As progress is made, the child forms still newer combinations from modified schemata. For example, a child may follow the ritual of sleeping after being exposed to the stimuli associated with sleeping (pillow, blanket, thumb sucking, etc.). Toward the end of the sensorimotor period, the child develops symbolic schemata and mental associations. These symbolic schemata enable a child to begin to pretend or make-believe in play. Some authors refer to symbolic play as make-believe play. Throughout the sensorimotor stage, play is individual or egocentric, and rules are not a part of it.

The preconceptual period within the preoperational stage marks the transition between practice play and symbolic play. At the preconceptual stage the child's play extends beyond the child's own actions. Also, new ludic symbols appear that enable children to pretend. At ages 4 through 7 (the intuitive thought stage), there is an advance in symbolic play. The child relates a story in correct order, is capable of a more exact and accurate imitation of reality, and uses collective symbolism (other people are considered in play). The child begins to play with one or more companions but also continues to display parallel play. In play the child can think in terms of others, and social rules begin to replace individual ludic symbols. For example, games of tag and games related to the hiding of a moving object appear. Although play is egocentric, opportunities for free, unstructured, and spontaneous play are important. Children at this level are not positively responsive to intuitive thought. There is an advancement from egocentricity to reciprocity in play. Therefore, opportunities for cooperative play become appropriate. It should be remembered that the collective symbolism associated with cooperative play is at its beginning in this period. Guessing games, games based on looking for missing objects, games of make-believe, and spontaneous games are stimulating for children during this stage. The fact that children are responsive to tag games, for example, indicates that they are beginning to play with others and to think of others in their play.

At the stage of concrete operations, children's play exhibits an increase in games with rules. Such rules may be "handed down," as in cultural games, or developed spontaneously. In addition, there is an expansion of socialization and a consolidation of social rules. Thus, the playing and construction of group games with rules becomes very attractive to children. As the child enters and moves through this period, play becomes less concerned with make-believe and pretending and becomes more concerned with "real" games. At this stage, play may be structured, social, and bound by rules. Although some children may be ready for such games by the seventh birthday, children retarded in cognitive development may not be ready for them until after adolescence, if then.

Causes of Mental Retardation

It is generally agreed that the origins of mental retardation can be traced to three factors:

- Organic or physical causes resulting mainly in severe and profound retardation and accounting for 10% to 15% of all individuals with mental retardation
- Severe stimulus deprivation resulting predominantly in mild and moderate retardation
- Natural distribution of intelligence within the human species (Reynolds & Birch, 1977), also resulting primarily in mild and moderate retardation

Organic or Physical Problems

Grossman (1977) identifies the following seven major organic or physical causes contributing to mental retardation:

1. Infections and intoxications
2. Trauma or physical injury
3. Metabolic or nutritional abnormalities

4. Gross brain disease (postnatal)
5. Unknown prenatal influence
6. Chromosomal abnormality
7. Gestational disorders

Infections and intoxications include *prenatal infection*, *postnatal infection*, and *intoxication*. Cases of prenatal infection would include mothers who contract rubella (German measles) within the first three months of pregnancy (the first trimester). Prenatal infections may also be viral or bacterial. The toxic subdivision includes toxemia of pregnancy, maternal phenylketonuria (PKU), hyperbilirubinemia (too much bile pigment in the blood), lead poisoning, and other toxic conditions.

Trauma or physical injury has five subdivisions including prenatal injury, mechanical injury at birth, prenatal hypoxia (lack of oxygen), postnatal hypoxia, and postnatal injury. Some examples are prenatal irradiation, difficulties in labor, prenatal placenta separation, massive hemorrhage, and other severe trauma such as that resulting from a fractured skull, contusions of the brain, or other injury.

Metabolic or nutritional abnormalities include *all disorders resulting from metabolic, nutritional, endocrine, or growth dysfunction* occurring either prenatally or postnatally. Examples include Tay-Sachs disease; lipoid (fat or fatlike substances) diseases; amino acid abnormalities such as PKU; carbohydrate abnormalities such as galactosemia and hypoglycemia; and endocrine diseases such as hypothyroidism, which causes cretinism.

Gross brain disease (postnatal) includes many disorders in which the etiology is unknown or uncertain. Examples include neurofibromatosis (multiple tumors of the skin, nerves, bones, or brain), tuberous sclerosis, new growths (tumors), and Huntington's chorea (characterized by progressive dementia and death).

Attributed to unknown prenatal influence are conditions presumed to exist at or prior to birth for which no known etiology has been established. Included in this category are cerebral malformation, anencephaly (partial or complete absence of the cerebrum, cerebellum, and flat bones of the skull), Cornelia de Lange syndrome (genetic growth disorder), microcephaly (abnormally small head), macrocephaly (excessively large head), and hydrocephaly (head enlarged with cerebral spinal fluid).

Chromosomal abnormalities include all types of *gene mutations*; *drug and other chemical effects on the chromosomes*; *viruses*, such as Cri-du-chat (cat cry syndrome); *various physical anomalies*, such as hypertelorism (widely spread eyes), epicanthal fold (fold of skin at the side of the eye), downward palpebral (eyelid) slant, low-set ears; and the *various trisomies*, including Down syndrome (trisomy 21), Klinefelter's syndrome, and Turner's syndrome.

Gestational disorders include all atypical gestational conditions such as prematurity (live infants delivered before 37 weeks from the first day of the last menstrual period), low birth weight, postmaturity (infant exceeding normal gestation period by 7 or more days), and other gestational disorders (Grossman, 1977).

Severe Stimulus Deprivation

Although there remain many unanswered questions surrounding the heredity versus environment argument, environment does affect the intellectual and personal development of infants and children. Stimulus deprivations caused by poverty, poor nutrition, poor education, parental absence, child abuse, and lack of appropriate gender role models have all been linked to mental retardation.

Natural Distribution of Intelligence

As stated previously, one of the criteria needed to determine whether an individual has mental retardation is "significantly subaverage general intellectual functioning," which is determined to exist when an individual scores 2 or more standard deviations below the mean on a standardized intelligence test. In a normal distribution, this would include 2% to 3% of the population.

Unfortunately, science's knowledge of the causes of mental retardation is so limited that a definite etiology can be assigned in only about 20% of cases and a possible etiology in another 20%. This means that 80% of cases remain unclear or unclassified. What is known, however, is that a child with mild mental retardation is more likely to come from a lower socioeconomic class than a nonretarded child. On the other hand, more severe levels of mental retardation do not relate to any one socioeconomic class. Likewise, specific causation can be attributed in very few cases of mild retardation, but a cause can almost always be identified in cases of severe retardation. Charges of racism and cultural bias abound. However, children born in poverty often must cope with greater incidence of poor nutrition, poor health and health habits, lack of social or intellectual stimulation, and lack of sensory and movement opportunities. They are the ones who are most prone to suffer from mental retardation with unspecified causes.

Characteristics of Individuals With Mental Retardation

Learning Characteristics

The area in which individuals with mental retardation differ most from other individuals is in cognitive behavior. The greater the degree of retardation, the lower the cognitive level at which the individual functions. Most adults with severe and profound mental retardation function at the sensorimotor cognitive stage, and adults with moderate mental retardation may be incapable of surpassing the preoperational substage. Adults with mild mental retardation may not be able to progress beyond the level of concrete operations, and adults with borderline mental retardation may be limited to simpler forms of formal operations.

Considerable research has identified the general differences in learning between children with and without mental retardation. Although the learning process and stages of learning are the same for both, children with mental retardation learn at a slower rate than nonretarded children and hence achieve less academically. The learning rate of children with mild mental retardation is usually 50% to 70% of the rate of nonretarded children, and the learning rate of children with moderate mental retardation is usually 30% to 50% of that of nonretarded children. Children with severe and profound mental retardation are generally incapable of traditional schooling. Although self-contained classes and separate schools for those children are found in most school systems, the primary educational objectives for this group involve mastery of the basic life skills and communication skills needed for their care. Whereas adults with severe mental retardation who function at a higher level can learn to dress, feed, and toilet themselves properly and can even benefit from sheltered workshop activities, those with profound mental retardation will most likely need close supervision and care throughout their lives.

Students with mental retardation do not retain learned information as well as their nonretarded peers. Therefore, *repetition of learned information and skills* is necessary to offset forgetting. Children with mental retardation are often less capable of applying past experience and previously learned information to new, though similar, tasks. Because they have difficulty generalizing, they are more likely to view each new task as a novel one. Concrete tasks and information are more easily learned and utilized than their abstract counterparts. Also, children with mental retardation are generally unable to attend to as many task cues or pieces of information as children of normal or above-normal intellect. *Instructions must, therefore, be concrete*, emphasizing only the most important task information. Because verbalization is more abstract than demonstration or manipulation, physical educators may find it advantageous to *accompany verbal instruction with the more concrete forms of instruction* when teaching students with mental retardation.

Despite these characteristics, educators must take care not to predict the limits of ability of a child with mental retardation. Teachers are cautioned not to impose their own limits on those children but rather to permit each child to progress along the developmental continuum of learning and skill acquisition at a rate and capacity appropriate to the individual.

Social/Emotional Characteristics

Although children with mental retardation exhibit the same ranges of social behavior and emotion as other children, they more frequently demonstrate inappropriate responses to social and emotional situations. Because they have difficulty generalizing information or learning from past experiences at the same rate or capacity as nonretarded children, they are more often exposed to situations they are ill prepared to handle. Children with mental retardation often do not fully comprehend what is expected of them, and they may respond inappropriately because they have misinterpreted the situation rather than because they lack appropriate responses.

Educational programs for children with mental retardation should always include experiences to help them determine social behaviors and emotional responses for everyday situations. Personal acceptance and development of proper social relationships are critical to independence. As with nonretarded individuals, the reason most individuals with mild and moderate retardation lose jobs is inadequacy of social skills, such as poor work habits and the inability to get along with fellow workers.

Physical and Motor Characteristics

Children with mental retardation differ least from nonretarded children in their physical and motor characteristics. Although most children with mental retardation evidence developmental motor delays, these seem to be related more to the cognitive factors of attention and comprehension rather than to physiologic or motoric deficits.

Generally, the greater the retardation, the more

lag in attaining major developmental milestones. As a group, children with mental retardation walk and talk later, are slightly shorter, and usually are more susceptible to physical problems and illnesses than other children. In comparative studies, children with mental retardation consistently score lower than nonretarded children on measures of strength, endurance, agility, balance, running speed, flexibility, and reaction time. Although many youngsters with borderline and mild mental retardation can successfully compete with their nonretarded peers, students with moderate mental retardation tend to fall 4 or more years behind their nonretarded peers on tests of physical fitness and motor performance.

In general, the fitness and motor performance of nonretarded children exceeds that of children with mild mental retardation, who in turn perform better than children with moderate mental retardation. The performance of boys generally exceeds that of girls, with the differences between the sexes increasing as the degree of retardation increases. Flexibility and balance seem to be the exceptions to the generalizations just stated. Whereas non-retarded girls show greater flexibility and balance than nonretarded boys, boys with mental retardation show greater flexibility and balance than girls with mental retardation. Also, children with moderate mental retardation exhibit more flexibility than children with mild mental retardation (Rarick, Dobbins, & Broadhead, 1976; Rarick & McQuillan, 1977). Down syndrome children tend to have hypotonic musculature and hypermobility of the joints, which permits them greater than normal body flexibility.

Many children with mental retardation are hypotonic and overweight. Disproportionate bodies pose many problems with body mechanics and balance. The "institutional" walk of the nonathletic child with mental retardation is characterized by a shuffling gait with legs wide apart and externally rotated for balance. Body alignment is in a total body slump. Club hands and feet, postural deviations, and cerebral palsy are all prevalent among youngsters with mental retardation; the physical educator must take them into consideration when planning the program for each child. See Figure 11.1.

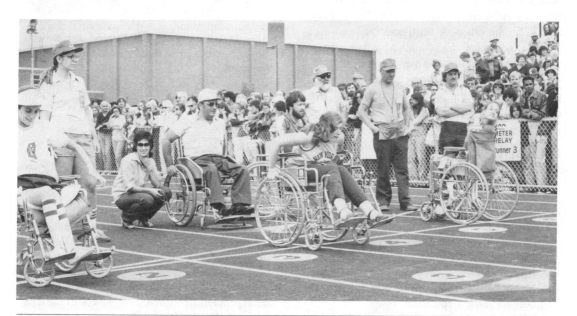

Figure 11.1 Many children with mental retardation have other conditions as well. Photo courtesy of Special Olympics International.

Down Syndrome

Down syndrome is the most prevalent genetic condition associated with mental retardation. One in 800 children is born with Down syndrome. In the United States, approximately 5,000 such children are born each year. Although fathers are genetically responsible for the abnormality in about 30% of all cases, women over the age of 35 present the highest risk (1 in 400) of having a Down syndrome child. At age 40 the risk increases to 1 in 110 births, and at age 45 the risk is 1 in 35 births.

Cause

Down syndrome results from one of three chromosomal abnormalities. The most common cause is trisomy 21, so named because of the presence of an extra #21 chromosome. This results in a total of 47 chromosomes instead of the normal 46 (23 chromosomes received from each parent). A second cause of Down syndrome is nondisjunction. This occurs when one pair of chromosomes fails to divide during meiotic cell division, resulting in 24 chromosomes in one haploid cell and 22 in the other. A third and rare cause of Down syndrome is translocation, which occurs when two chromosomes grow together so that, while appearing to be one chromosome, they actually contain the genetic material of two chromosomes.

Characteristics

Although there are over 50 clinical characteristics of Down syndrome, the most common signs are the following (see Figure 11.2):

- Short stature
- Poor muscle tone
- Hypermobility of the joints
- Slanting eyes with folds of skin at the inner corners (called epicanthic folds)
- White spots in the iris of the eyes

Figure 11.2 Special Olympics athlete with Down syndrome. Photo courtesy of Special Olympics International.

- Transverse crease on the palms
- Small nose with a flat bridge
- Short neck
- Small head
- Small mouth
- Sparse, fine hair
- Protruding, fissured tongue
- Broad hands and feet with stubby fingers and toes
- Excess skin at the nape of the neck

Down syndrome children also tend to have many health problems. Approximately 44% of these individuals develop congenital heart disease and

Table 11.4 Characteristics of the Child with Down Syndrome

Characteristics	Implications for movement experiences
Lag in physical growth. (Growth ceases at an earlier than normal age and generally results in shorter height and smaller overall stature.) Lag is evident in motor development.	The child may need to participate in activities geared for younger age groups.
The circulatory system is less well developed. Arteries are often narrow and thinner than normal, and less vascular proliferation is evidenced. Many children (especially boys) exhibit congenital heart disorders, heart murmurs and septum defects being the most common.	Although there is a need for the development of endurance, youngsters will have difficulty in endurance activities. It is necessary for all children to have a medical examination and for the instructor to develop a program with medical consultation.
Poor respiration and susceptibility to respiratory infections. (Underdeveloped jaw causes mouth to be too small for normal-sized tongue, inducing mouth breathing.)	Poor respiration may impede participation in endurance activities.
Perceptual handicaps.	Children may be clumsy and awkward. Activities to develop perceptual abilities should be emphasized.
Poor balance.	Since balance is important in most physical and motor activities, lack of balance will affect performance ability. Children need balance training.
Enjoyment of music and rhythmic activities.	The instructor should include rhythmic activities in the program to provide successful and enjoyable experiences and should use music as an aid in teaching.
Obesity.	General overall participation in activity as well as activities that enhance weight reduction are recommended.
Flabbiness. (Hypotonicity, particularly associated with newborn infants, develops with age.)	The instructor should provide opportunity for movement experiences at early ages and activities to increase strength at later ages.
Protruding abdomen, lack of muscle and ligament support around the joints, and pronated ankles.	Activities to enhance body alignment and to increase muscle and ligament support around the joints and abdominal exercises are recommended.
Ability to mimic.	Instructor should demonstrate activities and ask children to imitate them.

have a greater risk of developing leukemia. Bowel defects requiring surgery and respiratory infections are also common. Down syndrome individuals age more rapidly, and almost all who live beyond age 35 develop Alzheimer's disease. All individuals with Down syndrome have some degree of mental retardation. The degree can range from mild to profound; however, most function in the moderate-to-severe range. Table 11.4 describes the implications for movement experiences for children with Down syndrome. Individuals with Down syndrome are becoming increasingly integrated into our society and institutions—schools, health care systems, and the work force.

Physical Education Programming

The many medical problems of individuals with Down syndrome require medical clearance for activity participation and careful planning of the physical education program. Muscle hypotonia (low muscle tone) and hypermobility (above normal mobility) of the joints often cause postural and orthopedic impairments such as lordosis; ptosis; dislocated hips; kyphosis; atlantoaxial instability; flat, pronated feet; and forward head. Exercises and activities must not put undue stress on the body such that hernias, dislocations, strains, or sprains result.

Tests

Assessment is necessary to determine the status of a student with mental retardation. Children with mild to moderate retardation will, in many cases, be able to take the same tests as children without retardation. However, children with severe to profound mental retardation will often most appropriately be administered tests designed for their particular population.

Some norm-referenced tests have been developed specifically for use with people with mental retardation. Also, there are several appropriate content- and criterion-referenced tests that may be used to measure physical education abilities. These include tests associated with the Project ACTIVE Physical Fitness Test I (Vodola, 1978), the I CAN program (Wessel, 1979), the Ohio State University Scale of Intra-Gross Motor Assessment (Ohio State SIGMA) (Loovis & Ersing, 1979), the Special Olympics Sports Skills Guides (1985), and the Data Based Gymnasium (Dunn, Morehouse, & Fredericks, 1986). Consult chapter 4 for additional information dealing with testing.

Teaching Methods

Although many of the methods used in teaching nonhandicapped children can be applicable to those with mental retardation, certain methods are often stressed in the teaching of students with mental retardation. Reynolds and Birch (1977) recommend several techniques to increase teacher productivity and satisfaction; these are discussed in subsequent paragraphs.

Undercutting

A teacher should begin to teach well within the range of student skill and comprehension. If new tasks are too difficult and therefore frustrating, the teacher should drop back slightly until the student regains confidence.

Using Concrete Experiences

Hands-on experiences facilitate learning for individuals with mental retardation. The teacher should provide as many concrete learning experiences as possible. Demonstration, physical prompting, and manipulation of body parts are preferred over verbal instructions (see Figure 11.3).

Helping Children Set the Pace of Learning

By charting the student's progress, both teacher and student can often determine when a goal will

Figure 11.3 Physical manipulation is used to teach a pass in floor hockey. Photo courtesy of B. Slatas.

be accomplished (e.g., complete two laps around the track). Cooperative charting can provide motivation and direction to help a student estimate how long it will take to accomplish any new task, set personal objectives to accomplish a task within a reasonable margin of error, and identify practice techniques for reaching the objectives set.

Systematically Employing Principles of Reinforcement

Behavioral principles must be systematically employed and coordinated. Behaviors to be influenced must be pinpointed, and systems must be designed to promote change in the identified behaviors. An excellent example of a program that systematically employs behavioral principles in the teaching of youngsters with severe handicaps is the Data Based Gymnasium developed by Dunn, Morehouse, and Fredericks (1986).

Giving Children Choices

Giving choices to children with mild or moderate mental retardation is often an effective way to motivate them to achieve. Each choice must specify *what* is to be done, *when* it is to be completed, *where* the activity will take place, *with whom* it is to be completed, and *why* the task should be attempted. Contingency contracting between teacher and student is an agreement that when a certain task is completed, the student will be free to do one of several other appealing tasks. Offering choices gives students with mental retardation experience in self-control and self-determination.

Using Peer Instruction

One of the most exciting developments in special education programs is the use of other students (peer tutors) to help children with special needs. It is common for young children to rely on slightly older ones as role models. Cross-age tutoring is an excellent way of providing children with mental retardation with role models whom they can imitate.

Using Pupil Feedback

By observing students, a teacher obtains valuable information about their learning and performance. Because tests provide opportunity for the systematic observation of behavior, students should be tested frequently. For maximum validity, tests should be content- or criterion-referenced and should occur in the most "real" situation possible.

Giving Prompt Feedback to Pupils

There is substantial evidence that, the shorter the time lapse between student performance and feedback, the more learning is facilitated. This is especially true in the case of persons with severe and profound mental retardation.

Moving From Familiar to Unfamiliar

Because the student with mental retardation has difficulty with transfer of learning and has less flexibility of approach to a task, the progression from familiar to unfamiliar must take place gradually and be strongly reinforced. Tasks to be learned should be divided into small meaningful steps, presented sequentially, and then rehearsed in total, with as little change in order as possible. Teaching skills in the "real" environment, rather than in a simulated environment, is preferable.

Modeling Behavior

Children tend to imitate adults and other children they admire. They mold their own behavior to conform to the examples of others. Thus, modeling can serve as an important teaching technique.

Limiting Extraneous Stimuli

Teachers can facilitate the learning of students with mental retardation by decreasing extraneous stimuli and instructing them to focus on relevant information.

Invoking the High Interest/ Low Difficulty Principle

Children with mild and moderate mental retardation aspire to accomplishments often beyond their ability. Television coverage of major sporting events stimulates their desire to participate in high-level team sport competition. The physical educator can capitalize on this enthusiasm by designing modified versions of the sport that students can perform successfully.

Using Task Analysis

Breaking down skills into sequential tasks is an important instructional approach in working with children with mental retardation. Many planned programs discussed later in the chapter employ task analysis.

Being Consistent and Predictable

Consistency of teacher behavior helps establish and maintain a sound working relationship between teacher and students. When students know what to expect, they can plan their behaviors with the certainty of what the consequences will be. Children with mental retardation are often less flexible in accepting or adapting to new routines. Therefore, day-to-day consistency of class structure, teacher behavior, and expectations of students is important in optimizing their learning.

Education of Students in Mainstreamed Settings

Approximately 30% of all students with mental retardation are receiving some support services while in a mainstreamed class, and 56% are receiving specially designed instruction in separate classes within the school (U.S. Department of Education, 1986). Physical education teachers face the task of providing successful, enjoyable, and challenging learning experiences for all students in mainstreamed classes. Their teaching strategies must ensure that students with mental retardation will comprehend instructions and achieve success in the gymnasium. In addition to the teaching methods presented earlier, teachers can enhance effective integration by

- reducing the amount of uncertainty facing students who are integrated,
- shortening and simplifying instructions,
- using well-defined and distinctive cues,
- employing multisensory teaching strategies, and
- modifying instruction and activities by reducing the speed of skill execution and reducing the force required for successfully executing a skill.

Activities

In selecting activities for students with mental retardation, the physical educator should be aware of the games, activities, and sports enjoyed by children within the neighborhood and offered by local recreation agencies. These activities are appropriate choices for the physical education class. Communication with local recreation agencies can result in cooperative programming and facilitate successful integration of students with mental retardation into structured community-based play groups.

Selection of Activities According to Mental Age

Because students with mental retardation progress through the same stages of development as nonretarded children but at a slower rate, many professionals recommend that activity selection be geared to mental age. Mental age is determined by the following formula: Mental Age = IQ/100 × Chronological Age. However, while it is important to select and structure activities according to mental age, the physical educator must also be sensitive to the social ramifications of the activity. Older adolescents with mental retardation will not want to engage in "childish" games such as Duck, Duck, Goose or Fox and Squirrels.

Basic Activities

A particular need of children with mental retardation is to develop the motor skills and physical fitness levels they will require for optimal vocational training and successful use of leisure time. Rarick, Dobbins, and Broadhead (1976) recommend structuring physical education for educable mentally retarded students (with moderate mental retardation) so that 30% of the program is devoted to activities that develop muscular strength, 20% to development of gross body coordination, 5% to 10% to improvement of balance abilities, and 5% to 10% to improvement of flexibility.

Activities for Students With Mild to Moderate Retardation

Often students with mild mental retardation excel in sports, and sports may be their primary avenue for success and self-esteem. They are more likely to be mainstreamed in physical education classes than in any academic subject. Their physical and motor needs are generally like those of nonretarded students; therefore, physical education activities for students with mild mental retardation often will be the same as or similar to those for their nonretarded peers.

Generally, the following types of activities are best for persons with mild and moderate mental retardation:

- Individual rather than team activities
- Individual sports
- Activities involving music
- Activities requiring little emphasis on strategy, rules, or memorization
- Gross body movement activities (rather than fine motor coordination activities)
- Activities that provide constant movement rather than those requiring long periods of inactivity

While students with mild mental retardation often excel in physical education and sports, those with moderate mental retardation generally do not achieve high skill levels. Still, basketball, soccer, hockey, baseball, and dancing are activities often popular among adolescents with moderate mental retardation even though concepts of team play, strategy, and rules are difficult for them to learn. Highly skilled people with mild mental retardation can learn strategy and rules through concrete teaching experiences. Skill and sport activities like those fostered by Special Olympics yield success and enjoyment for older students with mental retardation.

Activities for Students With Severe and Profound Retardation

Individuals with severe and profound mental retardation are not generally placed into integrated or mainstreamed public school classes, but rather into special classes, schools, or institutions. Their level of mental and motor functioning is very basic. Their activity is generally characterized by little student interaction (i.e., parallel play), with most interaction occurring between teacher and student. School-age individuals with severe and profound mental retardation generally need a physical education program that emphasizes

- sensorimotor training,
- physical and motor fitness,
- fundamental skills, and
- movement patterns.

Sensorimotor programs involve the stimulation of a child's senses so that sensory channels are developed enough to receive information from the environment. Functional senses then permit the child to respond to the environment through movement and manipulation. In these programs, children are taught the normal infant motor progression of head control, crawling, grasping, releasing, sitting, creeping, and standing. Many students with severe and profound mental retardation do not walk before the age of 9, and many never become ambulatory. Individuals with profound mental retardation may not readily respond to their environment and may exhibit little or none of the curiosity that would motivate them to investigate the environment and learn. Even the most rudimentary skills must be taught.

Planned Programs

Several established programs are good resources for instructional processes and methods, assessment procedures, and activities relative to physical education and sport for individuals with mental retardation. Several of these, in fact, were originally designed for use with mentally retarded populations. In one of the first contributions, Thomas M. Vodola (1978) developed Project ACTIVE (*A*ll *C*hildren *T*otally *I*n*V*olved *E*xercising) (see chapter 10). Project ACTIVE includes

a systematic instructional process (test-assess-prescribe-evaluate), norm-referenced tests for the measurement of physical and motor ability, and a variety of other tests to help assess abilities in physical education. The project also provides many activity ideas for learning. Project ACTIVE is a National Diffusion Network (NDN) project sponsored by the U.S. Department of Education.

Another notable program is I CAN, designed under the leadership of Janet Wessel (1979) of Michigan State University. I CAN uses an achievement-based curriculum (ABC) model designed to improve the quality of physical education services to all children, including mentally retarded children. The I CAN ABC model provides criterion-referenced assessment evaluation in a variety of performance areas, as well as instructional resource materials to help children improve their abilities. The I CAN ABC process consists of the following steps: plan, assess, prescribe, teach, evaluate, and modify. The program offers extensive resources including activities for preprimary motor and play skills; primary skills; and sport, leisure, and recreation skills. All have direct relevance to the physical education programs for students with mental retardation. The I CAN program is reviewed in greater detail in chapter 10.

Littman and Leslie (1978) have developed a physical education enrichment program (PREP) that emphasizes the motor development, socialization, and language development of preschool children. Because the program gives much attention to play and gross motor development, it is particularly relevant for those who teach students with mental retardation. Closely related in both purpose and title is the PREP Play Program (Watkinson & Wall, 1979), designed to develop the play skills of young children with mental retardation. The program provides task-analyzed instructional sequences, curricular materials for the development of group play skills, and a systematic instructional model. The program is based on the assumption that, if play skills are developed, children will more likely become involved in play and reap the values of that involvement. Each target play skill

The Individual Motor Program
O.S.U. SIGMA and P.B.C. Cumulative Data-Profile

Name of Child _____ Sex _____

Birthdate _____ Height _____ Weight _____

Basic Motor Task	Date		Date		Date		Date	
	SIGMA Level	P.B.C. Level / B.O. / T.L.	SIGMA Level	P.B.C. Level / B.O. / T.L.	SIGMA Level	P.B.C. Level / B.O. / T.L.	SIGMA Level	P.B.C. Level / B.O. / T.L.
1. Walking	C / IT / IB		C / IT / IB		C / IT / IB		C / IT / IB	
2. Stair Climbing	C / IT / IB		C / IT / IB		C / IT / IB		C / IT / IB	
3. Running	C / IT / IB		C / IT / IB		C / IT / IB		C / IT / IB	
4. Throwing	C / IT / IB		C / IT / IB		C / IT / IB		C / IT / IB	
5. Catching	C / IT / IB		C / IT / IB		C / IT / IB		C / IT / IB	
6. Jumping	C / IT / IB		C / IT / IB		C / IT / IB		C / IT / IB	
7. Hopping	C / IT / IB		C / IT / IB		C / IT / IB		C / IT / IB	
8. Skipping	C / IT / IB		C / IT / IB		C / IT / IB		C / IT / IB	
9. Striking	C / IT / IB		C / IT / IB		C / IT / IB		C / IT / IB	
10. Kicking	C / IT / IB		C / IT / IB		C / IT / IB		C / IT / IB	
11. Ladder Climbing	C / IT / IB		C / IT / IB		C / IT / IB		C / IT / IB	

Comments:
Scoring Subscripts:
"C"—Completes all behavior criteria and trail criteria for that level.
"IT"—Refers to a performance in which trail criterion has not been completely accomplished.
"IB"—Refers to a performance in which the behavioral criterion(s) has not been completely accomplished.
"R"—Indicates a child refuses to participate in the assessment procedure.

Figure 11.4 Individual motor program recording form. *Note.* From *Assessing and Programming Gross Motor Development for Children* (p. 11) by E.M. Loovis and W.F. Ersing, 1979, Loudonville, OH: Ohio Motor Assessment Associates. Copyright 1979 by E. Michael Loovis and Walter F. Ersing. Reprinted by permission.

is broken down into specific, sequenced tasks. The culminating step in the sequence is the actual target skill that, when attained, enables children to play well in most environments.

A program that directly relates assessment and curriculum is the individual motor program (IMP) model, which was developed by Loovis and Ersing (1979). The IMP includes testing and instructional materials for preschool and school-age children with mental retardation. The IMP comprises two parts: the Ohio State University Scale of Intra-Gross Motor Assessment (SIGMA), and the performance-based curriculum (PBC). The Ohio State SIGMA is a criterion-referenced assessment of 11 basic gross motor skills; the PBC provides a sequence of progressive instructional experiences for each of the gross motor skills. A form that may be used to record present level of performance on each of the motor tasks is shown in Figure 11.4. Figure 11.5 presents a sample teaching-learning experience for youngsters working toward the attainment of Behavioral Objective #1, Level II: stair climbing.

An important program with particular relevance for individuals with severe and profound retardation is the Data Based Gymnasium (Dunn et al., 1986). The Data Based Gymnasium (DBG) offers a behaviorally oriented instructional model for teaching students with severe and profound handicaps, and a system for analyzing behavioral principles for the socialization of behaviors. Finally, DBG includes a game, exercise, and leisure sport

---

P.B.C. ACTIVITY: *STAIR CLIMBING*
Level: II

Behavioral Objective: #1

To ascend a series of 5 steps (*maximum 8 in. high*) using a two foot landing (*mark-time pattern*)— when standing at the bottom of a series of five (5) steps (*maximum 8 in. high*), the child, with or without the aid of the railing or wall, walks up using a two foot landing (*mark-time pattern*) two out of three times.

Teaching-Learning Experiences:
1. Child steps over objects, e.g., sticks, wands, ropes, etc., which are held at different heights.
2. Child walks up one step constructed from a mat(s) with assistance from a railing or wall.
   a. Height of step should increase gradually from approximately 2 to 8 in.
   b. Number of steps should increase gradually from 1 to 4. (*Activity desirable if fold-away mats are available.*)
   c. Gradually decrease assistance until child can walk unassisted.
   Note: A possible technique to facilitate stepping up onto the mat is stepping over a wand or stick held at mat level.
3. Child walks up incline board at least 2 ft wide with assistance from instructor or wall.
4. Child walks up one (then 2, 3, & 4) step(s) of normal size (8 in.) with assistance from a railing or wall.

Figure 11.5 Teaching-learning experiences for stair climbing. *Note.* From *Assessing and Programming Gross Motor Development for Children* (p. 43) by E.M. Loovis and W.F. Ersing (1979), Loudonville, OH: Ohio Motor Assessment Associates. Copyright 1979 by E. Michael Loovis and Walter F. Ersing. Reprinted by permission.

curriculum. Specific skills within the curriculum are broken down into tasks and steps sequenced as phases representing shaping behaviors (see Figure 11.6). Students are reinforced for successfully completing tasks that approximate the terminal or targeted behavior. The Data Based Gymnasium includes a clipboard instructional and management system that helps to identify present status, objectives, and progress on skill development.

A project begun in Arizona with the aim of helping general physical education meet the individual needs of exceptional learners is Project Physical Education Opportunity Program for Exceptional Learners (PEOPEL). PEOPEL (Irmer, Glasenapp, Norenberg, & Odenkirk, 1983) provides 36 units of instruction applicable to students in physical education. The units include basic performance objectives that have been task analyzed for use in individualized instruction. The task analysis and the use of student aids to individualize instruction make the program particularly suitable for teaching students with mental retardation.

The *Special Olympics Sports Skills Guides*

BASIC GAME SKILLS

Underhand Strike

Terminal Objective: The student will perform an underhand strike with the preferred arm and hit a volleyball which the student is holding with his opposite hand.

Prerequisite Skills: Gross Motor—Lower Extremity, C; Body Orientation, G.

Phase I   Student will perform an underhand strike at an 8 in. foam ball that is held by a teacher in front of the student's body at waist high level.

Phase II   Student will perform an underhand strike with the teacher's hand supporting the student's hand in front of the student's body with the 8 in. foam ball lying in the student's palm, waist high.

Phase III   Student will perform an underhand strike at an 8 in. foam ball which is held waist high by the student with the teacher's hand held halfway down the student's arm.

Phase IV   Student will perform an underhand strike with an 8 in. foam ball placed waist high with the teacher's hand placed on the student's elbow.

Phase V   Student will perform an underhand strike with a volleyball held waist high by the student, no assistance from the teacher.

           The following steps apply to Phase V.

           Steps:

           1. 8 in. foam ball
           2. 8 in. rubber ball
           3. 8 in. volleyball

Suggested Materials: An 8 in. diameter volleyball, rubber ball, and foam ball

Teaching Notes: 1. To perform this behavior, the student should swing the preferred arm backward with a clenched fist and then forward, striking the ball.

Figure 11.6 A task analysis of the underhand strike. *Note.* From *Physical Education for the Severely Handicapped* (p. 161) by J.M. Dunn, J.W. Morehouse, Jr., and H.D.B. Fredericks, 1986, Austin, TX: Pro-Ed. Copyright 1986 by Teaching Research. Reprinted by permission.

created by Special Olympics International are also helpful in the development of sports skills. Initially designed for children and adults with mental retardation, the guides are presented in a series of manuals that present long-term goals, short-term objectives, task-analyzed activities, sport-specific assessments, and teaching suggestions for various sports. Sports skills guides are now available for the following:

- Alpine skiing
- Aquatics (swimming and diving)
- Athletics (track and field)
- Basketball
- Bowling
- Canoeing
- Cross-country skiing
- Cycling
- Equestrian
- Gymnastics
- Floor and poly hockey
- Ice skating
- Motor activities program
- Roller skating
- Soccer
- Softball
- Table tennis
- Team handball
- Tennis
- Volleyball
- Weightlifting

The many planned programs discussed in this section are particularly relevant to people with mental retardation. However, because several have application for other populations in adapted physical education, they are presented in more detail in other chapters throughout this book.

Special Olympics

Special Olympics was created in 1968 by Eunice Kennedy Shriver and the Joseph P. Kennedy, Jr. Foundation. It is an international sports training and competition program open to individuals with mental retardation 8 years of age and older,

regardless of their abilities. The mission of Special Olympics is to provide year-round sports training and competition in a variety of Olympic-type sports for all children and adults with mental retardation.

Summer and Winter Special Olympics Games are held annually as chapter (state), sectional, area or county, and local competitions. International Summer Special Olympics Games, which take place every 4 years, began in 1975. International Winter Special Olympics Games, also held every 4 years, began in 1977. Additional Special Olympics competitions that include two or more sports are defined as tournaments. To advance to higher levels of competition in a particular year (i.e., from local through area and sectional to chapter competition), an athlete must have participated for a minimum of 8 weeks in an organized training program in the sport(s) in which he or she is entered for higher-level competition. To advance, an athlete must have placed first, second, or third at the lower level of competition in the sport(s). Instruction for 8-week training programs is provided in the *Special Olympics Sports Skills Guides*.

The showcase for acquired sports skills of Special Olympians in training is the many Special Olympics competitions held throughout the year. These competitions have the excitement, pageantry, fanfare, and color associated with Olympic games—including the parade of athletes, the lighting of the torch, the opening declaration, the flag raising, and the releasing of balloons. In addition to showcasing their skills, Special Olympians often have the opportunity to meet celebrities and local politicians, experience new sport and recreational activities through a variety of clinics, enjoy an overnight experience away from home with friends, and develop the physical and social skills necessary to enter school and community sport programs.

Two classifications of sport, official and demonstration, exist in Special Olympics. Official Special Olympics summer sports include

- aquatics,
- athletics,

- basketball,
- bowling,
- gymnastics,
- roller skating,
- soccer,
- softball, and
- volleyball.

Official winter sports include

- alpine and nordic skiing,
- figure and speed skating, and
- floor or poly hockey.

Demonstration Special Olympics sports include

- canoeing,
- cycling,
- table tennis,
- team handball,
- tennis, and
- weightlifting.

To provide consistency in training, Special Olympics uses the sports rules of the International Sports Federation (given the responsibility by the International Olympic Committee for handling the technical aspects of Olympic Games) to regulate a sport, except when those rules conflict with Official Special Olympics Sports Rules (1988).

Because of the wide range of athletic abilities among people with mental retardation, Special Olympics training and competition programs offer motor ability training, team and individual sports skills, modified competition, and regulation competition in most official and demonstration sports.

Special Olympics has developed three pioneer programs to help schools integrate into existing after-school sports programs, sports training, and competition for students with mental retardation. In the first program, School Sports Partnership, students with mental retardation train and compete alongside interscholastic athletes. Varsity and junior varsity athletes serve as peer coaches, scrimmage teammates, and boosters during competition. Athletes with mental retardation compete in existing interscholastic league competitions. For example, in a track and field meet, the varsity

100-meter dash is followed by a Special Olympics 100-meter dash. In distance races, all athletes start together. At the end of the meet, individual and school scores are tabulated for varsity and partnership teams. In team sports (soccer, softball, and basketball), partnership teams compete just prior to and at the same site as the varsity or junior varsity game.

The second program, Unified Sports leagues, creates teams with equal numbers of athletes with and without mental retardation. Unified Sports leagues can be part of a school's interscholastic, intramural, or community recreation sports program. Currently these leagues are established in six sports: bowling, basketball, softball, volleyball, soccer, and distance running.

The third program, Partners Clubs, brings together high school and college students with Special Olympics athletes to perform regular sport skills training and competition and to spend time enjoying other social and recreational activities in the school and community. The Partners Club should be a sanctioned school club with all the accompanying benefits.

All athletes with mental retardation should be able to earn school athletic letters and certificates, wear school uniforms, ride team buses to competitions, participate and be recognized in school award ceremonies, and represent their schools in Special Olympics local, area/county, and state competitions.

Safe Participation

If the physical educator plans activities appropriate to the academic, physical, motor, social, and emotional levels of children with mental retardation, there will be few contraindications for activity. Special Olympics has prohibited training and competition in certain sports that hold unnecessarily high risk of injury, especially injury that could have lifelong deleterious effects. Prohibited sports are the javelin, discus, and hammer throw; pole vaulting; boxing; platform diving; all martial arts; fencing; shooting; contact football and rugby; wrestling; judo; karate; nordic jumping; and trampolining. In addition, there is evidence from medical research that up to 10% of people with Down syndrome suffer from a malalignment of the cervical vertebrae C-1 and C-2 in the neck. This condition, called atlantoaxial subluxation, exposes affected individuals to the possibility of injury if they participate in activities that hyperextend or radically flex the neck and upper spine. The condition can be detected by a physician's examination that includes X-ray views of full flexion and extension of the neck. Physical education teachers are encouraged to follow the lead of Special Olympics in restricting individuals who have atlantoaxial subluxation from participating in activities which, by their nature, result in hyperextension, radical flexion, or direct pressure on the neck and upper spine. Such activities include

- certain gymnastics activities,
- diving,
- the butterfly stroke,
- the high jump,
- alpine skiing,
- heading the soccer ball, and
- any warm-up exercises placing undue stress on the head and neck.

Because many children with mental retardation, particularly those with Down syndrome, are cardiopathic, students *must* receive activity clearance from a physician. Appropriate activities within the limitations specified by the physician should then be individually planned.

Another common condition of individuals with mental retardation is muscular hypotonia or flabbiness. Infants with this condition are often called floppy babies. Although hypotonia decreases with age, it never disappears, and hernias, postural deviations, and poor body mechanics are prevalent because of insufficient musculature. The physical educator again must be careful in planning exercises and activities that are beyond the capabilities of individuals with muscular hypotonia, because they can lead to severe injury. Abdominal

and lower back exercises must be selected with care, and daily foot strengthening exercises are recommended.

Summary

Mental retardation is one of the most prevalent handicapping conditions. It is a condition that may be viewed from both psychometric and developmental perspectives. Mental retardation has numerous causes that result in varied characteristics influencing success and participation in physical education and sport. This chapter has suggested teaching methods, tests, and activities appropriate for this population and briefly reviewed selected planned programs relevant to youngsters with mental retardation. One of the major programs associated with physical education and sport is Special Olympics, which has made a significant impact on both instructional and competitive opportunities for children and adults with mental retardation. Most people with mental retardation have been and continue to be successfully involved in physical education and sport experiences.

Acknowledgment

Appreciation is extended to Joseph P. Winnick for writing the section on cognitive development and parts of the section on planned programs in this chapter.

Bibliography

Dunn, J.M., Morehouse, J.W., & Fredericks, H.D.B. (1986). *Physical education for the severely handicapped: A systematic approach to a data based gymnasium*. Austin, TX: Pro-Ed.

Grossman, H.J. (Ed.) (1977). *Manual on terminology and classification in mental retarda-*

tion. Washington, DC: American Association on Mental Deficiency.

Irmer, L.D., Glasenapp, G., Norenberg, M., & Odenkirk, B. (1983). *PEOPEL: Physical education opportunity program for exceptional learners* (6th ed.). Phoenix: Arizona Department of Education.

Karp, J. (n.d.). *Project ACTIVE: All Children Totally InVolved Exercising*. Kelso, WA: Kelso Public Schools [601 Crawford, Kelso, WA, 98626; pamphlet].

Kirk, S.A. (1972). *Educating exceptional children* (2nd ed.). Boston: Houghton Mifflin.

Littman, K.G., & Leslie, L. (1978). *Preschool recreation and enrichment programs (PREP)* (Vols. 1-3). Washington, DC: Hawkins & Associates.

Loovis, E.M., & Ersing, W.F. (1979). *Assessing and programming gross motor development for children*. Cleveland Heights, OH: Ohio Motor Assessment Associates.

Official Special Olympics sports rules. (1985). Washington, DC: Special Olympics.

Piaget, J. (1952). *The origins of intelligence in children*. New York: International Universities Press.

Rarick, G.L., Dobbins, D.A., & Broadhead, G.D. (1976). *The motor domain and its correlates in educationally handicapped children*. Englewood Cliffs, NJ: Prentice-Hall.

Rarick, G.L., & McQuillan, J.P. (1977). *The factor structure of motor abilities of trainable mentally retarded children: Implications for curriculum development* (DHEW Project No. H23-2544). Berkeley, CA: Department of Physical Education, University of California.

Reynolds, M.C., & Birch, J.W. (1977). *Teaching exceptional children in all America's schools*. Reston, VA: The Council for Exceptional Children.

Special Olympics sports skills guides. (1985). Washington, DC: Special Olympics.

U.S. Department of Education. (1986). *Eighth annual report to Congress on the implementation of the Education of the Handicapped Act* (DOE Publication No. 1986-491-151: 40210). Washington, DC: U.S. Government Printing Office.

Vodola, T.M. (1978). *Developmental and adapted physical education: A.C.T.I.V.E. motor ability and physical norms: For normal, mentally retarded, learning disabled, and emotionally disturbed individuals*. Oakhurst, NJ: Township of Ocean School District.

Watkinson, E.J., & Wall, A.E. (1979). *The PREP play program: Play skill instruction for young mentally retarded children*. Edmonton, Alberta, Canada: Physical Education Department, University of Alberta.

Wessel, J.A. (1979). *I CAN*. Northbrook, IL: Hubbard Scientific.

Winnick, J. (1979). *Early movement experiences and development: Habilitation and remediation*. Philadelphia: Saunders.

Resources

Written

Dunn, J.M., Morehouse, J.W., & Fredericks, H.D.B. (1986). *Physical education for the severely handicapped: A systematic approach to a data based gymnasium*. Austin, TX: Pro-Ed. This book provides an instructional approach for teaching severely and profoundly handicapped students.

Special Olympics. (1981-1989). *Sports skills guides*. Washington, DC: Author. This is a series of sport-specific instructional manuals. Each manual includes long-term goals, short-term objectives, skill assessments, task analyses, teaching suggestions, progression charts, and related information.

Audiovisual

Sacks, A. (Producer), & Delisa, J. (Director). (1983). *ABC Wide World of Sports 1983 inter-*

national summer Special Olympics games [Film and videotape]. Washington, DC: Special Olympics. This is a shortened version of the ABC Wide World of Sports coverage of the 1983 international games held at Louisiana State University, Baton Rouge, Louisiana. Track and field, swimming and diving, basketball, soccer, and volleyball are featured.

CHAPTER 12

Learning Disabilities

Diane H. Craft

Learning-disabled children form both the largest and least understood group of handicapped learners. It is likely that most teachers, whether in regular or adapted physical education, will teach many learning-disabled students in their career. This chapter is intended as an introduction to help teachers best meet the needs of children with learning disabilities.

There is no one profile of the learning-disabled child, but the following description may serve to bring the term to life. The learning-disabled child in a class may be that 9-year-old boy who seems intellectually bright but does poorly in school. He is the one who has difficulty reading and cannot consistently distinguish left from right or the letter *p* from the letter *b*. He seems clumsy and has difficulty with gross and fine motor tasks. His handwriting is almost unreadable, and he is the only child in the class who cannot skip, walk a balance beam, or change directions quickly in a tag game. When expected to do a difficult task, he frequently gives up before even trying. He seems to be such a puzzle!

Learning disabilities are often described in terms of the following four factors:

1. There is a discrepancy between intellectual potential and academic performance.
2. There are learning problems that are not due to mental retardation, emotional disturbance, or environmental disadvantage.
3. There is an uneven pattern within and among the areas of cognitive, affective, and/or motor development.
4. There may or may not be clear signs of central nervous system dysfunction.

Definition

The most widely used definition of *learning disability* is found in the regulations of PL 94-142, the Education for All Handicapped Children Act (1975).

Specific learning disability means a disorder in one or more of the basic psychological processes involved in understanding or in using language, spoken or written, which may manifest itself in an imperfect ability to listen, think, speak, read, write, spell or do mathematical calculations. The term includes such conditions as perceptual handicaps, brain injury, minimal brain dysfunction, dyslexia, and developmental aphasia. The term does not include children who have learning problems which are primarily the result of visual, hearing, or motor handicaps, of mental retardation, of emotional disturbance, or of environmental, cultural, or economic disadvantage (Section 121a.5(b)(9)).

The word *specific* has been added to indicate that each child has difficulty with only certain aspects of learning. For example, a child may have poor auditory memory but above-average visual memory. The learning disability is specific to certain functions.

The nature of learning disabilities is still unclear. Currently, work in the field of learning disabilities is based on empirical data documenting a discrepancy between a child's intellectual potential and actual academic achievement, but there is no theoretical base to explain the underlying causes of the educational discrepancy. Researchers in the field are challenged to develop theoretical constructs that explain the causes of learning disabilities. But while researchers are striving to meet this challenge, teachers and administrators who work with learning-disabled children daily have devised their own operational definitions of the condition. Most often their basis for identification of learning-disabled children is the discrepancy between a child's perceived ability and actual achievement. The *performance-potential discrepancy* is not part of the federal definition, but it is the single most agreed-upon benchmark of learning disabilities today.

In addressing the problem of defining learning disabilities, it is necessary to determine whether some children may not be learning disabled but, rather, teaching disabled. This suggests that the problem may not be entirely within the child but may also involve the curriculum in the schools or the inability of some people to teach.

Incidence

Because there is disagreement on what, exactly, constitutes a learning disability, it should be no surprise that there is disagreement about the prevalence of learning disabilities. The U.S. Department of Education indicates that two out of every five handicapped children are classified as having learning disabilities; this figure represents 4% of all school-age children. The ratio of learning-disabled boys to girls is at least 3:1.

Children classified as learning disabled in one state may not be so classified in other states. Some-times this classification is applied to children who don't fit neatly into other existing programs. Sometimes children who are mentally retarded are classified as learning disabled because it is a more acceptable term to parents or others. Schools may feel pressure to classify as learning-disabled students who are making poor progress in school, in order to receive additional federal funds for special education. Teachers may wish to have difficult children removed from their classes through the classification of learning disability; this furthers the notion that the reason for underachievement lies within the child rather than with the curriculum and the teaching method. All of these practices inflate estimates of the incidence of learning disabilities.

Suspected Causes

Any factor that causes dysfunction in one or more of the areas of the brain responsible for perceiving, integrating, and/or acting on information may contribute to learning disabilities. Suspected causes include neurological, genetic, and environmental factors. *Neurological factors* refer to cases of known or suspected brain damage caused by such things as infection, trauma to the skull, anoxia, and fetal alcohol syndrome. Some learning-disabled children may show hard or soft signs of neurological problems. *Hard signs* are results on EEG, reflex, and other tests, which experience has shown to be clear indicators of neurological damage. *Soft signs* are subjective results of neurological tests. The results may not be completely normal, but they are not sufficiently abnormal to support a conclusive diagnosis of neurological damage. Many learning-disabled children show soft signs of neurological damage. Central nervous system (brain) damage was originally thought to underlie all cases of learning disabilities, but this is no longer so.

Genetic factors are also suspected of causing learning disabilities because the incidence is higher among children whose parents and grandparents also had characteristics of learning disabilities. *En-*

vironmental factors such as stimulus deprivation, limited opportunity for motor experiences (e.g., running, jumping, climbing, coloring, and cutting), and lack of opportunity to develop academic readiness skills may also cause learning disabilities. Poor instruction and an inappropriate curriculum may be major contributors to some people's learning problems.

In summary, the causes of learning disabilities are largely unknown because the causes are probably multiple, cumulative, and interrelated, and therefore especially difficult to isolate and identify. Currently, practitioners can only focus on the observed behaviors while researchers seek further knowledge about the underlying causes of learning disabilities.

Problems in Information Processing Found in Learning-Disabled Children

Learning-disabled children seem to have difficulty in information processing. *Information processing* is the continuous cycle of four steps initiated by an *external stimulus*. These four steps are *sensory input, decision making, output* (the actual behavior), and using *feedback* for evaluation, planning of future sensory input, and decision making. Thus the fourth step, feedback, leads again to the first step, sensory input, restarting the cycle. The four events are diagrammed across the top of Figure 12.1. Information processing is described in greater detail in chapter 7.

Observation of the characteristics of learning-disabled individuals suggests a breakdown in one or more of the information processing steps. There can be various clusters of characteristics because different aspects of information processing may be affected in different individuals. One learning-disabled student may have difficulty attending to the relevant stimuli, while another individual may be able to attend but may have problems with directionality and with perception of spatial relationships when planning a movement. Both students have learning disabilities, but they may

exhibit different characteristics. The first student may appear hyperactive but coordinated; while the second, while not hyperactive, may instead appear clumsy and disorganized when moving. *There is no single description of the learning-disabled child.* Rather, each learning-disabled child may present a unique combination of learning problems depending on the steps of the information processing cycle that are affected.

Figure 12.1 diagrams many characteristics of learning disabilities and shows how they may indicate a breakdown in one or more of the steps of information processing. A problem with any one of the steps can affect the third step: output. The example used in Figure 12.1, throwing a ball, is intentionally different from the examples used in the following discussion of characteristics associated with learning disability. The use of more than one example is designed to elaborate on the concepts presented.

1. *Inattention* refers to difficulty focusing on the task at hand. Attention deficits seem to affect sensory input (the first step), decision making (the second step), and feedback (the fourth step) in information processing. Because an inattentive child may not be attending to the relevant stimuli, there may be inadequate stimulus reception and processing and thus inadequate learning. Inattentive children may not live up to their intellectual potential because they are not concentrating on the task. For example, a child with attentional problems may try to shoot a foul shot without really looking at the basket. After shooting, the child may not even look to see if the basket was made, thus failing to attend to the feedback that would lead to improved motor performance. The child's next attempt to shoot a basket may be as erratic as the first because little use has been made of the feedback provided by previous experience.

2. *Distractibility* suggests difficulty in ignoring extraneous stimuli in order to concentrate on the relevant stimuli of the task at

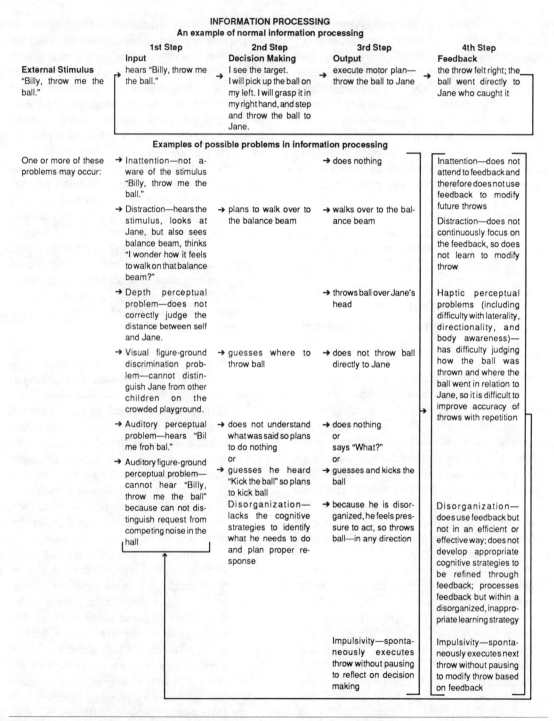

INFORMATION PROCESSING
An example of normal information processing

	1st Step Input	2nd Step Decision Making	3rd Step Output	4th Step Feedback
External Stimulus "Billy, throw me the ball."	hears "Billy, throw me the ball."	I see the target. I will pick up the ball on my left. I will grasp it in my right hand, and step and throw the ball to Jane.	execute motor plan— throw the ball to Jane	the throw felt right; the ball went directly to Jane who caught it

Examples of possible problems in information processing

One or more of these problems may occur:

Input / Decision Making problem	2nd Step (Decision Making)	3rd Step (Output)	4th Step (Feedback)
Inattention—not aware of the stimulus "Billy, throw me the ball."		does nothing	Inattention—does not attend to feedback and therefore does not use feedback to modify future throws
Distraction—hears the stimulus, looks at Jane, but also sees balance beam, thinks "I wonder how it feels to walk on that balance beam?"	plans to walk over to the balance beam	walks over to the balance beam	Distraction—does not continuously focus on the feedback, so does not learn to modify throw
Depth perceptual problem—does not correctly judge the distance between self and Jane.		throws ball over Jane's head	Haptic perceptual problems (including difficulty with laterality, directionality, and body awareness)— has difficulty judging how the ball was thrown and where the ball went in relation to Jane, so it is difficult to improve accuracy of throws with repetition
Visual figure-ground discrimination problem—cannot distinguish Jane from other children on the crowded playground.	guesses where to throw ball	does not throw ball directly to Jane	
Auditory perceptual problem—hears "Bil me froh bal."	does not understand what was said so plans to do nothing or guesses he heard "Kick the ball" so plans to kick ball	does nothing or says "What?" or guesses and kicks the ball	
Auditory figure-ground perceptual problem— cannot hear "Billy, throw me the ball" because can not distinguish request from competing noise in the hall			
	Disorganization— lacks the cognitive strategies to identify what he needs to do and plan proper response	because he is disorganized, he feels pressure to act, so throws ball—in any direction	Disorganization— does use feedback but not in an efficient or effective way; does not develop appropriate cognitive strategies to be refined through feedback; processes feedback but within a disorganized, inappropriate learning strategy
		Impulsivity—spontaneously executes throw without pausing to reflect on decision making	Impulsivity—spontaneously executes next throw without pausing to modify throw based on feedback

Figure 12.1 Throwing a ball viewed through an information processing model.

hand. Distractibility may affect sensory input (the first step) and use of feedback (the fourth step) in information processing.

Distractible children may fail to finish a task because other things have captured their attention. Given the task of throwing foul shots, distractible children may throw once and start to retrieve the ball. But while they are getting the ball, their attention is diverted by a wall chart, a person passing the gymnasium door, a child across the gym shooting baskets, or a comment made by an observer. They may not return to throwing foul shots until the teacher refocuses attention on the task. The slightest extraneous stimulation seems to distract these children so that they are unable to focus on one task for any length of time.

3. *Perceptual deficits* are frequently exhibited by learning-disabled children. Perception is the recognition and interpretation of stimuli received from the sense organs by the brain, and the motor response to the interpretation is perceptual-motor. Thus, perceptual deficits affect sensory input (the first step), decision making (the second step), and feedback (the fourth step) in information processing.

Many professionals see the identification of perceptual deficits as a prerequisite for labeling a child as learning disabled, but such an association has not always been substantiated by research (Kavale & Forness, 1985). Many, but not all, learning-disabled children have perceptual deficits. Perceptual problems may include visual, auditory, and haptic perception. Problems in *visual perception* involve difficulty with figure-ground discrimination, spatial relationships, and visual constancy and/or visual-motor coordination. Problems in *auditory perception* involve difficulty with figure-ground perception, auditory discrimination, sound localization, temporal auditory perception, and auditory-motor

coordination. Problems in *haptic perception* involve difficulty with laterality, directionality, body awareness, and tactile perception.

4. *Disorganization* is a random, haphazard approach to learning a task. Disorganized learning strategies may affect decision making (the second step) and feedback (the fourth step) in information processing. Typically, learning-disabled students have one or more of the following central processing problems. They may

- be unable to organize thoughts and materials logically;
- be unable to deal with quantitative and spatial concepts;
- be unable to see beyond the most superficial meanings or relationships, thus being concrete or stimulus-bound in their thinking;
- be unable to apply rules to problem solving;
- have difficulty in arriving at logical conclusions or predicting outcomes;
- be unable to make generalizations;
- be rigid in their thinking; or
- be unable to benefit from experiences that do not mesh with their overlearned existing language system.

Therefore, their ability to deal with novel situations is reduced considerably (Sutaria, 1985, p. 146).

Many learning-disabled students have difficulty *generating appropriate strategies* to guide their learning. Torgesen (1980) attributes the low performance of learning-disabled children on many tasks to the use of inappropriate or inefficient learning strategies rather than to structural or capacity limitations. Capable learners may spontaneously generate appropriate learning strategies. On observing a new step, a folk dancer may develop verbal cues for each move, which the dancer then repeats silently to guide the learning of the step. Many learning-disabled individuals do not spontaneously generate or use strategies such as verbal mediation to guide movement.

5. *Impulsivity* means acting before thinking about the consequences of the action, showing a lack of control or restraint of motor behavior or thought process. Impulsivity may affect all steps of information processing. It appears that impulsive children may not complete the process of gathering sensory input (the first step) before making a premature motor decision (the second step) and producing output (the third step). There is little consideration of the consequences of the action. After acting (output), the child may be already initiating the next action without pausing to process the feedback (the fourth step) that would help refine future actions.

Impulsive children display little inhibition when they wish to speak or act. Their ability to delay gratification is minimal. These children also show a low tolerance for frustration. On arriving at the gymnasium door with the class, impulsive children may see a ball on the floor across the room, run over, pick it up, and throw the ball wildly in the direction of the basket before reflecting on the fact that they are to do warm-ups when they first enter the gym.

Observable Behaviors

The previous section described problems in information processing. Each of these problems affects the output (step three), the behavior, of the learning-disabled child. The following paragraphs describe the affected behaviors. Every learning-disabled child presents a unique combination of these behaviors. Some of them may be exhibited by *all* children, to some degree, at one time or another. Only when these behaviors *typify* the child, *persist* over an extended period of time, and *interfere* with learning do they need special attention.

Academic/Learning Behaviors

Attention Deficit Disorder with Hyperactivity (ADD/H) is a behavioral characteristic of many students with learning disabilities. Children with ADD/H display difficulties attending to the task at hand. Characteristic behaviors found among hyperactive children and suggestions for managing their behaviors are presented in Table 12.1.

As every beginning teacher learns, it is better to distribute balls to all children in the physical education class only after giving directions on how the balls should be used. Children with ADD/H may be the first to throw the ball and run after it when they are expected to sit and listen to directions. Surprisingly, research has shown that hyperactive children are no more active than other children, but they are active in situations that demand high social compliance.

Dyslexia refers to reading achievement that is significantly below the level expected for the child's age, intelligence, and opportunities for reading instruction (Weiner, 1982). The delay in reading cannot be attributed to limited intelligence or poor instruction. Frequently, children with learning disabilities display dyslexia. Problems that contribute to difficulty in reading include:

- distractibility,
- inattention,
- use of inappropriate learning strategies, and
- perceptual problems.

Dysgraphia is the written counterpart of dyslexia. Common problems in writing include the kinds of disorganization, substitutions, and reversals found among learning-disabled children with dyslexia. Difficulty with fine motor coordination also contributes to messy or illegible written work.

Table 12.1 Attention Deficit Disorder with Hyperactivity (ADD/H)

Typical Characteristics:
• Overactive
• Distractible
• Impulsive
• Aggressive
• Erratic
• Uncoordinated

Children are described as hyperactive when they exhibit several of these characteristics to a greater degree than is found in the general population.

Medical treatment
• Administer daily doses of Ritalin or another stimulant.

Approach is recommended as a treatment of last resort but widely used. Stimulants are effective in decreasing hyperactive behavior but do not necessarily result in increased learning.

Nutrition management
• Prescribe modified diet that avoids sugars and additives.

Approach is based on belief that some hyperactivity may be related to allergies or sensitivity to certain foods and additives (Feingold, 1975).

Research does not support effectiveness of Feingold diet.

Behavior management and relaxation training
• Reward student for attending behavior; teach student tension reduction techniques.

Both approaches are based on the assumption that hyperactivity can be unlearned.

Both approaches address the behavior without seeking to explain underlying causes.

Stimulus reduction
• Teach hyperactive children in environment void of all distractions, i.e., windows covered, walls blank, students isolated in study carrels (Cruickshank, Bentzen, Ratzeburg, & Tannhauser, 1961).

Stimulus reduction in physical education could include teaching in small confined space, such as racquetball court, weight room, locker room, or corner of gym.

Research has not substantiated the superiority of the approach, but it remains popular with practitioners.

Motor Behaviors

There is no clear *motor profile* of the learning-disabled child. Some learning-disabled students are above average in motor performance and are even gifted athletes. Researchers have assessed the motor performance of learning-disabled children on a battery of perceptual-motor, reflex, and developmental scales. But among the 369 learning-disabled students studied, 12% were normal or above in motor performance, while 75% had moderate motor problems and 13% had severe motor problems (Sherrill & Pyfer, 1985). The children with severe motor problems were 2 to 3 years below expectations on all tests administered. Deficits were particularly pronounced in motor skills requiring

- motor planning using the hands,
- perceptual-motor development,
- hand control and speed, and
- balance.

Other studies have also concluded that children with learning disabilities have significant problems with tasks requiring balance and visual-motor and bilateral coordination (Bruininks & Bruininks, 1977; Haubenstricker, 1982).

Clumsy child syndrome is a term proposed by Arnheim and Sinclair (1975) to describe awkward and uncoordinated children. Many learning-disabled children fit the description of the "clumsy child." Specific descriptions of motor behaviors that contribute to the impression of a clumsy child are described in the following paragraphs.

Poor dynamic balance is a frequently documented characteristic of children with learning disabilities (Cinelli & DePaepe, 1984). Balance problems may be due to deficits in postural and equilibrium reflexes. In a review article, Rarick (1980) found that learning-disabled children frequently have hyperactive labyrinthine nystagmus and abnormal responses to vestibular stimulation. Poor balance may in turn contribute to frequent falling and an appearance of clumsiness.

Delayed motor development and immature basic motor skills such as inability to gallop, skip, or hop also characterize children with learning disabilities (Brunt, Magill, & Eason, 1983). The abnormal reflexes and perceptual problems noted previously could be factors contributing to these motor delays.

Immature fine motor skills presenting difficulty in cutting with scissors, tying shoelaces, writing,

and drawing can all characterize learning-disabled children.

Extraneous movements, arrhythmical patterns, difficulty controlling force, and *perseveration* also describe the movements of many learning-disabled children. *Extraneous movements* means the "inclusion of unnecessary movements which disrupt both temporal and serial organization of motor skills so that their execution no longer appears smooth and efficient" (Haubenstricker, 1982, p. 43). Flailing the arms while skipping is an extraneous movement. *Arrhythmical patterns* during motor performance refers to the inability to maintain a constant rhythm during a repetitive task such as finger tapping or rope jumping. A child may begin jumping rope in a smooth manner but within the first six jumps accelerates and adds extraneous movements until the rope tangles in the feet. *Difficulty controlling force* usually refers to using too much force for a given task. Typically, children with difficulty controlling force will kick a soccer ball far beyond their partner standing a few feet away. *Perseveration* means continuing to perform a movement long after it is required, such as dribbling a basketball after the signal to stop or repeating the same story long after everyone has stopped listening.

Inappropriate motor planning may underlie poor balance and problems with gross and fine motor skills. Many learning-disabled children have difficulty in developing a plan before starting to execute the movement. Such difficulty may reflect a lack of antecedent experiences and/or poor integrative ability. Misapplied force, premature or delayed responses, and inappropriate responses to complex sequences of stimuli all reflect problems in motor planning (Haubenstricker, 1982).

In an overview of the motor behaviors of learning-disabled children, inconsistency of performance is perhaps the hallmark. A child who has learned to gallop one week but cannot gallop the next week typifies the motor performance of many learning-disabled children. The variability of performance is at once the most frustrating and the most challenging aspect of learning disabilities.

Affective Behaviors

Some children with learning disabilities are well adjusted, happy, and self-confident. But research indicates that many such children have social and/or emotional difficulties. These are thought to be a result of living with a learning disability.

Lower self-concept characterizes learning-disabled children. The lower self-concept is thought to be the result of prolonged experiences of failure in school despite average or above intelligence. These children know that they are intelligent, yet they continue to fail in schoolwork that their equally intelligent peers can master. Learning-disabled students with perceptual problems, gross motor delays, and poor coordination show the lowest self-esteem. Physical fitness, motor skill, and athletic competence are key factors in determining the self-concept of handicapped children (Kahn, 1982). Thus, athletic incompetence and academic failure contribute to the low self-concept of uncoordinated learning-disabled children. Typically, the uncoordinated child is selected last when teams are chosen, an embarrassing experience that does not make any child feel wanted or valued.

Unhappiness and anxiety have been shown to be characteristics of learning-disabled children. Also, these children tend to have an external locus of control: They believe that external events such as luck and chance determine their performance, rather than their own ability and effort.

Social imperception has been found to characterize many learning-disabled children. A socially imperceptive person seems oblivious to the subtle verbal and nonverbal social cues that guide interpersonal relations. The imperceptive person may not note the cues of a furrowed forehead, a sidelong glance, a clenched jaw, or an incline of the body away from the speaker that may communi-

cate dissatisfaction with and desire to get away from the speaker. Frustrated because the speaker seems to be ignoring the listener's signals of displeasure with the conversation, the listener may finally shout, "Oh, just leave me alone!" and walk away, leaving the imperceptive speaker puzzled.

The social imperception and academic imperception (inability to identify relevant academic cues) observed in some learning-disabled children may share a common source. One learning-disabled first grade boy was observed to score a point in a playground game (an infrequent event for this uncoordinated child), after which he ran over to his cheering teammates and whacked two of them on the back with his hand. The teammates immediately stopped cheering the boy's play and instead yelled at him. It seems that the boy had seen ball players on television exchange congratulatory pats on the back after a good play. He was attempting to do the same but, not having perceived the cue that the pats should be soft, had hit his teammates instead. Such social imperception does little to boost an individual's popularity. As a result of social imperception, many learning-disabled children may be social outcasts with few friends.

Lack of goal direction or motivation also frequently characterizes individuals with learning disabilities. This lack of goal direction has been attributed to a history of academic failure but may also be due to an inability to perceive the relevant aspects of the skill to be learned (Wong, Wong, & LeMare, 1982).

At one time, learning disabilities were presumed to disappear after childhood. But research has shown that the disability can persist into adolescence and beyond. The motor characteristics may diminish in importance, and the social/emotional characteristics may become more apparent. Deficits in visual-spatial development, language and communication skills, memory and sequencing, attentional skills, and social and emotional skills may persist (Whyte, 1984). The poor self-concept developed through years of unhappy school experiences may be the most debilitating characteristic. The importance of remediating learning disabilities at an early age cannot be overemphasized.

Approaches to Remediation of Learning Disabilities

Children with learning disabilities form a very heterogeneous group. It is likely that learning disabilities have many different causes; it therefore follows that there could be many different ways of teaching (or treating) those with learning disabilities. Accordingly, there is currently no single approach that is universally supported, but rather there are several, each of which has been successful with some learning-disabled students and unsuccessful with others. For the sake of consistency, the physical educator should determine if there is an approach that is being used successfully in the child's classroom or home, then follow the same approach where practical.

Educational and Medical Approaches to Hyperactivity

Various educational and medical approaches proposed for teaching (and treating) learning-disabled students with ADD/H are addressed separately in Table 12.1. Many of these approaches are specific to hyperactivity and are not designed for use with learning-disabled children who are not hyperactive.

Multisensory Approaches

A number of *multisensory approaches* have been developed for use with learning-disabled students. Grace Fernald developed the VAKT approach in which the visual, auditory, kinesthetic, and tactile senses are used in reading and spelling. Children trace a word while saying it, then read the

word and write it from memory, and eventually use the word in writing stories. Similarly, Gillingham and Stillman refined Orton's VAK (visual, auditory, and kinesthetic) phonetic approach to teaching reading. Children look at a letter, make the sound of the letter, trace it, and use the letter in writing words.

Movement has long been recognized as a medium through which academic concepts can be reinforced. Children can practice reading by producing the movements printed on flash cards—for example, jump, hop, skip, touch something green, touch your right ear. They can learn shapes by forming their bodies into various shapes such as triangle, square, curve, and straight line. They can practice mathematics by keeping score in games like bowling and kickball, hopping in or throwing at numbered squares and then adding or subtracting the value of each square, and counting out pieces of equipment.

James Humphrey has written a series of books illustrating the use of active games to teach and practice academic concepts. One example is the book by Humphrey and Sullivan (1970) listed in the "Resources" section at the end of this chapter.

Psychoneurological Approach

The *psychoneurological approach* to treating learning disabilities is based on the assumption that there is underlying neurological damage—brain damage—in the child. A neurologist conducts an examination to determine the nature and location of the damage. Psychotropic drug therapy may be prescribed to decrease hyperactive, impulsive, and emotionally labile behavior so that the child is better able to attend to instruction. But the brain is most complex in structure and function and is only partially understood, so it is frequently not possible to determine and locate the neurological source of the learning disability. And even in cases where the source of the problem is identified, there is often no known drug treatment. Thus, for most learning-disabled children, this approach is of limited value. With a small number of children for whom surgery and/or medication *has* been prescribed, the neurological approach has resulted in substantial improvements in learning. Further information on the psychoneurological approach is presented in chapter 13.

Psychoeducational Approach

In the eclectic *psychoeducational approach*, the psychologist and teacher jointly plan an intervention program designed to teach the social and academic readiness skills the child needs to succeed at school and at home. The deficits in academic achievement and behavior are dealt with directly. Using the *life-space interview technique*, empathetic teachers talk with and listen to children in crisis to help them recognize that their behavior is a problem, understand the basis for their behavior, identify its consequences, and plan alternative behaviors that are more appropriate. Further discussion on the psychoeducational approach is presented in chapter 13.

Behavioral Deficit Strategy

The *behavioral deficit strategy* (also known as the learning disability approach) seeks to remediate specific disabilities in language, reading, writing, spelling, and mathematics through instruction. Instructional programs diagnose the specific problems and prescribe remedial instruction. One test used to diagnose specific problems is the Illinois Test of Psycholinguistic Abilities (ITPA). For example, in one test item the child is asked to listen to and repeat a string of numbers (3-7-5-1-8-4). Difficulty with this test item may indicate a difficulty in auditory sequential memory. Activities in which the child practices listening to and repeating directions orally may be prescribed—for example, "Pick up a ball, walk with it to your spot, and practice bouncing the ball." Social behavioral deficits are also addressed because it is thought that appropriate behavior will develop as the child experiences academic success.

Ecological Approach

The *ecological approach* is one of the few approaches to suggest that the learning disability may not have its source solely within the child but instead may result from the interaction between the child and the environment. In this approach, the curriculum, teaching methods, and home environment are all examined and revised to better meet the child's needs. For example, a hyperactive boy may be unable to remain seated for 30 min at a time as other children do. The ecological approach would not necessarily view the problem as with the child ("He won't sit still!") but rather as a problem between the child and the sanctions of the culture ("The culture says that *all* children have to sit in their seats for 30 min at a time. But *this* child needs to move more frequently!"). The classroom rules could be changed so that the hyperactive child has three assigned seating areas—at the desk, on the carpet, and at the activities table—and is allowed to change his seat freely among these areas when he feels the need to move.

Perceptual-Motor Approach

Kephart, Frostig, Barsch, Getman, and other theorists have each proposed that movement experiences can help children develop perceptual-motor skills, which in turn underlie and can enhance cognitive skills. These theorists each developed *perceptual-motor training programs* that use movement experiences to improve academic/cognitive performance. It is widely accepted that movement experiences are necessary for normal perceptual-motor development. But there is little documentation supporting theories that claim improving motor performance will improve academic/cognitive performance. Research over the past two decades has generally failed to support the effectiveness of Kephart's, Frostig's, Barsch's, and Getman's perceptual-motor training programs in improving academic/cognitive performance (Kavale & Mattson, 1983).

However, improvement of perceptual-motor

skills is an important goal in itself. As shown in Figure 12.1, efficient information processing is vital for skilled motor performance and develops readiness skills for academic achievement. Therefore, many physical educators include perceptual-motor activities in the curriculum for learning-disabled children.

Jean Ayres, an occupational therapist, addresses the hypothesized underlying causes of learning disabilities (1972). She posits that there is a lack of sensory integration. As shown in Figure 12.1, sensory integration occurs as part of sensory input (step one) and decision making (step two) in information processing (the perceptual-motor process). Ayres proposes a program of activities thought to promote the integration of sensory stimuli, which in turn should result in improved academic/cognitive performance. Ayres theorizes that development and integration of the visual, auditory, kinesthetic, vestibular, and tactile systems are necessary before the environment can be accurately interpreted. Typical sensory integration activities include tactile stimulation through rubbing of the body with different textures; vestibular stimulation through rolling, spinning, and balancing; and kinesthetic stimulation through a variety of activities, many of which focus on the use of scooter boards. Physical and occupational therapists frequently use Ayres' sensory integration techniques. Research on the effectiveness of sensory integration programs is equivocal to date. Usually, physical educators prefer the direct instruction approach in working with learning-disabled students.

Direct Instructional Programs

Physical education programs for learning-disabled children should focus on the development of successful movement experiences. Individualized instruction is accomplished through a series of steps: assess, plan, implement, and evaluate. First, the children are assessed to identify learning strengths and weaknesses. Second, remedial instruction is planned and instructional objectives are written. Third, the instructional program is im-

plemented. Finally, the children's progress toward the objectives is measured and the progress evaluated. Programs are modified on the basis of ongoing evaluation. The *direct instructional approach* is based on the assumptions that all children can learn and that learning is a function of instruction, not a function of the learner. Effective instruction provides teaching and nonteaching examples, small subskills (progressions), general strategies, and sufficient practice to reach automaticity. Specific teaching methods are presented in the following section.

Assessing the Skills of Learning-Disabled Children

The first step in teaching and in writing an IEP is determining the student's *present level of performance*. Administration of perceptual and motor tests is particularly useful. The Bruininks-Oseretsky Test of Motor Proficiency may be used to measure fine and gross motor coordination. The Ohio State University Scale of Intra-Gross Motor Assessment (OSU SIGMA) and Ulrich's Test of Gross Motor Development are both suitable for measuring the maturity of basic motor patterns. Other relevant tests include the Frostig Developmental Test of Visual Perception (measuring five components of visual perception) and the Purdue Perceptual-Motor Survey (measuring the four components of perceptual-motor development). Additional information on each of these tests may be found in chapter 4.

Teaching Learning-Disabled Children in Regular Physical Education Classes

Regardless of the educational approach to which one subscribes, some teaching methods are widely endorsed as appropriate for learning-disabled students. Many of the suggestions presented in this section are part of sound teaching techniques for *all* children. But, because learning-disabled students by definition have difficulty learning, the suggested techniques may be especially important for this population.

Education in the mainstream is recommended for any child who can *safely and successfully* participate in the regular physical education class. Many learning-disabled children have only mild behavioral or motor problems and thus can remain in regular classes. Others have severe learning problems that are best met in separate, adapted physical education classes. Assessment of each learning-disabled child's present level of performance will guide the teacher in recommending the best placement and determining at what level to begin instruction. Some children with learning disabilities who need practice in motor skills may be scheduled for an adapted physical education class in addition to the mainstreamed class. Others' needs may be met entirely within the regular class. Most of the teaching suggestions that follow apply to learning-disabled children taught in mainstreamed physical education classes.

1. *Use a behavior management program to teach impulsive, inattentive, and hyperactive children.* Such a program positively reinforces attending behavior to increase each child's learning and to create a more pleasant classroom environment.
2. *Use a highly structured, consistent approach to teaching.* Establish a routine that is repeated day after day and leaves nothing to chance. Whether in a mainstreamed or separate class, this may mean that every day, all students enter the gym and go to their spots, which are marked on the floor. Class always begins with an established warm-up routine, continues with the introduction and practice of new skills and participation in a game or dance, and concludes with a return to the same floor spots for the cool-down and review. Equipment is consistently arranged in the same location. Activities are always done in the same

order and facing the same direction. One warm-up may be used for several sessions to enable children to learn it well and anticipate the structure of the class. The teacher may wish to create an audiocassette tape of the warm-up routine, with music and verbal instructions. Thus freed from calling out instructions, the teacher may move among the students as they warm up, providing individual assistance to students with learning disabilities. Perceptual concepts such as laterality can be incorporated in the warm-up—for example, "Turn to the left as you run in place; twist to the right as you do sit-ups; stretch and reach to the ceiling with your left hand." There are few class rules, but they are well understood and applied equally to all students. Sample rules for young children could include:

- listen when others are speaking,
- keep your hands to yourself,
- wear sneakers, and
- *try* every activity.

3. *Select activities that emphasize moving slowly and with control to decrease hyperactivity and impulsivity.* Use "slow" races, with such challenges as "How slowly can you do a push-up? A forward roll?" Include instruction in relaxation. For example, dim the lights and ask all students to go to their floor spots and lie on their backs with eyes closed. Present relaxation activities through guided imagery ("Imagine that you are relaxing in a warm place under the hot sun.") or progressive relaxation ("Tense your right arm, hold it, now relax. Feel the tension flow from your arm. Feel how limp your arm has become.") Check that students are, in fact, relaxing by gently lifting a limb off of the floor to see if it feels loose and heavy. If it does, then the person is probably relaxed. These activities may help children who only seem to know the feeling of "fast" and "tense" learn the feeling of "slow" and "relaxed." Within

each lesson, alternate active games with relaxation training or passive games, using a format of work, rest, work, rest. The periods of rest are designed to give hyperactive students a chance to slow down before they become so excited that they are out of control.

4. *Teach in a quiet, less stimulating environment to decrease distractibility.* Keep the gymnasium neat, clean, and well ordered. Store out of sight any equipment not needed for the activity in progress. An isolated hallway, racquetball court, or enclave in the gym created by mats standing on end may help create visual isolation from other children. Facing the children toward the corner so that their backs are to the other activities in the gym also helps to decrease distractibility. Some learning-disabled children are simply too distractible to function in a regular class setting; they need an adapted physical education class with only a few members. Other learning-disabled children are only moderately distractible and can learn when mainstreamed into a regular physical education class.

5. *Reduce total class size to allow the teacher the extra time needed to work with these special children.* It is unfair to everyone when teachers are expected to teach large classes that include children with special needs without any additional support.

6. *Use peer tutors to further individualize instruction.* A mature classmate, an upper-grade student, or an adult volunteer may work with the one or two learning-disabled children. The peer tutor helps the learning-disabled children remain focused on the task through verbal prompts, such as asking, "And what do you do now?" Dividing the large class into small groups that work in separate areas of the gym also sometimes helps distractible children. Balance the number of hyperactive and hypoactive children in the group. Experi-

ment with various combinations of students to find the mix of personalities that works best.

7. *Use verbal mediation to teach especially disorganized, distractible children.* Verbal mediation is a strategy in which children are encouraged to plan aloud what they will do to focus attention on the task at hand. Distractible children may be coached to repeat directions aloud—for example, "First, I will get the ball from the box, then I will shoot foul shots until I score 10 points." If the children are off task, the teacher asks "What is the task you are to do?" and prompts them to refocus attention on the task at hand. On-task behavior is also reinforced. Praise children when they are attending to the task as expected. "Catch them being good."

8. *Provide appropriate learning strategies to help disorganized learners focus on the skill to be learned.* Plan the instructional objectives for each lesson and share these objectives with the students. This technique lets everyone know the behavior that is to be learned. For example, if the objective of the lesson is to throw a ball at one of several targets using a mature overhand pattern, tell this to the class. Together with the students, identify the critical elements of the mature throwing pattern. An example of a critical element may be to "step with the other foot as you throw."

Many learning-disabled students have difficulty selectively attending to the relevant aspects of the skill to be learned. Reinforce the relevant stimulus. For example, place footprints on the floor so that children standing on the footprints will have their sides to the target. Place a third footprint where the children will step as they transfer their weight during the throw, thus providing a visual cue. Provide verbal cues as well. Teach children to say aloud "step and throw" as a cue to transfer weight while releasing the ball. Also, teach children how to use feedback. For example, after the ball is thrown, ask children to identify where the ball landed in relation to the target ("The ball hit below the target.") and to identify what needs to change in the next throw ("I need to release the ball sooner."). The intent is to help learning-disabled children use feedback in perfecting future performances, a strategy that most nondisabled children use spontaneously. Explain objectives and provide learning strategies and cues to help focus the attention of disorganized learning-disabled children on the relevant aspects of the skill.

9. *In giving instruction, use more than one sense to teach students with perceptual problems.* Provide clear, concise verbal directions coupled with visual demonstrations and, where appropriate, physical assistance with the skill. If children with perceptual problems are not following directions, it may be that they do not understand them. Children may not follow the instruction to "skip around the outside of the circle" because they are unmotivated and uncooperative. But it may also be that they do not know how to skip, do not understand that the classmates holding hands form a circle, or do not know where the outside of the circle is located. Instruction in these concepts may be necessary before the children can follow the directions.

10. *Teach to mastery to enhance students' self-efficacy and self-concept.* Whether in a mainstreamed or separate class, avoid conducting a curriculum that only samples activities rather than providing practice until they are mastered. Task-analyze and use progressions to guarantee success at the early stages of learning. A data-based approach to instruction may be helpful in developing self-efficacy. Daily or weekly progress is recorded so that, even when

progress is slow and inconsistent, improvement over time can be demonstrated to the students.

11. *Eliminate embarrassing teaching practices that force comparisons among students.* Examples of such practices include posting the fitness scores of all class members and "choosing up teams" in front of the class. No one enjoys knowing that he or she was the last choice. Instead, recognize the "most improved" and good performances of learning-disabled students.

12. *Use a cooperative teaching style to increase students' social interaction and self-concept.* Most important, minimize highly competitive team games requiring precise, skilled responses, such as baseball, if these skills are beyond the capability of the child. Include team games only when the child has the skill to compete successfully. Also, avoid elimination activities in which skilled players get the most practice and unskilled players get the least practice. Similarly, avoid team games that require some to be "losers." Many of these children already see themselves as losers; teachers do not need to reinforce this concept. Cooperative games and competition against oneself are more appropriate alternatives, especially in the elementary grades. Cooperative activities in which children succeed by working together may be especially important, because they have been shown to increase social interaction. Games such as Crossover Dodgeball, Slowest Races, Cooperative Beach Ball and Volleyball, and Project Adventure challenges may be more appropriate than the traditional team sports. To decrease anxiety, individualize instruction so that a child does not have to perform a skill not yet mastered in front of classmates.

13. *Review previously acquired skills before teaching more advanced skills that require mastery at the basic level.* Anticipate that

learning-disabled children will often be inconsistent performers, particularly of skills taught during previous lessons. Daily review is important, as are opportunities for continued practice of newly acquired skills.

14. *Design a curriculum that includes activities in perceptual-motor skills, gross and fine motor skills, balance, and body awareness.* Be alert to the role that perception plays in motor skill performance. If children have difficulty catching, it may be due to perceptual problems in such areas as visual tracking or figure/ground discrimination, in addition to inadequate bilateral coordination or slow reaction times.

15. *To encourage motor planning, ask children to explain what they will do before moving.* This explanation will ensure that children are giving some advance thought to how and where they will move.

The preceding suggestions for activity selection and teaching strategies will help meet the needs of children with learning disabilities. Happily, many of these suggestions will also help the teacher best meet the needs of *all* of the students in the class.

Summary

The controversy over the definition, incidence, and causes of specific learning disabilities continues. Classification tends to be made on the basis of an educational discrepancy between a child's intellectual potential and actual academic achievement. It appears that many learning-disabled children have difficulty in the area of information processing. They may display inattention, distractibility, perceptual deficits, visual or auditory perception deficits, disorganization, and/or impulsivity. Their academic and learning behaviors may include attention deficit disorder with hyperactivity, dyslexia, and/or dysgraphia. Their motor behaviors tend to parallel the clumsy child syndrome and may include poor dynamic balance,

delayed motor development and immature basic motor skills, immature fine motor skills, extraneous movements, arrhythmical pattern, difficulty controlling force, perseveration, and/or inappropriate motor planning. Affective behaviors of learning-disabled children may include low self-concept, unhappiness and anxiety, social imperception, and/or lack of goal-direction. Physical educators often teach children with learning disabilities in a direct instructional approach through a noncompetitive, individualized curriculum presented in a structured, consistent, focused environment. This approach also helps teachers best meet the needs of nondisabled students. As a result, most learning-disabled children can be safely and successfully mainstreamed into the regular physical education class.

Bibliography

Arnheim, D.D., & Sinclair, W.A. (1975). *The clumsy child: A program of motor therapy.* St. Louis: Mosby.

Ayres, J. (1972). Types of sensory integrative dysfunction among disabled learners. *American Journal of Occupational Therapy, 26,* 13-18.

Bruininks, V.L., & Bruininks, R.L. (1977). Motor proficiency and learning disabled and nondisabled students. *Perceptual and Motor Skills, 44,* 1131-1137.

Brunt, D., Magill, R.A., & Eason, R. (1983). Distinctions in variability of motor output between learning disabled and normal children. *Perceptual and Motor Skills, 57,* 731-734.

Cinelli, B., & DePaepe, J.L. (1984). Dynamic balance of learning disabled and nondisabled children. *Perceptual and Motor Skills, 58,* 243-245.

Cruickshank, W., Bentzen, F., Ratzeburg, R., & Tannhauser, M. (1961). *A teaching method for brain-injured and hyperactive children: A demonstration pilot study.* Syracuse, NY: Syracuse University Press.

Feingold, B.F. (1975). *Why your child is hyperactive.* New York: Random House.

Haubenstricker, J.L. (1982). Motor development in children with learning disabilities. *Journal of Physical Education, Recreation and Dance,* **53**, 41-43.

Kahn, L.E. (1982). *Self-concept and physical fitness of retarded students as correlates of social interaction between retarded and nonretarded students.* Unpublished doctoral dissertation, New York University.

Kavale, K.A., & Forness, S.R. (1985). *The science of learning disabilities.* San Diego: College-Hill Press.

Kavale, K.A., & Mattson, P.D. (1983). One jumped off the balance beam: Meta-analysis of perceptual-motor training. *Journal of Learning Disabilities,* **16**, 165-173.

Rarick, G.L. (1980). Cognitive-motor relationships in the growing years. *Research Quarterly for Exercise and Sport,* **51**, 174-192.

Sherrill, C., & Pyfer, J.L. (1985). Learning disabled students in physical education. *Adapted Physical Activity Quarterly,* **2**, 283-291.

Sutaria, S.D. (1985). *Specific learning disabilities: Nature and needs.* Springfield, IL: Charles C. Thomas.

Torgesen, J.K. (1980). Conceptual and educational implications of the use of efficient task strategies by learning disabled children. *Journal of Learning Disabilities,* **13**, 364-371.

Weiner, I.B. (1982). *Child and adolescent psychopathology.* New York: Wiley.

Whyte, L.A. (1984). Characteristics of learning disabilities persisting into adolescence. *Alberta Journal of Educational Research,* **30**, 14-25.

Wong, B., Wong, R., & LeMare, L. (1982). Effect of knowledge of criterion task on comprehension and recall in normally achieving and learning disabled children. *Journal of Educational Research,* **76**, 119-126.

Resources

Written

Arrighi, M. (1985). Equal opportunity through instructional design. *Journal of Physical Education, Recreation and Dance,* **56**(6), 58-64. Several ideas for individualizing instruction are presented for use in classes with a wide range of skills.

Hayes, M. (1975). *"Oh dear, someone said learning disabilities": A book for teachers and parents.* San Rafael, CA: Academic Therapy. This book provides descriptions and discusses feelings regarding learning disabilities. It contains simulations of some learning disabilities suitable for use in undergraduate classes or with older children.

Humphrey, J., & Sullivan, D. (1970). *Teaching slow learners through active games.* Springfield, IL: Charles C. Thomas.

Lawrence, C., & Hackett, L. (1975). *Water learning: A new adventure.* Palo Alto, CA: Peek Publications. This is an inexpensive book full of ideas for teaching perceptual concepts using the medium of water. Curriculum ideas designed for children in preschool and primary grades are presented.

Audiovisual

Lawrence, C. (1972). *Splash* [Film]. Aptos, CA: Documentary Films. This 20-min, 16-mm sound/color film illustrates ideas for teaching perceptual concepts using the medium of water. It is a companion to the book *Water Learning.*

CHAPTER 13

Behavioral Disabilities

E. Michael Loovis

Scenario: Mike, John, and Dan are standing together shooting baskets. The time is 9:10 a.m. Mr. Rogers, the physical educator, turns toward the students and says, "It's time for our lesson—put your basketballs away." Mike says, "Not me." John says, "Not me." Dan says, "Not me." Mr. Rogers moves toward Mike. Mike feints a throw at Mr. Rogers. Mr. Rogers jerks back. He then rushes forward and quickly snatches the basketball from Mike. Mr. Rogers puts the basketball in the ball cart. Mike screams for the ball and says he wants to play with it. Mike moves toward Mr. Rogers and tries to snatch the ball from the cart. Mr. Rogers pushes him away. Mike kicks Mr. Rogers on the leg. He kicks him again and demands the return of his basketball. He kicks Mr. Rogers again. He pushes the metal ball cart at Mr. Rogers. Mr. Rogers jumps out of the way. Mike picks up a small metal chair and throws it violently. Mr. Rogers cannot move in time. The chair strikes his foot. Mr. Rogers pushes Mike down on the floor. Mike starts up. He pulls over the ball cart. Then he stops a moment. Mr. Rogers is picking up the ball cart. Mike looks at Mr. Rogers. Mr. Rogers moves toward Mike. Mike runs away. John wants his basketball. Mr. Rogers says "No!" John joins Mike in trying to pull over the ball cart and grabs basketballs from the cart.

Mr. Rogers pushes John away roughly. John is screaming that he wants to play with the basketballs. He moves toward the ball cart. John pulls the cart over and lets it crash onto the floor. Mike says he is going to the bathroom. Mr. Rogers asks Dan to close the gymnasium door. Dan reaches the door at the same time as Mike. Mike hits Dan in the face. Dan's nose is bleeding. Mr. Rogers walks over to Dan, turns to the others, and says that he is taking Dan to the lavatory. The time is 9:14 a.m.

This chapter discusses a student population whose educational opportunities have sometimes been and, in many circumstances, continue to be a concern. In the past these students have been referred to as emotionally disturbed, socially maladjusted, behavior disordered, and emotionally handicapped. Certain characteristics invariably associated with these students make them stand out. Not all of them exhibit the same characteristics; in fact, quite the opposite is true. Generally speaking, they can demonstrate behavior that is labeled hyperactive, distractive, or impulsive. Some of these students may exhibit aggression beyond what is considered normal or socially acceptable. Some may behave in a manner that is considered withdrawn; they may act immature or behave in ways that tend to highlight feelings of inadequacy. Another segment of this population may demonstrate behavior directed in a very negative way against society; these individuals are known as juvenile delinquents.

It was not until Bower (l981) that special education reached temporary agreement on the definition of *emotionally handicapped*. Bower's definition became so popular that it was included, with few changes, in the rules and regulations governing the implementation of PL 94-l42. Section 121a.5 of the rules and regulations defines "seriously emotionally disturbed" as follows:

(i) The term means a condition exhibiting one or more of the following characteristics over a long period of time and to a marked degree, which adversely affects educational performance:

(A) An inability to learn which cannot be explained by intellectual, sensory, or health factors;

(B) An inability to build or maintain satisfactory relationships with peers and teachers;

(C) Inappropriate types of behavior or feelings under normal circumstances;

(D) A general pervasive mood of unhappiness or depression; or

(E) A tendency to develop physical symptoms or fears associated with personal or school problems.

(ii) The term includes children who are schizophrenic (or autistic). The term does not include children who are socially maladjusted, unless it is determined that they are seriously emotionally disturbed (the Education for All Handicapped Children Act of 1975).

The terms *seriously emotionally disturbed* and *behaviorally disturbed* (BD) are used synonymously in this chapter. Identification of seriously emotionally disturbed individuals is perhaps the most perplexing problem facing school and mental health professionals. Therefore, it is beneficial to understand the three qualifiers that appear in the first paragraph of the federal definition, namely,

duration, degree, and adverse effects on educational performance.

1. *Long period of time*. This qualifier primarily excludes problems that conceivably could be construed as emotional disturbance but that are situational in nature and thus understandable or expected. For example, a death in the family, a divorce, or another crisis situation could alter behavior a way that makes it appear aberrant.

2. *Marked degree*. Under consideration here are the magnitude and duration of a behavior. Intensity of behavioral displays, such as loudness of response during an outburst, is considered. Also noted is the amount of time a student engages in a particular behavior—for example, the loud outbursts occurring frequently and lasting for much longer periods than would be considered normal.

3. *Adversely affects educational performance*. There must be a demonstrable cause-and-effect relationship between a student's behavior and decreased academic performance. This requires, at the very least, determining if students are performing at or near the level they would be expected to attain without behavioral disability.

Severely and Profoundly Disturbed

Severely and profoundly disturbed people are commonly grouped under the general heading of *psychotic*. Their behavior is sufficiently different, both qualitatively and quantitatively, from that of individuals said to be mildly or moderately disturbed to warrant a separate classification. Subsumed under the general term *psychotic* are two major conditions or disturbances in children. These conditions are *childhood schizophrenia* and *infantile autism*; the major difference between them is the age of onset. According to the third edition of the American Psychiatric Association's *Diagnostic and Statistical Manual of Mental Disorders*, commonly called DSM-III (American Psychiatric Association, 1980), infantile autism usually appears before the age of 30 months, while childhood schizophrenia is more likely to appear after the age of 12 years than between those ages.

Infantile Autism

Jenson and Young (1985) have identified major developmental and behavioral characteristics associated with infantile autism. They include

- lack of social responsiveness or an inability to relate socially to human beings,
- delayed language, including severe comprehensive and expressive linguistic difficulties,
- intellectual deficits, with particular difficulties in skills requiring verbal abilities,
- stimulus overselectivity; attending to only part of a relevant cue or in fact attending to an irrelevant cue, and
- self-stimulation, such as rocking, hand flapping, gazing at objects and lights, rhythmic manipulation of objects. (This category also includes self-injury; however, only about 5% to 10% of the autistic population engages in self-injurious behavior.)

Childhood Schizophrenia

As with infantile autism, there are specific characteristics that distinguish childhood schizophrenia from other types of childhood disorders. These characteristics include the following (Stainback & Stainback, 1980):

- Lack of contact with reality
- Development of own world
- Apparent denial of the human quality of people
- Inappropriate affect
- Body movements that appear bizarre

- Stereotyped actions
- Special knowledge about particular subjects
- Distorted time orientations
- Inappropriate speech structure and content

Behavioral Disabilities in Public School Settings

Just as a psychiatric frame of reference helps in better understanding students who are severely and profoundly behaviorally disturbed, a behavioral classification appears best for understanding the mild and moderately BD students who are more likely to be found in the public school setting. Perhaps the best work in dimensional classification has been done by Quay (1986). These studies have shown that several dimensions are consistently found in special education classes for emotionally disturbed students. More recently, a study by Von Isser, Quay, and Love (1980) reaffirmed the dimensions identified earlier. With only a few semantic differences the dimensions remain as follows:

1. *Conduct disorder* involves such characteristics as overt aggression, both verbal and physical; disruptiveness; negativism; irresponsibility; and defiance of authority—all of which are at variance with the behavioral expectations of the school and other social institutions.
2. *Anxiety-withdrawal* stands in considerable contrast to conduct disorders, involving, as it does, overanxiety, social withdrawal, seclusiveness, shyness, sensitivity, and other behaviors implying a retreat from the environment rather than a hostile response to it.
3. *Immaturity* characteristically involves preoccupation, short attention span, passivity, daydreaming, sluggishness, and behavior not in accord with developmental expectations.
4. *Socialized aggression* typically involves

gang activities, cooperative stealing, truancy, and other manifestations of participation in a delinquent subculture. (pp. 272-273)

In similar fashion, Dunn, Morehouse, and Fredericks (1986) have identified four areas of inappropriate behavior—behaviors that are self-indulgent, noncompliant, aggressive, and self-stimulatory or self-destructive—that may require behavioral intervention.

Causes of Behavioral Disabilities

Several factors conceivably having a causal relationship to BD have been identified; they include biological, family, and school factors. In addition, the state of insecurity and dissatisfaction resulting from unresolved problems or unfulfilled needs—in other words, frustration—will be examined as a cause of BD.

Biological Factors

According to Kauffman (1985), several biological aberrations may contribute to the etiology of BD. These include genetic anomalies, difficult temperament, brain damage or dysfunction, nutritional deficiencies, physical illness or disability, and psychophysiological disorders. With these factors identified, it is important to reiterate Kauffman's assertion that "in *nearly all* cases of mental illness (including psychosis) no reliable *direct* evidence of biological disease or disorder can be found" (p. 117).

Family Factors

Family relationships are viewed largely as contributory factors in the etiology of BD. This explains why such circumstances as broken homes, divorce, chaotic or hostile family relationships, absence of mother or father, and parental separation,

to name just a few, have the potential to produce situations in which youngsters are vulnerable to development of BD. It is also clear that there is not a one-to-one relationship between disruptive family relations and BD. Many youngsters find parental discord more injurious than separation from one or both parents. Research also points to a multiplier effect: When two or more factors are present simultaneously, there is increased probability that a behavior disorder will develop.

School Factors

It has become increasingly clear that, besides the family, school is the most significant socializing factor in the life of the child. For this reason, the school must shoulder some of the responsibility for causing BD. According to Kauffman (1985) schools contribute to the development of behavior disorders in several ways:

1. "School administrators, teachers, and other pupils may be insensitive to children's individuality.
2. Teachers may hold inappropriate expectations for children.
3. Teachers may be inconsistent in managing children's behavior.
4. Instruction may be offered in nonfunctional (i.e., irrelevant) skills.
5. Inappropriate contingencies of reinforcement may be arranged by school personnel.
6. Peers and teachers may provide models of undesirable conduct." (p. 164)

Frustration

When faced with a physical or psychological barrier that prevents accomplishment of a goal, the BD child may resort to behaviors that are considered maladaptive. These behaviors are diametrically opposed to those that society expects from children and adolescents. When goals are thwarted, individuals can respond in one of two

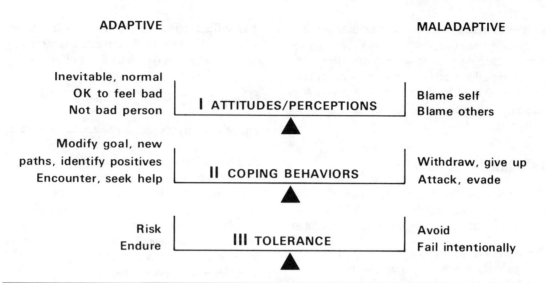

Figure 13.1   Three facets of adaptive frustration management. *Note.* From *Conflict in the Classroom: The Education of Emotionally Disturbed Children, Fourth Edition*, by Nicholas J. Long, William C. Morse, and Ruth G. Newman. Copyright © 1980 by Wadsworth, Inc. Used by permission of the publisher.

basic ways; Figure 13.1 illustrates the management of frustration associated with a goal-thwarting experience. In both the adaptive and maladaptive responses there are three facets. *Attitudes and perceptions* involve the attributions associated with a frustrating experience. Typically, children with BD either blame others or blame themselves for their inability to deal with stressful situations. Lacking effective *coping behaviors*, children with serious emotional problems tend to respond by either withdrawing/giving up or attacking/evading. In either case, the response is likely to reinforce distorted perceptions of self-esteem, trust, and peer relationships. The third facet of adaptive frustration management is *tolerance*. Barriers to the achievement of goals are present on a daily basis. The ability to cope with these frustrations is normally developed over time. An individual whose coping ability has failed to develop may either avoid situations that produce failure or fail intentionally, which further reinforces an already negative feeling of self-worth (Fagen, 1980).

Approaches

The conceptual models that serve as the basis for understanding and treating or educating students with behavioral disabilities are discussed more comprehensively in chapter 6. The following paragraphs highlight the psychodynamic, psychoeducational, psychoneurological, and behavioral approaches to teaching BD students.

Psychodynamic

The psychodynamic approach has as its central focus the improvement of psychological functioning. This improvement depends on helping individuals cope with deep-seated emotional problems that can result in impaired personal relationships, conflicting social values, poor self-concept, ability deficits, and antisocial habits and attitudes. Failure to alleviate the cause(s) of psychological dysfunction can lead to learning and behavioral difficulties. The psychodynamic approach uses a number of treatment modalities including psycho-analysis, counseling, play therapy, and group therapy. Because of its strong, primarily Freudian, psychological orientation, this approach is less likely to be used by teachers, and consequently its potential benefits in the educational setting are at best speculative.

Psychoeducational

The psychoeducational approach assumes that academic failure and misbehavior can be dealt with directly and therapeutically. Students are taught to

- acknowledge that they have a problem,
- understand why they are misbehaving,
- observe the consequences of their behavior, and
- plan an alternate response or way of behaving that is more appropriate.

Teachers are taught to anticipate a crisis and deal with it in a nonemotional manner. In crisis intervention, they use the major tool of the psycho-educational approach: the life-space interview. Life-space interviewing utilizes talking and experiencing to help students recognize and appreciate their feelings. It is especially effective in momentary crisis situations.

Psychoneurological

The major focus of the psychoneurological approach as it relates to behavioral disabilities is the reduction of those general behavioral characteristics such as hyperactivity, distractibility, impulsiveness, and emotional lability that make the management of behavior difficult at best. Presence of these characteristics is attributed to neuro-physiological dysfunction. The prescribed treatment for such dysfunction within the psycho-neurological model is drug therapy. The primary category of medication used to manage the behavior of school-age children is the psychotropic drugs. Chapter 6 discusses drug therapy in depth;

it is sufficient for this chapter to note that the primary advantage of drug therapy is its ability to make other interventions more effective.

Behavioral

The behavioral approach is an elaboration of learning principles such as those embodied in respondent conditioning, social learning theory, and operant conditioning. The term most commonly used to describe this approach is behavior modification. An extensive discussion of behavior modification and its principles, primarily reinforcement, is presented in chapter 6. The salient features of the behavioral approach are careful assessment of observable behavior; analysis of the effect of environmental stimuli, both those that precede a response (antecedents) and those that follow it (consequences); and systematic arrangement of the consequences in order to change a behavior, or at least its frequency. Within the behavioral model, the most rapidly emerging area having implications for students with behavioral disabilities is *cognitive-behavior modification* (Meichenbaum, 1977). With its emphasis on self-control techniques, it is a natural concomitant in programs that are attempting to move beyond the traditional Skinnerian concept of behavior management—for example, in the psychoeducational approach described earlier.

The Behaviorally Disturbed Youngster Mainstreamed

At the very core of effective instruction with BD students is an examination of the ways people communicate and a consideration of various alternatives to major conflict. According to the Positive Education Program (PEP) handbook (1980), "communication is effective when persons are able to (a) give and receive information clearly; and (b) use the information to achieve a desired result" (p. 113). Giving and receiving information clearly is a goal of effective interpersonal communication, which is based on two general communication processes. The first involves the technique of *active listening* (Gordon, 1970); the second process, *conflict resolution*, is discussed later in this section.

Active Listening

Three basic skills are essential to the technique of active listening. The first is attending, a physical act that requires the listener to face the person speaking, maintain eye contact, and lean forward, if seated. These actions communicate to the speaker that the listener is, in fact, interested in what is being said. Listening, the second component skill, means more than just hearing what is being said. It involves the process of "decoding," an attempt by the listener to interpret what has been said. Consider the following example:

Sender code: "Why must we do these exercises?"

Possible receiver decoding:

A. "He doesn't know how to perform them and is embarrassed to admit it."

B. "He's bored with the lesson and is anxious to get to the next class."

C. "He's unclear about why the exercises are necessary and is seeking some clarification."

Suppose that the most accurate decoding was A or C, but the listener decoded the message as B. A misunderstanding would result, and the communication process would start to break down. Situations like the one just portrayed occur frequently, with neither the speaker nor the listener aware that a misunderstanding exists. The question then becomes "What can be done to ensure that the correct message is being communicated?" The answer is contained in the third and final step of the active listening process.

The third component of active listening is responding. With this step the decoding process is completed as the listener sends back the results of his or her decoding in an attempt to ascertain if there are any misunderstandings. In effect, the listener merely restates the interpretation of the sender's message.

The communication process called active listening can help prevent misunderstandings, facilitate problem solving, and demonstrate warmth and understanding. As with any new skill, it requires practice for maximum effectiveness.

Conflict Resolution

Teaching students with BD entails a greater than average risk of confrontation as a way of resolving conflict. This does not imply that interpersonal confrontation need be punitive or destructive. On the contrary, a healthy use of confrontation provides the opportunity to examine a set of behaviors in relation to expectations and perceptions of others as well as to establish rules.

The goal of confrontation is resolution of conflicts through constructive behavior change. There are several necessary steps in reaching this desired goal through confrontation. They include

- making an assertive, confrontive statement (one that expresses honestly and directly how the speaker feels about another's behavior),
- being aware of common reactions to confrontation, and
- knowing how to deal effectively with these reactions.

Although assertive confrontation can be an effective means of resolving conflicts, it requires skillful use of each step in the process.

Verbal Mediation

A third communication technique is verbal mediation, which "usually involves having the child verbalize the association between his behavior and the consequences of that behavior" (PEP, 1980,

p. 131). Of particular importance in verbal mediation is having students take an active role in the process rather than passively hearing teachers make the association for them. The following situation illustrates verbal mediation:

> A student has just earned 10 min of free time by successfully completing the assigned drill at a circuit training station.
>
> Teacher: "What did you do to earn free time?"
>
> Student: "I followed directions and completed my work."
>
> Teacher: "Do you like free time?"
>
> Student: "Yes, it's fun."
>
> Teacher: "So when you do your work, then you can have fun."
>
> Student: "Right."
>
> Teacher: "Good for you! Keep up the good work."

In this example, the teacher has facilitated the student's verbal mediation of the positive association between the appropriate behavior and the positive consequence.

Physical Education and Sport Activities

It is generally acknowledged that children who have behavioral disabilities frequently exhibit deficits in physical and motor proficiency (Poindexter, 1969a). Clinical observations and some research evidence indicate that the perceptual-motor abilities of emotionally disturbed students are also below average. Llorens (1968) found evidence of specific deficiencies in two or more of the Ayres' syndromes in emotionally disturbed school-age children suspected of having perceptual-motor dysfunction. Poindexter (1969b) found that the performance scores of emotionally disturbed

children on the Kephart Perceptual-Motor Survey were less than those of a comparable group of youngsters without such disturbances.

With the exception of the perceptual-motor dysfunctions associated with the Ayres' syndromes, which apparently have a neurophysiological basis, motoric deficiencies in BD students are more often than not attributed to various indirect causes or factors. Behavioral characteristics like attention deficits, poor work habits, impulsivity, hyperactivity, feelings of inadequacy, and demonstration of aggressive behavior are examples of indirect factors that are blamed for poor motor performance rather than some innate inability to move well.

Exercise programs have been shown to exert a positive influence on disruptive behavior. As little as 10 min of jogging daily has produced a significant reduction in the disruptive behavior of children (Allan, 1980). Watters and Watters (1980) studied autistic boys and found that exercise decreased self-stimulatory behavior. This finding in itself is important, but its significance is enhanced when the results of Koegel, Firestone, Kramme, and Dunlap (1974) are considered. They found that suppression of self-stimulation causes an increase in other behaviors, such as spontaneous play. More recently, Kern, Koegel, Dyer, Blew, and Fenton (1982) examined the effect of jogging on self-stimulation and appropriate responding in autistic children. Their conclusions, that exercise reduced self-stimulatory behavior, confirmed previous research. Beyond that finding, they also demonstrated that exercise produced better responding during additional movement activities (e.g., ball playing) and during engagement in preschool-level academic tasks.

The nature of the physical education program for students with behavioral disabilities should correspond to their needs as revealed by formal and informal assessment. Currently, the Project ACTIVE Motor Ability Test, Level II (Karp, 1985) is the only standardized test specifically developed for use with this population. It is, however, applicable to mild cases of BD only and is not a valid instrument for use with individuals having severe or profound levels of BD. Assessment at these levels remains an area of great need.

In working with students who have mild behavior disabilities, educators should keep a basic but important instructional principle in mind: To the extent possible, methods of assessment and programs of physical activity should reflect what is traditionally suitable for the student population at large.

Movement Programs

Depending on students' developmental abilities and behavioral characteristics, they should be placed in the class that can best meet their needs. Regardless of placement, the type of programming chosen and the degree of peer interaction are two variables of considerable import. The first area of concern is the program itself. Because students with behavioral disabilities apparently lag in physical and motor abilities, the physical educator must provide them with appropriate developmental activities. The emphasis should be on physical conditioning, balance, and basic movement abilities. The development of fundamental locomotor and nonlocomotor movements will also require attention. In addition, it may be necessary to emphasize perceptual-motor activities because students with behavioral disabilities often demonstrate inadequacies in this area.

Many physical education programs use games as a means to accomplish goals and objectives established for individuals and classes. Because students with behavioral disabilities often lack fundamental skills, they frequently are incapable of demonstrating even minimal levels of competence in these games. In consequence of the inability to participate effectively, they have an increased tendency to act out—perhaps with verbal and/or physical aggression—or to withdraw, which further excludes them from an opportunity to develop skills. In an effort to promote the most positive

learning environment, Huber (1980) suggests the following guidelines for constructive use of games and sports with children who have behavioral disabilities: (a) adults should actively participate in games and should fulfill the role of umpire as well, (b) adults should participate in order to control negative peer interaction, (c) adults should model appropriate prosocial behaviors, (d) adults should provide opportunities to build physical coordination and skill, (e) adults should plan the game and discuss it before and after it is played, and (f) adults should be ready to modify the game if necessary to accomplish a specific objective for an individual or group.

Relaxation is another program component that deserves a special place in the normal movement routine of many students with BD. Making the transition from gymnasium to classroom can be difficult for students with hyperactive behavior. This difficulty is not a reason to eliminate vigorous activity from these students' programs; rather, it is a reason to provide additional time, a buffer, during which the students can use relaxation techniques they have been taught.

The ability *to play* effectively is crucial to success in physical education. Because games are a part of the physical education program for most students with BD, it is essential for teachers to be aware of the direct relationship between the type of activity chosen and the degree to which inappropriate behavior is likely to occur. Gump and Sutton-Smith (1955) studied the social interaction of emotionally disturbed children in a camp setting. They found that the type of programming chosen was directly related to the amount of aggression demonstrated during activity. Some of the specific variables that seemed to control aggression were reduced body contact, simpler rules, and fewer skill requirements. Not to be overlooked is the New Games approach, which has a cooperative rather than a competitive orientation. In light of the problems surrounding self-concept and the antisocial behavior exhibited by some students with BD, the least desirable situation is one that prescribes winners and losers or that rewards overly aggressive behavior.

Instructional Considerations

Mildly Handicapped Students

In physical education, behaviorally disabled students with higher levels of functioning can be taught with a humanistic approach. Generally speaking, the techniques suggested by Sherrill (1986) are applicable with this population. More specifically, the approach outlined by Hellison (1985) has immediate relevance for practitioners confronted with students who lack self-control and consequently present management problems. Hellison's four primary goals or developmental levels, *self-control, involvement, self-responsibility*, and *caring*, are instrumental in overcoming many current discipline and motivation problems in schools. (Hellison's levels are discussed in chapter 5.) Hellison has likewise identified five basic strategies that foster attainment of the developmental levels: teacher talk, modeling, reinforcement, reflection time, and student sharing. These strategies are designed to (a) prevent disruptive behavior, (b) deal with individual problems, (c) discourage disruptive behavior, and (d) resolve arguments.

Because self-control is basic to Hellison's approach, *teacher talk* (what teachers say to students) is very important. Examples of this strategy include

- conveying to students, either verbally on an individual or small-group basis or visually by posting signs in the gymnasium, that they are not to interfere with other students' rights (this is called the *first rule*);
- reviewing and prioritizing the rules used in physical education—for example, repeatedly reminding students of the *first rule*;
- teaching the levels; taking advantage of opportunities or "teachable moments" to emphasize a particular level;
- pointing out negative consequences—that is, sharing with students one's feelings and perceptions about what they are doing and what effect it has;
- transferring developmental levels to life outside the gym, which implies generalization of self-control to other situations, such as at home with family or in the neighborhood with friends; and
- confronting and negotiating, e.g., using the conflict resolution process described in chapter 6 as a means to reduce problems.

Modeling (what teachers do in the presence of students) is the second strategy. Teachers and coaches should (a) model self-control in their interactions with students and others, (b) model verbal "teases" in a manner that helps students distinguish between a verbal put-down and a joke, and (c) model self-control while participating occasionally in games with students.

Reinforcement strategies (what teachers do to strengthen specific student attitudes or behaviors) are used to demonstrate how to behave in a responsible manner and to reward self-control when it occurs. Examples of reinforcement include (a) giving praise for demonstrating good self-control or for making progress toward self-control, (b) conferring awards for achieving specified levels of self-control, and (c) providing rewards—for instance, granting a free-play day to students who demonstrate sufficient self-control during the week.

Reflection time (time students spend thinking about their attitudes and behaviors in relation to the developmental levels) is an opportunity for students to think about how well they have demonstrated self-control on any given day. Two examples of reflection time are self-evaluation and counseling days. In self-evaluation, students are asked to reflect either in writing or verbally on their self-control during the class period. Counseling sessions, on the other hand, are arranged individually and provide for a dialog about self-control as well as additional opportunities for reinforcement.

Student sharing (in which students are asked to give their opinions about some aspect of the program) is the final strategy. It promotes discussion of specific types of behavior that clearly interfere with the rights of others. This strategy involves students in discussing what constitutes self-control, and it encourages them to think about the consequences of violating the established self-control rules. It can incorporate the use of student juries.

Severely Handicapped Students

Severely handicapped students represent a different segment of the behaviorally disabled population, one that requires more intense programming efforts. This group, which has been characterized by Dunn et al. (1986), includes students who are self-indulgent, aggressive, noncompliant, and self-stimulatory or self-destructive. Using the basic steps of behavioral programming discussed in chapter 6, Dunn and associates developed the Data Based Gymnasium. This program incorporates behavioral principles in a systematic effort to produce consistent behavior on the part of adults who work with BD students and eventually to bring students' behavior under the control of naturally occurring reinforcers. To this latter end, instructors use natural reinforcers available in the environment—for example, praising a desirable behavior to strengthen it or ignoring an undesirable one to bring about its extinction. Tangible reinforcers such as token economies are introduced only after it has been demonstrated that the consistent use of social reinforcement or extinction will not achieve the desired behavioral outcome.

In an effort to equip teachers with a consistent treatment procedure, Dunn and associates have prescribed a set of consequences or rules of thumb that are applied to inappropriate behaviors. For each area of inappropriate behavior—for example,

self-indulgent behavior—there exists a specific rule of thumb. The intent of the rules of thumb is to make development and implementation of a formal behavioral program unnecessary.

Self-Indulgent Behavior

Behaviors in this category include crying, screaming, tantruming, and repetitive, irritating activities and noises. The rule of thumb for handling students who engage in self-indulgent behaviors is to ignore them until the behavior is discontinued and then to socially reinforce the first occurrence of an appropriate behavior.

Noncompliant Behavior

Noncompliant behaviors include instances when students say ''No'' when asked to do something. They also include forgetting or failing to do something because students choose not to do what is asked. In addition, noncompliance includes doing what is requested but in a less than presentable way. The rule of thumb for noncompliant behaviors is that teachers should ignore noncompliant verbalizations, lead noncompliant students physically through the task, or prevent students from participating in an activity until they follow through on the initial request. Compliance with any requests is immediately reinforced socially.

Aggressive Behavior

Verbal or physical abuse directed toward an object or a person is considered aggressive behavior. More specifically, hitting, fighting, pinching, biting, pushing, and deliberately destroying someone's property are examples of aggressive acts. The rule of thumb for aggressive behavior is that it is punished immediately with a verbal reprimand, and the offending student is removed from the activity. Social reinforcement is given when students demonstrate appropriate interaction with other persons or objects.

Self-Stimulatory Behavior

This category includes behaviors that interfere with learning because students become engrossed in the perseverative nature of the activities. Examples include head banging, hand flapping, body rocking, and eye gouging. As a rule of thumb, Dunn and associates recommend a formal behavioral program to deal with this type of behavior. An in-depth discussion of formal behavior modification principles and programs is presented in chapter 6.

Summary

The concept of behavior disabilities as used in this chapter corresponds to the concept of serious emotional disturbance as defined in PL 94-142. The psychodynamic, psychoeducational, behavioral, and psychoneurological approaches were examined for their effectiveness in habilitating students with behavioral disabilities. Suggestions were provided for teaching BD students in integrated physical education classes; effective interpersonal communication, specifically, active listening, conflict resolution, and verbal mediation was discussed. The work of Hellison and the contributions of Dunn and his colleagues were cited as effective approaches to physical education for students with behavioral disabilities.

Bibliography

Allan, J.I. (1980). Jogging can modify disruptive behaviors. *Teaching Exceptional Children,* **12,** 66-70.

American Psychiatric Association. (1980). *Diagnostic and statistical manual of mental disorders* (3rd ed.). Washington, DC: Author.

Bower, E.M. (1981). *Early identification of emotionally handicapped children in school* (3rd ed.). Springfield, IL: Charles C. Thomas.

Dunn, J.M., Morehouse, J.W., & Fredericks, H.D.B. (1986). *Physical education for the severely handicapped: A systematic approach to a data based gymnasium.* Austin: Pro-Ed.

Education for All Handicapped Children Act of 1975, § 121 a.5, U.S.C. § 1401 (1977).

Fagen, S.A. (1980). Adaptive frustration management. In N.J. Long, W.C. Morse, & R.G. Newman (Eds.), *Conflict in the classroom* (4th ed.) (pp. 228-233). Belmont, CA: Wadsworth.

Gordon, T. (1970). *Parent effectiveness training.* New York: The New American Library.

Gump, P., & Sutton-Smith, B. (1955). Activity setting and social interaction: A field study. *American Journal of Orthopsychiatry,* **25,** 755-760.

Hellison, D.R. (1985). *Goals and strategies for teaching physical education.* Champaign, IL: Human Kinetics.

Huber, F. (1980). A strategy for teaching cooperative games: Let's put back the fun in games for disturbed children. In N.J. Long, W.C. Morse, & R.G. Newman (Eds.), *Conflict in the classroom* (4th ed.) (pp. 323-327). Belmont, CA: Wadsworth.

Jenson, W.R., & Young, K.R. (1985). Childhood autism: Developmental considerations and behavioral interventions by professionals, families, and peers. In R.J. McMahon & R.D. Peters (Eds.), *Childhood disorders: Behavioral-developmental approaches* (pp. 169-194). New York: Brunner/Mazel.

Karp, J. (1985). *A.C.T.I.V.E.—All children totally involved exercising.* Kelso, WA: Kelso Public Schools.

Kauffman, J.M. (1985). *Characteristics of children's behavior disorders* (3rd ed.). Columbus, OH: Merrill.

Kern, L., Koegel, R.L., Dyer, K., Blew, P.A., & Fenton, L.R. (1982). The effect of physical exercise on self-stimulation and appropriate responding in autistic children. *Journal of Autism and Developmental Disorders,* **4,** 399-416.

Koegel, R.L., Firestone, P.B., Kramme, K.W., & Dunlap, G. (1974). Increasing spontaneous play by suppressing self-stimulation in autistic children. *Journal of Applied Behavior Analysis, 7*, 521-528.

Llorens, L.A. (1968). Identification of the Ayres' syndrome in emotionally disturbed children: An exploratory study. *American Journal of Occupational Therapy, 22*, 286-288.

Meichenbaum, D. (1977). *Cognitive-behavior modification: An integrative approach.* New York: Plenum.

Poindexter, H. (1969a). Motor development and performance of emotionally disturbed children. *Journal of Health, Physical Education and Recreation, 40*, 69-71.

Poindexter, H. (1969b). The status of physical education for the emotionally disturbed. In *Physical education and recreation for handicapped children: A study conference on research and demonstration needs* (pp. 14-20). Washington, DC: American Association for Health, Physical Education, and Recreation and the National Recreation and Park Association.

Positive Education Program (PEP). (1980). *Helping disturbed children.* Cleveland: Author.

Quay, H.C. (1986). Classification. In H.C. Quay & J.S. Werry (Eds.), *Psychopathological disorders of childhood* (3rd ed.) (pp. 1-34). New York: Wiley.

Sherrill, C. (1986). *Adapted physical education and recreation: A multidisciplinary approach* (3rd ed.). Dubuque, IA: Wm. C. Brown.

Stainback, S., & Stainback, W. (1980). *Educating children with severe maladaptive behaviors.* New York: Grune & Stratton.

Von Isser, A., Quay, H.C., & Love, C.T. (1980). Interrelationships among three measures of deviant behavior. *Exceptional Children, 46*, 272-276.

Watters, R.G., & Watters, W.E. (1980). Decreasing self-stimulatory behavior with physical exercise in a group of autistic boys. *Journal of Autism and Developmental Disorders, 10*, 379-387.

Resources

Written Materials

Dunn, J.M., Morehouse, J.W., & Fredericks, H.D.B. (1986). *Physical education for the severely handicapped: A systematic approach to a data based gymnasium.* Austin, TX: Pro-Ed. This text is a "nuts and bolts" approach to working with severely handicapped students in the physical education setting. It combines detailed information on learning theory with a variety of examples to illustrate the principles that are advocated for use in the gymnasium.

Goldstein, A.P., Sprafkin, R.P., Gershaw, N.J., & Klein, P. (1980). *Skillstreaming the adolescent: A structured learning approach to teaching prosocial skills.* Champaign, IL: Research Press. This is an innovative program designed to help adolescents develop competence in dealing with interpersonal conflicts, in increasing self-esteem, and in contributing to a positive classroom atmosphere.

Audiovisual

Foxx, R.M. (Producer). (1980). *Harry* [Videocassette and film]. Champaign, IL: Research Press. Dr. Richard M. Foxx demonstrates classic examples of fading, extinction, and time-out as well as almost every important principle of behavior modification during one-on-one treatment sessions with Harry. At the time this documentary was filmed, Harry was a 24-year-old mildly retarded person who had a history of severe self-abuse, which had defeated all attempts to educate him.

CHAPTER 14

Sensory Impairments

Diane H. Craft

Sensory impairments include conditions that affect the functioning of one or more of the senses: touch, taste, smell, vision, and hearing. By convention, the term refers to vision and hearing. It is these two senses upon which people depend heavily. This chapter will describe both visual impairments and hearing impairments, discuss the characteristics of individuals with these two sensory impairments, and offer suggestions for teaching physical education to these individuals.

Visual Impairments

The educational definition from the regulations of PL 94-142, the Education of All Handicapped Children Act (1975), states: "Visually handicapped means a *visual impairment* which, even when corrected, adversely affects a child's educational performance. The term includes both partially sighted and blind children [Section 121a.5(b) (1)]." Not every child with a visual loss needs special education; special services are required only when the visual loss interferes with learning.

There are at least three methods of classification to describe the remaining vision of people with visual impairments. These classifications are presented in Table 14.1.

Causes of Visual Impairments

There are scores of causes for visual impairment. While most causes can be directly related to the effects of aging, occasionally blindness originates before or at birth (*congenital*) or in childhood or later (*acquired*). The causes of blindness affecting young people will be emphasized here.

Disorders of the Retina

The *retina* is the nerve tissue at the back of the eye upon which the image of the outside world is focused for transmittal to the brain along the optic nerve. Several diseases can damage the retina, resulting in loss of sight. *Diabetic retinopathy* (diabetes-caused hemorrhaging on the retina), *macular degeneration* (damage to the center part of the eye, which provides detail and color in vision), *retinitis pigmentosa* (inherited disease leading to tunnel vision), *retinal detachment* (separation of the layers of the retina), *retinal vascular diseases* (associated with sickle-cell anemia), and damage caused by injury, drugs, or toxins are all forms of retinal damage.

Disorders of the Cornea, Lens, and Uveal Tract

The *cornea* forms the outer surface of the eye. Behind the cornea lie the aqueous, crystalline lens, and vitreous humor. The eye is encased in the uveal tract. In order for light from the outside world to focus on the retina, all of these structures must remain absolutely clear and without distortion. *Hazy cornea*, in which the cornea becomes cloudy, may result from herpes simplex virus,

Table 14.1 Classifications of Visual Impairments

Classification based on ability to read print

Total blindness	is the inability to read large print even with magnification. Braille is usually used for written communication.
Partial sight	is the ability to read print through the use of large-print books and/or magnification.
Visual impairment	refers to the range of vision encompassing total blindness and partial sight.

Classification based on visual loss after correction

Legal blindness (20/00)	is visual acuity of 20/200 or less in the better eye even with correction, or a field of vision so narrowed that the widest diameter of the visual field subtends an angular distance no greater than 20°.
Travel vision (5/200 to 10/200)	is the ability to see at 5 to 10 ft what the normal eye can see at 200 ft.
Motion perception (3/200 to 5/200)	is the ability to see at 3 to 5 ft what the normal eye can see at 200 ft. This ability is limited almost entirely to perception of motion.
Light perception (<3/200)	is the ability to distinguish a strong light at a distance of 3 ft from the eye but the inability to detect a hand movement at 3 ft from the eye.
Total blindness	is the inability to recognize a strong light that is shone directly into the eye.

Classification for sport competition[a]

B1	From no light perception at all in either eye up to light perception and inability to recognize objects or contours in any direction and at any distance.
B2	From ability to recognize objects or contours up to a visual acuity of 2/60 and/or limited visual field of 5°.
B3	2/60 to 6/60 (20/200) vision and/or field of vision between 5° and 60°.

[a]Classifications used by the United States Association for Blind Athletes (1986).

congenital syphilis, or even a minor accident such as a twig brushing the eye. *Cataracts*, in which the lens is opaque instead of clear, occur with aging but can also occur in infants of mothers who are infected with rubella during the first trimester of pregnancy. *Uveitis* is an inflammation of the uveal tract that accounts for 12% of all visual impairments. *Glaucoma* occurs when the intraocular fluid is unable to continuously drain from the eye. The resulting increase in pressure within the eye can lead to total blindness.

Refractory Error and Squint

The eye is designed so that the images from the environment are focused clearly on the retina. If the eye is shorter than normal (farsightedness or *hypermetropia*), longer than normal (nearsightedness or *myopia*), or irregularly shaped (*astigmatism*), then vision needs to be corrected through glasses, contact lenses, or surgery. *Accommodative squint* occurs when the two eyes are not focusing together. As a result, double vision or the suppression of the image from one eye, known as "lazy eye," can occur.

Disorders of the Visual Pathways

Tumors, blows to the skull, strokes, inflammation, or degeneration through diseases such as multiple sclerosis are possible sources of damage to the *optic nerve*, which is the pathway from the eye to the occipital cortex at the rear of the brain. Because nerves usually do not regenerate, any damage to the visual pathways is likely to be permanent.

Retrolental Fibroplasia

Many adults are blind today as a result of retrolental fibroplasia (RLF). In the 1940s and 1950s, many premature infants were placed in incubators filled with oxygen-enriched air. When an alarmingly large number of these infants became blind, it was found that the high concentrations of oxygen in the incubators caused blindness. RLF also seems to be associated with mild brain damage. Today this disorder occurs only rarely, when an incubator malfunctions.

Incidence

Currently there are about a half million people in the United States who are legally blind. Most of these people are over the age of 65 and have lost their vision through diseases associated with aging. But there are at least 44,000 children who are legally blind, with half of them having congenital blindness.

Characteristics of People With Visual Impairments

Although there is tremendous diversity among people with visual impairments, some characteristics seem to occur with greater frequency in this population than among sighted individuals. The characteristics described next are generalizations, and readers are cautioned to remember that any individual may differ considerably from the generalizations. Characteristics of individuals with visual impairments can be greatly influenced by such factors as the amount of usable vision, the age at which vision was lost, and the presence of other health problems and handicapping conditions.

Cognitive Characteristics

Vision plays a key role in the learning of many basic perceptions, concepts, and motor skills. Before the age of 2, infants develop the basis for body awareness, postural orientation, sensory integration, and motor patterns. If a congenitally blind infant is not stimulated to learn through senses other than vision, there may be subsequent problems in perception and cognitive development. Many infants born without vision show delays in these areas not shown by children who lose their sight later in life.

Affective/Social Characteristics

Stereotyped behaviors similar to those exhibited by some mentally retarded people are also more prevalent among congenitally blind children than among those who are adventitiously blind. These behaviors, also known as blindisms, are repetitive, purposeless movements like rocking forward and backward while seated or standing, waving the hands or flinging the fingers in front of the face, or digging the fingers into the eyes. Stereotyped behaviors are thought to provide stimulation to the person who does not receive visual stimulation by visual means, but they are socially unacceptable. These behaviors may reflect nervousness, so calm reminders such as quietly placing a hand on the shoulder to stop a person's rocking may be more effective than scolding. It is also possible to substitute acceptable behaviors that are incompatible with the stereotyped behavior, such as playing patty cake.

A cluster of three characteristics found in some people with visual impairments may present obstacles to socializing with sighted peers. People without vision often have passive, expressionless faces because they cannot learn to animate their faces by watching others. Similarly, some people with visual impairments may at times appear insensitive to the concerns of others. This reflects the fact that, lacking sight, they cannot respond to the nonverbal cues that communicate subtle feelings. Finally, some people with visual impairments may seem very talkative because they are uncomfortable with the pauses in conversation usually filled by nonverbal gestures. *Socialization* is enhanced when sighted people are helped to understand and accept these subtle differences.

Some people with visual impairments, whether they are congenitally or adventitiously blind, are fearful and dependent. These characteristics probably result not from the lack of vision, but rather from socialization. Well-intentioned parents and teachers may be *overprotective* of blind children who must live without the benefit of one of the senses. But this overprotection usually leads to reduced opportunities to freely explore the environment along with possible delays in perceptual, motor, and cognitive development. Most people who have been noted for their achievements despite their lack of sight share a fearless, devil-may-care attitude toward life. Readers are encouraged to read about the lives of Harry Cordellos, Charles Buell, and Helen Keller, as well as the controversial book by Robert Scott (1969) on socialized dependency of blind individuals, entitled *The Making of Blind Men*. Scott suggests that society expects blind people to be helpless and dependent and treats them accordingly. This treatment then *teaches* blind people to act in ways that fulfill the expectation. To counteract this patronizing societal attitude, it is extremely important that physical educators teach independence and self-sufficiency to blind students and expect them to exhibit those qualities.

Motor/Physical Characteristics

The lack of sight does not directly cause any specific motor or physical characteristics. But the reduced opportunity for movement that often accompanies blindness may result in unique patterns. As early as 12 weeks after birth, the movements of congenitally blind infants may differ significantly from those of their sighted peers. Data on the delay in developmental milestones among blind children are presented in Table 14.2. The reduced opportunity for rough-and-tumble play with parents, the parents' heightened protective instincts, the infant's own fear of being moved suddenly,

Table 14.2   Developmental Milestones in Motor Patterns Among Young Blind Children

Motor behavior	Expected age	Blind
Head up from prone	1 month	4 months
Elevates self on elbows	4 months	8.75 months
Reaches	3-5 months	8 months
Sits	6-8 months	8 months
Raises to sitting	8 months	11 months
Creeps	7 months	13 months
Stepping movements when supported	8.8 months	10.75 months
Stands by using furniture	8.6 months	13 months
Stands alone	11 months	13 months
Walks three steps	11.7 months	15 months
Walks alone	12-15 months	19 months

Note. From "Developmental Guidelines for Teachers and Evaluators of Multihandicapped Children" by M.B. Langley in *An Introduction to Assessment of Severely Profoundly Handicapped Children: Module III*, Austin, TX: Education Service Center, Region XIII. Adapted by permission.

the lack of visual motivation for movement, and the lack of opportunity to observe others moving may all contribute to motor delays among blind children. To minimize those delays, it is imperative to give visually impaired children the opportunity to move in a safe environment.

Among adventitiously blind people who were sighted for several years, motor delays are not usually observed. These people need corrective feedback from others as a substitute for the ability to visually monitor their own movements, so that skills once mastered do not deteriorate.

As a group, people with visual impairments show postural deviations. Again, this difference is pronounced among congenitally blind people who have never had the opportunity to see normal posture. It is also pronounced among people with partial sight, who may hold their heads in an unusual position to maximize vision. Corrective postural exercises may help remediate postural deviations. Body image and balance may also be poor among visually impaired students. This may be due to a lack of opportunities for the regular physical activity through which balance and body image are developed and refined.

Similarly, fitness levels of people with visual impairments are below those of their sighted peers. The performance of blind students on fitness tests varies with the degree of mobility required by a particular test item. Winnick (1985) found that blind students performed best in flexibility, arm strength, and muscular endurance, and worst in throwing. Other factors affecting the fitness level of visually impaired children are gender and age. Except in flexibility, visually impaired boys are more physically fit than their female counterparts. As expected, older children are more fit than younger ones.

As a group, blind students have fitness levels below those of sighted students, but there are many blind students who are more fit than their sighted peers. On fitness items that do not require mobility, 25% of blind youths exceed the median performance of sighted youths (Winnick, 1985). Harry Cordellos, a blind athlete, scored among the very highest of all individuals assessed for cardiovascular fitness at the Center for Aerobic Studies directed by Kenneth Cooper in Texas. The opportunity and the will to move, not the degree of vision, are the key factors determining an individual's level of performance. Buell found that overprotected blind children scored lower in tests of running, jumping, and throwing than neglected and non-neglected blind children. He concluded that neglect is preferable to overprotection in terms of motor performance (Winnick, 1985). These findings show that parents and teachers *must* provide visually impaired children with the opportunity to move.

Teaching Methods and Activities

The best practices for teaching visually impaired students differ little from those for sighted students in physical education. A teacher who uses methods that simultaneously meet the needs of both highly skilled and poorly skilled individuals will be better able to accommodate mainstreamed visually impaired students. Individualized instruction, following the model of assess, plan, implement, and evaluate, can accommodate a range of student abilities.

The first step in individualizing instruction is determining each student's present level of performance through assessment. Tests suitable for use with visually impaired students are described in Table 14.3. (Refer to chapter 4 for additional information on tests in the motor domain.) Using assessment as a basis for determining motor needs, the physical education teacher can plan goals and short-term instructional objectives for each student, modifying activities as needed.

Vision plays a prominent role in information processing (see the model described in chapters 7 and 12, and depicted in Figure 12.1). To the extent that vision is necessary for input (step 1), decision making (step 2), output (step 3), and feedback (step 4), information processing in people with visual impairments will be disturbed. It is the

Table 14.3 Tests for Visually Impaired Students

Test name	Area tested	Availability of norms
Physical Fitness Testing of the Disabled: Project UNIQUE (Winnick & Short, 1985)	Fitness	Norms available for students with visual impairments, ages 10-17
Buell Adaptation (1973) of AAHPERD Youth Fitness Test (1965 version)	Fitness	Norms available for students with visual impairments, ages 10-17
Ohio State University Scale of Intra-Gross Motor Assessment (OSU-SIGMA) (Loovis & Ersing, 1979)	Motor skills[a]	No norms available
Test of Gross Motor Development (Ulrich, 1985)	Motor skills[a]	Norms available only for students with sight, ages 3-10

[a]This test has not been specifically adapted to assess the motor or sport skills of blind participants. Currently no tests of motor or sport skills have been adapted for use with visually impaired students.

teacher's task to highlight other sources of sensory input, such as auditory, tactile, and kinesthetic, to compensate for diminished or absent visual input. For example, the task of throwing a ball at a target is heavily dependent on visual input and feedback. *Auditory cues* may be added for visually impaired students in compensation for the absent visual cues. A buzzer, radio, or other noisemaker can be placed behind the target to aid in locating the target (sensory input—step 1). Auditory cues may also be added to provide feedback about the throw (step 4). Tin cans used as a target will make noise when hit, thus providing auditory feedback that the throw was accurate. Also, the teacher or a fellow student may describe the accuracy of the throw ("You were 2 ft above and to the right of the target."). The information processing model may be a useful guide in adapting instruction for students with visual impairments.

Select Activities That Do Not Require Modification

When teaching physical education to blind students, it is most desirable to select activities that are not heavily dependent on visual input and feedback and thus require little or no modification. Examples of sports and activities in which a person with limited vision can participate without modification include

- folk and square dancing,
- rope jumping,
- tug-of-war and parachute play with young children,
- canoeing and tandem bicycling with a sighted partner in the front seat,
- crewing with a sighted coxswain,
- bowling and archery for a person with tunnel vision,

Figure 14.1 Playing goal ball.

- waterskiing using whistle signals, and
- cross-country skiing with a sighted partner.

Goal ball, shown in Figure 14.1, is a sport specifically designed for blind players. Introducing goal ball in a mainstreamed class may reverse the usual situation: Everyone wears blindfolds, so visually impaired students may outperform their sighted peers because of their increased opportunity to develop auditory perception (Kearney & Copeland, 1979).

Modify to Provide Kinesthetic Cues

Information processing can be facilitated by provision of *kinesthetic cues*. For blind students, the use of kinesthetic feedback is potentially a more efficient method of learning than the use of auditory feedback (Dye, 1983). In teaching a motor skill, the teacher can physically guide a child's body to the correct position to help the child learn. A scale model, such as a doll with movable joints

that children can feel, helps to convey the relationship of the body parts during a maneuver such as a jumping jack, forward roll, or cartwheel. Using different surfaces to mark playing areas can improve orientation in the gym. Mats can be arranged on the floor in front of a wall to signal the out-of-bounds area. Orientation in bowling is simplified through the use of a lightweight portable rail that is set up in line with the gutter to guide the bowler's approach.

Modify to Provide Auditory Cues

Modify visually dependent activities to provide additional auditory cues. For example, baseball can be modified to use a large ball that is hit as it bounces off home plate or a beeper ball with an audible buzzer inside. The first base coach calls out to direct the batter to the base. Make a playground ball audible inexpensively by inserting bells, then resealing the ball with a bicycle tire patch. For the benefit of both sighted and blind students, use precise, unambiguous verbal descriptions when giving feedback. Statements such as "Hold the racket 3 to 4 in. above your left shoulder" provide more feedback than "Hold the racket like this." Include visually impaired students during spectator events by assigning a student announcer to describe the action, much as a radio announcer describes a ball game. Selecting an announcer with a lively sense of humor can make the event more fun for everyone.

Enhance Visual Cues

Brightly colored balls, mats, field markers, and goals that contrast with the background will enable partially sighted students to use any *residual vision*. The nature of visual limitations varies greatly, so ask each partially sighted student what modifications will be most helpful. Some can see bright, multicolored objects under strong light best, while others (including people with albinism and glaucoma) need solid-colored objects under nonglare lights.

Adapted Sports

The last decade has seen a proliferation in competitive sports available for visually impaired athletes. The sports open to visually impaired athletes of any age through the United States Association for Blind Athletes include the following:

- Goal ball
- Women's gymnastics
- Men's wrestling
- Track and field
- Swimming
- Tandem cycling
- Judo
- Winter sports of downhill and cross-country skiing and speed skating
- Power and weight lifting

The sports of rowing and diving are close to adoption.

Classification for competition is based on residual vision (see Table 14.1). Rules for each sport are modified slightly from those established by the national sport organization. For example, track and field follows National Collegiate Athletic Association (NCAA) rules with these exceptions: Wire lane markers are used in sprints, sighted partners may be used on distance runs, hurdles are eliminated, and totally blind jumpers touch the high bar, then back off and use a one- or two-step approach.

Wrestling rules are modified slightly to require that opponents maintain physical contact throughout the match. Visually impaired wrestlers have a long history of victories and state championships against sighted opponents (Buell, 1966).

Women's gymnastics competition adheres to United States Gymnastics Federation rules except that totally blind vaulters may start with their hands on the horse and use a two-bounce takeoff; coaches on the balance beam may warn competitors when they near the end of the beam, and no jumps are used; floor exercise competitors may count their steps to the edge of the mat; and music may be placed anywhere near the mat to aid directionality.

Swimming also follows NCAA rules. Athletes count their strokes so that they can anticipate the pool's edge. A coach may also tap a swimmer to signal the approaching end of the pool. With the backstroke, flags hung low over the pool signal the end of the pool by brushing the swimmer's arms. When necessary, a spotter may use a paddle board to protect a swimmer's head.

Goal ball is a sport specifically for blind athletes. Two teams of three players each compete on a 18 m-by-8.5 m playing area to stop a rolled ball from crossing their end line. All players wear blindfolds, so they must listen for the rolling ball filled with bells. In this lively sport, players stretch, dive, or lunge to stop the oncoming ball with any part of their body.

Beep Ball is a popular modification of baseball; its rules are presented in chapter 25.

Hearing Impairments

Speaking as a deaf person I believe that the most effective "cure" for deafness is not medicine, mechanical or electronic devices nor the surgical blade, but understanding. And, ironically, understanding is free. Before we can develop understanding, however, we must create awareness. (Gannon, cited in Freeman, Carbin, & Boese, 1981, p. 189)

Definition

Hearing impairment is a term that indicates some malfunction of the auditory mechanism. Within the scope of hearing impairments are several types and degrees of hearing loss.

Deafness refers to a hearing loss that is disabling to an extent that hearing alone is insufficient for comprehension, with or without the use of a hearing aid. Another mode of communication is usually used by a deaf person. PL 94-142 defines *deaf* as having a hearing impairment so severe that the student is unable to process language through hearing, with or without the use of an amplification device. The loss must be severe enough to affect the student's educational performance adversely [Education for All Handicapped Children Act of 1975, Section 121a.5(b)(1)].

Hard-of-hearing means having a hearing loss that is disabling to an extent that understanding speech through the ear alone is difficult but not impossible. The hard-of-hearing person usually relies on amplification by a hearing aid and/or remedial help in communication skills. PL 94-142 defines *hard-of-hearing* as having a hearing impairment that may be permanent or fluctuating and that adversely affects the student's educational achievement or performance [Education for All Handicapped Children Act of 1975, Section 121a.5(b)(1)].

Most people with auditory losses are hard-of-hearing, not totally deaf. Two children may have the same degree and pattern of hearing loss but may utilize their residual hearing differently because of differences in age when hearing loss occurred, motivation, intelligence, presence of other handicapping conditions, or response to a training program.

The degree of hearing loss is described in *decibels (dB)*, as is the amount of residual hearing. The ability to detect sounds in the 0 to 25 dB range is considered normal for children. Ordinary conversation occurs in the 40 to 50 dB range, while noises in the 125 to 140 dB range are painfully loud. The *pure-tone audiogram* is the standard test used for measuring hearing. The audiogram is usually conducted by an *audiologist*, who is a nonmedical professional trained in hearing evaluation and hearing loss management. The audiogram tests the hearing in each ear at three frequencies—500, 1,000, and 2,000 hertz—that reflect the range of frequencies occurring in speech. The audiogram results indicate the average of the three speech frequencies for the better ear. Degrees of hearing loss are presented in Table 14.4.

The age at which the hearing impairment occurs can greatly influence the method of communication used by a hearing-impaired person. *Prelingual deafness* is the condition of people whose deafness was present at birth or originated at an age prior to the development of speech and language. *Postlingual deafness* refers to the condition of those who became deaf at an age following the spontaneous acquisition of speech and language (Moores, 1978). It is in the first three years of life that most children learn to understand and use language in the form of speech. For a child who experiences total hearing loss before learning to speak, the task of developing oral speech may be close to impossible. A prelingually deaf person trained in *speechreading* (lipreading) is usually no more proficient in that skill than an untrained hearing person. (Simulate this by turning off the sound while watching television and trying to follow

Table 14.4 Degrees of Hearing Loss

Hearing threshold	Degree of impairment	Difficulty understanding the following speech
27-40 dB[a]	Slight impairment	Faint speech
41-55 dB	Mild impairment	Normal speech
56-70 dB	Marked impairment	Loud speech
71-90 dB	Severe impairment	Shouted speech
Greater than 90 dB	Profound impairment	Any speech, even amplified speech

[a]Decibels.

what is being said.) Because of the difficulty most prelingually deaf people have in speaking and speechreading, many use sign language instead. In contrast, people who had already developed speech before the hearing loss occurred can usually retain intelligible speech, often with the help of remedial training. These people can also speechread with proficiency.

Incidence

The incidence of total deafness among children is approximately 1 in 1,000, but as many as 1 in 16 possess milder forms of hearing loss that can handicap them in school. Sometimes these children are regarded as slow learners or thought to have behavior problems when their inappropriate behavior is actually due to an undetected mild hearing loss.

Among deaf children, approximately two thirds have *congenital deafness* (present at birth), and one third have *acquired deafness* (developed sometime after birth). At least two of the leading causes of congenital deafness (rubella and Rh incompatibility) are now preventable. However, the expected decrease in the incidence of deafness has been offset by medical advances that enable more severely premature babies and children with meningitis and encephalitis to survive, but only

to have multiple disabilities, including deafness. Thus the incidence of deafness is not decreasing but instead changing to include many more multiply handicapped people.

Symptoms

Symptoms and behaviors that may indicate that a child has a hearing loss include

- lack of attention,
- turning or cocking of the head,
- difficulty in following directions,
- aggressive, stubborn, shy, or withdrawn behavior,
- reluctance to participate in oral activities,
- dependence on classmates for instructions,
- tendency to achieve best in small groups,
- disparity between expected and actual achievement,
- frequent earaches,
- fluid running from the ears,
- frequent colds and sore throats, and
- recurring tonsillitis (Winnick, 1979).

If an auditory loss is suspected, it should be assessed as soon as possible because early intervention is needed to minimize the handicap caused by deafness.

Types and Causes

There are three major types of hearing loss: conductive, sensorineural, and mixed. A *conductive* loss occurs when sound is not transmitted well to the inner ear. It is analogous to a radio with the volume on low. The words are faint, but there is no distortion. Conductive loss can be corrected surgically or medically because it is a mechanical problem in which nerves remain undamaged. Causes of conductive loss include

- wax plugs,
- injuries,
- allergies,
- malformed ears, and
- infection such as serous otitis media (middle ear effusion, often treated with a plastic tube placed in the eardrum for several months).

A *sensorineural* loss is much more serious and likely to be permanent. It is analogous to a radio that is not well tuned. The words may be loud, but they are distorted and garbled. Sensorineural losses affect fidelity as well as loudness, so there is distortion of sounds. While louder speech or use of a hearing aid may help voices be heard, the words still may not be understood. Typically, low-pitched vowel sounds are heard, but the high-pitched consonants such as *t, p,* and *k* are not heard clearly. This makes it difficult to distinguish between words such as *pop* and *top*. A *mixed* loss is a combination of both conductive and sensorineural losses. The conductive part of the loss may be permanent or temporary, as in the case of recurring ear infections.

Prenatal causes of sensorineural loss include

- maternal infections of rubella, glandular fever, and influenza;
- anemia during pregnancy;
- toxemia;
- allergy; and
- drugs.

The most prevalent prenatal cause of deafness between 1963 and 1965 was the *rubella* epidemic.

Now all young children are required to be immunized for rubella to protect women in the first trimester of pregnancy from exposure to the disease. But not all children have been reached, and there are still some occurrences of maternal rubella resulting in deafness, as well as blindness and mental retardation, in newborns.

Perinatal causes of sensorineural loss include

- *anoxia*, the lack of oxygen, and
- *kernicterus*, a depositing of bile pigments in the brain, usually due to Rh incompatibility between mother and infant.

Postnatal causes of sensorineural loss include

- infections such as mumps, measles, meningitis, encephalitis, and nose and throat infections that spread through the eustachian tube to the ear;
- injuries; and
- drugs such as streptomycin, neomycin, salicylates, and quinine.

Characteristics

Individuals who are classified as hard-of-hearing typically share the characteristics of the general population. Their hearing impairments usually are mild and do not present major obstacles to speech. But most people with profound postlingual deafness or severe or profound prelingual deafness may have unique characteristics due to communication problems. Those characteristics will be the focus of this section.

Language and Cultural Characteristics

The overriding characteristic of deaf individuals is not lack of hearing, but *difficulty in communicating* and the effect of that difficulty on social interaction. Please note that speaking and communication are not synonymous. Communication is the exchange of ideas. Speech is the means through which most people communicate, but writing and signing are also ways of communicating. Currently, the *Total Communication Method* (a combination of speech, residual hearing, fingerspelling, and sign language) is the preferred method of communication among deaf individuals. But the *oral-only method* (a combination of residual hearing, speechreading or lipreading, and speech) has also been popular.

The most common sign language used in the United States is the *American Sign Language* (ASL). Like English, ASL is a language with its own grammar and structure that can communicate subtle nuances of abstractions in addition to describing concrete objects. Most hearing people see only the signs that name objects and directions, illustrated in Figure 14.2, and are unaware of the subtlety of ASL and other sign languages.

Research has shown that a major factor in the language skills and adjustment of prelingually deaf people is whether they are exposed to language—in this case sign language—from birth. Significant language delays are found among deaf children with hearing parents. But language delays are *not* found among deaf children with deaf parents because these children have the opportunity to learn sign language as rapidly as their hearing peers learn speech.

Currently, most prelingually deaf children do not develop intelligible speech despite the best-known teaching methods. Thus, verbal communication between hearing and profoundly deaf people remains a major problem. Unfortunately, hearing people often view deaf people's use of Total Communication including sign language as a defect, not a difference. Professor Leo Jacobs (1974), a prelingual deaf person born of deaf parents, wrote:

I never noticed my own handicap nor came up against discrimination or unfair treatment until I began my own personal contacts with hearing people when I entered school. . . . I felt more handicapped from the treatment I received at the hands of hearing people than from my deafness. . . . The real ills of deaf people lie more with minority group dynamics than with their deafness (p.99). . . . They are

subject to the same problems that other minority groups face: the demand that the minority people come up to the expectations of the majority, and the majority's utter disregard for the real needs of the minority group. (p. 71)

Cognitive Characteristics

The difficulty and delay in language acquisition by deaf children is reflected in their academic achievement. Despite average intelligence, the mean reading level of deaf high school graduates is comparable to that of 9- or 10-year-old hearing children. Deaf students are substantially behind their hearing peers in other measures of achievement, too. Most tests are designed for hearing children and require a good working knowledge of written English. But even when appropriate tests are given, the performance of deaf students is still poor (Freeman, Carbin, & Boese, 1981). One reason is that deaf children have decreased opportunities for *incidental learning* because they cannot overhear conversations. Rarely do hearing parents, teachers, and friends sign when not addressing deaf children; so there is little opportunity to "oversee" conversations, and continuity with life's events is often missing. There is no chance to hear the argument that preceded a brother's crying, or to share the whispered excitement of classmates before a surprise party.

Behavioral Characteristics

The incidence of impulsivity seems to be greater among deaf than hearing children. This may be due to a deprivation of communication and incidental learning opportunities. Harris found that deaf children of deaf parents are significantly less impulsive than other deaf children; this suggests that the communication problem is at the root of impulsivity.

Among deaf children, 20% to 30% show behavioral disorders, compared to 7% to 10% of hearing children. This greater incidence of behavioral disorders may occur because the deaf children

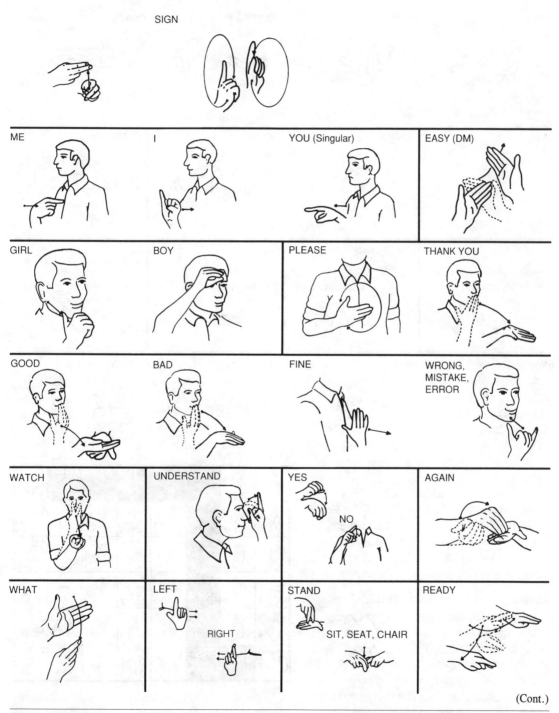

Figure 14.2 Signing for physical education. Reprinted by permission of the American Alliance for Health Physical Education, Recreation and Dance, 1900 Association Drive, Reston, Virginia 22091.

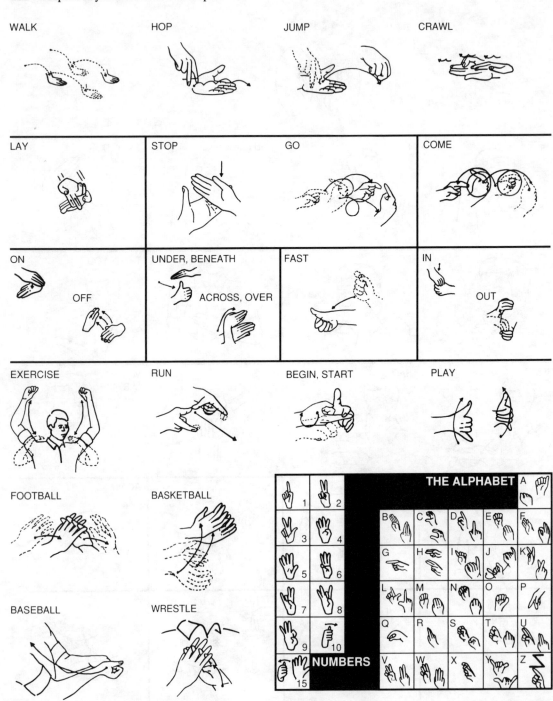

Figure 14.2 (Continued)

have not learned enough about what is expected of them and why and how to behave in approved ways (Freeman et al., 1981).

Motor Characteristics

In motor performance, there seems to be little difference between deaf and hearing children unless there is *vestibular etiology*. If damage to the *semi-circular canals* is part of the hearing impairment, the child will almost certainly have balance problems. These problems may in turn cause developmental and motor ability delays.

There do not appear to be any significant differences in static and dynamic balance between hearing students and hearing-impaired students without vestibular etiology. But balance is definitely poorer among children whose deafness results from meningitis, which causes vestibular damage. Research results concerning motor development and motor ability are less clear. Approximately half of the studies reviewed conclude that deaf children fall farther behind hearing peers in motor development with increasing age. But the other half of the studies indicate no significant differences in motor development between the two groups (Schmidt, 1985). Equally ambiguous results were found regarding motor ability. Half of the studies noted significant delays among hearing-impaired students, while half found no delays (Schmidt, 1985). One possible explanation for the discrepancy in findings may be variation in the number of hearing-impaired children with vestibular damage included in each study. Most studies on the motor performance of deaf children do not group those with vestibular etiology separately from other deaf children. Results indicating poor motor performance for deaf children as a group probably reflect the very poor performance of the children with vestibular etiology together with the average performance of the rest of the deaf children.

In a recent study using the Bruininks-Oseretsky Test of Motor Proficiency, Brunt and Broadhead (1982) found that deaf 7- to 14-year-old boys and girls did not do as well as hearing peers on static and dynamic balance tasks but did better than the hearing children on visual-motor skills. This result may be due to the deaf students' experience with sign language and fingerspelling, a system in which a unique hand and finger position corresponds to each letter in the alphabet.

Deaf students do not seem to differ from hearing students in physical fitness. There are no significant differences across age groups between hearing-impaired and hearing students on the body composition, strength, flexibility, power-speed, and cardiorespiratory endurance measures of physical fitness (Winnick & Short, 1986). Only in the power-strength item (sit-ups) do the hearing students perform significantly better than the hearing-impaired students. There are the usual differences in gender and age. In both hearing-impaired and hearing populations, boys are more fit than girls (except in tests of flexibility), and older children are more fit than younger ones. These findings indicate that physical educators can evaluate hearing-impaired students against the same fitness norms used with hearing students.

Schmidt (1985) and Winnick (1985) compared the motor performance of two groups of deaf students, one group educated in special schools for the deaf and another group who attended regular public schools. Both studies found that the deaf students in special schools performed significantly better than those mainstreamed into regular schools. While unproven, it is strongly suspected that deaf students in regular schools are not provided with sufficient opportunities for physical activity to allow them to fulfill their potential. Thus, their motor performance may be limited by discriminatory attitudes and practices in regular schools rather than by lack of ability.

Teaching Deaf-Blind Children

Children called deaf-blind are really *multisensory deprived* (MSD) individuals who lack effective use of both of the distance senses: vision and hearing. Although the term *deaf-blind* suggests that these people can neither hear nor see, this is seldom accurate. The overwhelming majority of deaf-blind children receive both visual and auditory input, but information received through these sensory channels is usually distorted. It is more accurate to state that these people are both hard-of-hearing and partially sighted. Only in a rare instance, such as Helen Keller's, is a person totally blind and profoundly deaf.

The problems of MSD children are complex. These children may

- lack the ability to communicate with their environment in a meaningful way,
- have a distorted perception of their world,
- lack the ability to anticipate future events or the results of their actions,
- be deprived of many of the most basic extrinsic motivations,
- have medical problems which lead to serious developmental lags,
- be mislabeled as retarded or emotionally disturbed,
- be forced to develop unique learning styles to compensate for their multiple handicaps, and
- have extreme difficulty in establishing and maintaining interpersonal relationships. (McInnes & Treffry, 1982, p. 2).

Multisensory deprivation presents serious obstacles to learning. MSD children can manipulate objects, but, because they do not receive clear visual or auditory feedback, they have difficulty anticipating the consequences of an action.

Until recently most MSD children were assumed to be profoundly retarded, institutionalized, and offered few educational opportunities. Deaf-blind children have shown substantial lags in social, emotional, cognitive, and motor development. Results of recently developed programs demonstrate that many of these children are not inherently profoundly retarded but only deprived of an opportunity to learn. But establishing an educational program for MSD children is not a task that can be undertaken in a haphazard way. Because these children have almost no opportunity for incidental learning, everything must be taught, including how to play. Programs for MSD children need *planned activities* leading to the accomplishment of *established objectives* that require the child to *problem solve, communicate, use residual vision and hearing*, and *exert control over the environment* (McInnes & Treffry, 1982). Movement should be at the base of the program because, through movement, deaf-blind children learn about themselves and the environment.

Deaf-blind students can participate in most sports on a recreational level. Weight lifting, dancing, roller skating, swimming, skiing, bowling, hiking, and canoeing are all possible. But in order to enjoy these and other sports, students need the prerequisite skills and immediate feedback on the success of their efforts. McInnes and Treffry (1982) suggest following these steps regardless of the child's current performance level:

1. Provide the opportunity to explore, manipulate, and become familiar with equipment and facilities.
2. Together with the child, demonstrate and model the response. For example, place the child's hand over the teacher's hands when paddling; once the child can follow the motion, place the teacher's hands over the child's hands when paddling. This step, analogous to demonstrating and modeling the desired behavior, is essential to provide security as well as skill development.
3. Provide immediate feedback on performance so the child can compare the performance with the model.
4. Explain and give the child time to prepare for the coming action. Surprise moves do not foster security and confidence.

The books listed under "Resources" at the end of the chapter provide more complete teaching and curriculum suggestions related to deaf-blind students.

Teaching Considerations

To the extent that information processing is dependent on auditory cues, hearing-impaired students will have difficulty learning. Yet movement is one area that is not heavily dependent on those cues. Usually visual cues can be substituted for the auditory cues that are distorted or absent. Few rules, pieces of equipment, facilities, or skills require modification. But, because deafness places profound limitations on verbal communication, teaching methods must be modified for hearing-impaired students. The following modifications are suggested for teaching deaf students in regular physical education classes.

1. Maximize the hearing-impaired students' ability to use auditory cues by teaching in a quiet gymnasium, without music playing in the background or others talking while directions are being given. Facilitate speechreading by providing good lighting and facing the students so that lips and facial expressions are fully visible.

2. Supplement verbal input and feedback by arranging for a hearing student to repeat or explain any instructions missed by the deaf student. (Even skilled speechreaders seldom understand more than 40% of the words in a conversation.) Use ample demonstrations, written copies of game directions and even lesson plans, and visual cues such as flashing lights to get attention. When outdoors, stand near hearing-impaired students and tap them on the shoulder to gain their attention. Develop easily visible signals for use when students are at the other end of the field. Learn as much sign language as possible, beginning with the signs presented in Figure 14.2. Some hearing students may also be eager to learn sign language and one-hand manual. It is assumed that a physical educator teaching full time in a school for the deaf where Total Communication is used would study to quickly acquire signing

skills. This teacher would both sign and speak all conversations.

3. Finally, promote acceptance of hearing-impaired students by enforcing classroom rules fairly with all students. Offering preferential treatment to hearing-impaired students does little to endear them to their classmates.

Mainstreaming Hearing-Impaired Students

An important objective of physical education for mainstreamed hearing-impaired students should be promoting *social interaction*. Physical education is the one area where verbal communication can be minimized and movement maximized. It is also an area where working together toward a common goal can be emphasized. For these reasons, physical education is one of the first areas into which hearing-impaired students are mainstreamed.

Integration of a deaf child into a hearing class should occur on the first day of the school year so that the child starts as one of the group. It is important to speak in a positive manner to the other students about hearing impairments and how best to communicate with the deaf child. Activities that foster cooperation but do not depend heavily on verbal cues should be planned. Be sure that the deaf child understands the activity before playing. At the same time, help hearing students understand that if the deaf children do not follow the rules it may be because they do not understand the rules, not because they are intentionally breaking them. Because of the teacher time needed to communicate with deaf children mainstreamed into a regular class, the total class size should be reduced.

For the benefit of all children in the class, design a curriculum that emphasizes cooperative and self-testing activities. It is not necessary to avoid team sports, but the games should be organized in a manner that meets the needs of each child in the class. Basketball, soccer, and football can all be played with two to four players per team, matched by skill level. With this approach, highly skilled players are challenged because they are competing against others of equal skill, while less skilled players are allowed to play on a level commensurate with their abilities. With few players on each team, all players have more practice time and thus learn faster. All children, including mainstreamed deaf children, will benefit from a curriculum that is individualized in the manner just described.

To promote social interaction, teach neighborhood games. Hearing children learn games like rope jumping, hopscotch, Four Square, and softball mostly by watching and listening to others play; such incidental learning is not available to deaf children. Teaching these games in physical education class helps deaf children understand and become skilled in them, thus increasing the chances that they will be included in neighborhood play.

Special Considerations

For most hearing-impaired individuals there are no restrictions on participation in physical education. But people with infections in the external or middle ear should avoid swimming until the infection has subsided. Children with tubes in their ears also need to stay out of the water until the tubes are removed. Children susceptible to earaches should avoid exposing unprotected ears to cold weather.

People with damage to the semicircular canals may wish to refrain from some activities. Because of balance problems and vertigo, these people should climb to heights, jump on the trampoline, or dive only if there are adequate safeguards to ensure that they will not be hurt as a result of a loss of balance. Tumbling activities that require rotation, such as dive-forward rolls, cartwheels, and handsprings, should be attempted only with close spotting. Activities that teach balancing skills in a safe situation *should* be included in the physical education curriculum. It is not possible to restore a damaged vestibular system, but it is possible to teach a person to make maximum use of visual and kinesthetic cues in balancing.

Tests

Very few physical education tests have been designed and normed specifically for hearing-impaired students. *Physical Fitness Testing of the Disabled: Project UNIQUE* by Winnick and Short (1985) is the most current such test available. It offers national norms established for 10- to 17-year-old hearing-impaired students on fitness items that have been modified slightly to compensate for the students' lack of hearing. The fitness items are the same as those for hearing students, but hand signals have been added. The norms for hearing-impaired and hearing students are the same with the exception of those for sit-ups.

Most other physical fitness tests can be administered to deaf students provided that visual cues are substituted for auditory cues (e.g., drop arm in addition to shouting ''go'' to signal the start of an event). The major modification involves the instructions for the test. Teachers must be very sure that deaf students understand each test item so that the results reflect ability and not lack of understanding. Refer to chapter 4 for additional information on tests in the psychomotor domain.

Adapted Sports

The sport skills of deaf athletes span the range found in the regular population, from unskilled to highly skilled. Deaf athletes are capable of competing as equals among hearing athletes, and some do with much success. As far back as 1883, deaf athletes were competing in professional sports. In that year Edward Dundon become the first deaf professional baseball player on record. Scores of deaf baseball players have followed his example. Hearing-impaired athletes have also excelled in such sports as swimming, wrestling, football, and bowling. At least eight deaf bowlers have bowled a sanctioned perfect game of 300. Deaf women have also excelled in sports. Kitty O'Neal has earned the title of Fastest Woman on Earth for her women's world speed records in waterskiing (104.85 mph), rocketpowered car driving

(512.083 mph), and quarter-mile car speed racing (395.54 mph). Some deaf athletes have gone on to coach hearing teams, like Albert Berg, who became the first football coach at Purdue University in 1887. But many deaf athletes choose to compete against each other under the auspices of the *American Athletic Association of the Deaf* (AAAD) and the *International Committee of Silent Sports* (CISS). The preference for competing among themselves reflects the socialization to feel more comfortable among other deaf individuals.

On the international level, the CISS sponsors 13 summer sports in which men and women compete:

- Cycling
- Swimming
- Basketball
- Men's wrestling
- Tennis
- Water polo
- Soccer
- Track and field
- Shooting
- Handball
- Table tennis
- Volleyball
- Badminton

On the national level, the AAAD actively promotes the sports of basketball, softball, and volleyball. The rules followed by AAAD and CISS are nearly identical to those used in other national and international competition. A few changes have been made to reflect participants' difficulty in hearing. A whistle is blown *and* a flag waved in team sports to stop play. In track and swimming events a gun is used by a starter, who stands down the track in front of the runners. The gun itself is filled with black smoke to make the shot easily visible to athletes who cannot hear it or feel the vibrations.

Any person who is hard-of-hearing or deaf is eligible to compete under the auspices of AAAD. Eligibility is determined through an audiogram, which must show a hearing loss greater than 55 dB in the better ear at the three frequency-pure tones of 500, 1,000, and 2,000 Hz. There are no further subclassifications based on degree of hearing loss, so an athlete with a moderate hearing loss may compete against an athlete with a profound hearing loss. This system is quite different from the many subclassifications found within competition for visually impaired and physically challenged athletes, and it serves to underscore the minimal influence that a hearing loss exerts on athletic achievement.

Summary

The characteristics of people who are legally blind depend in large part on the time when sight was lost and the degree of the loss. Most of the half million people in the United States who are legally blind have some sight remaining. To aid learning, the physical educator needs to enhance the visual cues while augmenting them with kinesthetic and auditory cues. Of the many skilled athletes who are blind, many choose to compete in sports through the United States Association for Blind Athletes.

One of the dominant characteristics of hearing impairments is difficulty in communication. The difficulty of interacting with hearing individuals through a common language has helped to create a separate deaf community. A primary goal in physical education may be to help ease this social isolation by encouraging deaf students to participate in sports and games with others.

Bibliography

Brunt, D., & Broadhead, G.D. (1982). Motor proficiency traits of deaf children. *Research Quarterly for Exercise and Sport,* **53**, 236-238.

Buell, C.E. (1966). *Physical education for blind children.* Springfield, IL: Charles C. Thomas.

Buell, C.E. (1973). *Physical education and recreation for the visually handicapped.* Washington, DC: American Association for Health, Physical Education and Recreation.

Dye, L.A. (1983). *A study of augmented modes of feedback used by blind children to learn a selected motor task*. Unpublished doctoral dissertation, New York University.

Education for All Handicapped Children Act of 1975, § 121a.5, U.S.C. § 1401 (1977).

Freeman, R.D., Carbin, C.F., & Boese, R.J. (1981). *Can't your child hear? A guide for those who care about deaf children*. Austin, TX: Pro-Ed.

Jacobs, L.M. (1974). *A deaf adult speaks out*. Washington, DC: Gallaudet College Press.

Kearney, S., & Copeland, R. (1979). Goal ball. *Journal of Physical Education and Recreation, 50*, 24-26.

Loovis, M., & Ersing, W. (1979). *Assessing and programming gross motor development for children* (2nd ed.). Loudenville, OH: Mohican Textbook.

McInnes, J.M. & Treffry, J.A. (1982). *Deaf-blind infants and children: A developmental guide*. Toronto, Ontario, Canada: University of Toronto Press.

Moores, D.F. (1978). *Educating the deaf: Psychology, principles, and practices*. Boston: Houghton Mifflin.

Schmidt, S. (1985). Hearing-impaired students in physical education. *Adapted Physical Activity Quarterly, 2*, 300-306.

Scott, R.A. (1969). *The making of blind men: A study of adult socialization*. New York: Russell Sage Foundation.

Ulrich, D.A. (1985). *Test of gross motor development*. Austin, TX: Pro-Ed.

Winnick, J.P. (1979). *Early movement experiences and development: Habilitation and rehabilitation*. Philadelphia: Saunders.

Winnick, J.P. (1985). The performance of visually impaired youngsters in physical education activities: Implications for mainstreaming. *Adapted Physical Activity Quarterly, 2*, 292-299.

Winnick, J.P., & Short, F.X. (1985). *Physical fitness testing of the disabled: Project UNIQUE*. Champaign, IL: Human Kinetics.

Winnick, J.P., & Short, F.X. (1986). Physical fitness of adolescents with auditory impairments. *Adapted Physical Activity Quarterly, 3*, 58-66.

Resources

Written

Lange, E. (1975). *Adapted physical education for the deaf-blind child*. Raleigh, NC: Department of Public Instruction. This curriculum guide addresses the teaching of physical education to deaf-blind children.

Sonkson, P.M., Levitt, S., & Kitsinger, M. (1984). Identification of constraints acting on motor development in young visually disabled children and principles of remediation. *Child: Care, health and development, 10*, 273-286. This article discusses possible reasons for delays in motor development among visually impaired children and suggests activities that may minimize the delays.

Audiovisual

Buell, C. (1965). *Physical education for blind children* [Film]. Madison: University of Wisconsin Film Library. The film shows physical education classes conducted specifically for visually impaired children, emphasizing the success these students can have in sports.

Charlton, R., & Joaquin, P. (1979). *Survival run* [Film]. Berkeley: Extension Media Center, University of California. The film is about Harry Cordellos, a superb athlete who happens to be blind.

Getting through: A guide to better understanding of the hard-of-hearing [Record]. (1971). Chicago: Zenith Radio Corp. The record simulates various types of hearing losses.

Grupp, M. (Producer). (1981). *Sign of victory* [Film]. New York: FilmMakers Library. The film presents the story of the championship girls' basketball team from the Rhode Island School for the Deaf.

CHAPTER 15

Cerebral Palsy, Amputations, and Other Orthopedic Impairments

David L. Porretta

Children and youth with cerebral palsy (CP), amputations, and Les Autres (a French term meaning "the others") impairments were once restricted from physical activity for fear that it would aggravate their conditions. Now, they are encouraged to participate in a great variety of physical education and sport activities. Educators and medical specialists alike now realize the benefits of physical activity for the development of physical and motor fitness, self-image, and socialization.

Cerebral Palsy

Cerebral palsy (CP) is a group of permanent disabling symptoms resulting from damage to the motor control areas of the brain. It is a nonprogressive condition that may originate before, during, or after birth, and that manifests itself in a loss or impairment of control over voluntary musculature. Depending on the location and the amount of damage to the brain, symptoms may vary widely, ranging from severe (total inability to control bodily movements) to very mild (only a slight speech impairment). Damage to the brain contributes to abnormal reflex development in the majority of individuals; this results in difficulty coordinating and integrating basic movement patterns. It is rare for damage to be isolated in a small portion of the brain. For this reason, the person commonly exhibits a multiplicity of other impairments, which may include mental retardation, seizures, speech and language disorders, and sensory and/or perceptual impairments (especially those involving visual-motor control). CP can result from a myriad of prenatal, natal, or postnatal causes. Some of the more common causes are rubella, Rh incompatibility, prematurity, birth trauma, anoxia, meningitis, poisoning, and brain hemorrhages or tumors.

Incidence

Approximately 700,000 Americans have CP, and, of this number, one third are under 21 years of age. Approximately seven infants are born with CP per 100,000 live births. Prenatal (congenital) CP constitutes about 60% of all cases.

Classifications

CP individuals typically exhibit a variety of observable symptoms, depending on the degree and location of brain damage. Over the years, classification schemes have evolved that categorize CP according to *topographical (anatomical site)*, *neuromotor (medical)*, and *functional* perspectives (of which the functional classification is the most recent).

Topographical

The topographical classification is based on the body segments afflicted. Classes include

- monoplegia—any one body part involved,
- diplegia—major involvement of both lower limbs and minor involvement of both upper limbs,
- hemiplegia—involvement of one complete side of the body (arm and leg),
- triplegia—any three limbs involved, and
- quadriplegia—all four limbs involved.

Neuromotor

In 1956, the American Academy for Cerebral Palsy adopted a neuromotor classification system to describe cerebral palsy (Minear, 1956). This system is composed of six types.

Spasticity. Spasticity results from damage to motor areas of the cerebrum and is characterized by increased muscle tone (hypertonicity), primarily of the flexors and internal rotators, which may lead to permanent contractures and bone deformities. Strong, exaggerated muscle contractions are common, and in some cases muscles will continue to contract repetitively. Spasticity is associated with a *hyperactive stretch reflex*. The hyperactive reflex can be elicited, for example, when muscles of the anterior forearm (flexors) are quickly stretched in order to extend the wrist. When this happens, receptors that control tone in the stretched muscles overreact, causing the stretched muscles to contract. This results in inaccurate and jerky movement, with the wrist assuming a flexed as opposed to an extended or midposition. If muscles of the upper limb are prone to spasticity, the shoulder will be adducted, the arm will be carried toward the midline of the body, and the forearm will be flexed and pronated. The wrist will be hyperflexed and the hand will be fisted.

Lower-limb involvement results in hip flexion, with the thigh pulling toward the midline, causing the leg to cross during ambulation. Lower-limb involvement causes flexion at the knee joint because of tight hamstring muscles. Increased tone in both the gastrocnemius and soleus muscles, along with a shortened Achilles tendon, contributes to excessive plantar flexion of the foot. A scissoring gait characterized by flexion of the hip, knee, and ankle along with rotation of the leg toward the midline is exhibited (Figure 15.1). With their narrow base of support, people with a scissoring gait typically have problems with balance and locomotor activities. Because of increased muscle contraction and limited range of motion, they may have difficulty running, jumping, and throwing properly. Mental retardation,

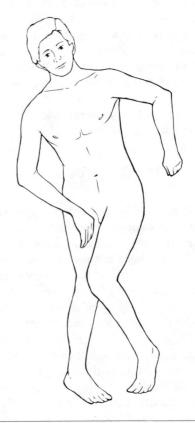

Figure 15.1 Person exhibiting spastic cerebral palsy.

seizures, and perceptual disorders are more common in spasticity than in any other type of cerebral palsy. Approximately 50% of all cerebral-palsied individuals are of this type.

Athetosis.   Damage to the basal ganglia (masses of gray matter located deep within the cerebral hemispheres of the brain) results in an overflow of motor impulses to the muscles, a condition known as athetosis (Figure 15.2). Slow, writhing movements that are uncoordinated and involuntary are characteristic of this type of cerebral palsy. Muscle tone tends to fluctuate from hypertonicity to hypotonicity; the fluctuation typically affects muscles that control the head, neck, limbs, and trunk. Severe difficulty in head control is usually exhibited, with the head drawn back and positioned to one side. Facial grimacing, a protruding tongue, and trouble controlling salivation are common. The individual has difficulty eating, drinking, and speaking. Because lack of head control affects visual pursuit, affected individuals may have difficulty tracking thrown balls or responding to quick movements made by others in activity situations. They will have difficulty performing movements that require accuracy, such as throwing a ball to a target or kicking a moving ball. A lordotic standing posture, in which the lumbar spine assumes an abnormal anterior curve, is common. In compensation, the arms and shoulders are placed in a forward position. Athetoids typically exhibit aphasia (impairment or loss of language) and articulation difficulties. This type comprises approximately 20% of the entire CP population.

Ataxia.   Damage to the cerebellum, which normally regulates balance and muscle coordination, results in a condition known as ataxia (see Figure 15.2). Muscles show abnormal degrees of

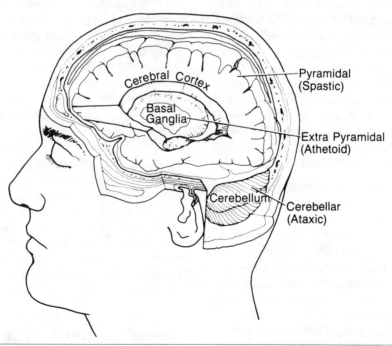

Figure 15.2   General areas of the brain involved in major neuromotor types of cerebral palsy. *Note.* From *Physically Handicapped Children: A Medical Atlas for Teachers* (2nd ed.) (p. 67) by E.E. Bleck and D.A. Nagel (Eds.), 1982, New York: Grune & Stratton. Copyright 1982 by Grune & Stratton. Reprinted by permission.

hypotonicity. Ataxia is usually not diagnosed until the child attempts to walk. When trying to walk, the individual is extremely unsteady because of balance difficulties and lacks the coordination necessary for proper arm and leg movement. A wide-based gait is typically exhibited. Nystagmus, a constant involuntary movement of the eyeball, is commonly observed, and those able to ambulate frequently fall. People with mild forms of ataxia are often considered clumsy or awkward. They will experience difficulty with basic motor skills and patterns, especially locomotor activities like running, jumping, and skipping. Ataxia occurs in about 10% of the CP population.

Tremor. Tremor results from damage to the basal ganglia and is characterized by involuntary rhythmic movement. Voluntary movements tend to increase shaking and trembling of the affected limb. Tremor can be classified as either non-intentional (continuous) or intentional (only when movement is attempted) in nature. Nonintentional tremor is uncommon in children. People who have cerebral palsy of the tremor type have greater success with gross motor than with fine motor movements. Unlike gross motor activities, where general movement patterns predominate, fine motor activities require precision of movement. As a result, activities such as writing, drawing, archery, or pistol shooting will be difficult. Only about 2% of all CP individuals exhibit tremor.

Rigidity. Rigidity is associated with diffuse damage to the brain, not damage to any specific area. It is considered a severe form of spasticity in which the stretch reflex is weak or absent. Severe hypertonicity and reduced range of motion are present, and affected individuals are usually quadriplegic. The elbows, knee joints, and spine tend to remain in an extended position. Flexion movements are, therefore, difficult, and the rigid limb exhibits greater resistance to slow than to rapid movement. Some activities, like certain dances that require the person to perform slowly while bending the limbs and trunk, will be difficult if not impossible. Severe mental retardation

is common; therefore, uncomplicated lead-up activities should be presented. Only about 2% to 4% of all CP individuals are affected by rigidity.

Mixed. When an individual possesses two or more of the above conditions in equal degrees, a rare mixed condition exists. People assigned to the mixed classification are usually quadriplegic and have both spasticity and athetosis equally. When no one type of CP predominates, the individual should be classified as mixed (Bleck, 1982).

Functional

A *functional classification* scheme is commonly used today in the field of education. According to this classification system, students are placed into one of eight classes according to the severity of the disability (see Table 15.1). Class I denotes severe impairment, while Class VIII denotes very minimal impairment. This scheme has important implications for physical education and sport, because individuals are categorized according to ability level. For example, participants in Classes VII and VIII may be good candidates for inclusion in regular physical education settings, especially for activities that require a significant amount of locomotion. Teachers and coaches can also use this system, as does the United States Cerebral Palsy Athletic Association (USCPAA), to assist in equalizing competition among participants. In activities requiring competition between two individuals, players of the same classification can compete against each other. In team activities, players of the same class can be placed on separate teams so that each team is composed of players of similar functional levels. These suggestions for equalizing competition can be followed in both integrated and segregated settings.

General Educational Considerations

From a medical standpoint, treatment for CP is aimed at alleviating symptoms caused by damage to the brain. This consists of treating both motor

Table 15.1   Functional Classification Scheme for Cerebral Palsy

	Class description	Mode of ambulation
I	Severe quadriplegia, spasticity mostly prevalent, limited trunk control, unable to grasp a softball, poor functional strength	Electric wheelchair
II	Severe to moderate quadriplegia, better upper extremity range of motion and coordination than Class I, poor functional strength and severe control problems in the upper extremities	Propels wheelchair with legs
III	Moderate quadriplegia, fair functional strength and moderate control problems in upper extremities and torso	Wheelchair for daily activities but may ambulate with assistive devices
IV	Moderate to severe problems in lower limbs, good functional strength and minimal control problems in upper limbs and torso	Wheelchair for daily activities but may ambulate with assistive devices
V	Good functional strength and minimal control problems in upper limbs	No wheelchair, may or may not use assistive devices
VI	Moderate to severe quadriplegia, greater upper limb involvement, less coordination/balance problems when running or throwing	Ambulates without walking devices
VII	Moderate to minimal hemiplegia, good functional ability in nonaffected side, walks/runs with a limp	Walks without assistive devices
VIII	Minimal hemiplegia, may have minimal coordination problems, good balance	Runs and jumps freely

Note. From *Sport and Disabled Athletes: The 1984 Olympic Scientific Congress* (Vol. 9), p. 119, C. Sherrill (Ed.), 1986, Champaign, IL: Human Kinetics. Copyright 1986 by Human Kinetics. Adapted by permission.

and other associated disabilities. Treatment for motor dysfunction usually entails developing voluntary muscle control, emphasizing muscle relaxation, and increasing functional motor skills. In some instances, braces and orthotic devices are used to help prevent permanent contractures or support affected muscle groups; this is especially true for those with spasticity. Surgery can be performed to lengthen contracted tendons (especially the Achilles tendon) or to reposition an unimpaired muscle to perform the movement of an impaired one. A repositioning operation known as the Eggar's procedure relieves flexion at the knee joint

and helps to extend the hip by transferring the insertion of the hamstrings from the pelvis to the femur. In rare instances, brain surgery can be performed to alleviate extreme hypertonicity. A procedure known as chronic cerebellar stimulation (CCS), in which electrodes are surgically implanted on the cerebellum, has recently been developed. This procedure has demonstrated improvement; however, long-range effects on the central nervous system have not yet been documented.

Because of central nervous system damage, many CP individuals exhibit abnormal reflex development, which interferes with the acquisition of voluntary movement. If abnormal reflex patterns are present, young CP children will most likely receive physical therapy designed to inhibit abnormal reflex activity in addition to enhancing flexibility and body alignment. As the student progresses in age, the emphasis is transferred to the development and attainment of functional motor skills.

Attention must also be given to the psychological and social development of CP individuals. The various disabilities associated with CP increase the possibility of adjustment problems. Because of the negative reactions that other people may have to their condition, CP individuals may not be socially accepted. As a result, guidance from psychologists or professional counselors should be sought for both parents and their children when emotional conflicts arise.

The primary concern should be for the *total* person. A team approach in which both medical and educational personnel work together with the parent and, when appropriate, the student, is recommended.

Amputations

Amputation refers to the loss of an entire limb or of a specific limb segment. Amputations may be categorized as either acquired or congenital. Acquired amputations can result from disease, tumor, or trauma; congenital amputations result from failure of the fetus to properly develop during the first 3 months of gestation. In most cases, the cause or causes of partial or total congenital limb absence are unknown. Generally, there are two types of congenital deformities. In one type, a middle segment of a limb is absent, but the proximal and distal portions are intact; this is known as *phocomelia*. Here, the hand or foot is attached directly to the shoulder or hip without the remaining anatomical structures present. The second type of deficiency is similar to surgical amputation, where no normal structures, like hands or fingers,

are present below the missing segment. In many cases, however, immature finger-like buds are present; this deficiency is usually below the elbow and unilateral.

Incidence

It has been estimated that more than 300,000 people in the United States are amputees, of whom more than two thirds are missing a lower limb. Of this number, about 7% are below 21 years of age. Unlike the general population of amputees, those below age 21 have a greater percentage of upper- than lower-limb losses. Congenital limb losses are approximately twice as prevalent as acquired losses for those under 21 years old.

Classification

Amputations can be classified according to the site and level of limb absence or from a *functional* point of view. The United States Amputee Athletic Association (USAAA) classifies amputations according to both the site of amputation and functional ability ("Competitive Classifications," 1985). Nine classes are identified as follows:

- Class A1—Double above the knee (AK)
- Class A2—Single AK
- Class A3—Double below the knee (BK)
- Class A4—Single BK
- Class A5—Double above the elbow (AE)
- Class A6—Single AE
- Class A7—Double below the elbow (BE)
- Class A8—Single BE
- Class A9—Combined lower plus upper limb amputations

According to this system, Class A8 represents functional ability greater than Class A1.

General Educational Considerations

In nearly all cases, a *prosthetic device* is prescribed and selected for the amputee by a team of medical specialists (Figure 15.3). The prosthetic device is designed to compensate, as much as possible, for the functional loss of the limb. Devices are chosen according to the size of the individual and the area and extent of limb absence. Most authorities favor the use of a prosthetic device as early as possible following the loss of the limb because the device tends to be more easily incorporated into the person's normal body actions than if it were introduced later. Learning to use a device takes time and effort, and some with more extensive lower-limb amputations need training with canes or crutches.

Limb-deficient individuals often have psychosocial needs that require attention. Many feel shame, inferiority, and anxiety when in a social setting—feelings that may result from the stares or comments of others. Individual counseling by a psychologist or professional counselor may be needed to foster healthy emotional functioning.

Les Autres

Muscular Dystrophy

Muscular dystrophy is actually considered a group of inherited diseases that are characterized by progressive, diffuse weakness of various muscle groups. Muscle cells within the belly of the muscles degenerate and are replaced by adipose and connective tissue. The dystrophy itself is not fatal, but secondary complications of muscle weakness predispose the person to respiratory disorders and heart problems. It is quite common for dystrophic individuals in advanced stages of the disease to die from a simple respiratory infection or as a result of myocardial involvement.

There are various types of muscular dystrophy, including the *facio-scapulo-humeral, limb-girdle*, and *Duchenne* types. The facio-scapulo-humeral type initially affects muscles of the shoulders and face and, in some instances, the hip and thigh. Life expectancy is usually normal because this type of dystrophy may arrest itself at any time. In limb-girdle muscular dystrophy, degeneration may begin in either the shoulder or the hip girdle, with eventual involvement of both. Unlike the facio-scapulo-humeral type, degeneration continues at a slow rate. Facio-scapulo-humeral dystrophy manifests itself during adolescence or adulthood. The limb-girdle type may be exhibited at any time from late childhood on, though it usually occurs during the teenage years. With both facio-scapulo-humeral and limb-girdle dystrophy, males and females are equally affected.

Duchenne muscular dystrophy is the most common of all dystrophies, appears in childhood, and affects more boys than girls. Symptoms may occur as early as age 3, or may not appear until the child is 10 years old. The Duchenne type is commonly

Figure 15.3 Child with prosthetic device. *Note.* From *Physically Handicapped Children: A Medical Atlas for Teachers* (2nd ed.) (p. 23) by E.E. Bleck and D.A. Nagel (Eds.), 1982, New York: Grune & Stratton. Copyright 1982 by Grune & Stratton. Reprinted by permission.

referred to as *pseudohypertrophic muscular dystrophy*. A pseudohypertrophic appearance, especially of the calf and forearm muscles, is the result of an excessive accumulation of adipose and connective tissues within the interstitial spaces between degenerated muscle cells. It is yet to be determined how this happens. In addition, there is atrophy and weakness of the thigh, hip, back, shoulder girdle, and respiratory muscles. The anterior tibialis muscle of the lower leg becomes extremely weak, resulting in a *drop* foot where the foot remains angled in a downward manner; thus, the individual is prone to falling. Steady and rapid progression of the disease usually leads to the inability to walk within approximately 10 years after onset. The child exhibits characteristics that include

- a waddling gait,
- difficulty in climbing stairs,
- a tendency to fall, and
- difficulty in rising from a recumbent position.

Lordosis frequently develops from weakness of the trunk musculature. As the disease progresses, the individual eventually becomes confined to a wheelchair and grows obese. In addition, contractures may form at the ankle, knee, and hip joints, and muscle atrophy is extensive. Death often results in about the third decade of life. At present, no treatment exists to stop muscle atrophy; any treatment given is basically symptomatic. A major treatment goal is to maintain ambulation as long as possible.

Physical education can play an important role in managing muscular dystrophy. Muscular strength and endurance activities programmed on a regular basis can have a positive effect on muscular development and can serve to counteract progressive muscular dystrophy. Particular attention should be given to the development of the lower leg, hip, abdomen, and thigh. For people with weak respiratory muscles, especially those confined to wheelchairs, breathing exercises and activities should be given priority and performed on a daily basis. Strength and endurance can be developed through aquatic activities, which utilize water as resistance. Performed on a regular basis, flexibility activities and exercises help to develop or maintain the person's range of motion so that permanent joint contractures do not develop; flexibility activities that help keep the child's attention may be chosen. Various dance movements are particularly helpful for improving flexibility. Arm and upper-body movements for those in wheelchairs can be performed to music. Postural exercises and activities help reduce lordosis and give the person an opportunity to perform out of the wheelchair.

Juvenile Rheumatoid Arthritis

Juvenile rheumatoid arthritis (JRA), or *Still's disease*, manifests itself in childhood. As with adult rheumatoid arthritis, the cause of JRA is unknown. Depending on the degree of involvement, JRA affects joint movement. Joints become inflamed, and the result is reduced range of motion. In some cases, permanent joint contractures develop and muscle atrophy is pronounced. Some authorities suggest that inflammation of the joints results from abnormal antibodies of unknown origin that circulate in the blood and destroy the body's normal structures. The disease is not inherited, nor does it seem to be a result of climate, diet, or patterns of living. It may manifest itself as early as 6 weeks of age. As many as 250,000 children possess the disease to varying degrees; it afflicts more girls than boys. JRA is characterized by a series of remissions and exacerbations (attacks). One cannot predict how long affected children will remain ill or the length of time they will be symptom-free. Generally, the prognosis for JRA is quite encouraging: Approximately 60% to 70% of children will be free of the disease with no permanent joint damage 10 years after onset. Others, however, will have severe and permanent functional disability.

At present, there is no cure for JRA. Treatment for severe periods of exacerbation consists of controlling joint inflammation, which is accomplished through medicine, rest, appropriately designed exercises, and, in some cases, surgery. During acute stages, complete bed rest is strongly recommended, and excessive weight bearing by inflamed joints should be avoided. In some instances, surgery may be performed to remove damaged tissue from the joint in order to prevent greater deterioration to bone and cartilage. Total hip replacements are now performed in some cases with great success.

Even during acute stages of JRA, joints should be exercised through the greatest possible range of motion at least once or twice a day so range of motion can be maintained. For individuals unable to exercise independently, teachers or therapists can provide partial or total assistance.

The physical education program should stress exercises and activities that help increase or maintain range of motion so that permanent contractures do not develop. Muscular strength and endurance activities should also be offered to decrease muscle atrophy. Isometric activities, such as hooking the fingers of both hands together and trying to pull them apart or placing the palms together and pushing, may be particularly helpful to encourage the development of hand muscles. Another hand exercise involves squeezing objects of various sizes and shapes. Most people with severe joint inflammation or deterioration should refrain from activities that twist, jar, or place undue stress upon the joints; activities like basketball, volleyball, and tennis may need to be modified accordingly.

Osteogenesis Imperfecta

Osteogenesis imperfecta, also known as *brittle bone disease*, is an inherited condition in which bones are imperfectly formed. An unknown cause produces a defect in the protein matrix of collagen fibers. The defect reduces the amount of calcium and phosphorous (bone salts), which in turn produces a weak bone structure. Bones are very easily broken. When healed, they take on a shortened, bowed appearance. Other affected body

parts that include collagen are joint ligaments, skin, and the sclera (white portion) of the eye. Joint tissues exhibit abnormal elasticity, the skin appears translucent, and the thinning sclera takes on a blue discoloration as the choroid (underlying eyeball) is exposed. There are two types of osteogenesis imperfecta: *congenital* (present at birth) and *tarda* (with later onset). The congenital type is severe, while the tarda type is mild. Many students with the severe form require the use of crutches or wheelchairs. There is no cure for the disease. At the present time, surgery is the most effective treatment; it consists of reinforcing the bone by inserting a steel rod lengthwise through its shaft.

Physical education activities such as swimming, bowling (with some modifications), and the use of Nerf or beach balls for striking and catching are safe to perform because they do not place undue stress upon the joints or bones. Because of abnormal joint elasticity, strength-building exercises and activities, which can increase joint stability, should be encouraged. This may be accomplished in a swimming environment. Most people with the disorder should not play power volleyball, basketball, or football unless the games are modified appropriately.

Arthrogryposis

Arthrogryposis (ar-throw-gry-po-sis), also known as *multiple congenital contractures*, is a nonprogressive congenital disease of unknown origin. Approximately 500 infants in the United States are born with arthrogryposis each year. The condition, which may affect some or all of the joints, is characterized by stiff joints (contractures) and weak muscles. Instead of normal muscle tissue surrounding the joints, fatty and connective tissue is present. The severity of the condition varies; an individual may be in a wheelchair or be only minimally affected. Limbs commonly exhibit deformities and can be fixed in almost any position. In addition, affected limbs are usually small in circumference, and joints appear large. Surgery, casting, and bracing are usually recommended for people with deformities. Most typically, upper limb involvement includes turned-in shoulders, extended and straightened elbows, pronated forearms, and flexed wrists and fingers; trunk and lower-limb involvement includes flexion and outward rotation of the hip, bent or straightened knees, and feet that are turned in and down. Other conditions associated with the disease include congenital heart defects, respiratory problems, and various facial abnormalities. Individuals with arthrogryposis almost always possess normal intelligence and speech.

Because people with this disease have restricted range of motion, their physical education program should focus on exercises and activities that increase flexibility. In addition, they should be taught games and sports that effectively make use of leisure time. In most cases, exercises and activities that are appropriate for arthritic individuals are also acceptable for those with arthrogryposis. Swimming, an excellent leisure activity, encourages the development of flexibility and serves to strengthen weak muscles surrounding joints. Other activities, modified when needed, may include miniature golf, bowling, shuffleboard, boccia, and track and field events.

Multiple Sclerosis

Approximately 500,000 people in the United States have multiple sclerosis (MS). It is a slowly progressive neurological disorder that may result in total incapacitation and death. The disease generally appears between the ages of 20 and 40, but it may manifest itself in young children or the elderly. It affects more women than men. MS is characterized by changes in the white matter covering (myelin sheath) of nerve fibers at various locations throughout the central nervous system (brain and spinal cord); the cause is unknown. The myelin sheath is destroyed and is replaced by scar tissue; a lesion may vary from the size of a pinpoint to about 1/2 in. in diameter. Individuals with

MS exhibit various symptoms, depending on the location of the damage. The most common symptoms are numbness, general weakness, double vision, slurred speech, staggering gait, and partial or complete paralysis. The early stage of the disease is characterized by periods of exacerbation followed by periods of remission. As scar tissue continues to replace healthy tissue, the symptoms tend to continue uninterrupted.

Because most people with MS are stricken in the most productive and enjoyable years of life, many are unable to cope emotionally with the disease. Additional stress results from the fact that there is no established treatment that can cure it. The main treatment objective is to maintain the person's functional ability as long as possible. Treatment should be directed toward preventing loss of range of motion (which would result in permanent contractures) and preserving strength and endurance. Many times the disease progresses to a point where the person needs braces or a wheelchair. Intensive therapy or physical conditioning during acute phases of MS may cause general body fatigue. Therefore, physical activities should be judiciously programmed for the MS individual.

Mild forms of physical activity that emphasize strength and endurance should be performed for short periods of time. However, the duration and intensity of the activity should be programmed according to the individual's exercise tolerance level. Activities such as bowling, miniature golf, and table tennis are acceptable if regular rest periods are provided. In addition, a variety of stretching exercises and activities are recommended to maintain adequate range of motion. Activities incorporating balance and agility components may prove to be helpful for those exhibiting staggering gait or varying degrees of paralysis. Many of these activities can be done in water.

Friedreich's Ataxia

An inherited neurological disease, Friedreich's ataxia usually manifests itself in childhood and early adolesence. It is characterized by progressive degeneration of sensory nerves of the limbs and trunk and may progress in either a slow or a rapid manner. When the disease progresses quickly, many people become wheelchair bound by the late teens and early twenties. Early symptoms may be poor balance and lack of limb and trunk coordination, resulting in a clumsy, awkward, wide-based gait almost indistinguishable from the gait of ataxic cerebral palsy. Fine motor control of the upper limbs tends to be impaired because tremors may be present. Atrophy is common in muscles of the distal limbs. Affected individuals typically exhibit slurred speech and are prone to seizures. Most will develop foot deformities such as clubfoot, high arches, and hammertoes, a condition in which the toes are curled because of tight flexor tendons of the second and third toes. As the disease progresses, spinal deformities such as kyphosis and scoliosis are common. The majority of individuals exhibit heart problems such as heart murmur, enlarged heart, and constriction of the aorta and pulmonary arteries. Visual abnormalities include nystagmus and poor visual tracking. Therapy consists of managing foot and spinal deformities and cardiac conditions. Medication may be prescribed to control cardiac, tremor, and seizure disorders.

Physical education activities should be planned to promote muscle strength and endurance and body coordination. Activities that develop muscles of the distal limbs such as the wrist, forearm, foot, and lower leg are recommended. The development of grip strength is essential for activities that utilize implements such as rackets and bats. Individuals exhibiting poor balance and lack of coordination are in need of balance training and activities that encourage development of fundamental locomotor movements. For those with fine motor control difficulties, activities may take the form of riflery, billiards, or archery. Remedial exercises are recommended for people with foot and spinal deviations. Games, exercises, and activities should be programmed according to individual tolerance

levels for those with cardiac conditions, and those prone to seizures should be closely monitored.

Myasthenia Gravis

Myasthenia gravis is a disease characterized by a reduction in muscular strength that may be minimal or severe. Even when strength is greatly reduced the individual still has enough strength to perform activities, but often this demands maximum or near maximum effort. In some cases, the disease is easily confused with muscular dystrophy because muscle weakness affects the back, lower extremities, and intercostal muscles. It affects twice as many females as males and occurs most often in the fourth decade, though some cases have shown that adolescent girls can exhibit the disease. Although the cause is not known, some authorities believe that nerve impulses are prevented from reaching the muscle fiber because of the production of an abnormal chemical compound at the distal end of the motor nerve.

One of the main symptoms is abnormal fatigue. Muscles generally appear normal except for some disuse atrophy. Weakness of the extraocular and lid muscles of the eye occurs in about one half of all cases; this results in drooping of the eyelid (ptosis) and double vision (strabismus). Because facial, jaw, and tongue muscles become easily fatigued, individuals may have problems chewing and speaking. Weakness of the neck muscles may cause the person not to hold the head erect. Back musculature may also be weakened; this leads to malalignment of the spinal column, which can further restrict movement. Muscle weakness makes the execution of the activities of daily living difficult and contributes to low levels of cardiorespiratory efficiency. The disease is not progressive; it may appear gradually, or it may be sudden. It commonly goes into remission for weeks, months, or years. Affected individuals, therefore, live in fear of recurrent attacks.

Physical education activities should focus on the development of physical fitness. Because people with myasthenia gravis fatigue easily, their activities should be programmed in a progressive manner and according to individual tolerance levels that take into account the duration, intensity, and frequency of the activity. When the muscles of respiration are weakened, breathing activities are strongly recommended. It is important to strengthen weak neck muscles, especially when the program includes such activities as heading a soccer ball or hitting a volleyball. Fitness levels can be maintained during acute stages through swimming activities incorporated into the program. Poor body mechanics resulting from weak musculature will ultimately affect locomotor skills; therefore, remedial posture exercises and activities should be offered.

Guillain-Barré Syndrome

Guillain-Barré syndrome (also known as *infectious polyneuritis* or *infectious neuronitis)* is a neurological disorder characterized by ascending paralysis of peripheral and cranial nerves. Spinal and cranial nerves are affected, which results in acute and progressive paralysis. Initially, the lower extremities become easily fatigued, and numbness, tingling, and symmetrical weakness are present. Paralysis, which usually originates in the feet and lower legs, progresses to the upper leg, continues on to the trunk and upper extremities, and finally affects the facial muscles. Symptoms usually reach their maximum within a few weeks. When initially affected, people involved in locomotor activities of an endurance nature, like distance running, typically find themselves stumbling or falling during the activity session as muscles of the feet and lower legs fatigue prematurely. The condition is frequently preceded by a respiratory or gastrointestinal infection, which suggests that a virus may be the cause. However, attempts to isolate a virus have not been successful. Some authorities believe that the syndrome is an autoimmune disease.

Guillain-Barré syndrome affects both males and females equally. It may affect both infants and the elderly but seems to cluster in childhood and middle age. While about one third of those stricken with the syndrome may die, the majority recover, either completely or with minimal paralysis. Acute stage treatment includes warm, wet applications to the extremities, passive range-of-motion exercises, and rest.

For people who have made complete recovery, no restrictions in physical activities are needed. However, some individuals who do not completely recover exhibit weakness in limb and respiratory muscles. Their activities can focus on maintaining or improving cardiorespiratory endurance and strength and endurance of unaffected muscles. When a significant amount of weakness remains in the lower extremities, activities may need to be modified accordingly.

Program Implications

All people with cerebral palsy, amputations, or Les Autres conditions can benefit from physical education and sport activities. The type and degree of physical disability, motor educability, interest level, and overall educational goals will determine the modifications and adaptations that are needed. With these factors taken into account, the instructional program can be individualized and personalized.

General Guidelines

A number of general guidelines can be applied to programs for people with cerebral palsy, amputations, and Les Autres conditions. The guidelines which follow pertain to safety considerations, physical fitness, motor development, psychosocial development, and implications for sports.

Safety Considerations

All programs should be conducted in a safe and secure environment in which students are free to explore the capabilities of their own bodies and to interact with surroundings that will nurture their physical and motor development. Activity areas should always be well padded for those who are considered clumsy or who ambulate with assistive devices.

More severely impaired students will need special equipment, such as bolsters (to support the upper body while in the prone position) or standing platforms (to assist them in maintaining a standing posture) to help them perform various motor tasks. However, students with mild impairment will need no specialized equipment. Because many physically disabled persons have difficulty maintaining an erect posture for extended periods of time, some activities are best done in a prone, supine, or sitting position. Bolsters can provide movement assistance in the prone position, while specially designed chairs or seats equipped with belts or straps can help in performing movements from a sitting position.

Because of abnormal muscle tone and reduced range of motion, many individuals with neuromotor involvement have difficulty moving voluntarily. The teacher may need to assist in the following ways:

- Getting the person into and out of activity positions
- Supporting the person during activity
- Helping the person execute a specific skill or exercise

The teacher may need to position students by applying varying degrees of pressure with the hands to key points of the body such as the head, neck, spine, shoulders, elbows, hips, pelvis, knees, and ankles. An example is applying both hands symmetrically to both of the individual's elbows in order to reduce flexion at the elbow joints. Finnie (1975) suggests that the ultimate aim of handling and positioning CP individuals is to continually encourage them to move as independently as possible. This is accomplished by gradually reducing the amount of support to key points

of the body over a period of time. Teachers should consult with therapists whenever possible in an effort to coordinate positioning procedures. In addition, teachers should closely monitor physical assistance that a disabled student receives from his or her peers. Peer assistance should be discouraged if it poses a safety risk.

Because all conditions described in this chapter are of medical origin, it is important that physical educators consult medical professionals when establishing programs to meet unique needs. This is especially important for students who are receiving physical or occupational therapy or who are convalescing under the care of a physician for their condition.

Physical Fitness

Reduced muscular strength, flexibility, and cardiovascular endurance levels are common in students with physical handicaps, especially in comparison to the normal population. Winnick and Short (1982) found that young people with CP or spinal neuromuscular conditions exhibited physical fitness levels significantly below those of normal youth. When compared to normal youth, youngsters with paraplegic spinal neuromuscular conditions generally exhibited significantly inferior scores on items that included grip strength, flexed-arm hang, and pull-ups. Compared to able-bodied youngsters, CP youth scored significantly lower on items that included sit-ups, leg raise, sit-and-reach, grip strength, flexed-arm hang, pull-ups, and standing long jump. When compared to youngsters with paraplegic spinal neuromuscular conditions, CP individuals had lower levels of fitness. Both groups were more variable in their performances when compared to normal youngsters. This variability is probably due to the wide range in the severity of each impairment. On muscular strength and endurance measures, CP youngsters generally performed between one and two standard deviation units below normal youngsters.

Winnick and Short (1982) found similar scores when comparing CP subjects to able-bodied youth on skinfold measures. Nevertheless, there was a trend for those with paraplegic spinal neuromuscular conditions to exhibit skinfold measures greater than those of able-bodied youth. Individuals with higher skinfold measures may be in greater need of continuous aerobic activities (such as running, swimming, or wheeling for distance) so that skinfold measures can be reduced.

In general, less severely impaired youngsters exhibited better fitness scores than those more severely impaired. Winnick and Short (1982) reported that, while nonimpaired youngsters increase fitness scores as they get older, this was not the case with the orthopedically impaired youngsters in their study. In fact, in some instances, fitness levels decreased as impaired youngsters increased in age. These data strongly suggest the need for physical fitness development with young, severely impaired people. Recommended tests for *assessing physical and motor fitness* in persons with CP, amputations, and Les Autres conditions include the following:

- Project UNIQUE Physical Fitness Test
- Hughes Basic Gross Motor Assessment
- Project ACTIVE Motor Ability Test for the Severely Multihandicapped

For students with low fitness levels, certain precautions may need to be taken as fitness programs are established. It is especially important that the teacher be sensitive to the frequency, intensity, and duration of exercises and activities. Fatigue may cause the child to become frustrated, which in turn adversely affects proper performance. The instructor should permit rest periods when endurance-related activities are offered. For example, players should be substituted during games of soccer or basketball. Because restricted movement is common for individuals whose conditions are described in this chapter, it is vitally important that strength and flexibility be developed to the maximum extent possible. Weak musculature and limited range of motion, if unattended, will lead to permanent joint contractures that result in significant loss of movement capability.

Motor Development

CP, amputations, and Les Autres impairments restrict individuals from experiencing normal movement patterns that are essential to normal motor development. As a result, delays in motor control and development are common. CP individuals typically exhibit motor delays because they either lack movement ability or have difficulty in controlling movements. Children with congenital amputations are frequently unable to execute fundamental movements in an appropriate manner. A child born with the absence of a lower limb, for example, may be delayed in acquiring locomotor patterns such as creeping, walking, and running. Conditions that result in muscle atrophy, like muscular dystrophy or Friedreich's ataxia, prevent individuals from developing the strength and endurance levels needed to perform fundamental movements.

Physical education programs should encourage the sequential development of fundamental motor patterns and skills essential for participation in games, sports, and leisure activities. When attempting to enhance motor development levels, the physical educator should be concerned primarily with the manner in which a movement is performed rather than with its outcome. The goal of every physical education program should be to encourage individuals to achieve maximum motor control and development. *Motor development tests* recommended for use with persons who have CP, amputations, and Les Autres conditions include the following:

- The Denver Developmental Screening Test
- The Bayley Scales of Infant Development
- Milani-Comparetti Developmental Chart

Psychosocial Development

Many people with CP, amputations, and Les Autres conditions lack self-confidence, have low motivational levels, and exhibit problems with body image. An appropriately designed physical education program can provide successful movement experiences that not only motivate students, but also help them gain the self-confidence needed to develop a positive self-image, which is vitally important for emotional well-being. A realistic body image can be developed when the physical education teacher does not expect students to perform skills and activities perfectly. Rather, it is more important that the student perform the activity as independently as possible with a specified degree of success. The teacher should promote the attitude that it is acceptable for students to fail at times when attempting activities because this is a natural part of the learning process. Physical activities perceived as fun and not hard work can motivate students to perform to their maximum potential.

Implications for Sports

Physical education teachers are encouraged to integrate into their programs many of the sport activities described in the "Adapted Sports" section of this chapter. For example, the club throw or thrust kick, two field events of the USCPAA, can be incorporated in a physical education program as a means of developing strength and can also offer opportunity for sport competition. Other events (included in USCPAA and USAAA sport programs) such as bowling, archery, cycling, and boccia can be taught with a view toward future competition or leisure activity. Team games and sports may include volleyball, softball, basketball, soccer, floor hockey, and touch football. Cosom hockey, a combination of ice hockey and basketball, can also be included in the physical education program especially for people in wheelchairs (Adams, Daniel, McCubbin, & Rullman, 1982). It is played either indoors or outdoors with lightweight plastic sticks and pucks or balls. Players attempt to hit the puck or ball past the opponent's goal.

Individual and dual activities may include tennis, table tennis, riflery, archery, badminton, fencing, horseback riding, weight lifting, gymnastics, billiards, and track and field. Another appropriate individual activity may be a wheelchair cross-country biathlon (Adams et al., 1982). The objective of this activity is to accurately shoot a BB gun at a target 15 ft away at two separate stations along a predetermined course 100 to 300 ft in length. The course is to be traversed as quickly as possible. Winter activities, including ice hockey, ice skating, downhill and cross-country skiing, tobogganing, and sledding, are also popular in northern regions.

Cerebral Palsy

CP individuals exhibiting inappropriate reflexive behavior typically have difficulty learning and performing various motor skills. When a child is receiving therapy, is it important for the physical educator to work in conjunction with therapists in an effort to foster the suppression of certain abnormal reflexes and the facilitation of righting and equilibrium reactions. While many physical education activities help in the development of righting and equilibrium reactions, others may elicit abnormal reflexes. When attempting to catch a ball, for example, the person may be unable to place both hands in front of the body because an abnormal reflex overrides this voluntary movement.

As the student gets older, it may become apparent that, even with therapy, inappropriate reflexes will not be inhibited. Professionals responsible for the student's physical education program must therefore pursue attainment of functional skills, including sport skills. Activities determined to be inappropriate at a younger age may be acceptable when the student is older if the activity is found to have functional value. The attainment of functional skills such as creeping, walking, running, and throwing is important to future skill development and should be incorporated into the student's program. Asking older CP students to repetitively perform activities that elicit unwanted reflexes will not aggravate the condition of cerebral palsy.

Because of either restricted or extraneous movements, a CP individual may exert more energy than a nonimpaired person to accomplish the same task. The added energy output requires a greater degree of endurance. As a result, the duration of physical activities may need to be shortened.

Strength

In addressing the development of strength, it is important to note that muscle tone imbalances between flexor and extensor muscle groups are common in CP persons. For those with spastic tendencies, flexor muscles may be disproportionately stronger than the extensors. Therefore, strength development should focus on strengthening the extensor muscles. For example, even though a student may have increased tone of the forearm flexors while at the same time performing poorly on pull-ups, one should not continue to develop forearm flexors as opposed to forearm extensors. The goal is to develop and maintain a balance between flexor and extensor muscles throughout all regions of the body. Isokinetic resistance exercises are particularly useful for developing strength, probably because they provide constant tension through the full range of motion and aid in inhibiting jerky movements that are extraneous and uncontrolled. Moving limbs in diagonal patterns when developing strength is preferable to exercising isolated muscles. Simple diagonal patterns, for example, moving the entire arm across the body in a diagonal plane, encourage muscle groups to work in harmony. Such movements can be elicited by involving individuals in a variety of gross motor activities that may include throwing, striking, or kicking movements.

Flexibility

Tight muscles in both the upper and lower limbs and the hip region contribute to reduced flexibility. If left unattended, restricted range of motion leads to contractures and bone deformities. Surburg (1986) recommends that more emphasis be placed on relaxing affected muscles than on stretching them. The instructor may wish to begin a flexi-

bility program session by helping students relax target muscle groups. When stretching exercises are used, they should be of a static, as opposed to a ballistic, nature, and they should be done both before and after strength and endurance activities. If an individual is participating in a ballistic type of activity such as a club throw, ballistic stretching can be used, but it should be preceded by static stretching. Stretching exercises for more severely affected body parts should be done on a daily basis. Therefore, students should be encouraged to perform stretching exercises on their own whenever possible.

Speed

Many CP students have difficulty with games and sport skills that include a speed component because quickly performed movements tend to activate the stretch reflex. However, an appropriate program can permit CP students to increase their movement speed. Speed development activities for CP individuals will differ little from those for the nonimpaired, except that such activities should be conducted more frequently than for the nonimpaired student: Daily activities are recommended. CP students should be encouraged to perform movements as quickly as possible but to perform them in a controlled, accurate, and purposeful manner. Activities having a speed component include throwing and kicking for distance, running, and jumping. Initially, the student should concentrate on the pattern of the movement while gradually increasing the speed of its execution. To develop arm and leg speed, the student can be asked to throw or kick a ball (or some other object) in a "soft" manner to a target; gradually, the throw or kick can increase in speed.

Motor Coordination

Varying degrees of incoordination (dyspraxia) are common in CP individuals and contribute to delayed motor control and development. Those who are significantly uncoordinated may have problems ambulating independently or with appliances and may need to wear protective headgear. Because they frequently fall, they should be taught, when appropriate, to fall in a protective manner. Because of abnormal movements and posture, CP individuals have difficulty with controlling balance and body coordination. Obstacle courses, horseback riding, bicycling and tricycling, and balance beam and teeter (stability) board activities can be offered to assist them in controlling movements.

Motor control difficulties notwithstanding, CP persons can learn to become more accurate in their performance. Many times the use of a weighted ball, bat, or other implement will assist in decreasing abnormal flailing or tremor movements. Adding weight to the implement helps in reducing exaggerated stretch reflexes, which, in turn, aids in controlling movement. CP individuals with motor control deficiencies resulting from athetoid, tremor, or ataxic tendencies can be expected to throw or kick for distance better and to exhibit freer running patterns than others who have limited range of motion due to spastic or rigid tendencies.

Loud noises and stressful situations increase the amount of electrical stimulation from the brain to the muscles; this tends to increase abnormal and extraneous movements, which, in turn, make motor activities difficult to perform. In an attempt to deal with this situation, students should be taught to concentrate on the activity to be performed. Individuals exhibiting spastic tendencies tend to relax more when encouraged to make slow, repetitive movements that have a purpose, while those with athetoid tendencies perform better when encouraged to relax before moving. Highly competitive situations that promote winning at all costs may tend to increase abnormal movements. Therefore, competitive situations may need to be introduced gradually. The teaching of relaxation techniques, which consciously reduce abnormal muscle tone and prepare the student for activity and competition, has been found to be beneficial. Another way to help CP individuals improve general motor control and coordination is to have them construct a mental picture of the skill or activity prior to performance. This technique, called mental imagery, may help to integrate thoughts with actions.

In motor skill development for CP students, the skills taught should be broken down into basic component parts and presented sequentially. This method is particularly useful for uncoordinated students seeking to learn more complex motor skills. However, because of the general lack of body coordination, activities should initially focus on simple repetitive movements rather than on complicated ones requiring many directional changes. Therefore, activities that help to develop basic fundamental motor skills and patterns, such as walking, running, jumping, throwing, catching, and so forth, should be taught.

Perceptual-Motor Disorders

Perceptual-motor disorders also contribute to poor motor performance. Because of these disorders, many CP children exhibit short attention spans and are easily distracted by objects and persons in the immediate environment. Activities may therefore need to be conducted in an environment as free from distractions as possible, especially during early skill development.

Visual perceptual disorders are common among CP students and can adversely affect activities and events that involve spatial relationships. These may include player positioning in team sports like soccer, remaining in lanes during track events, and determining distances between objects like boccia balls. Students may have difficulty with various accuracy and aiming tasks such as throwing, tossing, kicking, or pushing an object to a specified target, as well as with activities involving various degrees of fine motor coordination, such as crossbow target shooting, angling, or pocket billiards.

Amputees

In general, a physical education program for amputees can follow the same guidelines as one developed for able-bodied individuals. Aside from missing limb(s), the amputee is considered able bodied. However, the location and extent of the amputation(s) may require modifications in some activities.

Most amputees typically use prosthetic devices in physical education activities. A person with unilateral lower-limb amputation usually continues to use the device for participation in football, basketball, volleyball, and most leisure-time activities. In some situations, a unilateral AE or shoulder amputee may consider the device a hindrance to successful performance and discard it during participation; this is common in baseball or softball. Of course, in some activities the prosthetic device must be removed, as in swimming. Since 1978, the National Federation of State High Schools Association allows participating athletes to wear prosthetic devices for interscholastic football and wrestling (Adams et al., 1982). However, a device cannot be used if it is more dangerous to other players than a corresponding human limb or if it places the user at an advantage over an opponent. For football, the ruling is restricted solely to BK prosthetic devices; for wrestling and soccer, upper-limb and AK prostheses are allowed though their use is discouraged.

Physical Fitness

Like people with other physically handicapping conditions, amputees may need to increase their levels of physical fitness. Muscular strength and endurance and flexibility should be developed for all parts of the body. For a person with only a partial limb amputation, such as an ankle or wrist disarticulation, exercises and activities should be programmed to encourage the most normal possible use of the remaining limb segment. Individuals with bilateral BK or AK amputations often have lower cardiovascular endurance levels than upper-limb amputees because their locomotor activities may be severely restricted. To encourage cardiovascular development in these people, the physical educator should provide activities, such as marathon racing or slalom events, in which a

wheelchair can be used. Using an arm-propelled tricycle is also recommended. Swimming is an excellent cardiovascular activity; the effect of limb absence can be minimized by the use of flippers to aid in propulsion. Both unilateral and bilateral AK amputees have a tendency to be obese and, therefore, should be encouraged to follow a weight reduction diet along with a program of regular, vigorous physical activity.

Motor Ability

Limb deficiency can affect a person's level of motor ability. The absence of a limb most often affects the center of gravity, to a greater degree in lower-limb amputees than in upper-limb amputees. The result is difficulty with activities requiring balance. Developing both static and dynamic balance is crucial to the performance of locomotor skills such as walking, running, hopping, or, for that matter, sitting in a wheelchair. Activities that foster the development of balance and proper body alignment should be encouraged; these may include traversing an obstacle course, performing on a minitrampoline, or walking a balance beam. Speed and agility may also be adversely affected, especially in those with lower-limb deficiencies. People with unilateral AK and bilateral BK or AK amputations are most affected and may have difficulty in locomotor activities that require quick change of direction, such as basketball, football, baseball, soccer, and tennis.

While unilateral BK or BE amputees can participate most effectively in physical education and competitive sports, those with bilateral upper or lower amputations will have specific activity restrictions. Bilateral upper-limb amputees can successfully engage in activities that involve the lower extremities to a signficant degree—for example, skating, soccer, and running.

Unilateral AK amputees can effectively participate in activities such as swimming, waterskiing, snow skiing, weight lifting, and certain field events like the shot put and javelin, which do not place emphasis on locomotion. Those with bilateral BK amputations will be more limited in activities like track events, football, or basketball that involve jumping, hopping, or body contact. Bilateral AK amputees are much more restricted in their activities, usually relying part time on a wheelchair and using crutches at other times. Activities such as archery, badminton, riflery, and bowling, which can be performed from a sitting or prone position, are appropriate.

Integration

Unless people with CP, amputations, and Les Autres conditions are severely physically impaired, most can be safely and effectively integrated into regular physical education programs. Those with mild degrees of impairment are prime candidates for integration. In all cases, however, decisions about integration must be made on an individual basis. The impairments described in this chapter primarily affect physical functioning; aside from some instances of CP, mental impairments are rare. Most students with these conditions will understand verbal and written directions as well as rules and strategies for various games and sports. In certain cases, teachers may need to structure activities to suit the participants' abilities. For example, students impaired by CP, amputation, or other lower-limb deficiencies could play goalie in soccer or floor hockey and could pitch or play first base in softball.

Adapted Sports

At almost all age levels, people with CP, amputations, and Les Autres conditions now have the opportunity to become involved in competitive sports. The United States Les Autres Sports Association (USLASA), the USCPAA, and the USAAA have been organized to assist individuals in reaching their maximum potential in sport. All three organizations are members of the Committee on Sports for the Disabled (COSD) of the United States Olympic Committee and members of the

International Sports Organization for the Disabled (ISOD). USLASA, USCPAA, and USAAA offer a variety of sporting events that in many cases have been modified for specific disabilities. Athletes are able to participate in these events on the basis of their functional abilities.

Cerebral Palsy

Competition for CP athletes is based on the eight-level functional classification system described at the beginning of this chapter (see Table 15.1). Athletes are placed in a specific class through two testing procedures. In the first, a functional profile is established through observation and questioning regarding the person's daily living skills. The second testing procedure involves the measurement of speed, accuracy, and range of motion for upper extremity and torso function and, for ambulant athletes, the assessment of lower extremity function. Generally, athletes compete within their designated classes in a variety of events. Table 15.2 identifies competitive events and associated classification levels.

Each year the USCPAA holds a number of clinics for professionals and volunteers that focus on coaching, training, and officiating techniques. The association publishes a medically approved rules manual and a separate training guide.

Amputees

The USAAA, founded in 1981, fosters athletic competition among people with acquired or congenital amputations, including those with single-arm paralysis. There are several chapters of the USAAA across the country; the Eastern Amputee Athletic Association is the newest and largest.

Competition is based on the nine-level classification system previously described. People with combinations of amputations not specified in the classification system are assigned to the class closest to the actual disability. For example, a combined AK and BK amputee would be placed

Table 15.2 Classes Eligible for USCPAA Activities

Activities	Classes
Archery and bowling	I-VII
Bicycling	VII-VIII
Tricycling	II-VI
Cross country	VI-VIII
Horseback riding	I-VII
Power lifting (bench press)	I-VIII (according to weight)
Slalom	I-IV
Soccer	
Seven-a-side ambulant	VI-VIII
Wheelchair (team handball)	I-VI
Swimming	I-VIII
Table tennis	
Ambulatory	V-VIII
Wheelchair	I-IV
Target rifle shooting	I-VIII
Wheelchair boccia (individual and team)	I-II
Track	
20m electric chair	I
20m, 60m upper extremity thrust	II
60m, 200m, 400m (foot propulsion)	III
100m, 400m, 800m	IV, VII, VIII
100m, 400m	V
60m, 200m, 400m	VI
4 × 100m wheelchair shuttle relay	II-IV
4 × 200m ambulatory relay	V-VIII
Field events	
Distance throw (soft shot),	I-II
Precision throw (soft shot or club),	
Soft discus, high toss	
Shot put, club throw,	II
Distance kick, medicine ball thrust kick	
Club throw	II upper extremity, III-VI
Shot put, discus	II upper extremity, III-VIII
Javelin throw	IV-VIII
Long jump	VII-VIII

Note. From UCPA (1983). *NASCP-USA Classification and Sport Rules Manual* (2nd ed.), pp. 14-27. New York: UCPA. Adapted by permission of Grune & Stratton, Inc.

in Class A1, whereas a combined AE and BE amputee would be in Class A5. People with single-arm paralysis are tested for muscle strength of the arms and hands. The following movements are tested and scored on a scale from 0 to 5 (5 being the greatest function):

- Shoulder flexion, extension, abduction, and adduction
- Elbow flexion and extension
- Wrist dorsal and volar flexion
- Finger flexion and extension at the metacarpophalangeal joints
- Thumb opposition and extension

Classification for participants with single-arm paralysis is limited to A6 (AE) or A8 (BE).

USAAA competition takes place in track (100-, 200- and 400-m dashes and 800- and 1,500-m runs) and field events (shot put, discus, javelin, long jump, high jump), basketball, volleyball, lawn bowling, pistol shooting, table tennis, cycling, archery, weight lifting, and swimming (100-m backstroke, 400-m breaststroke, 100- and 400-m freestyle, and 4 × 50-m individual medley). Volleyball and basketball are offered in both sitting and ambulatory categories. In each sport, athletes of similar classifications compete against each other. In most sports athletes compete with prostheses, except for those with double AK or combined upper and lower amputations. In addition to USAAA competitions, amputees are eligible to compete in events sponsored by the National Wheelchair Athletic Association (NWAA), the National Wheelchair Basketball Association (NWBA), and the National Federation of Wheelchair Tennis (NFWT), as long as they have an amputation of the lower extremity and require a wheelchair.

Les Autres

Traditionally, the Les Autres movement was associated with cerebral palsy sports. Les Autres ath-

letes performed at the National Cerebral Palsy Games in 1981 and 1983 along with CP athletes. At the National Cerebral Palsy/Les Autres games in Michigan in 1985, they participated in their own separate competition. In 1988 USLASA held a national competition in Nashville.

Under USLASA auspices, athletes compete mostly in the same general event categories as USCPAA and USAAA athletes. Events include track and field, swimming, volleyball, basketball, and weight lifting. Recently USLASA has added a new class for athletes requiring the use of an electric wheelchair. The number of classes varies with the event. For example, athletes in field events are assigned to one of seven classes, while there are six classes for track events.

Summary

This chapter has described the conditions of cerebral palsy, amputations, and Les Autres impairments as they relate to physical activity and sport. Les Autres conditions discussed were muscular dystrophy, juvenile rheumatoid arthritis, osteogenesis imperfecta, arthrogryposis, multiple sclerosis, Friedreich's ataxia, myasthenia gravis, and Guillain-Barré syndrome. Physical and motor needs were described and program and activity suggestions presented. Recognizing the medical nature of these conditions, teachers and coaches are encouraged to plan activities on the basis of input from physicians and allied health professionals.

Bibliography

Adams, R., Daniel, A., McCubbin, J., & Rullman, L. (1982). *Games, sports and exercises for the physically handicapped* (2nd ed.). Philadelphia: Lea & Febiger.

Bleck, E. (1982). Cerebral Palsy. In E.E. Bleck

& D.A. Nagel (Eds.), *Physically handicapped children: A medical atlas for teachers* (2nd ed.). (pp. 59-132). New York: Grune & Stratton.

Competitive classifications by disability. (1985, Winter). *Palaestra*, 56-57.

Finnie, N. (1975). *Handling the young cerebral palsied child at home* (2nd ed.). New York: Dutton.

Minear, W.L. (1956). A classification of cerebral palsy. *Pediatrics, 18*, 841-852.

Surburg, P.R. (1986). New perspectives for developing range of motion and flexibility for special populations. *Adapted Physical Activity Quarterly, 3*, 227-235.

Winnick, J.P., & Short, F.X. (1982). *The physical fitness of sensory and orthopedically impaired youth* (Final Report, Project UNIQUE). Brockport, NY: State University of New York College at Brockport. (ERIC Document Reproduction Service No. ED 240 764)

Resources

Written

Sherrill, C. (Ed.) (1986). *Sport and disabled athletes: The 1984 Olympic Scientific Congress Proceedings* (Vol. 9). Champaign, IL: Human Kinetics. The book provides a current review of sport for disabled athletes. It includes a selection of papers presented at the 1984 Olympic Scientific Congress held at the University of Oregon at Eugene.

Audiovisual

IBM Corporation. *Here I am: The International Games for the Disabled* [Videotape]. Modern Talking Picture Service, 5000 Park Street North, St. Petersburg, FL 33709. This videotape covers the 1984 International Games for the Disabled on Long Island, New York, featuring over 1,700 athletes from 45 countries.

CHAPTER 16

Spinal Cord Impairments

Luke E. Kelly

Spinal cord impairments are conditions that result from injury or disease to the vertebrae and/or the nerves of the spinal column. These conditions almost always are associated with some degree of *paralysis* due to damage to the spinal cord. The degree of the paralysis is a function of the location of the injury on the spinal column and the number of neural fibers that are subsequently destroyed. Five such spinal cord impairments will be examined in this chapter: *traumatic injuries* to the spine resulting in *quadriplegia* and *paraplegia*, *poliomyelitis*, *spina bifida*, *spondylolysis*, and *spondylolisthesis*.

Classifications

Medical

As illustrated in Figure 16.1, spinal cord injuries are medically labeled or classified according to the segment of the spinal column (i.e., cervical, thoracic, lumbar, or sacral) and the number of the vertebra at or below which the injury occurred. For example, an individual classified as a C-6 complete would have suffered a fracture between the sixth and seventh cervical vertebrae that completely severed the spinal cord. The location of the injury is important because it provides some insight into the functions that may be affected as a result. The extent of the spinal cord lesion is

ascertained through muscle, reflex, and sensation testing.

The actual impact of a spinal cord injury is best understood in terms of

- what muscles can still be used,
- how strong these muscles are, and
- what can functionally be done with these muscles in the context of self-help skills (eating, dressing, grooming, toileting), movement (wheelchair, ambulation, transfers, bed), vocational skills, and physical education skills.

Figure 16.2 provides a summary of the major muscle groups innervated at several key locations along the spinal column, with implications for the movements, abilities, and physical education activities that may be possible with lesions at those locations. The functional abilities remaining are cumulative as one progresses down the spinal column. For example, an individual with a lesion at or below T-1 would have all the muscles and abilities shown at and above that level.

Sport

Sport organizations that sponsor athletic events for individuals with spinal cord impairments use different classification systems to equate athletes for competition. The most widely used system is the one developed by the National Wheelchair

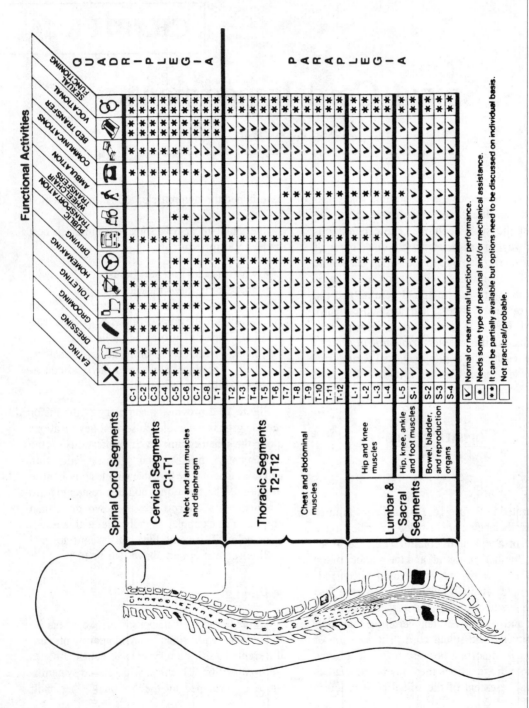

Figure 16.1 Functional activity for spinal cord injuries. *Note.* From *Games, Sports, and Exercises for the Physically Handicapped* (p. 150) by R.C. Adams, A.N. Daniel, J.A. McCubbin, and L. Rullman, 1982, Philadelphia: Lea & Febiger. Courtesy of the Harmarville Rehabilitation Center, Pittsburgh, Pennsylvania 15238. Reprinted by permission.

Lesion locations	Key muscles innervated	Potential movements	Associated functional abilities	Sample PE activities
C-4	Neck Diaphragm	Head control Limited respiratory endurance	Control of an electronic wheelchair and other computer/electronic devices that can be controlled by a mouth opening operated joystick.	Riflery Bowling
C-5	Partial shoulder Biceps	Abduction of the arms Flexion of the arms	Can propel a wheelchair with modified rims, can assist in transfers, can perform some functional arm movements using elbow flexion and gravity to extend the arm.	Swimming
C-6	Major shoulder Wrist extensors	Abduction and flexion of the arms Wrist extension and possibly a weak grasp	Roll over in bed, may be able to transfer from wheelchair to bed, improved ability to propel wheelchair independently, partial independence in eating, grooming, and dressing using special assistive devices.	Billiards Putting
C-7	Triceps Finger extensions Finger flexions	Stabilization and extension of the arm at the elbow. Improved grasp and release, but still weak	Independent in wheelchair locomotion, bed, sitting up, and in many cases transferring from bed to wheelchair. Increased independence in eating, grooming, and dressing.	Archery Crossbow Table tennis
T-1	All upper extremity muscles	All upper body Lacks trunk stability and respiratory endurance	Independent in wheelchair, bed, transfers, eating, grooming, dressing, and toileting. Can ambulate with assistance using long braces, pelvic band, and crutches.	Any activities from a wheelchair

(Cont.)

Figure 16.2 Potential functional abilities by select lesion locations.

Lesion locations	Key muscles innervated	Potential movements	Associated functional abilities	Sample PE activities
T-6	Upper trunk muscles	Trunk stability Improved respiratory endurance	Lift heavier objects because of improved stability. Can independently put their own braces on. Can ambulate with low spinal attachment, pelvic band, long leg braces, and crutches using a "swing" to gait but still depend on wheelchair as primary means of locomotion.	Track & field Bowling Weightlifting
T-12	Abdominal muscles and thoracic back muscles	Increased trunk stability All muscles needed for respiratory endurance	Can independently ambulate with long leg braces including stairs and curbs. Uses a wheelchair only for convenience.	Competitive swimming Marathon racing
L-4	Lower back Hip flexions Quadriceps	Total trunk stability Ability to flex the hip and lift the leg	Can walk independently with short leg braces and bilateral canes or crutches.	Some standing activities
S-1	Hamstring and peroneal muscles	Bend knee Lift the foot up	Can walk independently without crutches. May require ankle braces and/or orthodic shoes.	Normal PE

Figure 16.2 (Continued)

Athletic Association (NWAA). The NWAA system classifies athletes by functional ability into one of seven classes on the basis of their level of muscular functioning. The muscle testing and certification are performed by a physician. This classification system provides an efficient way of equating competition among a diverse group of athletes with varying types of spinal cord impairments. The classifications in the NWAA system are described in Figure 16.3.

NWAA CLASSIFICATIONS

Class IA
All cervical lesions with complete or incomplete quadriplegia who have involvement of both hands, weakness of triceps (up to and including grade 3 on testing scale) and with severe weakness of the trunk and lower extremities interfering significantly with trunk balance and the ability to walk.

Class IB
All cervical lesions with complete or incomplete quadriplegia who have involvement of upper extremities but less than IA with the preservation of normal or good triceps (4 or 5 on testing scale) and with a generalized weakness of the trunk and lower extremities interfering significantly with trunk balance and the ability to walk.

Class IC
All cervical lesions with complete or incomplete quadriplegia who have involvement of upper extremities but less than IB with preservation of normal or good triceps (4 or 5 on testing scale) and normal or good finger flexion and extension (grasp and release) but without intrinsic hand function and with a generalized weakness of the trunk and lower extremities interfering significantly with trunk balance and the ability to walk.

Class II
Complete or incomplete paraplegia below T1 down to and including T5 or comparable disability with total abdominal paralysis or poor abdominal muscle strength (0-2 on testing scale) and no useful trunk sitting balance.

Class III
Complete or incomplete paraplegia or comparable disability below T5 down to and including T10 with upper abdominal and spinal extensor musculature sufficient to provide some element of trunk sitting balance but not normal.

Class IV
Complete or incomplete paraplegia or comparable disability below T10 down to and including L2 without quadriceps or very weak quadriceps with a value up to and including 2 on the testing scale and gluteal paralysis.

Class V
Complete or incomplete paraplegia or comparable disability below L2 with quadriceps in grades 3-5.

Figure 16.3 NWAA classifications system. *Note.* From *Constitution and Rules: Training Techniques and Records* (p. 25) by National Wheelchair Athletic Association, 1977, Garden City, NY. Copyright 1977 by National Wheelchair Athletic Association. Reprinted by permission.

Conditions

Traumatic Quadriplegia and Paraplegia

Traumatic quadriplegia and paraplegia refer to spinal cord injuries that result in the loss of movement and sensation. Quadriplegia is used to describe the more severe form, in which all four limbs are affected. Paraplegia refers to the condition in which primarily the lower limbs are affected.

The amount of paralysis and/or loss of sensation associated with quadriplegia and paraplegia is related to the location of the injury (how high on the spine) and the amount of neural damage (the degree of the lesion). Figure 16.1 shows a side view of the spinal column, accompanied by a description of the functional abilities associated with various levels of injury. The functional abilities indicated for each of the levels should be viewed cautiously because the neural damage to the spinal cord at the site of the injury may be complete or partial. If the cord is severed completely, the individual will have no motor control or sensation in the parts of the body innervated below that point. This loss will be permanent because the spinal cord cannot regenerate itself. In many cases the damage to the spinal cord will only be partial, resulting in retention of some sensation and motor control below the site of the injury. In a case involving partial lesion, the individual may experience a gradual return of some muscle control and sensation over a period of several months following the injury. This is due not to regeneration of damaged nerves but rather to the alleviation of pressure on nerves at the injury site caused by bruising and/or swelling.

Incidence

It is estimated that approximately 10,000 people suffer spinal cord injuries each year. Among the major causes are falls, automobile accidents, athletic injuries (e.g., football, gymnastics, diving), and bicycle accidents. Unfortunately, a large percentage of these injuries happen to students of high school age, with the incidence being greater among males than females. It should be noted that, when spinal cord injury is suspected, proper handling of the patient immediately after the injury can play a major role in minimizing any additional damage to the spinal cord.

Bergeron (1982) outlines seven rules that should be followed whenever a head or spinal injury is suspected:

1. Always provide respiratory resuscitation or CPR as needed, even though the patient may have neck or spinal injuries. Use the modified jaw-thrust method for mouth-to-mouth resuscitation.

2. Always attempt to control serious bleeding, even though the patient may have neck or spinal injuries. Avoid, if possible, moving patients or any of their limbs.

3. Always consider that an unconscious accident patient has neck and spinal injuries until you can determine otherwise.

4. Do not attempt to splint fractures if there are any indications of neck or spinal injuries.

5. Never move a patient having neck or spinal injuries unless you must do so to provide CPR, reach life-threatening bleeding, or protect you and the patient from immediate danger at the scene.

6. Take measures to immobilize the patient's head, neck, and as much of the body as possible.

7. Monitor continuously all patients having neck or spinal injury. These patients will often go into shock. Sometimes these patients will have paralysis of the chest muscles and go into respiratory arrest. (p. 180)

Other emergency medical care resources are included in the reference list at the end of the chapter (American Academy of Orthopaedic Surgeons, 1981; Grant, Murray, & Bergeron, 1982).

Treatment and Educational Considerations

The treatment of individuals with spinal cord injuries usually involves three phases:

- Hospitalization
- Rehabilitation
- Return to the home environment

Although the three phases are presented as separate, there is considerable overlap between the treatments provided within each phase. During the hospital phase the acute medical aspects of the injury are addressed and therapy is initiated. Depending on the severity of the injury, the hospital stay can last up to several months. Many people with spinal cord injuries are then transferred from the hospital to a rehabilitation center. As indicated by its name, the rehabilitation phase centers on adjustment to the injury and mastery of basic living skills (toileting, dressing, transfers, wheelchair use, etc.) with the functional abilities still available. Near the end of the rehabilitation phase, a transition is begun to move the individual back into the home environment. In the case of a student, the transition involves working with parents and school personnel to make sure that they have the appropriate skills and understanding of the individual's condition and needs and that they know what environmental modifications will be required to accommodate those needs.

The abilities outlined in Figure 16.2 are those that can potentially be achieved by people with spinal cord injuries. Unfortunately, to achieve these abilities, individuals must accept their condition, not be hindered by any *secondary health problems*, and be highly motivated to work in rehabilitation. The implications of these factors are discussed below.

One of the major secondary problems associated with spinal cord injuries is *psychological acceptance* of the limitations imposed by the injury and the loss of former abilities. *Counseling* is usually a major component of the treatment plan during rehabilitation. It should be recognized that the rate of adjustment and the degree to which different individuals learn to cope with their disabilities varies tremendously.

People with spinal cord injuries are susceptible to a number of *secondary health conditions*. One of their most common health problems is pressure sores or *decubitus ulcers*. These are caused by the lack of innervation and reduced blood flow to the skin and most commonly occur at pressure points where bony prominences are close to the skin (buttocks, pelvis, and ankles). Because of the poor blood circulation these sores can easily become infected and are extremely slow to heal. The prevention of pressure sores involves regular inspection of the skin, the use of additional padding in troubled areas, and regular pressure releases (changes in position that alleviate the pressure). Individually designed seat cushions can be made and are used by many people to help better distribute pressure and avoid pressure sores. Keeping the skin dry is also important, because the skin is more susceptible to sores when it is wet from urine and/or perspiration.

A problem closely related to pressure sores is *bruising* of the skin. Because no sensation is felt in the limbs that are not innervated, it is not uncommon for them to be unconsciously bruised or irritated from hitting or rubbing against other surfaces. Injuries of this nature are quite common in wheelchair activities like basketball if appropriate precautions are not taken. Because these bruises are not felt, they can go unnoticed and eventually can become infected.

A third health problem commonly encountered in individuals with spinal cord injuries is *urinary tract infections*. Urination is controlled by some form of catheterization on an established schedule. Urinary infections occur when urine is retained in the bladder and backs up into the kidneys. Urinary tract infections can be very severe and usually keep the patient bedridden for a prolonged period of time, which is counterproductive for attitude, rehabilitation, and skill development. Bowel movements must also be carefully monitored to prevent constipation and incontinence. Bowel movements are usually controlled by a combination of diet and mild laxatives. In cases where bowel movements cannot be controlled by diet, a tube is surgically inserted into the intestine. The tube exits through a small opening made in the side and is connected to a bag that collects the fecal excretions.

Two other closely associated problems that frequently accompany spinal cord injuries are *spasticity* and *contractures*. Spasticity is an increase in muscle tone in muscles that are no longer innervated because of the injury. This increased muscle tone can nullify the use of other, still innervated muscles. The term *spasm* is frequently used to describe sudden spasticity in a muscle group that can be of sufficient force to launch an individual out of a wheelchair. The best treatment for spastic muscles is to stretch them regularly, particularly before and after rigorous activity. Contractures can frequently occur in the joints of the lower limbs if they are not regularly, passively moved through the full range of motion. A high degree of spasticity in various muscle groups can also limit the range of motion and contribute to contractures.

The last problem commonly associated with spinal cord injuries is a tendency toward *obesity*. The loss of function in the large muscle groups in the lower limbs severely reduces the caloric burning capacity of people with spinal cord injuries. Unfortunately, a corresponding loss in appetite does not also occur. Many individuals with spinal cord injuries tend to resume their habitual caloric intake or even to increase it because of their sedentary condition. Weight and diet should be carefully monitored to prevent obesity and the secondary health hazards associated with it. Once weight is gained, it is extremely difficult to lose.

A major key to success in rehabilitation and in accepting a disability is motivation. Many individuals with spinal cord impairments initially have great difficulty accepting the loss of previous abilities and subsequently are reluctant to work hard during the tedious and often painful therapy. Recreational and sport activities are commonly used in both counseling and therapy to provide reasons for working hard and distractions. A physical educator should be sensitive to the motivational needs of a student returning to a program with a spinal cord impairment. Although sport can be a motivator for many, it can also highlight the loss of previous skills and abilities.

The physical education teacher should anticipate needs in the areas of body image, upper body strength, range of motion, endurance, and wheelchair tolerance. These needs, together with the student's functional abilities, should be analyzed to determine what lifetime sport skills and wheelchair sports are most viable for future participation. These activities then become the annual instructional goals for the physical education program.

While an individual with a spinal cord injury is still learning to deal with the injury, the physical educator can assist by anticipating the person's needs and planning ahead. This may involve reminding the student to perform *pressure releases* at regular intervals (lifting the weight off the seat of the chair by doing an arm press on the arm supports of the chair, or just shifting the sitting position) or bringing extra towels to class to absorb extra moisture in the chair. Because spasticity and spasms are common, stretching at the beginning of class and periodically during the class is recommended. Finally, pads should be provided to prevent bruising in active wheelchair activities. As the student becomes accustomed to the condition, most of these precautions will become automatic habits. A student who has an external bag should be reminded to empty and clean it before physical education class. In contact activities, care should be taken to protect the bag from contact. For swimming, the bag should be removed and the opening in the side covered with a water-tight bandage.

Poliomyelitis

Poliomyelitis, commonly called *polio*, is a form of paralysis caused by a viral infection that affects the motor cells in the spinal cord. The severity and degree of paralysis vary with each individual and depend on the number and location of the motor cells affected. The paralysis may be temporary, occurring only during the acute phase of the illness (in which case the motor cells are not destroyed), or permanent if the motor cells are destroyed by the virus. Bowel and bladder control, as well as sensation in the involved limbs, are not affected in this condition.

Incidence

The occurrence of polio is rare in school-age children today because of the widespread use of the Salk vaccine.

Treatment and Educational Considerations

During the acute, or active, phase of the illness, the child is confined to bed. The illness is accompanied by a high fever and pain and paralysis in the affected muscles. After the acute phase, muscle testing is conducted to determine which muscles were affected and to what degree. Rehabilitation is then begun to develop functional abilities with the muscles that remain.

Depending on the severity of the paralysis, a child may require instruction in walking with crutches or long leg braces and/or using a wheelchair. When the lower limbs have been severely affected, it is not uncommon for bone deformities to occur as the child develops. These deformities can involve the hips, knees, ankles, or feet and frequently require surgery to correct.

Specific activity implications are difficult to provide for children with polio because their range of abilities can be so great. Physical educators need to accurately evaluate the abilities and limitations imposed by the condition for each student and then make appropriate placement and instructional decisions.

Many children with only one involved limb or mild involvement of two limbs will already have learned to compensate for the condition and will do fine in the regular physical education program. Others with more extensive or severe involvement may require a more restricted adapted physical education program. Care should be taken not to totally remove these children from regular physical education. Whatever the degree of involvement, these children have normal IQs, typical play interests, and the desire to be with their classmates.

Regardless of the physical education placement, the emphasis should be on optimal development of the muscles the student does have. Priority should be given to lifetime sport skills and activities that can be carried over and pursued for recreation and fitness when the school years are past. Swimming is an excellent example of an activity that promotes lifetime fitness, provides recreation, and prepares one for other activities such as sailing and canoeing.

Spina Bifida

Spina bifida is a congenital birth defect in which the neural tube fails to close completely during the first 4 weeks of fetal development. Subsequently, the posterior arch of one or more vertebrae fails to develop properly, leaving an opening in the spinal column. There are three classifications of spina bifida, based on which structures, if any, protrude through the opening in the spine.

Myelomeningocele is the most severe and, unfortunately, the most common form of spina bifida. In this condition the covering of the spinal cord (meninges), cerebrospinal fluid, and part of the spinal cord protrude through the opening and form a visible sac on the child's back (see Figure 16.4a). Some degree of neurological damage and subsequent loss of motor function are always associated with this form.

Spina bifida meningocele is similar to the myelomeningocele form, except that only the spinal cord covering and cerebrospinal fluid protrude into the sac (see Figure 16.4b). This form rarely has any neurological damage associated with it.

Occulta is the mildest and least common form of spina bifida. In this condition, the defect is present in the posterior arch of the vertebra, but nothing protrudes through the opening (see Figure 16.4c). No neurological damage is associated with this type of spina bifida.

Myelomeningocele   Meningocele   Occulta

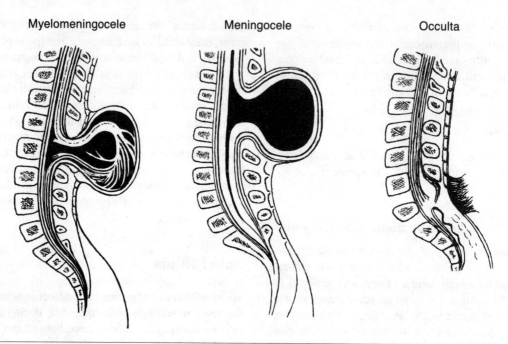

Figure 16.4 Diagram of the three types of spina bifida. *Note.* From "Spina Bifida" by G.G. Deaver, D. Buck, and J. McCarthy. In *1951 Year Book of Physical Medicine and Rehabilitation.* Copyright 1952 by Year Book Medical Publishers, Inc., Chicago.

Once detected soon after birth and surgically corrected, the meningocele and occulta forms of spina bifida have no adverse ramifications. The greatest threat in these conditions is from infection prior to surgery.

Incidence

Because some degree of neurological damage is always associated with the myelomeningocele type of spina bifida, it will be the form discussed in the remainder of this section. Approximately two children out of every 1,000 live births have spina bifida, and 80% of these children have the myelomeningocele form. The degree of neurological damage associated with spina bifida myelomeningocele depends on the location of the deformity and the amount of damage done to the spinal cord. Fortunately, spina bifida occurs most commonly in the lumbar vertebrae, sparing motor function in the upper limbs and limiting the disability primarily to the lower limbs. Bowel and bladder control are almost always lost. The muscle functions and abilities presented in Figure 16.2 for spinal cord lesions in the lumbar region can also be used to ascertain what functional abilities a child with spina bifida will have.

In addition to the neurological impairment associated with damage to the spinal cord, myelomeningocele is almost always accompanied by *hydrocephalus*. This is a condition in which the circulation of the cerebrospinal fluid is obstructed in one of the ventricles or cavities of the brain. If the obstruction is not removed or circumvented, the ventricle begins to enlarge, putting pressure on the brain and enlarging the head. If not treated, this condition can lead to brain damage and mental retardation, and ultimately to death. Today, hydrocephalus is suspected early in children with spina bifida and is usually treated surgically by insertion of a shunt during the first few weeks after birth (see Figure 16.5). The shunt, a plastic tube

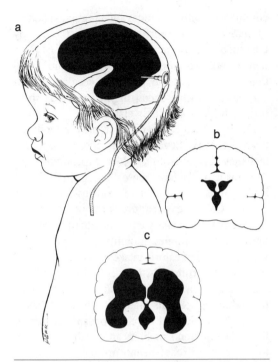

Figure 16.5 Illustration of a shunt being used to relieve hydrocephalus: a) the shunt in place, b) normal ventricles, c) enlarged ventricles.

equipped with a pressure value, is inserted into a ventricle and drains off the excess cerebrospinal fluid. The fluid is usually drained into either the heart (ventriculoatrial) or the abdomen (ventriculoperitoneal) to be reabsorbed by the body.

Treatment and Educational Considerations

As mentioned earlier, all forms of spina bifida are diagnosed and surgically treated soon after birth. The major treatment beyond the immediate medical procedures involves physical and occupational therapy for the child and counseling and training for the parents. The therapy has two focuses: using assistive devices to position children so that they parallel the developmental positions (sitting, crawling, standing, etc.) through which a normal child progresses, and maintaining full range of

motion and stimulating circulation in the lower limbs. In conjunction with their therapy, spina bifida children are fitted with braces and encouraged to ambulate. Even if functional walking skills are not developed, it is very important for the spina bifida child to do weight-bearing activities to stimulate bone growth and circulation in the lower limbs. Parents are counseled to try to provide the child with as normal and as many appropriate stimuli as possible. Many parents, unfortunately, frequently overprotect and confine their spina bifida children, which results in further delays in growth and development.

There are several important similarities and differences in the treatments of spina bifida and of the spinal cord injuries discussed earlier in this chapter. The similarities concern the muscle and sensation loss and the common problems related to these deficits:

- Bone deformities
- Postural deviations
- Pressure sores
- Bruising
- Urinary infections
- Obesity

The differences are related to the onset of the conditions; different circumstances result in different emotional and developmental ramifications.

Generally, children with spina bifida have fewer emotional problems dealing with their condition than do children with acquired spinal cord impairments, probably because the condition has been present since birth and they have not suffered the loss of any former abilities. However, this is not to imply that they do not become frustrated when other children can perform skills and play activities that they cannot because of their dependence on a wheelchair or crutches.

A second major ramification of the early onset of spina bifida is its effect on growth and development. The lack of innervation and subsequent use and stimulation of the affected limbs retards their physical growth. The result is a greater incidence of bone deformities and contractures in the lower limbs and a greater need for *orthotics* (braces) to help minimize these deformities and assist in providing functional support. A concurrent problem is related to *sensory deprivation* during the early years of development due to restricted mobility. This deprivation is frequently compounded by overprotecting parents and medical problems that confine the child to bed for long periods.

Children with spina bifida are vulnerable to infections from pressure sores and bruises. Pressure sores are most common in those who are confined to wheelchairs. Bruising and skin irritation are particular concerns for spina bifida children using crutches and long leg braces. These children have a tendency to fall frequently in physical activities and to be susceptible to skin irritations from their braces if the braces are not properly put on each time.

Bowel and bladder control present significant social problems for the spina bifida child during the early elementary school years. Bowel movements are controlled by diet and medication, which are designed to prevent constipation. Urination is commonly controlled today by a regular schedule of *catheterization*, performed during the day by the school nurse or an aide (see Figure 16.6). This dependence on others for help with personal functions and the inevitable occasional accident in class can have negative social implications for spina bifida children and their classmates.

Finally, spina bifida children have a tendency toward obesity. Several causes contribute to this tendency. The loss of the caloric expenditure typically made by the large muscle groups in the lower limbs limits the number of calories that can be burned. Caloric expenditure is frequently further limited by the sedentary environment of these children and their limited mobility during the early years. Control of caloric intake is essential to avoid obesity. Unfortunately, food is frequently highly gratifying to these children and is over provided by indulging parents and caregivers. Obesity should be avoided at all costs because it further limits the children's mobility and predisposes them to a variety of other health problems.

Spina bifida children will most likely be placed initially in some combination of adapted and regu-

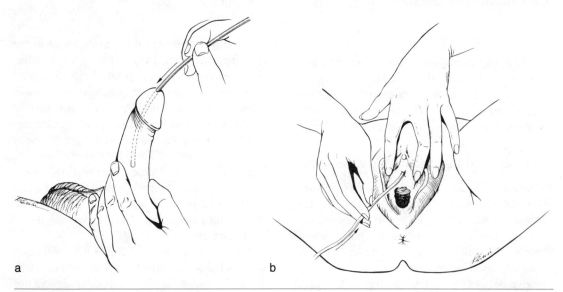

a   b

Figure 16.6 Illustration of male (a) and female (b) catherization procedures used to remove urine using a lubricated plastic catheter.

lar physical education during the early elementary years and will be fully mainstreamed into the regular physical education program by the end of the elementary years. It is important not to remove these children unnecessarily from regular physical education. They have normal IQs and the same play and social needs as the other students in their classes. On the other hand, the primary goal of physical education, to develop physical and motor skills, should not be sacrificed purely for social objectives. If the children's physical and motor needs cannot be met in the regular physical education, they should receive appropriate support and/or supplemental adapted physical education to meet these needs.

In summary, spina bifida children need to achieve the same physical education goals and objectives targeted for other students. Modifications will be needed to accommodate their mode of locomotion (crutches or wheelchair) and to emphasize their upper body development. Emphasis should be placed on physical fitness and the development of lifetime sport skills.

Spondylolysis and Spondylolisthesis

Spondylolysis refers to a congenital malformation of the neural arches of the fourth, or more commonly, the fifth lumbar vertebra. Individuals with spondylolysis may or may not experience any back pain, but they are predisposed to acquiring spondylolisthesis. Spondylolisthesis is similar to spondylolysis, except that in this condition, the fifth lumbar vertebra has slid forward. The displacement occurs because of the lack of the neural arch structure and the ligaments that normally hold this area in place. Spondylolisthesis can be congenital or can occur as a result of trauma to the back. It is usually associated with severe back pain and pain in the legs.

Treatment in mild cases involves training and awareness of proper posture. Individuals with spondylolisthesis frequently have an exaggerated lordotic curve in the back. In more severe cases,

surgery is performed to realign the vertebrae and fuse that section of the spine.

Medical consultation should be pursued before any students with spondylolysis or spondylolisthesis participate in physical education. Children with mild cases may be able to participate in regular physical education with emphasis on proper posture, additional stretching, and avoidance of activities that involve severe stretching or trauma to the back. In more severe cases, adapted physical education may be required to provide more comprehensive posture training and exercises and to foster the development of physical and motor skills that will not aggravate the condition.

Implications for Physical Education

Assessment is the key to successfully addressing the physical education needs of students with spinal cord impairments. Physical educators must work as part of a team to obtain the assessment data they need to provide appropriate instruction. By consulting with each other, the physical educator and the physical and/or occupational therapist can share essential information about their goals and objectives for each student. The physical therapist can provide pertinent information about the muscles that are still innervated and those that have been lost, the existing muscle strength and the prognosis for its further development, the range of motion at the various joints, and the presence or absence of sensation in the limbs. The physical and/or occupational therapist can also provide useful information about adapted appliances (e.g., a device to hold a racket when a grip is not possible) as well as practical guidance on putting on and removing braces, adjusting wheelchairs, positioning and the use of restraints in wheelchairs, lifting and handling the student, and making transfers to and from the wheelchair.

Within the domain of physical education, the physical educator must be able to assess the spinal cord–impaired student's physical fitness and motor skills. Only one currently available physical fitness test, the Project UNIQUE Physical Fitness Test (Winnick & Short, 1985), was designed specifically to accommodate individuals with spinal cord impairments and provides appropriate normative data for this population.

In general, spinal cord–impaired individuals have placed significantly below nonhandicapped students at their age level on physical fitness measures and in motor skill development. Winnick and Short (1985), for example, have reported that 52% to 72% of spinal cord–impaired individuals in their Project UNIQUE study had skinfold measures greater than the median value for same-aged nonimpaired subjects, and that only about 19% of the spinal cord–impaired girls and 36% of the boys scored above the nonimpaired median on grip strength. Winnick and Short (1984) have also reported that youngsters with paraplegic spinal neuromuscular conditions have generally lower fitness levels than normal youngsters of the same age and gender, and that these youngsters do not demonstrate significant improvement with age or show significant gender differences like those found among normal youngsters. These results should not be misinterpreted to mean that people with spinal cord impairments cannot develop better levels of physical fitness. Research has shown, on the contrary, that with proper instruction and opportunity to practice, these individuals can make significant improvements in physical fitness. The key is appropriate instruction and practice designed to address individual needs.

Fitness programs for individuals with spinal cord impairments should focus on flexibility, strength, and endurance training. While flexibility in all joints should be a goal, particular emphasis should be placed on preventing or reducing contractures in joints where muscles are no longer innervated. These situations require a regular routine of passive stretching that moves the joints through the full range of motion.

Strength training should focus on restoring and/or maximizing the strength in the unaffected muscles. Care must be taken not to create *muscle imbalances* by overstrengthening muscle groups when the antagonist muscles are affected. Most common progressive resistance exercises are suitable for spinal cord–impaired individuals with little or no modification. Posture and correct body mechanics should be stressed during all strength training activities.

One of the most challenging fitness areas with individuals who have spinal cord impairments is cardiorespiratory endurance. Work in this area is frequently complicated by the loss of the large muscle groups of the legs, which makes cardiorespiratory training more difficult. In these cases, the principles of intensity, frequency, and duration must be applied to less traditional aerobic activities that use the smaller muscle groups of the arms and shoulders. A number of wheelchair ergometers and hand-driven bicycle ergometers have been designed specifically to address the cardiorespiratory needs of spinal cord–impaired individuals. While it is more difficult to attain the benefits of cardiorespiratory training using the smaller muscle groups of the arms and shoulders, it is not impossible. There are a number of highly conditioned wheelchair marathoners who clearly demonstrate that high levels of aerobic fitness can be attained.

In addition to physical fitness and motor skill areas, physical educators should concentrate on *posture, body mechanics* and *weight control*. Individuals with spinal cord impairments frequently have poor body mechanics as a result of muscle imbalances and contractures. Exercises and activities that contribute to body awareness and alignment should, therefore, be stressed. Another secondary problem that contributes to poor posture and has a general negative effect on both physical fitness and motor skill acquistion is obesity. Obesity is, unfortunately, very common in individuals with spinal cord impairments, largely because the loss of the large muscle groups of the lower limbs diminishes their capacity to burn calories. Weight control is a function of balancing caloric intake with caloric expenditure. Because, in many cases, caloric expenditure is limited to a large degree by the extent of muscle damage and the subsequent activities that can be undertaken, the obvious solution is to control food intake.

In terms of sport skills, the most valuable activities are those that have the greatest carryover potential for lifetime participation. The selection of activities should provide a balance between warm- and cold-weather sports as well as indoor and outdoor sports. Preference should be given to sports that promote physical fitness and for which there are organized opportunities for participation in the community. Just about any sport (e.g., golf, tennis, swimming, skiing) can be adapted or modified so that individuals with spinal cord impairments can participate.

The goal of assessment is to obtain the most accurate and complete data possible so that the most appropriate placement and instruction can be provided. Physical educators must be willing to devote both the time and effort required to obtain this assessment data if they wish to help their students reach their maximum potential in physical education. Working cooperatively with a team is the key to maximizing staff efficiency and the benefits for the students.

Adapted Sport Activities

The roots of sport for people with spinal cord impairments can be traced back to the early 1940s, to two separate but similar events. Dr. Ludwig Guttman organized the first informal archery competition for spinal cord–injured patients at the Stoke Mandeville Hospital in England in July of 1948. This event has evolved into the present-day International Stoke Mandeville Games. At approximately the same time (1945) in the United States, the Paralyzed Veterans of America organized the first wheelchair basketball games. From these games evolved the National Wheelchair Basketball Association and the National Wheelchair Athletic Association.

Today, there are a large number of organizations that sponsor athletic programs and sporting events for individuals with spinal cord impairments. These organizations have evolved from the need to provide athletic and recreational opportunities to spinal cord–impaired individuals who want to participate in sport. The names and addresses of several of the larger, more prominent organizations are listed in the appendix.

The National Wheelchair Athletic Association (NWAA) is one of the oldest and most notable organizations sponsoring athletic events for people with neuromuscular impairments resulting from spinal cord injuries, spina bifida, or polio. The NWAA sponsors competitive events in pistol shooting, riflery, swimming, table tennis, weight lifting, archery, fencing, wheelchair slalom, and track and field. Competitors are classified into divisions by age and functional ability (see Figure 16.3). There are two age divisions: adult, for individuals aged 16 and older, and junior, for individuals 8 to 15 years old.

The National Handicapped Sport and Recreation Association (NHSRA) plays a major role in organizing and sponsoring both competitive and noncompetitive winter sports events for the handicapped. In addition, NHSRA is a leader in the development and dissemination of recreation and training materials related to sport and recreation for the handicapped. One example is the ''Fitness Is for Everyone'' program, which includes a series of aerobic dance videotapes designed especially to help individuals with paraplegia, quadriplegia, amputations, and cerebral palsy develop endurance, strength, and flexibility.

A number of special organizations sponsor athletic competitions in a specific sport. Although many of these organizations employ the NWAA classification system, the National Wheelchair Basketball Association (NWBA) has its own system. In the NWBA classification system, each player is classified as a I, II, or III, depending on the location of the spinal injury and the degree of motor loss. Each class has a corresponding point value of 1, 2, or 3. A team can comprise players in any combination of classes as long as the total point value for the five players does not exceed 12 and there are not more than three Class III players. The classifications are made according to certain criteria (National Wheelchair Basketball Association, 1986, p. 7).

National Wheelchair Basketball Association —— Classification System ——

Class I: Complete motor loss at T-7 or above or comparable disability where there is total loss of muscle function originating at or above T-7.

Class II: Complete motor loss originating at T-8 and descending through and including L-2 where there may be motor power of hips and thighs. Also included in this class are amputees with bilateral hip disarticulation.

Class III: All other physical disabilities as related to lower extremity paralysis or paresis originating at or below L-3. All lower-extremity amputees are included in this class except those with bilaterial hip disarticulation.

The NWBA classification system provides an excellent model for equating team sport competition in physical education classes that include mainstreamed students with spinal cord impairments. A similar classification system based on students' skill levels could also be designed and used in physical education classes.

In the past decade, wheelchair sports have evolved from primarily recreational events into events that are highly sophisticated and competitive. Many of the initial advances in wheelchair sports were the direct result of technical advances in wheelchair design and/or research related to the postural and body mechanics of wheelchair propulsion (see chapter 8). In recent years, attention has shifted to defining and improving training and conditioning programs for wheelchair athletes

(Crase, 1979; Curtis 1981a, 1981b, 1981c, 1982; Dawson, William, & Rape, 1980; Frey, 1975; Horvat, French, & Henschen, 1986; Skuldt, 1984).

Specialized, organized sport programs serve as an extension of the physical education curriculum. They provide spinal cord–impaired students with the same opportunity to gain the benefits and experiences all athletes derive from sport, and they act as an additional source of motivation. These activities also give participants an opportunity to meet and interact socially with others who have similar characteristics, interests, and needs. Finally, these sport experiences expose spinal cord–impaired students to positive role models who demonstrate the difference between having a disability and being handicapped. To maximize the probability that handicapped students will both attempt and succeed in sports, physical educators must ensure that the physical education curriculum provides both instruction in the fundamental sport skills and the appropriate transition from skill development to skill application in actual sport situations.

Summary

Individuals with spinal cord impairments need to achieve the same physical education goals as other students. To successfully meet the needs of these students, physical educators must have a thorough understanding of the nature of the impairments and the functional abilities that can be attained. They can then build on this knowledge base to determine the most appropriate placement and instructional programming for each student. Particular emphasis in the program should be placed on body awareness, physical fitness, and the development of lifetime sport skills. Adapted sports, using functional ability classification systems, provide excellent opportunities for individuals with spinal cord impairments to apply and practice the skills learned in physical education.

Bibliography

Adams, R.C., Daniel, A.N., McCubbin, J.A., & Rullman, L. (1982). *Games, sports, and exercises for the physically handicapped* (3rd ed.). Philadelphia: Lea & Febiger.

American Academy of Orthopaedic Surgeons. (1981). *Emergency care and transportation of the sick and injured* (3rd ed.). Menasha, WI: George Banta.

Bergeron, J.D. (1982). *First responder*. Bowie, MD: Brady.

Crase, N. (1979). Two conditioning courses: For wheelers. *Sports 'N Spokes, 5*, 21-22.

Curtis, K. (1981a). Wheelchair sports medicine part 1: Basics of exercise physiology. *Sports 'N Spokes, 7*(1), 26-30.

Curtis, K. (1981b). Wheelchair sports medicine part 2: Training. *Sports 'N Spokes, 7*(2), 16-19.

Curtis, K. (1981c). Wheelchair sports medicine part 3: Stretching routines. *Sports 'N Spokes, 7*(3), 16-20.

Curtis, K. (1982). Wheelchair sports medicine part 4: Athletic injuries. *Sports 'N Spokes, 7*(5), 20-24.

Dawson, G., William, S., & Rape, S. (1980). Heart rate and athletics. *Sports 'N Spokes, 6*, 13-14.

Frey, K. (1975). Strength training & wheelchair sports. *Sports 'N Spokes, 1*, 7-8.

Grant, H.D., Murray, R.H., & Bergeron, J.D. (1982). *Emergency care*. Bowie, MD: Brady.

Horvat, M., French, R., & Henschen, K. (1986). A comparison of male and female able-bodied and wheelchair athletes. *Paraplegia, 24*, 115-122.

National Wheelchair Athletic Association. (1979). *Rules of the National Wheelchair Athletic Association*. Woodside, NY: Author.

National Wheelchair Basketball Association. (1986). *1985-1986 NWBA rules and case book*. Lexington, KY: Author.

Skuldt, A. (1984). Exercise limitations for quadriplegics. *Sports 'N Spokes, 10*, 19-20.

Winnick, J.P., & Short, F.X. (1984). The physical fitness of youngsters with spinal neuromuscular conditions. *Adapted Physical Activity Quarterly, 1*, 37-51.

Winnick, J.P., & Short, F.X. (1985). *Physical fitness testing of the disabled*. Champaign, IL: Human Kinetics.

Resources

Written

Curtis, K. (1981a). Wheelchair sports medicine part 1: Basics of exercise physiology. *Sports 'N Spokes, 7*(1), 26-30.

Curtis, K. (1981b). Wheelchair sports medicine part 2: Training. *Sports 'N Spokes, 7*(2), 16-19.

Curtis, K. (1981c). Wheelchair sports medicine part 3: Stretching routines. *Sports 'N Spokes, 7*(3), 16-20.

Curtis, K. (1982). Wheelchair sports medicine part 4: Athletic injuries. *Sports 'N Spokes, 7*(5), 20-24.

This four-part series on sports medicine for wheelchair sports provides an excellent foundation for the beginning athlete and volunteer coaches working with wheelchair athletes for the first time.

Audiovisual

National Handicapped Sports and Recreation Association. (1986). *Fitness is for everyone* [Videotape]. Cleveland: Wyse Public Relations. NHSRA has developed a series of aerobic and strength-flexibility videotapes (each approximately 30 min in length) that are specifically designed for individuals with paraplegia, quadriplegia, cerebral palsy, and amputations. These are professionally made tapes. Each routine is demonstrated by a professional aerobics instructor and a person with a specific disability.

CHAPTER 17

Other Health–Impaired and Nonhandicapped Students in Adapted Physical Education

Paul R. Surburg

The heading of this chapter might lead the reader to expect that two distinct areas will be covered. When PL 94-142 was discussed in chapter 1, one of the 11 official handicapping conditions recognized as being included in that law was *other health impaired*. Nonhandicapped students' unique needs would seem to connote a different set of conditions and circumstances. Table 17.1 presents eight conditions, cited as "chronic or acute health problems," which qualify as other health–impaired (OHI) conditions (Education for All Handicapped Children Act of 1975). While some students having those conditions may be designated as handicapped, with IEPs developed for their specific needs, not all students with OHI conditions will be so designated.

There are two reasons that the designation of handicapped might not be applied to these students. First, a student with diabetes or asthma may not want to be labeled as handicapped or, in the vernacular of certain school settings, "a special ed student." In many states the OHI condition must be officially diagnosed by a physician; a family physician may be reluctant to confirm a diagnosis that could place a certain stigma upon the student. Parents often intercede with the phy-

Table 17.1 Incidence per 1,000 Persons of Other Health–Impaired Conditions as Cited in PL 94-142

Condition	Incidence
Cancer	250
Heart condition	120
Diabetes	10
Epilepsy	5
Asthma	3-6
Rheumatic fever	2
Sickle-cell anemia	2
Hemophilia	10

sician to prevent the label of handicapped from being imposed upon their child.

Second, in many states the development of an IEP exclusively for physical education is rare. In the absence of limitations that would hinder a student in the academic environment, the probability of establishing an IEP only for physical education is low. Nevertheless, while OHI students may not be designated as handicapped, regular and adapted physical educators must understand those students' conditions and the best way to provide meaningful physical education experiences for them.

Some nonhandicapped students also have unique needs that should be met in a physical education program. For example, a high school student who has Osgood-Schlatter's condition may not be able to engage in all types of physical education activities. A person with a broken leg may be temporarily limited in the physical education setting (see Figure 17.1). People with long-term disorders will benefit from physical education programs that are modified to meet their present unique needs. For many of these students an individualized physical education program (IPEP) is recommended (see chapter 3).

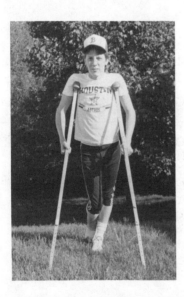

Figure 17.1 Student with a temporary limitation.

Ironically, the information offered in this chapter to help meet nonhandicapped students' needs may also be applicable to students designated as handicapped. A deaf student might break a leg, and information presented in the section on fractures would be useful for working with this student. Topics discussed under the heading of "Long-Term Disorders" are conditions that handicapped persons may exhibit. Thus the content of this chapter is applicable for both handicapped and nonhandicapped students.

Activity Injuries

Students may sustain activity or sport injuries in different settings. While some injuries may originate in a physical education class, more occur during free-time or recreational pursuits.

If an injury occurs in physical education class, immediate care should be provided in the RICE sequence: *Rest* should be given immediately to the injured part or joint. *Ice* or a cold application should be administered immediately and removed after a 20-min interval. Cold may be reapplied in 1 to 1-1/2 hr, depending upon the extent of injury. *Compression* and *Elevation* reduce internal bleeding and swelling. Unfortunately, in the recreational or free-time setting, these procedures are not always followed, and the injury may be exacerbated. Without the ice and compression, intra-articular pressure from the swelling may stretch structures such as ankle ligaments just as if a person had purposely twisted the joint. Some type of immobilization or rest is needed for musculoskeletal injuries; this rest facilitates healing and reduces the risk of prolonging recovery time.

Unless injured students are on an athletic team, there probably will be no type of rehabilitation service available to them. While physical educators cannot act in the capacity of athletic trainers, they may provide valuable assistance. If an injury is not being managed in an appropriate manner, the physical educator may recommend that the student see a physician or visit a sports medicine clinic. Many hospitals provide sports medicine services; these clinics or departments are staffed by sport physical therapists or athletic trainers.

If the injured student is progressing normally toward recovery, the physical education class may provide an opportunity for exercises or activities that will ameliorate the condition. See Tables 17.2

through 17.6 for activities or exercises for three joints—ankle, knee, and shoulder—frequently injured in sport and recreational activities.

Ankle

Ankle sprains are a risk for anyone who actively engages in sport or physical activity. Jumping and other movements may cause a person to roll over on the ankle and stretch the medial or lateral side of this joint. Eighty-five percent of all ankle sprains are of the *inversion* type, in which the ligaments on the lateral side of the ankle are stretched.

Table 17.2 provides an exercise protocol for inversion sprains after primary care and treatment have been administered. While eversion sprains are less frequent, this injury tends to be more serious and entail a longer recovery period. Most of the exercises listed in Table 17.2 could be used for an eversion sprain; the eversion exercises, however, should be eliminated.

While the primary focus of this chapter is on *activity* and *exercise*, the reader should be aware that other rehabilitative measures may have been or are currently being used. Hydrotherapy and/or cryotherapy are used to treat sprained ankles. Another mode of treatment or management, taping of the ankle, may be in evidence in physical education class. Sports medicine practitioners differ on the value, duration, and methods of taping or strapping. If ankle taping has been prescribed by sports medicine personnel, compliance by the student should be encouraged. The physical educator, however, should not make a practice of taping ankles, for this could set a precedent for a time-consuming practice.

Table 17.2 Rehabilitation Protocol for a Moderate Inversion Sprain of the Ankle

Stage	Activity	Purpose
I. Control and decrease swelling and pain	A1. Flexion, extension, and spreading of toes	A1. Work on intrinsic foot muscles and certain muscles that go across the ankle
	2. Exercises for noninvolved leg and upper extremities	2. Keep rest of body in good condition
	3. Crutch walking with touch weight bearing	3. Involve ankle in a minimal amount of motion, yet replicate as closely as possible a normal gait pattern
II. Begin restoration of strength and movement	B1. Ankle circumduction movements	B1. Involve ankle in the four basic movements of this joint
	2. Toe raises	2. Begin to develop plantar flexors

(Cont.)

Table 17.2 (Continued)

Stage	Activity	Purpose
	3. Eversion exercises—isometric then isotonic	3. Reinforce side of ankle that has been stretched
	4. Achilles tendon stretch in sitting position with toes in, out, and straight ahead	4. Improve dorsiflexion and slight inversion and eversion
	5. Shift body weight from injured side to uninjured side	5. Begin to retrain proprioception
III. Restore full function to ankle	C1. Ankle circumduction	C1. Continue to improve range of motion (ROM)
	2. Achilles tendon stretching in standing position	2. Work on dorsiflexion
	3. Eversion exercises	3. Improve strength for protection
	4. Plantar, dorsiflexion, and inversion exercises	4. Develop main muscle groups of ankle
IV. Restore full function to ankle	D1-4. As in previous stage	
	5. Tilt board exercises	D5. Work on proprioception
	6. Walk-jog	6-14. Develop functional and sport-specific activities
	7. Jog faster; stop	
	8. Run and sprint	
	9. Jog figure 8s	
	10. Run figure 8s	
	11. Cutting—half speed	
	12. Cutting—full speed	
	13. Run Z-shaped patterns	
	14. Backwards running	

Knee

A variety of conditions and situations involving the knee may affect physical education performance. Several exercise protocols are available to deal with these conditions and situations. The first program (Table 17.3) is for a person who has a *sprain of the medial collateral ligament*. This is a common injury because forces are applied to the lateral part of the knee with subsequent stretch-ing of ligaments on the medial side. In Table 17.3 a reference is made to the daily adjustable progressive resistive (DAPRE) program. This progressive resistance program (Table 17.4), developed by Knight (1979), can be used for other joints or body parts where rehabilitation or strength improvement is desired.

A third protocol (Table 17.5) is a *patella protection program* (Paulos, Rusche, Johnson, & Noyes, 1980). Because of the increased incidence

Table 17.3 Rehabilitation Protocol for a Medial Collateral Ligament Sprain

Stage	Activity	Purpose
I. Control and decrease swelling and pain	A1. Isometric contractions of quadriceps muscles (quad setting) and hamstring muscles	A1. Prevent atrophy of muscles around knee
	2. Straight leg raises and dorsiflex the ankles	2. Work quadriceps muscles and stretch triceps surae
	3. Walk on crutches	3. Provide a method of ambulation
	4. General conditioning exercises for other three extremities	4. Keep rest of body in good condition
II. Begin to restore strength and movement at knee joint	B1. Isometric contractions of quadriceps and hamstring muscles	B1. Help to keep muscle tone
	2. Begin active range of motion (ROM) exercises	2. Need to have full motion at the knee
	3. General conditioning exercises of other extremities	3. Keep rest of body fit
III. Restore full function to knee	C1. Do isotonic exercise (DAPRE)	C1. Need to have sufficient strength to do activities and protect knee
	2. Steps D5-15 as delineated in Table 17.2	2. Same as in Table 17.2

Table 17.4 Daily Adjustable Progressive Resistance Exercise (DAPRE)

Set	Weight	Repetitions
1	50% of working weight	10
2	75% of working weight	6
3	100% of working weight	Maximum
4	Determined by repetitions done in third set[a]	Maximum number determines working weight for next session

(Cont.)

Table 17.4 (Continued)

Working weight adjustments

Repetitions during third set[a]	Working weight for fourth set
0 - 2	Decrease 5 to 10 lb
3 - 4	Decrease 0 to 5 lb
5 - 7	Keep the same
8 - 10	Increase 2.5 to 5 lb
More than 10	Increase 5 to 10 lb

Repetitions during fourth set	Working weight for next session[a]
0 - 2	Decrease 5 to 10 lb
3 - 4	Keep the same
5 - 7	Increase 2.5 to 7.5 lb
8 - 10	Increase 5 to 10 lb
More than 10	Increase 10 to 15 lb

[a]From Knight, K. (1979). Rehabilitating chondromalacia patellae. *The Physician and Sportsmedicine*, **1**, 147-148.

Table 17.5 Patella Protection Program

Stage	Activity	Purpose
I. Decrease inflammation and atrophy	A1. Isometric exercises (10 repetitions for 10 s; 10 s relax)	A1. Develop quadriceps muscles
	2. Flexibility exercises for lower extremity	2. Keep appropriate range of motion (ROM) in all major joints of leg
II. Develop strength without pain	B1. Terminal extension exercises[a]	B1. Continue to develop quadricep muscles without undue stress on patello-femoral surfaces
III. Develop maximum strength and endurance	C1. Isotonic extension exercises relegated to 0 to 20°	C1. Maintain reduced stress on patello-femoral surfaces

Stage	Activity	Purpose
	2. Isotonic flexion exercises through full ROM	2. Flexion exercises do not put undue stress on patello-femoral surfaces
	3. Flexibility exercises continued	3. Need to have full ROM at this joint and appropriate level of flexibility for future activities
	4. Endurance exercises in the form of swimming or bicycle ergometer work	4. Endurance components, both muscular and cardiovascular, need to be developed for future activities
IV. Restore full function to knee	D1. Continue strength and endurance exercises	D1. Need to increase these components to be comparable with nonaffected extremity
	2. Work on balance activities	2. Develop proprioception for this extremity
	3. Work on activities that are specific to sports or recreational activities	3. Address concept of task specificity

Note. Adapted from Paulos, L., Rusche, K., Johnson, C., & Noyes, F.R. (1980). Patellar malalignment: A treatment rationale. *Physical Therapy,* **60,** 1624-1632.
[a]To be explained in text under the heading "Selected Exercises"

of patella chondromalacia and other knee-related problems, "short arc" exercise programs like this one are being used in strength development and rehabilitation programs. Short arc refers to knee movement in the last 5° to 25° of extension. This program could be used with students who have iliotibial band syndrome, patella tendonitis, Osgood-Schlatter's condition, patellar subluxation, and rheumatoid joint disease.

Shoulder

The shoulder is composed of several major joints; sternoclavicular, acromioclavicular, scapulocostal, and glenohumeral. In many instances, activity-related strains or overuse syndromes involve the glenohumeral joint. Rotator cuff impingement syndrome, tendonitis, bursitis, and other glenohumeral problems may benefit from a general mobilizing and conditioning program for this joint (Table 17.6). This program is *contraindicated* for students suffering from *anterior glenohumeral dislocation.* In its chronic form, this condition is sometimes referred to as a "trick shoulder."

Mobilization for this condition consists primarily of adduction and/or internal rotation exercises. During the immobilization stage, isometric exercises are the exercises of choice; following immobilization the exercise regimen may progress from isometric exercises, such as pulling against rubber tubing, to pulley or free-weight exercises that emphasize adduction and internal rotation. It should be noted that external rotation and abduction are movements associated with the mechanism of injury.

Table 17.6 Shoulder Exercise Protocol for the Glenohumeral Joint

I. During period of immobilization	A1. Isometric contractions of major muscle groups of shoulder	A1. Reduce muscle atrophy
	2. Isotonic wrist exercises of involved extremity	2. These muscles may be kept in condition without involving shoulder muscle
	3. General conditioning exercises for the other three extremities	3. These muscle groups should be kept in good condition
II. Mobilization of the shoulder	B1. Work on moving the shoulder through abduction and external rotation	B1. Begin to gain appropriate range of motion (ROM)
	2. Codman's exercise[a]	2. Begins to enhance four motions of the shoulder
	3. Wall climbing exercise	3. Help to develop abduction and external rotation
	4. Continue conditioning of other extremities	4. Improve body fitness
III. Development of shoulder	C1. Isotonic exercises that involve shoulder flexion, extension, abduction, adduction, medial rotation, and lateral rotation	C1. Develop muscles that cause specific motions
	2. Specific exercise involvement: bench press, pullovers, push-ups, parallel bar dips	2. Develop muscles for aggregate muscle action
	3. Resistance movements that replicate sport activities	3. Conform to the principle of specificity

Note. Not to be used with glenohumeral dislocations
[a]Explained in text under the heading "Selected Exercises"

Selected Exercises

This section describes selected exercises (see Tables 17.2 through 17.6) that may not be familiar to the reader. Table 17.2 refers to tilt-board exercises. The apparatus used with this exercise, which is available commercially or could easily be constructed, is basically a circle of 3/4-in plywood that is 1 ft in diameter (Figure 17.2). Attached to the center of the board is half of a pool ball or similiar wooden ball. Standing with both feet on the board, the user attempts to balance on the

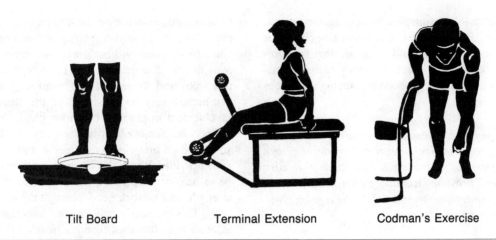

Tilt Board   Terminal Extension   Codman's Exercise

Figure 17.2 Selected exercises.

board. This apparatus could be used in a balancing task for nonhandicapped or handicapped students who need balance training.

Terminal extension exercises are listed as an intermediate strength exercise for quadricep development in the patella protection program (Table 17.5). Ideally, this exercise is done with a knee extension machine rather than a weight boot or weights wrapped around the ankle. The latter procedure causes a traction or pulling effect on the knee, which could stretch ligaments. Terminal extension exercises are initiated with the knee completely extended and resistance applied to the extremity (Figure 17.2). In subsequent exercise sessions, isotonic contractions are started with 5° of extension. Over a number of sessions, the degree of extension is increased until the person can extend against resistance through 25° of motion.

In Table 17.6 Codman's exercise is listed as an exercise to mobilize the shoulder. In this exercise, the participant bends over at the waist to achieve 90° of trunk flexion and holds on to a chair or the end of a table. In this position the arm of the affected side should hang in a relaxed state. The person initiates motion in a flexion-extension direction, then adduction-abduction, and finally circumduction. All of these motions are pendular

in nature without benefit of muscular contractions at the shoulder joint. Progressions in this exercise include wider circumduction motions and holding 2-1/2- and 5-lb weights as motions are performed (Figure 17.2).

Long-Term Disorders

This section will deal with several conditions that are classified as long-term disorders. The designation implies a condition or a problem that will last longer than 30 days. This time span is, to an extent, an arbitrary designation, because a third-degree ankle sprain (discussed in a previous section) may not be totally rehabilitated within these 30 days. Two conditions will be the primary focus here, but certain principles and procedures relevant to these conditions may be applied to the integration of students with other long-term conditions into regular physical education classes.

Fractures

While most bones may be fractured in various types of accidents, bones in the upper and lower extremities are often fractured in activity-related accidents—for example, in landing on an outstretched arm. While the focus of this chapter is activity, readers should be aware that fractures may result from other situations such as child abuse and pathologic bone weakening conditions like cancer.

For physical educators, the student with a fracture presents two challenges: first, developing a program for a student immobilized in a cast; second, providing assistance after removal of the cast to integrate the student into the regular physical education program.

The first challenge must be dealt with from the perspective that the *unaffected three fourths of the extremities* have normal movement. A student with a broken arm has no problem concerning ambulation and can easily maintain a high level of cardiovascular fitness. Strength development of three extremities can be pursued with only minimal modification or adaptation. With a broken arm, certain lifts such as the bench press would have to be eliminated, but development of the triceps of the nonaffected arm could be accomplished through other exercises, such as elbow extension exercises. Involvement of the affected arm should be predicated on recommendations from the physician and on good judgment. For example, any type of isometric exercise involving muscles immobilized in a cast should be approved by the physician. Exercises, isotonic or isometric, involving joints above or below the cast area should also have physician approval; this, however, does not mean that exercises are contraindicated for these joints.

Participation in physical education activities is based upon the nature of the activities in the unit. While a track unit may mean little restriction for the student with a broken arm, a unit on gymnastic activities may require considerable restriction. For the person with a broken radius of the nondominant arm, a badminton unit will need very little modification. An archery unit, while less demanding of vigorous activity, does require use of both upper extremities; the student could use a crossbow, which needs dexterity of one arm and could be mounted on a camera tripod. When unit activities preclude participation because of a fracture, physical fitness of the remaining three extremities may be the focus of the student's involvement in physical education class.

Once the *cast is removed*, the curricular focus should be on *integrating* the student into *normal class activities*. Part of this integration process may be to help develop range of motion, flexibility, strength, and muscular endurance in the affected limb. This assistance may be very important for students from low socioeconomic levels who may not have the benefit of appropriate medical services. Most students, regardless of socioeconomic background, can benefit from a systemic reconditioning program. Activities and exercises described in the earlier section entitled "Activity Injuries" may be incorporated into this program. The student's total integration into the regular physical education program is dependent upon a group of factors: the nature of the fracture, the extent of immobilization, the duration of the reconditioning period, and the nature of unit activities.

Osgood-Schlatter's Condition

A long-term condition that often presents a dilemma for the physical educator is Osgood-Schlatter's condition. *Not a disease*, as some books describe it, the condition involves incomplete separation of the epiphysis of the tibial tubercle from the tibia. O'Donoghue (1984) considers this condition to be more than just a single problem. Whether Osgood-Schlatter's condition is due to singular or plural causes, it affects primarily males aged 13 to 15; incidence among girls has increased in recent years (Strauss, 1984). The treatment varies from immobilization in a cast to restriction of explosive extension movements at the knee, such as jumping and kicking. Variation in treatment depends on the severity of the condition and the philoso-

phy of the attending physician concerning its management.

The physical educator should help the student with this condition *during both its stages*: (a) the acute stage of involvement and (b) the recovery stage. Because 60% to 75% of all cases are unilateral (Mital & Matza, 1977), affected students may be considered to have normal status for three fourths of their extremities. In essence, the approach discussed in the earlier section on fractures may be applied here. The comparison is applicable not only from a programmatic standpoint but also from a causality perspective, for with Osgood-Schlatter's condition there is a type of avulsion or fracture of bone from the tibial tuberosity. Involvement of the affected knee in activity must be based on a physician's recommendation. For example, certain physicians may approve isometric contractions of the quadriceps and stretching of the hamstrings in the affected extremity. Ankle exercises may also be considered appropriate for the affected limb. When all symptoms have disappeared and the physician has approved full participation, the student should begin a general mobilizing program in physical education class. Development of strength and flexibility of the affected limb should be part of the student's physical education program. Special attention should be given to the ratio of quadriceps to hamstring strength. The hamstrings should have 50% to 55% of the quadriceps' isotonic strength. The physical educator should evaluate (and improve where needed) the student's gait pattern following the occurrence of Osgood-Schlatter's condition.

Weight Control Problems

Many people associate weight control problems with the obese person going for the fourth serving at an all-you-can-eat smorgasbord. In reality there are *two types of weight control problems: overweight* and *underweight*. Both problems pose serious threats to a student's health.

Underweight

Only recently have the terms *anorexia nervosa* and *bulimia* become familiar to the general public. School staff and faculty, including physical educators, should realize that a coordinated effort among parents, student, physician, and school personnel is needed to deal with these problems.

Anorexia nervosa is a preoccupation with being thin that is manifested in willful self-starvation and may be accompanied by excessive physical activity. Most cases—95%—involve females, usually between the ages of 12 and 19. During the early stages both parents and student may be unaware that the condition is developing. As it progresses, the student becomes emaciated and hungry but denies the existence of the problem. Anorexia nervosa is not to be regarded lightly, for mortality rates range from 5% to 15% among diagnosed anorexics. Death is the result of circulatory collapse or cardiac arrhythmias due to electrolyte imbalance.

Bulimia is a condition associated with anorexia nervosa; it involves obsessive eating habits with ritualistic purging of ingested food by means of self-induced vomiting or laxatives. This practice also leads to electrolyte imbalance, impaired liver and kidney functioning, stomach rupture, tooth decay, and esophagitis.

The goals of treatment to promote weight gain in these conditions are simplistic in nature but challenging in execution. Hospitalization in a medical or psychiatric unit may be needed to initiate treatment, with a brief stay of 2 weeks or a longer period of several months to a year. Treatment consists of behavior modification, vitamin and mineral supplements, appropriate diet, and psychotherapy for the student and family. Low self-esteem, guilt, and anxiety are often part of the student's underlying problem.

The physical educator may be one of the first to recognize these problems. Anorexic or bulimic students present a profile of being compliant high-achievers. A preoccupation with thinness, apparent weight loss, and an increasing involvement in aerobic activities may be signs that referral to an appropriate health professional is needed. Whatever the stage of the student's disorder, physical education activities must be monitored to ensure an appropriate level of exertion. A caloric deficit—more calories being used than are taken in—should not be allowed to develop through or in conjunction with physical education activities. Fitness enhancement should be a gradual process, with strength gains achieved before cardiovascular endurance is attempted. Precautions or exercise contraindications for students with cardiovascular conditions, to be discussed in a subsequent section, are applicable in this situation. Dual and individual sports, some with certain modifications, are of suitable intensity and good for facilitating social interaction. A priority with the anorexic or bulimic student should be enhancement of self-esteem.

Overweight

A major health concern today is the number of overweight and obese students. Overweight is generally regarded as 10% over the appropriate weight, based on height and somatotype. Obesity is generally defined as at least 20% over appropriate weight. However, there are gender differences: Females may be considered obese when they exceed the appropriate weight by 30% to 35%; for males the range is 20% to 25%. One out of 10 school-age children is overweight. Both physical educators and adapted physical educators must cope with and provide suitable physical education experiences for overweight and obese students.

The cause of this condition is multifaceted in nature. While endocrine disorders may cause excessive weight gains, fewer that 10% of all cases can be attributed to this cause. Hypothalamic, pituitary, and thyroid dysfunction are causes of endocrine obesity. In the case of the hypothalamic dysfunction, damping of the hunger sensation does not take place, and a person feels hungry after consuming sufficient calories. Certain medications such as cortisone and adrenocortical steroids may produce the side effect of appetite elevation, with

concomitant weight gain. There seems to be a set of emotional factors that may result in overweight and obesity. Some people eat as a means of compensation or to reduce feelings of anxiety; others, however, eat excessively when content and happy.

Demographic variables related to obesity are gender, age, and socioeconomic level. Females are more likely than males to be obese at all age levels. The critical age range for obesity is between 20 and 50 years, and obesity is more prevalent among people from lower socioeconomic levels.

An increase in the number (hypertrophic obesity) or size (hyperplastic obesity) of the fat cells that make up adipose tissue may lead to obesity. There are two periods during which there are rapid increases in fat cell production: (a) the third trimester and the first year of life and (b) the adolescent growth spurt. Between these two periods the number of fat cells increases gradually. There is some evidence that vigorous exercise during childhood may reduce the size and number of fat cells (Saltin & Rowell, 1980).

Strategies for Weight Control

The physical educator is one member of a team who may help a student with a weight control problem. Just as exercise alone cannot remediate a weight problem, the physical educator alone cannot solve this problem. A team effort is needed, with the physician overseeing medical and dietary matters, the parents providing appropriate diet and psychological support, and the physical educator selecting the exercises and activities best for the obese or overweight student.

There are basically three ways to lose weight: diet, exercise, and a combination of the two. Diet alone is the most common method used by adults and is often the most abused method. The criterion frequently used to judge success with this approach is how quickly the maximum number of pounds can be lost. Certain fad diets, such as the Stillman and Scarsdale diets, may pose a health hazard for certain individuals. A crash diet may even trigger a starvation reaction, which causes the basal metabolic rate to diminish and may increase metabolic efficiency during physical activity. In this way, the body counteracts certain effects of the crash diet. A more gradual approach is a reduction of 500 calories a day, which in a week equals 3,500 calories—the number of calories needed to lose a pound of fat. Under the direction of a physician, an obese student may be on a diet that reduces intake by more than 500 calories per day.

Exercise helps with weight control, but it is a slow, difficult process if used as the sole method for weight reduction. On the other hand, exercise used in conjunction with a controlled diet may help to generate a negative caloric imbalance; this imbalance results when more calories are being used than are being consumed.

Physical Education and the Obese Student

A well-designed physical education program for overweight and obese students may contribute to increased caloric expenditure. There are, however, certain limitations or problems the physical educator must recognize and cope with in developing such a program.

Sherrill (1986) noted the following physical characteristics associated with obesity that may affect program planning:

- Distended abdomen
- Skeletal immaturity
- Mobility of fat rolls
- Edema
- Excessive perspiration
- Broad base in locomotor activities
- Galling between the thighs
- Fear of falling
- Postural faults
- Excessive buoyancy

Sherrill explains that the distended abdomen places excessive pressure on the diaphragm, with a resultant difficulty in breathing and a buildup of carbon dioxide. The consequence is a manifestation of drowsiness on the part of the obese student. The label of "lazy" may be an unfair designation, for this student has a physiological disadvantage.

The physical education program should be developed to provide successful experiences for the obese student. Activities that require lifting or excessively moving the body weight will not result in positive experiences. Gymnastic activities, distance running, rope climbing, and field events such as long jump may need extensive modification for the obese student. Gradual enhancement of endurance capabilities should be part of the student's program. Fast walking, bicycle riding, and certain swimming pool activities may help to develop aerobic endurance. Aquatic activities are usually deemed appropriate for many types of special populations; with the obese student activities such as water calisthenics may be quite appropriate because buoyancy may reduce stress on joints such as the knees, ankles, and feet. Excessive buoyancy may be counterproductive, as Sherrill (1986) points out, because this force may keep parts of the body out of the water, thus impeding the execution of certain swimming strokes.

Many of the typical units covered in a physical education class will need considerable modification for obese students. A basketball or football unit may center on developing certain fundamental skills such as passing, catching, kicking, and shooting. Softball may include the development of fundamental skills and involve modification of some rules—for example, allowing for courtesy or pinch runners. Dual and individual sports with modifications such as boundary or rule changes (i.e., the ball may bounce twice in handball) are appropriate activities. Golf, archery, and bowling need no modification, while tennis and racquetball may be feasible only in doubles play.

All curricular experiences should be oriented toward helping obese students *develop a positive attitude* toward themselves and toward activity. Physical education experiences—whether doing a caloric analysis of energy expenditures, learning to drive a golf ball, or being permitted to wear a different type of sport clothing than the typical gym uniform—should help obese students cope with their condition and should contribute directly or indirectly to the solution of the weight control problem. Finally, any strategy to improve self-image will help these students deal with their situation. Likewise, any strategy that changes the other students' attitude toward those with weight problems will facilitate integration of obese and overweight students into the social environment.

Diabetes Mellitus

Diabetes mellitus is a chronic disease characterized by insufficient insulin and disturbances of carbohydrate, protein, and fat metabolism. This disease affects approximately 11 million people in the United States. It is responsible for 50% of myocardial infarctions and 75% of all strokes; it is a major cause of new blindness and a causal factor for amputations (Duda, 1985). Ten percent of documented cases occur among school-aged children (Remein & Shields, 1962). This statistic has direct implications for physical education programs, because there is an excellent chance of having a diabetic student in class.

Insulin-dependent diabetes mellitus (IDDM) has, in certain cases, been linked to a viral origin; genetic or hereditary causes have also been associated with this type of diabetes. Also cited as a possible cause is an autoimmune reaction in which a virus may affect bodily cells and the immune system no longer identifies these cells as part of the body. These cells, which may be beta cells in the pancreas, are then destroyed or rejected by the body. Several factors seem to increase the likelihood of developing IDDM:

• Obesity
• Emotional stress
• Pregnancy
• Oral contraceptives
• Medications such as corticosteroids

There are *two types of diabetes*: (a) IDDM, also known as ketosis-prone or juvenile diabetes, and (b) non-insulin-dependent diabetes mellitus (NIDDM), also known as ketosis-resistant or maturity-onset diabetes. Insulin-dependent diabetes mellitus occurs most frequently before age 30 but may develop at any age. This type of diabetes requires daily insulin injections and dietary management. The treatment of non-insulin-dependent diabetes, by contrast, may be diet alone or in conjunction with insulin or hypoglycemic agents.

Because most school-age diabetics are insulin dependent, this section will deal exclusively with this form of the disease. With IDDM, pancreatic cells, particularly in the islets of Langerhans, degenerate and/or disappear; consequently, insulin production is diminished. Related complications are interference with the action of insulin at the cellular level, faulty storage of sugar in the liver, overproduction of sugar in the liver, and diminished utilization of sugar at the tissue level.

Insulin-dependent diabetes may become apparent dramatically, with ketoacidosis, or gradually with an asymptomatic status as in mild diabetes. With a deficiency of insulin the body cannot convert glucose to glycogen for storage in the liver, and an excess of sugar accumulates in the blood. Inadequate carbohydrate utilization also affects fat metabolism. When there is improper fat usage, waste products called ketones are formed, providing a condition called acidosis.

Symptoms of ketoacidosis or diabetic coma are extreme thirst; dry mucous membranes; labored breathing; weak and rapid pulse; sweet, fruity breath odor; vomiting; and high sugar content in the urine. This condition is a first-rank medical emergency and should be treated at a hospital with dosages of insulin and intravenous fluids for a dehydrated state.

Another condition that may be corrected more easily is insulin shock or hypoglycemia, which occurs when glycogen stored in the liver is depleted.

Symptoms of insulin shock *or* hypoglycemia *are fatigue, excessive perspiration, hunger, double vision, tremor, and absence of sugar in the urine. If this condition is not in an advanced stage, the ingestion of fruit juice, a candy bar, honey, or a carbonated (not diet) drink should rectify the sugar imbalance. When shock is severe enough to result in unconsciousness, an injection of glucagon or dextrose is used to elevate the glucose level in the blood.*

Physical Education and the Diabetic Student

The observation of certain procedures and protocols should ensure the diabetic student's successful involvement in physical education activities. Diabetes does not preclude exceptional achievement in sport activities, as evidenced by Ron Santo of the Chicago Cubs, Catfish Hunter of the New York Yankees, and tennis player Bill Talbert.

Both the student and physical educator must be aware of the interrelationship of diet, insulin intake, and exercise. The site of the insulin injection may depend on the kind of exercise planned. Insulin is a protein that cannot be taken orally because the digestive juices would destroy it; therefore, it must be injected subcutaneously. Injections are needed once or twice a day and should be administered at sites where the muscles are not used extensively in a sport or physical activity. Thus, for a student who is participating in track, the injection site should be the stomach rather than the legs. Another important consideration is the interaction between exercise and insulin dosage. There is an inverse relationship between the intensity of activity and the amount of insulin needed. A heightened level of activity

necessitates a reduction in insulin dosage. The physical educator must alert the diabetic student to any planned changes in kind or intensity of activity; in anticipation, the student will have to make appropriate adjustments in insulin dosage and/or diet.

Generally, the diabetic tries to keep three factors constant: *exercise, insulin usage*, and *diet*. A variation in one or more of these factors may precipitate a physiological imbalance. For example, a reduction in calories and an increase in exercise intensity may lead to insulin shock; an increase in calories and a reduction in insulin can lead to diabetic coma.

A diabetic student must constantly monitor the sugar level in the body. Several times a day the student will use a urine sample or blood test to evaluate the sugar level; the teacher should provide the time and privacy to conduct this test. A key to diabetes control is keeping the blood glucose level in the normal range. Close monitoring permits diabetics to determine how well they are managing their condition, and it is essential for safe participation in physical education or athletics.

There are some other factors or situations for both the physical educator and the diabetic to consider. A student involved in an intense exercise or training program should increase food intake rather than altering insulin dosage. Carbohydrate loading is not appropriate for diabetics; rather, they should take in carbohydrates during exercise because they lack the capacity for storing glycogen. As diabetics become older, circulatory problems may become a real concern. This should not exclude the school-age student from participating in contact or collision sports. Good skin care, however, should be encouraged by the physical educator.

Physicians today recognize the benefits for diabetics of participation in all kinds of physical activity including contact sports. Moreover, we live in a society that is increasingly aware of fitness, and physical fitness for the diabetic should be part of the physical education program.

Seizure Disorders

Seizure disorders, convulsive disorders, and epilepsy are terms used to describe a condition of the brain that is characterized by recurrent seizures. These episodes are related to erratic electrochemical brain discharges. It is estimated that 1% to 2% of the population have some type of seizure disorder; the incidence is higher in families that have a history of such disorders. Possible causes of epilepsy are severe birth trauma, drug abuse, congenital brain malformation, infection, brain tumor, poor cerebral circulation, and head trauma. Between 50% and 70% of all cases are idiopathic, with no known cause and no structural damage to the nervous system. The Epilepsy Foundation of America claims that, each year, 190,000 Americans sustain seizure-producing head trauma. This estimate was made during the era when the national speed limit was 55 mph; with an increase in the speed limit, the number of head injuries should increase as well.

Several systems have been developed to categorize seizure disorders. One approach dichotomizes this condition into generalized nonconvulsive and general convulsive seizures. Another system classifies seizures as grand mal, petit mal, jacksonian, focal epilepsy, psychomotor, jackknife seizures, and Lennox-Gastaul syndrome. The classification system endorsed by the Epilepsy Foundation of America has four categories: partial seizures, generalized seizures, unilateral seizures, and unclassified seizures.

Partial seizures originate from a localized area of the brain and usually are symptom specific. The traditional terms psychomotor and jacksonian would indicate seizures in this category. A jacksonian seizure begins as a localized seizure and may subsequently involve surrounding areas of the brain. It is manifested in jerky or stiff movements of an extremity, with tingling sensations in the limb. The seizure may start in a finger, spread to the hand, and finally affect the rest of the arm.

Sometimes a partial seizure of this type becomes a generalized tonic-clonic (grand mal) seizure.

The complex partial seizure may have different types of symptoms, but generally purposeless behavior is in evidence. The person may exhibit a glassy stare, produce undiscernible speech, engage in purposeless wandering, and emit strange noises. After this type of seizure a person may seem confused and is sometimes mistakenly thought to be drunk or on drugs.

Myoclonic, atonic, generalized tonic-clonic, and absence seizures are forms of generalized seizures. Absence seizures (petit mal), often found in children, usually last from 1 to 10 s. There are no overt manifestations, such as postural changes or interruption of activities, but there is a brief change in the level of consciousness. A teacher may mistake this change in consciousness for daydreaming or inattentiveness. This type of seizure rarely occurs during exercise. Myoclonic seizures are characterized by brief, involuntary quivers of the body sometimes occurring in rhythmic fashion. An atonic seizure is sometimes called "drop attack" because the person falls to the floor and is unconscious for a few seconds; this brief episode may result in injury from the fall.

A generalized tonic-clonic (grand mal) seizure is the most common type of seizure. In many people it is preceded by a warning or an aura, an experience such as a dreamy feeling, nausea, a visual disturbance, or olfactory sensations. Sensations of this nature are probably the beginning of abnormal brain discharges.

A generalized tonic-clonic seizure may begin with a guttural cry, loss of consciousness and falling to the floor, boardlike rigidity changing to quivering and jerking, wild thrashing movements, foaming at the mouth, labored breathing, and incontinence. This series of events may last from 2 to 5 min; the person regains consciousness, may be somewhat confused, and may feel sleepy and fatigued.

The following factors seem to promote the occurrence of seizures:

- Alcohol consumption
- Psychological stress
- Increase in blood alkalinity
- Hyperventilation
- Menstrual period
- Constipation
- Flashing lights of a certain velocity

While the cause of many seizure disorders has not been determined, treatment is highly successful. Approximately 80% of people with seizure disorders can control the conditions by using anticonvulsant drugs. Medications frequently prescribed for epileptics include phenytoin, phenobarbital, carbomazeprine, and primidone. Phenytoin (Dilantin) is prescribed for generalized tonic-clonic seizures because it does not produce the side effect of drowsiness. In females it may cause increased hair growth on the face and extremities. Phenobarbital (Luminal) is also used for generalized seizures but may produce hyperactivity with elementary-school-age students. For partial seizures ethosuximide (Zarontin) and trimethadione (Tridione) are often prescribed.

The following are first-aid measures for a generalized tonic-clonic seizure. If an epileptic has some warning or aura of an impending seizure, help the person into a supine position. Remove glasses and false teeth, if appropriate. Loosen tight-fitting clothes, and place a pillow or rolled-up cloth material under the head. If there is no warning, help the person into a lying position and follow the procedures just described; in addition, clear the area of hard objects. Do not attempt to restrain movements or force anything into the person's mouth, because tongue blades or other objects may break teeth and lacerate the mouth. If the mouth is open, some authorities advocate placing a soft object such as a clean, folded handkerchief between the teeth. Turn the head to provide an open airway and allow saliva to drain from the mouth. After the seizure subsides, the person should be told what happened, given reassurance, and, if tired, be allowed to rest.

If a seizure occurs, it is important to make a detailed written account of it. This information not only is important for the school system's incident reports but also provides input that lets the physician evaluate the severity and duration of the person's seizures and adjust drug dosages, if necessary.

Physical Education and Students With Seizure Disorders

Participation in physical education by students with seizure disorders has evolved through several stages. At one time physical education for this population was relatively passive, with activities like croquet, golf, and bowling being recommended. The next stage was a more vigorous program, with most activities being permitted except contact sports. Today, all activities including contact sports are deemed appropriate; the only stipulation is that the student's seizures be controlled (Livingston & Berman, 1974). The possibility of a blow to the head causing a seizure does not seem to be a valid reason for exclusion. Another misconception is that physical activity will precipitate seizures; in reality, physical activity may elevate the seizure threshold. The extent to which seizures are controlled through medication is the key factor in the selection of physical education activities.

Frequently, students with seizure disorders do not exhibit normal levels of physical fitness and motor skill development. While progress has been made toward controlling seizures, social factors such as protective parents and the stigma associated with a seizure disorder contribute to a passive lifestyle. Physical educators may help these students become more actively involved in sports and physical activity.

A major concern of the physical educator is the student's safety. While students with seizure disorders may engage in most activities, certain precautions should be observed. To engage in aquatic activities, which are often an object of concern, students should have their seizures under control. For swimming, the buddy system should be standard operating procedure. Also, the physical educator should be sure that the medication is not causing a side effect that may compromise safety procedures. If seizures are not controlled or side effects pose a risk, then activities such as weight training, gymnastics, and rope climbing must be modified or excluded from the student's program. However, because 80% of all students with epilepsy have their seizures under control, most students with seizure disorders may engage in a varied and beneficial physical education program.

Asthma

The student with asthma may be apprehensive about participating in physical education class. The regular or adapted physical educator should help to *alleviate this anxiety*; unfortunately, some physical educators have been inept in handling situations with asthmatic students. The purpose of this section is to provide guidance concerning the involvement of asthmatic students in physical education classes.

There are 9 million asthmatics in the United States; 50% of all cases begin in children under the age of 10. Twice as many males as females are affected by this condition.

While there are various theories concerning the types and causes of asthma, the mechanisms for the obstructive symptoms are (a) spasm of the muscular layer in the bronchial walls, (b) swollen mucous membrane, and (c) mucus secretions in the airways. All three conditions reduce the diameter of the bronchial passages and impede air flow.

Systems for classifying asthmatic disorders are oriented toward causation. One system reflects a dichotomy of causes. Extrinsic or allergic asthma occurs in children or adults who have a history of allergic reactions. These people are allergic to such offending substances as dust, pollen, animal danders, mold spores, and certain drugs. Intrinsic or nonallergic asthma may be induced by excessive exercise or may be psychosomatic in nature. Some authorities contend that a person may suffer from a combination of both extrinsic and intrinsic types.

The asthmatic may present symptoms ranging from brief episodes of wheezing, shortness of breath, and coughing to breathlessness, which will cause the person to talk in one- to two-word sentences, to tighten neck muscles with inhalation, and to exhibit a blue or gray coloration of lips and nail beds. When a student with asthma has difficulty breathing, the physical educator should help establish an upright position with shoulders relaxed, advise the student to drink a lot of fluids, provide reassurance, and encourage the student to take appropriate medication if one has been prescribed for such occasions. The school nurse, parent, or physician should be notified if a prescribed medication does not seem to be effective.

Physical educators, especially, should be aware of a condition known as either *exercise-induced asthma* (EIA) or *exercise-induced bronchospasm* (EIB). Exercise of high intensity or duration seems to precipitate muscular contraction of the bronchial tubes, which results in an asthmatic attack. A commonly accepted hypothesis is that intrathoracic airways are cooled during exercise by air that has not been completely warmed. This is related to abnormal increases in the rate and depth of breathing because the coolness affects airway mast cells, which liberate bronchoconstrictive substances.

The following factors influence the occurrence of EIA:

- Exercise intensity
- Type of exercise

- Interval versus sustained exercise
- Absence of warm-up
- Condition of air
- Use of preexercise medication

The implications of these factors for the physical education setting will be reflected in guidelines presented in the section called "Physical Education and the Asthmatic."

Medication and Asthma

Recent advances in medication have helped markedly to prevent EIA and have permitted asthmatics to be active in physical education and sport. Aerosol medication acts rapidly on the prime target area, the lungs. Cromolyn sodium and beta adrenergic agonists such as terbutaline are often the agents of choice, used singularly or in combination before exercise. These drugs should be administered 30 min to an hour before physical education class or sport participation. A word of caution must accompany the use of these pharmacological agents. First, there is concern among physicians that aerosols may be used to excess, and some recommend oral medication for children and certain adolescents. Excessive aerosol use can have deleterious effects; a relationship has been established between excessive use and an increase in mortality rate of asthmatics in Great Britain. Second, the use of certain drugs is prohibited in high-level competition. For example, use of isoproterenol or ephedrine would disqualify an athlete from Olympic competition.

Physical Education and the Asthmatic

Integration of the asthmatic student into the physical education class should follow these guidlines:

1. Consult the school nurse and/or the records to ascertain the status of the student's asthmatic condition. If no up-to-date information is available, a conference should be scheduled with the committee on adapted physical education. (See chapter 3 for a discussion of this committee.)
2. Together with the student, discuss feelings about exercise and collectively develop goals for physical education.
3. Conduct warm-up activities at the beginning of each class before bouts of vigorous activity. The purpose is to increase the body temperature until a mild sweat is developed. Warm-up might consist of walking, jogging, light mobilizing activities, and even some strengthening activities.
4. Classes should last from 30 to 40 min; shorter classes and interpolated rests should initially be the program for the unfit student.
5. If possible, asthmatic students should have class or engage in physical activity four or five times a week.
6. Gradually increase the level of exercise intensity. With an interval training regime, exercise intensity may be elevated to 70% of maximum heart rate. Rest intervals should be only brief enough to reduce the heart rate to 50% of maximum.
7. Administer preexercise medication as prescribed by the physician.
8. Establisn emergency procedures for coping with EIA episodes.
9. End each class with a cool-down period. At no time should vigorous activity be stopped abruptly. The student should at least walk around the gymnasium until the heart rate returns to within 20 beats per minute of the resting level.
10. Short-burst (anaerobic) or short-duration activities should be the predominant type of curricular activity for asthmatic students. For example, softball is a short-burst activity; soccer would not fall into this category.
11. While general strengthening exercises are valuable for the asthmatic, special emphasis should be placed on developing abdominal,

trunk, and shoulder muscles. Gymnastics may serve as a valuable adjunct to this strength development phase.

12. Class participation should emphasize cooperative endeavors and enjoyment of team play rather than winning.

13. Aquatic activities provide many benefits. Conducted in a warm, damp environment, they promote control of breathing and involve numerous muscle groups.

14. Other activities that emphasize breath control may be incorporated into the student's curriculum. Karate and various forms of dance are valuable in this regard.

15. A healtnful environment should be maintained. The physical educator should regularly clean and air gym mats, and students should be responsible for keeping their gym clothes, lockers, and gym shoes clean. Mats, shoes, and lockers harbor molds and dust.

16. While specific breathing exercises are a topic of controversy, activities that stress exhalation may be of value in a physical education class. Blowing Ping-Pong balls while on a gym scooter or in a swimming pool may help expiration and facilitate airflow out of the lungs. To help prevent hyperventilation, make sure students exhale twice as often as they inhale. Other activities that emphasize exhalation are balloon relays, blowing tissues in the air, and laughing.

17. Whether a student is on the gym floor, in the swimming pool, or on the softball field, provision should be made for disposing of coughed-up mucus. Tissues, some type of spittoon, or other convenience should be available for the asthmatic student.

18. Finally, a well-conducted physical education program should not only help students learn to pace themselves but also help them experience the joy of physical activity.

Cancer

Approximately 350,000 Americans die of cancer each year; it is second only to cardiovascular disease as a cause of death. While cancer is often associated with advancing age, it is a leading cause of death among children. Only accidents claim more victims among this age group.

Cancer is usually categorized according to the tissue that is affected. Malignant tumors of connective, muscular, or bone tissue are called sarcomas, while neoplasms of the epithelial tissue that covers surfaces, lines cavities, and constitutes glands are referred to as carcinomas. A clear understanding has not been established concerning the mechanisms of cell division; cancer cells differ in size and multiply more rapidly than normal cells. This uncontrolled, rapid growth may originate at a primary site and spread, or metastasize, to other locations of the body. Certain substances such as asbestos, nitrogen mustard, and cigarette smoke have been identified as carcinogenic in nature. Among school-age students, leukemia and tumors of the central nervous system are the most frequently occurring forms of cancer. Bone tumors are more common in children than adults, with peak ages between 15 and 19 years.

Treatment of neoplasms involves one or a combination of these therapeutic approaches: surgery, radiation, and chemotherapy. Surgery is used to remove a bulky tumor, relieve pain, correct obstructions, and/or reduce pressure on surrounding structures. Radiation is applied to impede cell multiplication and destroy cancerous cells; it may reduce tumor mass and help with pain control. Ionizing radiation (gamma rays) and particle radiation (beta rays) are targeted at the cellular deoxyribonucleic acid (DNA). Radiation therapy may be delivered through external beam radiation or isotope implants. Chemotherapy involves a variety of drugs to inhibit tumor growth or impede metastasis. Chemotherapeutic agents inhibit cell growth by interacting with DNA, competing with metabolites, preventing cell reproduction by altering protein synthesis, and changing chemical susceptibility. While certain drugs may be effective in certain situations, chemotherapy may cause side effects of pain, anemia, loss of hair, vomiting, and dermatitis.

A holistic approach for the terminally ill person is *hospice care*, which includes comprehensive physical, psychological, social, and spiritual care. Good hospice care emphasizes coordinating efforts of health care staff, maintaining quality of life in a homelike environment, and providing emotional support for both patient and staff. In several large cities hospice programs have been established for children with leukemia.

Physical Education and the Student With Cancer

The involvement of the student with cancer in physical education is predicated on the following factors: the student's health status, the importance of physical activity as perceived by the oncologist, the kind of support available from parents, and the willingness of physical educators to cope with this type of student. The student with cancer would be eligible for the benefits of PL 94-142 under the category of other health–impaired conditions.

Exercise as a maintenance or restorative technique for cancer patients holds promise. Buettner and Gavron (1981) reported that men and women who had a history of cancer benefited from an 8-week aerobic training program. When a sedentary control group was compared to the exercise group, the latter group exhibited significant improvement on five physiological measures. Another study compared an exercise group receiving chemotherapy for breast cancer with a control group (Winningham & MacVicar, 1985). Subjects in the exercise group exhibited more improvement on a graded exercise test than did the control group. Participants reported that their

feelings of nausea decreased as the exercise session progressed.

While participation in exercise and physical education programs may be beneficial, each student's needs must be dealt with individually. The type of cancer, its status, and the general condition of the student determine the extent and intensity of the program. The physician must have input concerning the nature and intensity of activities. A person with lung cancer will definitely have respiratory restrictions, and a student with osteogenic sarcoma, a type of bone cancer, may not be allowed to jog or even walk because of a risk of fractures. While the physical well-being of a student with cancer cannot be minimized, psychological well-being is important as well. Being mainstreamed into physical education and succeeding in this environment may greatly improve the student's self-image. To help minimize self-consciousness, the physical educator may let the student wear a ball cap or other head covering in class if hair loss has resulted from the medical treatment. Other variations in gym attire should be allowed when dermatological side effects are evident.

There may be days when chemotherapy or its side effects preclude active involvement in many activities. The following symptoms or situations are contraindications for exercise: pain in the legs or chest, unusual weakness, nausea during exercise, vomiting or diarrhea a day before class, sudden onset of labored breathing, dizziness or disorientation, and intravenous chemotherapy administered a day before class.

On other days the student may be able to engage in many physical education activities.

Adaptations discussed in other sections of this book may be appropriate for students with certain types of cancer. The student with leukemia may profit from program modifications recommended for an anemic student or one with a cardiovascular problem. Adaptations for a student with Perthes disease or other orthopedic problems may be appropriate for the student with a bone tumor. A student with a tumor of the central nervous system may need the same adaptations as one who has cerebral palsy or muscular dystrophy. The key to physical education for the student with cancer, as for all students with unique needs, is the IEP.

Cardiovascular Disorders

The cardiovascular system, which comprises the heart, arteries, veins, and lymphatic system, may be considered the life-giving transportation system of the body. Disorders of this system appear during all stages of development and age periods. The following are major categories of cardiovascular disorders: congenital acyanotic defects, congenital cyanotic defects, acquired inflammatory heart disease, valvular heart disease, degenerative cardiovascular disorders, cardiac complications, and vascular disorders. An estimated 25 million Americans have some type of cardiovascular disease. While heart disease is the leading cause of death in people over 25, it is the sixth leading cause of death among people in the 15- to 25-year age range.

A student with a cardiovascular disease or problem may be covered by PL 94-142 under the designation *other health impaired*. While IEPs including physical education may be developed for certain students with cardiac conditions, other students with this type of condition may be integrated into regular physical education without the benefit of an IEP. In both situations, the physical educator must know how best to involve students who are or have been afflicted with some type of cardiovascular problem. This section will orient the reader to some cardiovascular problems commonly found among school-age or preschool-age children and will recommend procedures and techniques for the delivery of physical education services to these students.

Rheumatic Fever and Rheumatic Heart Disease

A condition included in the broader designation of acquired inflammatory heart disease is rheumatic heart disease. Rheumatic fever is a systemic inflammatory disease of children that may occur following an untreated or inadequately treated streptococcal infection. Rheumatic heart disease is the name given to the cardiac manifestations of rheumatic fever; it is estimated that 500,000 young people between the ages of 5 and 19 are affected by this condition.

Rheumatic fever, which usually follows a strep throat, may be a hypersensitive reaction to the streptococcal infection, in which antibodies produced to combat the infection affect specific tissue locations and produce lesions at the heart and joints. Approximately 1% to 3% of strep infections develop into rheumatic fever. Some common symptoms of rheumatic fever are polyarthritis, motor awkwardness (chorea), pancarditis (myocarditis, pericarditis, and endocarditis), skin rash, and subcutaneous nodules near tendons or bony prominences of joints. While most of the symptoms are transitory in nature, the destructive effect of rheumatic fever lies in pancarditis, which develops in up to 50% of cases. Endocarditis causes a scarring of the heart valves, which may result in a stenosis or narrowing of valve openings; this scarring may also prevent the valve leaflets from completely closing, which causes a regurgitation between heart chambers. Both situations cause the heart to work more intensely, and if the damage is quite severe, congestive heart failure may occur. The mitral valve is more often affected in girls and the aortic valve in boys.

Treatment of rheumatic fever and rheumatic heart disease begins with eradicating the streptococcal infection, relieving symptoms, and preventing recurrence of the strep throat or rheumatic fever. During the acute stage of the disease, penicillin is often prescribed along with aspirin. With active carditis, bed rest may be indicated for as long as 5 weeks. Following the acute stage, penicillin may be prescribed to prevent recurrence. With severe valve damage, repair or replacement may be the treatment of choice. The integration into physical education classes of the student who has had rheumatic fever or rheumatic heart disease will be discussed under the heading "Physical Education and Cardiovascular Conditions." The physical educator may help with a very important aspect of combating rheumatic fever or rheumatic heart disease—namely, preventive measures. If a student in a physical education class presents symptoms of a cold with a severe sore throat, the student should be referred to the school nurse or advised to obtain a throat culture. A strep throat must be treated with antibiotics to ensure that it does not lead to rheumatic fever.

Physical Education and Cardiovascular Conditions

Determining the *appropriate intensity level* for students with cardiovascular disorders is the key to their integration into a physical education class. An affected student who is attending school should be involved in some type of physical education program. Numerous systems have been developed to classify individuals with cardiovascular disorders into groups that provide a baseline for activity selection. The American Heart Association recommends the following functional classification system (Love & Walthall, 1977):

- Class I—Patients with cardiac disease not resulting in limitation of physical activity. Ordinary physical activity does not cause undue fatigue, palpitation, dyspnea, or anginal pain.
- Class II—Patients with cardiac disease resulting in slight limitation of physical activity who are comfortable at rest. Ordinary physical activity results in fatigue, palpitation, dyspnea, or anginal pain.

- Class III—Patients with cardiac disease resulting in marked limitation of physical activity who are comfortable at rest. Less than ordinary physical activity causes fatigue, palpitation, dyspnea, or anginal pain.
- Class IV—Patients with cardiac disease resulting in inability to pursue any physical activity without discomfort. Symptoms of cardiac insufficiency or of anginal syndrome may be present even at rest. If any physical activity is undertaken, discomfort is increased.

Physicians often refer to this system in recommending exercise programs. The level of intensity, at least initially, should be based on the recommendation of the physician.

A more sophisticated approach to assessing exercise capacity is based on metabolic equivalents (MET). One MET is the equivalent of the basal oxygen requirement of the body at rest, or 3.5 milliliters (mL) of oxygen per kilogram (kg) of body weight per minute. If a person's maximum MET capacity is determined to be 7.0, the exercise prescription for a person with a heart condition is approximately 70% of this value or 4.9 MET units. Using this information the physical educator may consult a table that recommends appropriate activities for different MET levels (Table 17.7).

While physical education programs for students with cardiovascular problems must be personalized, the following suggestions should help in the implementation of each student's program:

1. Secure approval of the general framework of the physical education program (see chapter 3).
2. Increase gradually the level of intensity of all exercises and activities.
3. Stop all activity following pain in the sternal area, palpitation of the heart, cyanic appearance of the lips and nail beds, swelling of the ankles, or labored breathing.
4. Provide appropriate rest periods.

5. Reduce the intensity level of an activity if elementary children are squatting between activities or high school students are standing and breathing through their mouths.

6. Monitor pulse rate by comparing pre-exercise, exercise, and postexercise rates.

7. Reduce the intensity of certain exercises by having students perform them in a lying position.

8. Monitor carefully aquatic activities, which cause students to use a considerable number of muscle groups, thus placing greater demands on the cardiovascular system.

9. Reduce the highly competitive aspects of certain sport activities, which may elevate stress levels.

10. Modify programs according to climatic conditions: Hot and/or humid weather, for example, necessitates a reduction in intensity level.

11. Include a warm-up period. Part of every student's program, it is even more important for students with cardiovascular problems.

12. Caution against extremes in temperature variations of ingested fluids.

13. Provide assistance in weight management. Added poundage places additional stress on the cardiovascular system.

14. Understand the possible interactions between medication and activity.

15. Modify intensity levels by the following means:

    a. playing doubles in tennis and badminton and using the boundaries of the singles court;

    b. using courtesy runners in softball and kickball;

    c. allowing the ball to bounce more than the usual number of times in racquetball, volleyball, and tennis; and

    d. reducing the velocity of balls by using a beachball in place of an official volleyball and using whiffle balls rather than regulation balls.

Table 17.7 Metabolic Equivalents for Selected Activities

METs[a]	Activities
3 - 4	Archery
	Bowling
	Billiards
	Croquet
	Table tennis
5 - 6	Dancing (jitterbug, etc.)
	Golf (pulling cart)
	Roller skating
	Swimming (2 mph)
	Tennis (doubles)
7 - 8	Basketball (5-person teams)
	Cycling (10 mph)
	Running (12 min/mi)
	Tennis (singles)
	Touch football
9 - 10	Cycling (13 mph)
	Handball
	Racquetball
	Running (10 min/mi)
	Squash

[a]Metabolic equivalent (METs) is the body's basal oxygen requirement at rest.

Anemia

Anemia is a condition marked by a reduction in erthrocytes (red blood cells) or in the quality of hemoglobin, which is associated with oxygen transport throughout the body. A reduction in the oxygen-carrying capabilities of the blood necessitates increased cardiac output to compensate for the reduced amount of oxygen provided at the cellular level.

Anemia may be an inherited condition or may be caused by hemorrhaging and dietary deficiencies. Hemorrhagic anemia may result from infections, severe trauma, postoperative or postpartum bleeding, and coagulation defects. Iron deficiency anemia is prevalent in young children, preadolescent boys, pubescent girls who are experiencing their first menstrual periods, and premenopausal women. Iron is a main component of hemoglobin and is needed in the production of red blood cells. Lack of adequate stores of iron in the body leads to depleted erythrocyte mass and decreased hemoglobin concentration.

Sickle-cell anemia occurs most commonly, but not exclusively, in black Americans. It results from defective hemoglobin, which causes red blood cells to have a sickle shape. This condition is linked to a recessive trait that produces defective hemoglobin molecules. About 1 in 10 black Americans carries this abnormal gene; this situation is referred to as sickle-cell trait. If both parents have the trait, the chances are one in four that their child will have the disease. It is estimated that 1 in every 400 to 600 black children has sickle cell anemia. Hypoxia seems to affect the abnormal or defective hemoglobin molecules in the red blood cells, which become insoluble. An end result is an elongation or sickle-like appearance of these erythrocytes. This sickling effect may result in cell destruction and may impair circulation in capillaries and small blood vessels. A vicious cycle may be set up, with circulation impairment causing anoxic changes, which may lead to additional sickling and obstruction. To date, treatment consists mainly in management of symptoms, with hospitalization for severe aplastic crises. In these crises, blood transfusions, oxygen administration, and fluid ingestion are used. Symptoms accompanying sickle-cell anemia are jaundice, labored breathing, aching bones, chest pains, swollen joints, fatigue, and leg ulcers.

Physical Education for the Anemic Student

Many of the guidelines provided in the section dealing with *cardiovascular disorders* are applicable for the student with any type of anemia. The physical educator may be the first person to suspect that a student has anemia, observing lethargy, lack or loss of strength and endurance, irritability, and early onset of fatigue.

Excusing the anemic student from physical education is *not an appropriate option*, because lack of activity will aggravate the condition. It should be apparent to all concerned—parents, physician, physical educator, and student—that a modified program of physical activity is in the student's best interest. Intensity levels in all activities must correlate with the student's physiological status. Initially, activities such as bowling and archery may be suitable. Conditioning may mean walking around the track and lifting light weights such as dumbbells. As the student's fitness improves through medical intervention and modified activity, the intensity level of activities may be elevated.

For the student with sickle-cell anemia a coordinated effort between the physician and the physical educator is needed to design a safe and effective program. The physician must provide guidance on the level of intensity of physical fitness efforts, and the physical educator must select appropriate motor activities. Even with motor activities that stress balance, hand-eye coordination, and agility, the physical educator must note any sign of cardiorespiratory distress such as rapid pulse; labored breathing; pale lips, tongue, or nail beds; and any complaint of pain. Underwater swimming is usually avoided, and jumping activities should not be excessive because of possible joint inflammation. Both the student and the physical educator should monitor the condition of the student's skin, because skin ulcers may be a problem with this disorder.

Hemophilia

Hemophilia is a hereditary bleeding disorder resulting from the inability of the blood to coagulate properly because of a deficiency of certain clotting factors. Hemophilia is the most common X-linked genetic disease and affects 1.25 in 10,000 live male births. Because of the genetic mode, females act as carriers; they have a 50% chance of transmitting the defective gene to each male child. There is also a 50% chance that each female child will likewise be a carrier of this defect.

Hemophilia A, which affects over 80% of all hemophiliacs, is caused by a deficiency of coagulation Factor VIII. Another type of hemophilia is sometimes called Christmas disease, or hemophilia B, resulting from a deficiency in Factor IX. The absence or deficiency of certain clotting factors is the reason for the vernacular designation, *bleeder's disease*.

Hemophilia may be classified as mild, moderate, or severe. The mild form may not appear until adolescence or adulthood. Its symptoms are a tendency to bruise, frequent nosebleeds, bleeding gums, and hematomas. Moderate hemophilia causes symptoms similar to those of the mild type, but bleeding episodes are more frequent, and there is occasional bleeding into the joints. Severe hemophilia is marked by spontaneous bleeding or severe bleeding after minor injuries. Bleeding into joints and muscle is more extensive than with the moderate type and causes pain, swelling, and extreme tenderness. Peripheral neuropathies may result from bleeding near peripheral nerves, with subsequent pain and muscle atrophy.

Physical Education for the Hemophilic Student

The hemophilic student may derive both physical and social benefit from participating in physical education if appropriate precautions and modifications are in place. The student's physician should provide guidance on suitable physical education activities. Besides providing input on curriculum, the physician may wish to be informed (or instruct that the school nurse be informed) if certain injuries to the head, neck, or chest occur. Some of these injuries may require special blood factor replacement. The physician may alert the physical educator to watch for signs of severe

internal hemorrhage, which may include severe pain or swelling in joints and muscles, joint stiffness, and abdominal pain. Hemophilic students should *wear a medical identification tag or bracelet at all times*. Because blood transfusions carry the risk of infection with hepatitis, the physical educator may observe early symptoms of that disease: headache, vomiting, fever, nausea, pain over the liver, and abdominal tenderness. At no time should a student with hemophilia take aspirin, because this drug exacerbates the tendency to bleed.

If a hemophilic student sustains some type of trauma, apply ice bags and pressure to the injured area and elevate the part if possible. The student should be restricted from activity for 48 hours after the bleeding is under control.

Activities that enhance physical fitness should be part of the hemophilic student's program. Swimming is an excellent activity for enhancing cardiorespiratory endurance, muscular strength, and flexibility without subjecting the student to possible trauma. Jogging or fast walking may be used to develop aerobic capacities. If a student has had a problem with bleeding in a joint such as the knee, isometric rather than isotonic exercises may be used. Contact and collision sports such as football, basketball, and soccer are contraindicated. However, developing certain skill components of these sports, such as passing a football and shooting free throws, is desirable. Dual and individual sports such as tennis, archery, and golf are fine; racquetball is not an appropriate sport because of the risk of being hit by the ball.

Acquired Immunodeficiency Syndrome

Acquired Immunodeficiency Syndrome (AIDS) is a very serious health disorder that has reached epidemic proportions. It is caused by an infection with Human T-Cell Lymphotropic Virus Type III

(HTLV-III), which is known as Human Immuno-deficiency Virus (HIV). As a result of HIV, people with AIDS have *defective immune systems* and cannot combat certain types of infections or rare malignancies. Certain individuals infected with HIV do not contract AIDS but develop a set of symptoms called AIDS-related complex (ARC). While some of these people may appear healthy, they are capable of transmitting AIDS to others.

The HIV virus has been found in such body fluids as blood, seminal fluid, vaginal secretions, saliva, and tears. It has not been documented that the last two fluids transmit this virus, or that the disease can be airborne or spread by casual contact. Casual contact is defined as contact other than (a) sexual contact or (b) contact between mother and child during gestation or breast feeding.

Two causal factors are associated with AIDS-infected children: (a) birth to a mother who has this disorder and (b) receiving blood or clotting factors containing HIV. It is not clear if the number of elementary-age children with AIDS will increase appreciably. While blood screening techniques have improved, a certain number of hemophilic children may still acquire AIDS. At present the number of mothers with AIDS is on the increase, and their offspring will swell the number of preschool-age children with AIDS. High school students, particularly from inner city schools, will probably show an increase in AIDS because of intravenous drug use.

Physical Education and the AIDS Student

The physician, in consultation with parents and school officials, will determine the student's placement in the school setting and in the physical education class. Most state departments of health will allow a student to attend school if the student behaves acceptably (e.g., does not bite) and has no skin eruptions or uncovered sores. If any of these conditions are seen in physical education classes, the student should be removed from class immedi-ately and sent to the appropriate school official. The same procedure should be followed if the student has a fever, a cough, or diarrhea.

The nature of the physical education program for students with AIDS depends on their physical capacities and motoric abilities. Because some students with AIDS are hemophiliacs, the information provided in the sections on hemophilia and other cardiovascular problems is applicable to them. *If there is a bleeding episode* in a physical education class because of an accident, an injury, or a situation related to a hemophilic condition, *appropriate hygienic procedures* should be followed. Blood or any body fluid should be treated with caution. Rubber gloves should be worn for cleaning up spills of any body fluid, and blood-soaked articles should be placed in leakproof bags for disposal or washing.

While appropriate hygienic practices are required, AIDS necessitates fewer adaptations and modifications for students than some other types of handicapping conditions. It is essential to separate the hysteria and misinformation from the established facts.

Summary

The focus of this chapter has been certain conditions that, under PL 94-142, are designated as *other health impaired*. Cancer, rheumatic heart disorders, diabetes, asthma, hemophilia, and acquired immunodeficiency syndrome are included in this category. Some students with these conditions (for example, students with asthma) may not have formal IEPs but may need certain modifications or adaptations in physical education. Activity injuries and long-term disorders such as fractures and Osgood-Schlatter's condition are not covered by the designation *other health impaired* but may limit a student's involvement in physical education class. Both nonhandicapped and handicapped students may have to cope with such conditions; suggestions for appropriate physical education experiences have been provided for these students.

Bibliography

Buettner, L.L., & Gavron, S.J. (1981, November). *Personality changes and physiological effects of a personalized fitness enrichment program for cancer patients*. Paper presented at the Third International Symposium on Adapted Physical Activity, New Orleans.

Duda, M. (1985). The role of exercise in managing diabetes. *The Physician and Sportsmedicine, 13*, 164-170.

Education for All Handicapped Children Act of 1975, § 121a.5, U.S.C. § 1401 (1977).

Knight, K. (1979). Rehabilitating chondromalacia patellae. *The Physician and Sportsmedicine, 7*, 147-148.

Livingston, S., & Berman, W. (1974). Participation of the epileptic child in contact sports. *Sports Medicine, 2*, 170-173.

Love, H.D., & Walthall, S.E. (1977). *A handbook of medical, educational, and psychological information for teachers of physically handicapped children*. Springfield, IL: Thomas.

Mital, M.A., & Matza, R.A. (1977). Osgood-Schlatter's disease: The pain puzzler. *The Physician and Sportsmedicine, 5*, 60-73.

O'Donoghue, D. (1984). *Treatment of injuries to athletes*. St. Louis: Mosby.

Paulos, L., Rusche, K., Johnson, C., & Noyes, F.R. (1980). Patellar malalignment: A treatment rationale. *Physical Therapy, 60*, 1624-1632.

Remein, Q.R., & Shields, F.A. (1962). *Diabetes fact book*. Washington, DC: United States Public Health Service.

Saltin, B., & Rowell, L.B. (1980). Functional adaptation to physical activity and inactivity. *Federation Proceeding, 39*, 1506-13.

Sherrill, C. (1986). *Adapted physical education and recreation: A multidisciplinary approach* (3rd ed.). Dubuque, IA: Wm. C. Brown.

Strauss, R.H. (Ed.) (1984). *Sports medicine and physiology*. Philadelphia: Saunders.

Winningham, M.L., & MacVicar, M.G. (1985). Response of cancer patients on chemotherapy to a supervised exercise program. *Medicine and Science in Sports and Exercise, 17*, 292.

Resources

Ankle sprains: A round table (1986). *The Physician and Sportsmedicine, 14*, 101-118. This is a discussion among prominent physicians and a sport physical therapist concerning types of sprains, keys to injury, treatment of both stable and unstable ankles, and prevention of sprain.

Duda, M. (1985). The role of exercise in managing diabetes. *The Physician and Sportsmedicine, 13*, 164-170. A question-and-answer format provides excellent coverage of the involvement of diabetes in exercise. This article provides answers to questions that may be raised by teachers or students regarding the role of exercise for the diabetic.

Morton, A., Fitch, K.D., & Hahn, A.G. (1981). Physical activity and the asthmatic. *The Physician and Sportsmedicine, 9*, 51-60. This article covers three areas: (1) the role of exercise in provoking an asthmatic attack, (2) aerobic fitness in the treatment of asthma, and (3) medications used to prevent asthmatic attacks.

Orenstein, D.M., Henke, K.C., & Cerny, F.J. (1983). Exercise and cystic fibrosis. *The Physician and Sportsmedicine, 11*, 57-63. This article provides excellent background material concerning cystic fibrosis and focuses on the value of exercise for the student with this condition.

Parcel, G.S. (1986). *Basic emergency care of the sick and injured*. St. Louis: Mosby.

Ritter, M.A., & Albohm, M.J. (1987). *Your injury: A common sense guide to sports injuries*. Indianapolis: Benchmark Press. This book covers sport- and activity-related injuries. It provides insights concerning the symptoms of these injuries, procedures to follow and avoid, and modifications of activities or exercises.

Surburg, P.R. (1985). Osgood-Schlatter's condition and the forgotten student. *The Physical Educator, 42,* 186-189. This article includes an in-depth discussion of this condition and strategies to involve the affected student in physical education classes during the different stages of the disorder.

Developmental Aspects
of Adapted Physical Education

Part IV includes chapters that present and discuss components of physical fitness, motor development, and body mechanics and posture. This information is intended to build on foundational knowledge related to growth and development. In these chapters, special consideration is given to the influence of handicapping conditions on development, learning, and performance.

CHAPTER 18

Physical Fitness

Francis X. Short

Professional physical educators are well aware of the value of physical fitness. They recognize that physical fitness is important for improved health, a more attractive appearance, and increased physical performance. Physical educators, however, must also be aware that as important as physical fitness is for the general population, it has greater significance for people with handicapping conditions. For instance, a person who has a paraplegic spinal cord injury has a greater need for upper body strength and endurance training for wheelchair propulsion and transfers; a person with spastic cerebral palsy has a greater need for flexibility training because hypertonic muscles restrict movement; and people with visual impairments and mental retardation have a greater need for cardiorespiratory endurance and weight loss training because of the sedentary lifestyle frequency associated with these conditions.

This chapter presents information on fitness, including definitions, principles for development, and considerations for people with unique needs.

Definition

A universally acceptable definition of physical fitness does not exist. Traditionally, physical fitness has been defined as ''the ability to carry out tasks with vigor and alertness, without undue fatigue, and with ample energy to enjoy leisure-time pursuits and to meet unusual situations and unforeseen emergencies'' (Clarke & Clarke, 1978, p. 32). More recently, physical fitness has been conceptualized as a ''multifaceted continuum extending from birth to death'' and has been operationally defined by the tests used to measure it (AAHPERD, 1980). These tests fall into two broad categories: (1) those purporting to measure physiological or health-related aspects of fitness and (2) those purporting to measure athletic or performance-related aspects of fitness.

Although there is a distinction between health-related and performance-related fitness, one should not necessarily be considered more important than the other. For school-age youngsters, fitness for optimal health and fitness for success in sports and games are both sound educational goals. Moreover, despite the conceptual differences, there is some practical overlap between the health and performance aspects. For instance, although body composition is considered to be a health-related component of fitness, athletic performance, with few exceptions, also is enhanced by a reduction in adipose tissue. Similarly, the sit-up test can be classified as either a health- or performance-related test item, depending on the rationale for its use. For these reasons a more comprehensive approach to physical fitness is taken in this chapter. Here physical fitness is conceptualized as having both health and performance aspects and is operationally defined by test items that measure body composition, muscular strength and endurance, flexibility, and cardiorespiratory endurance.

Components

Because there is no universally acceptable definition of physical fitness, the reader should not be surprised to learn that the components attributed to physical fitness vary somewhat from authority to authority. The components discussed in this chapter are those presented in the definition just mentioned and are consistent with a training model suggested by Winnick and Short (1985). Each component is defined in the following paragraphs, along with common methods of assessment.

Body Composition

Body composition refers to the degree of leanness or fatness of the individual. Anthropometric measures such as skinfold and girth measurement and height and weight assessment can be utilized in field settings to gather information on body composition.

Muscular Strength and Endurance

As used here, muscular strength and endurance is a rather broad component of physical fitness encompassing a number of primarily performance-related aspects including strength, muscular endurance, speed, and power. *Strength* is the amount of force that can be exerted by one or a group of muscles in a single contraction. We can measure strength by using dynamometers or tensiometers, or by recording the maximum amount of weight that can be lifted in a single repetition. *Muscular endurance* refers to the ability to sustain a muscular contraction or contractions of a submaximal nature. Sit-ups and flexed-arm hang are examples of field-based tests of muscular endurance. *Speed* is the ability to execute or repeat a movement rapidly. It is a performance-related aspect of fitness that is dependent upon muscle elasticity, neuromuscular coordination, strength and endurance, and effective utilization of the anaerobic energy systems of the body (Winnick & Short,

1985). Speed is usually measured by having students run a short distance (e.g., 50 yd) as fast as possible. *Power* is often defined as the amount of force that can be generated by a muscle or muscle group in a given period of time. Consequently, power encompasses elements of both strength and speed. In fact, Winnick and Short (1984) used the terms power-strength, power-speed, and power-endurance to distinguish among power-related factors in a study involving field-based measures of physical fitness. Traditionally, power has been assessed through such test items as the standing long jump, the vertical jump, or an object throw of some kind (Figure 18.1).

Figure 18.1 Jim Mastro, gold medal winner among blind athletes at the 1984 International Games for the Disabled, demonstrates the power-strength requirements of the shot put.

Flexibility

Two types of flexibility are generally discussed in the professional literature: static or extent flexibility and dynamic flexibility. Static flexibility refers to the range of motion around one or a sequence of joints. Dynamic flexibility is the resistance in a joint to movement. Because degree of flexibility is specific to the various joints in the body, a single test cannot reflect overall flexibility. Instruments such as goniometers and flexometers have been used to measure flexibility, but a popular field measure currently being used is the sit and reach test, which is an indicator of trunk-hip flexibility.

Cardiorespiratory Endurance

Cardiorespiratory endurance is defined as the ability to perform large-muscle or whole-body activities continuously for a sustained period. A number of factors contribute to efficient cardiorespiratory functioning, including the ability of the heart to pump blood, the ability of the veins and arteries to carry the blood, the ability of the respiratory system to process oxygen to the blood, and the ability of the muscles to utilize the oxygen delivered by the blood. A number of indices of cardiorespiratory endurance, including maximal oxygen consumption, are used in laboratory settings; however, distance runs are appropriate measures in field settings.

Physical Fitness Programming

Whether programming for students with or without handicapping conditions, the physical educator must first ask, *"Physical fitness for what purpose?"* In other words, the initial step in programming is identifying the components of physical fitness to be developed to help the student attain specific goals and objectives in physical edu-

cation. For students with handicapping conditions, physical fitness programming can range from fitness for basic stability (sitting, kneeling, etc.) to fitness for competitive sport participation. In effect, a continuum of performance-related physical fitness exists, and different components of fitness will be emphasized for each step on the continuum. Figure 18.2 identifies five "links" in a performance-related fitness continuum. Links are used to indicate that some overlap exists between successive levels. Teachers may find the continuum a helpful guideline in targeting fitness components for development. Each link is discussed separately in the following paragraphs.

A Physical Fitness Continuum

Basic stability is the ability to independently support the body against the force of gravity. Physical fitness for basic stability might be an appropriate goal for youngsters with more serious handicaps whose current level of motor functioning consists primarily of lying on the floor or on a mat. Progressions at this link range from lying to sitting to kneeling to standing. Physical fitness for basic stability should emphasize the development of strength and endurance of the muscles necessary for the skill being taught, usually the "antigravity" muscles (abdominals and extensors of the spine, hip, knee, and ankle). Because motor development proceeds in a cephalocaudal direction ("head to tail"), the instructor should target for physical development those muscles that are prerequisite to the desired motor activity. For example, consider the student whose current level of performance is simply "prone lying." If the

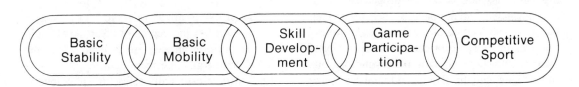

Figure 18.2 Continuum of performance-related physical fitness.

long-range goal is "independent kneeling," the physical educator should first attempt to develop strength and endurance of the neck extensors. This strategy eventually should allow the youngster to independently raise the head from the mat, which is the first milestone in the developmental sequence leading to independent kneeling. Selective flexibility training is also necessary at this link on the continuum. If long sitting (legs out straight) is being taught, increased hamstring or low back flexibility may be necessary; if the student is being taught to kneel, the hip flexors may require additional flexibility training.

Basic mobility refers to the development of rudimentary locomotor abilities characterized by progressions from crawling to creeping to walking. The physical educator should continue to pay attention to those components of muscular strength/endurance and flexibility that are prerequisite to a particular locomotor pattern. Flexibility training should attempt to guarantee that sufficient range of motion exists to allow the mobility pattern being taught. Development of muscular strength and endurance should continue to reflect the demands of the skill. For instance, if creeping is being taught, the deltoids, triceps, and hip flexors must be targeted for development.

Skill development is the link in the continuum where students possess necessary levels of physical fitness to support the development of the fundamental movement patterns such as running, jumping, throwing, and kicking. If sufficient levels of flexibility are maintained, the primary emphasis of the physical fitness program should be the development of power-related aspects of muscular strength and endurance. Many of the fundamental movement patterns require rapid and/or explosive muscular action for proper execution. Fundamental locomotor patterns such as hopping, skipping, and leaping all have a "flight phase" that can only be accomplished with powerful muscle contractions. Success in throwing, kicking, and striking activities is related to muscle power as well.

Game participation refers to the incorporation of the fundamental movement patterns in game contexts. At this link in the continuum, the development of physical fitness should be balanced among the four general components of fitness so that the student may participate in a variety of activities. Attention to cardiorespiratory endurance and body composition, therefore, is introduced at this point. Improved cardiorespiratory endurance will enable the student to participate for longer periods of time in aerobic activities, and reduction of body fat generally will enhance performance in most games.

Competitive sport is the last link of the fitness continuum. When teachers and coaches are developing fitness programs for individuals at this level, they must specifically identify the components that are necessary for success in the particular sport activity and devise training programs to enhance performance. Developing physical fitness as part of the sport training of athletes with handicapping conditions has received increased attention in recent years, and many improvements in performance have been attributed to improved training (see Figure 18.3).

Principles for Development

A complete review of the principles of physical fitness development is beyond the scope of this chapter. Even the beginning physical educator, however, must understand that the progressions for the development of physical fitness revolve around the concepts of intensity, duration, frequency, and mode. These are the variables that the teacher must consider and manipulate when developing physical fitness programs.

- *Intensity* essentially refers to "how much"; it describes the degree of effort that should be made in an exercise to bring about the desired training effect.
- *Duration* essentially refers to "how long"; it describes the length of time an exercise

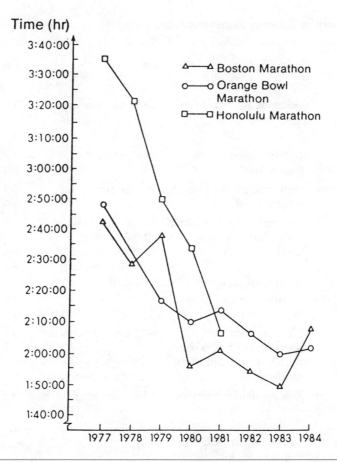

Figure 18.3 Winning wheelchair marathon times for male competitors. *Note*. From "Training and Fitness Programs for Disabled Athletes: Past, Present, and Future" by R. Steadward and C. Walsh. In *Sport and Disabled Athletes* (p. 5) by Claudine Sherrill (Ed.), 1986, Champaign, IL: Human Kinetics. Copyright 1986 by Human Kinetics. Reprinted with permission.

should be performed at a given level of intensity.

- *Frequency* essentially refers to "how often"; it describes the number of times per week the exercise should be performed at given levels of intensity and duration.
- *Mode* essentially refers to "what kind"; it describes the type of exercise to be performed.

These four training variables differ for the various components of fitness. A summary of recom-

mended levels of intensity, duration, and frequency for the four components of fitness is presented in Table 18.1.

Physical Fitness for Students With Unique Needs

The principles established for the development of physical fitness in the general population are also appropriate in most cases for the development of

Table 18.1 Summary of Training Recommendations

Component	Intensity	Duration	Frequency
Body composition	Moderate	20-30 min per session	3-5 days per week
Muscular strength/ endurance			
Strength	4-10 repetitions[a] (heavy load)	10 s or less	3 times per session; 3-5 days per week
Muscular endurance	Minimum 20 repetitions[a] (lighter load)	30 s or more	2-3 times per session; 3-5 days per week
Speed	Maximal or near maximal (7/8) effort (moderate load)	1-30 s (emphasis on alactic system) 30-180 s (emphasis on lactic acid system)	1-3 times per session (at least 1 repetition per set); 3-5 times per week
Power	10-20 repetitions[a] executed (moderate to heavy load)	30 s or less	2-3 times per session; 3-5 days per week
Flexibility	5-10 repetitions at approximately 10% over-stretch or to point of dis-comfiture	6-12 s per repetition	3 times per session; 3-7 days per week
Cardiorespiratory endurance	75% maximum heart rate	20-40 min per session	3-5 days per week

[a]Recommendations are for isotonic or isokinetic activity.

physical fitness in individuals with unique needs. This is particularly true for students with sensory, cognitive, or emotional disabilities, as well as for nonhandicapped students with low fitness. It should be emphasized, however, that when students begin programs with low levels of fitness, the intensity and duration of the activity may need to be reduced. Programs for those with low fitness should be characterized initially by limited intensity and duration followed by gradual progression. For example, recent research suggests that even general gross motor activity (without regard to aerobic demands) may have a positive impact on the cardiovascular functioning of profoundly handicapped children, provided the activities are performed on a regular basis (Mulholland & McNeill, 1985).

The term *regular basis* also has important implications for adapted physical education. Canadian researchers, for instance, recently reported that, following a rigorous training program, a group of sightless adolescents was found to have aerobic power and body composition test scores that were comparable to those of normally sighted individuals. Following a 10-week summer vacation, however, these scores deteriorated to levels previously reported for untrained blind adolescents and well below the values for the normally sighted (di Natale, Lee, Ward, & Shephard, 1985). One implication is that students with handicapping conditions must understand the value of regular physical activity and teachers must give the students training ideas that are "transportable," that is, ideas that can be used outside the school environment.

Instructors who work with persons with unique needs may have to modify methodology in order to achieve satisfactory results. For instance, with students who have auditory impairments, a teacher will need to employ some alternate form of communication when describing activities; more demonstration may be necessary with students who are mentally retarded; and a behavior modification program may be necessary to increase the motivation of a student with an emotional problem.

In some cases, the *way* an activity is performed may need to be modified. For example, students with visual impairments can, and should, participate in running activities as long as some form of guidance is provided. For short-distance running (to develop power and speed), a guide wire or a rope is usually an appropriate way to supply the necessary guidance. For running over a longer distance (to develop cardiorespiratory endurance or to lose weight), tactual guidance provided by a sighted partner is usually the recommended method. Another way to modify an activity is to reduce its complexity by eliminating or adapting rules to increase participation by students with handicapping conditions. (Readers are referred to other chapters for more specific discussions of modifications of methods and activities.)

In the development of physical fitness programs in adapted physical education, the most significant modifications in intensity, duration, frequency, and mode will be made for students with physical handicaps. Considerations in fitness programming for those students, therefore, are discussed in greater detail in the following paragraphs. Although they are written specifically with the physically handicapped person in mind, the reader may find that some of the material can be generalized to other students who exhibit poor fitness.

Weight Loss and Cardiorespiratory Endurance

Because many of the activities suggested for both weight loss and cardiorespiratory endurance are similar, they are combined here for discussion pur-

poses. As noted in the introduction to this chapter, youngsters with handicapping conditions frequently have a unique need to improve body composition and to increase cardiorespiratory endurance because of their sedentary lifestyle. The general implication, therefore, is that continuous, whole-body activities need to be provided when these conditions exist.

When students are in wheelchairs, participation in whole-body activities may not be possible or practical. One physiological consequence of a spinal cord injury, for instance, is reduced maximum oxygen uptake. One reason for this is that oxygen uptake is directly proportional to the amount of muscle mass involved in an activity (Astrand & Saltin, 1961). Because propelling a wheelchair involves a more specific group of muscles than, say, jogging, it will be more difficult for a student in a wheelchair to obtain maximum oxygen uptake values that approach those of the able-bodied student. This is not to suggest that positive changes in cardiorespiratory endurance and body composition cannot be effected in the person with a spinal cord injury. The teacher should recognize, however, that the effectiveness of a continuous aerobic training program conducted in a wheelchair may be limited by the muscular strength and endurance of the student's arms and shoulders. A small student pushing a standard wheelchair, for example, might not be able to push that chair long enough to tax the cardiorespiratory system or burn a significant number of calories. Consequently, the teacher must consider modifying the mode of activity.

Swimming is an excellent medium for enhancing physical fitness, particularly for students with physical handicaps. In cases where students have loss of muscle function or coordination, flotation devices may have to be provided so that exercise can be maintained for sufficient duration. Activities such as lap swimming and aerobic water games can enhance both body composition (when weight loss is indicated) and cardiorespiratory endurance. For students who use crutches or other assistive devices for ambulation, walking laps in chest-deep water may also be an appropriate activity. The water simultaneously provides the support necessary for independent ambulation and the resistance necessary to increase the intensity of the task.

Bicycling activities also should be considered. When a student has sufficient leg function, stationary bikes and three-wheelers can be useful in designing a continuous activity of moderate to high intensity. In cases where the legs are impaired but the arms remain unaffected, adapted, hand-propelled bicycles can be used.

Finally, the physical educator may wish to incorporate "mat activities" into the exercise program. Activities that require the student to pull the body along a mat are sometimes very challenging. In fact, having a student with cerebral palsy creep or crawl to a cone placed only 10 to 15 ft away may meet the intensity and duration requirements to elicit a training effect.

Muscular Strength and Endurance

Research indicates that the muscular strength and endurance of most people with handicapping conditions is below those of their able-bodied peers. This is true despite the fact that, in many instances (muscular dystrophy being a notable exception), muscle physiology is normal and consequently, the muscles of impaired youngsters will respond appropriately to training as long as innervation is intact.

When there is complete loss of muscle function due to spinal cord injury, no improvement in muscular strength and endurance can be attained through exercise. For people with partial loss of muscle function, exercise is recommended; however, the intensity of the activity must be modified radically. *Active* and/or *assistive* exercises, therefore, may have to be used in place of resistive excercises, although the overload principle must still be maintained to produce a training effect. An active exercise is one in which the participant independently works a muscle through the range of motion, with gravity providing the only resistance. An assistive exercise is one in which the participant works through the range of motion with some form of outside assistance. (A third alternative to resistive exercise is *passive* exercise, in which another individual moves the participant's limb through the range of motion. Because no muscle action is involved on the part of the participant, passive exercise is not recommended for the development of muscular strength and endurance, but it can be used to enhance flexibility.)

Principles of active and assistive exercise should also be applied to students who do not have nerve damage but who are unable to overcome even minimal resistance in exercise. For a student who is unable to do a sit-up, for instance, an inclined board can be used so that the student does "downhill" sit-ups. This is a less intense, assistive exercise where gravity provides the assistance. A pull-up task can also be modified with the use of an inclined board. By lying on a scooter placed on the inclined board, the student can perform pull-ups in a way in which the effects of gravity are reduced. It should be noted that, as levels of intensity are established for pull-ups or other tasks where the body provides resistance, the student's body weight and that of any braces or prosthetic devices being worn must be considered. The intensity of the task is more demanding for those who are heavier or who are wearing orthopedic devices.

Many muscular strength and endurance exercises can be done in a pool or on a mat. Teachers should be careful, however, to position the student in such a way that the targeted muscles are exercised at the most appropriate intensity. Knee flexion (hamstring) exercises, for example, are more difficult in a prone position than in a side-lying position because gravity provides more resistance when one is prone. Positioning of the student is also a consideration when reflexes are a problem. Activities that are appropriate for specific positions must be designed individually. An example would be exercises that allow the head to remain in the midline for an individual who exhibits the asymmetrical tonic neck reflex, a condition where turning the head in either direction causes extension of the limbs on the "face" side of the body and flexion of the limbs on the "skull" side.

When developing muscular strength and endurance, the physical educator must guard against creating muscular imbalances within the individual's body. Whenever possible and appropriate, therefore, both agonists and antagonists should be exercised. Muscular imbalance is a particularly important issue for students with spastic cerebral palsy. Ordinarily, attention should be given to the development of the extensors, abductors, and supinators of the student with spasticity because the flexors, adductors, and pronators tend to be hypertonic and dominate their antagonists. Muscle imbalance is also a problem for people with spinal cord injuries. For those with spinal cord injuries, muscular strength and endurance activities should be selected to improve or maintain proper body alignment and to improve the capacity of the functional muscles. For quadriplegics exercise will usually involve the anterior deltoid, biceps, and lower trapezius; for paraplegics exercise can be expanded to include the shoulder depressors (e.g., pectorals), triceps, and latissimus dorsi (O'Sullivan, Cullen, & Schmitz, 1981). Mat activities, including modified push-ups, modified pull-ups, and log rolling, are usually appropriate for students with spinal cord injuries.

The student with cerebral palsy requires some additional considerations with regard to muscular strength and endurance. Because of inefficiency of movement, individuals with cerebral palsy may tire more rapidly than other students in the class. Consequently, the duration of the activity may have to be modified; this is especially true with both muscular endurance and cardiorespiratory endurance activities. When possible, isokinetic exercises are recommended over isotonic or isometric exercises because, with the former, resistance varies throughout the range of motion. Isokinetic exercise supplies a constant tension to the muscle commensurate with muscle contraction, allowing for a more controlled exercise.

McCubbin and Shasby (1985), for instance, have reported that isokinetic exercise can effectively improve torque and speed of movement in the elbow extensors of adolescents with cerebral palsy. Finally, the physical educator should recognize that power training for speed creates special problems for the student with cerebral palsy; attempts to move quickly often result in uncontrolled movements that produce inefficiency. When rapidly performed exercises appear to be counterproductive, the best way to develop speed might be by increasing flexibility, improving the quality of the desired movement pattern, and *gradually* requiring faster execution of controlled movements. Because the development of speed is so complex in students with cerebral palsy, the teacher should consider increasing the frequency of training (in addition to its intensity) for best results.

Precautions
—— and Contraindications ——

Although the vast majority of students with handicapping conditions require no special precautions when participating in vigorous physical activity, some do. Following is an overview of specific precautions and some contraindications for selected handicapping conditions.

Amputations: Physical educators should be aware that a prosthetic device may traumatize the remaining portion of the limb, the stump, during vigorous physical activity. The stump should be examined regularly for bruises; use of a stump sock to reduce skin irritation is recommended.

Cystic Fibrosis: Salt tablets should be available, particularly when vigorous physical activity is conducted in hot weather (Adams, Daniel, McCubbin, & Rullman, 1982). The perspiration of a person with cystic fibrosis is unusually salty and can deplete the body of sodium chloride.

Diabetes: Physical activity must be coordinated with diet and insulin. Because a delicate balance exists among these three variables, it is recommended that exercise be performed on a daily as opposed to an intermittent basis. Exercise is contraindicated, of course, when the person is hypoglycemic (has low blood sugar). In addition, particular caution should be exercised to protect the diabetic from scrapes, bruises, and blisters because increased risk of infection is a problem associated with diabetes.

Down Syndrome: Approximately 17% of youngsters with Down syndrome exhibit atlantoaxial instability, a condition in which there is unusual mobility between the first and second cervical vertebrae. Exercises or activities that require or cause neck flexion may injure the spinal cord. All Down syndrome children should be x-rayed to determine if they have atlantoaxial instability (Cooke, 1984).

Glaucoma: Weight lifting is usually contraindicated for individuals with glaucoma because of the potential danger of increasing the pressure in the eyeball (French & Jansma, 1982).

Heart Disease: Physical educators should be able to identify the symptoms of heart disease, including uncomfortable breathlessness and persistent palpitation with physical activity; pain in the chest, shoulder, or arms; and swelling in the legs and ankles. Physical activity is contraindicated in the presence of any of these symptoms (Adams et al., 1982).

Juvenile Rheumatoid Arthritis: Activities or exercises that jar the joints of the body should be avoided. Activities conducted in place generally are more appropriate than those that require running.

Muscular Dystrophy: Physical activity is usually recommended as part of the treatment program for a youngster with muscular dystrophy. Some experts, however, caution about exercising to *fatigue* because it is thought that fatigued muscles allow greater amounts of the muscle enzyme creatine phosphokinase (CPK) to escape into the bloodstream, thereby hastening the progression of the condition (Adams et al., 1982).

Seizure Disorders: Because the occurrence of seizures is unpredictable, activities and exercises should be analyzed to guarantee that the student is not placed in a potentially dangerous situation should a seizure occur.

Spinal Cord Injury: Some people with spinal cord injuries have problems with thermoregulation; one consequence is that they do not dissipate heat from the body very well. When continuous activities are conducted in hot weather, therefore, participants should be provided with shade, wet towels, water to drink, sunscreen, hats, and any other items designed to reduce body temperature.

Figure 18.4 Shade and wet towels help to cool down athletes with spinal cord injuries.

Flexibility

As with other components of physical fitness, research suggests that the flexibility of students with handicapping conditions generally is inferior to that of their able-bodied peers. Although flexibility training is important for all students, its incorporation into physical fitness programs for physically disabled students is highly recommended. Increased flexibility will allow for improved functional movement and will help to combat contractures, a condition characterized by shortened muscles that may result in some physical deviation. Contractures are associated with a number of conditions including muscular dystrophy, juvenile rheumatoid arthritis, amputation, spinal cord injury, and cerebral palsy.

When contractures are already present or when other severe restrictions in flexibility exist, the frequency and duration of training must increase significantly. In these instances it is recommended that flexibility training be provided at least three times per day and the duration of the training be up to 30 to 45 min per session (Winnick & Short, 1985). When this type of schedule is recommended, however, flexibility training will probably go beyond the scope of physical education (regular or adapted), and students must take responsibility for their own flexibility exercises outside of the school environment. For instance, youngsters with cerebral palsy whose legs are severely adducted should assume an abducted posture while doing homework or watching television at home, or should become involved in appropriate recreation programs such as horseback riding.

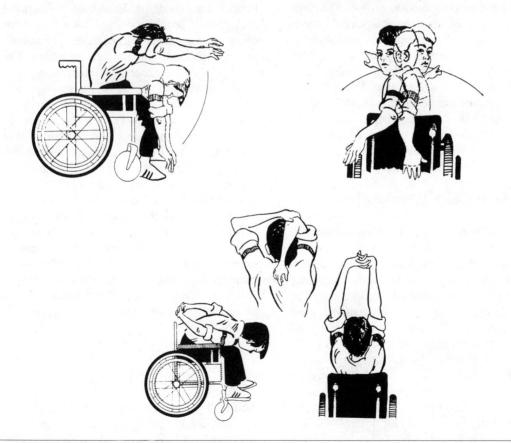

Figure 18.5 Examples of flexibility exercises for students in wheelchairs. *Note.* From ''Flexibility'' by K. Rusling. In *Training Guide to Cerebral Palsy Sports* (3rd ed.) (pp. 62-63) by J.A. Jones (Ed.), 1988, Champaign, IL: Human Kinetics. Copyright 1988 by Jeffrey A. Jones. Reprinted with permission.

The physical therapist can serve as a valuable resource to the physical educator in identifying muscular imbalances and selecting appropriate activities for the development of flexibility. The flexors, adductors, and pronators, for instance, are usually the muscle groups requiring the greatest attention in development of flexibility among individuals with spastic cerebral palsy. For those with spinal cord injuries, flexibility of the arms and shoulders is important for functional efficiency. Attention to trunk flexibility, however, is not always recommended for those with spinal cord injuries because increased range of motion may interfere with necessary trunk stability (O'Sullivan et al., 1981).

Physical therapists also can provide additional flexibility training when the goals and objectives of the student's program cannot be met in physical education or when severe restrictions in flexibility prohibit the student from attaining other objectives in physical education. When there is complete loss of muscle function about a joint and passive exercise is needed to improve flexibility, it is recommended that the physical educator refer the student to the physical therapist.

General Considerations

When developing programs of physical fitness, the physical educator should be aware of students' initial levels of fitness and select activities accordingly. In all cases the procedure should be to start slowly and progress gradually. Students should be taught to warm up prior to a workout and warm down afterward. The physical educator should motivate students to pursue higher levels of fitness by keeping records, charting progress, and providing awards. Selecting enjoyable activities will also help to maintain interest in physical fitness; for instance, charting a class's cumulative running distances on a map for a "cross-country run" will be more interesting and motivating than simply telling them to "run three laps." The physical educator should also be a good role model for students; this includes staying fit and participating in class activities whenever possible. Finally, the physical educator should view physical fitness as an ongoing part of the physical education program and not just one unit of instruction. Even though different units will be taught throughout the year, activities within a unit (exercises, games, drills, etc.) should be arranged to enhance, or at least maintain, physical fitness.

Summary

Physical fitness is critical to the person with a handicapping condition. In addition to improved performance, health, and appearance, high levels of fitness can foster independence, particularly among individuals with physical handicaps. The goals of a fitness program for individuals with unique needs will depend upon the type and severity of the handicapping condition and current levels of physical fitness. Performance-related fitness for basic stability, basic mobility, skill development, game participation, and competitive sport are all reasonable goals in adapted physical education. Teachers must understand that, with few exceptions, students with handicapping conditions will exhibit a favorable physiological response to training. In many cases the recommendations for intensity, frequency, and duration of exercise do not differ significantly from those made for the nonhandicapped. The mode, or type of activity, however, frequently must be modified to provide the students with an appropriate workout.

Bibliography

Adams, R.C., Daniel, A.N., McCubbin, J.A., & Rullman, L. (1982). *Games, sports, and exercises for the physically handicapped*. Philadelphia: Lea & Febiger.

American Alliance for Health, Physical Education, Recreation and Dance (1980). *Health related physical fitness test manual*. Reston, VA: Author.

Astrand, P.O., & Saltin, B. (1961). Maximal oxygen uptake and heart rate in various types of muscular activity. *Journal of Applied Physiology,* **16**, 977-981.

Clarke, H.H., and Clarke, D.H. (1978). *Developmental and adapted physical education*. Englewood Cliffs, NJ: Prentice-Hall.

Cooke, R.E. (1984). Atlantoaxial instability in individuals with Down's syndrome. *Adapted Physical Activity Quarterly,* **1**, 194-196.

di Natale, J., Lee, M., Ward, G., & Shephard, R.J. (1985). Loss of physical condition in sightless adolescents during a summer vacation. *Adapted Physical Activity Quarterly,* **2**, 144-150.

French, R.W., & Jansma, P. (1982). *Special physical education*. Columbus, OH: Merrill.

McCubbin, J.A., & Shasby, G.B. (1985). Effects of isokinetic exercise on adolescents with cerebral palsy. *Adapted Physical Activity Quarterly,* **2**, 56-64.

Mulholland, R., & McNeill, A.W. (1985). Cardiovascular responses of three profoundly retarded, multiply handicapped children during selected motor activities. *Adapted Physical Activity Quarterly,* **2**, 151-160.

O'Sullivan, S.B., Cullen, K.E., & Schmitz, T.J. (1981). *Physical rehabilitation: Evaluation and treatment procedures*. Philadelphia: F.A. Davis.

Steadward, R., & Walsh, C. (1986). Training and fitness programs for disabled athletes: Past, present, and future. In C. Sherrill (Ed.), *Sport and disabled athletes* (pp. 3-19). Champaign, IL: Human Kinetics.

Winnick, J.P., & Short, F.X. (1984). Test item selection for the Project UNIQUE Physical Fitness Test. *Adapted Physical Activity Quarterly,* **1**, 296-314.

Winnick, J.P., & Short, F.X. (1985). *Physical fitness testing of the disabled*. Champaign, IL: Human Kinetics.

Resources

Armchair aerobics [Videotape]. Port Washington, WI: The Fitness Firm. This aerobics videotape is designed for the physically disabled person.

Fitness is for everyone [Videotape]. Washington, DC: National Handicapped Sports and Recreation Association. This includes six 30-min videotapes on exercise for disabled persons.

Reach for fitness [Videotape]. Irvine, CA: Karl-Lorimar Home Video. This is a Richard Simmons videotape with exercises for the physically challenged person.

CHAPTER 19

Motor Development

Bruce A. McClenaghan

The acquisition of motor skills is a developmental process that begins early during the prenatal period and continues throughout life. Developmental studies have supported the premise that the ability to move efficiently is acquired in a sequential and orderly manner. Ability to perform motor skills is dependent upon both the integrity of the neurological and musculoskeletal systems and the complex interaction of maturation and experience. Deficiencies in any of these factors can result in impaired motor function. For example, the learning-disabled child frequently exhibits some degree of motor impairment resulting from an inability to receive and process sensory information, while the child with cerebral palsy has difficulty moving body segments in a coordinated manner because of an impaired central nervous system.

This chapter will review developmental theory and apply the principles of motor development to the teaching of children with a variety of motor impairments.

Principles of Motor Development

Numerous authors have presented models to depict the manner in which motor skills are acquired and refined. Regardless of the specific author, several principles appear to be common.

Developmental Sequence

Children acquire the ability to move in a sequential and orderly manner, progressing from simple, isolated body actions to highly complex and coordinated motor skills. This developmental process tends to proceed in a head-to-foot, *cephalocaudal*, and trunk-to-extremities, *proximodistal* manner.

Developmental Rate

Although the sequence of motor skill acquisition is well documented and dependent upon the maturation and integrity of the neurological and musculoskeletal systems, the rate at which children pass through this sequence is dependent upon the individual.

An important consideration in a discussion of developmental rate is the concept of *critical periods*. McGraw (1939) concluded from her early developmental work that there are periods in the developmental process in which the acquisition of a particular skill may be greatly enhanced through repetitive experience. In more recent works, Seefeldt (1975) and Oyama (1979) have referred to these times as "sensitive periods." The exact role of these critical periods with children who have impairments is not known. It appears, however, that children who exhibit a generalized developmental delay may also experience a delay in these periods when motor skills can be most

315

readily learned. As a rule, the earlier a motor impairment can be identified and remedial activities provided, the greater the chance for improving performance.

Developmental Order

Neuromuscular coordination of the large muscles responsible for postural control and gross movements of the extremities is developed before coordination of the muscles responsible for more precise movements. In addition, movements that require similar action of one set of extremities on both sides of the body, *bilateral*, are refined before actions that require the movement of an arm and leg on the same side, *unilateral*. *Cross-lateral* actions, requiring the simultaneous movement of opposing limbs, represent a more difficult task requiring complex neurological control and are thus the last to be acquired.

Movements in specific directions (planes) also appear to be acquired at differing times in the developmental process. Movements in the *sagittal* direction (forward and rearward) tend to develop before those in the *frontal* plane (side to side). Actions in the *transverse* plane (rotation) develop only after movements in the sagittal and frontal planes are well established.

These simple principles can provide the basis for the design of experiences to help children refine motor skills. For example, the principle of developmental sequence makes it obvious that an advanced skill cannot be learned until the child has acquired the prerequisite movements associated with that skill. Thus, we should not attempt to play volleyball until the subskills of serving, digging, setting, and spiking are learned. Similarly, these subskills cannot be learned until fundamental actions such as body weight transfer, trunk rotation, vertical jumping, and so on have been acquired.

Developmental Stages

Most developmental theories are based on the premise that, with aging, children demonstrate readily observable changes in behavior. These changes are frequently referred to as *developmental milestones*. Authors have grouped these milestones into *developmental stages*, thus providing a model of the developmental process.

With maturation, children exhibit increasingly complex behaviors as they broaden their ability, increase their level of functioning, and become more skilled. At each stage of development children exhibit similar generalized behaviors, although each child represents a unique set of genetic endowments and experiences. Generalized stages of development—infancy, childhood, and adolescence—provide a basis for charting the acquisition of motor skills.

Developmental changes can be observed in both the mechanical characteristics of movement (*process characteristics*) and the level of performance (*product characteristics*). Researchers and instructors have used both process and product characteristics to define developmental changes. For example, one can generalize that the time (product) it takes to run a 50-yd dash decreases with age during childhood. Developmental studies also have shown that there are definite changes in the mechanical qualities (process) of the run during this period, contributing to the improved performance. Product characteristics provide the instructor with normative data for judging a student's level of performance. Frequently this information is used to determine if a child is performing at an age-appropriate level. With children exhibiting motor delays, this information alone is of limited value because it is often already known that their performance is below age level.

Process characteristics may be applied similarly, in that they allow the user to determine the level of performance. These mechanical descriptors, however, provide additional information that can contribute to instruction. While product characteristics identify only the age level of functioning, process characteristics identify not only age level but also the mechanical qualities of the performance. This additional information allows the instructor to pinpoint specific factors contributing to reduced performance. For example, when the skill being evaluated is throwing a ball for distance, it is insufficient to know only that the child's performance is 2 years behind established norms. This information indicates only that this child needs additional experience throwing a ball for distance, something that simple observation would have indicated. It is important for the instructor to know not only that the child's performance is below age level, but also that the reason for the performance lag is a lack of trunk rotation and forward shift in body weight.

Two approaches have been used to describe process characteristics of a motor performance (Ulrich, 1987). Seefeldt and Haubenstricker (1982) described the action of the total body, while Halverson (1983) and Roberton (1984) described the actions of individual body segments.

The regularity of the developmental process has allowed researchers to chart the sequential changes that occur as a result of age and experience. As children mature they move through these changes in much the same order. The rate of sequential change, however, appears to differ among children (Roberton, 1984). Thus, the child who is motorically delayed because of a central nervous system impairment will acquire motor skills in the same developmental sequence as the child without an impairment. But the rate of development may be slowed by the impairment, and the child's ultimate motor potential may be lower than that of the nonimpaired child.

Several authors have identified the stages that children pass through in acquiring mature and efficient motor skills (Gallahue, 1982; Roberton, 1984). Table 19.1 presents a summary of these developmental stages, relating the age-based general developmental stages and the function-based stages of motor development.

Reflex Stage

Motor behavior begins early during the prenatal period (at approximately 7.5 weeks) when the fetus exhibits the first signs of movement (Hooker, 1952). Several early studies attempted to positively correlate these prenatal movements with later post-

Table 19.1 Stages of Motor Development

General developmental stage	Stage of motor development
Adolescence	Skill
Childhood	Fundamental movement pattern
Infancy	Prepattern
Prenatal	Reflex

natal motor ability (Richards & Newberry, 1938; Walters, 1965).

Once a child is born the earliest movements that can be elicited consist of reflexes, involuntary movements resulting from various kinds of stimuli. Reflexive actions are frequently classified as *primitive reflexes*, those that are used to sustain early life, and *postural reflexes*, actions that resemble later voluntary movements and are used to support the body against gravity or allow movement.

This early reflexive behavior exhibited by the infant is frequently used as a diagnostic tool in determining the integrity of the central nervous system. It has been demonstrated that in nonimpaired children, motor development is characterized by a regular sequence in which reflexes appear, mature, and disappear (Paine et al., 1964). In children with motor impairment there is a tendency for primitive reflexes to persist, while the appearance of higher levels of motor activity is delayed. Cratty (1979) noted that, when a reflex is elicited, if it is uneven in strength, too weak, or too strong, some neurological dysfunction may be suspected. Similarly, if a reflexive action is not inhibited by the central nervous system and continues to be exhibited for too long a period, or if a reflex fails to appear at all, the examining physician may suspect some type of neurological impairment. Tables 19.2 and 19.3 summarize common primitive and postural reflexes, approximate

Table 19.2 Primitive Reflexes of the Newborn

Reflex	Onset	Inhibition	Stimulus	Behavior
Moro	Birth	3rd month	Supine position: Sudden loud noise near infant's head. Rapid or sudden movement of infant's head.	Stimulation will result in extension of the infant's extremities, followed by a return to a flexed position against the body.
Tonic neck (asymmetrical)	Birth[a]	6th month	Supine position: Neck is turned so head is facing left or right.	Extremities on side of body facing head position extend, those on side opposite flex.
Tonic neck (symmetrical)	Birth[a]	6th month	Supported sitting: Flexion or extension of infant's head.	Extension of neck will result in extension of arms and flexion of legs. Flexion of neck will result in extension of arms and flexion of legs.
Grasping	Birth	4th-6th month	Supine position: Stimulation of the palm of the hand or the ball of the foot.	Stimulation will result in a grasping action of the fingers or toes.
Babinski	Birth	6th month	Supine position: Stimulation by stroking the sole of the foot.	Stimulation will result in extension of the toes.
Sucking	Birth	3rd month	Supine or supported sitting: Stimulus applied directly above or below the lips.	Touching area of mouth will result in a sucking action of the lips.

[a]Not seen in all children.

Table 19.3   Postural Reflexes of the Newborn

Reflex	Onset	Inhibition	Stimulus	Behavior
Labyrinthine righting	2nd month	12th month	Supported upright position: Tilting of trunk forward, rearward, or to side.	Infant will attempt to keep head in an upright position by moving head in opposite direction from tilt.
Supportive reactions	4th month (arms) 9th month (legs)	12th month	Prone or upright supported: Movement of the child's extremities toward a surface.	Extension of the extremities to a position of support.
Pull-up	3rd month	4th month	Upright sitting supported by hands: Tilting of child from side to side and front and back.	Infant will flex arms in an attempt to maintain equilibrium.
Stepping	2nd week	5th month	Supported upright position: Infant is held in upright position and soles of feet are allowed to touch a surface.	Definite stepping action of only the lower extremities.
Crawling	Birth	4th month	Prone unsupported position: Stimulus is applied to sole of one foot.	Crawling action exhibited by both the upper and lower extremities.
Swimming	Birth	5th month	Prone held over water: Infant is held over or in water.	Swimming movements elicited in both the upper and lower extremities.

times of their onset and inhibition, associated methods of stimulation, and expected motor responses.

As voluntary movements begin to take the place of these early reflex actions, reflexes remain very important to the performance of motor skills. Voluntary control of a motor skill is usually limited to the initiation and regulation of speed, force, range, and direction and the termination of the movement (Gowitzke & Milner, 1980). The performer does not control the action of individual muscles. Functional features of the movement, such as stabilization of the joint and relaxation of the antagonists, are controlled by reflex actions. We frequently observe these underlying reflexes when teaching a child a new skill. For example, when a child is attempting a forward roll or a dive from the side of the pool, righting reflexes must be overcome before the skill can be successfully performed. The child's initial instinct is to right and extend the body rather than to roll, which results in an inappropriate action. Underlying reflex action also can be used to improve performance of a motor skill. For this reason, the stretch reflex is often used to facilitate the performance of a motor skill. A skilled tennis player visually monitors the flight of the ball and times the backswing so that the stretch of the shoulder muscles can contribute to the forward swing of the racquet.

Reflexes also play an important part in motor rehabilitation. The role of the instructor working with a motor-impaired individual frequently can be categorized as *facilitatory* or *inhibitory* in nature. Facilitatory techniques are used when additional neuromuscular stimulation is needed to perform the desired action, while inhibitory techniques are used to reduce the action of the neuromuscular system. For example, the child with cerebral palsy often has difficulty inhibiting the action of primitive and postural reflexes. These reflexes frequently impede and distract from the performance of voluntary movements. An objective in working with the cerebral palsy child is to use techniques that will inhibit or control this excessive reflex activity. Obviously, with the

spastic cerebral palsy child, ballistic movements of the extremities should be avoided because they would stimulate an already overactive stretch reflex; the result would be increased spasticity. For this reason, various inhibitory techniques should be used in an attempt to decrease activity of the musculature.

By contrast, these same ballistic movements can be used with a child who has hypotonicity in the muscles of the extremities. Rapid movement of the extremity will increase muscle tone and may result in better performance. Numerous examples of facilitatory techniques are available in athletic performance. For instance, the athlete uses the tonic neck reflex to assist in performing an overhand throwing action. Before performing a ballistic contraction of a muscle, the athlete stretches the muscle by moving the limb in the direction opposite the intended line of movement. This same technique may be used with the child who has difficulty in voluntarily moving a limb.

Reflex Inhibition/Prepattern Stage

During infancy the central and peripheral nervous systems mature and develop, which results in an inhibition of reflexes and increased voluntary control over the musculature. The exact role of postural reflexes in the development of similar voluntary movements is still being debated (Thelen, 1980).

During this stage of motor development children gain the ability to resist gravitational force, walk independently, and manipulate objects with their hands. These early voluntary movements form the basis for the development of more complex motor patterns during the early childhood period. It is important to emphasize that, although the "normal" child acquires these abilities rather early in life, the child with a motor impairment may have difficulty progressing beyond this stage of development.

During the initial 2 years of life, the neurological system rapidly matures and the child exhibits increased voluntary control over the antigravity muscles. Control over these muscles significantly contributes to the development of locomotor skills. Crawling is often the infant's first attempt to move from one location to another. Cratty (1975) noted that crawling often begins as a mistake rather than an attempt at purposeful movement. First attempts at crawling frequently result from the child reaching forward with one hand to obtain an object, losing equilibrium, and falling forward. Early crawling involves the use of the arms only to slide the trunk forward and appears at approximately the 6th month. As voluntary control, strength, and stability skills progress, the child begins to incorporate the legs into the crawling action. Early attempts at this creeping pattern are characterized by deliberate movement of one limb at a time (Gallahue, 1982). As this action is refined, the movements are coordinated into a more efficient and repetitive movement.

Acquisition of upright walking passes through a series of increasingly complex stages, beginning with the first uncoordinated steps and ending with a highly integrated and refined action involving the processing of sensory information and the coordination of multiple body segments. Children usually make early attempts at walking when held upright. Limbs are held in a position of flexion as the child performs a rapid, unrhythmical stepping motion. As the movement matures, the infant is able to bear more weight on the lower extremities, the base of support is narrowed, and stride length and speed increase. The stepping action becomes rhythmical as the infant makes initial contact with the heels of the feet. The arms swing in a controlled manner in opposition with the legs. Sutherland (1984) has done extensive study of normal and pathological gait patterns in humans. Figure 19.1 illustrates the changes observed in the walking pattern during the first 3 years of life.

Manipulative abilities also are refined during this early period of child development. Prior to the development of voluntary manipulative behaviors, the infant is limited to exploring the exter-

nal world through vision. An important step in the developmental process, therefore, is the refinement of the ability to reach and make contact with objects. Before the 3rd month of age the infant makes no definite attempts to reach for objects. During the 4th and 5th months, visual attention is integrated with the reaching task as the infant attempts to make contact with objects. Similarly, around the 4th month, early forms of a voluntary grasp may be observed. The first attempts at grasping objects are not possible until the palmar grasp reflex is inhibited. Halverson (1931, 1932), in an early study using filmed records of children grasping a 1-in red cube, identified the steps involved in acquiring an efficient grasping action. He noted that at approximately 5 months of age children exhibited a "primitive squeeze" where the object was actually pressed against the body or the opposite hand. At approximately 6 to 7 months the children refined a palm grasp, where the object was pressed against the palm of the hand by all the fingers. The thumb had become increasingly important in the grasping action by 8 months, and during the next several months the thumb and forefinger began to coordinate. By 13 months it was noted that the children were able to control and manipulate the object with the fingertips and thumb.

The ability to voluntarily release an object is acquired after the grasp has been mastered. Early attempts at releasing an object involve crude forms of a throw, often resulting from a vigorous shaking of the object. By the time the child is 14 months of age, early forms of a voluntary release may be observed. At approximately 18 months the infant has mastered a well-coordinated reach, grasp, and release (Halverson, 1937).

The acquisition of upright locomotion and efficient manipulative behaviors marks the transition into the next stage of motor development. Not all development progresses in such a smooth and sequential manner. Children who have motor impairments may experience difficulty acquiring one or more of the early voluntary movements. For example, visually impaired children are

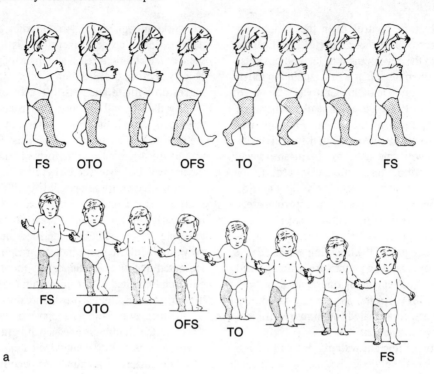

FS   OTO   OFS   TO   FS

FS   OTO   OFS   TO   FS

a

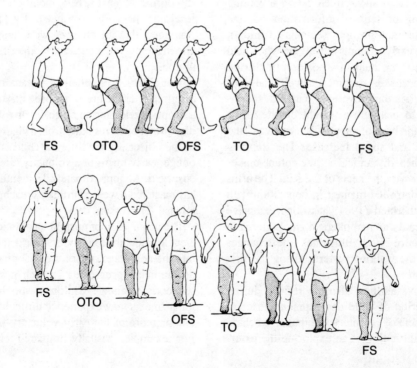

FS   OTO   OFS   TO   FS

FS   OTO   OFS   TO   FS

b

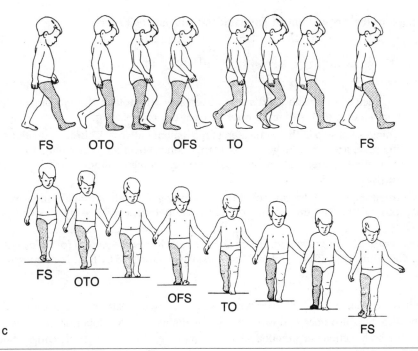

Figure 19.1   Developmental acquisition of walking during the a) first, b) second, and c) third year of life. FS = foot strike, OTO = opposite take-off, OFS = opposite foot strike. *Note*. From *Gait Disorders in Childhood and Adolescence* by D.H. Sutherland, 1984, Baltimore: Williams & Wilkins. Copyright 1984 by Williams & Wilkins. Reprinted by permission.

normally delayed in acquiring upright gait. This delay in walking is often attributed to poor stability skills and the lack of visual stimulation. The instructor working with these children must take into account the normal sequence of development to plan appropriate remedial strategies that will enhance the acquisition of motor skills.

Fundamental Movement Pattern Stage

The period of early childhood (2 to 6 years) appears to be critical in the development and refinement of motor skills. During this period the voluntary movements acquired during the reflex inhibition/prepattern stage are further refined and sequenced together to form *movement patterns*. These patterns form the basis for later advanced motor skills. During the period of early childhood,

children acquire fundamental movement patterns by gradually integrating a greater number of actions into a coordinated and refined pattern. Running, for example, requires the performer to synchronize arm and leg action with stability skills.

Several authors have developed methods for qualitatively evaluating the developmental changes in movement patterns during this period (McClenaghan & Gallahue, 1978; Roberton, 1984). Each of these authors has identified the developmental changes that occur in movement patterns during early childhood. McClenaghan and Gallahue defined three steps that are readily observable in the refinement of fundamental movement patterns (Table 19.4).

It is often difficult to observe and evaluate the qualitative changes that are occurring in the performance of a movement while it is being performed. To facilitate this process, several authors

Table 19.4 Steps in the Acquisition of Fundamental Movement Patterns

Step	Description
Initial	Characterized by the child's first observable attempts at the movement. Many of the components and actions of a refined pattern are missing.
Elementary	Transitional step in the acquisition of movement patterns. Coordination and performance improve, and the child gains progressive control over the movement. More components of a refined pattern are integrated into the movement, although often performed incorrectly.
Mature	Integration of all the components of the movement patten into a well-coordinated, purposeful act. The movement resembles the pattern exhibited by a skilled performer.

Note. From *Fundamental Movement Patterns: A Developmental and Remedial Approach* (p. 79) by B.A. McClenaghan and D.L. Gallahue, 1978, Philadelphia: Saunders. Copyright 1978 by B.A. McClenaghan. Adapted by permission.

(McClenaghan & Gallahue, 1978; Roberton, 1984) have broken the movements down into readily observable body actions or components. During the performance, observational attention is directed to the individual body actions. This approach allows for the possibility that individual components (such as arm or leg action) may develop at differing rates (Roberton, 1984).

Although it is not the purpose of this chapter to duplicate the work by these authors, for clarity, the following paragraphs offer an example of the developmental sequences. For additional information on developmental progression, readers are referred to several works included in the bibliography at the end of the chapter (Gallahue, 1982; McClenaghan & Gallahue, 1978; Roberton, 1984; Wickstrom, 1983).

In our example, the acquisition of the overhand throwing pattern will be used to illustrate the various stages of development. The overhand throwing pattern involves propelling an object into space by using the arm and hand in an over-the-shoulder pattern. This movement, when performed in the mature pattern, requires the sequencing of a number of body segments into a coordinated and purposeful movement. Numerous authors have described the qualitative changes that occur in the throwing pattern with age (McClenaghan & Gallahue, 1978; Roberton & Halverson, 1984; Wild, 1938). When the developmental sequence of a movement pattern is described, the movement should also be described in terms of its phase and body action.

Most motor skills can easily be divided into phases (Table 19.5) whose names describe the purpose of the movements that take place during the phase. For example, the overhand throwing pattern can be broken down into phases as follows: The initial rearward action of the arm and turning of the trunk away from the intended target are included in the preparatory phase; the forward rotation of the trunk, transfer of body weight, and forward motion of the arm characterize the action phase; and the absorption of the throwing motion as the arm crosses in front of the body is contained in the follow-through phase of the movement pattern.

The overhand throwing pattern also can be divided into the actions of individual body segments. This movement pattern comprises actions of the hand/arm, trunk, and leg. These movements, when combined into a coordinated action, constitute the throwing motion. Dividing the overhand throwing pattern into segmental actions

Table 19.5   Phases of a Movement

Phase	Description
Preparatory	Movements directed away from the intended direction of motion. The purpose of this phase is to place selected muscles and joints in the best position for the generation of force.
Action	Movement in the intended line of action. This phase accomplishes the primary purpose of the action.
Follow-through	All movements occurring after the primary purpose of the action has been achieved. This phase is often used to absorb the forces generated during the action phase of the movement.

allows the observer to accurately evaluate the quality of the performance and readily identify segments of the movement that are being performed incorrectly. Figure 19.2 shows how this pattern can be evaluated using developmental information. Other movement patterns may be similarly divided into developmental sequences. This information is particularly valuable in working with children who have progressed through the reflex inhibition/prepattern stage of development.

Knowledge of the developmental acquisition of fundamental movement patterns is of limited value in working with children confined to wheelchairs. Although some of the information can be helpful in instruction (for example, hand position while catching), much is not directly applicable to this population. At present there is little information relating to the developmental acquisition of wheelchair motor skills.

Motor Development Theory and the Handicapped Child

Motor development theory is based on observations of normal children as they mature and refine motor skills. This information, if applied correctly, can provide insights into the influence of various impairments on the acquisition of motor skills, common characteristics of children exhibiting motor impairments, and ways in which the principles of motor development can be applied in an instructional setting.

Causes of Motor Impairments

As previously discussed, the ability to efficiently perform motor skills depends on the integrity of the motor system and the complex interaction between maturation and experience. Rarely are the motor impairments exhibited by handicapped children related solely to a deficiency in the motor system or an experiential deprivation. Rather, the motor delay is usually the result of some impairment to the motor system compounded by a lack of opportunity to participate in structured physical activities.

The human motor system is an extremely complex array of neural tissue that receives a continuous stream of stimuli from objects and events in the environment, processes this information, and provides appropriate stimuli to the muscles to move in a coordinated and purposeful manner. Major components of this system include a variety of sensory receptors, which are located throughout the body and provide input; the central nervous system, which is involved in processing of sensory information and production of motor stimuli;

Throwing

Initial Stage

Arm Action	The throwing motion is performed mainly from the elbow, which remains in front of the body. The throw consists of a pushing action. At the point of release, the fingers are spread. The follow-through is forward and downward.
Trunk Action	The trunk remains perpendicular to the target throughout the throw. There is very little shoulder rotation during the throwing motion. The child tends to move slightly backward as the throw is made.
Leg-Foot Action	The feet remain stationary, although there may be some purposeless shifting of the feet during preparation for the throw.

Elementary Stage

Arm Action	The arm is swung in preparation, first sideward-upward and then backward to a position of elbow flexion where the ball is brought to a position behind the head. The arm swings forward in a high over-the-shoulder action. The follow-through is forward and downward. The wrist completes the throw, and the ball is controlled more by the fingers.

Trunk Action   The trunk rotates toward the throwing side during the preparatory phases of the throw. As the arm initiates the throwing action, the trunk rotates back toward the nonthrowing side. The trunk flexes forward with the forward motion of the throwing arm.

Leg-Foot Action   The performer steps forward with the leg that is on the same side as the throwing arm. There is a forward shift in the body weight.

Mature Stage

Arm Action   The arm swings backward in preparation for the throw. The throwing elbow moves forward horizontally as it extends. The thumb rotates in and downward and therefore ends up pointing downward. At release the fingers remain close together.

Trunk Action   During the preparatory phase of the throw, the trunk is markedly rotated to the throwing side and the throwing shoulder drops slightly. As the forward motion begins, the trunk rotates through the hips, spine, and shoulders. The throwing shoulder rotates to a position in line with the target.

Leg-Foot Action   During the preparatory phase of the throw, the weight is on the rear foot. As the trunk rotates, the weight is completely shifted with a step on the foot that is on the nonthrowing side of the body.

Figure 19.2 Segmental actions of overhand throw by developmental level. *Note.* From *Fundamental Movement: A Developmental and Remedial Approach* by B.A. McClenaghan and D.L. Gallahue, 1978, Philadelphia: Saunders. Copyright 1978 by Bruce McClenaghan. Reprinted by permission.

and the musculoskeletal structures, which provide support and allow movement. These major components are interconnected through a vast array of nerves that transmit electrical impulses to and from the central nervous system. Ghez (1981) has identified three primary roles of the motor system:

- Channeling of information received from sensory receptors or from memory stores to appropriate motor neurons
- Accurately controlling the degree of contraction of each muscle according to the intended purpose of the movement

- Coordinating the action of the muscles (synergy) into their appropriate role (agonist, antagonist, or stabilizer)

The extent to which deficits in the motor system will affect the performance of motor skills depends on the location and extent of the impairment. For example, children with impairment at the sensory receptor level of the motor system are often delayed in the acquisition of motor skills. Thus, visually impaired children experience delayed development of physical skills, particularly those skills that depend on mobility and locomotion (Winnick, 1985). Similarly, learning-disabled children also appear to experience deficits in the development of motor skills. Bruininks and Bruininks (1977) noted that children tested on the Bruininks-Oseretsky Test of Motor Proficiency exhibited delays in activities requiring body equilibrium, visual-motor control, and bilateral coordination.

A central nervous system impairment may have a more direct influence on motor development. Children identified as mentally retarded perform less proficiently than normal peers on measurements of static and dynamic strength, power, coordination, balance, and agility (Rarick, 1973). Moderately retarded children also appear to be markedly inferior in the development and refinement of fundamental motor patterns (Hemmert, 1979). While the mentally retarded child shows a delayed acquisition of motor skills and lower performance levels compared to the nonretarded, the child with cerebral palsy is greatly influenced by the inability to inhibit reflex activity. Although both these impairments may be classified as central in origin, their influence on the developmental process and the performance of motor skills varies greatly. Similarly, the individual who is spinal cord injured will be severely restricted in the ability to move, with the nature and degree of restriction depending on the location and extent of the impairment.

Impairments to the musculoskeletal segments can also influence acquisition of motor skills. The child missing a limb because of a congenital defect or an acquired amputation will need to compensate for that loss, either through adaptation of the movement or through the use of a prosthetic device. Even with the great advances made in the design of artificial limbs, their ability to duplicate normal function is often limited. Degenerative neuromuscular diseases interrupt the normal flow of information to and from the central nervous system, which often results in an impaired ability to perform motor skills.

The extent to which an enrichment program of motor experiences (the adapted physical education program) can improve motor performance depends on the exact nature of the child's impairment. It is important to determine whether the impairment reflects primarily a delay in development, caused by a lack of experiences, or a neurological or structural deficit. Children who are delayed have the potential to achieve normal levels of function over an extended period of enrichment. A deficit, on the other hand, implies a permanent impairment that may limit the child's potential to achieve normal levels of motor ability. If a delay is suspected, steps are taken to enhance the learning environment in an attempt to facilitate the developmental process. Children exhibiting deficits must also be provided an enrichment program designed help them compensate for the impaired ability.

Rarely does a motor impairment result solely from either a delay in development or a motor deficit. Rather, a motor impairment is often the result of a deficit that is compounded by delayed development. The instructor needs to identify the areas of ability that will respond most to an enrichment program while developing alternative skills in areas impaired by a deficit.

Behaviors Associated With Motor Impairment

Although each child with a motor impairment is unique, the behaviors resulting from that impairment often may be classified according to the type of motor problem involved. This is not to imply that all motor-impaired children exhibit each of these behaviors but, rather, that these children often exhibit one or a combination of them. Table 19.6 summarizes behaviors commonly seen in motorically impaired children.

The extent to which children exhibit one or more of these characteristic behaviors varies with the nature and severity of the impairments. For instance, many children exhibit clumsiness but have not been found to have any specific neurological impairment. The cerebral palsy child, in contrast, exhibits more observable behavior associated with a severe neurological impairment and is readily classified according to the kind of motor behavior exhibited.

Individualizing Instruction

Adapted physical education, like other special education programs, provides a continuum of services designed to individualize instruction to meet the needs of all students (see chapter 2). Important steps in this process include

- identification of student needs,
- development of appropriate instructional objectives, and
- presentation of remedial activities.

The adapted physical educator spends considerable time and effort in identifying motor deficiencies. Often this results in attention being focused on the negative aspects of the child's behavior

Table 19.6 Characteristic Behaviors Associated With Motor Impairment

Classification	Description
Generalized clumsiness	A general inability to exhibit efficient coordination, balance, and/or agility. This behavior is often the result of some unidentified neurological deficit (Sherrill, 1986).
Apraxia	The inability to plan a motor act, resulting in uncoordinated movement.
Abnormal muscle tone	Excess (hypertonia) or lack (hypotonia) of muscle tone, resulting in the inability to efficiently perform movement patterns.
Athetosis	Impairment of inhibition, manifested by more or less continuous, purposeless movements (Halpern, 1978).
Dysmetria	Inability to control spatial, temporal, and control force production of a movement (Halpern, 1978).
Dyssynergia	Impaired coordination of muscular action (Halpern, 1978).
Dysrhythmia	Difficulty organizing time and performing movements that have a rhythmical pattern (Eichstaedt and Kalakian, 1987).
Perseveration	Persistence of a movement after it is concluded. Inability to cease a movement at a command to stop. Difficulty shifting from one movement to another.
Dissociation	Inability to perceive the whole from its parts. In motor skills, manifested in difficulty sequencing individual body actions into a movement pattern.
Inconsistency	Inconsistent performance on different trials.
Equilibrium deficits	Inability to maintain postural stability while maintaining a static position or moving. Inability to shift weight forward, rearward, and side to side.

rather than the positive. Using a developmental approach to instruction, the adapted physical educator can build on the skills the student possesses to develop and refine more advanced behaviors. The focus of this approach is on the positive aspects of the child's ability.

Identification of Student Needs

Often, the individual working with children who have special needs is required to formally evaluate a student's present level of functioning. This can easily become a full-time task in the absence of strategies to expedite the assessment process. Although the IEP (individualized education program) procedure lends itself to the use of product measures, these records sometimes provide little information valuable for instruction and for the correction of motor impairments. Norms are useful for documenting the level of a child's performance but frequently do not provide insight into the cause of a reduced level of performance. For this reason, it is recommended that process characteristics be used in addition to product measures when a handicapped child's motor performance is being evaluated for teaching purposes.

Process characteristics can quickly and accurately be assessed through systematic observation. The validity of this assessment technique is highly dependent upon the manner in which the observation is performed. The main prerequisite for accurate observation and assessment of motor abilities is the observer's knowledge of developmental theory and familiarity with the sequential stages of motor skill acquisition.

The most common assessment method using a developmental stages approach is criterion-referenced evaluation, discussed in chapter 4. With this technique a child's performance is judged against a preestablished standard, not according to the performance levels of others. The various developmental stages and the sequential acquisition of motor skills at each stage form the criteria for assessment. Age-referenced standards related to motor development for both handicapped and nonhandicapped youngsters are available in the literature.

Development of Instructional Objectives

Developmentally established criteria can also be used in writing instructional objectives for a particular child. In a developmentally sequenced criterion list, the next criterion level beyond the child's present level of functioning becomes the objective that will be the focus of instructional emphasis.

Presentation of Remedial Activities

A thorough understanding of developmental theory gives an instructor insight into activities that can help improve motor performance. Developmental theory is best used with a task analysis approach to instruction. Task analysis is the process of breaking a skill down into subparts and then presenting these to the student in a developmentally appropriate sequence. The extent to which the instructor must break a skill into its parts depends on the student's ability level and the complexity of the skill to be learned. For example, normally developing children learn to throw with a mature, overhand throwing action by watching others perform the movement and imitating their action. Because of the skill level of the performer and the low complexity of the movement, learning through demonstration-imitation is sufficient to refine the movement pattern. When there is a change in the skill level of the performer and/or the complexity of the movement, the method of presentation must be modified.

Highly complex skills such as gymnastic routines are traditionally presented to beginning learners in a part-by-part manner. Subskills are presented, practiced, and combined until the movement resembles the desired action. With such highly complex movements, it would be of limited value to have the student attempt the skill before being able to successfully complete the subskills that make up the total movement. That approach could result in continued performer failure and, ultimately, withdrawal from the activity.

To children exhibiting motor impairments, the simplest of movements can represent highly complex actions. For this reason, overhand throwing is not learned through simple observation and practice. Rather, the skill must be broken into its components and presented in parts.

Awareness of developmental sequences gives the instructor greater understanding of the kinds of movement observed in a classroom. The child who "chops" at a thrown ball instead of swinging, and the child who runs without a flight phase are common examples of difficulty with the acquisition of motor skills.

Developmental information can also help the teacher design instructional activities. For example, the severely impaired child who cannot sit independently but who demonstrates good head and neck control is ready for activities to develop the adequate postural control that will lead to independent sitting.

Summary

The acquisition of motor skills is a developmental process that continues throughout a lifetime. The teacher working with children who have difficulty developing efficient motor skills has a unique opportunity to significantly influence an individual's ability to function.

A thorough knowledge of developmental principles and the sequence of motor skill acquisition will give the teacher the background necessary to work with all children, regardless of their impairment. It is important to recognize that not all children have the same potential to perform motor skills. It is unrealistic, therefore, to expect all children to achieve the same level of performance, regardless of the enrichment activities provided.

Our primary objective must be to help children achieve their full developmental potential.

Bibliography

Bruininks, V.L., & Bruininks, R.L. (1977). Motor proficiency and learning disabled and non-disabled students. *Perceptual and Motor Skills,* **44**, 1131-1137.

Cratty, B.J. (1975). *Remedial motor activity for children*. Philadelphia: Lea & Febiger.

Cratty, B.J. (1979). *Perceptual and motor development in infants and children*. Englewood Cliffs, NJ: Prentice-Hall.

Eichstaedt, C.B., & Kalakian, L.H. (1987). *Developmental/adapted physical education: Making ability count*. New York: Macmillan.

Gallahue, D.L. (1982). *Understanding motor development in children*. New York: Wiley.

Ghez, C. (1981). Introduction to the motor systems. In E.R. Kandel & J.H. Schwartz (Eds.), *Principles of neural science* (pp 429-442). New York: Elsevier North Holland.

Gowitzke, B.A., & Milner, M. (1980). *Understanding the scientific bases of human movement*. Baltimore: Williams & Wilkins.

Halpern, D. (1978). Therapeutic exercise for cerebral palsy. In J.V. Basmajian (Ed.), *Therapeutic exercise* (3rd ed.) (pp. 281-306). Baltimore: Williams & Wilkins.

Halverson, H.M. (1931). An experimental study of prehension in infants by means of systematic cinema records. *Genetic Psychology Monographs,* **10**, 112-125.

Halverson, H.M. (1932). A further study of grasping. *Journal of Genetic Psychology,* **7**, 41.

Halverson, H.M. (1937). Studies of the grasping responses in early infancy. *Journal of Genetic Psychology,* **51**, 437-449.

Halverson, L. (1983). *Observing children's motor development in action*. Eugene, OR: Microform Publications.

Hemmert, T.J. (1979). An investigation of basic gross motor skill development of moderately retarded children and youth. (Doctoral dissertation, Ohio State University, 1978). *Dissertation Abstracts International, 39*, 4809a.

Hooker, D. (1952). *The prenatal origin of behavior*. Lawrence, KS: University of Kansas Press.

McClenaghan, B.A., & Gallahue, D.L. (1978). *Fundamental movement patterns: A developmental and remedial approach*. Philadelphia: Saunders.

McGraw, M. (1939). Later development of children specially trained during infancy. *Child Development, 10*, 1-19.

Oyama, S. (1979). The concept of the sensitive period in the developmental studies. *Merrill-Palmer Quarterly, 25*, 83-103.

Paine, R.S., Brazelton, T.B., Donovan, D.E., Dorbaugh, J.E., Hubbell, J.P., & Sears, E.M. (1964). Evolution of postural reflexes in normal infants and in the presence of chronic brain syndrome. *Neurology, 14*, 1037-1048.

Rarick, G.L. (1973). Motor performance of mentally retarded children. In G.L. Rarick (Ed.), *Physical activity: Human growth and development* (pp. 225-256). New York: Academic Press.

Richards, T.W., & Newberry, H. (1938). Studies in foetal behavior. *Child Development, 2*, 79.

Roberton, M.A. (1984). Changing motor patterns during childhood. In J.R. Thomas (Ed.), *Motor development during childhood and adolescence* (pp. 48-86). Minneapolis: Burgess.

Roberton, M.A., & Halverson, L. (1984). *Developing children—Their developing movement*. Philadelphia: Lea & Febiger.

Seefeldt, V. (1975). *Critical learning periods and programs of early intervention*. Paper presented to the National Convention of the American Alliance for Health, Physical Education and Recreation, Alantic City.

Seefeldt, V., & Haubenstricker, J. (1982). Patterns, phases, or stages: An analytical model for the study of developmental movement. In J.A.S. Kelso & J.E. Clark (Eds.), *The development of movement control and coordination* (pp. 309-318). New York: Wiley.

Sherrill, C. (1986). *Adapted physical education and recreation: A multidisciplinary approach* (3rd ed.). Dubuque, IA: Wm. C. Brown.

Sutherland, D.H. (1984). *Gait disorders in childhood and adolescence*. Baltimore: Williams & Wilkins.

Thelen, E. (1980). Determinants of amounts of stereotyped behavior in normal human infants. *Ethology and Sociobiology, 1*, 141-150.

Ulrich, B.D. (1987). Developmental perspectives of motor skill performance in children. In D. Gould & M.R. Weiss (Eds.), *Advances in pediatric sport sciences: Vol. 2. Behavioral issues* (pp. 167-168). Champaign, IL: Human Kinetics.

Walters, C.E. (1965). Prediction of post-natal development from foetal activity. *Child Development, 33*, 801-808.

Wickstrom, R. (1983). *Fundamental motor patterns* (3rd ed.). Philadelphia: Lea & Febiger.

Wild, M. (1938). The behavior pattern of throwing and some observations concerning its course of development in children. *Research Quarterly, 9*, 20-24.

Winnick, J.P. (1985). The performance of visually impaired youngsters in physical education activities: Implications for mainstreaming. *Adapted Physical Activity Quarterly, 2*, 292-299.

Resources

Gallahue, D.L. (1982). *Understanding motor development in children*. New York: Wiley. This text contains some excellent photographs of children performing motor skills at various developmental levels.

Payne, V.G., & Isaacs, L.D. (1987). *Human motor development: A lifespan approach.* Mountain View, CA: Mayfield. Chapters of particular interest in this book include "Infant Reflexes and Stereotypes," "Voluntary Movements of Infancy," "Fine Motor Development," and "Fundamental Movements of Childhood."

Sherrill, C. (1986). *Adapted physical education and recreation: A multidisciplinary approach.* Dubuque, IA: Wm. C. Brown. This text applies developmental information to the teaching of children exhibiting motor impairments.

CHAPTER 20

Body Mechanics and Posture

Luke E. Kelly

The term *good posture* implies appropriate alignment of body segments and body mechanics. Optimal body mechanics are desirable because they allow individuals to maximize their efficiency and minimize the strain placed upon the body—both of which are important for safe and successful performance in physical education and sport. Posture refers to appropriate body mechanics, whether the body is stationary or moving; it should not be thought of only as correct body alignment in standing or sitting. Good posture is a relative term. There are acceptable variations among individuals due to differences in body build and composition, and there are marked deviations that clearly require professional attention and remediation. The purpose of this chapter is to provide the physical educator with the knowledge and skills to identify postural deviations and, where appropriate, to remediate them in physical education.

Mild postural deviations are quite common and can often be remediated through proper instruction and practice in physical education. It is estimated that 70% of all children have mild postural deviations and that 5% have serious ones. The prevalence of serious postural deviations is, unfortunately, much greater among handicapped students.

Poor posture can result from any one or combination of factors such as ignorance, environmental conditions, genetics, physical and/or growth abnormalities, or psychological conditions. In many cases children are unaware that they have poor postures because they do not know what correct postures are and how their postures differ. In other cases, postural deviations can be traced to simple environmental factors such as poorly fitting shoes. In handicapped students, poor posture can be caused by factors affecting balance (e.g., visual impairments), neuromuscular conditions (e.g., spina bifida and cerebral palsy), or congenital defects (e.g., bone deformities and amputations). Finally, poor posture can occur as a result of attitude or self-concept. Pupils who have a poor body image or lack confidence in their ability to move tend to display defensive postures that are characterized by poor body alignment.

Physical educators should play an important role in the identification and remediation of postural deviations in all students. The physical educator is often the one educator in the school with the opportunity and background to identify and address postural problems. Unfortunately, postural screening and subsequent remediation are overlooked in many physical education programs. This is ironic, because the development of kinesthetic awareness and proper body mechanics is fundamental to teaching physical education and is clearly within the domain of physical education as defined by PL 94-142.

Several excellent general posture screening tests are available that can be used easily by physical educators and that involve minimal preparation and equipment to administer. Three examples, referenced at the end of this chapter, are the

Posture Grid (Adams, Daniel, McCubbin, & Rullman, 1982), the Iowa Posture Test (Scott & French, 1959), and the New York Posture Rating Test (New York State Education Department, 1966). Posture screening should be an annual procedure in all physical education programs. Particular attention should be paid to handicapped children because of their generally higher incidence of postural deviation. The appropriate school personnel, as well as the parents or guardians of all children identified as having present and potential postural problems, should be informed and requested to pursue further evaluation. The instructor can remediate most mild postural deviations within the regular physical education program by educating the children about proper body mechanics and prescribing exercises that can be performed both in and out of class. Sample exercises are described at the end of this chapter.

The purpose of the remainder of the chapter is to review some of the specific postural deviations that occur in the spinal column and lower extremities. Implications for adapted physical education, as well as procedures for assessment and remediation, will be discussed for each deviation.

Spinal Column Deviations

Viewed from the back, the spinal column should be straight with no lateral (sideways) curves. Any lateral curvature in the back is abnormal and is referred to as *scoliosis*. Viewed from the side, the spinal column has two mild curves. The first natural curve occurs in the thoracic region, where the vertebrae are concave forward (curving slightly in a posterior or outward direction). An extreme curvature in this region is abnormal and is known as *kyphosis*. The second natural curve occurs in the lumbar section, where there is mild forward convexity (inward curvature) of the spine. An extreme curvature in this region is also abnormal and is called *lordosis*. An exaggerated lumbar curve in lower elementary-age children is natural but should disappear by the age of 8.

Scoliosis

Lateral deviations in the spinal column are generally classified according to whether the deviation is *structural* or *nonstructural*. Structural deviations are generally related to orthopedic impairments and are permanent or fixed changes in the alignment of the vertebrae that cannot be altered through simple physical manipulation, positioning, or exercise. Nonstructural or functional deviations are those in which the vertebrae can be realigned through positioning and/or removal of the primary cause—such as ignorance or muscle weaknesses—which can be remedied with practice and exercise.

Structural scoliosis is also frequently classified according to the cause of the condition. Although scoliosis has many possible causes, the two most common are labeled *idiopathic* and *neuromuscular*. Idiopathic means that the cause is unknown. Neuromuscular means that the scoliosis is the result of nerve and/or muscle problems.

Structural idiopathic scoliosis occurs in approximately 2% of all school-age children. The onset of scoliosis usually occurs during the early adolescent years, when children are undergoing a rapid growth spurt. This form of scoliosis is characterized by an S-shaped curve, usually composed of a major curve and one or two minor curves. The major curve is the one causing the deformity. The minor curves, sometimes referred to as secondary or compensatory curves, usually occur above and/or below the major curve and are the result of the body's attempt to adjust for the major curve. Although both genders appear to be equally affected by this condition, a greater percentage of females have the progressive form that becomes more severe if not altered. The cause of this progressive form of scoliosis is unknown, but there is some evidence that suggests a possible genetic link in females.

A second type of structural scoliosis, more commonly found in severely handicapped children, is caused by neuromuscular problems. This form of scoliosis is usually characterized by a C-shaped curve. In severe cases this form of scoliosis can lead to balance difficulties, pressure on internal organs, and seating problems (pressure sores) for students in wheelchairs.

Nonstructural scoliosis can be the result of a number of causes and can be characterized by either an S- or a C-curve. The primary causes can be broadly classified as either skeletal or muscular. An example of scoliosis with a skeletal cause would be a curve that has resulted from one leg being shorter than the other. An example of scoliosis with a muscular cause would be a curve that has resulted because the muscles on one side of the back have become stronger than the muscles on the other side and have pulled the spinal column out of line. Fortunately, nonstructural scoliosis can usually be effectively treated by identification and correction of the cause—that is, inserting a lift in the child's shoe to equalize the length of the legs or strengthening and stretching the appropriate muscle groups in the back.

Assessment of Scoliosis

Early identification is extremely important for both structural and nonstructural scoliosis so that help can begin and the severity of the curve can be reduced. Scoliosis screening should be conducted annually for all children, particularly from the 3rd through the 10th grade, when the condition is most likely to occur. If a child is suspected of having scoliosis, the parents or guardians as well as other appropriate school personnel should be notified and further evaluation conducted. Students suspected of having scoliosis should be monitored more frequently, approximately every 3 months, to ascertain if the condition is progressing. A scoliosis assessment, which can be performed in less than a minute, involves observing the student shirtless. The assessments should be done individually, and by an assessor of the same gender as the children being assessed, because children of these ages are usually self-conscious about the changes occurring in their bodies and about being seen undressed.

To perform a scoliosis assessment, check the symmetry of the child's back while the child is standing and then when the child is bent forward. First, with the child standing erect, observe from a posterior view for any differences between the two sides of the back, including the following points (see Figure 20.1, rows A-D):

1. Does the spinal column appear straight or curved?
2. Are the shoulders at the same height, or does one appear higher than the other?
3. Are the hips at the same horizontal distance from the floor, or does one appear higher than the other?
4. Is the space between the arms and trunk equal on both sides of the body?
5. Do the shoulder blades protrude evenly, or does one appear to protrude more than the other?

Then ask the child to perform the Adam's position, bent forward at the waist to approximately 90° (Adam's Test; see Figure 20.2). Examine the back from both a posterior and an anterior view for any noticeable differences in symmetry, such as curvature of the spine or one side of the back being higher or lower than the other, particularly in the thoracic and lumbar regions.

Care and Remediation of Scoliosis

The treatment of scoliosis depends on the type and the degree of curvature. As mentioned earlier, nonstructural scoliosis can frequently be corrected when the cause is identified and the condition remediated through a program of specific exercises and body awareness. With structural scoliosis, the treatment varies according to the degree of curvature. Children with mild curvatures (less than 20°) are usually given exercise programs to keep the spine flexible and are monitored on a regular basis to make sure the curves are not becoming more severe.

Children with more severe curves (20°- 40°) are usually treated by means of braces or orthotics, which force the spine into better alignment and/or prevent it from deviating further. The Milwaukee

POSTURE RATING CHART

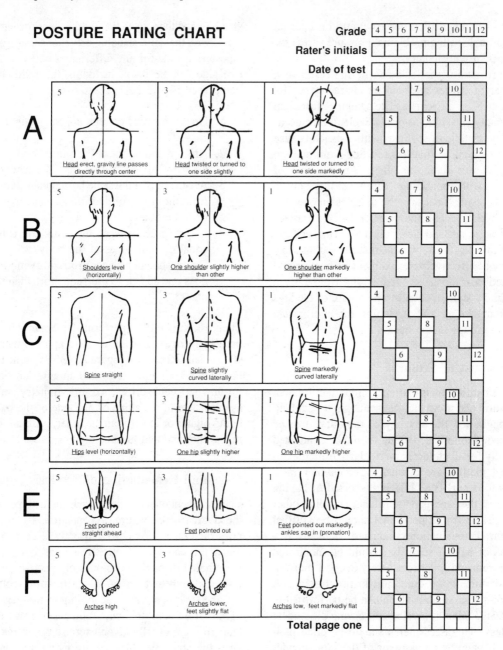

Grade	4	5	6	7	8	9	10	11	12
Rater's initials									
Date of test									

A

5	3	1
Head erect, gravity line passes directly through center	Head twisted or turned to one side slightly	Head twisted or turned to one side markedly

B

5	3	1
Shoulders level (horizontally)	One shoulder slightly higher than other	One shoulder markedly higher than other

C

5	3	1
Spine straight	Spine slightly curved laterally	Spine markedly curved laterally

D

5	3	1
Hips level (horizontally)	One hip slightly higher	One hip markedly higher

E

5	3	1
Feet pointed straight ahead	Feet pointed out	Feet pointed out markedly, ankles sag in (pronation)

F

5	3	1
Arches high	Arches lower, feet slightly flat	Arches low, feet markedly flat

Total page one

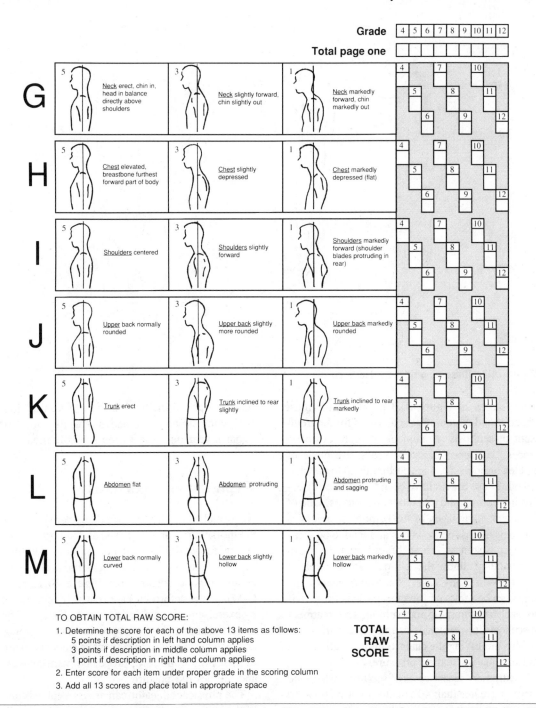

Figure 20.1 The New York State Posture Rating Chart. *Note.* From *New York State Physical Fitness Test for Boys and Girls Grades 4-12* by New York State Education Department, 1966, Albany, NY. Copyright by New York State Education Department. Reprinted by permission.

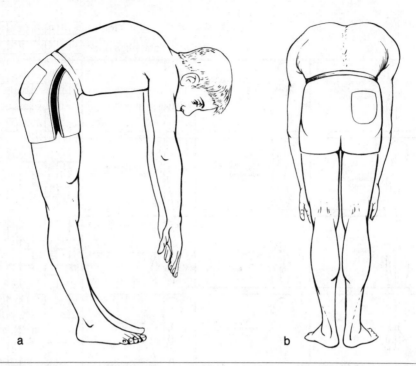

Figure 20.2 Illustration of the Adam's position.

brace shown in Figure 20.3 is one of the most effective and commonly used braces for the treatment of scoliosis. A number of more cosmetic braces, developed in recent years, are made of molded orthoplast and are custom fitted to the individual. These braces have been found to be effective in treating mild and moderate curves. One of the major advantages of the orthoplast braces is that they are less conspicuous and tend to be worn more consistently. These braces must be worn continuously until the child reaches skeletal maturity—in many cases, for 4 to 5 years. The brace can be removed for short periods for activities such as swimming and bathing. The treatment of scoliosis in wheelchair-bound persons may also involve modifying the chair to improve alignment and to equalize seating pressures.

In extremely severe cases of scoliosis, where the curve is greater than 40° or does not respond to bracing, surgery is employed. The surgical treatment usually involves fusing together the vertebrae in the affected region of the spine by means of bone grafts and the implantation of a metal rod. Following surgery, a brace is typically worn for about a year until the fusion has solidified.

Kyphosis and Lordosis

Abnormal concavity forward (backward curve) in the thoracic region (kyphosis) and abnormal convexity forward (forward curve) in the lumbar region (lordosis) are usually nonstructural and the result of poor posture (see Figure 20.1, rows G-M). These deformities are routinely remediated by exercise programs designed to tighten specific muscle groups and stretch opposing muscle groups and by education designed to make students aware of their present posture, proper body mechanics, and the desired posture.

The physical educator can assess kyphosis and lordosis by observing children under the conditions described previously for scoliosis screening, but from the side view. Look for exaggerated

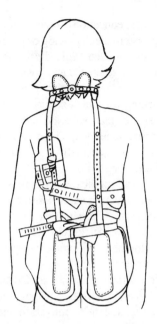

Figure 20.3 Illustration of the Milwaukee brace. *Note.* From *Games, Sports and Exercises for the Physically Handicapped* (p. 42) by R.C. Adams, A.N. Daniel, J.A. McCubbin, and L. Rullman, 1982, Philadelphia: Lea & Febiger. Copyright 1982 by Lea & Febiger. Courtesy of Milwaukee Children's Hospital. Reprinted by permission.

curves in the thoracic and lumbar regions of the spinal column. Kyphosis is usually characterized by a rounded appearance of the upper back. Lordosis is characterized by a hollow back appearance and a protruding abdomen.

Structural kyphosis, sometimes referred to as Scheuermann's disease or juvenile kyphosis, is similar in appearance during the early stages to the nonstructural form described earlier, but it is the result of a deformity in the shape of the vertebrae in the thoracic region. While the cause of this vertebral deformity is unknown, it can be diagnosed by X rays. This form of kyphosis is frequently accompanied by a compensatory lordotic curve. The prevalence of this deformity is not known, but it appears to affect both genders equally during adolescence.

Early detection and treatment of structural kyphosis through bracing can result in effective remediation of the condition. The treatment typically involves wearing a brace continuously for 1 to 2 years until the vertebrae reshape themselves. A variety of braces and orthotic jackets have been developed for the treatment of this condition. The Milwaukee brace used for the treatment of scoliosis is considered one of the more effective braces for treating this form of kyphosis.

Implications for Adapted Physical Education

As discussed earlier, physical educators can play a major role in screening for postural deviations in the spinal column. Children identified as having mild, nonstructural posture problems should receive special instruction and exercises to remediate their problems. Following are several general guidelines that should be considered whenever a physical educator is designing, implementing, or monitoring an exercise program to correct postural deviations.

1. Establish and follow policies and procedures for working with students suspected of having structural or serious postural deviations of the spinal column.

2. In an exercise program to remediate a postural deviation, the general objective is to strengthen the muscles used to pull the spinal column back into correct alignment and to stretch or lengthen the muscles that are pulling the spinal column out of alignment. The stretching program should be performed at least twice a day, and muscle strengthening exercises should be performed at least every other day. A number of different exercise and stretching routines should be developed to add variety and keep the exercise routine interesting. Setting the exercise routines to music and establishing reward systems are also recommended, especially for students who are not highly motivated to exercise.

3. All exercise and activity programs should begin and end with stretching exercises, with greatest emphasis on static stretching. Stretches should each be performed five times and held for a count of 15.

4. The exercise program should be initiated with mild, low-intensity exercises that can be easily performed by the children. The intensity of the exercises should be gradually increased as the children's strength and endurance increase.

5. In most cases, individual exercise programs should be initiated and taught in adapted physical education. After the student has learned the exercise routine it can be performed in the regular physical education class and monitored by the regular physical education teacher. First, explain to the student the nature of the postural deviation being addressed, the reasons that good posture is desirable, and the ways in which the exercises will help. The exercises should then be taught and monitored until it is clear that the child understands how to perform them correctly. The importance of making the student aware of the difference between the present posture and the desired posture cannot be overemphasized. Many children with mild postural deviations are simply unaware of the problem and, therefore, do not even try to correct their posture. Mirrors and videotape are useful media for giving students feedback on posture. When working with visually impaired students, the teacher will need to provide specific tactile and kinesthetic feedback to teach them the feeling of the correct postures. Cratty (1971) has described a tactile posture board, composed of a series of movable wooden pegs projecting through a vertical board, which can be placed along a student's spine to provide tactual feedback related to both postural deviations and desired postures.

6. Children should follow their exercise programs at home on the days they do not have physical education. Some form of monitoring system, such as a log or progress chart, should be used. Periodically the children should be evaluated and given feedback and reinforcement to motivate them to continue working on their exercise programs.

7. Exercises that make the body symmetrical are recommended. The use of asymmetric exercises, especially for children being treated for scoliosis, should be used only following medical consultation.

8. When selecting exercises to remediate one curve (i.e., the major curve), take care to ensure that the exercise does not foster the development of another curve (i.e., the minor curve).

9. The exercise program should be made as varied and interesting as possible to maintain the student's motivation and involvement. Alternating between routine exercises and activities like swimming and rowing will usually result in greater compliance with the program. Motivation is an even greater concern with mentally retarded students, who may not comprehend why they need to exercise or why better posture is desirable; they will require more frequent feedback and reinforcement. Showing students random polaroid snapshots is a good technique for keeping their attention on their posture and rewarding them when they are displaying the desired posture.

10. Students wearing braces such as the Milwaukee brace can exercise and participate in physical education, though activities that cause trauma to the spine (e.g., jumping and gymnastics) may be contraindicated. As a general rule, the brace will be self-limiting.

Recommended Exercises

Using the guidelines just presented and drawing on an understanding of the muscles involved in a spinal column deviation, a physical educator should be able to select appropriate exercise and activities. The following lists include sample exercises for the upper and lower back that can be used in the remediation of the three major spinal cord deviations discussed in this chapter. These exercise lists provide examples and are far from complete. Several resources that provide additional exercises and more detailed descriptions of their performance are listed at the end of this chapter.

Sample Upper Back Exercises

1. *Symmetrical* swimming strokes such as the backstroke and the breaststroke. If a pool is not available, the arm patterns of these strokes can be performed on a bench covered with a mat. Hand weights or pulley weights can be used to control the resistance.
2. Rowing using either a rowboat or a rowing machine. The rowing action can also be performed with hand weights or pulley weights.
3. Various arm and shoulder lifts from a prone position on a mat. Small hand weights can be used to increase resistance.
4. Hanging from a bar. This is a good stretching exercise.
5. Lateral (sideways) trunk bending from either a standing or a kneeling position. Forward bending should be avoided.

Sample Lower Back Exercises

1. Any form of correctly performed sit-ups commensurate with the student's ability. Emphasis should be placed on keeping the lower back flat and performing the sit-ups in a slow, continuous action, as opposed to performing a high number of repetitions. Raising of the hips and sudden jerky movements should not be allowed.
2. Pelvic tilt. This can be done from a supine position on a mat or standing against a wall.
3. Alternating or combined knee exchanges (bringing the knee to chest) from a supine position on a mat.
4. Doing a bicycling action with the legs from a supine position on a mat.

5. Leg lifts. Any variation of leg lifts is appropriate as long as the lower back is kept flat and pressed against the floor.

Lower Extremity and Foot Disorders

Deviations in the alignment of the hips, legs, and feet are common and can result in pain, loss of efficiency, and other postural problems. The correct alignment of the hips, legs, and feet is shown in Figure 20.4. The assessment of postural alignment of the lower extremities is included in the general posture screening instruments presented in the first part of this chapter.

The purpose of this section is to review some of the common deviations found in the hips, legs, and feet. Many of these problems are related and frequently occur together. As with the spinal column deviations discussed earlier, deviations in the alignment of the lower extremities can be either structural or nonstructural. Structural deviations are usually caused by skeletal or neuromuscular problems, which may be congenital or acquired. Nonstructural deviations are typically the result of muscle imbalances that, if not treated, may eventually become structural deviations.

Hip Deformities

Four common deformities occur at the hip joint. The first two (coxa valga and coxa vara) are the result of the angle between the head of the femur and the shaft of the femur and can occur in anyone. The third and fourth deformities involve hip dislocations, which are caused by congenital abnormalities in the formation of the hip joint or are acquired because of either trauma or gradual deformation of the hip joint.

Coxa Valga

The alignment of the upper leg is the result of the way the head of the femur articulates with the hip socket and the angle between the head of the femur

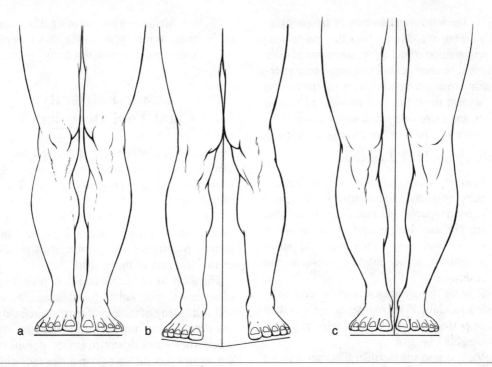

Figure 20.4 Illustration of alignment of the lower extremities: a) normal, b) knock-knees, and c) bowlegs.

and the shaft of the femur. In *coxa* (hip) *valga* (out), the angle between the head of the femur and the shaft is greater than normal, which results in the upper leg appearing abducted or bowed. The increased angle also causes the affected leg to be longer. This condition is structural and usually congenital and cannot be affected by attention, exercise or activity in physical education.

Coxa Vara

This deformity is the opposite of coxa valga. In *coxa vara*, the angle between the head of the femur and the shaft is smaller than normal, which results in the upper leg appearing bent inward or in a knock-kneed appearance. This condition, more common than coxa valga, can be either congenital or acquired. The acquired form, which occurs most frequently in males during the adolescent growth spurt, is usually caused by trauma or dislocation of the hip. If identified early, the condition

is usually treated by several weeks of abstention from weight bearing. If the condition is allowed to progress, bracing and surgery may be required to correct it.

Hip Dislocations

Hip dislocation is the situation in which the head of the femur is separated from the hip socket. Hip dislocations can be classified as either congenital or acquired. Congenital dislocations, sometimes refered to as developmental hip dislocations, result from deficits in prenatal development and abnormal birth conditions. The cause of this condition is unknown, but there is some relatively strong evidence of a hereditary link. The condition is more prevalent in females and occurs most frequently in the left hip.

Depending on the severity of a congenital hip dislocation, it may be detected immediately after birth or, in mild cases, not until the child begins to walk. Other observable symptoms are decreased range of adduction of the hip on the affected side and asymmetical fat folds on the upper legs. If the condition is not detected early, older children exhibit additional symptoms of exaggerated lordotic and scoliotic curves, pain, and fatigue. Treatment of congenital hip dislocations varies with the degree of the dislocation and the age at which it is detected. In mild cases involving very young children, dislocation can be successfully treated with splints. In more severe cases, a combination of casts, traction, and even surgery may be required.

In most cases, congenital hip dislocations will have been treated and remediated before the child enters school and will require no special attention in physical education. Occasionally, a case will be encountered where the condition was detected late and the child needs attention in the area of postural training and conditioning of the muscles in the hip region. The physical educator should consult with the appropriate medical personnel to coordinate the child's physical education objectives with the objectives being worked on in rehabilitation.

Acquired hip dislocations can be either acute or gradual. Acute dislocations are caused by trauma or injury to the hip. Gradual dislocations are caused by a progressive deformation of the hip joint and are common in many children with neuromuscular conditions such as cerebral palsy and spina bifida, who spend a majority of their time sitting in wheelchairs. These children are born with normal hip joints which are gradually deformed because of unbalanced muscle forces placed on the joint. Hip dislocations in these children frequently occur with very little associated pain. When the hip is dislocated, the affected leg will appear shorter and will be rotated inward in a scissoring position. Physical educators should be aware of these signs and of the potential for this problem in the neuromuscularly handicapped children they serve. The physical educator should consult regularly with the medical personnel on the status of students with potential hip dislocations and on physical education activities that might aggravate this condition and that, therefore, should be avoided.

Hip dislocation conditions can be treated prior to the actual dislocation by surgery that cuts the muscles, tendons, and/or nerves of the muscles exerting the inappropriate force on the joint. This usually involves the adductor muscles and tendons and the obturator nerve. After the hip has actually been dislocated, more extensive surgery involving restructuring of the hip joint is required.

Knee Deformities

A number of alignment problems referred to as knee deformities are the result of muscle imbalances, compensatory actions resulting from hip deviations, or abnormalities in the lower leg (tibia and fibula).

Bowlegs

Bowlegs or *genu* (knee) *varum* (inward) is the condition in which there is an inward bowing of the legs, resulting in the knees being separated when the ankles are touching (Figure 20.4c). The bowing can occur in either the femur or the tibia but is most common in the tibia. One or both legs can be affected. This condition is a common nonstructural problem in many young children, usually correcting itself by the time a child reaches the age of 3. If the condition has not corrected itself by that age, it must be treated with braces or it will most likely become a permanent structural deformity. This structural deformity is frequently accompanied by compensatory deformities in the feet. By school age, bowlegs cannot be remediated by activity or exercises in physical education. The physical educator's major responsibility, when the condition is suspected in the lower elementary grades, is to refer the child to a physician for possible treatment through bracing. Most children with this deformity, although sometimes appearing awkward in their movements, can successfully participate in all regular physical education activities.

Knock-Knees

Knock-knees is the opposite of bowlegs. In this deviation the lower legs bow outward, with the result that the ankles are forced apart when the knees are touching (Figure 20.4b). This condition is usually nonstructural and common in very young children, and it frequently corrects itself. In young children, the deviation can be treated through bracing. If not treated, the deformity will eventually become structural. Knock-knees is a common postural deviation in obese children. Poor alignment of the knee results in a disproportionate amount of weight being borne by the medial aspect of the knee and predisposes the joint to potential strain and injury. Physical educators should carefully consider this point when selecting physical education and/or athletic events for students with this condition. Activities that increase the possibility of trauma to the knee—such as jumping from heights, running on hard or uneven surfaces, and/or games and sports where the knees could be hit laterally—should be carefully evaluated.

Tibial Torsion

Tibial torsion is the result of an inward rotation of the lower leg (tibia). This condition can result in toeing in or can be caused by a foot deformity. The condition, caused by a muscle imbalance that twists the tibia inward, frequently occurs in young children who are in a non-weight-bearing position for a prolonged period as a result of injury or illness. When it is not contraindicated by the injury or illness, children should be encouraged to bear weight on their legs each day. Attention should be focused on maintaining the legs in proper alignment and stretching the muscles that pull the tibia inward. If identified early in children, this deformity can be treated through bracing. In more severe cases a combination of surgery and bracing may be required.

Knee Flexion Deformity

Knee flexion deformity is common in children with neuromuscular handicaps such as cerebral palsy who are confined to wheelchairs. It is characterized by the legs being permanently bent or contracted in a sitting position. This condition can be painful, makes the legs harder to manage, and prevents the children from using standing tables or attempting ambulation even with the aid of braces and crutches. The condition is initially treated with splints and typically requires surgical lengthening of the hamstring tendons in which their insertions are repositioned. Physical educators can assist in preventing this condition by encouraging wheelchair-bound students to move their knees through the full range of motion. This might mean having the students leave their wheelchairs and perform a stretching routine on a mat while the other class members are doing other stretching exercises.

Foot Deformities

Although foot deformities can be caused by skeletal and neuromuscular abnormalities, the majority are caused by compensatory postures required to offset other postural misalignments in the legs, hips, and spine. As a result, the feet are typically the most abused structure in the body. Most foot deformities in children are identified and treated before they enter school. Occasionally mild deformities can go unnoticed by parents and will be identified by the physical educator when the student complains of pain or avoids certain activities in physical education.

Physical educators should review the medical files and be aware of any students who have foot deformities. In most cases, the students will require no special consideration and will be able to participate normally in the regular physical education setting. When appropriate, the physical educator may need to monitor specific students to make sure they are wearing their braces and/or orthotics and performing any exercises prescribed by their physicians. Several of the common foot deformities found in children are described in the following paragraphs to provide physical educators with a basic understanding of the conditions and how they are treated.

Clubfoot

Clubfoot or *talipes* refers to a number of deformities in the foot in which the foot is usually severely twisted out of shape. This condition is usually congenital or acquired as the result of a neuromuscular condition. The term *talipes* is usually followed by one or more descriptors indicating the nature of the deformity: *equinus* (toe walking caused by tight heel cords), *calcaneus* (opposite of equinus and caused by loose heel cords, resulting in the foot being flexed), *varus* (toes and sole of the foot are turned inward, causing the individual to walk on the outside edge of the feet), and *valgus* (toes and sole of the foot are turned outward, causing the individual to walk on the inside edge of the feet). Mild forms of the conditions are treated with braces and orthopedic shoes. More severe forms require a combination of corrective surgery and braces.

Pronation

Pronation is a foot deformity in which the individual walks on the medial (inside) edge of the feet. The condition is frequently accompanied by toeing out. Pronation is usually acquired and can be remediated, if identified early, through corrective shoes and exercises.

Flatfoot

Flatfoot or *pes planus* may be acquired or congenital and may be the result of a fallen or flat longitudinal arch. Flatfoot is considered a postural deviation only when it is acquired as a result of poor body mechanics. In such cases, the structure of the foot is altered, which reduces its mechanical efficiency in absorbing and distributing force. This postural deviation, in turn, can cause pain in the longitudinal arch and result in other postural deviations as well. This condition is common in visually impaired and obese children. Treatment can involve prescriptive exercises and orthotics (inserts in the shoes).

Hollowfoot

Hollowfoot or *pes cavus*, the opposite of flatfoot, is characterized by an extremely high longitudinal arch. This condition is usually congenital and is frequently associated with clubfoot. As in pes planus, the change in alignment of the foot due to the extremely high arch reduces the foot's ability to absorb and distribute force. The condition can be treated with orthopedic shoes and, in severe cases, with surgery.

Morton's Toe

Morton's toe refers to a deformity caused by a fallen metatarsal arch. The fallen arch puts pressure on surrounding nerves, which makes this condition very painful. The condition is caused by a disproportional amount of weight and stress being placed on the ball of the foot over a prolonged period of time. The treatment usually involves identifying and removing the cause, introducing appropriate exercises, and inserting an arch support in the shoe.

Hallux Valgus

Hallux valgus is a condition in which the big toe is bent inward toward the other toes. The condition is caused by pressure forcing the big toe inward, usually as a result of poorly fitting shoes. If the condition persists a bunion forms, and eventually a calcium deposit builds up on the head of the first metatarsal. Treatment involves removing the bunion and calcium deposit and fitting the individual with appropriate shoes.

Summary

All children can benefit from good posture and body mechanics to safely and efficiently participate in physical education and athletics. Poor posture and body mechanics predispose children to potential injury. Physical educators, given the nature of their position and preparation, can play an important role in the identification and remediation of postural deviations. Postural screening should be an annual event in all physical education programs. Awareness and understanding of proper body mechanics should be taught to all children so that they may monitor and evaluate their own postures.

Bibliography

Adams, R.C., Daniel, A.N., McCubbin, J.A., & Rullman, L. (1982). *Games, sports and exercises for the physically handicapped*. Philadephia: Lea & Febiger.

Cratty, B.J. (1971). *Movement and spatial awareness in blind children and youth*. Springfield, IL: Charles C. Thomas.

New York State Education Department (1966). *New York State physical fitness test for boys and girls grades 4-12*. Albany, NY: Author.

Scott, M.G., and French, E. (1959). *Measurement and evaluation in physical education*. Dubuque, IA: Wm. C. Brown.

Resources

Audiovisual

Scoliosis screening for early detection [Film]. Minneapolis: Multi Video International.

Spinal screening [Film]. Chicago: Scoliosis Research Society.

These are two excellent films that describe the various types of spinal deviations that can occur in children and techniques for conducting spinal cord deviation evaluations.

Other

Posture Grid (1982). In R.C. Adams, A.N. Daniel, J.A. McCubbin, & L. Rullman, *Games, sports and exercises for the physically handicapped* (pp. 171-179). Philadelphia: Lea & Febiger.

Iowa Posture Test (1959). In M.G. Scott & E. French, *Measurement and evaluation in physical education* (pp. 414-421). Dubuque, IA: Wm. C. Brown.

New York Posture Rating Test (1966). In *New York State physical fitness test for boys and girls grades 4-12*. Albany, NY: New York State Education Department.

These are three examples of posture screening tests that are readily accessible to physical educators and are applicable for use in physical education classes.

Activities for Students With Unique Needs

Part V, the final part of the book, covers activities associated with adapted physical education and sport. It includes separate chapters on elementary games and activities, developmental and remedial exercises and activities, rhythms and dance, aquatics, team sports, individual and dual sports, and winter sports. Although the exact topical coverage of each chapter is influenced by the nature of the activities discussed, there are several common threads. First, to the extent relevant and appropriate, the chapters identify skills, lead-up activities, modifications, and variations. In many instances these include ideas associated with or procedures presently used in established organized sport programs. Second, some chapters provide information on organized sport programs. Third, most of the chapters address the integration of handicapped and able-bodied youngsters in activities.

The reader's attention is directed to the many techniques that can be used, separately or in combination, in adapting activities. These include, but

are not limited to, modifying or reducing skill or effort demands of an activity; "giving handicaps"; sharing responsibilities; providing physical assistance or assistive devices; reducing space and/or distance requirements; modifying facilities, equipment, or rules; and modifying activities to emphasize abilities and exclude the use of elimination as a feature of a game or activity. These and other techniques have many interesting applications. Examples include striking stationary rather than moving objects, throwing light rather than heavy objects, striking with large rather than small implements, bowling with a handrail guide or ramp, playing on a shortened field, using hand rather than foot cranks or pedals to move a tricycle, running or responding to a sound cue rather than to a visual cue, and changing rules to permit the use of a guide wire in track. Of course, the list of applications is virtually endless. In reading the chapters, record all the techniques for modifying activities that you can find; then use these techniques in adapting activities for your students.

CHAPTER 21

Elementary Games and Activities

Diane H. Craft

Games characterized by a low level of organizational requirements, such as those organized spontaneously by neighborhood children, are important for the socializing skills they impart to their participants. In addition, these games provide opportunities for improving and refining physical fitness and motor and sports skills. Too often children with handicapping conditions do not participate in these neighborhood games and thus miss out on their benefits.

This chapter offers specific suggestions for modifying games to accommodate children with disabilities, suggestions that can also be applied to other activities not mentioned here. In considering the suggestions, remember that individuals with the same disability can be so diverse that no single modification will accommodate all students.

Modifying Games of Low Organization

Tag

Tag games are characterized by one or more children trying to catch the other children who try to avoid being tagged by the ones who are "it." If tagged, a child then becomes the new "it" and tries to tag others.

Playing in a smaller area will make it easier for "it" to tag other children. Playing on a hard surface will enable children in wheelchairs to participate. For children with cardiac or respiratory conditions or for those with low fitness, provide "safe" areas where players may choose to sit and rest for a moment before returning to the game. Locate the safe area to the side of the playing area and mark it by placing a carpet square or base on the ground. Discourage its overuse by children who do not require rest.

When some players are in wheelchairs, it may be necessary to have the ambulatory ones run with a partner to slow the game to a speed that is accessible to all players. To equalize competition for any children in the group who have single-leg disabilities, everyone else may be required to hop instead of run, as shown in Figure 21.1.

Tag is not an elimination game. In fact, the least skilled players often get the most practice because they tend to be easier to tag and are frequently "it." To ensure that no one child is "it" for too long, a time limit may be introduced: If "it" has not succeeded in tagging another player after 1 min, "it" chooses another child to become "it."

Have the one who is "it" wear a brightly colored pinny and carry bells so that children with hearing and visual impairments can hear or see "it" coming. To discourage arguments about whether or not a child was actually tagged, all players could wear flag football flags. To tag another player, "it" would need to pull off that child's flag.

Variation: In Freeze Tag, children run to avoid being tagged by "it." When tagged, a child must stop on the spot and remain motionless until a teammate frees the child by touching. The child

Figure 21.1 In a tag game, competition is equalized by having the ambulatory child hop while chasing others using motorized wheelchairs. Printed with permission.

is then unfrozen and resumes playing the game. A variation of Freeze Tag is Tunnel Tag, in which tagged children must stand with feet spread until a teammate frees them by crawling between their feet. To increase the pace and excitement of both Freeze Tag and Tunnel Tag, two teams may be formed. One team is "it" while the other team tries to avoid being tagged. When all players on one team have been tagged, the teams switch roles.

There is an elimination aspect to both Freeze Tag and Tunnel Tag. The slower children will be tagged and spend much of their time waiting to be freed instead of getting cardiovascular exercise and practicing running and dodging skills. A time limit could be imposed so that the chasers and fleers change roles every 2 min instead of continuing until the chasers have tagged everyone.

SPUD

In SPUD, all children gather close around "it," who is holding a ball. "It" throws the ball high into the air while shouting the name of another player. All those whose names were not called run away from the ball as fast as possible. The person whose name was called hurries to catch the ball, then yells "stop," at which time the other children must stop running and freeze in place. The person holding the ball may take three giant steps in the direction of any player, then try to hit that player with the ball. The target person may dodge the ball, provided that the feet do not move. If hit, the person becomes the new "it" and gets a letter of the word "SPUD." If not hit, the person who threw the ball becomes the new "it" and acquires a letter. The cycle repeats, with the new "it" throwing the ball into the air while calling another player's name. The first person to get the four letters *S-P-U-D* loses, and the game ends.

For most children, no modification of the game is needed because SPUD usually is played with a large playground ball rather than a small hard ball that would hurt if it struck a player. A ball containing a buzzer or bells could be used when visually impaired children are playing. The other children could be required to make noise so that the visually impaired child with the ball could hear where to aim.

For children with ambulatory problems or slow reactions, the ball could be placed on the ground instead of thrown into the air; this change would make it easier for the child to get the ball and call "stop." To prevent the other players from running so far away that they are out of hitting range, the playing area could be reduced to a small circle, or the children could be required to hop instead of run to get away.

In SPUD, much of the time is spent watching while one person tries to hit another with the ball. Rest periods are thus already part of the game, making further modification unnecessary.

Because SPUD is played until one person gets all four letters, there is no time when some children are eliminated while others continue to play. However, if one child is continually the loser because of lower skills, modifications could be made to equalize competition—for example, some children might need to get *S-P-U-D-D-E-R*.

With hearing-impaired children, who may not be able to respond when others call their name, have "it" also point to the person whose name is called. Signing the person's name could be substituted for calling the name if all players are familiar with sign language.

Variations: There are numerous variations of SPUD in which items within a category are called out instead of players' names. At the beginning of the game a category is selected, such as colors, numbers, cars, or countries. Each child secretly chooses an item within the category. For example, if the category is colors, "it" throws the ball into the air and calls out "blue." Any child who secretly chose the color blue must catch the ball. If no child (or two children) chose blue, then "it" must again throw the ball into the air and call a different item from the category until "it" calls an item that one child has selected. In all other respects, the game is identical to the original game described previously.

Capture the Flag

Two teams are formed, each with a territory and a flag to protect at the rear of the territory. Each team tries to penetrate the other team's territory, grab the flag, and carry it to their own territory, thus winning the game. Players are safe when in their own territory. But any time they are in the opponent's territory, they can be tagged and sent to the jail located within and to the side of the other team's territory. Here they wait until the end of the game or until freed by a teammate running to the jail and touching them. Jailed teammates may form a chain by touching each other, and if one jailed teammate is freed, all the others in the chain are free as well.

The "flag" to be captured may be almost any object such as a sock, pinny, or Indian club. If children who use wheelchairs or walkers are playing the game, the flags may be placed on top of a cone at waist height so that they are easier to reach. Use brightly colored objects as flags, and have the teams wear pinnies of contrasting colors to aid players with visual impairments.

Success in the game depends on the team strategy of distracting the opponents guarding the flag while a teammate sneaks in to steal it. Children who learn more slowly than their peers may have difficulty in following the team strategy, thus requiring direct instruction in its use. For children who are not yet mentally capable of learning the strategy, assign a teammate to coach them on what to do, substitute a simpler game, or have them play with younger children who are playing not by strategy but in a free-for-all approach.

Players usually run continuously in Capture the Flag. To accommodate children who must limit their exertion, allow substitution at the player's request. To equalize competition for children with ambulatory problems (including those who use wheelchairs, walkers, or prostheses), require other children to jump instead of run or to play with one leg tied to a partner's, as in a three-legged race. Children who have ambulatory problems or who must limit their exertion may wish to guard their team's flag rather than venture into the opponent's territory.

Capture the Flag entails elimination in that the less skilled players may be tagged early in the game and spend most of their time watching the play from jail. To reduce the time any individual spends in jail, set a limit of two players in jail at one time. When a third player is caught, the first one in jail may leave, with safe passage back to the home territory.

Marco Polo

Marco Polo is often played in the shallow water of backyard and community pools. One person is "it" and tries to tag any other player, who then becomes "it." This game differs from other games of tag in that the one who is "it" wears a blindfold. "It" regularly shouts "Marco," to which all other players must momentarily stop and respond "Polo." Thus, sound is the means for locating other players in the pool. At all times, the division between the deep and shallow ends of the pool must be clearly marked with buoys, so that the blindfolded player cannot accidentally wander into the deep end.

To accommodate children who move slowly in the water, decrease the playing area when they are "it" and expand the area when they are not "it." Allow children who must limit their exertion to rest during alternate rounds of the game. As in all activities, children with sickle-cell anemia should avoid holding of the breath, as when swimming under water.

To modify Marco Polo to accommodate visually impaired players, make a rule that everyone must wear a blindfold or that "it" must talk continuously while searching for others. To equalize competition for children who have limited use of their legs (such as those with spina bifida), require all players to move using only their arms. Because blindfolds are used, Marco Polo relies heavily on auditory perception. Thus the game may be totally inappropriate for hearing-impaired children.

Four Square

Four Square is a ball game played with four people on a flat, hard surface at least 6 ft by 6 ft, such as a driveway or sidewalk. The playing area is marked with a large square, which is then further divided into four smaller squares. The four squares are numbered, and a player stands in each one. The person in the fourth square is designated as the leader, who names a skill to perform with the ball that one or more of the other players must imitate until the leader makes a mistake. For example, the leader may announce the skill of "tea party" and select one other player with whom to bounce the ball back and forth until the leader says stop. If the leader misses the ball, then the other player becomes the leader. If the other player misses, the leader remains in charge of the game and selects another skill to perform with a different player. Other skills include "around the world" (the leader bounces the ball into each of the other squares, and those players must catch the ball and bounce it back into the leader's square) and "spike" (the leader bounces the ball forcefully into another player's square, challenging the other to catch the ball without leaving the square).

The size and color of the ball can be varied. A large, soft ball, such as a 12-in. playground ball that is partially deflated, results in a slow rebound and a slower pace of play. A beach ball is not recommended because it is too soft to bounce well and so light that it is difficult to catch. A small, hard ball such as a racquetball results in a fast, high rebound, quickening the pace of the game and making it challenging for even highly skilled players. When four people of similar skill play together, the skill complexity is self-regulating. Groups of less skilled players may choose to gently bounce the ball to each other, while more highly skilled players will spike the ball into the very corners of each other's squares.

Children who use wheelchairs can participate in Four Square if the playing areas of their squares are limited to the distance that they can reach without moving their wheelchairs. The rules may also be modified to require that the ball be bounced within an arm's length of players in wheelchairs. Children who must limit their exertion can play from chairs located in the squares. To equalize competition, all four players could be seated in chairs. This modification still provides all players with practice in eye-hand coordination. Because Four Square is a ball activity that relies heavily on vision, it may not be appropriate for children with visual impairments that would prevent them from visually tracking the ball. When teaching Four Square in a class that includes one or more children with visual impairments, it might be best to offer all class members a choice of two or more alternative activities such as rope jumping or plastic pin bowling.

New Games

Recent years have seen a concern about some of the values taught through traditional competitive games and the possible negative impact of these values on children's development. Out of this concern new or cooperative games have evolved. The *new games* are an attempt to humanize contemporary games. These *cooperative games* are presented as a positive alternative to competitive games, which always have a winner but must also have losers. In new or cooperative games everyone works together toward a common goal. Everyone wins! No one loses! The emphasis in new games is on acceptance and sharing, eliminating the fear of failure among participants (Orlick, 1978). The new games are characterized by minimal equipment; flexible rules; a loosely organized, nonjudgmental atmosphere; and fun and success.

Four essential components of a successful new game are *cooperation, acceptance, involvement*, and *fun* (Orlick, 1978). These four components can be of benefit for all children but may be especially so for children with handicapping conditions. Cooperation requires working together with others. No one person, whether labeled "normal" or "handicapped," can thrive totally independently of others. Cooperative games can help children realize that it is too simplistic and inaccurate to categorize "normal" children as independent and "handicapped" children as depen-

dent. Cooperative games foster the concept that all people are *interdependent*.

Acceptance involves recognizing the value of each person's contribution toward the common goal. Games that promote acceptance foster a positive self-concept and may thus be particularly beneficial for children who have low self-concepts.

Involvement promotes a feeling of belonging, contribution, and satisfaction. Historically, children with handicapping conditions have been excluded from participation with "normal" children. Either they attended separate schools or they were made the permanent scorekeepers in regular schools. New games involving everyone counter the historical practice of exclusion and instead encourage inclusion and a sense of belonging.

Fun is the main reason that children play games. New games enhance fun for *all* children because the fear of failure or rejection and the impulse toward destructiveness are reduced.

Following are some examples of new games and adaptations. All of the examples are from Orlick's *Cooperative Games and Sports Book* (1978); I have added the modifications. For more extensive listings of new and cooperative games, refer to Orlick's book and the other resources following this chapter and chapter 5.

Cooperative Musical Hoops

Cooperative Musical Hoops is a nonelimination variation of Musical Chairs (Orlick, 1978). In the competitive game, the child who does not find an unoccupied chair is eliminated. But in the game of Cooperative Musical Hoops, all children work together to ensure that each one is included in a hoop. Thus, the game is well suited for introducing the concept of cooperation to very young children.

Hoops, instead of chairs, are scattered around the floor. There is one fewer hoop than the number of players. Children run, walk, jump, hop, push wheelchairs, or otherwise move around the gym while music plays. When the music stops, players rush to stand inside a hoop. Because there are fewer hoops than players, two or more players must share a hoop. Each time the music stops another hoop is eliminated until as many as eight children share a hoop, often giggling and laughing as they try to hold each other inside the remaining hoops (Figure 21.2).

Children with various disabilities can participate in the game without adaptation. The game's cooperative nature will encourage children to help classmates who may not be able to see the hoops or hear the music. The no-lose emphasis of the game virtually eliminates arguing and does not threaten the fragile self-concept of many behavior-disordered children.

Frozen Beanbag

Frozen Beanbag is a game of helping that is appropriate for young children (Orlick, 1978). Each child tries to move around the gym while keeping a beanbag balanced on the head. Children can be asked to walk, run, skip, hop, walk backward, and so on. A child whose beanbag falls off is frozen and must not move until another child picks up

the fallen beanbag and places it back on the frozen child's head. Helpers must replace classmates' beanbags without losing their own (Figure 21.3). The teacher can reinforce the importance of helping others at the end of the game by asking, "How many people did you help unfreeze?" Rhythmic background music can add to the enjoyment of the game.

Children with disabilities can enjoy playing Frozen Beanbag with few modifications. Visually impaired children may need verbal cues from others in locating dropped beanbags and replacing them on other children's heads. Because children in wheelchairs may not be able to reach beanbags on the floor, the rules can be modified to allow the "frozen" children to hand the dropped beanbags to their wheelchair-bound helpers, who must then replace the beanbags on the owners' heads without dropping their own. It is unlikely that any modification will be needed for hearing-impaired, learning-disabled, or behavior-disordered children to participate because the noncompetitive nature of the game facilitates the inclusion of children of differing abilities.

Figure 21.2 Cooperative Musical Hoops.

Figure 21.3 Frozen Beanbag.

Nonelimination Simon Says

In the traditional game of Simon Says, one child leads the activity, selecting movements that the other children must mimic only after the command "Simon Says do this" is given. Anyone who mimics a movement after the command "Do this" (without the words "Simon Says") is eliminated from the game. In Nonelimination Simon Says, in contrast with the traditional game, two games are played simultaneously. If eliminated from one game, a child merely joins the other, similar game in progress. The least skilled player may switch several times from one game to the other and back again but will never be eliminated. Thus, all children are involved in play at all times.

Minor adaptations in Nonelimination Simon Says may be needed for children with unique needs. Those with movement limitations may attempt to imitate each movement but not duplicate it exactly when that is not physiologically possible. The instructions "Simon Says do this" or simply "Do this" can be signed while spoken to include hearing-impaired children. A description of the movement, such as "Simon Says touch your right ear," can be added for visually impaired children. The game may be especially instructive for learning-disabled and mentally retarded children with perceptual deficits. The game can be structured to provide practice in the perceptual concepts of body part identification, laterality, and directionality as well as colors and shapes. Commands might include "Simon Says: touch your knuckles . . . touch your right ear with your left hand . . . smile at the person on your left . . . touch something purple . . . stand on a square on the floor." The game can also be played in pairs, allowing the teacher to place children with slower reactions together to give them a chance to think through each command before the leader gives the next one. Children with quick reactions can be paired so that they may play the game at a rapid pace that is challenging to them.

Sticky Popcorn

Sticky Popcorn is a cooperative game well suited to 4- and 5-year-old children who enjoy imagination games and practicing the basic motor skill of jumping. The game begins with children scattered across the play area, pretending they are kernels of sticky popcorn. They jump around the area in search of other kernels of popcorn. When they contact another kernel, they stick together, and now jump around together in search of still more kernels. Soon the entire group is one large popcorn ball.

Everyone, regardless of disability, can add imagination to the game by pretending to turn on the popper, pour in the oil, add the popcorn, and then slowly start popping as the kernels get hot. While most children with disabilities can play the game without modification, nonambulatory children can "pop" from their wheelchairs or on a mat, attracting other kernels of popcorn to them. Children with visual impairments can begin the game stuck together.

Long, Long, Long Jump

Older children can enjoy the cooperative challenge of Long, Long, Long Jump. The goal is to jump collectively as far as possible. The first person begins at the starting line and jumps as far as possible. The second person then begins the jump where the first person lands, and so on, until each child has added to the collective jump. The game can be played repeatedly, with the group striving to improve on the previous distance jumped. The cooperative nature of the game encourages the skilled players to coach the less skilled ones in jumping technique to improve the whole group's performance.

The game may be modified slightly to include children who are physiologically unable to jump. Children in wheelchairs could substitute the distance traveled in one push of a stationary wheelchair, children on mats could substitute the distance rolled, and children with walkers could use the distance covered by the walker in two steps.

Collective Score Volleyball

A host of traditional games can be transformed into cooperative games through a change from team scores to collective scores. Volleyball is an example. Instead of forming two teams that compete against each other for the higher score, the two teams work together for the highest number of consecutive hits. Collective Score Volleyball provides practice in sharing the ball among teammates and setting up teammates for good hits. Frequently, a few players on each team seek to dominate the game. Additional rules may discourage this practice and provide a chance for everyone to play the ball. These rules could include requiring three hits on one side before the ball is sent over the net, requiring at least one boy and one girl to hit the ball before it goes over the net, or requiring everyone on a side to hit the ball before sending it over the net. (This last suggestion works best with small teams of three or four players.) Another variation is to time how long the ball is

kept in the air rather than to count the number of hits. Rules such as these give all players an opportunity to practice their volleyball skills.

Further modifications may be made to suit the skill levels of the players. For beginning players and those with movement difficulties, a slow-bouncing ball such as a beach ball may be better than a regulation volleyball because it provides more time to react and respond to the direction of the ball. As skill and speed are developed, a Nerf volleyball may be substituted, then a regulation volleyball.

Project Adventure

Project Adventure is a physical education curriculum, developed in the Hamilton-Wenham Regional School District in Massachusetts, that seeks to apply to public education some of the educational concepts of Outward Bound. The program is described in *Cowstails and Cobras: A Guide to Ropes Courses, Initiative Games, and Other Adventure Activities* (Rohnke, 1977). The physical activity curriculum seeks to combine "a joyful sense of adventure, a willingness to move beyond previously set limits and the satisfaction of solving problems together" (p. 5).

Learning goals of Project Adventure participants are:

1. to increase a sense of personal confidence,
2. to increase mutual support within a group,
3. to increase the level of agility and physical coordination,
4. to increase the sense of joy in one's physical self and in being with others, and
5. to increase familiarity and identification with the natural world. (Rohnke, 1977, pp. 7-8)

The developers of Project Adventure argue that real adventure is hard for most young people to find. Yet there is much to be learned from real adventure that can generalize to overcoming everyday obstacles. The opportunity for commitment to performance where the outcome is uncertain is a healthy decision-making process. Challenges such as the Ropes Course, group initiative activities, and games are used to achieve these goals.

The Ropes Course is perhaps the most salient feature of the Project Adventure curriculum. It is a maze of cables, pegs, logs, platforms, boards, and ropes that offers a range of challenging activities. Usually the course includes lower and higher elements. Typical lower-element challenges, where participants are close to the ground, include the Tension Traverse, in which a person tries to cross the space between two trees or poles by walking on a wire; the Wild Woosey (Figure 21.4), in which two people cross on divergent wires by leaning on each other for support; Flea Leaps, in which a person leaps from tree

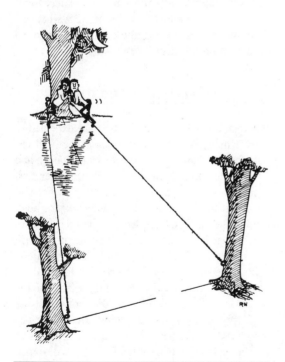

Figure 21.4 Wild Woosey. *Note.* From *Cowstails and Cobras* (p. 35) by K. Rohnke, 1977, Hamilton, MA: Project Adventure. Copyright 1977 by Project Adventure. Reprinted by permission.

stump to tree stump; and the Swinging Log, in which a person walks across a free-swinging balance log. Typical higher-element challenges include climbing an inclined log, walking across a two-lane bridge, and rappelling (lowering oneself down a wall or over a cliff by using ropes).

Higher-element challenges are usually safer than lower-element challenges because the participant is on a belay, a rope-friction arrangement used to stop a fall. But few people initially feel safe when over 50 ft above the ground. Books on ropes courses provide directions for their construction and use. It is not the situation in which to learn through trial and error, so *the reader is strongly advised also to obtain first-hand instruction from an experienced person before attempting Project Adventure activities*. The element of danger in the activities becomes all too real when safety measures are not fully understood or implemented.

Another aspect of Project Adventure is group initiative games, which present problems that require the combined physical and mental strength of the group for solution. A few examples of these games follow.

All Aboard

Typical of group initiative games is All Aboard (Figure 21.5), in which the object is to get as many people as possible on a platform. Each person must have at least one foot off the ground and all together must hold the balanced pose for at least 5 s. Usually a group of 12 to 15 people can squeeze onto a 2 ft-by-2 ft platform built about 18 in. above the ground.

Punctured Drum

Punctured Drum (Figure 21.6) requires a 55-gallon drum with approximately 120 punctures for a group of 12 participants. The goal is to fill the drum to overflowing, while using only parts of the participants' anatomies to plug the many nail-size holes.

Figure 21.5 All Aboard. *Note.* From *Cowstails and Cobras* (p. 67) by K. Rohnke, 1977, Hamilton, MA: Project Adventure. Copyright 1977 by Project Adventure. Reprinted by permission.

Figure 21.6 Punctured Drum. *Note.* From *Cowstails and Cobras* (p. 68) by K. Rohnke, 1977, Hamilton, MA: Project Adventure. Copyright 1977 by Project Adventure. Reprinted by permission.

Reach for the Sky

Collectively the group attempts to place a mark as high as possible on a wall or a large, smooth tree trunk. Much cooperation and planning is required to get group members high up the wall or tree. The group is not allowed to use the wall or tree to aid in climbing, but only for support.

The Wall

The intent of this game is to get all of the group members over a 12-ft wall with maximum speed and efficiency, but without the use of aids. Once people have gone over the wall, they may not simply walk around the wall to help others. Only by again scaling the wall may someone return to help others, after which the person must scale the wall yet again to finish the game. For safety, only three people are allowed to top of the wall at one time. When descending, the climber must touch each step on the back of the wall.

Preschool Education

Between birth and age 5 children are expected to master many of the *readiness skills* that will enable them to learn in the typical kindergarten and first-grade curriculum. Most children enter first grade with an awareness of their own bodies and the ability to manipulate objects and move the body through space. They also have mastered the basics of language and are able to concentrate on one task for several minutes. These and other readiness skills are prerequisites for developing the skills of reading, writing, and computing. Many of the readiness skills are learned without formal instruction, through incidental learning. But in the last few decades there has been increased emphasis on formal instruction in preschool programs designed to develop these skills.

Preschool education refers to programs specifically designed for young children, typically between 2 and 5 years of age. The goals are to provide children with the environment and instruction needed for each one to develop as fully as possible in the cognitive, affective, and motor domains. While such programs may be offered as enrichment for most children, there are some children who learn more slowly or in different ways and *need* a preschool program if they are to progress as much as possible. Preschool programs for children with disabilities are a response to the recognized need for *early intervention* to minimize the negative effects of a disability.

Teaching a preschool program entails the four steps followed at other educational levels: assess, plan, implement, and evaluate. First, each child is assessed to determine strengths and weaknesses. Areas to assess in the psychomotor domain include physical fitness, motor development and motor skills, posture and body mechanics, and play behaviors.

Physical fitness assessment of preschool children should encompass strength and endurance and body composition. Does the child have the strength to pull him- or herself up from a sitting position to a stand? Does the child have the endurance to play actively for many minutes without stopping because of breathlessness? Is the child's body composition normal, or is it excessively fat or lean?

Motor development and motor skill assessment should address reflexive movement, basic motor skills, and perceptual-motor functioning. The primitive and postural reflexes that were so necessary at birth must mature and then must be inhibited to allow the refinement of voluntary movement. Physical educators working with preschoolers can assess the maturity of primitive and postural reflexes using Tables 19.2 and 19.3. Activities to aid in the inhibition of reflexes may be planned with the physical therapist.

Motor skills, which are developed and refined during the preschool years, can be assessed formally or informally. To assess motor skills physical educators may use one of the several formal instruments discussed in chapter 4, including the Ohio State University SIGMA and the Test of Gross Motor Development, or the three-phase approach developed by McClenaghan and Gallahue and described in Table 19.5. Developmental motor milestones may also be assessed by means of the Bayley Scales of Infant Development or the Denver Developmental Screening Test, also discussed in chapter 4. A more practical approach to assessment may be to informally observe preschool children at play, using one or more of these assessment instruments to guide the observation. For example, at snack time the teacher notes whether the children use the palmar or pincer grasp for picking up finger food and whether they consistently use one hand in preference to the other. On the playground the teacher observes whether the children have a mature run or an immature run, using the Ohio State University SIGMA or McClenaghan and Gallahue's phases as a guide. Kephart (see chapter 4) offers guidelines for assessing perceptual-motor functioning.

Body mechanics and posture may be assessed through informal observation or the use of posture charts. Because young children have not yet developed the spinal curves characteristic of adults, it is not always appropriate to use adult charts as a guide.

A fourth area to assess is play behaviors, as an indicator of social maturation. Four common stages of preschool play are (a) *solitary play* (1- to 2-year-olds), in which the child is self-absorbed, playing alone; (b) *parallel play* (2- to 3-year-olds), in which the child may play alongside other children and may even use the same materials, but with little social interaction; (c) *associative play* (3- to 4-year-olds), in which the child informally interacts with other children for brief periods; and (d) *cooperative play* (4- to 5-year-olds), in which the child plays with one or more other children, taking turns and later learning to follow the rules of low-organization games. The physical educator may observe each child at play in the presence of other preschoolers to assess the play behaviors.

Following the assessment of the reflexes, motor skills, posture and body mechanics, and play behaviors of each child, a curriculum is planned and implemented to help each child reach the next level in development. The goal of preschool is to enhance children's learning—in a manner that develops a love of learning and in a setting full of happiness and affection that helps establish a basic feeling of well-being (Hendrick, 1980). The program is comprehensive, emphasizing cognitive, affective, and motor development. Meeting the goal does not usually require a separate preschool program only for children with disabilities, nor is it necessary to label a child as disabled. But it is necessary to *individualize instruction* for each child. When teaching a child who learns slowly, it may be necessary to present tasks in smaller steps that are carefully sequenced; provide simple, concise directions along with demonstration and the chance to learn while doing; repeat learned tasks to enable the child to experience success; teach using several senses in an environment with reduced distractions; and consistently reinforce good behavior. It is also necessary to use equipment that is accessible and challenging to all children. The accessible playground developed by Dr. Louis Bowers, shown in Figure 21.7, provides an opportunity to practice a wide variety of motor skills, but it also offers partially enclosed spaces for quiet games and secret conversations.

Physical educators can draw on a variety of curricula in teaching preschoolers. These programs include the Project PREP Play Program, the I CAN ABC model for preprimary and primary motor and play skills, and the performance-based curriculum (PBC) that is part of the Ohio State University SIGMA assessment. These programs are discussed in chapters 4 and 11.

The final step in teaching is evaluation. Each child is reassessed to determine if the program that was planned and implemented has been successful. Usually the tests or informal observations used in the assessment can be readministered for evaluation. Using the results, the teacher decides how to modify the curriculum to better teach each child.

The importance of preschool education for children with disabilities is becoming widely recognized. People are realizing that many conditions resulting in severe handicaps could have been minimized through early intervention. The trend in federal and state legislation is to provide a quality preschool program to any child with a disability. Physical educators need to become better

Figure 21.7 One of the accessible playgrounds developed by Dr. Louis Bowers. Reprinted by permission.

prepared to contribute to preschool education. More than at any other time in life, movement is the basic means of learning in the preschool years. Physical educators need to assist in helping these young people learn to move efficiently.

Summary

This chapter presented modifications of low-organization games such as Tag, SPUD, Capture the Flag, Marco Polo, and Four Square typically played spontaneously among neighborhood children. Sometimes children with disabilities are not included in spontaneous play, perhaps because they lack skill or knowledge of the game. Teaching the appropriate rules and skills during physical education can help prepare disabled children to participate in and be welcomed into neighborhood games.

New games also have a place in the physical education curriculum. Nonelimination Simon Says, Frozen Beanbag, and Long, Long, Long Jump are a few such games that foster the values of cooperation and interdependence. The Project Adventure curriculum seeks to develop personal confidence through activities that offer students real adventures.

The chapter concluded with a discussion of preschool education. As the importance of preschool education to children with disabilities becomes recognized, physical educators need to prepare to teach at this level.

Bibliography

Hendrick, J. (1980). *The whole child: New trends in early education* (2nd ed.). St. Louis: Mosby.

Orlick, T. (1978). *The cooperative sports and games book*. New York: Pantheon Books.

Rohnke, K. (1977). *Cowstails and cobras: A guide to ropes courses, initiative games, and other adventure activities*. P.O. Box 100, Hamilton, MA 01936: Project Adventure.

Resources

Written

Gilliom, B. *Basic movement education for children: Rationale and teaching units*. Reading, MA: Addison-Wesley. This book provides an excellent introduction to movement education followed by many specific lesson plans for implementing a movement education curriculum.

High profile (1981) and *Teaching through adventure* (1976). Hamilton, MA: Project Adventure. These two publications describe additional adventure programs. Also, training workshops specifically aimed at designing a Project Adventure program appropriate for people with special needs are available through Project Adventure, P.O. Box 100, Hamilton, MA 01936, (508)468-1766.

Littman, K.G., & Leslie, L. (1978). *Preschool recreation enrichment program (PREP)*. Washington, DC: Hawkins and Associates, Distributors. These manuals describe how to plan, train staff for, and implement a preschool program for children with disabilities.

Audiovisual

Bowers, L., & Klesius, S. (Writer, Director, Producer). (1982). *I'm special: Places to play* [Videotapes]. Fifteen-min modules present accessible alternatives to traditional playgrounds. There are 14 modules, each addressing a different aspect of special physical education for children.

Other

Voyageur Outward Bound is a program offering canoe expeditions, wilderness camping, and rock climbing to people with moderate to severe disabilities such as cerebral palsy, hearing impairments, amputations, paraplegia, and congenital defects. For information contact Voyageur Outward Bound, 10900 Cedar Lake Road, Minnetonka, MN 55343, (800)328-2943.

Developmental and Remedial Exercises and Activities

David L. Porretta

This chapter discusses developmental and remedial exercises and activities that can be incorporated into physical education and sport programs. Although many of the activities presented are of an individual nature, they can and should be used in a group setting whenever possible. This not only motivates participants to develop physically, but encourages them to socialize with each other as well.

Relaxation

The primary focus of relaxation is the conscious control of the body and its various functions. When used appropriately, relaxation activities help people with physical and motor needs to consciously release muscular tension in various regions of the body.

Many individuals with handicapping conditions are particularly in need of relaxation training. For people with increased muscle tone or general hyperactive behavior, relaxation techniques used *prior* to gross motor or sport activities prepare them to perform to the best of their ability. For cerebral-palsied individuals exhibiting increased muscle tone, relaxation training helps to reduce abnormal muscle tone, thereby allowing greater controlled movement capability. Some people have difficulty returning to a relatively calm pre-

performance state, especially after highly competitive or exciting activities. This is common for those exhibiting hyperactive or perseverative behavior. In such cases, relaxation techniques used as an immediate *follow-up* to gross motor or sport activities prepare for the return to a normal resting state by helping to bring about a reduction in many physiological responses like heart rate, breathing, and muscle tenseness. Relaxation following vigorous physical activity is particularly helpful in public school settings, where students must return to a normal resting state in order to resume sedentary classroom activities. There are cases, however, where relaxation activities should not be offered: People who are lethargic or have low levels of physical vitality do not need them.

A number of relaxation methods have proven to be successful. Some of the more popular, which will be discussed in the following subsections, include the Jacobson relaxation method, the imagery (association-set) method, and a relatively new method known as biofeedback. Two Eastern methods, hatha-yoga and tai chi (tie jee), while not discussed in detail, are also excellent forms of relaxation that focus on the concept of mental, spiritual, and physical health. Both of these methods advocate the harmonious functioning of mind and body. Hatha-yoga emphasizes maintaining specific body positions, whereas tai chi emphasizes the feel of moving from one position to the other. Relaxation activities may use one of these methods exclusively or may combine varying aspects of two or more of them. This choice is left to the discretion of the teacher or coach and, where appropriate, the student. The manner in which the methods are taught and the amount of time devoted to their use will depend greatly upon the student's age and the degree and type of handicapping condition, as well as the type of gross motor activity to be performed.

Jacobson's Relaxation Method

The Jacobson method of relaxation was first developed over 50 years ago by Edmund Jacobson, a physician interested in tension control (Jacobson, 1970). Jacobson's method, still popular today, is based on consciously relaxing tense muscles. Information on the state of muscle activity is sent via proprioceptors to the arousal system located in the reticular area of the brain. Muscle relaxation brings about a reduction in neural activity of the reticular area, thereby reducing one's level of arousal.

The Jacobson method involves voluntarily contracting and then relaxing a specific group of muscles three times in succession. This is done progressively; the individual contracts and relaxes various muscle groups in a prescribed manner in a specified order. The progression begins with muscle groups in the left arm and then the right arm, followed by the left leg and then the right leg, proceeding to the trunk, back, neck, and finally the face. The individual focuses on one region of the body at a time. Once a region, such as the right arm, has been relaxed, muscles in that region should stay relaxed as the relaxation progresses to subsequent regions of the body. Initially, progressive relaxation training should be done with the eyes closed from a supine position with legs together, arms at the sides, and palms facing upward. Once the technique has been learned in this position, the individual can use it in a sitting position.

Jacobson found that his method was effective for relaxing mentally retarded children. Today the method is successfully used to relax hyperactive individuals and those with conditions such as cerebral palsy, learning disabilities, and emotional disturbances.

The following is a sample relaxation routine showing how the Jacobson method can be used prior to adapted physical education and sport activities. The session takes approximately 10 min once participants have had an introduction to the method. This sample session incorporates a slight modification based on the method suggested by Harris (1986). Before the session begins, the instructor has participants lie in a supine position on a mat, arms to the sides, and eyes closed, and tells them to tense muscles for 10 s and then relax them for 30 s on command. Pillows placed under the knees, elbows, and neck can be used to support key parts of the body. If time permits, the sequence can be repeated.

Sample of a —— Relaxation Routine ——

"Make a tight fist with your dominant hand, now tighten your lower arm and now your upper arm, hold . . . now relax."

"Make a tight fist with your nondominant hand, now tighten your lower arm and now your upper arm, hold . . . now relax."

"Wrinkle the forehead, press the head against the floor, turn head as far to the right as possible (pause) and as far to the left as possible (pause) . . . now relax."

"Now wrinkle the muscles of the face, making a big grimace or frown, close eyes tightly, purse lips, press tongue against roof of mouth, hunch shoulders, hold . . . now relax." (Give instructions quickly so the tension build-up is continuous.)

"Next arch the back, take a deep breath and hold . . . relax."

"Next take a deep breath and push the stomach out as you inhale, hold . . . relax."

"With the dominant foot, pull the foot and toes backward to the shin bone, tighten shin muscles, hold . . . relax. Curl toes, tighten calf muscles, thigh, and buttocks, hold . . . relax."

"With the nondominant foot, pull the foot and toes backward to the shin bone, tighten shin muscles, hold . . . relax. Curl toes, tighten calf muscles, thigh, and buttocks, hold . . . relax."

Imagery (Association-Set) Relaxation Method

Imagery is a method of relaxation in which the individual produces a mental picture or image conducive to a relaxed state. This method is also known as *association-set, mind-set,* or *autogenic training* because the user voluntarily produces a mental image and continues to focus upon it. The image can be generated internally by the individual, or it can be suggested by the teacher or coach. Mental images may be elicited by words, phrases, or quiet music. The type of image used depends on age, mental capacity, and personal preference. Young children respond well to words and phrases such as melting like the snow, floating like a cloud, or sleeping like a kitten; for older children and adults various colors or scenic surroundings (e.g., lying on the beach) help produce a relaxing state. This method is best used in a restful environment free from noise or other distractions, with participants in a sitting or recumbent position with eyes closed. Imagery relaxation may be of limited benefit in some cases, especially for students who have mental retardation, emotional disturbances, or central nervous system damage so severe as to interfere with the production of and continued focus on a realistic image.

Recently, sport psychologists have employed imagery as a means of improving the performance of athletes. With this method, athletes produce a mental picture of themselves successfully performing a particular skill or feat during competition (e.g., scoring a soccer goal). Imagery holds great promise for enhancing the performance of handicapped athletes and is now receiving increased attention from coaches and researchers alike.

Vealey (1986) recommends using imagery training daily for approximately 10 min. It can be used either before the practice or game, to create a proper frame of mind for participation, or afterward, to reemphasize key situations or plays. Imagery exercises are specific to the activity or sport and must, therefore, be tailored to each participant's need. The following exercise, suggested by Vealey for enhancing performance, is the type recommended for use in adapted physical education or sport programs.

Sample of Imagery Training

"Either sit or lie comfortably with eyes closed. Begin by placing yourself in a relaxed state by slow deep breathing of one to two minutes. Now, choose a piece of equipment in your sport such as a ball, racquet, club, etc. Try to imagine very fine details of the object. Turn it over in your hands and examine every part of the object. Feel its outline and texture. Now imagine yourself performing with the object. First focus on seeing yourself very clearly performing an activity. Visualize yourself repeating the skill over and over. Next try to hear the sounds that accompany this particular movement. Listen carefully to all the sounds that are being made as you perform this skill. Now put the sight and sound together. Try to get a clear picture of yourself performing the skill and also hear all of the sounds involved" (Vealey, 1986, p. 217).

Biofeedback

Biofeedback is a recommended form of relaxation therapy. A relatively new procedure, biofeedback uses a combination of modern technology and individual training to bring about physiological changes in such parameters as heart rate, body temperature, and muscular activity through conscious control. Through training, an individual can learn to reduce abnormal muscle tension. However, because of the lack of supporting research, it remains uncertain whether the clinical use of biofeedback is significantly better than muscle relaxation therapy in reducing hyperactivity (Winnick, 1984).

Through the use of sophisticated electronic technology, a body signal like a muscle impulse is picked up by way of electrodes strategically placed on or in the muscle and is fed back to the person in the form of a tone, light, or number representing the muscle impulse. The person then tries to alter the intensity or duration of the signal, which in turn changes the physiological response. Finally, through practice, the person is taught to consciously control the response (muscle impulse) with the aim of reducing muscular tension (Figure 22.1).

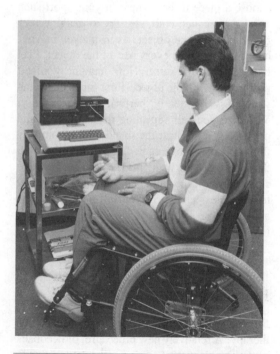

Figure 22.1 Reducing muscular tension through biofeedback.

Until recently, biofeedback has been employed primarily in medicine and psychotherapy. Realizing its great potential for the self-regulation of muscle responses in handicapped people, teachers and coaches are now utilizing biofeedback as a method of relaxation. Although it has limits as a practical tool for physical education classes, its use as a training device in competitive sport settings is virtually unlimited. Because of the complexity of the electronic technology and the training methodology, however, biofeedback to promote better performance can best be used outside the regular class or practice period. It is recommended that biofeedback training initially be conducted three to four times per week for a period of approximately 30 to 40 min. As one becomes more proficient in controlling the specific body functions of concern, training can be conducted less frequently for a period of 10 to 15 min. In addition, the participant should be instructed to supplement biofeedback training with progressive relaxation activities at home. When voluntary control is obtained at the desired level, monitoring by the biofeedback apparatus will no longer be needed.

The following is a description of a sample program to obtain muscle relaxation of the dominant upper arm. The person is seated comfortably in a chair. Surface electrodes are then placed on the person's biceps muscle. When the feedback apparatus is on, the person will begin to hear a clicking sound. Initially, the person should be allowed time to experiment with controlling the clicking sound. For example, the trainer might ask the person, "What makes the clicking more frequent? What makes the clicking less frequent? What happens when you think of throwing a ball as far as you can? What happens when you think of your arm floating on water?" Further directions are as follows:

"Tighten your muscle very hard. As you tighten your muscle, you should hear the sound of the biofeedback machine increasing in the number and frequency of clicks. Now, try to completely relax the muscle. As you relax, the number and fre-

quency of clicks should diminish. (The tightening and relaxing of the muscle should be repeated so that the person can actually feel the muscle contracting and relaxing.) Now, think of how limp and heavy your entire arm can be. Concentrate on reducing the clicking sound to a lower and lower level. Remember, you are in control of your muscles.''

The person is to repeat the phrase ''my arm is limp and heavy'' three times aloud and then to repeat the phrase silently. If concentration should happen to be completely lost, ask the person to rest for a short time and try again.

Physical Fitness

This section describes exercises and activities directed toward the development or remediation of physical fitness components crucial to successful performance in physical education and sport. In recognition of individual needs, modifications of exercises and activities are also presented. Many of the exercises and activities presented can be performed in an aquatic environment: Water provides buoyancy, which assists in movement, and also a degree of resistance for developing muscular strength and endurance.

The exercises and activities described fall into four areas (components) of physical fitness: flexibility, muscular strength and endurance, cardiorespiratory endurance, and body composition. Exercises and activities related to the fitness component of body composition will be presented in conjunction with cardiorespiratory activities because many of the latter activities also promote the regulation of fatness. Exercises and activities that develop cardiorespiratory endurance also provide the frequency, intensity, and duration levels needed to increase caloric expenditure and thus help reduce body fat. In the sections that follow, exercises and activities for the flexibility and the muscular strength and endurance components are grouped according to areas of the body targeted. Often these exercises can be performed to music;

this helps maintain participants' interest. Individuals with mental disabilities respond particularly well to exercises using music. This section includes muscular strength and endurance exercises not typically found in weight training programs. Specific weight training exercises that utilize additional resistance (other than body weight) will be described in a subsequent section called ''Weight Training and Body Building.''

Flexibility

Exercises to develop flexibility are usually performed from a stationary position and are designed to improve joint range of motion and prepare the individual for more vigorous physical activity. Upper body and upper extremity exercises may include the following:

- Head rotations
- Arm circles
- Arm hang from a horizontal bar
- Wrist circles
- Bracing the shoulders

Exercises and activities for the trunk, hips, back, and thighs may include the following:

- Trunk rotations
- Elephant walk
- Leg lifts from a prone position or lying on right or left side
- Toe touches performed from a sitting position
- Alternate knee flexion from a supine position
- Bent-knee sitting position with back against wall
- Head-and-chest raise from a prone position
- Frog posture (Figure 22.2)

Lower leg and ankle exercises and activities may include the following:

- Toe circles from a sitting position
- Dorsiflexion stretch
- Walking on heels, toes, lateral aspect of foot, or medial aspect of foot
- Curling and extending toes

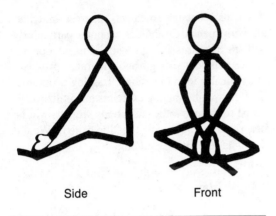

Side   Front

Figure 22.2 The frog posture.

In some instances, individuals with partial paralysis or very poor range of motion will need to be assisted through an exercise by the teacher or coach. Students unable to exercise in a standing position, particularly those with cerebral palsy, may perform the exercises from a sitting or lying position. In flexibility exercises for cerebral-palsied individuals, Surburg (1986) suggests placing a greater emphasis on relaxing target muscle groups than on stretching them. In addition, it may be helpful for some students—for example, those with juvenile rheumatoid arthritis—to perform exercises in a therapeutically warm pool.

Muscular Strength and Endurance

To increase the amount of force a specific muscle or muscle group can exert and the length of time it can continue working, muscular strength and endurance exercises can be used. Exercises and activities to develop the upper body and upper extremities may include the following:

- Modified push-ups (performed with knees touching the floor)
- Chin-ups with a horizontal bar, done from a supine position on the floor
- Flexed-arm hang
- Floor ladder pull (Figure 22.3)
- Straight-arm support (Figure 22.4)
- Squeezing balls of various sizes with both hands
- Crab walk
- Rope climbing
- Seal crawl
- Medicine ball throw
- Tug-of-war

Trunk, hip, back, and thigh exercises may include the following:

- Bent-knee sit-ups with arms folded across chest
- Squat-jumps
- Partial curl-ups

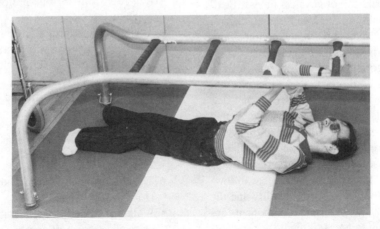

Figure 22.3 Performing on the floor ladder.

Figure 22.4 Performing a straight arm support from a wheelchair.

Exercises and activities for lower legs and ankles may include the following:

- Heel raises
- Foot dorsiflexion
- Moving an object (like a heavy ball or toy) across the floor with medial and lateral aspects of the foot

Students with unilateral upper limb amputations can perform one-arm push-ups from a kneeling position, while those with greater initial strength can do regular push-ups with one arm by turning the body from the prone to the side position. Individuals in wheelchairs can perform pull-ups, chin-ups, flexed-arm hang, and straight-arm support exercises from the chair. Various weighted objects can be substituted for a medicine ball. Tug-of-war

can be played from a standing, sitting, kneeling, or prone position on the floor. Those with poor abdominal strength can do bent-knee sit-ups on an inclined mat, where the head and shoulders are placed at the top of the incline, or they may wish to use the arms to assist with sit-ups. Students with poor overall strength and endurance can do the crab walk supported by a scooter. Heel raises and the foot dorsiflexion exercise can be performed from a standing, sitting, or lying position. A partner or the instructor can help by providing resistance with the hand to either the instep (dorsiflexion exercise) or the ball of the foot (heel raises).

Cardiorespiratory Endurance and Body Composition

For efficient heart and lung function and for adequate caloric expenditure, exercises and activities usually incorporate full body movement sustained over a long period of time. Exercises and activities may include the following:

- Mountain climbing or hiking
- Inverted cycling
- Roller skating over distance
- Bench stepping
- Rope skipping
- Walking or jogging on a treadmill (Figure 22.5)
- Jogging in place
- Jogging over distance
- Swimming over distance
- Wheeling over distance
- Jumping jacks
- Obstacle course
- Fitness trails
- Cross-country skiing
- Canoeing or sculling over distance
- Exercycling (Figure 22.6)
- Bicycling or tricycling
- Jumping on a trampoline
- Arm pedaling (Figure 22.7)
- Speed bag

- Tag games
- Scooter activities
- Relays
- Aerobic dance routines

Students who are visually impaired may have difficulty with activities that require running or moving specified distances without assistance. Increasingly, schools are using treadmills and exercycles as part of cardiorespiratory development for youngsters with disabling conditions, especially those with visual impairments. With such equipment, the duration and intensity of the exercise can easily be set. Activity partners can provide assistance in jogging, while guide ropes may be helpful for distance swimming. In addition, a visually impaired person can run alongside a bike being pedaled by a sighted person, holding the bicycle's handlebar with one hand. People in wheelchairs can increase their cardiorespiratory endurance by participating in wheelchair mara-

Figure 22.6 Exercycle. Photo courtesy of McIver School, Greensboro, NC. Printed with permission.

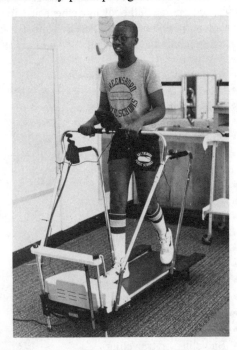

Figure 22.5 Walking on a treadmill. Photo courtesy of McIver School, Greensboro, NC. Printed with permission.

Figure 22.7 Arm pedaling exercise. Printed with permission.

thoning or using an arm ergometer (Figure 22.7), a hand-propelled tricycle, or a speed bag. For individuals with asthma or cardiopathic conditions, activities on an intermittent basis—similar to an interval training regimen—are advised. Here, activities that require running short distances, like softball and volleyball, are preferable to continuous running activities.

Breathing Exercises and Activities

For students with asthma, cystic fibrosis, or other conditions resulting in abnormal respiration or weak respiratory muscles (especially those with muscular dystrophy), breathing exercises and activities are of paramount importance. Breathing exercises and activities help asthmatic people in getting air into and out of the lungs; for those with cystic fibrosis, these exercises and activities help in eliminating excess mucus from the respiratory tract. Appropriately designed exercises can assist in increasing vital lung capacity and allowing the cardiorespiratory system to work more efficiently and effectively. The respiratory muscles (such as the intercostals, major and minor pectorals, diaphragm, and abdominals) are exercised, and this enhances the movement of air into and out of the lungs.

Following are some examples of breathing exercises and activities that can be incorporated into any adapted physical education program. For students with upper respiratory dysfunction, it is recommended that exercises and activities be conducted either daily or every other day for a period of 20 to 30 min. Frequency of the activity will depend on individual need. Breathing activities, as opposed to exercises, provide enjoyment, motivation, and competition for those who need daily sessions.

Forward Flexion—From a sitting or standing position and with arms relaxed, slowly bend forward at the waist while exhaling through the mouth. Bending forward as far as possible, forcefully expel as much air as possible and hold for a count of three. Slowly bring the trunk and head to an upright position while inhaling through the nostrils. This can be repeated as many times as desired.

Chest Expander—In a supine position with hips and knees flexed (so that the feet are flat on the floor and approximately 12 in. from the buttocks), place one hand on the chest and the other on the abdomen. Inhale slowly through the nostrils, trying to expand only the chest to the maximum extent possible. Hold for a count of two or three and then slowly exhale through the mouth with pursed lips until air is expelled. This can be repeated as many times as desired.

Elbow Rotation—From a sitting or standing position, place fingers on the shoulders so that elbows are bent and out to the sides. At the same time, slowly move both elbows in a circular fashion. Beginning with an upward and then backward motion of the elbows, inhale through the mouth. As elbows complete the circle and move downward and to the front, exhale through the mouth. This can be repeated as many times as desired.

Balloon Keep-Up—Two players stand facing each other about 3 feet apart. One player tosses a balloon in the air directly in front of the other player. The players alternate in blowing the balloon toward each other. They attempt to keep the balloon in the air for as long as possible without letting it hit the ground or touching it with the hands or body.

Ping-Pong Soccer—Two players sit facing each other at the ends of a small table (approximately 3 to 4 ft long). A Ping-Pong ball is placed in the middle of the table. On command, each player attempts to move the ball toward the opponent's goal with forceful breaths of air. A goal is scored when the ball falls off the opponent's side of the table. Players are not allowed to rise from the sitting position.

Lights Out—Each player sits at the end of a long table directly in front of a lighted candle. The player attempts to blow out the flame at progressively greater distances. The player extinguishing the flame at the greatest distance is the winner.

Breathing Activities in an Aquatic Environment—Breathing activities in water are popular and are most helpful in motivating students. Some activities include fully inhaling and exhaling air in neck- or shoulder-deep water, blowing bubbles with face submerged in waist-deep water, and blowing a Ping-Pong ball across the width of the pool or over a specified distance.

Weight Training and Body Building

Weight training programs utilize various exercises designed to develop muscular strength and endurance of specified muscle groups. In addition, many people seek to develop muscular power through weight training. The development of power is important for games and sports that require explosive movements like the long jump or spiking in volleyball.

Weight training is a very popular form of physical activity and is found in a variety of programs and environments. It is commonplace in health clubs, fitness centers, and recreational facilities as well as in schools. Some individuals use weight training for the purpose of bodybuilding (developing maximum muscle size and definition), while others use it for developing and maintaining physical fitness. Weight training is taught as an activity in many physical education programs, and it is commonly included as part of overall conditioning regimens for athletes at all competitive levels in nearly every sport.

Physical rehabilitation programs regularly incorporate weight training exercises to help people regain muscular strength and endurance following traumatic injury or illness. Anyone who has experienced physical rehabilitation can attest to the importance of weight training in restoring appropriate levels of muscular strength and endurance. Many physically disabled individuals continue to pursue weight training following medically prescribed rehabilitation programs. In fact, weight lifting (of which the bench press is the most popular activity) is a sanctioned event in all levels of NWAA, USCPAA, USLASA, and USAAA competition.

Isokinetics and Accommodating Resistance Training

A form of weight training that has recently become popular is *isokinetics*. In isokinetic training, the rate at which the exercise is performed can be controlled and direct, automatically variable resistance provided throughout the full range of movement. With this type of training, the resistance automatically increases or decreases in a manner directly proportional to increases or decreases in muscle force. Isokinetic training can closely match normal speeds of performance while, at the same time, producing lower incidences of muscle and joint pain following workouts. Nautilus equipment, which incorporates principles similar to those of isokinetic training, can be adjusted to allow for very fast or very slow movements (Figure 22.8).

Figure 22.8 Using a Nautilus machine for exercise.

This type of training, involving accommodating resistance, has tremendous possibilities, especially in developing muscles for specific sports that require powerful and fast movements. In Nautilus training, Westcott (1983) suggests that optimum strength gains can be realized with only one set of 8 to 12 repetitions with maximum weight for each exercise, as opposed to three sets recommended for training *isotonically*. Even though it is costly, some school districts and recreation centers and most athletic clubs now have isokinetic or accommodating-resistance equipment. Nautilus equipment is popular and offers a number of advantages. It can be adjusted to fit persons of various sizes and physiques; it is safe, durable, and designed so that the user has control over the exercise. Training partners are recommended, especially for physically disabled persons, but are not necessary for operating the machine. Unlike with free weights, once the user is positioned in the machine, the movement pattern is fixed and inflexible.

Other Forms of Weight Training

In addition to Nautilus-type equipment, weight training can be performed with free weights, a Universal gym, or various weighted objects. These methods seem to be the most feasible and cost-effective to date. Most schools and recreational and training facilities now have, in addition to free weights, at least one Universal gym. Universal gym equipment is arranged so that a number of people can perform a variety of exercises in a relatively small area. The Universal gym is preferable to the use of free weights in weight training programs for handicapped individuals for the following reasons:

- It is safer than free weights because weights cannot be dropped on the floor, nor can one lose balance, as when lifting a heavy barbell.
- It saves time because weights can be changed by the simple use of a pin, whereas free

weights must be continually placed on or removed from bars.
- It is convenient, especially for individuals with physical disabilities such as amputation or paralysis.

Most weight training exercises can be performed with Universal gym equipment. Exercises that develop the upper body and upper extremities include the following:

- Military press
- Bench press
- Pull-downs
- Bicep curls
- Forearm curls

Exercises that develop the back, hip, and abdomen include the following:

- Bent-knee sit-ups with arms folded across chest, on inclined board
- Back arch

Lower extremity exercises include the following:

- Leg press
- Knee extensions
- Knee curls
- Foot plantar flexion

In a weight training program for children of elementary school age, various weighted objects can be used in place of free weights or Universal gym equipment. Stuffed animals, beanbags, or balls are desirable because the weight of these objects can initially be light and adjusted in small increments.

Modifications of Weight Training Exercises

People with unilateral upper- or lower-limb amputations can perform modified exercises with one limb. For example, a unilateral upper-limb amputee may find it easier to perform a military press using a dumbbell instead of Universal equipment. Those with below-the-elbow, below-the-knee, or wrist or ankle disarticulations can exercise with free weights strapped to the remaining limb segment. Most people in wheelchairs can perform exercises in their chairs (except for the bench press, where assistance may be needed for transfer and the person may need to be strapped to the bench).

Recommendations for Developmental and Remedial Activities

The following general program recommendations, designed to enhance performance, have been taken in part from Winnick and Short (1985).

- Exercises and activities with a rehabilitative purpose should be conducted under the supervision of a physician and in coordination with physical therapists, occupational therapists, and/or other professional support personnel.
- Program activity sessions should take place on a regular rather than a sporadic basis.
- A variety of exercises and activities should be offered to allow as many parts of the body as possible to be active.
- Exercises and activities should be based on individual needs as determined by the person's present level of performance.
- The frequency, intensity, and duration of activity sessions should be programmed on an individual basis according to the person's tolerance level. AAHPERD (1980) suggests that activity levels should not be increased more than 10% each week.
- More severely impaired individuals may need exercises and activities with greater frequency than can be offered within the adapted physical education program. Therefore, exercises and activities performed at home or outside of the program are encouraged.

Summary

This chapter dealt with exercises and activities for relaxation and physical fitness. It stressed the importance of relaxation in preparing people both physically and psychologically for activity, and in assisting in the recovery from activity. The second portion of the chapter focused on exercises and activity modifications that can improve physical fitness levels in persons with unique needs. Finally, along with an overview of weight training and body building, program principles as well as exercises and activities that can be appropriately modified for persons with unique needs were presented.

Bibliography

American Alliance for Health, Physical Education, Recreation and Dance (1980). *Health related physical fitness manual*. Washington, DC: Author.

Harris, D. (1986). Relaxation and energizing techniques for regulation of arousal. In J. Williams (Ed.), *Applied sport psychology: Personal growth to peak performance* (pp. 185-207). Palo Alto, CA: Mayfield.

Jacobson, E. (1970). *Modern treatment of tense patients*. Springfield, IL: Charles C. Thomas.

Surburg, P. (1986). New perspectives for developing range of motion and flexibility for special populations. *Adapted Physical Activity Quarterly*, **3**, 227-235.

Vealey, R. (1986). Imagery training for performance enhancement. In J. Williams (Ed.), *Applied sport psychology: Personal growth to peak performance* (pp. 209-234). Palo Alto, CA: Mayfield.

Westcott, W.L. (1983). *Strength fitness: Physiological principles and training techniques*. Newton, MA: Allyn and Bacon.

Winnick, J.P. (1984). Recent advances related to special physical education and sport. *Adapted Physical Activity Quarterly*, **1**, 197-206.

Winnick, J.P., & Short, F.X. (1985). *Physical fitness testing of the disabled*. Champaign, IL: Human Kinetics.

Resources

Written

Basmajian, J. (1983). *Biofeedback: Principles and practices for clinicians* (2nd ed.). Baltimore: Williams & Wilkins. This book covers the underlying principles of biofeedback and its use as a means for dealing with various disorders.

Brosnan, J. (1982). *Yoga for handicapped people*. London: Souvenir Press. This book describes how yoga can be performed by handicapped people with a variety of disabilities. Specific exercises and positions are included, along with illustrations.

Audiovisual

Richard Simmons Reach Foundation (n.d.). *Reach for fitness* [Videotape]. Karl-Lorimar Home Video: Irvine, CA. This 40-min video was developed in conjunction with leading physicians and health educators for physically impaired persons. Disabled individuals are shown performing a variety of exercises.

CHAPTER 23

Rhythms and Dance

Patricia L. Krebs

Rhythmic movement and dance are integral parts of life, as natural as walking or swaying to music. Historically, rhythmic movement and dance for handicapped populations has been called dance therapy. The American Dance Therapy Association, Inc. (ADTA) defines dance/movement therapy as "the psychotherapeutic use of movement as a process which furthers the emotional and physical integration of the individual. Dance therapy is distinguished from other utilizations of dance . . . by its focus on the nonverbal aspects of behavior and its use of movement as the process for intervention" (Sherrill, 1986, p. 356). Therapy is conducted by certified dance therapists and, in some ways, is similar to adapted dance.

As used here, adapted rhythms and dance refers to a dance curriculum designed to meet the unique needs of individuals with specific learning, behavioral, or motor problems. This definition parallels the definition of adapted physical education. Like adapted physical education, adapted rhythmic movement and dance instruction begins with an assessment of the individual's present level of performance. From this information, long-term goals, specific short-term behavioral objectives, special services, and other parts of the student's individual education program (IEP) may be developed.

What makes rhythmic movement and dance look and feel different from other parts of the physical education curriculum is not its methods or content, but how and why it is used by the student. Whereas sports and games generally use move-

ment in functional, task-oriented ways, dance uses movement for expressive communication. The uniqueness of this expression and communication is the quality that gives rhythmic movement and dance its identity and distinguishes it from games and sports (Logsdon et al., 1984).

Many motor patterns and skills that evolve with the normal growth and maturation of able-bodied children may be nonexistent or develop as splinter skills in children with unique needs. Thus, their participation in rhythm and dance activities may be frustrating, if not impossible. However, through a well-developed rhythm and dance experience, their needs can be met in a successful, satisfying manner.

Rhythm is functionally important to life processes and movement skills. The human heart beats to a predisposed rhythm. Breathing follows a certain rhythm. Speaking, walking, running, hopping, and skipping are distinguished as much by their rhythms as by their unique movements.

Rhythm involves three components: tempo (speed), pattern (even or uneven beats), and accent (emphasis). Walking and running differ primarily in tempo (speed). Different patterns (beats) can be illustrated by a comparison of walking and skipping. Whereas walking involves a consistent pattern of slow beats each time a step is taken, skipping interrupts this pattern with a fast hop between two slow walking steps, producing an inconsistent pattern of slow-fast-slow (step-hop-step). Accent is best illustrated in language. When speaking, we accent (emphasize) particular syllables in a word and particular parts of a sentence. A person who does not use much vocal emphasis speaks in a monotone voice.

Dance is a combination of movement and rhythm where movement qualities, movement components, and rhythmic movement are purposefully integrated. Dance has a beginning, middle, and end. In dance, the body is the instrument. Dance evolves as a natural progression of expression as an individual acquires movement and rhythmic skills. A person must build a strong repertoire of movement and rhythmic skills to become successful in dance.

Teaching Progression of Rhythm and Dance

Laban (1963) grouped movement into 16 basic movement themes. Each theme represents a movement idea that corresponds to a stage in the progressive unfolding of movement in the growing child. Preston (1963) simplified and reorganized Laban's themes into 7 movement themes for organizing and developing educational dance content:

- Theme 1—Awareness of the body (total body actions and actions of individual body parts)
- Theme 2—Awareness of weight and time (contrasting qualities)
- Theme 3—Awareness of space (areas, directions, levels, pathways, and extensions)
- Theme 4—Awareness of flow of movement (use of space and time)
- Theme 5—Awareness of adaptation to partners and small groups (simple forms of relationships)
- Theme 6—Awareness of body (emphasis on elevation, body shapes, and gestures)
- Theme 7—Awareness of the basic effort actions (rhythmic nature of time, weight, and space)

The themes approach can be used to give teachers guidelines for dance progression. Once children learn the basic content of a theme, experiences are designed to combine material from previous themes with the newly learned content. Table 23.1 outlines a dance program that begins in kindergarten and continues through sixth grade. Solid lines indicate when a theme is developmentally most appropriate in a physical education program. Starred lines denote a theme that may be appropriate but is used less frequently. Dotted lines represent material with more advanced themes to increase complexity in a physical education experience (Logsdon et al., 1984).

Suggested Rhythm and Dance Activities

Basic Rhythmic Activities and Action Songs

Simple rhythmic activities and action songs are used to teach the seven movement themes to young children. In early rhythmic experiences, the teacher follows the lead of the child and maintains a beat that corresponds to the rhythm of the child's movement. Later the teacher presents a rhythm that challenges children to alter their normal rhythm of movement and follow an externally presented rhythm. Children who have temporal perception problems or mobility impairments often experience difficulty moving to an externally imposed rhythm. In this case, the teacher may spend more time permitting the student to move to a variety of self-initiated rhythms. Storytelling through dance and mime will often attune the student to the rhythmic qualities necessary to portray a story, word, or animal. Students can also use rhythmic instruments to accompany their own rhythmic movements.

Action songs prescribe certain body movements to accompany the words of a song. Movements may involve isolated body parts (Themes 2, 3) or total body movement (Themes 1, 4, 6, 7). Action songs can combine locomotor and axial move-

Table 23.1 Suggested Dance Progression by Theme and Age

Theme	5	6	7	8	9	10	11	12
Age in years								
1. Awareness of the body			_____		**************************			
2. Awareness of weight and time			_____			****************		
3. Awareness of space					_____		********	
4. Awareness of flow	• • •	_____						**
5. Awareness of adaptation to partners and small groups	• • • • • • •	_____						
6. Awareness of the body	• • • • • • • • • •	_____						
7. Awareness of the basic effort actions	• • • •	_____						

Note. From *Physical Education for Children: A Focus on the Teaching Process* (2nd ed.) (p. 161) by B.J. Logsdon, K.R. Barrett, M.R. Broer, R. McGee, M. Ammons, L.E. Halverson, and M.A. Roberton, 1984, Philadelphia: Lea & Febiger. Copyright 1977 by Lea & Febiger. Adapted by permission.

ments with rhythms. Some action songs involving isolated body movement (Themes 2, 3) are "If You're Happy and You Know It, Clap Your Hands," "Itsy Bitsy Spider," "Head, Shoulders, Knees, and Toes," and "So Early in the Morning." Action songs with words involving total body coordination (Themes 1, 4, 6, 7) include "Looby-Loo," "Pop Goes the Weasel," "Farmer in the Dell," "Mexican Hat Dance," "Skip to My Lou," "London Bridge," "Sing a Song of Sixpence," "Go Round and Round the Village," and "Ten Little Indians."

Ballroom, Folk, and Square Dance

Ballroom, folk, and square dances are social dances that children and adults can enjoy once they have mastered the seven movement themes. Ballroom dances include the waltz, fox-trot, cha-cha, rumba, tango, samba, mamba, meringue, polka, jitterbug, and rock-and-roll. Ballroom dances are generally uncomposed. The male partner sets the rhythm, decides what steps are to be used, and controls his female partner's direction and progression around the floor; the female responds to her partner.

Folk dances are international. They are composed dances that have set routines and a uniformity of movement. Folk dances are very popular worldwide and are valued for the insights they offer into ethnic culture and political history. They are mirrors reflecting the cultural traditions and social influences of preceding periods. Folk dances illuminate what peoples have played, valued, admired, and worked to achieve.

Square dance is indigenous to the United States, with a similarity in the fundamental forms of movement and techniques that ensures uniformity across the country. However, square dance has a different "accent" in each section of the U.S.

Aerobic Dance

Aerobic dance combines the benefits of a good cardiovascular workout with the appeal of dance and music. It borrows steps from every dance form and uses any beat—pop, folk, rock, ethnic, country, or classical. The aerobic dance movement sweeping the country is simple enough that dancers can learn the steps as they perform them. Basic locomotor and nonlocomotor movements are combined in movement patterns that flow into each other without stopping.

Modern Dance

Modern dance is one of four types of creative dance, which also includes jazz, tap, and ballet. The dance ideas of Ruth St. Dennis and Ted Shawn led to the birth of modern dance. Disciples of the Dennishawn School and Dance Company, Martha Graham, Doris Humphrey, and Charles Weidman, as well as Germany's Hanya Holm, nurtured and developed American modern dance into its present form.

The uniqueness of modern dance is that the stimulating force of the movement lies in the rhythm of the body and the thoughts and emotions of the dancer. The modern dancer does not interpret music and move to it, but rather selects or composes music, words, and/or sounds that will best stimulate the expressive movement of the body (Brown & Sommer, 1969).

Modern dance, then, is the ideal creative dance form for individuals with handicapping conditions. Modern dance recognizes individuality and takes into consideration all of a person's capacities and abilities. Because modern dance is an expression of feelings and meanings, dancers learn to understand movement principles and to develop a keen kinesthetic sense that lets them create their own expressive movements (see Figure 23.1). Modern dance classes generally explore the creative potential of the individual's movement through carefully structured exercises in axial, locomotive, and relaxation techniques; joint mobility; muscle strengthening; dexterity; falls; partner work; and movements with objects.

Because modern dance focuses on individual

Figure 23.1 Ballerina Monika Valgemae has a significant hearing impairment. Gallaudet University Photo. Printed with permission.

expression in movement, little adaptation is necessary. Students create movements within their own realm of ability. The challenge of modern dance is to develop students' awareness of their movement possibilities and to help them express feelings and emotions through movement. The following are some creative techniques:

- Wearing masks (The personality portrayed must be demonstrated through body shape and movements. The mask prevents students from showing changing facial expressions.)
- Mime
- Improvising with and without props
- Acting out stories or sketches
- Acting out stories to music
- Using props to convey mood

Contemporary Age-Appropriate Rhythmic and Dance Activities

As mentioned at the beginning of the chapter, rhythmic movement and dance are an integral part of life and of the normalization process. The individual must build a strong repertoire of movement and rhythmic abilities to be successful in dance.

Primary Group

Primary-age children are able to perform walks of various kinds, march, run, hop, jump, skip, gallop, slide, swing, and clap their hands. Children of this age love action songs, rope jumping, hopscotch, rhythmic movement with percussive instruments, mimetics, and simple folk dances. Popular action songs include "Farmer in the Dell," "Head, Shoulders, Knees, and Toes," "Ring Around the Rosie," "Sing a Song of Sixpence," "Looby Loo," "Here We Go 'Round the Mulberry Bush," "Baa Baa Blacksheep," "I'm a Little Teapot," and "Twinkle Twinkle Little Star." Girls play Snake and High Waters with the jump rope and learn hopscotch to a variety of chants. Children often play with toy percussive instruments like drums, bells, tambourines, maracas, and triangles. At family and social gatherings, children often dance the alley cat, the hokey pokey, and the bunny hop. Games like follow the leader, Mother-May-I, Charlie-Over-the-Water, Red Rover, Statues, and Whistle Stop involve many rhythmic qualities.

It is important for primary-age children with handicapping conditions to participate in these play experiences with able-bodied children as much as possible to help facilitate dance and rhythmic learning. These primary rhythmic activities help children discriminate among tempos (Theme 2); create patterns of body movement (Theme 4); create movements for imaginative play by imitating animals, people, or things (Themes 1, 2, 3, 4); dramatize nursery rhymes, poems, songs, and stories; differentiate between even and uneven rhythms (Theme 2); change direction at the end of each phrase of music (Theme 3); and express lightness and heaviness of the music through body movements (Theme 2).

Middle and Upper Elementary School Children

At this age, children begin to work cooperatively in small groups (Theme 5). Therefore, they enjoy rhythmic movement with objects (e.g., hoops, wands, balls), gymnastics, group stunts, and social dancing (Themes 5, 6, 7). Some children become interested in creative dance (tap, ballet, jazz, modern) and ballroom dance. Many attend weekly dance lessons to become proficient dancers and have aspirations of becoming the next Ginger Rogers, Fred Astaire, Debbie Allen, Gregory Hines, Mikhail Baryshnikov, or Cynthia Gregory. Basic dance steps, dance positions, and dance formations should be introduced to students early. Simple folk dances and square dance figures, as well as mime and improvisations both with and without props (Theme 6), provide adolescents with the fundamentals to learn more complex dance movements. Table 23.2 shows the basic two-step task analyzed for effective teaching.

A visual presentation can facilitate learning for students with hearing impairments. A texture display may assist students with visual impairments by enabling them to feel the step sequence with their hands and then replicate the pattern with their feet.

Adolescents

While interest in creative or ballroom dance wanes for many students, adolescence brings the new social demands of dating and learning the latest "craze," be it dancing to popular rock or learning

Table 23.2   Task Analysis of the Basic Two-Step

Step	Action
1	Step forward on the left foot.
2	Close the right foot to the left foot and take the weight on the right foot.
3	Step forward on the left foot.
4	Step forward on the right foot.
5	Close the left foot to the right foot and take the weight on the right foot.
6	Step forward on the right foot.
7	Repeat Steps 1 through 6, 5 times.
8	Using drum accompaniment, add rhythm of quick-quick-slow.
9	Using drum accompaniment, repeat steps 1 through 6 with new rhythm, 5 times.
10	Using recording with 2/4 or 4/4 time, perform basic two-step for the duration of the recording.

to break-dance. If the basic dance steps, positions, and formations have been learned and the student has developed a keen kinesthetic sense of the body through modern dance techniques, then dancers at this age can master more complex variations of basic dance steps and learn to express the style and mood of dance.

In general, students find pleasure in performing a few simple steps, varied by changes in rhythm, direction, style, and tempo. Those who have discovered the art of dancing enjoy learning more intricate dance patterns and personally set a high standard on form. In adolescence, students are ready to learn proper body carriage for dancing, techniques of leading and following, and dance etiquette, and to create their own dance compositions.

Modifying
Rhythm and Dance Activities

With minimal modification, individuals with handicapping conditions can experience the pleasure and joy of rhythmic and dance activities.

When teaching students with mental impairments, it may be necessary to emphasize demonstrations and manual guidance and minimize verbal explanations. Directional arrows, footprints, and picture signs placed on the floor can be used to help students learn movement sequences. When teaching action songs to children with mental retardation, it is important to select songs with simple melodies that are within the students' vocal range and with short intervals of frequently repeated phrases. It is best to teach words and melody first and then teach dance steps and/or actions without partners or groups. It may be necessary to slow the tempo of the music when teaching a dance step (Crain, 1981). When students with mental retardation are learning social dances, it is best that the music have a strong beat, easy rhythm, and simple music phrases that are frequently repeated. Likewise, dance sequences should be short and well within the comprehension and physical tolerance level of the students.

When presenting new dances to mentally retarded students, first let them listen to the entire record or piece of music. Next students can clap the rhythm. Finally, they may be asked to perform the required actions. Each part of the dance sequence should be taught separately and then the parts combined into a whole sequence. The tempo of the music can be slow as students learn dance parts and combine them into a sequence. The tempo then can be gradually increased as the students increase their skill.

In teaching square dance, it is desirable to use an experienced caller who can follow the pace of the students. Records with singing calls may be too fast and the "square dance patter" too confusing for students to follow.

Mentally retarded youngsters will often have difficulty with the self-expression, interpretations, and creative movement responses required in modern dance. Therefore, the modern dance teacher may need to use a command instructional style within a highly structured environment. In a structured environment there are clearly defined boundaries, and each student is assigned a space in which to perform the prescribed movements. The teacher choreographs movements and the students practice them in the formation prescribed by the teacher. To be perceived by students, contrasting activities will often initially require exaggeration of differences. Strategically placed colors or items may be needed to direct students. Movement phrases may have to be subgrouped for initial learning, then regrouped later for students who have problems sequencing movements and processing multipart directions.

Mobility-impaired children may need to substitute swaying, swinging, walking, sliding, twisting, turning, and balancing steps for more complex or fast-paced dance steps. The instructor may need to substitute wheelchair and crutch ambulation for locomotor skills or have an able-bodied assistant push a student's wheelchair. Crutch or cane tapping can be substituted for hand clapping if necessary. Upper-body, arm, and head movements may be substituted for leg movements (Kindel, 1986). When necessary, the tempo of the music may be slowed and the timing of coordinated steps adjusted to suit the abilities and experience of the students.

To allow more time to complete a square dance figure, music can be added. Often the trimming (chorus) is repeated by the caller and/or the dancers until all dancers have completed the figure. A live caller who can follow the pace of the group is better than a recording (Szyman, 1976). Mobility-impaired children can make the following adapted responses to common square dance calls:

- Honor your partner: Bow heads.
- Do-si-do: Take one step forward and one step back.
- Do-si-do paso: Partners place left crutches together and circle. Then corners place right crutches together and circle.
- Allemande left: Corners move counterclockwise around each other, maintaining eye contact.
- Grand right and left: Partners face, pass to right of partner so backs face; pass to left of person facing you and continue passing alternately right and left until you meet your partner again.
- Swing: Partners circle clockwise around male partners.

Students can be paired to enhance their aerobic abilities. For example, if paired with someone in a wheelchair, a student with balance problems can use the wheelchair for stability while helping to maneuver the partner's chair. In teaching social dance to students with mobility impairments, dancers should be encouraged to maintain eye contact because physical contact between dancers may be limited or eliminated. Leads, the calling of the steps, should be given verbally by either the male or female partner. Timing in giving and successfully following verbal leads takes much practice and needs to be taught throughout the social dance unit. Movements should be kept small, with ample room between dancers. When teaching a new dance, maintain a distance of two wheelchairs, or one adult crutch, between dancers. As dancers become more skilled, this distance can be decreased. Table 23.3 describes waltz steps for dancers who use wheelchairs.

Social-integrative wheelchair dancing originated in the Federal Republic of Germany in 1974. The

Table 23.3 Waltz Steps for Dancers in Wheelchairs

Step	Counts	Man	Woman
Basic	1,2,3	F	B
	1,2,3	B	F
Box step	1	F	B
	2,3	Turn R 90°	Turn L 90°
	1	F	F
	2,3	Turn L 90°	Turn R 90°
	1	B	F
	2,3	Turn L 90°	Turn R 90°
	1	F	F
	2,3	Turn R 90°	Turn L 90°

Note. F = Forward; B = Backward; R = Right; L = Left. From *Dance for Physically Disabled Persons* (p. 11) by K. Hill, 1976, Reston, VA: American Alliance for Health, Physical Education, Recreation and Dance. Adapted by permission.

movements of the wheelchair and the step-combinations of the "pedestrian" are coordinated so that the couple dances in harmony. Wheelchair users rhythmically roll forward and backward, start and stop the chair, turn at different speeds, and move head, shoulders, arms, and upper body. Their able-bodied partners perform the regular dance steps and help their partners to stop, roll, turn, and display their skill.

Students with mobility impairments often exhibit very creative modern dance movement; however, because these students generally cannot move about as freely or quickly as their able-bodied peers, the modern dance teacher will often need to decrease the number of repetitions, slow the tempo of the music, and simplify patterns of movement (Harris, 1979).

Visually impaired students will need to follow continuous sound to have a sense of the direction in which to move. Surface textures may be placed on the floor to establish boundaries, and brightly colored tape or mats may be used to emphasize direction and space. A sighted or partially sighted student can be paired with a totally blind partner. Visually impaired dancers may put their hands on a partner's shoulders or hips to receive the kinesthetic sensations of time, space, and size concepts.

Formations such as circle, line, or square should be used to help students better orient themselves to various dances. Backward, forward, and side steps may be substituted for more complex movement patterns. To learn dance patterns, students can move their hands on the floor to simulate movements. It is important that acoustics be good and competing noises eliminated so that participants can clearly hear the music and lyrics.

To prevent accidents, dances can be modified so that partners either continually touch one another (thus coordinating movements) or stay totally separate from one another in their own defined spaces. All dancing should take place away from walls or other obstacles.

Teachers can use percussion instruments and music to help hearing-impaired students feel and respond to vibrations. Students can place their hands on a piano or phonograph to feel vibrations and establish rhythm. They should also recite the words of a song as they clap to the beat. When teaching, the instructor can demonstrate dance steps and count beats by using a percussion instrument if necessary. Dance steps should be demonstrated with the instructor's back to the students so they can easily mimic right and left movements. It may also help to have hearing-impaired students put their hands on the shoulders or hips of another to experience the rhythm.

Students with hearing impairments can follow music by clapping, stamping, or vocalizing beats and rhythms. They should wear shoe taps to help establish and maintain rhythm. Gallaudet University, a university for hearing impaired students, offers courses in dance (see Figures 23.2 and 23.3). Folk and square dances can be performed in a line or square to allow all to see and follow

Figure 23.2 Gallaudet Dance Company tap dancers. Lonnelle Crosby, Lily Chin, Sherry Rome, and Sandara Carroll (l-r) have significant hearing losses. Gallaudet University photo. Printed with permission.

Figure 23.3 Ms. Sue Gill-Gould of the Gallaudet Dance Company performs at the National Art Gallery in Washington, D.C. Ms. Gill-Gould has a hearing impairment. Gallaudet University photo. Printed with permission.

the leader, and speakers should be placed directly on a wood floor to increase the intensity of the vibrations and bass tones.

Dance and rhythmic movement are often used in therapy for children who have a lessened capacity to effectively relate to others. Dance therapists use rhythmic movement and dance in a group setting to help each member relate to the group. Spontaneous dance is often used to elicit conflicts and imaginations unrestricted by reality (Bender & Boas, 1941). Action songs can provide socially acceptable outlets for aggression, hostility, and frustration, whereas pantomime and mimetic activities let children relate events from their own past and express innermost thoughts and ideas. For the child with a behavioral disability, dance may be most helpful in social adjustment and appropriate expression of feelings.

Dance and Rhythmic Movement in Sport Programs

The connection between dance and sport skills has been clearly recognized. Knute Rockne required Notre Dame football players to enroll in dance classes. Woody Hayes incorporated dance procedures into the practice schedule of Ohio State University football players, and Lynn Swann of the Pittsburgh Steelers attributed his outstanding athletic abilities to 14 years of study in dance. Dance and sport share many movement skills and motor competencies including balance, breathing, weight transfer, centering, and the efficient use of time, space, and energy (Minton & Beckwith, 1986).

The sport most directly related to dance is gymnastics. Floor exercise routines require dance and dance transitions between tumbling moves. Also, the centering and balance learned from ballet are necessary for working on a 4-in.-wide balance beam. Ballet moves such as the plié, tendu, dégagé, rond de jambe, grand battements, relevé,

port de bras, and jump are the same moves that help the basketball player, diver, and ice or roller skater improve his or her jumps and extensions.

The United States Association of Blind Athletes (USABA) sanctions women's gymnastics for its athletes. Events include floor exercise, balance beam, uneven bars, vaulting, and all-around. The rules and policies for USABA competition in women's gymnastics are similar to those adopted by the United States Gymnastics Federation (USGF) and by the International Federation of Gymnastics (FIG).

Sports that involve rhythmic movements and dance in Special Olympics include gymnastics, figure skating (singles, pairs, and ice dancing), and roller skating (free style and dance couples). While the rules of an international sports governing body are used, modifications are provided to limit the complexity of routines and the difficulty of moves (*Official Special Olympics Summer/Winter Sports Rules*, 1988).

Summary

Rhythmic movement and dance are important movement forms of communication and creative expression. Adapted dance is a modified dance curriculum using instruction designed to meet the unique needs of individuals. Basic rhythmic skills, such as locomotor and axial movements, are prerequisite to successful dancing. Ballroom, folk, and square dances are important socialization and integration vehicles for students with handicapping conditions. The highly popular aerobic dance combines simple locomotor and nonlocomotor activities that are fun and exhilarating. Modern dance recognizes individuality and takes into consideration all the capacities and abilities of students, so little adaptation is necessary for individuals with different abilities. Because of the many values associated with rhythms and dance, physical educators must ensure opportunities for attaining full potential through a complete program of dance instruction.

Bibliography

Bender, L., & Boas, F. (1941). Creative dance in therapy. *American Journal of Orthopsychiatry, 2*, 235-245.

Brown, M.C., & Sommer, B.K. (1969). *Movement education: Its evolution and a modern approach.* Reading, MA: Addison-Wesley.

Crain, C. (1981). *Movement and rhythmic activities for the mentally retarded.* Springfield, IL: Charles C Thomas.

Harris, C.G. (1979). Dance for students with orthopedic conditions. *AAHPERD Practical Pointers, 2*, 1-22.

Hill, K. (1976). *Dance for physically disabled persons: A manual for teaching ballroom, square and folk dances to users of wheelchairs and crutches.* Reston, VA: American Alliance for Health, Physical Education, Recreation and Dance.

Kindel, M. (1986). Wheelchair dancer. *A Positive Approach: A National Magazine for the Physically Challenged*, Premier Issue, 41-43.

Laban, R. (1963). *Modern education dance* (2nd ed.). Revised by L. Ullman. New York: Frederick A. Praeger.

Logsdon, B.J., Barrett, K.R., Broer, M.R., McGee, R., Ammons, M., Halverson, L.E., & Roberton, M.A. (1984). *Physical education for children: A focus on the teaching process* (2nd ed.). Philadelphia: Lea & Febiger.

Minton, S., & Beckwith, B. (1986). Dance and sport. The elusive connection. *Journal of Physical Education, Recreation and Dance, 57*(5), 26-27.

Official Special Olympics summer/winter sports rules (revised). (1988). Washington, DC: Special Olympics International.

Preston, V. (1963). *A handbook for modern educational dance.* London: McDonald and Evans.

Sherrill, C. (1986). *Adapted physical education and recreation.* Dubuque, IA: Wm. C. Brown.

Szyman, R. (1976). Square dancing on wheels. *Sports 'N Spokes, 2*, 5-7.

Resources

Audiovisual

Caplow-Lender, E., & Harpas, L. (Speakers) (1982). *Special dancing on your feet or in your seat* (Recording No. EL0102). Atlanta: Educational Record Center. This recording offers dance/movement activities for people of all ages with special needs and a variety of music for people with physical limitations or developmental deficiencies.

Caplow-Lender, E., Harpas, L., & Samberg, S. (Speakers) (1977). *Special music for special people* (Recording No. EL0985). Atlanta: Educational Record Center. This recording provides creative physical activity for leaders working with physically handicapped, perceptually disabled, and emotionally disturbed people. Special material has been included for the geriatric recreation field. There are dances, exercise programs, creative activities, and rhythmic games. The activities described provide adaptations for nonambulatory participants.

CHAPTER 24

Aquatics

E. Louise Priest

Aquatics provides many of the best lifetime activities available to people with unique needs, particularly because most activities are individual in nature and easily adapted. Aquatic activities can be therapeutic, educational, recreational, and sport-participatory, and thus offer a broad scope of benefits to people with handicapping conditions. Aquatics itself is an extremely varied field, with activities ranging from simple learn-to-swim programs to aquatic sports such as canoeing, water-skiing, scuba diving, sailing, and other types of boating. Competitive programs are available in most of these sports. Both competitive and non-competitive programs offer individuals opportunity for peer interaction, achievement, success, improved self-concept, and lessened evidence of (and effect of) impairment. In aquatics, these programs also offer a lifetime activity. This chapter covers two basic areas: (a) swimming and (b) other aquatic activities.

Swimming

When asked to define swimming, most people will describe a stroke such as the crawl or the breast-stroke. Swimming, in actuality, is moving independently through the water, and as so defined, it is a skill within reach of most people.

Some general benefits of swimming are the same for all people, both disabled and nondisabled.

These benefits include improved cardiovascular fitness, increased muscle strength and flexibility, and improved general physiological function. While these benefits can accrue to all participants, they may be of much greater importance to disabled persons, who may have a functional deficit in one of these areas. They may also be more readily achieved in the aquatic environment. American Red Cross materials (1977) state that a person with balance problems may find walking much easier in the water because of the support of the water and the buoyancy of the body. These two factors, buoyancy and support, are doubly important when weight-bearing activities are impossible or inadvisable. There are, in fact, many individuals who can engage in aerobic levels of activity only in the water; thus swimming can be essential to the development of fitness and a healthy lifestyle. In addition, flexibility and muscle strength can often be increased by aquatic activity, and these factors are most important to daily living skills.

Some components of psychomotor development are also important to consider in the context of aquatics. Many children have deficits in perceptual-motor performance—such factors as balance, kinesthetic awareness, eye-hand coordination, and the like—and aquatic activities can be used to improve performance in these areas. In fact, structuring aquatic classes around components of perceptual-motor performance can be therapeutic for a disabled child and concurrently be developmental for a nondisabled child: The approach is thus a logical one for use in a mainstream setting.

Safety is an important consideration as well. Swimming ability is essential for safe participation in all other water sports. All participants in aquatic sports should learn to swim and to be comfortable in the water, as well as learning simple self-help and rescue skills (see Figure 24.1). The teaching of safety skills is important in all aquatic programs. In fact, the safety of the participants must be of primary concern; according to the American Red Cross (1974), it is absolutely essential that there be a lifeguard on duty at all times in aquatic programs.

General Teaching Suggestions

Every teacher must have a degree of expertise in task analysis: the process of analyzing a task or skill and identifying its component parts. Often an aquatic skill cannot be taught effectively until the teacher understands the component parts and their effects upon the performance of the whole skill. An example is the beginner skill of recovery from the prone float. Superficially, it might seem to be an action that could be elicited by the simple command "stand up." Many beginners have trouble, however, in initial stages because they omit some of the component parts of the action or do them in the wrong sequence.

The Task: Recovery from the prone float
The Components:

1. Tuck of legs
2. Downward thrust of extended arms
3. Extension of legs to bottom of pool
4. Lift of head
5. Straightening of trunk to balanced stand

Doing the actions in proper sequence makes the skill easy; doing them out of sequence makes it

Figure 24.1 Learning about safety equipment. Photo courtesy of Fairfax Co. (VA) Parks.

harder or impossible. When teaching this skill to any student, it may be necessary to incorporate several steps into each component. For example, the learner may do the tuck and extension of the legs while holding the poolside with both hands, then with one hand, then while holding the teacher's hands, then while being held at the waist by the teacher. Similarly, the arm action may be practiced with decreasing support, before being combined with the tuck and stand. This analysis and sequencing of components is absolutely essential to teaching in adapted programs.

Much of the motor performance and adapted physical education literature will be helpful to the aquatics teacher in understanding how the body moves, and that information can be utilized in teaching aquatic skills. Aquatic teaching materials that contain some information on task analysis include *Adapted Aquatics*, American Red Cross (1977a); *Methods in Adapted Aquatics*, American Red Cross (1977b); *Swimming and Aquatic Safety*, American Red Cross (1981); and *Competitive Swimming for New Champions*, Van Rossen and Woodrich (1979).

Knowledge of reflexology and other aspects of human development can be extremely useful to the swimming teacher. Sometimes a reflex pattern can look very much like a fear response, and it can be important for the teacher to discriminate between the two and react appropriately. Some individuals who have cerebral palsy or are developmentally delayed exhibit reflexes that are normal in very young children but are sometimes misinterpreted when seen in older children. Knowledge of reflexes can also be useful in eliciting a desired response. For example, if a cerebral-palsied child has one leg extended and one leg flexed, stimulation of the sole of the foot of the flexed leg will cause the leg to extend. This extensor thrust reflexive reaction can be used to cause leg extension. Some cerebral-palsied people retain a "startle reflex" throughout their lives, and any sudden loud noise (and some other stimuli) will cause them to extend and then flex the arms. This reflex would not indicate fear of the water per se, but the movement pattern is sometimes in-terpreted as that. Swimming teachers with students who are developmentally delayed or have cerebral palsy are well advised to learn about reflexes and human development sequences.

Adapting Swimming Skills

Adapting swimming skills to individuals of varying capabilities requires several competencies on the part of teachers. The aquatics teacher must understand swimming skills and the actions that are effective in balancing and moving a body through the water. The teacher must also, of course, understand specific handicapping conditions and how they affect an individual in swimming (or in motor skills in other aquatic activities). Of primary importance is the teacher's competency in individual assessment—the ability to look at student movement, assess capabilities, and say, "I believe I can teach *this* skill with *this* or *that* adaptation or change." Of course, not all skills will need to be adapted; many students can perform aquatic skills with *no* adaptations. In fact, *most* impaired people could do most aquatic skills if instruction were based on goals, not on the methods of achieving those goals. (For instance, the skill "flutter kick for 50 yd" is not achievable by a paraplegic or a double-leg amputee. But if the requirement were stated in terms of the *goal*—"move 50 yd independently"—the method of doing so would be irrelevant, and the paraplegic and the amputee could achieve that goal.)

The purpose of adaptation in aquatics is to facilitate movement through the water. This is done by either (a) adjusting the student's body position or (b) increasing the effectiveness of propulsive action. An adaptation may also necessitate deletion of a skill component, as in the deletion of the breaststroke kick for amputees or paraplegics. In any case, the stroke or skill is adapted to the student's ability.

Looking at physical disability and inferring incompetence (both physical and mental) is a common—and very bad—habit. The aquatic educator must learn to think in positive terms, to look at an individual and say, "This person can move this way, so he or she can do these skills or do this skill in this way.'' For example, in assessing an individual with limited shoulder and elbow flexibility, the teacher should not think, ''Well, I can't teach the back crawl to this person,'' but rather, ''The beginner crawl will give this person mobility.'' Even such things as residual reflexive actions can be used in positive rather than negative ways.

Adapting may also mean incorporating the use of flotation aids, or weights for counterbalance: These somewhat simple modifications may greatly enhance the swimmer's balance and movement capacity. Any change or adaptation that helps the swimmer achieve is appropriate. The nature of the change becomes critical only in those agency or competitive programs that require that skills be performed in specific ways.

Orientation to Water

If a student is hesitant to enter the water for any reason, there are several things an instructor can and must do.

1. Provide support, either tactile or artificial. The student may need to feel the handclasp of the instructor, to be reassured that help is there. Sometimes, artificial supporters such as water wings or foam mats, with the instructor standing close by, will be effective (see Figure 24.2).
2. Do simple, common activities first. Usually, walking in the water and maintaining contact with either the poolside or the instructor is a useful activity for developing ''water comfort.'' For the young child, toys and sponges are often most helpful in facilitating water orientation. The student who cannot walk can be supported in slow patterns of movement.
3. Continue to provide support until the student can regain balance in the water when it is lost.

As research has shown (Lawrence & Hackett, 1975; Priest, 1976b, 1976c), many games of low

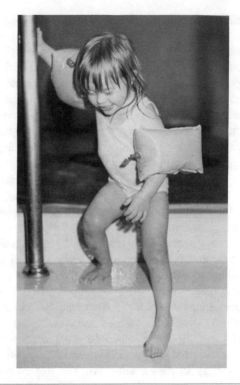

Figure 24.2 Arm band flotation aids can be useful. Photo courtesy of the American Red Cross.

organization and movement exploration activities are easily adapted to the aquatic environment and are useful in facilitating water orientation for children. The following activities are fun, and at the same time they enhance participants' social, emotional, and physical development. The challenge can be enjoyed by both able-bodied swimmers and those with various impairments, because the required movements and concepts can be adapted to the swimmers' abilities.

Obstacle Course

An obstacle course may be set up in a pool with equipment such as

- a post or standard to go around;
- a hoop or snapwall to go through;

- two ropes, one to go under and one to go over; and
- several hoops or snapwalls to go in and out.

Negotiating the obstacle course is enjoyable and helps reinforce basic movement concepts. A non-ambulatory child may be carried through the course, and a child who is hesitant may be accompanied by the teacher. However, maximum benefit from the standpoint of movement exploration will be derived only if a child does the activity or movement independently. These are some benefits of the obstacle course:

- It reinforces concepts of around, in/out, over/under, up/down.
- It improves ability to follow directions.
- It sharpens awareness of the environment and objects in it.
- It improves the child's ability to move through water in varying directions.

Dive and Collect Relay

For this group game, a variety of sinkable objects are tossed into the pool. At the start signal, players sit or surface dive and collect as many objects as possible, until all are collected or a stop signal is given. The player with the most objects wins. The relay incorporates an academic remediation element if the players are asked to identify the object. This game

- enhances fine motor control,
- improves ability to follow directions,
- enhances target location ability,
- enhances spatial orientation,
- improves ability to open eyes and swim under water, and
- improves breath control.

Object Relay

In this relay a variety of objects are placed on the pool deck in two matching stacks, one for each team. The leader stands in the pool at any distance from the side, holding two hula hoops floating in the water. The leader gives a directive to the first students in line, such as "Bring me something that floats; ready-go." The child chooses the object and takes it to the hula hoop. A new directive is given for each team member. In addition to promoting water comfort, this activity

- enhances discrimination among certain objects,
- exposes children to competition on a simple level,
- requires following a task with several steps,
- teaches different and faster methods of moving, and
- improves understanding of the buoyancy of objects.

Prebeginner Level Skills

For some disabled persons, it is advisable to use a skill breakdown that yields more simple skills than those of the traditional beginner level. Such a skill breakdown usually includes such actions as

- entering and leaving the pool with assistance,
- walking in the water with assistance,
- walking in the water unassisted,
- bobbing up and down to chin level,
- blowing bubbles with the mouth and nose in water,
- entering and leaving the pool unassisted,
- putting the face in the water and blowing bubbles,
- kicking the legs while assisted,
- kicking the legs while being "towed" by the instructor,
- sitting on the pool bottom assisted,
- sitting on the pool bottom and regaining standing balance assisted, and
- sitting on the pool bottom and regaining standing balance unassisted.

It is important to reinforce completion of the skill with specific feedback. In teaching the prebeginner skills, and in moving from these into beginner and more advanced skills, the instructor should take into consideration the motor complexity of a skill. For instance, a synchronous bilateral activity, one in which both arms or both legs move in the same plane and at the same time, is more easily executed (or at a lower developmental level) than is an alternating bilateral activity. Thus, the American or Australian crawl stroke is more complex motorically than are the elementary backstroke and the breaststroke. The crawl is, in fact, a very complex motor activity: The arms are moving in one alternating activity and the legs moving in a different alternating activity while, in addition, the head is moving in a very specified way and in a different rhythm. It is a demanding stroke motorically, and some individuals with developmental delay would find other strokes easier to execute.

Facility Considerations

There are several aspects of a facility that can affect an individual's participation in aquatic activities. Water and air temperatures, especially if they are below 82 °F, can adversely affect a student who is new to water experience. A water temperature of 86° to 90 °F is desirable, with air temperature a few degrees higher. These higher temperatures are especially beneficial for individuals who have cerebral palsy and for very young children. However, they are not recommended for people with multiple sclerosis, for whom the water temperature should be 85 °F or lower.

Few pools in the United States are built for easy access. Even many newer pools are not ideally constructed. Fortunately, adaptations can be made with removable ramps and other devices, and equipment (see Figure 24.3) is available for facilitating transfers and water entry.

The ideal teaching facility has different water depths, so that swimmers of any height can touch the bottom while walking. Some pools are designed with an adjustable bottom. With a portion

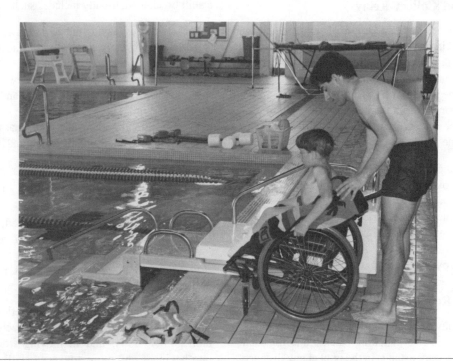

Figure 24.3 Transfer Tier to aid water entry. Photo courtesy of Triad Technologies.

of the bottom constructed to move up and down on hydraulic lifts (see Figure 24.4), the water depth can be easily and rapidly varied. This feature is ideal in programs for persons who have motor performance deficits.

Many other devices have been developed to accommodate smaller individuals in pools lacking sufficient shallow water. Some devices are available commercially. An example is the Tot Dock, designed for adapting a deep-water pool for use by small children (see Figure 24.5). Constructed and assembled in sections, the Tot Dock can be varied in size and in height.

For information on other aspects of facility

Figure 24.4 Pool with an adjustable bottom. Photo courtesy of the New York State School for the Blind, Mr. Robert Seibold, Superintendent and Coordinator. Reprinted with permission.

Figure 24.5 A Tot Dock to provide shallow water.

design that should be considered and modified if necessary, consult the list of resources at the end of this chapter.

Specific Techniques

Some impairments can cause difficulties for students in water adjustment and skill performance. The effects of the impairments will be discussed briefly in this section, with suggestions for helping the teacher adapt the skill so that the student can be successful. Obviously, all impairments cannot be dealt with here. Where effects or appropriate teaching methods are similar, impairments are grouped. Although generalization is necessary, it should always be remembered that no generalization applies to all individuals within a group. For this and other reasons, actual practice teaching of students with unique needs is a necessity. As stated by Dunn and Harris (1979) and Priest (1983), hands-on experience is essential for beginning teachers.

Cerebral Palsy

The extent to which cerebral palsy affects an individual in the water depends on the degree of involvement. A severely involved person will have problems with breath control, balance, coordination, and lack of flexibility. In addition, the person may have extreme hip flexion and exhibit some reflex patterns that make swimming more difficult. Warm water (90 °F plus) is highly desirable. Assessing the student's movement capability on land will help the teacher know what movements to expect in the water; however, many people who use a wheelchair for mobility on land can walk unaided in the water. This independent mobility is greatly rewarding to the individual and may in fact contribute to greater independence on land. Generally speaking, the teacher should follow these guidelines with cerebral-palsied students:

- Assess the student's ability to control head position. The prone position is unsafe, and even the supine position difficult, until the student can (a) control breathing, (b) lift the head voluntarily and independently, or (c) signal the teacher for lift to an upright position.
- Let the student adjust to the water in a vertical position. The vertical position is usually most restful for individuals with cerebral palsy.
- Spend time during each lesson on breath control. This is difficult for many individuals with cerebral palsy because of involvement of the oral musculature.
- Be aware that the student with cerebral palsy will probably be more comfortable on the back because of breathing freedom, but will have less effective movement patterns in that position because of limited shoulder and arm flexibility and increased hip flexion. Thus, it is better to start the student in supine position, then—when breath control is effective—move to prone position for greater mobility.
- Be alert to balance problems. A student who cannot recover a balanced stance when balance is lost must be worked with on a one-to-one basis.
- Work toward increasing range of motion and mobility. Most individuals will be non-buoyant, and the use of buoyancy aids may be desirable (see Figure 24.6). Many cerebral-palsied people are unable to do a motionless float but can nevertheless swim effectively.

It is important to encourage independent action: walking and swimming with or without flotation devices or aids. The general physical fitness level may be low, and specific activities to increase strength and endurance should be included in the aquatic program. Severely involved students will have limited range of movement and, sometimes, immobile joints and contractures. Teachers must be able to assess differing movement patterns and establish attainable goals.

Mental Retardation

The most common characteristic of mental retardation is slowness in learning; thus, the main effect

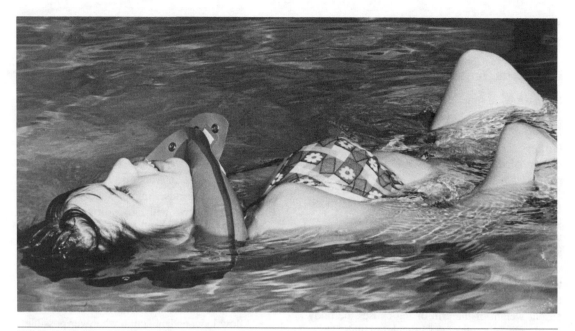

Figure 24.6 Head support with flotation to facilitate independence. Photo courtesy of the American Red Cross. Printed with permission.

of the impairment in aquatics may be a necessary modification in the style and approach of the teacher. Where learning is slow, more repetition is necessary; where attention span is limited, a greater variety of activities must be included. Lawrence and Hackett (1975) and Priest (1976a) have demonstrated aquatic activities to be useful in academic reinforcement. Mildly and moderately mentally retarded people usually have the motoric ability to do most swimming skills. The teacher may need to simplify some terminology or descriptions to allow for lower cognitive functioning. However, the movement patterns and skills may need no adaptation. A reminder here: Even in simplifying, age-appropriate vocabulary should be used.

In contrast with the mildly retarded, individuals who are severely or profoundly retarded usually do have motoric involvement. (The motoric deficit may be due partially to inactivity.) They also have greater difficulty in learning, so repetition is essential. A multisensory approach is most effective,

utilizing stimulation of as many senses as possible in the learning situation. These students may also have speech deficits, and swimming teachers should utilize parallel talk, describing aquatic activities while guiding the individual through them.

Water adjustment will be less rapid, ordinarily, because of the fear of new situations. The teacher needs to be reassuring, while spending much time on water adjustment and facility orientation. Tactile modeling, guiding the student's body part through a movement pattern, will be effective. Fear of new situations is not unusual, but conversely, because some severely retarded individuals seem to lack self-preservation awareness, extra care must be taken for their safety.

Most mentally retarded individuals will be capable of skills found in the traditional (American Red Cross or YMCA) courses. As the Special Olympics program has shown, many can excel in both skill and competition. U.S. Synchronized Swimming, the national governing body for that sport, reports that several states have synchronized swim teams for mentally retarded persons.

Orthopedic Impairments

Similarities in functional problems and in teaching considerations make it convenient to group these impairments under a common heading. Orthopedic impairments may adversely affect a person's balance, buoyancy, and range of movement in aquatic activities.

Balance. Most humans float in a vertical position, with the water at about eye level. Most of us also can learn to float in a supine position, or at least lie in that position with a minimum of motion. Once learned, balance is relatively easy to maintain. A person who has an arm or a leg missing will not float as easily in this position: The absent weight of the arm or leg causes the body to roll, with the side of the amputation high. Thus, the person must apply the principles of counterbalance, turning the head to the side of the amputation and swinging the remaining arm out to provide some support. Counteracting an undesirable action or effect with another action or movement is a necessary principle in aquatics for a person with an orthopedic impairment. This may be as simple as turning the head and lifting an arm, or it may involve the need for more forceful sculling with the arms to overcome the drag of nonfunctional legs and the like. Balance in the water changes as body composition changes, and balance must be relearned if the body changes drastically.

Buoyancy and Range of Movement. Orthopedic impairments affect buoyancy also. A person with no legs will float higher in the water than a person who has paralyzed legs: Both individuals will have to adjust the direction and force of their arm pull to compensate and achieve a comfortable position. Some people find that, because of a gain in weight (adipose tissue), they have too much buoyancy for swimming in ways previously learned, and must change their head position or arm pull in compensation.

Most people with lower body involvement have stronger upper bodies because their arms are used more. Some, however, have decreased general strength and greater susceptibility to fatigue. Activities to improve cardiovascular efficiency are often advisable. Sensory responses may be low or absent in the extremities of paraplegics and quadriplegics, and weight-bearing activities may be inadvisable for some individuals. The aquatic instructor should follow these guidelines:

- Individualize instruction. This is absolutely essential because impairments differ, and every "body" will move differently.
- Provide support until balance is learned and until the student can recover to an upright position from prone or supine.
- Spend time on water adjustment and watermanship. Comfort in the water is important.
- Be alert to signs of fatigue and chilling.
- Allow independent action wherever possible. Don't overprotect.

Individuals with orthopedic impairments should learn all basic strokes, determining from experience which they prefer or can do more easily. Any adaptation is acceptable. Generally speaking, students with good upper body strength and shoulder flexibility will do well with the crawl stroke and backstroke, and those with balance difficulty will do less well with the sidestroke. A stroke with underwater recovery, such as the elementary backstroke or beginner crawl, will be more easily executed by an individual with either balance or buoyancy difficulties.

Sport participation and competition today are such that people with orthopedic impairments have almost unlimited opportunity to compete and to excel (see Figure 24.7). A strong foundation of swimming skill and watermanship will help ensure their safety as they participate in available water sports.

Seizure Disorders

Most seizures can be controlled by medication, and people with seizure disorders participate in

Figure 24.7 A scuba diver: orthopedically impaired and *able*. Photo courtesy of Curt Barlow. Printed with permission.

most aquatic activities. The medical community is not in agreement about the effect of head-impact sports on seizure incidence, but a few physicians say that diving should be avoided. Some individuals find that increased fatigue affects them adversely, and aquatic instructors need to be aware of the fatigue level of their students. There does seem to be general agreement that people who are subject to seizures should not scuba dive (although some do), but other water sports are not a problem. It is obvious, however, that a person whose seizures may not be controlled should be accompanied by (or have near) someone who knows how to handle a seizure in the water. If an individual has a grand mal seizure while in the water, the instructor, guard, or aide should do the following:

- Support the person, keeping the head above water and tilted back to maintain an open airway.

- Keep the person away from the poolside and any equipment.
- Remove the person from the water after the seizure, using a mat or appropriate lift.
- Place the person on his or her side, and allow to rest briefly.
- Provide private rest if desired.
- Tell the person (if an adult) or the parent or supervisor (if a child) that the seizure occurred.

In many aquatic programs, a person who has a seizure is not allowed to return to the water the same day. That is not always the case, however, and instructors need to know the policies of the program in which they are teaching. It is always true, however, that someone who has multiple seizures, especially if the seizures last 10 min or more, is in danger of status epilepticus. If this occurs, the person should certainly not return to the water, and medical help should be obtained.

Other than the possibility of a seizure, epilepsy will probably have little effect on an individual's participation in aquatic activities. There is no need to adapt skills, but there is need for the aquatic instructor to know how to handle the seizure emergency.

Vision and Hearing Impairments

Vision or hearing loss does not essentially affect a person in the performance of aquatic skills. Students having these sensory impairments create a challenge in communication for the aquatic instructor. When one sensory capacity is impaired, communication through the other senses must be maximized.

Visual Impairment. Blind students should be given the opportunity to measure their environment by walking around the pool and dressing rooms and learning the shape and location of things through auditory and tactile input. When there is doubt about whether or not help is needed, it is important to ask. Some blind people are self-reliant and prefer to function independently, while others will appreciate and accept help with some tasks. Generally speaking, people with visual impairment will not be able to profit visually from demonstrations but will benefit from tactile modeling (having the motion guided by the instructor's hands, or feeling the action while someone else is executing it). In aquatics, as in all activities for the visually impaired, the teacher must speak with verbal accuracy and specificity. Teaching suggestions for use with visually impaired persons can be found in *Adapted Aquatics*, American Red Cross (1977a); *Aquatics for Special Populations*, YMCA of the USA (1987); and *Aquatic Recreation for the Blind*, Cordellos (1987).

Hearing Impairment. People with impaired hearing rely heavily on visual cues and are particularly adept at imitating actions they view. The hearing-impaired child who uses manual communication will usually delight in teaching sign language words to the teacher who does not know that language. Children with hearing impairment usually have no motoric or perceptual motor problem other than the hearing deficit and can become skilled swimmers. Some must wear ear molds while swimming.

There are various schools of thought regarding education for hearing-impaired individuals, and it is important that the aquatics program not conflict with the educational or therapeutic program. If children are enrolled in an oral program (where manual communication is not taught), it is essential that, in the swimming program, only those signs essential to safety be used. Teachers should speak clearly, and with normal lip movement, to facilitate speechreading. When speaking to hearing-impaired students, teachers must remember to face the student and to have the student face them. Demonstrations are essential, because fewer than one third of the speech sounds in the English language are visually discernible, and teachers cannot assume that even adept speechreaders will understand all of what is said to them. Additional teaching suggestions may be found in American Red Cross (1977) and YMCA (1987) materials.

Swimming as a Competitive Sport

Not everyone, whether disabled or able-bodied, wishes to participate in competitive events. For many people, the feeling of individual achievement, mastery of a skill, and a sense of independence provide exhilarating rewards. There are, after all, several kinds of competition, and competition with oneself in achieving a goal may be all the competition some people desire. Some, however, may wish to compete with others, and swimming competitively can have great rewards.

People with disabilities have opportunities to compete in swimming at local, regional, national, and international levels. The National Wheelchair Athletic Association (NWAA), the national governing body for regional and national competition wheelchair events, has rules and guidebooks available for many sports, including swimming. Many authors, including Miller (1985), have shown that wheelchair sports have been effective in motivating disabled adults and in contributing to public awareness of disabled people as people of ability.

In swimming, as in other competitive sports for disabled persons, participants are classified according to degree of disability. The NWAA classification system is presented in Figure 16.3. Competition is regulated by classification to maintain fair competition for people with all degrees of disability, in both men's and women's divisions. In wheelchair sports, rules are kept as close as possible to those used in regular amateur competition. National rules are used, with only minimal adaptation. (For the classification system used for athletes with cerebral palsy, see Table 15.1.)

Other Aquatic Sports

Water sports offer disabled persons greater independence, enhanced leisure and recreation activities, and opportunity to develop their abilities in an increasing variety of ways. Disabled persons are participating in almost all water sports, and for most of them, little adaptation is needed. According to the U.S. Coast Guard, more than 100,000 physically handicapped persons participate in boating activities in the United States. Coast Guard surveys show that paraplegics, amputees, hearing-impaired, blind, and partially sighted people operate power boats, race sailboats, and paddle canoes and kayaks on rivers and in wilderness areas—most with few modifications. Since the mid-60s, physically impaired people have engaged in scuba diving and waterskiing. Rowing and sculling have gained recently in popularity through the active participation and promotion of some championship rowers who are disabled. Whole books are devoted to some of these activities, and it is not possible to thoroughly cover all aquatic sports in one chapter. However, the more popular activities will be discussed in this section. The list of resources at the chapter's conclusion will guide those interested to further appropriate reading.

Lead-Up Skills for Boating Programs

Skills needed for operation of boats are type-specific—that is, a person needs one type of skill for paddling a canoe and another skill for sailcraft. However, there are some generalized lead-up skills, many of which can be taught in pools.

Use of Personal Flotation Devices (PFDs)

Federal law requires either the use of a personal flotation device (PFD) by every passenger or the availability of one for every passenger in every craft. In order to effectively use a PFD, a person must first understand its importance and then be able to wear it properly. All students should be given an explanation and demonstration of PFD use. Students who are too physically impaired to take an active part in this process should still be

encouraged to give accurate instructions to whoever is helping them with the PFD and should always check to see that it is properly secured.

Students should also have the opportunity to learn for themselves that the PFD will really keep them afloat in deep water. From practicing a back float in shallow water while wearing the PFD, the student should progress to floating in deep water and eventually to falling off the dock or deck into deep water until he or she is comfortable in relying on, and convinced of the necessity for, the PFD.

Craft Familiarization

Canoes, kayaks, and small sailboats can be brought to the pool for initial familiarization. This is often done in colder climates or where initial instruction takes place in winter to prepare for outdoor participation.

Boarding and Debarking

Boarding and debarking and even elementary handling techniques can be taught in a pool or on quiet water. Boarding and debarking are often the most difficult part of boat operation for disabled people.

Capsize Procedures

Practice of capsize procedures can be difficult, and the initial trial should be closely supervised by the instructor. Although an able-bodied individual might be able to react quickly when a craft capsizes to avoid getting hurt, a boater who is physically impaired, cannot see or hear, or has slower mental processes may be at a disadvantage. A supervised capsize of a stationary craft, with the instructor either on board or in the water, is a good way to start. The instructor initiates the capsize by submerging the near gunwale. As the boat comes over, the instructor catches the far gunwale to keep it from hitting any of the students and then assists them to supporting positions on the craft. This procedure results in a much slower capsize, giving the students a chance to understand what is happening and to react accordingly. As the students become familiar with what occurs during a capsize, the instructor can let them tip their crafts independently in simulation of an actual emergency.

Canoeing and Kayaking

Canoeing and kayaking experiences can vary from a quiet and leisurely paddle on a lake to an exhilarating and breathtaking ride through the rapids of a giant river, and people with handicapping conditions do both of these things. Participation in the sport requires the ability to sit and maintain balance and the ability to use the arms and hands. White water kayaking and canoeing require better balance and upper body control than activities on flat water. Many amputees and paraplegics are expert white water kayakers and participate in demanding wilderness trips. Backrests or special seats are often used to reduce fatigue and aid balance. Basic canoeing and kayaking skills are best taught in warm pools, although in warm climates many programs are conducted completely out-of-doors. There is competition, including Olympic competition, in paddling sports, but most canoeing and kayaking, for both disabled and able-bodied people, is done for personal challenge and enjoyment. Adaptive equipment includes such items as high-back seats, custom-made hand grips and mitts, devices for one-arm paddling, and special docks with loading slings. There are hundreds of local canoe clubs that now have persons with disabilities among their membership. The American Canoe Association, Outward Bound, and Vinland Center all have programs that actively support the involvement of disabled persons in this sport. There are also excellent programs sponsored by universities, the Department of Education, and organizations such as the Council for Exceptional Children.

Sailing

Sailing offers freedom; fresh air; the exhilaration of speed, motion, and the sounds of the sea; and an opportunity to either participate or compete on equal terms with able-bodied people. Small sailboats can be handled with ease by many disabled people, and there are amputees and paraplegics who ocean race. Sailing instruction has been available to blind people for years in England, Canada, and the United States.

It is often true that, for those with handicapping conditions, the only uncomfortable or risky part of sailing is getting on and off the boat. Boats, piers, and embarking procedures and facilities, like so many things in our society, were made for individuals having unimpaired mobility. Mobility is useful in other aspects of small-boat sailing: handling the tiller, coming about, and changing positions to effect trim, to name a few. Nevertheless, obstacles can be overcome and adaptations made, so that disabled people can sail competently. In England, several special seats have been developed, which allow easy movement from one side of the boat to the other. The British Sports Association for the Disabled (1983) has done considerable work in the area of aquatic sports, and its book, *Water Sports for the Disabled*, is a fine reference on many aspects of aquatic sports, sailing in particular.

Rowing

Rowing is often seen as an ''Ivy League'' sport, largely associated with east coast colleges. While colleges and prep schools in that region often do have rowing teams, the activity is certainly not confined there. Recreational rowing is growing greatly in popularity, and colleges all over the United States have rowing teams. Stoll (1986) reported on a program of U.S. Rowing, the national governing body for the sport. Through its program Rowing in the Mainstream, U.S. Rowing is actively working to propagate the sport by initiating programs that are community centered and accessible to all populations. Most of the communities selected had rowing programs, but none of the programs combined the activities of able-bodied and mobility-impaired individuals. Rowing in the Mainstream is an outgrowth of an earlier University of Michigan program, called Freedom on the River, which involved amputees, quadriplegics, and other mobility-impaired individuals. The boats used in these rowing programs are stable recreational shells. For use by disabled persons, the shells are outfitted with a fixed molded fiberglass seat, a seat belt, and a chest strap for those with high-level spinal injuries. Mitts and straps are used for quadriplegics.

Rowing can be excellent exercise. Enjoyment of this sport certainly is not limited to east coast college students but can be available to anyone, disabled or able-bodied.

Waterskiing

Opportunities for disabled persons to engage in waterskiing have been expanding for more than 20 years. Blind people and amputees have skied in many clubs for years, and the development of the sitz ski (a sled-like device) and the ski seat opened the sport to paraplegics. In general, a strong back and strong legs are desirable for skiing, although many single-leg amputees and unilateral amputees ski well. Both the American Water Ski Association and the British Disabled Water Ski Association have ongoing activities and instructors trained to teach skiing to disabled persons. Cordellos (1981) says that it was the excitement, freedom, and movement of waterskiing that changed his life. In his earlier work (1976), Cordellos discussed both waterskiing and sailboarding for the blind, as well as many other water sports. Organizations such as the Christian Family Ski School in Winter Haven, the Cypress Gardens Ski School, and the Water Ski Club of San Francisco teach waterskiing to the blind and other disabled persons on a regular basis. Since 1983,

Norway has conducted international ski competition, including trick skiing, for blind athletes. Slalom, barefoot, and jump skiing are well within the capacity of blind water-skiers.

Wide tow bars, or two bars that can be coupled and detached, are often used in teaching blind or amputee skiers. Ski booms are used for more advanced practice. A sling device attached to a harness around the shoulder is used by some single-arm amputees, thus equalizing the pull between the arm and the body. (There is a quick release device for both the skier and the boat operator.)

Scuba Diving

The number of disabled people involved in scuba diving has increased considerably in the past few years, although there have been diving clubs for the disabled since the early 70s. While both the medical and diving communities posed considerable resistance to the entrance of disabled persons to the sport, scuba diving proved to be an area (Priest 1985) where disabled persons intended to be involved, regardless of opposition. While it may be true that people subject to seizures should not engage in scuba diving, many other disabilities do not interfere with safe participation. Scuba is, of course, a high-risk sport, and particularly because more research is needed on several factors, the risks need to be made clear to participants. However, as Robinson (1986a) has shown, some of the greatest hurdles to overcome have been the attitudes of society about disabled persons. As she has also shown (Robinson 1986b), there are many effective techniques for adapting skills and equipment to enable people with disabilities to enjoy the underwater world (see Figure 24.8). With modified techniques and equipment, risk can be maintained within acceptable limits.

One of the problems surrounding the involvement of disabled people in scuba diving has been the wording of course requirements in the training programs of certifying agencies. A 50-yd flutter

Figure 24.8 Scuba diving with disabilities—an accessible adventure sport. Photo courtesy of Curt Barlow. Printed with permission.

kick is manifestly impossible for a paraplegic or a quadriplegic. Priest (1985) and others have suggested that criteria should be reworded to reflect performance goals rather than specific skills. In an example of this concept, the British Sub-Aqua club specifies a "level of competence" to be expected of disabled divers. The competencies include the following:

- Ability to drive to the dive site
- Ability to look after diving equipment
- Ability to swim unaided, dive, adjust equipment, perform safety exercises, swim in the company of a buddy diver, execute a controlled ascent, and swim to a boat on the surface

Scuba diving for disabled persons is now being actively encouraged by certifying agencies such as the National Association of Underwater Instruc-

tors (NAUI), the Professional Association of Diving Instructors (PADI), and the YMCA in the U.S. and Canada. The Handicapped Scuba Association in California continues to promote scuba for disabled persons through activities, films, and printed materials. Scuba diving is an example of a sport providing personal challenge in a unique environment.

Summary

This chapter has offered an overview of aquatics for individuals with special needs. The benefits of aquatics have been stressed, teaching suggestions given, and some specific handicapping conditions examined in relation to function in the water. In addition to swimming, other aquatic sports have been discussed, including boating, waterskiing, and scuba diving. In these and other physically demanding sports, disabled individuals have shown ingenuity in adaptation, stamina and tenacity in participation, ability to overcome physical and psychological obstacles, and tremendous drive for achievement. Aquatic sports, with all their concomitant benefits, are pathways to achievement and normalization in the lives of disabled persons.

Bibliography

American Red Cross. (1974). *Basic rescue and water safety*. Washington, DC: Author.

American Red Cross. (1977a). *Adapted aquatics*. New York: Doubleday.

American Red Cross. (1977b). *Methods in Adapted Aquatics*. Washington, DC: Author.

British Sports Association for the Disabled. (1983). *Water sports for the disabled*. West Yorkshire, England: EP Publishing.

Cordellos, H. (1981). *Breaking through*. Mountain View, CA: Anderson World.

Cordellos, H. (1987). *Aquatic recreation for the blind*. Berkeley, CA: LaBuy Printing.

Dunn, J., & Harris, J. (Eds.) (1979). *Physical education for the handicapped: Meeting the need through inservice education*. Corvallis, OR: Oregon State University.

Lawrence, C., & Hackett, L. (1975). *Water learning, a new adventure*. Palo Alto, CA: PEEK Publications.

Miller, B. (1985). Coaching the wheelchair athlete. *National Aquatics Journal,* **1**(2), 10-12.

Priest, L. (1976a). Academic remediation in aquatics. *Therapeutic Recreation Journal,* **X**(2), 35-37.

Priest, L. (1976b). Movement exploration in aquatics. *Therapeutic Recreation Journal,* **X**(2), 35-37.

Priest, L. (1976c). Developmental pool activities for fun. *Challenge,* **11**(3), 5.

Priest, L. (1979). Integrating the disabled into aquatics programs. *Journal of Physical Education and Recreation,* **50**(2), 57-59.

Priest, L. (1983). Instructor training in adapted aquatics. *National Association for Girls and Women in Sport Guide*. Reston, VA: American Alliance for Health, Physical Education, Recreation and Dance.

Priest, L. (1985). Diving for the disabled. *National Aquatics Journal,* **1**(1), 14-15.

Robinson, J. (1986a). Diving with disabilities. *National Aquatics Journal,* **2**(1), 8-9.

Robinson, J. (1986b). *Scuba diving with disabilities*. Champaign, IL: Human Kinetics.

Stoll, E. (1986). Rowing in the mainstream. *National Aquatics Journal,* **2**(3), 8.

Van Rossen, D., & Woodrich, B. (1979). *Competitive swimming for new champions*. New York: McGraw-Hill.

Winnick, J.P., & Short, F.X. (1981). *Special athletic opportunities for individuals with handicapping conditions*. Brockport, NY: State University of New York.

YMCA of the USA. (1987). *Aquatics for special populations*. Champaign, IL: Human Kinetics.

Resources

Written

American Red Cross. (1981). *Swimming and aquatic safety*. Washington, DC: Author. This book describes all skills in the American Red Cross swimming program, with teaching suggestions for instructors.

Council for National Cooperation in Aquatics. (1986). *Swimming pools: A guide to their planning, design, and operation*. Champaign, IL: Human Kinetics. This comprehensive book on planning and operating swimming pools has a chapter on pools for disabled persons.

deVarona, D. (1984). *Hydro-aerobics*. New York: Macmillan. An aquatic exercise program devised and used by deVarona is explained in detail.

Krasevec, J., & Grimes, D. (1984). *Hydrorobics*. Champaign, IL: Leisure Press. Water exercise is defined and explained, with an individual exercise program outlined in detail.

Audiovisual

Allen, J. (Director), & Priest, L. (Technical Advisor). (1974). *Focus on ability* [Film]. Washington, DC: American Red Cross. The film offers an overview of the benefits of aquatic activity for disabled persons, with teaching suggestions for instructors.

Handicapped Scuba Association. (1986). *Freedom in depth* [Videotape]. San Clemente, CA: Author. An action-packed film about disabled scuba divers, made by disabled scuba divers.

Lawrence, C. (Producer). (1969). *Splash* [Film]. Saratoga, CA: Active Learning Films. This production shows benefits of aquatic activities and academic reinforcement through aquatics for severely handicapped children.

Other

American Canoe Association, 8580 Cinderbed Rd., Suite 1900, Newington, VA 22122. This membership organization promotes canoe and kayak education and participation.

American Red Cross, 17th and D Street NW, Washington, DC 20006. The American Red Cross develops aquatic materials and promotes aquatic education and instructor training through 3,000 local chapters.

American Water Ski Association, 799 Overlook Drive, P.O. Box 191, Winter Haven, FL 33882. This organization promotes waterskiing and safety education for recreational waterskiing.

Council for National Cooperation in Aquatics, 901 West New York Street, Indianapolis, IN 46223. This is a nonprofit educational organization promoting all aspects of aquatics and aquatic education. A quarterly journal is available to members.

Handicapped Boaters Association, P.O. Box 1134, Ansonia Station, New York, NY 10023. This association develops materials and promotes programs in boating for disabled persons.

Handicapped Scuba Association, 1104 El Prado, San Clemente, CA 92672. The HSA conducts training programs for scuba instructors and disabled divers.

National Association of Underwater Instructors, P.O. Box 14650, Montclair, CA 91763. This certifying agency for scuba instructors develops resource material for instructors.

Professional Association of Diving Instructors, 1243 East Warner Avenue, Santa Ana, CA 92705. Another certifying agency for scuba instructors, this association develops resource material for instructors.

United States Coast Guard Office of Boating Safety, 400 Seventh Street SW, Washington, DC 20560. The Coast Guard office develops materials, gives grants for programs and materials, and promotes safe boating in all coastal waterways.

U.S. Rowing, 201 S. Capitol, Suite 400, Indianapolis, IN 46223. The national governing body for competitive rowing in the U.S. promotes recreational and competitive rowing.

United States Synchronized Swimming, 201 S. Capitol, Suite 510, Indianapolis, IN 46223. The national governing body for synchronized swimming in the U.S. develops materials and promotes the sport.

YMCA Scuba Program, 6083 Oakbrook Parkway, Norcross, GA 30093. This agency regulates and promotes the teaching of scuba diving in YMCAs.

CHAPTER 25

Team Sports

David L. Porretta

Team sports are a popular way for disabled individuals to become involved in physical activity. In mainstreamed settings, impaired individuals have excelled and continue to excel in amateur as well as professional team sports, and many interscholastic and recreational sport programs encourage participation of disabled persons on an integrated basis.

Mainstreamed sport competition is especially encouraged for people with auditory impairments. In sports like floor hockey, basketball, and volleyball, which are played in a relatively small area, few modifications need to be made. In volleyball, the beginning or ending of play may be signaled by an official pulling the net. On the other hand, sports played out-of-doors on a large field may require somewhat more modification. For instance, in football and soccer, flags and hand gestures can supplement whistles as signals. For deaf football players, a bass drum on the sideline may signal the snap of the ball instead of the quarterback's verbal cadence. There are teams composed entirely of deaf players who compete against nonimpaired individuals.

A number of organizations now provide sport programs for disabled athletes. The American Athletic Association for the Deaf (AAAD), one such organization, offers competition solely for those with hearing impairments. Team events include volleyball, soccer, and basketball, in which athletes are classified according to gender and degree of hearing loss. These sports are regularly featured at the World Games for the Deaf and follow international sports federation rules with some minor adjustments. Because few modifications are needed for hearing-impaired people to effectively participate in team sports, the focus in the remainder of this chapter will be on people with other types of disabilities.

Other sport organizations, such as the United States Cerebral Palsy Athletic Association (USCPAA) and the National Beep Baseball Association (NBBA), have been formed to meet the needs of disabled individuals for segregated sport competition. Beep baseball, goal ball, wheelchair soccer, and wheelchair softball are relatively new team sports that have been designed for players with disabilities. Official rules for these sports are described in this chapter.

Basketball

Basketball is a popular activity in both physical education and sport programs. It incorporates the skills of running, jumping, shooting, passing, and dribbling. Varying or modifying skills, rules, and/or equipment can allow disabled individuals to effectively participate in the game. Generally speaking, most ambulatory persons can participate in basketball with few or no modifications. However, those with severe mental impairments or mobility problems may need more restrictive settings, including segregated competition—for example, wheelchair basketball for people in wheelchairs.

Game Skills

Shooting and Passing

Bounce passing is advised for partially sighted players because the sound of the bounce lets them know from what direction the ball is coming. Bounce passing also provides more time for players with unilateral upper limb involvement to catch the ball. One-hand shots and passes should be encouraged for players who use crutches or have upper-limb amputations. Players in wheelchairs find the one-hand pass useful for long passes; when shooting at the basket, however, they often prefer the two-hand set shot (especially for longer shots) because both arms can put more force behind the ball. For people with ambulation difficulties, a net placed directly beneath the basket during shooting practice facilitates return of the ball. Players with upper-limb involvement may find it helpful to trap or cradle the ball against the upper body when trying to catch a pass.

Dribbling

For players with poor eye-hand coordination or poor vision, dribbling can be performed with a larger ball. For those having poor body coordination, it may be necessary to permit periodic bouncing while running or walking, although they can dribble the ball continually when standing still. Players in wheelchairs may need to dribble to the left or right of the chair and carry the ball in the lap when wheeling.

Lead-Up Games and Activities

Horse

Two or more players may play this shooting game, competing against each other from varying distances from the goal. To begin the game, a player takes a shot from anywhere on the court. If the shot is made, the next player must duplicate the shot (type of shot, distance, etc.). Failure to make the shot earns that player the letter H. If, however, the second player makes the shot, an additional shot may be attempted from anywhere on the court for the opponent to match. Players attempt shots that they feel the opponent may have difficulty making. The first person to acquire all of the letters H-O-R-S-E loses.

Spot Shot

This activity involves shooting a playground ball in any manner to a basket approximately 45 in. high from six different spots on the floor, ranging from 2 to 5 ft away. Two shots are attempted from each spot, for a total of 12 shots. The player's score is the number of shots made.

Other Activities

Other basketball lead-up activities may include bouncing a beach ball over a specified distance, shooting a playground ball into a large barrel, or dropping a tennis ball into a large container.

Variations and Modifications

Sport

In Special Olympics competition, the game follows rules developed by the Fédération Internationale de Basketball Amateur (FIBA) for all multinational and international competition (Special Olympics, 1986). The only significant modifications to play are the following:

- Each team member must play at least one quarter of the game.
- Fouls are called only in rough contact.
- Games consist of 6-min quarters.
- Players are allowed to shuffle the feet while holding the ball as long as they do not change direction.

- Players can take one extra step when gaining possession of the ball.
- Players are not allowed to position themselves around the key during a free throw in an attempt to rebound a ball that misses the basket.

The National Wheelchair Basketball Association (NWBA) has also modified the game for people confined to wheelchairs (Figure 25.1) (NWBA, 1980). These are the major rule modifications:

- The wheelchair is considered part of the player.
- Players must stay firmly seated in the chair at all times, especially during a jump ball.
- Offensive players may not remain in the key more than 5 s.
- Dribbling consists of simultaneously wheeling the chair and dribbling the ball (however, the player may not take more than two consecutive pushes without bouncing the ball).

- Three or more pushes results in a traveling violation.
- The ball is awarded to the other team if the footrest or antitip casters of the player's wheelchair touch the floor while the player has possession of the ball.
- The feet (especially those with some remaining function) may not be used to aid the player at any time.

Skill Events

Special Olympics offers shooting, passing, and dribbling skills competition. In field goal shooting competition, athletes shoot the ball in any manner from any distance on the court. For each basket made, the athlete receives one point. Two 30-s trials are given, and the best total score of the two trials is counted.

In speed passing competition, the athlete passes the ball in any manner (as long as it is thrown and

Figure 25.1 Wheelchair basketball. Photo courtesy of *Sports 'N Spokes* magazine. Printed with permission.

caught in the air from behind a restraining line) against a wall 7 ft 10 in. away. Passes that bounce between the wall and the line do not count. One point is awarded for each time the ball hits the wall and is caught. The best score of two 30-s trials is counted.

Dribbling competition requires the athlete to dribble the ball past five cones (10 ft apart) in a figure-eight pattern. When the last cone is reached, the athlete continues back to the starting line. One point is awarded each time the midpoint of the cone is reached.

Other Variations and Modifications

Game rules may be simplified by reducing the types of fouls players are allowed to commit. A playground ball may be used, and the basket can be lowered and/or enlarged. The game area may be restricted to half court for players with mobility impairments, such as those using lower-limb prostheses. Shorter play periods and frequent substitutions may be incorporated into the game for players with cardiac or asthmatic conditions. Lighter-weight balls can be used by those with insufficient arm strength.

Floor Hockey

The game of floor hockey is gaining popularity in physical education and sport programs across the country. Game skills include stick handling (fielding, passing, and dribbling the puck) and running. With appropriate variations and modifications, the game can be played by most disabled individuals.

Game Skills

Stick Handling

In order to facilitate better fielding, passing, shooting, and dribbling, the poly hockey stick blade can be enlarged for players with motor control problems or visual impairments. The size and length

of the stick are important factors for some disabled individuals. Lighter sticks should be available for smaller players and those with muscle weaknesses, and shorter sticks for those in wheelchairs.

When passing or shooting on goal, visually impaired players can push the puck with the stick rather than attempting a backswing before striking the puck. They will find playing with an enlarged and brightly colored puck very helpful. It is also helpful if a coach or a sighted teammate calls to them when the puck is passed in their direction.

Players with crutches may use the crutch as a stick to strike the puck as long as sufficient balance can be maintained. Those with crutches or leg braces can hit the puck more successfully from a stationary position. Players with unilateral upper-limb deficiencies or amputations can control the stick with the nonimpaired limb because sticks are light in weight. However, for those with poor grip, arm, or shoulder strength, the stick can be secured to the limb with a Velcro strap. Wheelchair players may need to stress passing or shooting rather than trying to dribble past opponents. When moving the chair, they usually place the stick in the lap.

Lead-Up Games and Activities

Shooting Activity

The player attempts 10 shots on goal from a distance determined by the teacher or coach. A goalie is not used. However, Indian clubs, tires, or cones are placed at various locations along the goal line. The player must score a goal without hitting the objects.

Puck Dribble Race

The player starts the race from behind a starting line. On command, the player dribbles the puck as quickly as possible in a forward direction for a distance of 32 ft 6 in.

Other Activities

Additional activities may include pushing a puck to the goal as fast as possible using a shuffleboard stick, kicking the puck with the feet as fast as possible to the goal, dribbling the puck as quickly as possible around a circle of cones, and shooting a sock stuffed in the shape of a ball (sock ball) with a poly hockey stick under table legs and into a large box turned on its side.

Variations and Modifications

Sport

As played under Special Olympics rules (Special Olympics, 1986), floor hockey is very similar to ice hockey. The game can be played on any safe, level, properly marked surface 39 ft 6 in. by 79 ft 9 in. Six players compose a team (one goalkeeper, two defenders, and three forwards). All players wear helmets and distinctive team markings. Players use sticks that resemble broom handles, except for the goalie, who uses a regulation ice hockey goalkeeper's stick. The goalie must wear a mask and helmet; pads and gloves are optional. The puck is a circular felt disc (approximately 8 in. in diameter) with a hole in the center. The end of the stick is placed in the hole in order to control the puck. Face-offs, offsides, and minor and major violations are part of the game. Games consist of three 9-min periods of running time, and the clock is stopped every 3 min to exchange lines. For penalties and "frozen" puck situations, the clock is also stopped.

Poly hockey, very similar to floor hockey, is also played in Special Olympics competition. The number of players is the same as in floor hockey, and all must wear helmets. However, poly hockey is played on a gymnasium floor used for basketball. Equipment includes a plastic hockey set, a set of goals, and a goalie mask. Positions include two forwards, two defenders, a center, and a goalie. Forwards must remain on their offensive side of the floor and defenders must stay on their defensive side. The center is the only player to move the full length of the court. Three 8-min

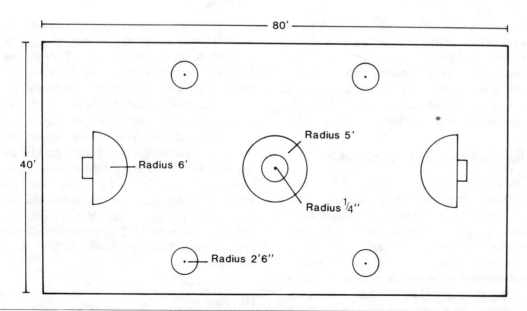

Figure 25.2 Floor hockey court. *Note*. From *Official Special Olympics Sports Rules* (p. 147) by Special Olympics, 1986, Washington, DC: Joseph P. Kennedy, Jr. Foundation. Copyright 1986 by Special Olympics. Printed with permission.

periods compose a game. Penalties are similar to those called in floor hockey (Figure 25.2).

Skill Events

Special Olympics offers skills competition in puck control, shooting for accuracy, and passing. In the puck control event, the athlete stickhandles the puck past six cones (10 ft apart) for a distance of 68 ft 3 in. and then shoots the puck at the goal. The time elapsed from the beginning of the event to the shot on goal is subtracted from 25. One point is also subtracted for each cone missed, and 5 points are added to the score if the goal is made.

In the shooting-for-accuracy event, the athlete takes five shots from directly in front of the goal from a distance of 16 ft 3 in. The goal is divided into the following point sections: 5 points for a shot entering the goal in either of the upper two corners, 3 points for a shot entering the goal in either of the lower two corners, 2 points for a shot entering the goal in the upper middle section, 1 point for a shot entering the goal in the lower middle section, and 0 points for a shot not entering the goal.

The passing event requires that the athlete make five passes from behind a passing line located 26 ft from two cones placed 39 in. apart. The athlete is awarded 5 points each time the puck passes between the two cones, while 3 points are awarded whenever the puck hits a cone. The total score is the sum of the scores for the five passes made.

Other Variations and Modifications

In order to accommodate players with varying ability levels, the game may be played on a smaller playing surface and with larger or smaller goals. To make the game less strenuous, a whiffle ball, a sock ball, a yarn or Nerf ball, or a large reinforced beanbag may be used. If players have impaired mobility, increasing the number of players on each team may be helpful. Body contact can be eliminated for players with bone or soft tissue conditions like juvenile rheumatoid arthritis or osteogenesis imperfecta. Penalties may be imposed on players who deliberately bump into opponents in wheelchairs.

Soccer

Soccer is included in many physical education and sport programs. Skills in soccer include running, dribbling, kicking, trapping, heading, and catching (goalie only) the ball. Because of its large playing area and continuous play, soccer requires stamina. However, the game can be varied or modified so that disabled persons can participate in any setting. For those with very minimal impairments (e.g., mild learning disability), no modifications in the game are necessary. Where integration is not possible or feasible, Special Olympics and USCPAA provide segregated competition for individuals in this popular sport.

Game Skills

Kicking

Whether for dribbling, passing, or shooting, the skill of kicking is of paramount importance in the game of soccer. People with upper-limb amputations can learn to kick the ball effectively, but they may have difficulty with longer kicks because the arms are normally abducted and extended to maintain balance. Individuals with unilateral lower-limb amputations may use a prothesis for support when passing or shooting the ball. Players may be unable to kick the ball with a prosthetic device; however, crutches can be used to "kick" the ball. Wheelchair users will be able to dribble the ball by using the footrests of the chair to contact the ball and push it forward. They can also be allowed to throw the ball because they do not have use of the lower limbs.

Heading

Most players can learn to head the ball successfully, although heading should not be encouraged for players with conditions such as hydrocephaly or atlantoaxial instability. Mentally handicapped as well as visually impaired players may find using a balloon or beach ball helpful for learning to head because these balls are soft and give players time to make body adjustments prior to contact with the ball. Players with upper-limb amputations can be very effective in heading the ball. Wheelchair players will be able to head the ball effectively as long as it comes directly to them. However, the distance the ball can be headed will be limited because the chair's backrest and the sitting position limit the player's ability to exert force on the ball.

Trapping and Catching

Most players can effectively learn to trap the ball. Foam balls are good to use with players who are hesitant to have the ball hit the body. Wheelchair users may have some difficulty trapping because the sitting position impedes the reception of the ball on the chest and abdomen. However, some players learn to trap the ball in their laps. When playing goalie, those in wheelchairs can catch effectively as long as upper-limb involvement is minimal. Most one-arm players will find it difficult to catch while in the goalie position. In this case, they should be encouraged to slap, trap, or hit the ball instead of trying to catch it.

Lead-Up Games and Activities

Circle Soccer

The game may be played on a playground with two teams, preferably of 8 to 10 players each. Each team forms a semicircle, and then both teams join to form a complete circle approximately 30 ft in diameter. Players of each team try to kick a soccer ball below shoulder level past their opponents. After each score, players on both teams rotate one position to the right. A team scores 1 point each time the ball passes the opponents' semicircle, and 1 point is scored against a team that uses their hands to stop the ball.

Accuracy Kick

This activity involves kicking a playground ball into a goal area 5 ft wide (with flag-sticks at each end) from a distance of 10 ft. A player is allowed three kicks from either a standing or a sitting position. The player receives 3 points each time a ball is kicked into the goal, 2 points each time the ball hits a flag-stick but does not pass through the goal, and 1 point each time the ball is kicked in the direction of the goal but does not reach the goal. Following three kicks, players' scores are compared.

Other Activities

Additional activities may include heading a beach ball into a large goal area from a short distance, dribbling a soccer ball in a circular manner around stationary players as fast as possible, throwing the ball in-bounds for distance, keeping a balloon in the air by kicking it, punting the ball for distance, and scooter soccer.

Variations and Modifications

Sport

Recently, modifications in the sport of soccer have been introduced by the USCPAA. That organization has developed rules for competition in both wheelchair soccer and seven-player soccer (NASCP, 1979). Games are open to both sexes and are composed of two 25-min periods.

In wheelchair soccer (Figure 25.3) (called wheelchair team handball in international competition) all players must participate in nonelectric wheelchairs except Class I athletes. As a result, for the other classes, chair movement must be accomplished by use of the hands and/or feet. The following modifications apply to wheelchair soccer:

- Teams are composed of at least nine players each.
- Teams must include at least one player from

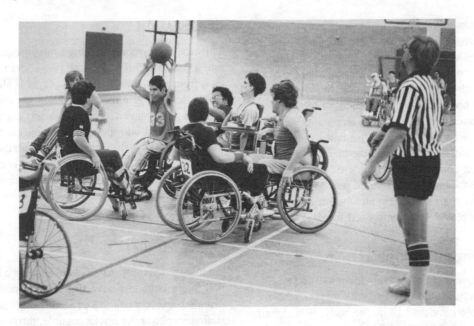

Figure 25.3 Wheelchair soccer. Photo courtesy of Jerry McCole and the Dallas Riders Disabled Sports Association. Printed with permission.

each of the Classes I, II, III, and VI, along with any combination of players from Classes IV through VI.

- The game may be played either indoors or out-of-doors on a hard surface suitable for wheelchairs.
- Boundaries have the same dimensions as for a basketball court.
- A 10-in. rubber playground ball is used.
- The goal area is 5 ft 6 in. high, 9 ft wide, and 4 ft deep.
- The wheelchair, an affected limb, and/or the body can be used to move the ball.
- Dribbling the ball with one or both hands is permitted.
- A maximum of 3 s is permitted for a player to hold or maintain possession of the ball before attempting a pass, dribble, or shot on goal.
- Fewer but not more than nine players are allowed on the playing area at one time.
- Unnecessary roughness and holding or running into another wheelchair results in penalties.

Ambulatory players (those without assistive devices) are eligible to play seven-player soccer, known in international competition simply as soccer. Rules generally follow Fédération Internationale de Football Association (FIFA) standards. Along with the seven-player limit, the modifications are as follows:

- The playing field dimensions are to be a maximum of 27 by 55 yd.
- Teams must be composed of at least one Class VI and no more than four Class VIII players.
- An out-of-bounds ball is returned to play by a kick.

In Special Olympics, the sport is played as Six-A-Side Soccer, and rules follow FIFA standards (Special Olympics, 1986). The following modifications are applied:

- The field dimensions must be a maximum of 146 ft by 178 ft 9 in. and a minimum of 52 ft

by 84 ft 6 in. (the recommended size is 130 ft by 162 ft 6 in.).
- The goal area must be 6 ft 6 in. high and 13 ft wide.
- The duration of the game is two 15-min halves.
- There are no offsides.

Skill Events

Special Olympics offers skill competition in passing, dribbling, and shooting. In the passing event, the player dribbles a soccer ball a distance of approximately 55 ft to a passing line. At the line, the player must bring the ball under control and pass it between two cones approximately 4 ft apart and about 18 ft from the pass line. Two sets of cones are located at a 45° angle from the pass line; the player has the option of passing to either set of cones.

The dribbling event requires players to dribble past five cones (8 ft 11 in. from each other) in a figure-eight pattern for a distance of 53 ft 7 in. The athlete's score is determined by subtracting from 50 the time taken to dribble the above distance.

In the shooting event, the player kicks the ball to a goal from a distance of approximately 40 ft. Point values are given to various locations within the goal, with higher values being assigned to areas directly inside either goal post. The player's score is the total of the scores on five shots.

Other Variations and Modifications

For a simplified game, fewer than 11 players can participate and field dimensions can be reduced. For players with low stamina, a partially deflated ball (which does not travel as fast as a fully inflated ball) can be used, and frequent rest periods, substitutions, or time-outs can be incorporated into the game. A soft Nerf or foam soccer ball can be used; in some cases, a cage ball can replace a soccer ball. Players with upper limb deficiencies may be allowed to kick the ball in-bounds on a throw-in. Additional players may be situated along the sidelines to take throw-ins for their teams.

Penalty kicks may also be employed for penalties occurring outside of goal areas. To avoid mass conversion on the ball, players can be required to play in specific zone areas.

Softball

Softball uses the skills of throwing, catching, fielding, hitting, and running. With certain modifications, the game can be played in an integrated setting by most disabled persons, though visually or mobility-impaired players may find competing in a segregated setting more appropriate. The National Wheelchair Softball Association (NWSA) sponsors competition for athletes in wheelchairs, while NBBA sponsors competition for blind players.

Game Skills

Throwing

Visually impaired people will throw with better accuracy if the person receiving the ball communicates verbally with the thrower. For players with small hands or hand deformities the use of a smaller or foam ball is recommended. Cerebral-palsied individuals, because of control problems, may find using a slightly heavier ball more advantageous. Individuals with lower limb disability will be able to throw the ball quite well. However, they will have difficulty throwing for distance because rotation of the body may be limited. A player with one upper limb will be able to throw the ball without much difficulty.

Catching

Visually impaired players will more easily learn to catch if a large, brightly colored ball is initially rolled or bounced. A beep baseball, described in this section under the heading ''Sport,'' will be most helpful. Wheelchair users and those with crutches or with braces may wish to use a large

glove. Players with one upper limb will be able to catch with one hand as long as eye-hand coordination is well developed. A glove is helpful to most one-arm players who have a remaining segment of the absent limb, provided they have mastered the technique of catching the ball and then freeing it from the glove for a throw. (After the catch, the player removes the glove with the ball by placing it under the armpit of the limb segment. The hand is then quickly drawn from the glove to grasp the ball for a throw.)

Fielding

An oversize glove can facilitate fielding for players with poor eye-hand coordination. Fielders should face in the direction from which the ball is being hit, and visually impaired players should be encouraged to listen for ground balls moving along the ground. Visually impaired players and those with assistive devices or in wheelchairs can be paired with sighted, able-bodied players for assistance in fielding. In most cases, the assisting player can direct the visually impaired teammate in intercepting the ball. While a fielder in a wheelchair should be able to intercept the ball independently, the assisting player can retrieve it from the ground after interception and hand it to the disabled player for the throw.

Batting

Fait and Dunn (1984) describe a modified batting technique for visually impaired players. Players batting right handed position themselves by kneeling on the left knee with the left shoulder facing the pitcher. The hands grasp the bat approximately 4 to 5 in. apart, with the left hand lower on the bat handle than the right hand. The batter is ready to strike the ball when the bat is brought backward approximately 3 in. from and parallel to the ground. As the pitcher rolls the ball, the batter brings the bat forward to strike it.

Players with one upper limb will be able to bat as long as the nonimpaired limb possesses enough strength to hold and swing a bat. To facilitate hitting, the player may use a lighter bat, grasping it not too close to the handle. Players in wheelchairs or on crutches must rely more on arm and shoulder strength for batting because they will be unable to shift their body weight from the back leg to the front leg to provide power for the swing. Plastic bats with large barrels will be helpful for people with poor arm and grip strength or poor eye-hand coordination. In this case, a large whiffle ball must be used.

Lead-Up Games and Activities

Home Run Softball

The game is played on a softball field with a pitcher, a catcher, a batter, and one fielder. The object of the game is for the batter to hit a pitched softball into fair territory, then run to first base and return home before the fielder or pitcher can get the ball to the catcher. The batter is out when three strikes are made, a fly ball is caught, or the ball reaches the catcher before the batter returns home.

Lead-Up Team Softball

The game is played in any open area, with six players constituting the team. Players position themselves in any manner approximately 12 ft from each other. To begin play, the first player throws the ball to the second player. Each player attempts to catch the softball and throw it (in any manner) accurately to the next one. The sixth player, on catching the ball, attempts to throw it into a target 3 ft by 3 ft, from a distance of 13 ft. Following that throw, players rotate positions until each player has had an opportunity to throw the ball to the target.

Other Activities

Additional activities may include throwing beanbags in an underarm manner through a hoop suspended from the floor, hitting balls for distance from a batting tee, punching a volleyball pitched in an underarm manner, keeping a balloon in the air by hitting it with a plastic stick, and batting a ball suspended from the ceiling or a tetherball pole.

Variations and Modifications

Sport

Beep baseball, specifically designed for the visually impaired athlete, has recently gained popularity. It is sanctioned by the NBBA. The object of the game is for the batter to hit a regulation 16-in. softball equipped with a special sound-emitting device and to reach base before an opposing player fields the ball. (The Telephone Pioneers of America distribute the balls nationwide. To obtain one, contact the local telephone company and request the address of that organization.) Teams are composed of seven players, two of whom are sighted. The sighted players are the pitcher and catcher, who play for their own team. The pitcher throws the ball in an underarm motion to the batter in an attempt to ''give up'' hits. The catcher assists the batters by positioning them in the batter's box, and also retrieves pitched balls. On defense, both sighted players stand in the field and assist their teammates in fielding the ball by calling out the name of the defensive player closest to the ball. The sighted players cannot field balls themselves. A batter gets five strikes before being called out. Each side has three outs per inning; there are six innings to an official game.

Upon hitting the ball beyond the 40-ft foul line, the batter runs to one of two cone-shaped bases (at least 48 in. high) located 90 ft from home plate. Bases contain battery-powered, remotely controlled buzzers; an umpire determines which buzzer is to be activated once the ball is hit. To score a run, the batter must touch the appropriate base before an opposing player cleanly fields the ball. However, if the opposing player fields the ball before the batter reaches base, the batter is ''out'' (Figure 25.4).

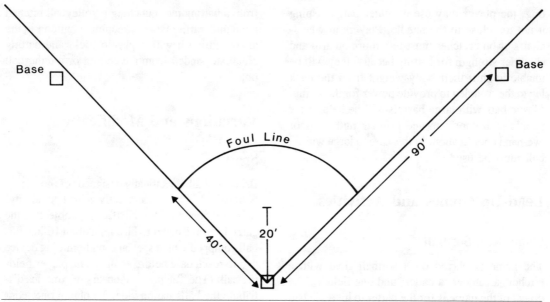

Figure 25.4 Beep baseball field.

The game of softball has been modified for players in wheelchairs by the NWSA. The game is played under the official rules for 16-in. slow-pitch softball with the following modifications ("Wheelin' Softball," 1977):

- All players must be in wheelchairs with foot platforms.
- The field is a smooth, level surface of blacktop or similar material.
- Bases should be placed 50 ft from each other.
- The pitcher should be positioned 28 ft from home plate.
- One-foot-square bases should be flush with the playing surface.
- Players are not allowed to leave their chairs to gain an advantage in catching or stopping a hit ball or to field a thrown ball.
- All base runners are awarded one base if a throwing error occurs and the ball leaves the playing area.

The game of softball is also modified for Special Olympics play (Special Olympics, 1986). Although the game follows Fédération Internationale de Softball (FIS) rules, the following modifications are used:

- The diamond consists of baselines 61 ft 9 in. in length, with the pitcher's rubber 45 ft 6 in. from home plate.
- Any batted ball that does not cross the "neutral zone" line (marked in the form of an arc 45 ft 6 in. from home plate) will be designated as a foul ball.
- A restricted-flight softball must be used.
- A batting tee placed directly behind home plate will be used in place of a pitched ball.
- All players must stand behind the "neutral zone" before the ball is hit.
- A time limit of 1 hr 15 min should be set for all games.

Skill Events

Special Olympics offers skill competition in throwing, hitting, fielding, and base running. In the throwing event, the object is to throw a softball as far as possible. Three attempts are given, and the player's score is the distance of the longest throw (measured from the restraining line to the point where the ball first touches the ground). A distance throwing event is also offered in competition sponsored by NWAA, which includes the Junior National Wheelchair Games. Similar events sponsored by USCPAA include a beanbag toss and an Indian club throw for distance.

The hitting event requires the player to bat for distance by hitting a softball off a batting tee. Three attempts are allowed, and the longest hit is the player's score. The distance is measured from the tee to the point where the ball first touches the ground.

For the fielding event, the player must throw a softball to a target (19 ft 6 in. high by 10 ft 1 in. wide) on a wall from a distance of 10 ft 9 in. The ball is then caught in the air or on one bounce as it rebounds from the wall. The player attempts to make as many catches as possible in 30 s. The player's best score from two 30-s trials is counted.

In the base running event, the player must start at home plate, run around the bases, and return home as fast as possible. The time needed to run the bases is subtracted from 60 to determine the point score. The best of two trials is counted.

Other Variations and Modifications

To accommodate players' varying ability levels, the number of strikes a batter is allowed can be increased. For example, players may swing until they hit the ball. In some cases, fewer than four bases can be used. Half-innings may end when three outs have been made, six runs have been scored, or 10 batters have come to bat. In addition, lighter-weight and large-barreled bats may be used. For players with poor eye-hand coordination, like those with cerebral palsy, the ball may be hit from a batting tee and/or a larger ball may be used. When some players are at bat, the ball may be rolled to them down a groove or tube-like channel. A walled or fenced area is recommended for players with mobility impairments so that distances to be covered during the game can be shortened. Shorter distances between bases can be employed, as well as a restricted-flight softball,

which travels a limited distance when hit. In addition, a greater number of players on defense may be allowed, especially if players have mobility problems. The game can also be modified so that it is played in a gymnasium with a whiffle ball and bat.

Football

Football utilizes the skills of passing, catching, kicking, blocking, and tackling. Most individuals can participate effectively in football or some variation of it. The regulation game of tackle football can be played by people with mild impairments who are in good physical condition. A small number of partially sighted players do participate on high school and collegiate teams. However, totally blind people will be unable to play the regulation game. Those with unilateral amputations either below the knee or above or below the elbow will be able to participate in regulation football as long as their prostheses do not pose a safety risk. Flag or touch football is more commonly offered in physical education and recreation sport programs. Most mentally impaired individuals, except those with severe or profound impairments, can safely be integrated with mainstreamed players. Individuals with conditions such as juvenile rheumatoid arthritis, osteogenesis imperfecta, or significant physical impairment may find modified, segregated participation more suitable.

Game Skills

Passing

Partially sighted players are able to pass the ball as long as distances are short and receivers wear bright-colored clothing. For players with poor grip strength, pronounced contracture of the hand or wrist, or crutches, a softer and smaller ball may be used to facilitate holding and gripping. People in wheelchairs will be able to effectively pass the ball if they have sufficient arm and shoulder strength. Wheelchair users will find it almost impossible to perform an underhand lateral pass while facing the line of scrimmage; therefore, this type of pass must be performed while they face the receiver.

Catching

Partially sighted and blind players should be facing the passer when attempting to catch the ball. Instead of trying to catch with the hands, players should be encouraged to cradle the ball with both hands or to trap the ball in the midsection. The ball should be passed from short distances without great speed; a foam ball can be used for safety purposes. Players who have unilateral arm deformities or amputations or who use crutches should catch the ball by stopping it with the palm of the nonimpaired hand and trapping it against the body. Wheelchair users will be able to catch effectively if the ball is thrown accurately; confinement to a chair limits one's range in catching. Wheelchair users and those on crutches will be much more successful in catching when the entire body faces the passer.

Kicking

Blind and partially sighted players may be encouraged to practice punting without shoes so they can feel the ball contacting the foot. In learning this punt, players should be instructed to point the toes (plantar flex the foot) while kicking. A player with unilateral arm amputation can punt the ball by having it rest in the palm of the nonimpaired hand. A punting play may begin with the player already holding the ball instead of with a snap from center.

Lead-Up Games and Activities

Kickoff Football

The game is played on a playground 30 by 60 yd by two teams of approximately six to eight players each. The object of the game is to return the kickoff as far as possible before being touched. The football is kicked off, as in regular flag football, from the center of the field. The player with the ball returns it as far up the field as possible without being touched by members of the opposing team. The team returning the ball may use a series of lateral passes to advance it; forward passes are not permitted. Play stops when the ball carrier is touched. The other team then kicks off from the middle of the field. The winner is the team advancing farthest up the field.

Football Throw Activity

A player attempts to pass a football from a distance of 30 ft through the hole of a large rubber tire suspended 4 ft from the ground on a rope. Ten attempts are given; the player's score is the number of successful passes out of 10.

Other Activities

Other lead-up activities may include placekicking the ball over a suspended bar or rope from varying distances, centering the ball to a target for accuracy, performing relays in which players hand the ball off to each other, and guessing the number of throws or kicks it will take to cover a predetermined distance.

Variations and Modifications

Sport

Wheelchair football is gaining popularity for many disabled persons. The game is played on a hard, flat surface 30 by 60 yd and, with few exceptions, is very similar to touch football. Rule modifications (Brasile, 1975) are as follows:

- Each team is composed of six on-the-field players.
- The ball carrier (not the wheelchair) must be touched above the knees with two hands simultaneously.
- All players on the team are eligible pass receivers.

- Blocking by ramming the wheelchair into the opponent's wheelchair from a front angle is allowed, while blocking into the larger rear wheel constitutes "clipping."
- A team must gain 15 instead of 10 yd for a first down.
- Ball throwing is substituted for kicking, and the kicking team must announce this to the defensive team through the referee before breaking the huddle.
- Extra point tries (which are taken from the 3-yd line) earn 2 points for a successful run and 1 point for a successful pass.

Skill Events

Various skill events can be offered. One is a passing-for-distance event, where players throw a football as far as possible. Three attempts are given, and the total distance covered (measured in feet and inches) in the three throws constitutes the player's score.

A catching event may require a player to run a specified pass pattern (e.g., down and out) and catch the ball. Five attempts are given, with the total number of catches constituting the player's score.

In a field goal kicking event, players attempt to placekick a football over a rope suspended 8 ft from the ground between two poles 50 ft apart. Kicks may be attempted from 5, 10, 15, 20, or 25 yd from the rope. Ten kicks are given, and players may kick from any or all of the five distances. Points are awarded according to the distance kicked. The points are as follows: 1 point for a 5-yd kick, 2 points for a 10-yd kick, 3 points for a 15-yd kick, 4 points for a 20-yd kick, and 5 points for a 25-yd kick. The total number of points accumulated from 10 kicks is the player's score.

Other Variations and Modifications

Simplified game situations that include only the performance of specific game skills can be used. For example, the game may be played to allow only passing plays. The field can be both shortened and narrowed, and the number of players on each team can be reduced. In addition, first-down yardage can be reduced to less than 10 yd, and more than four downs can be used to make a first down. For partially sighted players, a plastic football containing bells or a brightly colored foam ball may be used. The game may also be played with a kickball or volleyball by people of low skill. Individuals with arm or leg deformities as well as those with visual impairments can play most line positions in touch football.

Volleyball

Volleyball is a popular game included in most programs. Game skills include serving, passing, striking, and spiking the ball. Most disabled persons can be integrated into the game. However, for players with severe or profound mental impairments, or those with significant visual or mobility impairments, the game may require modifications.

Game Skills

Serving

Disabled players can learn to serve quite effectively. It will be helpful to begin with an underhand serve: The nondominant hand is beneath the ball, supporting it in front of and away from the body, while the dominant hand (fisted) strikes the ball in an underhand motion. Very young players or those with insufficient arm and shoulder strength can move closer to the net. As players develop coordination abilities, they can switch to the overhand serve. Players with one functional arm can serve overhand effectively by tossing the ball into the air with the nonimpaired arm and then hitting it with the same arm. Wheelchair users will be able to perform both the underhand and overhand serves, though for the underhand serve, it is important to be in a chair without armrests.

Striking

Visually impaired players can competently hit the ball with two hands if the ball is first allowed to bounce. This gives the player more time to visually track the ball. Because of limited mobility, players in wheelchairs—like those on crutches—will need to learn to return the ball with one hand. However, wheelchair players can use both hands to return a ball within their immediate area. As these players become more adept in predicting the flight of the ball over the net, they will be able to make a greater percentage of returns. Wheelchair participants will be more successful in returning the ball from the back court unless the net is lowered.

Lead-Up Games and Activities

Keep It Up

The game is played by teams forming circles approximately 15 to 20 ft in diameter. Any number of teams, of about six to eight members each, may play. To begin the game, a team member tosses the volleyball into the air within the circle. Teammates, using both hands, attempt to keep hitting the ball into the air (it must not hit the ground). A player may not strike the ball twice in succession. The team that keeps the ball in the air the longest scores 1 point, and the team with the most points wins the game.

Serving Activity

A player hits a total of 10 volleyballs, either underhand or overhand, over a net and into the opposite court. Point values are assigned to various areas within the opposite court, with areas farther away from the net having higher values. The player's score is the point total for all 10 serves.

Other Activities

Additional activities may include setting a beach ball or large balloon to oneself as many times as possible in succession, serving in the direction of a wall and catching the ball as it returns, and spiking the ball over a net that is approximately 1 ft higher than the player.

Variations and Modifications

Sport

The United States Amputee Athletic Association (USAAA) and the United States Les Autres Sports Association (USLASA) offer team sport competition in volleyball. In USAAA competition, six players from each team participate on the court. A point system is used to allow for equal distribution of players' abilities. Players are assigned 1, 2, 3, or 4 points according to two criteria: (a) classification into one of nine classes (see chapter 15) and (b) the results of a muscle strength test. At all times, players on the court must represent a total of 13 or more points. Sitting volleyball is offered for players in classes A1 through A9, while standing volleyball is played by athletes in classes A2 through A4 and A6 through A9.

The following rules (Cherenko, 1978) apply to the game of wheelchair volleyball:

- The court dimensions are 20 by 40 ft, and the net is set at a height of 6 ft.
- A team is composed of six on-court players (five players face the net to pass or spike the ball, while the sixth player is the setter and plays at the net in order to receive passes and set up spikers).
- A team is allowed a maximum of three contacts to return the ball over the net.
- A side-out is called if one big wheel of a chair crosses the center line or a player or chair touches the net during play.

Skill Events

Special Olympics competition includes skill events such as volleying, passing, and serving. In volley competition, the athlete attempts to volley the ball in an overhead manner above a line marked on a wall 11 ft from the floor. Play begins with the athlete tossing the ball against the wall and then volleying the ball as many times as possible in 1 min. If ball control is lost, the player must again toss the ball against the wall and continue volleying. Two 1 min trials are given, with 1 point awarded for each successful volley. The total number of successful volleys above the line for both trials constitutes the final score.

Passing competition requires the athlete to stand approximately 1 to 3 ft behind the end line and pass a ball, which has been thrown by another player into the athlete's own side of the court. The athlete's side of the court is divided into three areas of equal size, with a point value assigned to each area. Five points are awarded for a pass landing in the area closest to the net, 3 points for a pass landing in the middle third area, and 1 point for a pass landing in the area closest to the end line near the athlete. For passes that land on a line, the higher point value is awarded. The athlete's final score is the total of points scored in five attempts.

Serving competition requires the athlete to serve a ball into the opponent's side of the court. That court is divided into areas of equal size, and a point value is assigned to each area. One point is awarded for a serve landing in the area of the opponent's court closest to the net, 3 points are awarded for a serve landing in the middle third area, and 5 points for a serve landing in the area closest to the opponent's end line. For serves that land on a line, the athlete receives the higher point value. The final score is the total number of points made in 10 serves.

Other Variations and Modifications

Volleyball is easily modified for most disabled players. Most often, court dimensions are reduced, the net lowered, and the serving line brought closer to the net to accommodate the varying abilities of players. Balls may be permitted one bounce before players attempt to return them over the net, or an unlimited number of hits by the same team may be allowed before the ball is returned. Players with arm or hand deficiencies can be allowed to

carry on a hit or return. To serve, players may throw the ball over the net rather than hitting it, and they may catch the ball before returning it. Players may experience greater success by using a large, colored beach ball. Foam balls or cage balls can also replace the volleyball. Players with mobility problems, such as those using crutches or walkers, may play the game from a seated position, or the number of players on each team may be increased.

Goal Ball

Goal ball, a sport developed in Europe, was created primarily for visually impaired persons to increase auditory tracking ability, agility, coordination, and team-mindedness. The game is played in a silent arena where blindfolded players attempt to score goals by rolling a ball across an opponent's goal line. Game skills are throwing, shot blocking, and ball control. Males and females compete separately. To remove any advantages for partially sighted players, all players are blindfolded, even those who are totally blind. A hard rubber ball weighing approximately 4.5 lb for men and 3.5 lb for women is used. The ball used by male players is about the size of a basketball, while for women it is about the size of a volleyball. Each ball contains five to seven bells that allow players to track it during play. Balls may be purchased from the American Foundation for the Blind, 15 West 16th Street, New York, NY 10011.

Coaches are not permitted to communicate with their players outside of halftime or one of two official time-outs. Spectators must also remain silent so that players may hear the ball. However, the rules permit communication between players in the form of talking, finger snapping, and/or tapping on the floor.

The game consists of two 5-min periods. Running time is not used; rather, the clock is stopped at various points in the game for specific purposes (e.g., a scored goal or out-of-bounds play). Whistles are used to communicate clock times to players. Each team is allowed a total of five players, with only three players on the court at any one time and the two remaining players available for substitution. Substitutions are permitted only during time-outs or at halftime.

Players must remain within their respective play zones. Court boundaries are marked with white tape 3/4 in. wide. Tape with various textures is used so that players can distinguish boundaries and zones (Figures 25.5).

Play begins with a throw by a designated team. During the game, the ball may be thrown into play by any player. The ball must be rolling once it arrives in the opponent's throwing area; otherwise, a bouncing ball infraction is called. The ball may be passed twice before each throw on goal.

All three players may play defense. Defensive players may assume a kneeling, crouching, or lying position to contact the ball, but they cannot drop onto the playing surface until the ball has been thrown by an opponent. Defenders may move laterally within their team area. However, they cannot rush forward into the throwing area to intercept the ball except to follow a deflection.

Game Skills

Throwing

Throwing can be accomplished easily by most players. The ball is usually thrown in an underhand manner so that it rolls along the ground. Individuals with poor upper body strength or poor motor control may need to use a lighter ball.

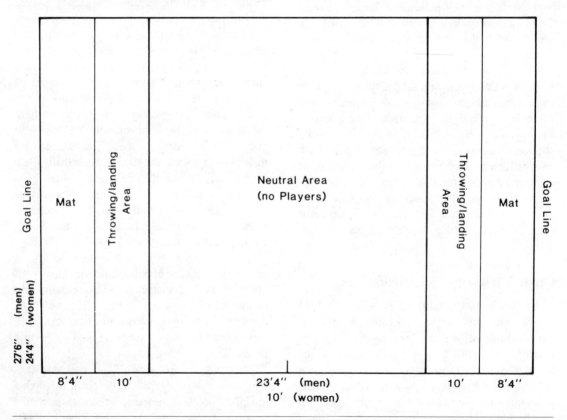

Figure 25.5   Goal ball arena.

Players with one arm can effectively throw the ball, while orthopedically impaired players who use scooters may need to push the ball with both hands along the ground rather than throwing it in an underhand motion. In other cases, players on scooters can "throw" the ball by striking it with a sidearm motion when it is located at their side.

Blocking and Ball Control

Blocking and ball control are essential skills because defensive players must stop the ball from entering the goal area. Once the ball is blocked, it is brought under control with the hands so that a throw can be made. It may be helpful to have mentally retarded players see the ball when learning the skill of blocking so that they can more effectively coordinate body movement with the sound of the ball. Players with amputations can wear prosthetic devices to assist in blocking, as long as the ball will not damage the device or vice versa. Wheelchair participants playing on scooters can effectively block balls when in the prone position.

Lead-Up Games and Activities

Heads-Up

This game involves one-on-one competition in a regulation goal ball arena. Play begins with players positioning themselves in their half of the arena. A player is given possession of the ball with the object of scoring a goal. The ball must be continuously rolled as the offensive player moves about; the player cannot carry the ball at any time. The defensive player can take control of the ball from the offensive player by deflecting or trapping a shot on goal. The first player to score three goals wins the game.

Speedy

This game involves two teams of three players each who play within an enclosed area. Players on each team assume a crouching or kneeling position and form a triangle with a distance of 12 ft between players. Players position themselves on small area rugs and face the middle of the triangle. On command, a player designated to begin the game rolls a goal ball as quickly as possible to the player on the immediate right, who controls the ball and throws it to the next player on the right, and so on. In the event the ball is not controlled by a player to whom it was thrown, that player must retrieve the ball and return to the area rug before throwing to the next player. Each time the ball returns to the player who started the game, a point is scored. The team scoring the most points in 1 min wins the game. Teams compete one at a time so that players can hear the ball.

Other Activities

Other activities may include throwing for accuracy to the goal and passing the ball as quickly as possible between two players for a specified period of time.

Variations and Modifications

Sport

Although it was developed over 30 years ago, goal ball is now gaining popularity in the United States and has become an official competitive sport of the U.S. Association for Blind Athletes (USABA). People with other types of disabilities as well as nondisabled people can participate in the game as long as blindfolds are worn.

Other Variations and Modifications

The game may be modified by increasing or decreasing the size of the play arena and the number of players on a side. People with mobility problems may play on scooter boards, and for those with poor upper-arm and shoulder strength, a lighter-weight ball may be used.

Integration

Most disabled players can be successfully and safely integrated into the regulation sports of basketball, floor hockey, soccer, football, softball, and goal ball as long as certain techniques are applied. One technique is to match abilities and positions; teachers and coaches should attempt to assign specific positions on the basis of ability levels of players. In football, mildly mentally retarded players possessing good catching skills could play end positions, while others with good speed could play the backfield. Players with cardiopathic conditions or those with limited mobility could play goalie in sports like soccer and floor hockey. Players with upper-arm impairments can serve as placekickers in football. In specific instances, a physical disability can be used to advantage. For example, Tom Dempsey, whose partial amputation of the kicking foot allowed for a broader surface with which to kick the ball, was a very successful placekicker in the National Football League.

The teacher or coach can also enhance integration by teaching to the players' abilities. When teaching or coaching mentally retarded players, one should emphasize concrete demonstrations more than verbal instructions. Verbal instructions, when used, should be short, simple, and direct. It is important to follow this technique when coaching first and third base in softball. In football and basketball, the use during game situations of a few simple plays that have been overlearned can encourage success. In sports like football or basketball, which require players to carry or move a ball, the player holding the ball can shout or call out to help the partially sighted player with ball location. In softball, players with unilateral upper-limb deficiencies should be instructed to "choke-up" and use a lighter-weight bat in order to swing effectively at the ball. In volleyball, players with unilateral upper-limb impairment can participate well as long as a one-hand serve is taught.

Modification to equipment can also foster integration. The teacher or coach can place audible goal locators in goal areas in sports such as basketball, soccer, and floor hockey for players with visual impairments. In addition, brightly colored balls or pucks may be used. Goals, when used, can be brightly painted or covered with tape. For example, the crossbar and goal posts in soccer could be brightly painted. In games played on an indoor court, such as floor hockey or basketball, mats may be placed along the sidelines in order to differentiate the playing surface from the out-of-bounds area. Players wearing prosthetic devices may participate as long as they adapt the devices according to regulations regarding their use.

Summary

This chapter described the more popular team sports included in physical education and sport programs. Team sports included in USCPAA, USLASA, USABA, NBBA, Special Olympics, NWBA, AAAD, and USAAA competition were also discussed. Game skills, along with variations and modifications specific to each sport, were identified. Also presented were lead-up games and activities, as well as rules and strategies, corresponding to those found in programs for able-bodied individuals. Finally, suggestions for integrating disabled persons into sport were offered.

Bibliography

Brasile, F.M. (1975). Football wheelchair style! *Sports 'N Spokes,* **1**, 1-2.

Cherenko, D. (1978). Volleyball. *Sports 'N Spokes,* **4**, 17-18.

Fait, H., & Dunn, J. (1984). *Special physical education: Adapted, individualized, developmental* (5th ed.). Philadelphia: Saunders.

National Association of Sports for Cerebral Palsy. (1979). *NASCP-USA constitution, rules, classification and national records sports manual.* New York: Author.

National Wheelchair Basketball Association. (1980). *1980-1981 constitution, by-laws, and executive regulations of the National Wheelchair Basketball Association*. Lexington, KY: Author.

Special Olympics. (1986). *Official Special Olympics sports rules*. Washington, DC: Joseph P. Kennedy, Jr. Foundation.

Wheelin' softball. (1977, September). *Sports 'N Spokes*, **3**, 15.

Resources

Written

Cowin, L., Sibille, J., & O'Riain, M. (1984). Motor soccer: The electric connection. *Sports 'N Spokes*, **10**, 43-44. This article describes the game of soccer adapted for players in electric wheelchairs. The game is played on a basketball court with a large rubber ball, and wheelchairs are equipped with specialized polyethylene bumpers.

Guttman, L. (1976). *Textbook of sport for the disabled*. Oxford, England: Alden Press. This text details various sports for physically and sensory impaired athletes along with sport organizations that sponsor competition.

Special Olympics. *Sports skills program* (rev. ed.). Washington, DC: Author. Separate manuals have been published for basketball, hockey, soccer, softball, and volleyball. Manuals include goals and objectives, skill assessment, task analyses, team tactics, modified games, and rules.

Audiovisual

Goal ball: An introductional videotape [Videotape]. (n.d.). Winnipeg, Manitoba, Canada: Communication Systems Distribution Group, University of Manitoba. This tape examines the sport of goal ball. It can be purchased or rented.

Here I am: The International Games for the Disabled [Film or videotape]. (1985). New York: Bradley-Kriegeskotte Associates. The production features the 1984 International Games for the Disabled. Games, rules, and sport adaptation are presented. Specific events include goal ball, volleyball, and wheelchair soccer.

The making of champions—Basketball [Film]. (1984). Washington, DC: Special Olympics. A 16mm film based on basketball fundamentals and the Sports Skills Instructional Program.

This is soccer: Teamwork [Film]. (1981). Washington, DC: Special Olympics. The film describes the game and team tactics.

CHAPTER 26

Individual and Dual Sports

E. Michael Loovis

This chapter presents a variety of individual and dual sports in which people with unique needs can participate successfully. Participation in these sports will be analyzed from two perspectives: within the context of sanctioned events sponsored by sport organizations, and as part of physical education programs in the schools. In terms of organized competition, discussion will be limited to the rules, procedural modifications, and adaptations that are currently in use and that are the only currently approved vehicle for participation. The remainder of the chapter will be a compendium of modifications or adjustments for a variety of sports. The incorporation of each sport by major sports organizations will be discussed, if applicable.

Tennis

Because of the nature of the game itself and the available variations and modifications, tennis or some form of it can be played by all but the most severely disabled people. Because the game can be either a singles or a doubles event, the skill requirements (both psychomotor and cognitive) can be modified in numerous ways to encourage participation. Regardless of the variations or modifications, the basic objective of the game remains the same: to return the ball legally across the net and to prevent one's opponent from doing the same.

Sport Skills

Typically, tennis can be played quite adequately with the ability to perform only the forehand and backhand strokes and the service. For the ground strokes, good footwork (for ambulatory players) or effective wheelchair mobility (Figure 26.1) along with good racquet preparation—moving the racquet into the backswing position well in advance of the ball's arrival—is fundamental to execution. Under normal circumstances, movement into position to return the ball and racquet preparation are performed simultaneously.

Lead-Up Activities

Adams, Daniel, McCubbin, and Rullman (1982) describe an elementary noncourt lead-up game, *Target Tennis*, that is appropriate for wheelchair-bound as well as ambulatory students and that can be played indoors with limited space. Basically, the players position themselves behind the end zone line, which is 10 ft from a target screen. The screen has five 10-in.-diameter openings, which serve as the targets. The player tosses a tennis ball in the air and, with an overhand swing, attempts to bounce the ball midway between the end zone line and the target so that the ball goes through one of the five openings. A bonus serve is permitted for every point scored. No points are awarded if the ball bounces twice.

Special Olympics provides four developmental

Figure 26.1 Wheelchair tennis competitor. Photo courtesy of Brad Parks. Printed with permission.

events that can serve as lead-up activities. They are *target serve, target bounce, racquet bounce*, and *return shot* (Special Olympics, 1985). In target serve, the athlete attempts to serve as many balls as possible into the opponent's service court. Target bounce consists of having the athlete bounce a tennis ball on the playing surface using one hand; the score is the highest number of consecutive bounces in two trials. In racquet bounce, the athlete bounces the ball off the racquet face as many times consecutively as possible; the score is the most consecutive bounces in two trials. Return shot involves attempting to return a tossed ball over the net and in-bounds; the score is the total for two trials.

Variations and Modifications

Sport

In 1980 the National Foundation of Wheelchair Tennis (NFWT) was founded to develop and spon-

sor competition in that sport. The rules for wheelchair tennis are the same as for regular tennis except that the ball is allowed to bounce *twice* before being returned (Parks, 1980). The first bounce must land in-bounds, while the second bounce may land either in-bounds or out-of-bounds.

Other Variations and Modifications

If mobility is a problem, the court size can be reduced to accommodate the disabled person. This might be accomplished by having able-bodied players defending the entire regulation court while disabled players defend only half of their court. It could likewise be accomplished by permitting players to strike the ball on the second bounce. Variations in the scoring system can facilitate participation. An example is scoring by counting the number of consecutive hits, which, in effect, structures the game as cooperative rather than competitive. If the disabled player has extremely limited mobility, then the court could be divided into designated scoring areas, with those closest to that player receiving higher point values. Racquet control may be a concern for some students because the standard tennis racquet may be too heavy. There are several solutions to this problem, including shortening the grip on the racquet, using a junior-size racquet, or substituting a racquetball racquet. In the case of an amputee, the racquet can be strapped to the stump, provided there is a functional stump remaining to allow for effective leverage and racquet use.

If mobility and/or racquet preparation are problematic, then reduction of court size, at least initially, will assist in learning proper racquet positioning and stroking because footwork will be minimal. If still unsuccessful, the player can be placed in the appropriate stroking position with the shoulder of the nonswinging arm perpendicular to the net. At this point, all that is necessary is to stride into and swing at the ball.

In service, the ball is routinely tossed into the air by the hand opposite the one holding the racquet. In preparation for striking the ball at the optimal height, the racquet is moved in an arc from a position in front of the body down to the floor and up to a position behind the back. At this point the racquet arm is fully extended to strike the ball as it descends from the apex of the toss. For some individuals who lack either the coordination or strength to perform the service as described, an appropriate variation is to bring the racquet straight up in front of the face to a position in which the hand holding the racquet is approximately even with the forehead or slightly higher. Although serving in this manner reduces speed and produces an arc that is considerably higher than normal, it does allow for service on the part of some players who might otherwise not learn to serve correctly. To accomplish the toss, a single-arm amputee may grip the ball in the racquet hand by extending the thumb and first finger beyond the racquet handle when gripped normally and holding the ball against the racquet. The ball is then tossed in the air and stroked in the usual way. A double-arm amputee having the racquet strapped

to the stump uses a different approach. The ball lies on the racquet's strings, and with a quick upward movement the ball is thrust into the air to be struck either in the air or after it bounces.

Table Tennis

Like tennis, table tennis or some version of it can be played by all but the most severely disabled person. It too can be played in singles or doubles competition, and, although the requisite skills are less adjustable than in tennis, the mechanical modifications that are available make this sport quite suitable for disabled people. Regardless of the variations and modifications, the basic objective of the game remains the same: to return the ball legally onto the opponent's side of the table in such a way as to prevent the opponent from making a legal return.

Sport Skills

As in tennis, the basic strokes are the forehand and backhand. Unlike in tennis, the service is not a separate stroke. A serving player puts the ball in play with either a forehand or a backhand stroke. The ball is required to strike the table on the server's side initially before striking the table on the receiver's side. In addition, servers must strike the ball outside the boundary at their end of the court.

Lead-Up Activities

Appropriate for use in physical education programs is an adapted table tennis game that originated at the Children's Rehabilitation Center, University of Virginia Hospital. Two or four people can play this game, called *surface table tennis*. The game involves hitting a regulation table tennis ball so that it moves on the surface of the table and passes through a modified net. The net is constructed from two pieces of string attached 1/2 in. apart to the top of official standards, and two or three pieces of string 3/4 in. apart at the bottom (Adams et al., 1982). At the start of play, the ball is placed on the table. A player then strikes it so that it rolls through the opening in the net into the opponent's court. Points are awarded to the player who last made a legal hit through the net. Points are lost when a player hits the ball over the net either on a bounce or in the air, when the ball fails to pass through the net, or when a player hits the ball twice in succession.

Another lead-up game, *Corner Ping-Pong*, was developed at the University of Connecticut (Fait & Dunn, 1984). It is played in a corner, with an area 6 ft high and 6 ft wide on each side of the corner. One player stands on either side of the center line. The server drops the ball and strokes it against the floor to the forward wall. The ball must rebound to the adjacent wall, then bounce onto the floor of the opponent's area. If the server fails to deliver a good serve, one point goes to the opponent. The ball may bounce only once on the floor before the opponent returns it. The ball must be stroked against the forward wall within the opponent's section of the playing area so that it rebounds to the adjacent wall and onto the floor in the server's area. Failure to return the ball means a point for the server. Scoring is similar to that for table tennis. Each player gets five consecutive serves. A ball that is stroked out of bounds is scored as a point for the other player. Game is 21 points, and the winner must win by two points.

Variations and Modifications

Sport

Table tennis is included as a sport in competitions offered by both the National Wheelchair Athletic Association (NWAA) and the United States Cerebral Palsy Athletic Association (USCPAA), formerly the National Association of Sports for Cerebral Palsy. Competition is based on the rules established by the United States Table Tennis Association. Some modifications are permitted. In

NWAA competition, the following rules apply (NWAA, 1986):

- Competitors' feet may not touch the floor.
- Athletes in certain classes (1A, 1B, and 1C) may have the racquet secured to their hands, may serve with or without upward projection of the ball, and are not penalized for volleying a ball that would otherwise clearly miss the table.

The following rules are used in USCPAA competition (NASCP, 1983):

- Wheelchair participants who mobilize their wheelchairs through use of the feet (Class II) may touch the ground.
- A serve must cross the baseline between the sidelines at the receiver's end to be good. The server may bounce the ball once before serving it. Players are allowed one illegal serve in a match (they may serve the ball again); all other serving violations mean a point for the receiver.
- Ambulatory competitors (Classes V through VIII) may use the table for support or balance; however, if the table moves, the player forfeits that point.

Other Variations and Modifications

Several assistive devices are available for individuals with severe disabilities such as muscular dystrophy and other disorders that weaken or affect the shoulder. The *ball bearing feeder* (Figure 26.2) provides assistance for shoulder and elbow motion by using gravity to gain a mechanical advantage and makes up for a loss of power resulting from weakened muscles. Another device is the *tenodesis splint* (Figure 26.3), which takes advantage of effective wrist extension. It is a functional brace that stabilizes the hand in a manner that facilitates thumb and finger opposition. The *bi-handle paddle*, which consists of a single paddle with handles on each side, was designed to encourage greater range of motion for participants in adapted

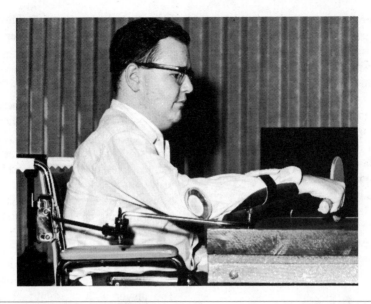

Figure 26.2 Ball bearing feeder. *Note.* From *Games, Sports, and Exercise for the Physically Handicapped* (3rd ed.) (p. 210) by R.C. Adams, A.N. Daniel, J.A. McCubbin, and L. Rullman, 1982, Philadelphia: Lea & Febiger. Copyright 1982 by Lea & Febiger. Reprinted by permission.

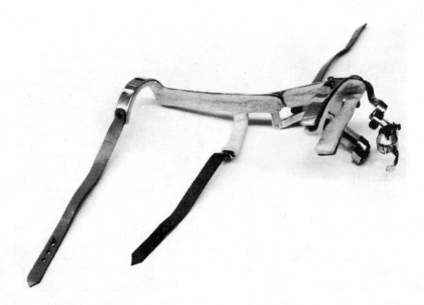

Figure 26.3 Tenodesis splint. *Note.* From *Games, Sports, and Exercise for the Physically Handicapped* (3rd ed.) (p. 211) by R.C. Adams, A.N. Daniel, J.A. McCubbin, and L. Rullman, 1982, Philadelphia: Lea & Febiger. Copyright 1982 by Lea & Febiger. Reprinted by permission.

table tennis. Its greatest asset is increased joint movement resulting from the bilateral nature of hand and finger positioning. A *strap-on paddle* has been designed for players with little or no functional finger flexion or grasp. The paddle is attached to the back of the hand with Velcro straps. The major disadvantage is that it precludes use of a forehand stroking action. Another device, the *space ball net* (Figure 26.4), can replace the paddle for blind players (Fait & Dunn, 1984). This device, held in two hands, consists of a lightweight metal frame that supports a nylon lattice or webbing. The net is large enough and provides an adequate rebounding surface to make participation by blind people feasible.

Figure 26.4 Space ball net.

Angling

Sport Skills

Angling is the use of casting and fishing skills. None of the contemporary sports organizations for disabled people sponsors competition in angling, and it is likewise not found very often in physical education programs. It is more likely to be used as a recreational sport. The American Casting Association (ACA) is the governing body for tournament fly and bait casting in the United States.

It sets the rules by which eligible casters may earn awards in registered tournaments.

Lead-Up Activities

In terms of lead-up activities, there are at least two casting games that deserve mention. *Skish* involves accuracy in target casting at various distances. Each participant casts 20 times at each target. One point is awarded for each direct hit (plug landing inside a target or similar goal). Three targets can be used simultaneously to speed up the game, with players changing position after each has had 20 casts at a target. The player with the greatest number of hits at the end of 60 casts is the winner. The second game, *speed casting*, is a variation of skish. Each player casts for 5 min at each target. The player with the high score at the end of 15 min is the winner (Adams et al., 1982).

Variations and Modifications

The major assistive device for use in angling is the *freehanderson recreation belt* (Figure 26.5),

Figure 26.5 Freehanderson recreation belt.

Individual and Dual Sports **437**

a specially designed harness into which one inserts rod and reel. This permits reeling and fighting fish one-handed.

Archery

Sport Skills

Under normal circumstances, shooting the longbow is a six-step procedure. The steps, in order of occurrence, are assuming the correct stance, nocking the arrow, drawing the bowstring, aiming at the target, releasing the bowstring, and following through until the arrow makes contact with the target. One or more of these steps may be problematic and may require some modification in the archer's technique.

Variations and Modifications

Sport

Target archery is an athletic event sponsored by USCPAA, NWAA, and USAAA. These groups observe the rules established by the International Archery Federation, with certain modifications.

The following are modifications that may be employed to encourage participation by individuals in wheelchairs (NWAA, 1986):

- Quadriplegic archers (Class 1A, 1B, or 1C) may use compound bows; if they do, they compete in the adaptive equipment division.
- Archers may use an adaptive equipment archery body support.

Modifications shared by both the NWAA (1986) and the USCPAA (NASCP, 1983) include

- the use of mechanical devices for stabilizing the bracing of the bow and the release of the string (for these archers, assistance in placing the arrow in the bow is permitted); and
- the use of an adjustable arrow rest and arrow plate and a draw check indicator on the bow, provided they are not electric or electronic and do not offer any additional aid in aiming.

Other Variations and Modifications

Several assistive devices are available to aid the archer who has a disability. These include (1) the *bow sling*, commercially available from most sports shops, which helps stabilize the wrist and hand for good bow control; (2) the *below-elbow amputee adapter device* (Figure 26.6), which is

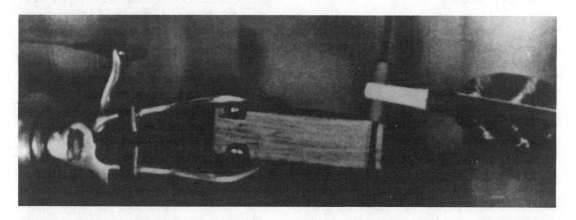

Figure 26.6 Amputee adapter device. *Note.* From *Games, Sports, and Exercise for the Physically Handicapped* (3rd ed.) (p. 241) by R.C. Adams, A.N. Daniel, J.A. McCubbin, and L. Rullman, 1982, Philadelphia: Lea & Febiger. Copyright 1982 by Lea & Febiger. Reprinted by permission.

held by the terminal end of the prosthesis and requires a slight rotation of the prosthesis to release the string and the arrow; and (3) the wheelchair *bowstringer*, which consists of a post buried in the ground with two appropriately spaced bolts around which the disabled archer places the bow in order to produce enough leverage to string it independently (Adams et al., 1982). Additionally, the *vertical bow set* can accommodate individuals with bilateral upper-extremity involvement (Wiseman, 1982).

Other program adjustments include use of the crossbow with the aid of the tripod assistive device for bilateral upper-extremity amputees. Various telescopic sights are also commercially available for the partially sighted archer.

Although the United States Association for Blind Athletes (USABA) does not sponsor competition in archery, there are several modifications (Hattenback, 1979) that can facilitate participation by individuals with visual impairments. These include

- using foot blocks to ensure proper orientation with the target,
- placing an audible goal locator behind the target to aid in directional cuing,
- using a brightly colored target for partially sighted individuals, and
- placing balloons on the target as a means of auditory feedback.

Badminton

None of the existing sports organizations for people with disabilities sponsors competition in badminton. The game is, however, ideally suited for individuals with disabilities and is played routinely in physical education.

Sport Skills

Badminton can be played quite adequately using only the forehand and backhand strokes and the underhand service. Beyond these strokes, development of the clear, smash, drop shot, and drive will depend on the ability of the participant.

Lead-Up Activities

There are at least two lead-up games that deserve mention. *Loop badminton* (Fait & Dunn, 1984) is played with a standard shuttlecock, table-tennis paddles, and a 24-in. loop that is placed on top of a standard 46 in. in height. The object of the game is to hit the shuttlecock through the loop, which is positioned in the center of a rectangular court 10 ft long and 5 ft wide. Scoring is done as in the standard game of badminton. Loop badminton is well adapted for individuals with restricted movement who wish to participate in an active game that requires extreme accuracy. A second modified game is called *balloon badminton* (Adams, Daniel, & Rullman, 1975). In this game a balloon is substituted for the shuttlecock, and table-tennis paddles are used instead of badminton racquets. The game can also be played by people with visual impairments if a bell is placed inside the balloon to aid in directional cuing.

Variations and Modifications

Some standard modifications are routinely used; these include, but are not limited to, reducing court size, strapping the racquet to the stump of the double-arm amputee, and using Velcro on the rim of the racquet and on the shuttlecock to aid in retrieval. Several assistive devices are used to facilitate participation in badminton. The *extension-handle racquet* involves splicing a length of wood to the shaft of a standard badminton racquet. This is helpful for a wheelchair player or one with limited movement. Another device is the *amputee serving tray* (Figure 26.7). Attached to the terminal end of the prosthesis, it permits easier service and promotes active use of the prosthesis.

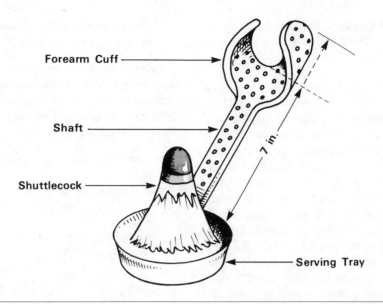

Forearm Cuff

Shaft

Shuttlecock

7 in.

Serving Tray

Figure 26.7 Amputee serving tray. *Note.* From *Games, Sports, and Exercise for the Physically Handicapped* (3rd ed.) (p. 251) by R.C. Adams, A.N. Daniel, J.A. McCubbin, and L. Rullman, 1982, Philadelphia: Lea & Febiger. Copyright 1982 by Lea & Febiger. Reprinted by permission.

Bowling

Bowling is an activity in which both ambulatory and wheelchair-bound people can participate with a high degree of success. Usually the ambulatory bowler demonstrates a procedure that incorporates the following actions: approach (which may be modified if lower extremity involvement exists); delivery, including the swinging of the ball; and release. A wheelchair-bound bowler will eliminate the approach and will either perform the swing and release independently or will use a piece of adapted equipment to assist in this part of the procedure.

Lead-Up Activities

Special Olympics (1985) sponsors two developmental events that qualify as lead-up activities. The two events are *target roll* and *frame bowl*.

Target Roll

This event consists of rolling three 30-cm-diameter playground balls between two flagpoles that are 1.5 m apart and 3 m from a rolling line. Bowlers may stand or sit, as long as they are behind the rolling line. Likewise, they may use one or both hands to roll the ball, provided it is released behind the rolling line. The ball must be rolling when it passes between the flagpoles in order for the roll to be legal. Points are awarded according to the following system: 5 points for each roll that goes between the poles without touching them, 4 points for each roll that touches a pole but continues between the poles, 2 points for each roll that touches a pole but does not continue across the goal line, and 1 point for each roll that goes in the direction of the flagpoles but does not hit anything. Additionally, bowlers receive 5 bonus points for rolling three consecutive balls between the flagpoles without touching the poles. The score is the aggregate result from all the rolls.

Frame Bowl

In this event the bowler rolls two frames and has two 30-cm-diameter plastic playground balls per frame. The object is to knock down the greatest number of plastic bowling pins from a traditional 10-pin triangular formation. The lead pin is set 5 m from a restraining line. Bowlers may either sit or stand and may use either one or both hands to roll the ball; the ball must be released behind the restraining line. Pins that are knocked down are cleared between the first and second rolls; pins are reset for each new frame. A bowler's score equals the number of pins knocked down in two frames. Five bonus points are awarded when all pins are knocked down on the first roll of a frame, and 2 bonus points are awarded when all remaining pins are knocked down on the second roll of the frame.

Variations and Modifications

Sport

Bowling is a sanctioned event in the competitions of USCPAA and Special Olympics. The USCPAA (NASCP, 1983) has developed the following procedures and/or rules for its competition:

- There are four divisions: two chute (ramp) and two nonchute.
- Nonchute divisions include Class III through VIII bowlers who do not use specialized equipment; the returnable ball handle is permitted in these divisions.
- Chute divisions are for Class I through VI bowlers using specialized equipment. There are two divisions: closed chute, for Class I and II bowlers, who need assistance with equipment (wheelchair, chute, or ball), and open chute, for Class III, IV, V, or VI bowlers, who do not require assistance with

their equipment (once on the chute the bowler must independently push the ball).

Special Olympics (1985) sponsors competition in bowling and follows the rules established by the American Bowling Congress and the Women's International Bowling Congress. Modified rules for use in Special Olympics are as follows:

- Ramps and other assistive devices are permitted.
- Bowlers using ramps shall compete in separate divisions and only against other ramp bowlers.
- Bowlers are permitted to bowl three consecutive frames.

Other Variations and Modifications

There are several assistive devices currently in use by ambulatory bowlers. The *handle grip bowling ball* (shown in Figure 3.2 on page 41), which snaps back instantly upon release, is ideal for bowlers with upper-extremity disabilities and for individuals with spastic cerebral palsy, especially those who have digital control difficulties. The American Bowling Congress has approved the handle grip ball for competitive play. Upper extremity amputees who use a hook can utilize an *attachable sleeve* made of neoprene to hold and deliver a bowling ball. The sleeve can be made to compress by use of a spring and to expand for release with the identical action used to open the conventional hook. *Stick bowling*, which is similar to use of a shuffleboard cue, was designed for individuals with upper-extremity involvement, primarily grip problems. The American Wheelchair Bowling Association (AWBA) permits stick bowling in its national competitions, provided the bowlers apply their own power and direction to the ball.

Wheelchair-bound bowlers have several assistive devices that facilitate participation. Although not approved by the AWBA for national competition, *ramp* or *chute* bowling has become extremely popular with severely disabled bowlers. The counterpart of stick bowling for the wheelchair-bound bowler is the *adapter-pusher device*, which was originally designed for wheelchair bowlers lacking sufficient upper-arm strength to lift the ball. The *handlebar-extension accessory*, used in conjunction with the adapter-pusher device, assists ambulatory bowlers who lack sufficient strength to lift the ball.

Although USABA does not sponsor competition in bowling, there are several modifications that can enhance participation in the sport by people with visual impairments. These modifications include

- the use of a bowling rail for guidance,
- the use of an auditory goal locator placed above or behind the pins, and
- a scoring board system that tactually indicates the pins that remain standing after the ball is rolled.

Fencing

Sport Skills

Fencing as a competitive event for people with disabilities began with the Stoke Mandeville Games in Stoke Mandeville, England. The object is to score by touching the opponent's target and to avoid being touched. Because of a lack of participants, fencing as a sanctioned event for disabled athletes in the United States is nonexistent. Several years ago it was an exhibition event for NWAA but subsequently was discontinued. If fencing is included in physical education, a number of variations and modifications make participation in this activity feasible for those with disabilities.

Variations and Modifications

Sport

Competition in fencing for wheelchair-bound individuals is normally conducted according to the rules of the International Stoke Mandeville Games Federation (1984). Among the modified rules that have been written to ensure equal opportunity for all participants in wheelchair fencing, the following are important to note:

- A fencing frame must be used.
- Fencers with significant loss of grip or control of the sword hand may bind the sword to the hand with a bandage or similar device.
- Fencers cannot purposely lose their balance, leave their chairs, rise from their seats, or use their legs to score a hit or to avoid being hit; the first offense is a warning, with subsequent offenses penalized by awarding one hit for each occurrence; accidental loss of balance is not penalized.
- The legs and the trunk below the waist are not valid target areas.

Other Variations and Modifications

Fencing is ordinarily conducted on a court measuring 6 ft by 40 ft; however, to accommodate wheelchair participants, it is suggested either that the dimensions of the standard court be changed to 8 ft by 20 ft or that a *circular* fencing court with a diameter of 15 to 20 ft be used (Adams et al., 1982). Blind fencers will require a smaller, narrower court, which may conceivably be equipped with a guide rail (Fait & Dunn, 1984).

Basically, the only piece of adaptive equipment is the lightweight sword, which permits independent participation especially for individuals with upper-extremity disabilities. In cases where no modification is necessary, the épée is recommended for ease of handling rather than the foil or sabre (Orr & Sheffield, 1981).

Horseback Riding

The North American Riding for the Handicapped Association, which originated in 1969, is the primary advisory group on riding for the disabled in the United States and Canada. It does not, however, sponsor competition. Handicapped riders compete nonetheless in the Annual Handicapped Riders Event of the Devon Horse Show. This competition is sponsored by the Bryn Mawr Rehabilitation Hospital Volunteer Association and the Thorncroft Equestrian Center of Malvern, Pennsylvania.

Sport Skills

The Cheff Center in Augusta, Michigan, houses the largest therapeutic riding program in the world, in both size and number of students. Students are scheduled five days a week. On the average, 150 students per week ride at the center. Additionally, courses are offered for people who wish to become certified as riding instructors for the handicapped. Horseback riding involves, among other skills, mounting, maintaining correct positioning on the mount, and dismounting. At the Cheff Center disabled students receive a six-phase lesson. The phases include *mounting, warm-up, riding instruction, exercises, games*, and *dismounting* (McCowan, 1972). A word about mounting, especially as it relates to the size of the horse, is important. Horses should be suitably sized—that is, small—because children are less likely to be fearful of smaller animals. In addition, smaller horses permit helpers to be in a better position for assisting unbalanced riders; the shoulder of the helper should be level with the middle of the rider's back.

Lead-Up Activities

Several possibilities exist for the use of games in the context of horseback riding instruction. The origin of some of these games is *pole bending*, which is common in Western riding and is used to teach horses how to bend and teach riders how to perform the movement. One game that encourages stretching of the arms involves placing quoits over the poles; this activity is conducted in relay fashion, with two- or three-person teams competing against each other. Another game consists of throwing balls into buckets placed on a wall or pole. The traditional game of Green Light, Red Light can be played as a way of reinforcing certain maneuvers, such as halts, which are taught to riders.

Variations and Modifications

Sport

Both USCPAA and the Special Olympics support the Annual Handicapped Riders Competition of the Devon Horse Show. It includes six riding divisions with various classes for physically handicapped, learning-disabled, mentally retarded, and visually and/or hearing-impaired competitors.

Participants are placed in one of two categories: a closed class for riders who can only sit on the back of a walking horse with an aide, and an open equitation class with jumping and a musical kur for advanced riders. Physically disabled riders are classified according to the USCPAA system, while mentally retarded and learning-disabled riders are classified as novice, intermediate, and advanced in riding ability (Heavens, 1985). Scoring is performed by two judges, with each participant having the opportunity to score 100 points. Judging comprises individual scores for equitation, balance, and general impression. The rider's score is the average of the scores assigned by the two judges.

Other Variations and Modifications

Mounting is the single most important phase of a riding program for disabled persons. Because for some disabled persons the typical method of mounting is impossible (i.e., placing the left foot in the stirrup, holding onto the cantle, and springing into the saddle), there are alternatives based on the riders' abilities. Several basic types of mounting procedures are used with disabled riders; these range from totally assisted mounts, either from the top of a ramp or at ground level, to normal mounting from the ground (McCowan, 1972).

Once mounted, individuals with disabilities have available to them numerous pieces of special equipment that can make riding an enjoyable and profitable learning experience. One commonly used item is an *adapted rein bar*, which permits riders with a disability in one arm to apply sufficient leverage on the reins with the unaffected arm to successfully guide the horse; it is faded as soon as the rider learns to apply pressure with the knees. Another adaptation is the *Humes rein*, consisting of large oval handholds fitted on the rein; this allows individuals with involvement of the hands to direct the horse with wrist and arm movement. *Body harnesses* are used extensively in riding programs for the disabled. They consist of web belts approximately 4 in. wide with a leather handhold in the back, which a leader can hold onto to help maintain a rider's balance. Most disabled riders also use the *Peacock stirrup*, which is shaped like a regular stirrup except that only one side is iron while the other side has a rubber belt attached top and bottom. This flexible portion of the stirrup releases quickly in case of a fall, reducing the chance that a foot could get caught. The *Devonshire boot* is used frequently if a rider has tight heel cords or weak ankles. Designed much like the front portion of a boot, it prevents the foot from running through the stirrup, and consequently it encourages keeping the toes up and heels down, which can be invaluable if heel cord stretching is desirable.

Gymnastics

Gymnastics has enjoyed considerable popularity in recent decades because of its visibility in the Olympic Games. As a result, individuals with disabling conditions have likewise begun to participate in gymnastic programs where opportunities have been available. For example, people with orthopedic involvements can participate and have participated in gymnastics programs for able-bodied as well as disabled persons (Winnick & Short, 1985).

Sport Skills

Beyond possessing the physical attributes necessary to participate in gymnastics (e.g., strength, agility, endurance, flexibility, coordination, and balance), participants must learn to compete either in one or more single events or in all events, referred to as the all-around. Under normal conditions men compete in the following events: pommel horse, rings, horizontal bar, parallel bars, and floor exercise. Women compete in balance beam, uneven parallel bars, vaulting, and floor exercise. In both men's and women's competitions, participation in all events qualifies athletes for a chance to win the all-around title.

Lead-Up Activities

The closest thing to lead-up activities related to gymnastics can be found in the Special Olympics Sports Skills Program and in select developmental events that are offered as part of the Special Olympics Games. In its sports skills program manual, *Gymnastics* (Special Olympics, n.d.), general conditioning exercises with emphasis on flexibility and strength are recommended. Doubles tumbling and balance stunts are also suggested. As an introductory experience, educational gymnastics, which uses a creative, problem-solving approach, can be used to teach basic movement concepts. This could eventually enable participants to compete in more advanced forms of gymnastic competition. Beyond these suggestions, the Special Olympics program (1985) incorporates developmental events that include the *wide-beam walk, bar hang, tumbling*, and *modified floor exercise*.

Variations and Modifications

Sport

Competition in gymnastics is offered by AAAD, the United States Association of Blind Athletes (USABA), and Special Olympics. The USABA offers gymnastics competition; however, it is for women only. Competition is held in balance beam, uneven parallel bars, floor exercises, vaulting, and the all-around event. With few exceptions, USABA follows the rules established by the Women's Technical Committees of the United States Gymnastics Federation. The USABA (1986) has developed the following procedures and modifications for its competition:

- Competitors are classified according to their degree of impairment and their ability level.
- Spotters and coaches may be present during routines and may provide verbal assistance during balance beam and vaulting events. There is a 0.5 deduction if contact is made with a coach or spotter during a routine.
- Balance beam and vaulting horse may be lowered.

The AAAD offers gymnastics events for men in floor exercise, parallel bars, rings, horizontal bars, pommel horse, and horse vault. As recently as the 1974 World Games for the Deaf, women competed in floor exercise, beam, horse, and uneven bars. Following the 1974 games, women's gymnastics was discontinued at the international level because of a lack of participants. Events are conducted according to the rules established by the International Federation of Gymnastics.

Gymnastics is offered in the Special Olympics games. Events for men include vaulting, parallel bars, pommel horse, high bar, rings, and free exercise. Women's events include vaulting, uneven parallel bars, balance beam, and floor exercise. Both men and women can compete in the all-around competition. Additionally, women can compete in rhythmic gymnastics in the following events: ribbon, ball, rope, hoop, and clubs. No significant modifications of the rules are required, and each participant's performance is judged according to the rules established for that event by the United States Gymnastics Federation (Special Olympics, 1985).

Other Variations and Modifications

Few modifications are used in gymnastics competition. If gymnastics is used in physical education programs, all of the modifications observed by the sports organizations in the conduct of their competitions would be valid.

Wrestling

The sport of wrestling requires considerable strength, balance, flexibility, and coordination. If disabled individuals possess these characteristics and if they can combine a knowledge of specific techniques with an ability to demonstrate them in competitive situations, then there is no reason that wrestling cannot be a sport in which disabled persons experience success.

Sport Skills

Wrestling consists of several fundamentals and techniques that are essential for success. These include *takedowns, escapes and reversals, breakdowns and controls*, and *pin holds*. When learned and performed well, these maneuvers assist in accomplishing the basic objective in wrestling, which is to dominate opponents by controlling them and holding both of their shoulders to the mat simultaneously for 1 s.

Lead-Up Activities

The development of specific lead-up activities for wrestling has apparently not been an area of creative activity. If lead-up activities are desirable, then one can conceivably use certain traditional elementary physical education self-testing activities that have some relationship to wrestling. Two such activities are listed in the following paragraphs.

Hand Wrestling

While standing, two people face each other and grasp right hands; each person raises one foot off the ground. On signal, each attempts to cause the other to touch either the free hand or foot to the ground.

Indian Leg Wrestle

Two people lie side by side but facing in opposite directions. Hips are adjacent to the partner's waist. Inside arms and legs are hooked. Each person raises the inside leg to a count of three; on the third count they bend knees, hook them, and attempt to force the partner into a backward roll.

Variations and Modifications

Sport

Both USABA and AAAD sponsor wrestling competitions. The USABA competition takes place in one division known as the Open Division and is contested according to international freestyle wrestling rules. Competition is held at the following weight classes: 91, 98, 105.5, 114.5, 125.5, 136.5, 149.5, 163, 180.5, 198, 220, and unlimited. The 91 and 98 weight classifications are reserved for competitors between the ages of 13 and 18. Competition is governed by the rules of United States of America Wrestling. The following modifications have been instituted to render conditions more suitable for visually impaired athletes:

- All authorized signals utilized by the referee must be given both verbally and visually at the same time when cautioning/warning or awarding points to either wrestler.
- Opponents begin the match in the neutral standing position with finger touch. Initial contact is made from the front unless waived by both competitors. When contact is broken, the match is interrupted and restarted in the neutral position at mat center (USABA, 1986).

Both Greco-Roman wrestling (which prohibits holds below the waist and use of the legs in attempting to take opponents to the mat) and freestyle wrestling are sanctioned events in competitions governed by AAAD. These events are conducted according to the rules established by the International Federation of Wrestling.

Other Variations and Modifications

Wrestling is not for everyone. For people with disabilities who want to attempt this sport, there are several modifications that can be used. For those with lower-extremity difficulties that prevent ambulation, all maneuvers should be taught from the mat with emphasis on arm technique. Bilateral upper-extremity involvement will probably restrict participation in all but leg wrestling maneuvers. After removal of protheses, single-arm amputees can participate with emphasis placed on arm maneuvers.

Track and Field

Sport

Because all of the major sports organizations for the disabled offer competitive opportunities in track and field, this section will focus on the rules modifications that have been enacted in order to make participation maximally available. For each organization the track portion will be discussed first, followed by the field events. No attempt will be made to examine sport skills, variations and modifications, and lead-up activities, except as related to Special Olympics.

National Wheelchair Athletic Association (NWAA)

Track and field competitions are governed by the rules of The Athletic Congress (TAC). The NWAA sponsors a classed division for field events and classed and open divisions for track events. Classes include 1A, 1B, 1C, II, III, IV, and V. All classes compete in 100-, 200-, 400-, 800-, and 1,500-m races; class IA also competes in a 60-m race. Relays are run at 400-, 800-, and 1,600-m distances. The open division competes at the same distances and also runs a 5,000-m race. In field events all classes compete in discus, shot put, and javelin, except class 1A, which substitutes the club throw for the javelin event. Additionally, all classes compete in the pentathlon, which consists of five individual events. Three events—javelin, shotput, and discus—are similar across all classes. Classes 1A, 1B, and 1C race at 100- and 800-m distances, while classes II through V race at 200- and 1,500-m distances.

The NWAA (1986) has designated the following specific rules:

- Wheelchairs with rigidly attached handrims are the rule in national championships; local competitions may waive this rule by including a separate competitive division for wheelchairs with handrims or equivalent devices that are not rigidly attached to the large wheel; the use of chain-driven or geared equipment is not permitted in any sanctioned NWAA competition.
- Batons are not exchanged in relay races; incoming racers use their hand to touch the back, shoulder, arm, or hand of the outgoing racer.
- Competitors may not secure any portion of their bodies to any part of the wheelchair in any fashion.
- Approved hold-down devices can be used to stabilize chairs of competitors in field events; sitting on the wheel is specifically prohibited; raising both buttocks from the seat before releasing the implement is illegal.
- Competitors in the club throw can hold and throw in any manner, including overhand or underhand or a combination; however, the throw can only be made with one hand.

United States Association for Blind Athletes (USABA)

International Amateur Athletic Federation rules are employed in track and field competitions. Within the USABA structure there are three visual classifications: B1, B2, and B3. The following events are provided for males and females across all three classes: 100-, 200-, 400-, 800-, and 1,500-m races. In addition, women run a 3,000-m race, while men run 5,000 m; there is also a 4 ×

100-m relay for men and women with combined visual classes. Both men and women in all three classes compete in long jump, high jump, discus, javelin, and shot put; men also compete in triple jump. There is a pentathlon consisting of the long jump, javelin, discus, 100 m, and either an 800-m race for women or a 1,500-m race for men. The pentathlon is contested by all classes and by men and women. A 10,000-m road race, open to all USABA classifications as well as the general public, may also be held. The USABA (1986) has determined that the following rules modifications are necessary in order to provide more suitable competition for visually impaired athletes:

- Guide wires are permitted for B1 athletes in 100-m races.
- Guides are allowed for B1 and B2 athletes in 200-m through 5,000-m events. When guides are used, there is an allowance of two lanes per competitor.
- Competitors may also decide what form guidance will take. They may choose an elbow lead, a tether, or to be free; at no time will the guide push or pull the competitor, nor will the guide ever precede the athlete.
- Acoustic aids are permitted for B1 and B2 athletes in field events; takeoff areas in the jumping events must be marked with bright, contrasting colors.
- Class B1 athletes use an astride position to commence the triple jump event; B1 high jumpers may touch the bar as an orientation prior to jumping.
- Class B1 shot put, discus, and javelin throwers may enter the throwing circle or runway (runup track) only with the assistance of a helper, who must leave the area prior to the first attempt.

American Athletic Association for the Deaf (AAAD)

Track competition for men includes races at standard distances from 100 m through 25-km road racing. It also includes 110- and 400-m hurdles,

3,000-m steeplechase, and 20-km walk. Along with the standard field events, AAAD provides competition in pole vaulting and hammer throw. Women's competition in track and field parallels that described for women in USABA with one exception, the 100-m hurdle.

Special Olympics

Special Olympics offers a greater number and diversity of track and field events than any other sport organization for people with disabilities. Included in the list of possible events that can be offered at a sanctioned competition are 50-, 100-, 200-, 400-, 800-, 1,500-, 3,000-, and 5,000-m races. There are walking races of 100, 400, and 800 m, as well as a 2-km walk. Additionally, there is a mile run along with 4 × 100- and 4 × 400-m relays. In field competition the following events are contested: long jump, high jump, standing long jump, shot put, softball throw, and pentathlon. There are also track and field events for wheelchair athletes. International Amateur Athletic Federation rules are employed in competitions sanctioned by Special Olympics (1985). Modifications to those rules include the following:

- In running events a rope or bell can be utilized to assist athletes who are visually impaired; a tap start can only be used with an athlete who is deaf and blind.
- In race walking events, athletes are not required to maintain a straight support leg while competing.
- In the softball throw, athletes can use any type of throw; they may throw from a stationary position or make a short run to the restraining area.

Special Olympics comes closer than the other organizations to describing lead-up activities. It does so through the provision of five developmental events, including the *10-m assisted walk, 25-m walk, ball throw, 10-m wheelchair dash,* and the *frisbee throw for distance.* Because most of these events are self-explanatory, only the frisbee throw will be described in more detail. In the frisbee throw for distance, athletes take three throws from within a throwing area, using either hand and any throwing motion. The best score in terms of distance is recorded. All competitors use a 109-gram frisbee. If none is available, then everyone uses frisbees of the same weight.

United States Cerebral Palsy Athletic Association (USCPAA)

Competition sanctioned by the USCPAA is governed by rules established by TAC. Events are contested via a seven-class system and consist of races as short as 20 m for Class I athletes in electric wheelchairs up to 800 m for Class VII and VIII. There is a 4 × 100-m wheelchair shuttle relay for Classes II through IV and a 4 × 200-m ambulatory relay for Classes V through VIII. The following events constitute the field portion: shot put, discus, javelin, club throw, and long jump. Additional events include the *precision club throw, soft shot, distance kick,* and *medicine ball thrust.* Modifications of rules used to ensure equitable competition include the following:

- Alternate lane assignments are used for all running events by Class V athletes because of their potential wide crutch gait.
- Baton exchanges and touches are not required in relays; the athlete or the front axle of the wheelchair must remain entirely behind the exchange zone starting line until the advancing athlete enters the exchange zone.

The USCPAA (NASCP, 1983) incorporates the following additional modifications in its field events:

- An attendant or a mechanical device may hold the chair in place; however, attendants may not sit inside the throwing area or in front of the stop board.
- The club throw, soft shot (6-in. square cloth weighing a maximum of 5 oz), and soft discus (webbed nylon material weighing 2.25 oz) are used for some classifications.

- Precision club throw and soft shot are included as events for some participants. A target of eight concentric rings is placed on the ground. The object of the event is to accurately throw the implement at the target. Each ring has a point value; the total for six throws is the final score. Competitors will throw from a distance of 6 ft from the bull's-eye.
- Distance kick and medicine ball thrust are offered for Class II athletes who cannot engage in routine throwing events. In the distance kick a 13-in. playground ball is placed on a foul line; the competitors initiate a backswing and then kick the ball forward while remaining seated in their chairs. Distance of the kick is the criterion. In the medicine ball thrust, a 6-lb medicine ball is used. Competitors may not kick the ball; rather the foot must remain in contact with the ball throughout the entire movement until release.

Beyond the traditional track and field events sponsored by the sports organizations for the disabled, there are several special events that are unique to these competitions. NWAA, USCPAA, USABA, and AAAD hold pentathlons. Additionally, the USABA sponsors a standard marathon competition. The NWAA and the USCPAA offer *slalom course* competition. According to NWAA (1986), the slalom course is no longer than 100 m, with no single straightaway longer than 5 m. It contains a series of obstacles (i.e., ramps, tilt boards, curbs), directional changes (minimally 10 directional changes of 180° each), and varied surfaces (including gravel, grass, and water).

Golf

Golf has not been incorporated into the major sport competitions for individuals with disabilities. However, it is an activity that can be included in physical education programs for individuals with any of a variety of disabilities.

Sport Skills

Golf, as it is normally played, requires a person to grasp the club and address the ball using an appropriate stance. Being able to swing the golf club backward, then forward through a large arc including follow-through is also a requisite task.

Lead-Up Activities

An appropriate lead-up activity is miniature golf. This very popular version of golf is quite suited to disabled persons. For many, this may represent the extent to which the golf experience is explored. Holes should range from 8 to 14 ft from tee mat to hole with a width of 3 ft, which accommodates reaching a ball lying in the center of the course from a wheelchair.

Variations and Modifications

Sport

At present only USCPAA offers competition in golf. It is an exhibition event that was added to the 1985 National Games when those games were expanded to include Les Autres athletes. Traditionally, Les Autres athletes have not been served by the major organizations governing sports for individuals with disabilities. Of the nearly 800 athletes who attended the 1985 USCPAA National Games held at Michigan State University, only three participated in golf and all three were Les Autres (Jones, 1986).

Other Variations and Modifications

Because of various limitations experienced by disabled persons, the essential sport skills are often problematic. Fait and Dunn (1984) have detailed many practical considerations necessary for successful golf participation by the disabled person. These include

- using powered carts for those who lack stamina to walk around the golf course but who can physically play the game;
- utilizing left-handed clubs for a right-handed player whose arm is missing or incapacitated, or vice versa;
- sitting on a chair for players who cannot balance on one crutch or who are unable to stand; those using a chair or sitting in a wheelchair should have the chair turned so they are facing the ball;
- eliminating the preliminary movement of the club (waggle) for blind golfers because this could produce an initial malalignment of the club with the ball. Additionally, information about distance to the hole can be provided by tapping on the cup or by telling golfers how far they are away from the cup; and,
- for some wheelchair players, using extra long clubs in order to clear the foot plates.

The *Putter Finger* is an assistive device that consists of a molded rubber suction cup designed to fit on the grip end of any putter. It is used to retrieve the ball from the hole (Adams et al., 1982). Another adaptation that enables blind golfers to practice independently was developed by Huber (personal communication, January, 1971). Three pieces of material, all of which produce different sounds when struck, are hung about 15 to 20 ft in front of golfers while they practice indoors. Golfers are instructed about the positions of the different pieces of material and the sound made by each. Because feedback about the direction of the ball's line of flight is available, they can determine whether the ball went straight, hooked, or sliced.

Weight Lifting

Weight lifting, more specifically *power lifting*, has developed over the years as an extremely popular sport for people with disabilities. In this chapter

power lifting as a sport is distinguished from routine weight training.

Sport Skills

Three events are usually considered in power lifting; these include the *bench press, squat*, and *deadlift*. Participants are classified by weight; however, braces and other devices are not counted in the total weight. The NWAA makes adjustments to recorded weight according to the site of an amputation.

Sport

Competitive power lifting programs are offered by NWAA, USCPAA, USAAA, and USABA. All organizations but one restrict their competitions to the bench press. The USABA (1986) sanctions three events: bench press, squat, and deadlift. Each organization has certain specific rules that accommodate its athletes. Some of the more significant modifications are the following:

- A Universal weight machine is used in place of free weights; one or more coaches can hold the legs of the competitor to provide balance and to restrain involuntary movement, but this assistance cannot involve the hips (NASCP, 1983).
- Strapping the legs above the knees to the bench is permissible as long as it is done with the strap provided by the organizing committee (NWAA, 1986).

Cycling

Cycling, whether bicycle or tricycle, is a useful skill from the standpoint of lifelong leisure pursuit. It can likewise be a strenuous sport that is pursued for its competitiveness. To compete, participants must develop a high level of fitness and learn effective race strategy.

Sport Skills

Cycling requires the ability to maintain one's balance on the cycle and to execute a reciprocal movement of the legs to turn the pedals. Beyond these two variables, which for some people are no small concern, all that remains is to determine whether riding is a leisurely pursuit or a competitive event for which training and conditioning are paramount.

Variations and Modifications

Sport

The AAAD sponsors three events, which include a 1,000-m sprint, a road race, and a time trial race on the road. The USAAA offers two events, a 25-km and a 50-km, in an open class category. The USCPAA sponsors both bicycle and tricycle events: There are three tricycle events, each conducted at 1,500 m for Classes II/III, IV/V, and VI; there are two bicycle events, each conducted at 5,000 m for Class VII and VIII athletes. The following specific rule modifications are in effect in USCPAA competitions (NASCP, 1983):

- Hand-propelled cycles are permitted.
- Spotters may accompany riders; they are not permitted to coach or perform pacing functions.

The USABA (1986) offers five events at each of two distances. These include 40-km tandem for men and women, 40-km tandem mixed (men/women), and 40-km single for men and women; the same events are also provided at a distance of 10 km. With few exceptions the rules for USABA cycling are the same as those for the United States Cycling Federation. The exceptions are as follows:

- The pilot (front rider) in tandem riding events must be sighted, with vision to exceed 20/200; the stoker (back rider) can be from any vision class.

- Single riders must have a visual classification of B2 or B3.
- There are *racing classes* with competition taking place in one division and with no separation by visual class.
- Both the 10- and 40-km courses will adhere to the following specifications: a mostly flat, paved road course that does not cross itself and that is clearly marked with chalk and closed to at least one lane of traffic.
- At 40 km, if there are more than 10 riders, a staggered start is used; at 10 km bikes are started at intervals of 30 s.

Special Olympics offers cycling as a demonstration sport. Events consist of 1-, 3-, and 5-km races as well as a 4 × 1-km relay race. Additionally, two developmental events can be offered: a 400-m race and a 100-m slalom. All events are governed by the rules established by the International Federation of Amateur Cycling (Special Olympics, 1985).

Other Variations and Modifications

Riding a bicycle can be a difficult task, especially for the disabled person. Individuals with impaired balance or coordination may require some adaptation of the cycling activity. Three- and four-wheeled bicycles with or without hand cranks can facilitate cycling for disabled persons. If riding a two-wheeled bicycle is the desirable approach, then training wheels suitable for full-size adult bikes can be constructed. Additionally, tandem cycling can be used in cases where total control of the bicycle is beyond the ability of the disabled person, as with the visually impaired.

Boccie

Boccie, the Italian version of bowling, is generally played on a sand or soil alley 75 ft long and 8 ft wide. The playing area is normally enclosed at the ends and sides by boards that are 18 in. and 12 in. high, respectively.

Sport Skills

The game requires that players roll or throw wooden balls in the direction of a smaller wooden ball or "jack." The object is to have the ball come to rest closer to the "jack" than any of the opponent's balls. To do this, players try to roll balls in order to protect their own well-placed shots, while knocking aside their opponents' balls.

Lead-Up Activities

The New York State Games for the Physically Challenged have adopted a new game, *Crazy Bocce*, as a demonstration activity. This game consists of throwing two sets of four wooden balls alternately into various size rings for specified point totals. Three smaller rings sit inside one large ring, which is 13 ft in circumference. Points are awarded only if the ball remains inside a ring. If the ball lands inside the large ring (but not in any of the smaller rings), 1 point is awarded. If the ball lands inside the small blue or red ring, 2 points

are earned. The other small ring is yellow, with a point value of 3. The game is usually played with the large ring placed in a small wading pool (see Figure 26.8). The large ring can also be attached to swimming pool sides, using a suction cup attachment that is provided. The game can also be played in the snow, on the beach, on the lawn, and on carpet. Crazy Bocce can be played and enjoyed by young and old alike (A. Conforti, personal communication, January 18, 1988).

Variations and Modifications

Sport

Both individual and team boccie are sanctioned events in the national competition of the USCPAA. Major modifications to the rules include these:

- The court is laid out on a gymnasium floor or asphalt surface and measures 12.5 m by 6 m.

Figure 26.8 Playing Crazy Bocce. Photograph courtesy of A. Conforti. Printed with permission.

- Assistants to players with impaired vision who need light or sound signals may enter the playing court during the game, but they must leave the court immediately after the throw.
- Players who have difficulty holding or placing the balls can receive assistance; however, they must throw, kick, or roll the ball independently.
- All balls must be thrown, rolled, or kicked into the court; assistive devices may be used if accepted by the referee prior to the game (NASCP, 1983).

Individual and team boccie are governed by identical rules, with the following major exceptions that apply to the individual sport:

- Competition is for Class I male and female athletes only.
- Competition consists of three rounds as compared to six rounds in the team event.

Other Variations and Modifications

There are several ways to modify boccie for participation by people with disabilities. A major concern is a lack of sufficient strength to propel the ball toward the jack. In such cases, substitution of a lighter object, such as a Nerf ball or balloon, or reduction of the legal court size would facilitate participation. Another area of concern is upper extremity involvement, which could prohibit rolling or throwing the boccie ball. This concern can be overcome if the individual is permitted to kick the ball into the target area or perhaps, as in regular bowling, to use a bowling cue/stick or even the bowling chute.

Integration

The variations and modifications that have been highlighted in this chapter reflect what is considered good practice in physical education as well as in sanctioned sports programs. For example, limiting the play area is an adaptation technique used in several sports such as tennis, badminton, and boccie.

Individual and dual sports provide a unique opportunity for encouraging *integration* of disabled people with their able-bodied peers. From elementary school through high school, variations and modifications can be utilized to alter a sport in subtle ways—for example, maintaining physical contact while wrestling. As a result of this approach, disabled students can participate and/or compete in regular physical education and sport programs and not only derive the benefits of instruction in activities that are themselves normalizing, but also receive that instruction in the least restrictive environment. Because of the reduced temporal and spatial demands of most of the individual and dual sports, there is every reason to believe that success in activities such as those highlighted in this chapter will be readily attainable within integrated settings.

Summary

For the most part, this chapter presented individual and dual sports that are currently available as part of the competitive offerings of the major sport organizations serving disabled athletes. In each case, the particular skills needed in the able-bodied version of the game or sport were detailed. Additionally, lead-up activities, as well as variations and modifications for use in competitive sport or for use in physical education programs, were suggested. Space limitations prevented discussion of other games and sports such as riflery and air pistol, shuffleboard, darts, and billiards. Information on riflery, air pistol, shuffleboard, and billiards can be found in the text by Adams, Daniel, McCubbin, and Rullman (1982), which is among the resources listed at the end of this chapter.

Bibliography

Adams, R.C., Daniel, A.N., McCubbin, J.A., & Rullman, L. (1982). *Games, sports, and exercises for the physically handicapped* (3rd ed.). Philadelphia: Lea & Febiger.

Adams, R.C., Daniel, A.N., & Rullman, L. (1975). *Games, sports, and exercises for the physically handicapped* (2nd ed.). Philadelphia: Lea & Febiger.

Fait, H.F., & Dunn, J.M. (1984). *Special physical education* (5th ed.). Philadelphia: Saunders.

Hattenback, R.T. (1979). Integrating persons with handicapping conditions in archery activities. In J.P. Winnick & J. Hurwitz (Eds.), *The preparation of regular physical educators for mainstreaming* (pp. 50-54). Brockport, NY: State University of New York, College at Brockport.

Heavens, T.L. (1985). Everyone is a winner at the sixth annual handicapped riders event. *Palaestra,* **1**(4), 28-32.

International Stoke Mandeville Games Federation. (1984). *Official rules for wheelchair fencing.* Aylesbury, United Kingdom: Author.

Jones, J. (1986). The 1985 national cerebral palsy/Les Autres games—A director's perspective. *Palaestra,* **2**(2), 20-27.

McCowan, L.L. (1972). *It is ability that counts: A training manual on therapeutic riding for the handicapped.* Olivet, MI: The Olivet College Press.

National Association of Sports for Cerebral Palsy. (1983). *Classification and sport rules manual.* New York: Author.

National Wheelchair Athletic Association. (1986). *Official rulebook of the National Wheelchair Athletic Association.* Colorado Springs, CO: Author.

Orr, R.E., & Sheffield, J. (1981). Adapted épée fencing. *Journal of Physical Education, Recreation and Dance,* **52**(6), 42, 71.

Parks, B.A. (1980). *Tennis in a wheelchair.* Newport Beach, CA: National Foundation of Wheelchair Tennis.

Special Olympics (n.d.) *Gymnastics.* Washington, DC: Author.

Special Olympics. (1985). *Official Special Olympics sports rules.* Washington, DC: Author.

United States Association for Blind Athletes. (1986). *Official 1986 Rules.* Beach Haven Park, NJ: Author.

Winnick, J.P., & Short, F.X. (1985). *Physical fitness testing of the disabled.* Champaign, IL: Human Kinetics.

Wiseman, D.C. (1982). *A practical approach to adapted physical education.* Reading, MA: Addison-Wesley.

Resources

Written

Adams, R.C., Daniel, A.N., McCubbin, J.A., & Rullman, L. (1982). *Games, sports, and exercises for the physically handicapped* (3rd ed.). Philadelphia: Lea & Febiger. This excellent resource provides in-depth suggestions concerning traditional and nontraditional games and sports that are suitable for participation by disabled persons. Included are suggestions for modifying existing sport or game structures, rules, and procedures.

Jones, J.A. (Ed.) (1984). *Training guide to cerebral palsy sports* (2nd ed.). New York: National Association of Sports for Cerebral Palsy. This manual shares the collective expertise of 40 individuals who actively engage in the training and conditioning of athletes with cerebral palsy. Topics range from training techniques in specific sports to flexibility, endurance training, and adaptive aerobics.

Wessel, J. (1979). *I CAN—Sport, leisure, and recreation skills*. Northbrook, IL: Hubbard. This program consists of four content modules that are designed to function independently or to supplement individualized physical education programs. Two of the modules, dance/individual sports and backyard/neighborhood activities, cover several of the sports and activities discussed in this chapter (e.g., badminton, bowling, gymnastics, and track and field).

Audiovisual

Kaufman, M. (Producer/Director). (1985). *Choosing victory* [Videotape]. Chicago, IL: Films Incorporated. This film was sparked by the announcement that two exhibition wheelchair races had been scheduled for the final day of track and field competition at the 1984 Summer Olympics. The film profiles the lives, careers, and training of five men and women whose drive and ambition have propelled them to success in their personal lives as well as in competitive sports.

CHAPTER 27

Winter Sport Activities

Luke E. Kelly

A major goal of physical education for both handicapped and nonhandicapped students is to provide the knowledge, skills, and experiences they need to live healthy and productive lives. At the completion of their high school physical education program, students should have the basic physical fitness and motor skills required to achieve this goal. It would be logical to assume that the emphasis on various sport skills in the school curriculum would reflect the students' needs in terms of carryover value and the likelihood of continuing participation after the school years. However, one area, that of winter sport skills, is frequently underrepresented in the physical education and sport curriculum. This is a serious omission for all students and especially disabled students. In many parts of the country, the winter season is the longest season during the school year. Winter sport activities provide opportunities for disabled people to

- maintain or improve their physical fitness levels,
- participate in many social/community recreation activities, and
- pursue athletic competition.

Failure to provide disabled youngsters with winter sport skills limits their recreational options during the winter months, which, in turn, may both affect their fitness and isolate them from many social activities and settings.

The purpose of this chapter is to introduce the reader to a number of winter sport activities that can be included in physical education and sport programs for persons with disabilities. It is not within the scope of this chapter to cover in detail how each winter sport skill should be taught. Instead, general guidelines are provided, along with a brief description of each winter sport activity and some specific adaptations for various disabled participants.

The disabled person, given proper instruction and practice, can pursue and successfully participate in a variety of winter sports such as *alpine* (downhill) skiing, *cross-country* skiing (nordic), *ice skating*, *ice picking*, *sledding*, *curling*, and *hockey*. Instructional programs for the disabled should be guided by equal attention to safety, motivation (fun), and skill development. Safety concerns should encompass the areas of physical and motoric readiness, appropriate clothing and equipment, and instructor qualifications.

Alpine Skiing

Downhill skiing is a winter sport in which most disabled individuals can participate with little or no modification. Skiing frees disabled people from many of the limitations that hinder their mobility on land and allows them to move with great agility and at great speeds. For many individuals with physical, mental, and sensory impairments, skiing offers a unique opportunity to challenge their environment.

The key to learning to ski is controlling one's weight distribution and directing where the weight is applied on the surface (edges) of the skis. The goal of any introductory ski program is to provide students with the basic skills needed to enjoy and safely participate in the sport. The basic skills of downhill skiing can be grouped into six categories:

1. Independence in putting on and taking off one's equipment
2. Independence in using rope and chair lifts
3. Falling and standing
4. Walking (sidestepping, herringbone)
5. Stopping (wedge, parallel)
6. Turning (wedge, parallel)

Instruction

It is strongly recommended that actual ski instruction be preceded by a conditioning program and the development of basic skills such as falling and standing. When the actual ski instruction begins, the skill sequence must be matched to the needs and abilities of the learners to both ensure safety and maximize enjoyment. While independent recovery (standing back up on one's skis) is ultimately a required skill for independent skiing, it may not be appropriate to concentrate on this skill during early learning. For many disabled individuals, learning to stand up on skis is very strenuous and often a frustrating experience. Students who are made to master this skill first are likely not to experience much success or fun and will soon become disenchanted with the idea of learning to ski. Initial instruction should focus on learning actual skiing skills such as a wedge stop, and the instructor should provide assistance to compensate for the lack of other skills, such as the ability to independently recover from falls. This form of instruction will provide students with confidence and some of the thrills of moving on skis. As skill and enjoyment increase, the students will become more motivated to work on mastering the other essential skills such as independent recovery.

Assistive Devices

A number of assistive devices have been developed to offset some of the limitations imposed by various handicapping conditions or to compensate for the general low fitness and/or poor motor coordination found in many disabled individuals. The most commonly used device is the *ski-bra* (Figure 27.1), which is mounted to the tip of the skis and serves two primary functions. First, it stabilizes the skis while still allowing them to move independently. Second, it assists the skier in

Figure 27.1 Photograph of a ski-bra. Photo courtesy of David Burton, Children's Rehabilitation Center, University of Virginia. Printed with permission.

positioning the skis in a wedge position, which improves balance and facilitates stopping and turning. The ski-bra can be used as a temporary learning device for any skier (e.g., mentally retarded, visually impaired, orthopedically impaired) during the early stages of learning, to assist with balance and control of the skis. The ski-bra may also be used as a permanent assistive device for individuals with lower extremity orthopedic impairments who lack sufficient strength and/or control of their lower limbs.

Canting wedges are another common modification used to assist disabled skiers. Small, thin wedges are placed between the sole of the ski boot and the ski. The wedges adjust the lateral tilt of the boot and subsequently affect the distribution of the weight over the edges of the skis. Canting

wedges are commonly used to assist skiers who have trouble turning to one side or the other.

Outriggers (Figure 27.2) are common assistive devices used by skiers with amputations and other orthopedic impairments who require additional support primarily in the area of balance. The outriggers are made from a Lofstrand crutch with a short ski attached to the bottom. The ski on the end of the crutch can be placed in a vertical (up) position and used as a crutch or positioned in a horizontal position for use as an outrigger. *Three-track* and *four-track* skiing are common terms used to describe the use of outriggers. Three-track skiing refers to individuals who use only one ski and two outriggers—for example, single-leg amputees; four-track skiing refers to those who use two skis and two outriggers.

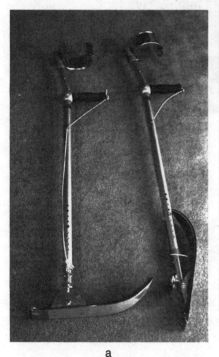

a

b

Figure 27.2 Outriggers: a) the right outrigger is in the down position for skiing; the left outrigger is in the up position and can be used as a crutch; b) an above-the-knee amputee skiing with outriggers. Photos courtesy of Mark Andrews, Centre for Health Sports Therapy—Centre for Disabled Skiing Instruction. Printed with permission.

Sit-skiing may be more accurately described as a form of sledding, but it is included here because it is performed on ski slopes and is the method used by paraplegics and quadriplegics to ski. Sit-skiing involves the use of a special sled (Figure 27.3). The paraplegic person is strapped into the sled, which contains appropriate padding and support to hold the skier in an upright sitting position. The top of the sled is covered by a water-repellent nylon skirt to keep the skier dry. The bottom of the sled is smooth, with a metal runner or edge running along each side. Skiers control

a

b

Figure 27.3 Sit-skiing sleds. A) side view of a sit-skiing sled. Photo courtesy of Mark Andrews, Centre for Health Sports Therapy—Centre for Disabled Skiing Instruction. Printed with permission. B) a sit-skier skiing while being tethered to the ski instructor. Photo courtesy of Chip Jones, Centre for Health Sports Therapy—Centre for Disabled Skiing Instruction. Printed with permission.

the sled by shifting their weight (over the edge) in the direction they want to go. A single kayak-type pole or two short poles can be used by the skier to assist in balancing and controlling the sled. Special mittens are available to allow individuals with limited grip strength to hold on to the poles. For the protection of both the sit-skier and other skiers on the slope, the beginner sit-skier should always be tethered to an experienced ski instructor. Modified sit-skis are also available and can be used by paraplegic persons for cross-country skiing.

Ski instructors use various forms of physical assistance to help and guide skiers with different disabilities. Instructors must be able to provide sufficient physical assistance during early learning to ensure both safety and success. Providing physical assistance to a moving beginner skier requires specific skills that must be learned and perfected. As the disabled skier's skills increase, the instructor must also know how to gradually fade out the physical assistance to verbal cues and eventually to independence.

In addition to the more universal assistive devices described above, there are numerous other devices that have been created to address specific needs of disabled skiers. Special prosthetic limbs, for example, have been developed to allow single- and double-leg (mono-ski) amputees to ski. Many of these devices are homemade by ski instructors trying to help specific individuals. Watching a national handicapped ski competition will clearly demonstrate that there is no limit to the devices that can be created to assist the disabled skier.

Cross-Country Skiing

Cross-country skiing in recent years has become a very popular winter sport. It is an excellent physical fitness and recreation activity. Because both the arms and the legs are used in cross-country skiing, this activity develops total body fitness. Two other advantages of the sport are that it costs nothing after the initial equipment is pur-chased and that it can be done almost anywhere (e.g., golf courses, parks, open fields). The major disadvantage of cross-country skiing for the disabled person, when compared to downhill skiing, is that the skier must create the momentum to move. This difference eliminates many more severely orthopedically impaired persons who lack either the strength or the control to generate the momentum needed to cross-country ski. However, because the activity is performed on snow and does not require that the feet actually be lifted off the ground, many individuals with cerebral palsy who have difficulty walking (shuffle gait) can success-fully cross-country ski.

A complete cross-country skiing outfit (skis, poles, shoes, and gaiters) can be purchased for approximately $150.00. Waxless (fishscale or step pattern) skis are recommended over wax skis for beginners. Waxless skis require no maintenance or preparation prior to use, and they provide more than sufficient resistance and glide for learning and enjoying cross-country skiing.

Initial instruction should take place in a relative-ly flat area with prepared tracks. Most beginning cross-country skiers tend to simply walk wearing their skis, using their poles for balance. This, un-fortunately, is incorrect and very fatiguing. The key in learning to cross-country ski is getting the feel of pushing back on one ski while the weight is transferred to the front foot and the front ski is slid forward. Instructors should focus on demon-strating this pattern and contrasting it with walk-ing. A very effective technique is to physically assist the beginning skier through this pattern so that the learner can feel what it is like. This works particularly well with mentally retarded and visually impaired skiers. Visually impaired cross-country skiers must be accompanied by sighted partners who usually ski parallel to them and in-form them of upcoming conditions (e.g., turns, changes in grades). The forward push and glide technique is the preferred pattern for the disabled skier, as opposed to the more strenuous and skill-demanding skating technique used by world-class nordic skiers.

Competitive Skiing for the Disabled

Skiing for the disabled is sponsored by a number of sport associations that conduct local, state, and national skiing competitions. Three of the largest and most prominent sponsors of ski competitions are Special Olympics, which sponsors competitions for mentally retarded people; the National Handicapped Sports and Recreation Association (NHSRA), which sponsors national skiing competitions for individuals with orthopedic and visual impairments; and the United States Association for Blind Athletes (USABA), which sponsors an annual national competition for blind skiers.

Special Olympics sponsors local, state, and national ski competitions. Competition is offered in both alpine and nordic events. The alpine events include downhill, giant slalom, and slalom races. The nordic events include the 100-m, 500-m, 1-km, 3-km, and 5-km races, as well as a 3 × 1-km relay. Athletes are classified for competition into one of three classes—novice, inter-

mediate, or advanced—on the basis of preliminary time trials in each event. There are no age or gender divisions. Special Olympics also offers developmental (noncompetitive/participation) alpine and nordic events. The developmental alpine events include a 10-m glide and a 10-m ski walk. The nordic developmental events include a 10-m pole walk (no skis), a 10-m ski walk (no poles), a glide event, and a 30-m snowshoe race.

NHSRA sponsors the Handicapped National Ski Championships each year. The nationals are preceded by a series of regional meets where athletes must qualify for the nationals. The national meets involve competition in three categories: alpine (downhill, slalom, giant slalom), nordic (5-km, 10-km, 15-km, 20-km, 30-km, biathlon, and relays), and sit-skiing (as listed for alpine and nordic). Athletes are classified according to the site and severity of their disability and the type of adapted equipment used in skiing. Orthopedically impaired skiers are divided into eight classes, described briefly as follows (U.S. Ski Association, 1989).

——— Classification of Orthopedically Impaired Skiers ———

Class 1—4-track: disability of both legs, skiing with outriggers and using two skis or one ski using a prosthesis

Class 2—3-track: disability of one leg, skiing with outriggers and one ski

Class 3—Two skis with poles: disability in both legs

Class 4—Two skis with poles: disability in one leg

Class 5—Two skis with no poles: disability of both arms or hands

Class 6—Two skis with no poles: disability of one arm or hand

Class 7—Disability of combination of arm and leg (athletes can use equipment of their choice)

Class 8—Any skier using a mono-ski and short outriggers

Visually impaired skiers are divided into three classes on the basis of visual acuity with maximum correction. The classifications are as follows (U.S. Ski Association, 1989).

——— Classification of Visually Impaired Skiers ———

Class B1—Totally blind: can distinguish light and dark but not shapes

Class B2—Partially sighted: 20/600 acuity or visual field of less than 5°

Class B3—Partially sighted: visual acuity between 20/600 and 20/200 and/or field of vision between 5° and 20°

The USABA, for its national ski competition, uses the three vision classifications just described for NHRSA. USABA offers giant slalom and downhill alpine events as well as 5-km, 10-km, and 25-km nordic events. Separate competitions are offered for each gender within each classification; there are no age divisions. Sighted guides are used in all of the events to verbally assist the blind skiers. USABA also sponsors approximately five nordic skiing training camps each year to promote skiing for visually impaired people. In addition to the USABA, Blind Outdoor Leisure Development (BOLD) provides satellite training programs in downhill skiing, and the Ski for Light organization sponsors approximately 20 weekend nordic ski instructional programs around the country each year.

In addition to the classifications just described, there are three age divisions: ages 0 through 18 (juniors), ages 19 through 40, and age 41 and over (seniors). Separate competitions are offered for each gender in each age division except when there are not enough participants of one gender to compose a heat. The same classifications apply for both alpine and cross-country skiing. The only difference between the men's and women's events is that females are limited to the 5-km and 10-km cross-country events.

Sit-skiing competition is conducted only in the United States, and, therefore, athletes competing in this category are not classified according to the international classification system. Sit-skiers are classified into one of two groups. Group 1 is composed of athletes with disabilities in the lower limbs, with injury between T5 and T10 inclusive. (Athletes with higher injuries, above T5, typically are not able to sit-ski.) Group 2 is for athletes with all other disabilities resulting from injury below T10 and conditions such as spina bifida, amputation, cerebral palsy, polio, and muscular dystrophy.

Ice Skating

Ice skating is another inexpensive winter sport that is readily accessible in many regions of the country. Most disabled individuals who can stand and walk independently can learn to ice skate successfully. For those who cannot, a modified form of ice skating, ice picking, is available. While skating is common in many areas on frozen lakes and ponds or water-covered tennis courts, the preferred environment for teaching ice skating is an indoor ice rink. An indoor rink offers a more moderate temperature and a better quality ice surface, free from the cracks and bumps commonly found in natural ice. Ice rinks can frequently be used by physical education programs during off times such as daytime hours on weekdays.

Properly fitting skates are essential for learning and ultimately enjoying ice skating. Ice skates should be fitted by a professional experienced in working with and fitting disabled individuals. Either figure or hockey skates can be used. The important consideration is that the skates provide good ankle and arch support so that the skater's weight is centered over the ankles and the blades of the skates are perpendicular to the ice when the skater is standing.

As discussed earlier in this chapter, instruction should be guided by safety and success. The greatest obstacle in learning to ice skate is the fear of falling. Although falling while first learning to skate is inevitable, steps can and should be taken to minimize the frequency and severity of the falls and, consequently, the apprehension. At the same time, the early stages of learning must be associated with success, which gives learners confidence that they will be able to learn to skate. It is recommended that padding be used around the major joints most likely to hit the ice during a fall. Knee and elbow pads reduce the physical trauma of taking a fall and also provide a form of psychological security that alleviates the fear of falling. When teaching mentally retarded adults to ice skate, I have used football pants with knee, hip, and sacral pads along with elbow pads and have found them to be very beneficial during the early stages of learning.

The locomotor skill of ice skating is very similar to walking. The weight, the center of gravity, is basically transferred in front of the base of support and from side to side as the legs are lifted and swung forward to catch the weight. The back skate is usually rotated outward about 30° to provide some resistance to sliding backward as the weight is transferred to the forward skate. Because success during the early lessons is essential, one-on-one instruction from an experienced instructor is highly recommended.

The primary aid used in teaching ice skating is physical assistance. Some individuals with orthopedic and neuromuscular impairments may benefit from the use of polyproplylene orthoses to stabilize their ankles. Ankle-foot orthoses arc custommade and can be worn inside the skates. The most universal skating aid is the Hein-A-Ken skate aid (Figure 27.4). This device does not interfere with the skating action of the legs, and it provides the beginning skater with a stable means of support independent from the instructor. The skate aid can be used for temporary assistance during the early stages of learning for students who need a little additional support or confidence; it can also be a more permanent assistive device for skaters with more severe orthopedic impairments. I have found it beneficial to add some foam padding to the top support bar in the front of the skate aid to further reduce the chance of injury from falls. It skate aids are not available, chairs can be used in a similar fashion.

Ice picking is a modified form of ice skating in which the participant sits on a sledge, a small sled with blades on the bottom, and uses small poles (picks) to propel the sledge on the ice. Ice picking can be performed by almost anyone and is particularly appropriate for individuals who only have upper limb control (e.g., paraplegics or those with spina bifida). Ice picking is an excellent activity for developing upper body strength and endurance. All skating activities and events (speed skating and skate dancing) can be modified and performed in sledges. Because both able-bodied and disabled individuals can use the equipment, ice picking offers a unique way to equalize participation and competition in integrated settings.

Figure 27.4 A beginning skater using a Hein-A-Ken skate aid. *Note.* From *Games, Sports, and Exercise for the Physically Handicapped* (3rd ed.) (p. 241) by R.C. Adams, A.N. Daniel, J.A. McCubbin, and L. Rullman, 1982, Philadelhia: Lea & Febiger. Copyright 1982 by Lea & Febiger. Reprinted by permission.

Special Olympics sponsors ice skating competitions in two categories: figure skating and speed skating. The figure skating events include singles, pairs, and ice dancing; the speed skating events include the 100-, 300-, 500-, 800-, and 1,000-m races. For each event, athletes are divided into three classifications—novice, intermediate, and advanced—on the basis of preliminary performance and time trials. Developmental (noncompetitive/participation) ice skating events are also offered. These include the slide for distance, the 10-m assisted skate, the 10-m unassisted skate, and the 30-m slalom.

The USABA sponsors two speed skating events (5,000- and 10,000-m) in conjunction with the national ski competition. Blind skaters are assisted by sighted guides who provide verbal cues from in front of, beside, or behind the blind skater.

Sledding and Tobogganing

In snowy regions of the country, sledding and tobogganing are two common recreational activities that are universally enjoyed by both children and adults. Many disabled individuals, however, avoid these activities because they lack the simple skills and confidence needed to successfully take part in them. The needed skills and confidence can easily be addressed in a physical education program. Given proper attention to safety and clothing, almost all disabled children can participate in sledding and tobogganing. Sleds and toboggans can be purchased and/or rented at minimal cost. Straps and padding can be added to commercial sleds and toboggans to accommodate the specific needs occasioned by different handicaps. Even the most severely disabled can experience the thrill of sledding or tobogganing when paired with an aide who can control and steer the sled.

Hockey

Ice hockey is a popular winter sport in the northern areas of the United States and is the national sport of Canada. The game is played by two teams who attempt to hit a puck into the opposing team's goal using their hockey sticks. Hockey is a continuous, highly active, and exciting sport. Because of these features, numerous modifications and adaptations have been made to ice hockey to accommodate disabled players. The major modifications include

- playing the game on a solid, less slippery surface, like a gymnasium floor or tennis court;
- using soft plastic balls, plastic pucks, or doughnut-shaped pucks instead of the traditional ice hockey pucks;
- using shorter and lighter sticks made of plastic, which are more durable, easier to handle, and less harmful to other players;
- changing the boundaries, the number of players per team, and the length of the playing periods to accommodate the ability of the players; and
- changing the size of the goals.

Modifications can easily be made to permit sticks to be held by physically impaired players or used from wheelchairs. A wide range of abilities can be accommodated in a game if the teams are balanced and the players' abilities matched to the various positions.

Special Olympics sponsors local, state, and national competition in two versions of hockey: floor hockey and poly hockey. These two games are basically the same except for the sticks and pucks used in each. In floor hockey, a stick similar to a broomstick with a vinyl coating on the end is used in conjunction with a doughnut-shaped puck. In poly hockey, plastic sticks similar to regular hockey sticks are used along with a plastic puck shaped like a regulation puck. The goalkeeper in both versions uses a regular hockey goalie stick. Although there are some minor variations in the skills related to each version due to the differences in equipment, the basic skills are the same for both games.

Sledge hockey is a modified form of ice hockey played on sledges. The only difference from the regulation game of ice hockey is that the game is played from a sledge and the puck is struck with a modified stick called a pick (see Figure 27.5). The pick is approximately 30 in. in length. On one end it has metal points that grip the ice and allow the athlete to propel the sledge. The other end, called the butt, is rubber coated. The butt end of the pick is held while the sledge is being propelled. When the athlete wants to hit the puck, the hand is slid down the shaft of the pick to cover the spiked end, and then the butt end of the pick is used to strike the puck.

Figure 27.5 Sledges and picks used in sledge hockey. Photo courtesy of Mike Andrews. Printed with permission.

Sledge hockey is an excellent recreational and fitness activity. Using sledges is also an ideal way of equating able-bodied and orthopedically impaired students in the same activity.

Logical modifications should be made to the regulation game of hockey to accommodate beginners, such as reducing the playing area, increasing the number of players on each team, increasing the size of the goal, playing without goalkeepers, or changing the size or type of puck (e.g., substituting a playground ball). The goal of all modifications should be to maximize participation and success in the basic sledge and hockey skills while gradually progressing toward the regulation game.

Curling

Curling is a popular recreational activity and sport in Europe and Canada. The playing area is an ice court 46 yd long and 14 ft wide, with a 6-ft circular target, called a *house*, marked on the ice at each end. The game is played by two teams of four players, with pieces of equipment called *stones* (a kettle-shaped weight 36 in. in circumference and weighing approximately 40 lb, with a gooseneck handle on top). A game is composed of 10 or 12 rounds called *heads*; a round consists of each player delivering (sliding) two stones. Players on each team alternate delivering stones until all have been delivered. After each stone is delivered, teammates can use brooms to sweep frost and moisture from the ice in front of the coming stone to keep it straight and allow it to slide farther. At the end of a round, a team scores a point for each stone they have closer to the center of the target than the other team. The team with the most points at the end of 10 or 12 rounds is the winner. If the score is tied, an additional round is played to break the tie.

Curling can easily be modified to accommodate individuals with just about any disability. The distance between the houses and the weight of the stones can be reduced to facilitate reaching the targets. The size of the targets can also easily be increased to maximize success. Audible goal locators can be placed on the houses to assist visually impaired players. The sweeping component of the game may be difficult to modify to include nonambulatory and visually impaired players. In these cases, mixed teams could be formed of players with different disabilities so that each team had a few members who could do the sweeping. Finally, assistive devices like those used in bowling (ramps and guide rails) could be used to help the severely disabled and visually impaired players deliver the stones.

Summary

Winter sports, in general, are excellent all-around activities. They develop motor skill, strength, and physical fitness while at the same time providing participants with functional recreational skills they can use for the rest of their lives. For many disabled individuals, winter sports performed on snow and ice allow them to move with agility and speed not possible under their own power on land. Winter sports, therefore, should be an essential component in the physical education and sport programs of all students, and especially disabled students. For this reason, activities have been discussed in this chapter with particular focus on ways to modify them for people with unique needs.

Bibliography

Adams, R.C., Daniel, A.N., McCubbin, J.A., & Rullman, L. (1982). *Games, sports and exercises for the physically handicapped*. Philadelphia: Lea & Febiger.

United States Ski Association. (1989). *Alpine skiing competition guide*. Park City, UT: Author.

Resources

Written

Adams, R.C. (1978). Therapeutic implications of ice skating. *Journal of Physical Education and Recreation, 49*, 56-57.

Axelson, P. (1984). Sit-skiing. *Sports 'N Spokes, 9*, 28-31.

Baldwin, E.R. (1972). *Cross-country skiing handbook*. Toronto, Ontario, Canada: Pargurian Press.

Caldwell, J. (1976). *The new cross-country ski book* (4th ed.). Brattleboro, VT: Stephen Green Press.

Cob, M. (1975). Skiing is for everyone. *Therapeutic Recreation Journal, 9*, 18-20.

Cottrell, J. (1980a). *Special Olympics dry land ski school*. Washington, DC: Joseph P. Kennedy, Jr. Foundation.

Cottrell, J. (1980b). *Skiing for everyone*. Winston-Salem, NC: Hunter.

Crase, N. (1983). 1983 National handicap ski championships. *Sports 'N Spokes, 9*, 36-39.

Hayes, D. (1972). *Ice hockey*. Dubuque, IA: Wm. C. Brown.

Heller, M. (Ed.). (1979). *The skier's encyclopedia*. New York: Paddington Press.

Krag, M.H., & Messner, D.G. (1982). Skiing for the physically handicapped. *Clinics in Sports Medicine, 1*, 319-332.

McKinley, N. (1982). The wilderness experience. *Sports 'N Spokes, 7*, 10-12.

O'Leary, H. *The Winter Park amputee ski teaching system*. Winter Park, CO: Winter Park Handicap Ski Program. This "how-to" manual describes the program used to teach people with amputations how to ski. This manual is a must for anyone planning to work with amputees in a ski program. Winter Park is an excellent resource for up-to-date information and techniques for teaching skiing to disabled persons.

Orr, L.F. (1983). Cross-country sled skiing. *Sports 'N Spokes, 9*, 18-20.

Physical Education and Recreation for the Handicapped Information and Research Utilization Center. (1974). *Challenging opportunities for special populations in aquatic, outdoor, and winter activities*. Reston, VA: American Alliance for Health, Physical Education and Recreation.

Plain, C.S. (1986). *Sledge hockey and ice picking*. Unpublished graduate project, State University of New York, College at Brockport. This resource provides a step-by-step approach for teaching the skills involved in sledge hockey and ice picking. Sample drills and activities are provided, as well as suggested modifications and adaptations that can be made to accommodate various disabilities.

Rappoport, A. (1982). Sledge hockey: The alternative to ice hockey for the disabled. *Sports 'N Spokes, 7*, 24-25.

Seaton, D.C., Schmottlach, N., Clayton, I.A., Leibee, H.C., & Messersmith, L.L. (1983). *Physical education handbook* (7th ed.). Englewood Cliffs, NJ: Prentice-Hall.

Sinclair, N. (1975). Cross-country skiing for the mentally handicapped. *Challenge, 10*, 1, 8.

Sledge Hockey Ice Picking Association. (1984). *Official sledge hockey rules and regulations manual*. Alberta, Canada: Author.

Special Olympics. (n.d.) *Alpine skiing sports skills instructional program*. Washington, DC: Joseph P. Kennedy, Jr. Foundation.

Special Olympics. (n.d.) *Hockey sports skills instructional program*. Washington, DC: Joseph P. Kennedy, Jr. Foundation.

These two manuals provide a "how-to" approach for teaching the basic skills involved in alpine skiing and hockey. Teaching suggestions, as well as sample drills and activities, are provided for each skill.

Other

Camp Holiday Trails—Center for Disabled Skiing Instructors, Alpine and Nordic Programs, P.O. Box 5806, Charlottesville, VA 22905.

Colorado Outdoor Education Center for the Handicapped, P.O. Box 697, Breckenridge, CO 80424.

The 52 Association, 441 Lexington Avenue, New York, NY 10017.

International Council on Therapeutic Ice Skating, P.O. Box 4541, Winter Park, FL 32793.

National Blind Organization of Leisure Development, 533 East Main Street, Aspen, CO 81611.

Skating Association for the Blind and Handicapped, Inc., P.O. Box 1629, Buffalo, NY 14216.

Ski for Light—HEALTHsports, Inc., 1455 West Lake Street, Minneapolis, MN 55408.

Vinland National Center, 3675 Ihduhape Road, Loretto, MN 55357.

Winter Park Handicapped Ski Program, Box 313, Winter Park, CO 80482.

Appendix

Organizations Related to Adapted Sport

American Athletic Association for the Deaf
3916 Lantern Drive
Silver Spring, MD 20902

American Blind Bowling Association
3500 Terry Drive
Norfolk, VA 23518

American Hearing Impaired Hockey
1143 West Lake Street
Chicago, IL 60607

American Wheelchair Bowling Association
15858 Larkspur Lane
Menomonee Falls, WI 53051

American Wheelchair Table Tennis Association
166 Haase Avenue
Paramus, NJ 07652

Braille Sports Foundation
75-25 North Street
Minneapolis, MN 55426

Canadian Wheelchair Sports Association
333 River Road
Ottawa, Ontario
Canada K1L8H9

Handicapped Scuba Association
1104 El Prado
San Clemente, CA 92672

International Wheelchair Road Racers Club, Inc.
30 Myano Lane
Stamford, CT 06902

Kirkwood Instruction of Blind Skiers Foundation
P.O. Box 138
Kirkwood, CA 95646

National Beep Baseball Association
512 8th Avenue NE
Minneapolis, MN 55413

National Foundation of Wheelchair Tennis
15441 Redhill Avenue, Suite A
Tustin, CA 92680

National Handicapped Sports and Recreation
  Association
Farragut Station
P.O. Box 33141
Washington, DC 20033

National Wheelchair Athletic Association
3617 Betty Drive, Suite S
Colorado Springs, CO 80907

National Wheelchair Basketball Association
110 Seaton Building
University of Kentucky
Lexington, KY 40506

National Wheelchair Racquetball Association
815 North Weber
Colorado Springs, CO 80903

National Wheelchair Softball Association
P.O. Box 22478
Minneapolis, MN 55422

North American Riding for the Handicapped
  Association
111 East Wacker Drive
Chicago, IL 60601

Paralyzed Veterans of America
801 18th Street NW
Washington, DC 20006

Special Olympics, Inc.
1350 New York Avenue NW
Washington, DC 20005

U.S. Amputee Athletic Association
Suite 149A
Belle Forest Circle
Nashville, TN 37221

U.S. Association for Blind Athletes
UAF/USC Benson Building
Columbia, SC 29208

U.S. Blind Golfers' Association
225 Baronne Street
New Orleans, LA 70112

U.S. Cerebral Palsy Athletic Association
34518 Warren Road, Suite 264
Westland, MI 48185

U.S. Deaf Skiers Association, Inc.
56 West 84th Street
New York, NY 10024

U.S. Deaf Tennis Association, Inc.
3102 Lake Avenue
Cheveryl, MD 20785

U.S. Les Autres Sports Association
1101 Post Oak Boulevard
Houston, TX 77056

U.S. Deaf Volleyball Association
3019 Halsey Avenue
Arcadia, CA 91006

U.S. Quad Rugby Association
811 Northwestern Drive
Grand Forks, ND 58201

U.S. Wheelchair Racquet-Sports Association
1941 Viento Veraro Drive
Diamond Bar, CA 91765

Wheelchair Sports Foundation
c/o Benjamin H. Lipton
40-24 62nd Street
Woodside, NY 11377

This appendix was developed by Patricia Krebs
and Joseph P. Winnick.

Author Index

Subject Index

About the Authors

Diane H. Craft received a doctorate in Adapted Physical Education (APE) from New York University in 1980. She is an associate professor of physical education at the State University of New York, College at Cortland. Her main responsibility is preparing teachers to instruct all children in their classes, including those with disabilities. As part of her work, she directs a U.S. Department of Education APE training grant.

Luke E. Kelly received his doctorate in adapted physical education from Texas Woman's University. He is the program area director of health and physical education, including the graduate program in adapted physical education, at the University of Virginia as well as the national director of Project I CAN-ABC. Dr. Kelly is actively involved in adapted physical education research in the areas of qualitative assessment of motor skills, curriculum design and evaluation, computer application, applications of social learning theory, and exercise compliance in the treatment of obesity.

Patricia L. Krebs received a doctorate in physical education from the University of Maryland in 1979. Formerly professor in the undergraduate and graduate adapted physical education program at Adelphi University in New York, Dr. Krebs is now director of the education-outreach project for Special Olympics International. Her main responsibilities are developing Model Special Olympics sport training and competition programs as part of the physical education and after-school sport programs in schools.

E. Michael Loovis is an associate professor of health, physical education, and recreation at Cleveland State University. His major interest in teacher education is the continuous professional development of career teachers to enable them to teach students with disabilities in the least restrictive environment. He has received federal, state, and foundation support to provide this needed training. His current research focus is the relationship between toy play and associated movement behavior in preschool children with disabilities.

Bruce A. McClenaghan is director of the Motor Rehabilitation Laboratory at the University of South Carolina, where he is on the faculty of the Department of Exercise Science. He earned his doctorate from Indiana State University, where his interest in motor development resulted in the publication of his first text. Currently his research is directed toward evaluating the effects of selected rehabilitation techniques on motor performance of the impaired child.

David L. Porretta received a doctorate in physical education from Temple University in 1981 and is now an associate professor of physical education at East Carolina University. He teaches in the area of adapted physical education, and his research focuses on the learning of motor skills by handicapped individuals.

E. Louise Priest is executive director of the Council for National Cooperation in Aquatics (CNCA). She has worked as a professional in aquatics for the YMCA, the American Red Cross, and CNCA. She spent 7 years at American Red Cross National Headquarters developing aquatic materials, including the text *Adapted Aquatics*. In her current position she developed the *National Aquatics Journal* and is its managing editor. A graduate of the University of Southern Indiana, she did graduate work at George Mason University in Virginia.

Sarah M. Rich is an associate professor at Ithaca College, Ithaca, New York. Her major teaching responsibilities are adapted physical education and therapeutic recreation. She earned a doctorate in adapted and developmental physical education from Texas Woman's University in 1981. Dr. Rich is the coach of the Mavericks, a beep baseball team, and is the travel director for the Senior Center in Ithaca.

Francis X. Short is an associate professor in the Department of Physical Education and Sport at the State University of New York, College at Brockport. He teaches courses in adapted physical education and growth and development and also coaches the women's intercollegiate volleyball team. He has authored and coauthored a number of publications and presentations related to physi-

cal fitness and the disabled. Dr. Short holds degrees from Springfield College and Indiana University.

Paul R. Surburg is a professor of physical education at Indiana University and director of the adapted physical education program. He is a licensed physical therapist and has published research and pedagogical articles in sports medicine. His other research area is the motor functioning of mentally handicapped persons, with a focus on factors influencing information processing.

Joseph P. Winnick is a professor of physical education and sport at the State University of New York, College at Brockport, where he also is coordinator of undergraduate and graduate specializations in adapted physical education. Dr. Winnick has been involved in several research activities and has gained national prominence as a result of studying the physical fitness of individuals with handicapping conditions. He has been involved in many service activities to benefit individuals with handicapping conditions in physical education and sport and has been an advocate for rights and opportunities for those individuals for several years. Dr. Winnick has been a consultant to the U.S. Department of Education and several colleges and universities. For recreation, he enjoys racquetball, softball, and basketball.